JOHN *m.* (2) Isabella of Angoulême
(1199–1216)

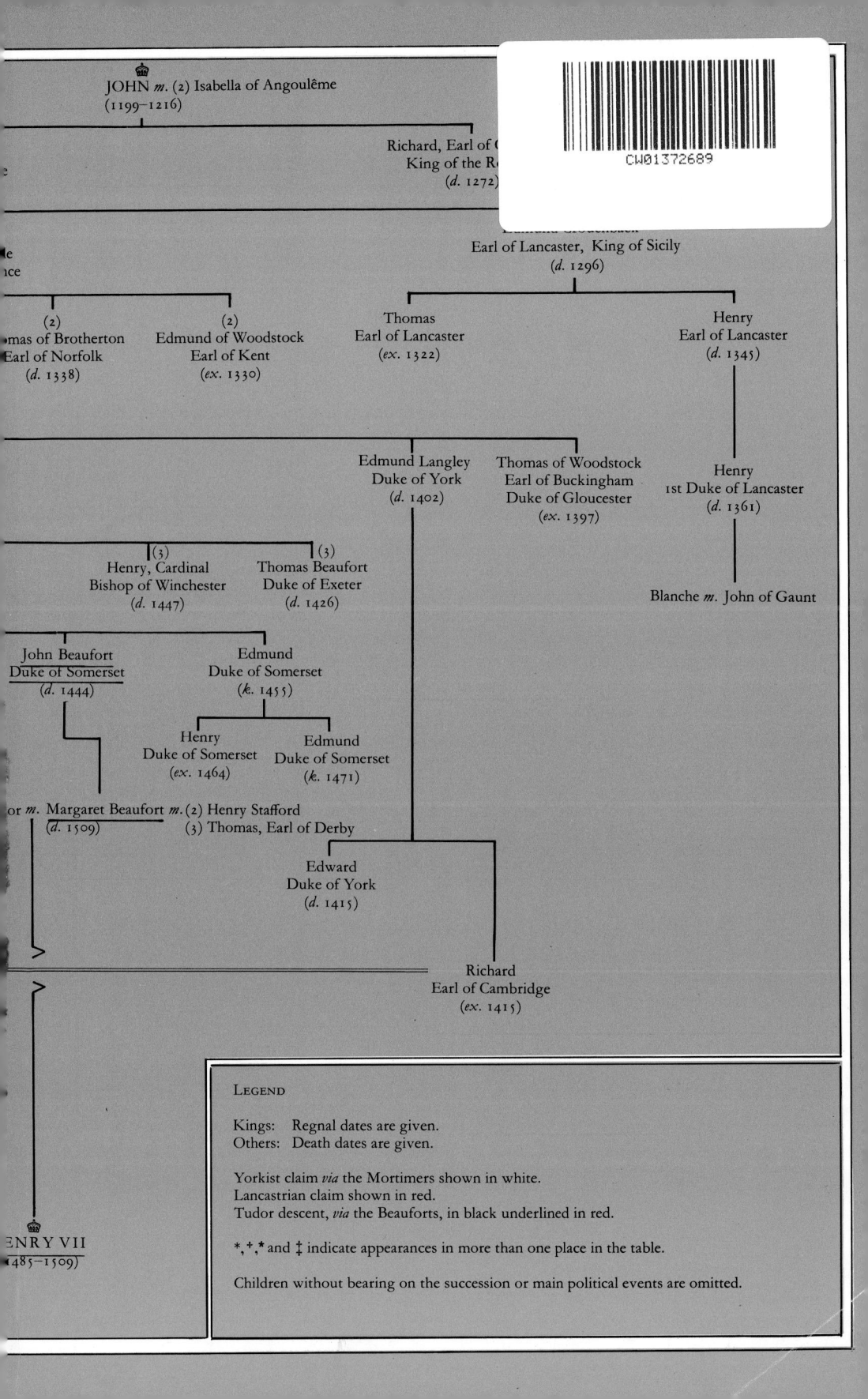

Richard, Earl of C...
King of the R...
(d. 1272)

Earl of Lancaster, King of Sicily
(d. 1296)

(2)   (2)
...mas of Brotherton   Edmund of Woodstock   Thomas   Henry
Earl of Norfolk   Earl of Kent   Earl of Lancaster   Earl of Lancaster
(d. 1338)   (ex. 1330)   (ex. 1322)   (d. 1345)

Edmund Langley   Thomas of Woodstock   Henry
Duke of York   Earl of Buckingham   1st Duke of Lancaster
(d. 1402)   Duke of Gloucester   (d. 1361)
                        (ex. 1397)

(3)   (3)
Henry, Cardinal   Thomas Beaufort
Bishop of Winchester   Duke of Exeter
(d. 1447)   (d. 1426)

Blanche *m.* John of Gaunt

John Beaufort   Edmund
Duke of Somerset   Duke of Somerset
(d. 1444)   (k. 1455)

Henry   Edmund
Duke of Somerset   Duke of Somerset
(ex. 1464)   (k. 1471)

...or *m.* Margaret Beaufort *m.* (2) Henry Stafford
        (d. 1509)   (3) Thomas, Earl of Derby

Edward
Duke of York
(d. 1415)

Richard
Earl of Cambridge
(ex. 1415)

Legend

Kings: Regnal dates are given.
Others: Death dates are given.

Yorkist claim *via* the Mortimers shown in white.
Lancastrian claim shown in red.
Tudor descent, *via* the Beauforts, in black underlined in red.

*, +, * and ‡ indicate appearances in more than one place in the table.

Children without bearing on the succession or main political events are omitted.

HENRY VII
(1485–1509)

A History of Parliament

By the same author

The Power of Parliament

The Coronation of Edward the Confessor: reconstruction of one of the 13th century wall paintings in the Painted Chamber. Painted by E. W. Tristram, it is based on water colour copies made in 1819 of the originals after their discovery beneath layers of whitewash and before the destruction of the Painted Chamber by fire.

A HISTORY
OF PARLIAMENT

—— * ——

THE MIDDLE AGES

Ronald Butt

CONSTABLE · LONDON

First published in Great Britain 1989
by Constable and Company Limited
10 Orange Street London WC2H 7EG
Copyright © 1989 by Ronald Butt
Set in Monophoto Garamond 11pt by
Servis Filmsetting Limited, Manchester
Printed in Great Britain by
St Edmundsbury Press Limited,
Bury St Edmunds, Suffolk

British Library CIP data
Butt, Ronald
A history of parliament: the Middle Ages
1. England and Wales. Parliament. 1216–1485
I. Title
328.42′09

ISBN 0 09 456220 2

TO THE MEMORY OF MY PARENTS
HERBERT AND CLARE BUTT

Contents

		page
	Illustrations	ix
	Acknowledgements	xi
	Abbreviations	xiii
	Preface	xv
	The Palace of Westminster	xxi
1	Prelude to Parliament: from Witan to Magna Carta	1
2	Henry III: the Emergence of Parliament	65
3	Edward I: King, Law and Parliament	117
4	Edward II: Parliament and Opposition	175
5	Edward III: The Rise and Influence of the Commons	231
6	Richard II: Parliament and the Crown's Authority	355
7	Henry IV: Parliament and a Hobbled King	451
8	Henry V: Parliament Pays for Glory	485
9	Henry VI: Parliament, Faction and Civil War	495
10	Edward IV: The King's Independence	567
11	Edward V and Richard III: Parliament and Usurper	614
	Select Bibliography	635
	Index	639

Illustrations

colour frontispiece
The coronation of Edward the Confessor (*English Heritage*)

between pages 200 and 201
The old palace of Westminster (*Ashmolean Museum, Oxford*)
Westminster Hall (*Photo: Hulton Picture Library*)
The Parliament of Edward I (from an engraving, after a Tudor original in the Royal Library, Windsor, *courtesy of Peter Jackson*)
The Painted Chamber (*PSA Crown Copyright*)
The coronation of Edward the Confessor (*Society of Antiquaries of London*)
The battle of Judas Maccabeus (*Society of Antiquaries of London*)
The White Chamber (from *Antiquities of Westminster*, J. T. Smith, 1807)
The Chapter House (*English Heritage*)
Sculpture of the Virgin Mary, Chapter House, Westminster (*Courtauld Institute*)
Sculpture of the Archangel Gabriel, Chapter House, Westminster (*Courtauld Institute*)

between pages 424 and 425
Effigy of Edward III (*National Portrait Gallery*)
Richard II (*Dean and Chapter of Westminster*)
Ruins of St Stephen's Chapel (*PSA Crown Copyright*)
Parliament Roll for April 1354 (*Public Record Office Crown copyright. Reproduced by permission of Controller of H.M. Stationery Office*)
Interior of the medieval Painted Chamber (*Society of Antiquaries of London*)
Parliament Roll, 1394 (*Public Record Office Crown copyright. Reproduced by permission of Controller of H.M. Stationery Office*)
Effigy of Henry IV (*National Portrait Gallery*)
Henry V (*National Portrait Gallery*)
The Jewel Tower (*English Heritage*)
Henry VI (*by gracious permission of H.M. the Queen*)
Edward IV (*by gracious permission of H.M. the Queen*)

Acknowledgements

I should like to acknowledge two particular debts. The first is to my publisher Ben Glazebrook for his great patience and tolerance as I have repeatedly taken up work on this book only to have to put it down again for long periods under pressure of other work and obligations.

Second, I owe thanks beyond measure to my son Edmund for the patience, interest and historical understanding with which he has helped me in checking successive drafts during the final two years of writing this book, and especially in guarding quotations and footnotes from intruding error. Not least, he has told me when what I had written needed to be clearer and I owe very many improvements of explanation to discussing them with him. I am very grateful for the innumerable weekends and evenings he has sacrificed to this book, but above all for his enthusiastic companionship in the work.

Abbreviations

B.I.H.R.	British Institute of Historical Research
B.J.R.L.	Bulletin of the John Rylands Library
Camden Soc.	Camden Society
Dignity of a Peer	Reports from the Lords' Committees . . . touching the Dignity of a Peer, 5 vols. (London, 1820–29)
E.H.D.	English Historical Documents (followed by volume number.)
E.H.R.	English Historical Review
Fryde and Miller	Historical Studies of the English Parliament, edited by E.B. Fryde and Edward Miller, 2 vols., 1970.
Foedera	Rymer's *Foedera* Record Commission vols. i–iv, 1816–33.
L.Q.R.	Law Quarterly Review
Rolls. Ser.	Rolls Series
Rot. Parl.	*Rotuli Parliamentorum*, vols 1–6 (1767)
Stat. R.	Statutes of the Realm (11 vols.) (Record Commission, 1810–28)
T.R.H.S.	Transactions of the Royal Historical Society

Preface

The purpose of this book is to describe the growth of the medieval Parliament by placing it in a continuous narrative of political history which is as fully sustained for the periods between Parliaments as during them. The idea for the book was conceived over fifteen years ago after I had completed *The Power of Parliament*, a study of the post-war Parliament in the context of its historical evolution. I had been struck by the fact that, although Parliament is the central theme of constitutional histories, there was no narrative history describing how it emerged and evolved from politics. There is, of course, the great publicly funded History of Parliament which is still being written and which concentrates in detail on the individual members of Parliaments in successive periods, their biographies, interests, political connections and constituencies. These volumes give short accounts of the governments and the political background of the periods they survey. But their immediate concern is not with Parliament as an agent and instrument in the unfolding of political history. Nor, because of its vast scale, is the official History of Parliament designed for the general reader. (The only volumes so far dealing with the medieval period are those covering the period from 1439 to 1509, which were published in 1936.) There exists no general survey of parliamentary history as a whole. A.F. Pollard's *Evolution of Parliament*, published in 1920, might be said to have approached that category but its approach was analytical rather than narrative and although it was a brilliant study, it was criticized for insufficient understanding of the medieval Parliament.

Yet there is a vast scholarly literature on particular episodes and aspects of parliamentary history from the thirteenth century onwards. Every episode and almost every aspect of its development has been investigated in detail. Scholars have scrutinized its origins and often disputed their conclusions, debating the extent to which its original function as the king's highest court remained its dominant feature for its first century or more. They have tried to determine what precisely distinguished a medieval Parliament from a 'great council' of more or less the same composition and they have discussed the importance, or otherwise, of the Commons in early parliamentary history. The influence of Parliament in legislation, the Commons' control over taxation and the development of parliamentary procedures have all been closely analysed. The surviving records and the mass of work on them by medieval historians provide a wealth of information about what the medieval Parliament was and did, and also about how it grew. It is an absorbing and often vivid story of great dramatic, human, political and constitutional interest. Parliament was the product of practical politics, not an artefact of constitutional theory. The work which has perhaps come closest to describing the organic political growth of Parliament has been (despite its title) the three volume *Constitutional History of England*, written at the end of the last century by the great medievalist Bishop Stubbs. This was on a firmly chronological basis and consistently related constitutional change to the domestic and foreign politics, in the wider sense, which brought it about.

In general histories of particular periods, of course, Parliament has a prominent place. Yet in respect of the medieval centuries they tend to discuss it principally in separate sections devoted to the constitution, with occasional references in the political narrative at points where Parliament connects most directly with the major events of the time. In one sense, this approach is understandable. Although it was during the Middle Ages that Parliament established the rights over taxation, privileges and procedures which were to be the basis of its future power, its sittings were of short duration. The political events which determined what happened in Parliament generally took place off the parliamentary stage. Parliament's influence on the greater questions of politics was occasional and usually, though by no means invariably, marginal. Yet if the medieval Parliament is regarded principally in terms of constitutional history and only occasionally in political terms, its history can too easily appear to the twentieth century mind as much less real than the battles, the depositions of kings and even the social history of the time. The continuity of parliamentary history during the medieval period will seldom be more than glimpsed and the important continuity of Parliament from the Middle Ages to our own time will not be understood.

The men who went to Parliament travelled long distances in difficult conditions and felt themselves, Commons as well as Lords, to be taking part in great events as, indeed, they often were. Kings did not take the trouble to call them together simply to make a show. The Lords were powerful men who had to be consulted if government was to be successful, especially in times of war. The Commons formed a bridge between the ruler and the communities he ruled. What the king could learn from the knights and burgesses elected to Parliament about their distant constituents' concerns and especially about their willingness to pay taxes was of great practical importance to him. What the men who went to Westminster could tell their constituents about the decisions solemnly taken by the king in Parliament was important in securing their acceptance. It is true that we know little, though we know something, of what Lords and Commons said when deliberating separately among themselves; the official records usually tell us directly only what happened on the formal occasions of full Parliament when the Commons came before the king and Lords in the Parliament chamber. Nevertheless, in doing so they are often remarkably vivid. Much material exists which can help to bring the medieval Parliament to life, especially if its proceedings are set in their broader political context.

It was because of external political pressures that Parliaments were summoned. This was true whether the cause of summons was the king's wish to enable those with grievances to petition him in Parliament for redress in the interests of more effective government, whether he wanted a solemn occasion for his law-making, or whether he needed money for war. It was true also when Parliament was summoned to give constitutional respectability to a usurper. Whatever the political reasons for summoning particular Parliaments, the accumulation of meetings gradually created an institution accepted as necessary to government.

From its origins to the present day the history of Parliament is seamless. This, therefore, is a narrative of that virtually uninterrupted continuity, beginning with a discussion of the parliamentary idea in the centuries before Parliament existed. It has been written with both the general reader and students in mind. My original intention had been to attempt to cover the entire history of Parliament in a single volume but it eventually became clear that this could only be done in a manner too cursory to meet the purpose. I therefore hope that the present volume will be the first of two, and in the final chapter of this book I have explained my reasons for choosing 1485 as the division between the medieval and modern periods.

By quoting extensively from the original sources, and particularly from the rolls of Parliament, I have tried as far as possible to let the past speak for itself and to allow it to communicate directly with readers. The Parliament rolls are anything but simply dry and formal accounts by officials, though they were written by clerks obedient to the men with power and they could sometimes be doctored for political purposes. From the reign of Edward II, the rolls begin to be increasingly informative politically. They record the opening addresses of chancellor-bishops (which were something between sermons and king's speeches), the statements of Speakers, and the petitions of aggrieved subjects which often reveal an alarming lack of law and order, sometimes reciting in detail sensational cases of outrage. The contents of the rolls offer a window into the conditions of medieval society outside Parliament, recording the anxieties of the Commons, conditions imposed in exchange for taxation, quarrels between magnates and, on rare occasions, words spoken by the king's own mouth. Details of impeachments and attainders and the disingenuous legitimatizing of *coups d'état* are duly written down in the orotund official jargon of the time. With solemn detachment, the rolls record the rightful claim of any king who has just assumed power and the lack of right of the one lately ousted.

I am very conscious, however, of my temerity in attempting to tackle and interpret so large and complex a subject and in treading on the same ground as the many distinguished scholars who have devoted themselves to particular aspects of medieval parliamentary studies. But part of the justification for this book is, I hope, that it will bring something of their specialist work and learning as a whole to the general reader.

I have adopted a basically chronological form because we tend to understand better why things happen if we see the order in which they happen. At various points in the narrative, however, I have paused to summarize the stage reached in the development of Parliament within the constitution, to describe its practices and procedures at that particular time and sometimes to give a broader account of the people, their social condition and the land which Parliament represented. But the continuous political growth of Parliament is the theme of the book and its core is, therefore, not so much the origins of Parliament in the thirteenth century, as its political development in the fourteenth when it became an accepted part of the political process. The years from the accession of Edward II in 1307 to the deposition of Richard II in 1399 were those in which Parliament began to assume its characteristic form and influence, and of those ninety-two years the most important were the long reign of Edward III when the Commons first became an indispensable part of Parliament because the king depended on them to finance his wars.

We cannot, therefore, understand the rise of the Commons under Edward III without some knowledge of the French wars. It is equally impossible to make sense of the crises in Parliament under Richard II without some account of the characters of the men concerned. The same is true at every stage of the medieval Parliament. To interpret parliamentary history during the long and confused reign of Henry VI we must understand something of the character of the king himself, the nature of the struggle among the magnates and the impact of the French war. Likewise, Richard III's single Parliament is only of interest when it is placed in the context of that most extraordinary of usurpations. In this book each king has his own chapter (with the exception of Edward V who never ruled) on the principle that every one of them was as much a head of government as a modern prime minister, each stamping his own mark for good and ill on his reign.

The dramatic interest of medieval parliamentary history steadily intensifies as the records illuminate with increasing brightness the detail of how things happened as well as what happened. But through the stark contrast between the externals of medieval politics and those of our own time we are also offered something more. Together with the unbroken thread of continuity between then and now, the differences can help us to understand the urge for power common to all societies more clearly than may be possible simply by contemplating our own over-familiar political ideas and practices.

Note on quotations: In quotations from original sources, those in Latin or Norman French are given in translation. I have, however, sometimes added in brackets the quotation (or an essential part of it) in the original language. This is partly because it may be useful for history students. But the principal reason is that the original modes of expression can help to give life to what is being described, which is why I have also given in their unmodernized form those quotations from sources written in English. The precise way in which people speak and the flavour of their words and formulations can give an insight into the way they think.

In Norman French quotations I have generally extended words which the clerks conventionally abbreviated by means of suspensions and contractions. They are given in a full form, normally one that would have been current at the time. For example, *ñre* becomes *nostre* (*notre*); *v̄re* becomes *vostre* (*votre*); *ple* becomes *parle*; *plement* becomes *parlement* and so on. Abbreviations in Latin quotations are similarly extended. In quotations from middle English I have generally retained the 'y' used in the printed parliamentary rolls to stand for the runic 'thorn' Þ, signifying the 'th' sound. But in some passages, where there is a risk of confusion (for instance with 'y' as in the second person plural 'ye' or as in 'yassent' for 'the assent') I have altered the symbol to 'th'. Where 'z' is printed for the Middle English symbol 'ȝ' as in 'zour' (your) I have retained it.

As well as giving references to the original source of quotations, I have also added references to modern printed collections of documents where they are most accessible, including those in translation. A general note on references is in the select bibliography.

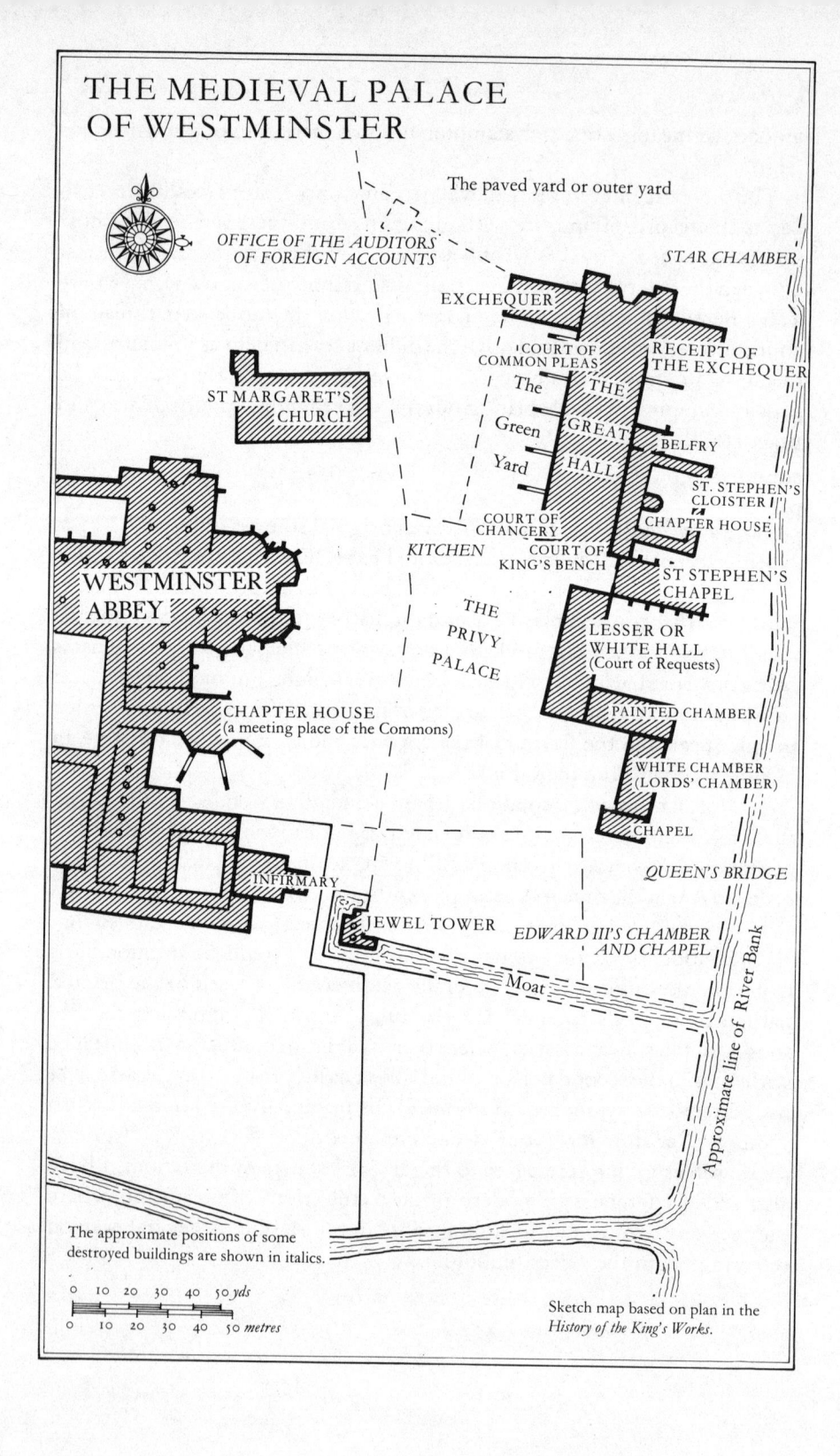

THE MEDIEVAL PALACE OF WESTMINSTER

The paved yard or outer yard

OFFICE OF THE AUDITORS OF FOREIGN ACCOUNTS

STAR CHAMBER

EXCHEQUER

ST MARGARET'S CHURCH

COURT OF COMMON PLEAS

RECEIPT OF THE EXCHEQUER

The Green Yard

THE GREAT HALL

BELFRY

ST. STEPHEN'S CLOISTER

COURT OF CHANCERY

CHAPTER HOUSE

KITCHEN

COURT OF KING'S BENCH

ST STEPHEN'S CHAPEL

WESTMINSTER ABBEY

THE PRIVY PALACE

LESSER OR WHITE HALL (Court of Requests)

PAINTED CHAMBER

CHAPTER HOUSE (a meeting place of the Commons)

WHITE CHAMBER (LORDS' CHAMBER)

CHAPEL

INFIRMARY

QUEEN'S BRIDGE

JEWEL TOWER

EDWARD III'S CHAMBER AND CHAPEL

Moat

Approximate line of River Bank

The approximate positions of some destroyed buildings are shown in italics.

0 10 20 30 40 50 yds
0 10 20 30 40 50 metres

Sketch map based on plan in the *History of the King's Works*.

The Palace of Westminster

The old Palace of Westminster was roughly divided into the 'great palace,' of which the centre was Westminster Hall, and the 'privy palace' which extended south of it. The 'great palace' included the law courts in Westminster Hall, the Exchequer and other buildings used for the administration of government to which there was public access. The privy palace housed the king, the queen, officials of the royal household and favoured noblemen. The most ancient of the medieval buildings were those of the privy palace, from which Old Palace Yard has derived its name.

The first Palace of Westminster was built for Edward the Confessor. Nothing of it remains. It was replaced by buildings constructed piecemeal by Norman and Plantagenet kings. Of these only three survived the great fire of 1834. These were Westminster Hall, the now heavily restored crypt of St Stephen's chapel and the Jewel Tower, which was built on land belonging to the Abbot of Westminster, outside the precincts of the palace proper, to house the king's wardrobe and jewels.

Westminster Hall was by far the largest building of the old palace. Built by William Rufus in the last decade of the 11th century, it was 240 feet long and 67 feet wide. It was, and is, the largest medieval hall in England, though Rufus himself was said to have regarded it as 'too big for a chamber and not big enough for a hall.' The structure of Rufus's original walls, refaced, is still substantially intact at the lower levels below the present great windows. But the Hall was substantially reconstructed by Richard II between 1394 and 1401, the work being finished in the reign of his supplanter, Henry Bolingbroke. Its outstanding new feature was the magnificent hammer beam roof weighing 660 tons and made of oak from Hampshire which had been transported to Westminster by river from Chertsey.

The great hall, however, was not a place of normal parliamentary assembly. Throughout the middle ages and up to the 18th century its most regular use was as the home of the law courts. The court of common pleas sat at the north end of the hall by the west wall and near the entrance to the Exchequer. The chancery and the king's bench were on a dais at the southern end, near St Stephen's chapel, with a bench which may have gone from wall to wall and with a marble chair on which the chancellor usually sat. This seat was also used by kings at their coronation banquets and both

Edward IV and Richard III seated themselves on it as a symbol that they had taken possession of the throne. For the great hall was also the scene of many state and dramatic occasions, including the gathering at which Richard II was deposed. But in parliamentary terms its only normal use was as the place where the preliminary proclamation of the opening of Parliament was made and where the 'Cry' was heard against carrying weapons or playing games during Parliament.

The buildings normally used for meetings of Parliament itself at Westminster were all to the south of the great hall, through which they were approached by Lords and Commons. They were in origin part of the king's home, Parliament being summoned to assemble where the king lived, that being the seat of government.

Immediately south of the great hall, and more or less in alignment with it, was the White Hall or Lesser (as distinct from the Great) Hall. This is only recorded once as having been used for a parliamentary purpose, when the Commons were instructed in 1368 to go to *'la Petite Sale.'* The Lesser Hall became the Court of Requests for the hearing of petitions but in 1801 it was adapted to become the new House of Lords to accommodate the enlarged peerage after the union with Ireland.

To the south east of the White, or Lesser, Hall was the Painted Chamber (*Camera Depicta*) where Parliaments were normally opened, Commons as well as Lords being present. This room had been the bedchamber or great chamber of Henry III and had been built on the basis of an existing 12th century structure. (It was also reputed to be the site of the room in which Edward the Confessor had died.) The Painted Chamber was 80 feet 6 inches long, 26 feet wide and 31 feet 9 inches high. It was paved with glazed tiles, had an embossed and boarded ceiling, a doorway to a small chapel and derived its name from magnificent wall paintings. Near the door was painted the aphorism '*Ke ne dune ke ne tine ne prent ke desire.*' (*Qui ne donne ce qu'il tient, ne prend ce qu'il desire*). After the fifteenth century the paintings were neglected and were eventually covered with whitewash, remaining concealed until what was left of them was revealed in 1819. Water colour copies were made by Edward Crocker and Charles Stothard from which reconstructions of the original were made by Professor Ernest Tristram (1882–1952). These hang in the present Palace of Westminster. The most notable of them is 'The Coronation of St Edward the Confessor,' the 13th century original of which was over Henry III's bed in the Painted Chamber.

Medieval Parliaments at Westminster were opened in the Painted Chamber with a speech on behalf of the king by the chancellor or some other minister, who declared the causes of summons. To these opening assemblies the Commons, or some of them, came before the king and Lords.

Afterwards, the Lords departed to a comparatively small room known as the White Chamber (not to be confused with the White Hall) just south of the Painted Chamber. This was a two storey building built, or rebuilt, by Edward II. The upper room became known as the Parliament House and then the House of Lords, which it remained until the peers moved to the former Court of Requests (the White Hall) in 1801. It was in the small White Chamber that the Lords deliberated on their own or with the king present, and to which the Commons (represented by a delegation headed by the Speaker) were summoned when it was necessary to call them back to appear before king and Lords after the opening ceremony in the Painted Chamber.

The Commons' own meeting place for most of the medieval period was not in the Palace of Westminster itself. In the earlier decades of the fourteenth century they used the Painted Chamber after it had been vacated by the full Parliament. But after 1352, apart from the one occasion when they are known to have been despatched to the Lesser Hall, they used the Chapter House of Westminster Abbey, the Painted Chamber being left for their committee meetings with the Lords. From 1397, however, the refectory of Abbey is their generally recorded meeting place and they ceased to use the Chapter House.

Three other buildings in the palace which were associated with Parliament must be mentioned. The finest jewel of the cluster of buildings at the heart of the palace was the high gothic chapel of St Stephen, inspired by the Sainte Chapelle in Paris, begun by Edward I and completed by Edward III. It replaced a Norman chapel said to have been built by King Stephen. It was parallel with the Painted Chamber from which it was separated by cloisters. After the Reformation, St. Stephen's Chapel was to be given to the Commons as their House in the reign of Edward VI. With its gothic ornamentation panelled over, it then remained the House of Commons until it was burned down in the great fire of 1834 which destroyed most of the rest of the old Palace as well.

Beyond the White Chamber, or Parliament House, was the Prince's Chamber, which was perhaps the room to which the Black Prince, just before his death, called the Commons in order to obtain a grant from them. Another room occasionally mentioned in the parliamentary records is Marcolf's chamber where the triers of Gascon petitions met and which was also the scene of the dispute between Richard II and Gloucester. It is thought to have lain near the river. A feature of the palace was the clock or bell tower in a paved yard north of Westminster Hall.

CHAPTER 1

——— * ———

Prelude to Parliament: from Witan to Magna Carta

I

PARLIAMENT had no sudden genesis. It arose gradually from the medieval court and council where Plantagenet kings consulted the great men of their realm to secure support and offered their people justice. Yet the deepest parliamentary roots lay in the consultative customs of the Anglo-Saxon people from the time of their first settlement in England. In primitive societies as much as in advanced states, government needs the consent of those whose opposition could undermine it. Attempts to rule simply by force are almost invariably thwarted sooner or later by the rise of greater force. The purpose of consultation, however, is not only to seek consent but to obtain information. Effective government in any kind of society requires wrongs to be put right, and this cannot be done unless the ruler is made aware of what needs remedy, and what kind of remedy seems advisable. The need for advice, support and information was as real for the kings who ruled the first separate English kingdoms among the forests of their new land as it is in twentieth century Britain.

In the earliest history of the English people, the communities and kingdoms were those of kindreds and tribes. Kings governed kindreds; the two words have a common derivation.[1] In such closely knit groups, some of which were at first probably little more than very extended families, both kings and those who counselled them would naturally act within the constraints imposed by the traditions and the law which they received from their forbears. As in any other society, the decisions reached, and the law

[1] 'King' has perhaps too grand a sound to our ears to convey an accurate description of early Anglo-Saxon leaders. 'Chief' might seem to serve better, but 'king' is the English word and we must use it.

that was declared, had in the last resort to be protected by the sanction of force. But this no more diminished the importance of consultation and consent for them than it does for us. From the earliest centuries when there was a number of Anglo-Saxon kingdoms, to the single English kingdom under the royal house of Wessex, there is written evidence that consultation was a persistent characteristic of a king's government and of his declarations of law. The six centuries between the arrival of the first pagan Anglo-Saxons and the conquest of their Christian descendants by William of Normandy saw the making of a civilization which was as remarkable for the effectiveness of its political administration as it was for its artistic achievement. Counsel and consent, custom and law, were at the heart of it.

Custom and the facts of power would indicate whom the king should consult, and in what manner. His natural advisers were the elders; the men of strength, standing, influence, experience and knowledge, who were known as the Witan. They were the Anglo-Saxon forerunners of the Norman and Plantagenet kings' court and council, and of the Parliament which was to grow from the post-Conquest council. The early Plantagenet Parliament (in which the king or the government acting in his name was central) was the highest court of the land in the judicial sense. It was also the occasion for law-making by the king and for tax-granting by his subjects. Perhaps most important, the medieval Parliament became the means by which the king consulted the 'representatives' of the political nation of the time. These attributes of the medieval parliament also appertained in some degree to the Norman and Plantagenet council. They were even more characteristic of the pre-Conquest Witan which was the guardian of the custom of the early English people and can be said to have acted in a sense as their representative.

The word 'representative' in this context, however, carries no implication of any elective process, since a lack of election does not necessarily mean a lack of representation. The idea that individuals or classes can only be represented by someone in whose election they themselves have taken part is a comparatively recent notion in parliamentary history. Edmund Burke defined 'virtual representation', as existing where there was 'a communion of interests, and a sympathy in feelings and desires between those who act in the name of any description of people, and the people in whose name they act, though the trustees are not actually chosen by them.' He thus expressed a concept of parliamentary representation which held throughout the 17th century struggle for parliamentary liberties, and persisted at least until the first Reform Bill.[1] If the principle of virtual representation can be applied to the parliaments of the 18th century with

[1] Burke's *Works*, Vol. III: Letter to Sir Hector Langrishe, 1797.

their rotten boroughs, there seems to be no logical reason for resisting its application to the earliest assemblies of the English nation – even though only those men whom the king chose, or felt obliged to choose, were present. By the same logic, there seems to be no justification for denying some genuine parliamentary attributes to the Witan, the king's chosen councillors of Anglo-Saxon England, who deliberated in the light of a strong concept of the age-old law of the 'folk'.

A meeting of the Witan, like a meeting of Parliament, was an occasion for political deliberation and law-making, and it cannot be denied some attributes of representation, provided that term is used free of any anachronistic idea of election or choosing by those represented. Yet it was usual not long ago to resist connecting the Witan with Parliament. This was partly in reaction against those 19th century historians who claimed much greater and more precise representative influence for the Witan than it had possessed, and who over-emphasized the practices of pre-Conquest government as the fount of all our liberties. (The myth of the free institutions of the Anglo-Saxons, and of their corruption by the Norman Conquest, had likewise been used as propaganda by 17th century parliamentarians against the Stuarts.) The true connection between the institutions and customs of pre-Conquest England and the emergence of Parliament became lost for too long in a sterile argument between the pro-Saxon and the pro-Norman schools of history, the one seeing in pre-Conquest history the origins of all English civic virtues, and the other finding no substantial contribution, and indeed little that was meritorious, in Anglo-Saxon society.[1] We have progressed beyond this way of thinking, and now recognize the remarkable cultural, artistic and intellectual achievements of the early English people, not least their gift for government and administration. Yet until comparatively recently the older historical arguments left their mark on our view of parliamentary history.[2] We do not hesitate to accept the emergence of Parliament from the great

[1] This attitude was expressed in its most ludicrous form by Carlyle when (slavishly following the 12th century Norman bias of William of Malmesbury) he described the Anglo-Saxons as 'a gluttonous race of Jutes and Angles capable of no grand combinations; lumbering about in pot-bellied equanimity.'

[2] In his *Evolution of Parliament* (1920) Professor A. P. Pollard wrote: 'Even English liberties appeared in an alien guise and there is hardly a word or phrase in the law and custom of the British constitution that is Anglo-Saxon in origin. To the "liberty of the subject" the Anglo-Saxon tongue has only contributed the article and the preposition; and "vote", "franchise", and "suffrage" are all extraneous terms. Court, council, and parliament, judge and jury, inquest and verdict, alike come from abroad; and the Englishman cannot perform a single civic or legal duty, or exercise a single political function, from parish court to parliament, without using a word or expressing a thought unknown to his Anglo-Saxon forbears. It was this vast importation that made it possible to construct our English state out of the raw

council of Norman and Plantagenet kings, but still sometimes shy away from associating Parliament with the Witan for fear of being accused of historical sentimentality. Yet between the Normans' council (*consilium*, or applying a later term to it, *magnum consilium*) and the Anglo-Saxons' Witan, there was no essential difference of function or composition. The Witan had no elective element, but neither had the enlarged Norman or Plantagenet council, or the first Parliaments. It was not until Parliaments had existed for nearly a century that elected representatives became a necessary part of them. In some respects, the Witan were more representative than the early Plantagenet enlarged councils or Parliaments. For the pre-Conquest councils included thegns who were of a lower status than the narrow class of baronial tenants-in-chief who comprised, with the prelates and officials, the Norman or Plantagenet king's enlarged council. In addition, the Witan were more representative of the wider community in the sense that, unlike the Norman baronage, they were of the same race and tradition as the majority, and used the same language.

Together, king and Witan were the highest authority in the nation, whether the nation was one of the earlier separate kingdoms (sometimes no bigger than a single shire of a later time) or the single kingdom of the English which was gradually created after Alfred by the supremacy of the royal house of Wessex. The Witan were in either case a largely aristocratic body, though they also included the king's household officials and retainers. There is no warrant for reading any 'democratic' implications into the occasional enlargement of meetings of the early Witan by applauding 'folk' present on important and dramatic occasions. Yet as well as the Witan in the earlier Anglo-Saxon period, there did exist popular local assemblies, the 'folkmoots', where men could invoke the law, and where an accommodation could be reached between a claim for dues sought by the king's officials, and a man's own calculation of what he owed. There was, however, no more any legislative function in these early popular local assemblies than there was a popular element in the Witan. Yet both Witan and folkmoot prepared the ground for the emergence of Parliament.

If the meeting of the Witan was the forerunner of the king's great council, from which Parliament grew, the folkmoots were the ancestors of the shire courts, created by the Anglo-Saxons, and continued by the Norman Kings,

---

material of Anglo-Saxon tribes' (Pollard, p. 6). Yet it does not follow that the origin of political institutions is necessarily indicated by the language in which they are named. The Normans, as the governing class, brought their language to the institutions of government. But they relied heavily on the administrative system they took over, which was far in advance of anything they had known in Normandy. It is very doubtful for instance whether the Domesday book could have been produced in the duchy.

in which the first representatives of the Commons in Parliament were chosen. Indeed, in many cases, the unit of administration known as the shire was a development of earlier tribal divisions, or had even been a separate kingdom. Long before the Norman Conquest, the shire courts had largely lost whatever popular element had been attached to them in the time of the early English settlements. As the number of ordinary peasant freeman gradually declined in Anglo-Saxon England, the shire courts came to be dominated by the class of thegns, who were often possessed of considerable land and were not altogether unlike the later knights, serving the king or other greater men such as ealdormen or, later, earls. Before the Conquest, the shire courts had already become an extension of the king's power, and were presided over by the sheriff (or shire-reeve) who was the king's official. Nevertheless, the shire court never lost the attribute of being deemed to represent the freemen of the community of the shire as a whole, and it was in this capacity that later medieval kings were to use it as their instrument for keeping the peace and administering the law in the district, as well as for selecting freely chosen knights to do service in Parliament.

In the earliest separate kingdoms, and also later in the single kingdom of the English, the Witan met only when they were summoned by the king. The Witan were the wise ones, in the sense that they were the ones that 'knew' – the men with the knowledge to advise the king.[1] Knowledge meant then, as it continued to mean in parliamentary history, not simply the wisdom or the background of understanding which enabled them to comment on what the king proposed to do, but the knowledge, which he might otherwise lack, about what needed to be done. Parliament has remained an invaluable channel of communication through which a government learns, particularly through its own supporters, of changes in the tide of public opinion and of new problems requiring solution. But today a government has many other means of communication to inform it. A thousand years ago, and for centuries thereafter, a king had only two means of gaining information about the state of his kingdom; through his counsellors, and through his own travel about its sparse and scattered settlements. Anglo-Saxon kings combined both methods available to them of gaining information. They travelled extensively and persistently through the vast forests of the land and from time to time they assembled meetings of the Witan as they went from place to place.

From the earliest years of the Anglo-Saxon period, there were nobles, freemen, and serfs, but the broad basis of Anglo-Saxon society had at first been the free peasant landowner, or landholder. By the time of the Norman

---

[1] 'Wita' means one who knows (the plural is witan); cf the sense of both the modern German *wissen* and the modern English 'wise' and 'wisdom'.

Conquest, most of the free peasantry, who had originally had no lords between themselves and the king, had gradually lost independence through the practice of commendation. This was an arrangement by which the less powerful landholder (whether thegn or freeman) surrendered his independence and gave personal service, or paid dues, to a more powerful lord in return for protection, whether because of economic or other pressures.[1] Yet despite the spread of this dependent quasi-feudal relationship, the Anglo-Saxons retained a deep-rooted tradition of freemen's rights, a respect for the law, and an ineradicable conviction that the most important acts of government, and particularly the function of law-making or law-declaring, were naturally carried out with the advice of the Witan who counselled the king.[2] (The word 'witenagemot', meaning a meeting of the Witan, was not, however, commonly written before the 11th century.) The Witan, when they met, included the king's immediate retainers, officials and household ministers, who provided him with advisers sufficient for ordinary daily purposes. These regular officials would have been as much the nucleus of any meeting of the Witan as they were later of the Norman king's council. But a meeting of the Witan was much more than that.

It was a vaguely composed assembly sometimes larger, sometimes smaller according to place and circumstances. Comparatively large gatherings of notables often played a decisive part in settling important questions, and in approving law-making. Bede tells us that when King Edwin of Northumbria had been brought by Paulinus almost to the point of abandoning paganism and accepting Christianity, he still felt that he should 'confer with his chief men and counsellors' before his final decision. 'Holding a council with his Witan' (*habito enim cum sapientibus consilio*), he asked each one what he thought of the new teaching. In response, one of the noblemen (in one of the most poetic similes in English history) likened a man's life to the brief flight of a sparrow through the firelit hall in winter, while the king, his ealdormen and thegns sit at supper. If, said this nobleman, Christian teaching brought greater certainty about what went before, and what is to follow this brief life, it seemed right that it should be followed. 'Other elders and counsellors of the king continued in the same manner', Bede tells us, and it seems clear that on this occasion, the Witan

---

[1] The agreement involved in commendation was, however, often breakable and renewable. It varied in terms from one case to another, and it did not involve either submission to a lord's jurisdiction or the holding of land in strict fief from a lord, which was to be the essential attribute of feudalism proper. It seems to have been less formal than the feudal tie.

[2] '... the earliest English Communities were primarily communities of law.' J. E. A. Joliffe, *Constitutional History of Medieval England*, p. 6.

were freely deliberating before a decision involving the highest policy was taken.[1] Edwin was baptized at York in the year 627 on the eve of Easter.

The most consistently used function of the Witan, however, was that of assenting to legislation, that is to say to the process of discovering and declaring the law as it was deemed to have long existed. The first English settlers had brought with them from Germany a system of laws and customs, with penalties for breaking them, and also a process for trying lawsuits, at first before the folkmoot, and later at the shire or hundred court. When it seemed to an Anglo-Saxon king that the law, or part of it, should be declared, enlarged or codified for the sake of certainty and clarity, he issued his code with the advice of the knowledgeable and powerful counsellors whose consent was needed. For instance, when King Wihtred of Kent issued a code of law, probably in the year 695, he called together (as the prologue to the enactment put it) 'a deliberative assembly of leading men... There with the consent of all, the leading men devised these decrees and added them to the lawful usages of the people of Kent...'[2] Likewise, the laws of King Ine of Wessex (in about 694) were enacted by 'Ine, by the grace of God, king of the West Saxons, with the advice and with the instruction of ... (my bishops) along with all my ealdormen and the chief councillors (Witan) of my people...'[3] The formula used by this early king of Wessex is not so very different from the preamble of a statute in the 20th century.[4]

Towards the end of the ninth century, Alfred composed a much more comprehensive code of law (based on the codes of former kings) for the English in Wessex and beyond it. 'I, then, Alfred, king, gathered these (laws) together, and commanded many of those to be written which our forefathers observed, those which seemed to me good; and many of those which seemed to me not good, I rejected them, by the counsel of my Witan, and ordained otherwise. For I dared not set in writing at all many of my own, because it was unknown to me what would please those who would come after us. But those which I found anywhere, which seemed to me most just, either of the time of Ine, my kinsman, or of Offa, king of the Mercians, or of Ethelbert, who first among the English received baptism, I collected here, and omitted the others. Then I, Alfred, king of the West Saxons,

[1] Bede's *Ecclesiastical History of the English People* (Edited by Colgrave and Mynors) Oxford Medieval Texts; Book II, Chapter 13 (OUP 1969); also *English Historical Documents, c500–1042*, ed. Dorothy Whitelock, Vol. I, p. 671–2 (second ed.).

[2] *E.H.D.* Vol. I, p. 396.

[3] *E.H.D.* Vol. I, p. 399, and Stubbs, *Select Charters*, (in Anglo-Saxon, with translation) p. 67.

[4] 'Be it enacted by the Queen's Most Excellent Majesty, by and with the advice and consent of the Lords Spiritual and Temporal, and Commons in this present Parliament assembled, and by the authority of the same, as follows....'

showed these to all my Witan, and they then said they were all pleased to observe them.'[1]

It appears, then, that Alfred, not unlike a modern government, himself prepared and proposed his law code (with the help of his permanent writing office) after which it was given the legal force he felt it needed by the consent of the Witan, in much the same way as a Parliament today is asked to pass legislation prepared by ministers and their officials. From the preamble to this law code, it seems clear that the Witan on this occasion was a body with a much larger, wider and more 'representative' attendance than the inner council who would have helped the king to draw up the law. In other words, it was a deliberative assembly. Further, although in the composition of such codes, the king was in theory merely declaring the existing law of the folk, he was also in reality making law. If Alfred dared not write much that was new, at least he could add something to what had gone before. There are some important provisions in his laws which are not derived from any known source, and which may therefore be original.[2]

The importance of the Witan in ratifying agreements and assenting to declarations of the law is instanced time and time again in the preambles to the decrees and treaties of Anglo-Saxon kings. The prologue to the treaty of 886 between King Alfred and the Danish King Guthrum, which established the boundary of the Danelaw and other agreed terms of peace, stated: 'This is the peace which King Alfred and King Guthrum and the councillors of all the English race and all the people which is in East Anglia have all agreed on and confirmed with oaths, for themselves and for their subjects, both for the living and those yet unborn, who care to have God's grace or ours. . . .'[3] It would be hard to deny the representative overtones of this declaration. Again, the terms in which King Athelstan (924–939) announced a series of penalties for law-breaking is revealing: 'I, King Athelstan, make known that I have learnt that our peace is worse kept than I should like . . . and my councillors say that I have borne it too long. . . . Now I have concluded, along with the councillors who have been with me at Christmas at Exeter. . . .'[4] This seems to be a clear reference to the meeting of the large council which was probably customary at Christmas and at other great annual festivals. Indeed, under Athelstan there was (to judge from the names of the witnesses to his charters) a great enlargement to include, not merely the ecclesiastics, the ealdormen (governors of shires whose offices

---

[1] Stubbs, *Select Charters*, pp. 69–70 (extract in Anglo-Saxon, with translation); also in E.H.D. Vol. I, pp. 408–16 (translation).
[2] F. M. Stenton, *Anglo-Saxon England* Third Edition (p. 276).
[3] Select Charters, p. 72.
[4] E.H.D. Vol. I, p. 422.

tended to become hereditary) and king's thegns, but also magnates from every part of a realm which now included the re-absorbed Danish lands.

For instance, a meeting of the Witan at Luton in 931 included the two archbishops, two Welsh princes, seventeen bishops, fifteen ealdormen, five abbots and fifty-nine *ministri* (the Latin version of thegns).[1] The normal attendance at a gathering of the Witan in Athelstan's reign was, however, about 60 or 70, laymen and clerics, and the principal change compared with earlier times was the greatly increased number of laymen, compared with clerics, who came from all parts of the enlarged realm with which the king had to keep in touch. Though each one of the Witan was dependent on the king's nomination, such gatherings seem to have been very like national assemblies, with Danish names as well as English now recorded, and many localities 'represented'. Throughout the Anglo-Saxon period, kings recorded the obligation they felt to act with the approval of the Witan, though the notice any king took of that assembly, and the ability of the Witan to inhibit any of his actions, must have depended on the strength or weakness of each king and his advisors. What cannot be doubted is that discussion and advice were considered to be natural in Anglo-Saxon society when important matters affecting the nation were in question. '. . . I have been inquiring with the advice of my councillors, both ecclesiastical and lay, first of all how I could most advance Christianity. . . . First, then, it seemed *to us all* (my italics) most necessary . . .' wrote King Edmund I (939–946) in the prologue to his code concerning the blood-feud.[2] Similarly, the law code issued by King Edgar (959–975) at Andover begins with the statement: 'This is the ordinance which King Edgar determined with the advice of his councillors, for the praise of God and for his own royal dignity, and for the benefit of all his people. . . .'[3] Edgar, the stability of whose reign in many respects represents the peak of the Anglo-Saxon monarchy in all England, left behind him a lasting tradition of itinerant inquiry and consultation which persisted after the Conquest. The 12th century monkish chronicler, Florence of Worcester, wrote of the king's travels 'winter and spring' throughout the realm, and of his diligent search to find how the laws were kept and whether the poor were oppressed.[4]

As well as being a deliberative and law-consenting national assembly of notables, the Witan were frequently consulted before extraordinary taxation was levied. That, however, did not happen often. In anything like normal circumstances, Anglo-Saxon kings were expected to live off the

---

[1] This seems to be one of the fullest surviving lists: Stubbs, *Constitutional History* (5th ed.), Vol. 1, p. 140.
[2] *E.H.D.* Vol. I, p. 428.
[3] *Ibid*, p. 431.
[4] *Chronicon ex Chronicis* (year 975) ed. B. Thorpe English Historical Society (1848).

food-rents and other customary dues from their lands. The only evidence of general taxation raised by the king and the Witan is that concerning the 'heregeld' (a tax to support the army) during the reign of Ethelred the Unready, and the Danegeld to pay the Danes for peace. (Whatever its political unwisdom, the Danegeld at least testified to the remarkably effective centralized administration under the old English monarchy which made its levy feasible.) Thus the Anglo-Saxon Chronicle for the year 1002 states that 'the King and his councillors determined that tribute should be paid to the fleet and peace made with them on condition that they should cease their evil doing . . .' Again, in 1012: 'In this year, Ealdorman Eadric and all the chief councillors of England, ecclesiastical and lay, came to London before Easter . . . and stayed there until the tribute, namely 48,000 pounds, was all paid. . . .'

A much more regular function of the Witan was giving consent to the issue by the king of charters authorizing the transfer of land. It is the lists of individual 'signatures' or marks to these charters which provide most of the available evidence of the composition of meetings of the Witan. Throughout the old English period, kings regularly made grants of 'bookland' under royal charter, as distinct from the 'folkland' held by custom. Whereas the customary services and food-rents for folkland were in the ordinary way paid to the king, a charter could transfer their benefit to another lord, perhaps as a reward for service he had given to the king. (The king, however, would normally reserve to himself the duty of service in the fyrd, the national military muster, in respect of such land.) The creation of bookland, which had originated in donations to the church, provided evidence of a 'title' to land held by its new lord who could both collect the dues from it and pass it on to his heirs.

The charters recording the transfer of bookland (which were normally in Latin) are known as diplomas, in distinction from writs, which were simpler documents in English, witnessed by the king's seal and conveying his instructions or information to the local authorities. Athelstan's diplomas were written in elaborate and decorated Latin to mark their importance and it was probably as more than passive witnesses that each member of the Witan present set his or her (for sometimes the king's wife or mother was present) name to each charter. When a king gave away part of the source of his income (his peasant's food-rents) it concerned the community as a whole. Such charters were made at meetings of the Witan in all parts of England. Their named witnesses included Welsh princes, archbishops, bishops, ealdormen (and later the earls who superseded the ealdormen as provincial governors in Cnut's reign) and thegns. From the earliest charters of the separate kingdoms, through the golden age of the old English monarchy from Alfred to Edgar, and up to the Norman Conquest, the witness lists testify to the spread of interests and functions represented by large meetings of the Witan. Almost always, the marks of witnesses testified that they had 'consented' as well as 'subscribed.'

In such lists the 'official' element (that is to say, the ealdormen or later the earls, with the king's own thegns) predominated, and usually the greater number of those present at a gathering of the Witan came from comparatively near the meeting place. With the difficulties of travel, this was bound to be so and it is not surprising that there were always comparatively few representatives from the north. Even so, the Witan could sometimes have a more 'national' character as is suggested by a document stating that a council of Ethelred II, held at Cookham in Berkshire, was attended by thegns 'from far and wide, both West Saxons and Mercians, Danes and English.'[1] A detailed analysis of attendances of the Witan in the reign of Edward the Confessor made by Tryggvi Oleson, suggests that the normal witenagemot of the time would include the king, the queen (and the queen-mother before the king's marriage), archbishops, bishops, earls from all over the country and thegns.[2] The ecclesiastics provided 42 per cent of the attestations, and the earls 15.4 per cent (a high proportion of the total number of earls). Most of the earls travelled with the king on his progresses. The thegns made up 36 per cent of the non-royal attendants, but unlike the earls, the majority of thegns in England were not present, to judge from the signature 'marks'. It was Sir Frank Stenton's opinion that this might be explained by the fact that 'the length of a list of witnesses was determined by the size of the parchment on which the charter was written', so that there might have been no room for the less important thegns to make their marks alongside their written names. Stenton therefore considered that the written lists over-emphasize the official element in the assembly.[3] Oleson contested this on the grounds that the scribes would first inscribe the charter, and only afterwards cut the parchment, so that probably all the thegns present made their signature marks. Whichever of these views is correct, it seems clear from Oleson's analysis of the 'signatures' that those thegns who did make their marks were almost invariably from the shires round about the place where the meeting of the Witan was held. This suggests an aspect of the assembly which seems to enhance its ability to reflect local opinion, even allowing for the preponderance of 'official' thegns who were beholden to the king.

[1] Stenton, op. cit., p. 551.
[2] Tryggvi J. Oleson, *The Witenagemot in the Reign of Edward the Confessor*, OUP.
[3] Stenton, op. cit., p. 543.

Coming from all over England, the earls would have been able to convey something of opinion in their more distant parts. They, like the king's close thegns and officials, seem to have travelled with the king wherever he went. But most of the thegns needed to make up a witenagemot were provided by those who could conveniently join the king on his progress at particular places, that is by those who came from comparatively nearby. It was inevitably so since travelling distances in England were huge, and habitations were separated by vast stretches of forest. It would be far too disruptive for thegns from all over the country to travel to every witenagemot, though some might do so on extraordinary occasions. It was simpler for the king to travel to successive regions in turn (living off his own lands as he went) and dealing with any local matters on the spot. In each place, therefore, the king could deliberate with thegns (many of them his local officials) who could not only acquaint him with local problems, but might also be said indirectly to provide a sample of the opinions of the loosely-knit class of thegns as a whole. In this way, there could always be enough thegns from different places at any Witan to give the meeting some flavour of 'virtual representation', and there were penalties for a failure to attend a summons. The large number of places at which the Witan are known to have assembled is indicative of the mobility of Anglo-Saxon kings. Between 900 and 1066, meetings of the Witan are recorded at over fifty different places, almost all of which were in the south of England, although very occasional gatherings took place in a few northern towns, including Lincoln, Nottingham and York.[1]

London was the most often used place of assembly, and Winchester another, although neither of these places favoured by the royal household was a capital city in anything like the sense now conveyed by the term. Most of the meeting places were towns, royal palaces or hunting-seats in Wessex, many of them in the west country, and on occasions an assembly of the Witan seems to have travelled on with the king from one palace to another.[2] A royal palace with a large hall, the bishops and the ealdormen or earls being seated, was obviously the most convenient meeting place. It was perhaps at a general meeting of the Witan, although it could have been at a smaller gathering of the boy king Edward's immediate councillors, that a disaster struck in 978. The Anglo-Saxon Chronicle for that year records that 'the leading councillors of England fell down from an upper story at Calne, all except the holy archbishop Dunstan, who alone remained standing on a

---

[1] H. R. Loyn, *The Governance of Anglo-Saxon England*, pp. 100–106, which includes a sketch-map charting the Witan's meeting places.
[2] H. R. Loyn op. cit. p. 104.

beam; some were severely injured there, and some did not escape with their lives'.

The witenagemot was not, then, a corporate body with clearly defined composition.[1] Yet to assert on that account that it had no sort of parliamentary function would be to take a pedantic view of what constitutes parliamentary activity. For the early Plantagenet Parliaments were equally fluid in composition. It would be equally illogical to take a dismissive view of the Witan's 'parliamentary' attributes on the grounds that only political exigencies and never constitutional obligation led to their meeting. This was also true of those 13th century meetings of the great council of the Plantagenets, which are not on that account refused the description of Parliament. The same applies if parliamentary attributes are denied the Witan on the grounds that their assembly consisted only of those whom the king chose or felt obliged to summon. That was also to be true of the Parliaments of Henry III. There is room for argument about which assemblies did and did not constitute Parliaments under Henry III and Edward I according to contemporary definition. But it was not the election of knights or burgesses, or any other particular composition which first produced a Parliament but its functions. Above all, since the principal functions of Parliament over the greater part of its history have been the giving of consent and, in one form or another, representing the governed, it would be wrong to see the Witan as lacking parliamentary characteristics. For they too exercised these functions after the manner of their time. If anything, a gathering of the Witan was more 'representative' of the political nation as a whole (to the limited extent that the nation might wish to be represented) than the feudal tenants-in-chiefs, judges and king's officials which were to constitute the first Parliaments.

The meetings of the later Witan, held on the progresses of an itinerant king, took place in a wide area from Exeter and Gloucester, to Nottingham, Winchester, Sandwich and London. Whether there were regular ceremonial crown-wearings at Christmas, Easter and Whitsun before the Conquest, comparable to those of William the Conqueror, is not wholly clear. But there were probably some special meetings at these festivals, and there were certainly assemblies of the Witan at times of important political decision, and also when it was necessary to recognize a new king. The reign of Edward the Confessor provides a notable insight into the political importance of the Witan, in the matter of the out-lawing and the in-lawing of Earl Godwin. The ambitions of this earl, who had been promoted by the

---

[1] 'In a very real sense, then, there is no such thing as a witenagemot, there are only witan. There is no council, there is only counsel.' Oleson, op. cit. p. 61.

late Danish king Cnut from obscure origins, played a large part in the politics of the Confessor's reign. Godwin's power was an unhappy legacy which Edward had to accept though the king had great personal reason for hating Godwin who was suspected of being implicated in the murder of Edward's brother. In 1051, however, Godwin over-reached himself in an act of defiance against the king. In that year, some men of Count Eustace of Boulogne, who was passing through Dover, killed a townsman and created a brawl in which more lives were lost and property was damaged. Eustace fled to the king at Gloucester, and the half-Norman Edward ordered Godwin to punish the town which was in Godwin's earldom of Wessex. Not unreasonably, in the circumstances, Godwin refused. Instead, he assembled an army. But other earls, with their men, rallied to the king. A truce was arranged and a meeting of the Witan was held in London. When Godwin refused to appear before the Witan without guarantees, he was declared an outlaw, and forced into exile with his sons, including the future King Harold. It was in Godwin's absence that Duke William of Normandy paid Edward a visit, when some recognition of William as his heir may have been made by the childless king.

In 1052, however, Godwin and his sons returned to England with military strength. They attracted support and eventually their army and the king's confronted each other outside London. Both sides, however, wanted to avoid civil war. 'Then it was decided that wise men (that is, men from the Witan) should go between the parties, and they made a truce on both sides.' After this, there was 'a meeting of the Witan, and Godwin was given (back) his earldom unconditionally'. (Anglo-Saxon Chronicle, versions C and D.) Or, in another version (Anglo-Saxon Chronicle E): 'Then a big council was summoned outside London and ... Earl Godwin expounded his case and cleared himself before King Edward ... and before all his countrymen. ...' If the assembly of the Witan which had outlawed Godwin had acted at Edward's behest, this second gathering had clearly taken an initiative which the humiliated King could not possibly have welcomed. It had no doubt acted partly in response to Godwin's military strength. But the Witan's final decision in Godwin's favour also reflected the increasing unpopularity of the Norman-French party at Edward's court (the king's mother was Emma of Normandy) during Godwin's absence. Policy was reversed and Edward could not resist it. Promising 'the full benefit of the laws to all people', the Witan outlawed those Frenchmen of whose loyalty they could not be assured. After Godwin's death in the following year, the dominant political figure for the rest of the reign was his son Harold.

Edward was without children and there was no adult candidate for the succession from the royal house of Wessex. In the final years of his reign there began the remarkable sequence of interlocking events which led to the Norman invasion. The exile of Harold's brother Tostig (at the insistence of the Northumbrians of his earldom) turned him into an enemy whose invasion, with Harold Hardrada of Norway in September 1066, was to make it much harder for Harold to resist William successfully a few weeks later. The sea voyage of Harold some two years before Edward's death, when he fell into William's hands, and was said to have promised the throne to the Norman duke, seemed also to have the mark of fate on it. Finally, there was the fact that Edward died when he did, on January 5, 1066; had he survived until his nearest male relation had become adult, the old English monarchy might have outlasted him.

Edward died at Westminster, just after the consecration of his new abbey there. As he had been ill for some time, there was opportunity for a large number of the Witan to assemble, though there remains no record of who was present. In any case, a larger than ordinary gathering of the Witan would have been customary for the Christmas meeting. The question for the Witan was who should succeed. Was it to be Edgar the Atheling, the grandson of Edmund Ironside, who had lately been brought back from exile into which his family had been driven when the Danish Cnut had taken the throne of all England on Ironside's death? He was the nearest heir of the blood, but he was only 13. Or was it to be William (who was related only by marriage to the English royal house, his great-aunt Emma having been the wife of Ethelred), or Harold, the most powerful man in England? The Anglo-Saxon monarchy had been hereditary in the royal family of Wessex, apart from the interruption by conquest of the Danish kings, but the crown did not always descend by strict primogeniture. The presumption was that a king should be succeeded by his eldest son, provided that son was capable of ruling. If on the other hand the son was too young, which was the usual reason for bending the succession, the crown would pass to the closest and most suitable blood relation, in most cases a brother of the late king. Subsequently the succession might or might not revert to the more direct line. In such circumstances, the Witan must have had an important influence on the succession. Yet to say that they possessed anything like a right of election as we understand the term would be to go far beyond the evidence. Nor did they exercise any right of deposition.

Sometimes the Witan would simply have to acquiesce in the facts of power politics, and accept a king imposed by force. Thus, on the death of Edmund Ironside, who had been forced to divide the kingdom between himself and the Danish Cnut, the Anglo-Saxon Chronicle simply recorded laconically: 'In this year, King Cnut succeeded to all the kingdom of England.' No reference was made to the Witan. When, after the Danish interlude, Edward the Confessor returned to England and obtained the throne, the Chronicle observed that 'all the people then received (another version says "chose") Edward as king, as was his natural right.' If, by observing strict succession, the crown would pass to an heir who was too young, or who was in some other way incapable, the first and decisive moves determining who should be the next king were probably made by members of the royal family in agreement with the most powerful of the Witan. The succession would then be recognized by the Witan, a procedure which was something far from election. If the heir by primogeniture was obviously suitable to succeed, there can have been no role for the Witan except formally to acknowledge him as king.

There is no evidence that the Witan set about nominating a candidate for the succession in January 1066, or debating the succession. When Edward died it must have seemed clear straight away that Edgar the Atheling was unsuitable to face the expected challenge from Duke William. A regency would not have commended itself to the thinking of Anglo-Saxon England. The man accepted as having the capacity to rule should be given the authority of kingship, just as the king in name should be capable of ruling. There was no near kinsman to take Edgar's place, and to the Witan which had so recently seen the royal line set aside by Danish kings, there must have seemed nothing shocking in accepting Harold Godwinson to represent the native English and defend them from foreign attack. Edward himself seems to have recognized this on his deathbed, and his action in bringing back the heirs of Edmund Ironside suggests that he may already have abandoned whatever intention he may have had of promoting William's succession.[1]

The Chronicle says that Earl Harold 'succeeded to the realm of England, just as the king had granted it to him, and as he had been chosen (by the Witan, or some of them) to the position.' The probably contemporary *Vita Aedwardi Regis* records the dying king as saying to Harold: 'I commend this woman (the queen, who was Harold's sister) with all the kingdom to your protection.'[2] The Witan assented, and to the extent that their assent was necessary in pre-Conquest England, the likelihood is that on such an occasion their essential function was to give legitimacy to the only succession which made political sense.

Several conditions were needed for succession to the old English throne.

---

[1] Edmund Ironside's heirs were his son, Edward the Exile, who died almost immediately on being brought back to England; and Edward's two younger children, Edgar the Atheling, and Margaret who married the king of Scots, whose daughter married Henry I, thus connecting by blood the Norman and Plantagenet kings with the Wessex dynasty.

[2] *Vita Aedwardi Regis* (Anon.) Edited by Frank Barlow (Nelson, 1962).

Prelude to Parliament: from Witan to Magna Carta

The candidate should have the nearest possible blood relationship to the previous king compatible with other qualifications. He should be of the old Wessex dynasty if at all possible, but he must be capable of ruling, his succession, where possible, should have the approval of his predecessor, and he should be acknowledged as king by the Witan. The last three of these conditions were fulfilled when Harold became king despite the claim by blood of the boy Edgar the Atheling. Nine months later, after he had been killed and the English defeated at Hastings, an attempt was made to restore the crown to the old line. Those of the Witan who were then in London, led by Archbishop Aldred of York and the Earls Edwin and Morcar chose Edgar the Atheling as king. But it was too late to solidify English resolve. After William had laid waste the countryside in a huge circle around London, Edgar tacitly abdicated and came out to submit to William, who was accepted as king. On Christmas Day he was crowned in Westminster Abbey and the old English state came to its end.

Reading the laws and utterances of the old English kings, and the chronicles of their times, it is impossible not to be struck by the strong sense of political responsibility of the rulers to the ruled which comes to us across the centuries. The Anglo-Saxon king was custodian of the law, custom and justice, and in some degree the Witan shared that custodianship with him. He consulted them on great law-giving and political occasions as a matter of course, and in a manner which shows the enlarged Witan to have been something much more substantial than either his personal servants or potentially threatening feudal magnates whose strength he must heed.[1] The Anglo-Saxon king was not generally a ruler in a state of tension with his nobles or people and the Witan were limited by, and represented, the custom of the people.[2] The Norman council of tenants-in-chief functioned in a very different political atmosphere. Yet gradually the old processes of consultation, consent and a concern for the law revived, and from the 13th century onwards found their expression through parliamentary representation. It is hard not to believe that the peculiar strength of the parliamentary ideas of consent and representation, and of the rights of freemen, owed more than can be proved to the political characteristics of kingship and of the Witan in the old English state.

---

[1] 'There are very few matters of importance to the state on which an Anglo-Saxon king cannot be shown to have consulted his council.' Stenton, op. cit. p. 552.

[2] 'Its weaknesses are apparent. Its composition was indefinite and gave too little influence to the nobility of northern England. It was dependent on the king for the right to meet and it cannot have possessed any idea of inherent unity. But in however narrow a form, it gave the character of a constitutional monarchy to the Old English state.' Stenton, op. cit. p. 554.

II

The fate of the nation in 1066 was determined by coincidences and accidents of personality so extraordinary that if they were fiction they would seem much more dramatic than convincing. If Edward the Confessor had not been childless, or if his nearest kinsman had been more than a boy, the Norman invasion might not have been attempted, or might at least have met with greater resistance by both leaders and people. If chance had not forced Harold to fight at Stamford Bridge immediately before Hastings, his generalship against the Normans might have been more effective, and even if the English had been defeated in that first battle, they might have been in better shape to offer sustained resistance to William afterwards. On the other hand, if the Normans had landed before the Norwegians, and Harold had succeeded in beating them in Sussex, the battle-weary English might afterwards have succumbed to the Scandinavians in the north. The momentous cultural link between England and France would then, in all probability, never have been forged. Above all, so risky a venture as the transport of the Norman army across the sea, with its horses which were crucial to the Norman victory, would never have been attempted by a leader with less determination than William, and even under him might well have failed. The whole direction of English history was changed by the fact that this remarkable man existed, and by the circumstances that aided him.

Yet these accidents on the narrative surface of history seem, as so often happens, to have fulfilled some deeper current of historical inevitability. Despite their great cultural tradition and their maturity in government, the English people, or at least their leaders, appear to have lost their political vigour and cohesion. Whether because of the deep-rooted divisions inherited from their recent internal wars and the conquest of Cnut; or because of the enervating and precarious peace of Edward's reign, and the deterioration of the royal house of Wessex, the English seem to have lacked the will to resist a self-confident challenger. Their failure to offer any coherent resistance after Hastings was more significant than their defeat in the battle itself. All they achieved after Hastings was enough resistance to ensure their own destruction as part of the political nation. Despite the good fortune that had assisted William, the English nobility seem to have fallen into a condition in which they would have needed luck not to be somebody's prey.

So, with the vigour of their recent Viking past given form and organization by their latinized veneer, the Normans subdued a more mature civilization and planted a new, and parvenu, military aristocracy in place of the old English nobility. The consequences for the nation's political development were profound. Here it is worth taking into account another 'if'. Had the English accepted William without resistance instead of making him fight for the crown, both at Hastings and later, it is possible that he, like Cnut, might have ruled more like an English king and less as a conqueror. In that event, the English landed classes might not have been almost entirely dispossessed for the benefit of the Normans, as they were by the end of William's reign. A smaller number of Norman landholders might have been anglicized more quickly, and political institutions, including the king's council, would have developed differently. As it was, England became a land of two races: French (as the Normans usually called themselves in England) and English, the first ruling the second. It was a country under military occupation, and although the Norman infusion was small in numbers, it had radically altered the national culture, language and political structure by the time the two peoples had merged into one. As a conqueror, William was able to impose a political unity on his mixed English, Danish and Norman subjects of the kind that the Anglo-Saxon kings, even when they made their most advantageous treaties with the Danish settlers, had never achieved, or even sought.

Yet William claimed to be the rightful heir of Edward the Confessor, and the preserver of the laws of Edward's time, and at the start of his reign he appeared willing to work with the old order. He retained the old English episcopate for several years, even using the services of the Anglo-Saxon Archbishop Stigand of Canterbury, schismatic and pluralist though that prelate was alleged by the Normans to be. William also kept a number of Anglo-Saxon earls on his council. Such men were needed at first to teach the new king and his servants the ways of the English administration. An early charter of William's reign shows Anglo-Saxon and Norman prelates and nobles, whose names are given as witnesses, side by side in council.[1] This harmony, however, did not last. Perhaps it could not. As castles went up throughout the land, and heavy taxes were levied; as the lands of Englishmen killed at Hastings and Stamford Bridge were given to Normans, nothing could disguise the English subjection. In the years 'immediately after the Conquest,' as the author of the *Dialogue of the Exchequer* wrote a century later, 'the conquered English used secretly to lie in wait for the suspect and hated race of Normans and clandestinely slay them in woods and secret places...' After 'exquisite torments' had failed to

---

[1] *E.H.D.* Vol. II, 1042–1189, ed. by David C. Douglas & George W. Greenaway. (2nd ed.) pp. 644–646.

stop this, the King ordered that 'the hundred in which Norman was found slain should be sentenced to pay a large sum to the Exchequer... unless the killer appeared or his identity was revealed by his flight. This was done, they say, in order that everyone should hasten to punish such crimes or to surrender the guilty to justice...'[1] This much abused process, known as the murder fine or the presentment of Englishry, was not abolished until the reign of Edward III, when an act of Parliament repealed it. During William's absence in Normandy, the oppression of his two regents, his half-brother Bishop Odo and William Fitz-Osbern, stimulated the first of a series of ill-coordinated rebellions with which England was riven from 1068 to 1072, and which completed the ruin of the English thegnhood.

These rebellions were put down with punitive ferocity, and the north of England was so laid waste that at the end of the reign much of it was still desolate. It was this period of rebellion which brought about the wholesale dispossession of landed Englishmen. By the end of the reign, when the Domesday survey set down the facts about land possession, stating from whom all land was held, and who held it in Edward's time, only about 8 per cent of land remained in English hands. Of the considerable number of tenants-in-chief, or barons, who held their land directly from the king, only two seem to have been Englishmen, and they were not large landholders. About half the land in England was in the hands of the King's Norman followers, and half of this was concentrated in the possession of only ten magnates. Of the rest of the land, one fifth was the king's demesne, and another quarter was held by the church. Thus a closely knit foreign aristocracy was established in England and, with it, a new feudal relationship which was different in one fundamental sense from the system of commendation by which an Anglo-Saxon would give his service in return for a more powerful man's protection. The basis of the new order was land. Every man held his land from someone under the king (at least in theory) though it was not a very neat structure and barons sometimes held land from other barons. The outstanding feature of the system was the *servitium debitum* which obliged the landholder to furnish the king with a stated number of trained and equipped knights, who were simply equestrian soldiers. They too had land, the knight's fee, in return for their service.

With such a huge transfer of land to a small and alien military aristocracy, and the replacement of almost all the Anglo-Saxon bishops by Normans or other foreigners within a few years of the Conquest, the style of government and the kind of consultation practised inevitably changed. Yet William

---

[1] *Dialogus de Saccario*, I, x, edited by Hughes, Crump and Johnson, p. 99. Extract printed in Stubbs, *Select Charters* pp. 218–219.

introduced few new institutions. He continued to use the shire and hundred courts: indeed, the sheriff after the Conquest became a more powerful figure than he had been before it.[1] The Conqueror largely maintained the laws of his predecessors, his own distinctive contribution to penal history being the forest law which imposed ferocious penalties on anyone killing game in any forest, whether it was on the king's land or not. The forest law was the source of grievance which was to be a recurrent subject of petitions in the earlier years of Parliament. In the conduct of government, the king's council or court was also, on the face of it, a continuation from the witenagemot which it replaced, fulfilling the same functions and also being dependent on the king for its summons.

In reality, however, there was a profound difference between the Norman *curia regis* or *concilium*, and the old Witan. For the Norman council was essentially feudal in composition and of foreign origin. It was a baronial assembly of tenants-in-chief, even prelates now being present principally in their capacity as tenants. It had neither the traditions nor the customs of the older gathering. We possess no detailed knowledge of the Norman council's deliberations; yet they must have been very different in atmosphere from those of the Witan. The attitude of new masters speaking a language different from that of the mass of the people was bound to produce a different relationship between the nobility and the common people. This difference was heightened by the rapid decline in the status of the old Anglo-Saxon freemen, and the fall of many of them into serfdom. The most important political relationship was now between king and barons and it tied them together in reciprocal support. King and magnates were bound together by the shared interest in the Conquest and the deliberations of the council were dominated by that fact. Yet eventually, there were to emerge from the 'contractual' element in the relationship between king and barons political tensions which would bring about constitutional changes of fundamental significance for the development of Parliament. The Norman feudal order itself was to become the source of the first challenge to the power of the post-Conquest crown and its claims were to lead to the writing of the statement of liberties in Magna Carta of which Parliament came to be the guardian.

It is also possible to discern under the Conqueror an incipient distinction between the king's wider consultative council of magnates (which would eventually seek to maintain some kind of control over his successors) and his ordinary court, or inner council of officials and close baronial associates. From the larger baronial council there emerged in later times the *magnum*

---

[1] The 'hundred' was a territorial unit of administration and jurisdiction, with its own hundred court, at a lower level than the shire.

concilium and Parliament. The business of the larger council was advice. The smaller council was the executive arm of the king's government. The distinction is far from clear cut, and the words *concilium* (or *consilium*) and *curia* were interchangeable. When William I held a council of any sort it would, indeed, generally be described as holding a court. Both the (greater) council and the (smaller) court were aspects of the same body and of the same process of advising the king. The men present at either sort of meeting were those whom the king had chosen to counsel him in given circumstances. Sometimes the *curia regis* of everyday government would be enlarged by adding to the household officials and to the king's ordinary baronial associates other barons drawn in for special occasions. At other times there would be a full assembly of tenants-in-chief, which it is convenient to describe as a great council, though this was a term not generally used until much later. Yet whatever form it took at particular times, the court or council could perform the same sort of functions. It could be an advisory body, a court of law (both in the judicial sense and in the sense of declaring the law) and an executive. The distinction we make between a law court, legislation, administration and advice would not then have been understood. The king's court was omnicompetent. Whether at a great council which was an advisory, consultative and political occasion, or at more routine meeting of the king's court, the same sort of people were present, though the balance between magnates and officials would be different. Even so, the germ of distinction that was emerging between the smaller and the larger sort of assembly under William I was strong enough to develop further under his two sons.[1]

From the *curia regis*, in its everyday form, grew the royal chancery which produced writs and charters. The Anglo-Saxon kings had a writing-office, but William appears to have introduced the official known as the chancellor. The *curia regis* also inherited responsibility for the remarkably efficient administrative and financial system of the old English kings. Another later offshoot from the *curia* was the court and the payments office of the Exchequer, where the fiscal and financial business of the kingdom was settled and the sheriff accounted to the crown for the taxation and dues he had received from his shire. These dues included the king's income, or *feorm*, from his demesne in each shire, and also the shire's contribution to Danegeld, which William had revived, the king's feudal dues from the shire, and various fines due to the crown. (The amounts paid to the king

---

[1] '... the same body, whether large or small, was a royal council, a court of justice, or a general assembly, according to the needs of the moment; it exercised executive, judicial, or legislative functions alternatively without clear discrimination.' J. F. Baldwin, *The King's Council in England during the Middle Ages*, p. 4 (1913).

through the Exchequer in each case were those which remained after each sheriff had deducted the king's and his own, expenses.) In short, the *curia regis* was the very distant ancestor of the modern executive, the Cabinet acting for the authority of the crown. It was also developing embryonic government departments, the chancery, the treasury and the Exchequer.

The greater council, on the other hand (the larger body of feudal counsellors) was the ancestor of the representative element in government, Parliament. Yet William's great baronial council, being separated from the majority of the people by the harsh fact of conquest, cannot have had the same self-identification with the folk and the custom of the folk as the Witan had possessed. In any case the style of government in Normandy had been very different from the traditions in England. A small military state of comparatively recent foundation, the duchy seems to have been ruled by personal decisions of the duke tempered by outbursts of baronial rebellion. The council which advised the Norman dukes consisted of kinsmen and personal adherents, who seldom differed from their leader and were largely dependent on him. Some of the characteristics of this personal government were no doubt carried over into the government of England, particularly in the aftermath of conquest. In the Norman king's council in England, William's word was law, whatever the feelings of the council. In 1070 or 1071, a court held in Somerset heard a plea from Bishop Wulfstan (one of the two Anglo-Saxon survivors among the episcopate) against the Norman archbishop of York concerning some disputed property. Wulfstan would not use the time available to him to rebut his opponent's case; instead he preferred to pray and say the holy offices. When the king asked him what counsel he had obtained, he replied simply: 'My counsel is with you.' On hearing this, despite the Norman sympathies of the council present, the king gave his verdict for Wulfstan.

The assembling of the tenants-in-chief in the great council took place largely on formal and comparatively infrequent occasions. The only version of the Anglo-Saxon chronicle to survive after 1079 (continuing doggedly to record events in the vernacular) has left us a famous description of William on such occasions. 'Also he was very dignified. Thrice he wore his crown every year, as often as he was in England; at Easter he wore it at Winchester; at Whitsuntide at Westminster; at Midwinter (Christmas) at Gloucester; and then were with him all the rich (powerful) men over all England, archbishops and bishops, abbots and earls, thegns and knights.'[1] Such ceremonial meetings gave William the opportunity to consult with all the important men of the land, and would be an occasion for settling baronial disputes. Sometimes important decisions of policy were also taken. At

[1] Anglo-Saxon Chronicle, 1087, the year of William's death.

Christmas 1085 when the king wore his crown and was 'with his court for five days' (the archbishops and clerics holding a parallel synod) the Chronicle records that 'after this the king had deep discussion with his council about this country – how it was occupied or with what sort of people.' The 'deep discussion' could have been in the greater council, or in meetings of the smaller everyday council augmented by some of the most important magnates. But it is quite likely that it was in the larger gathering, and perhaps in their deliberations about property, that the questions recorded in the Chronicle were first raised. The outcome was the great inquisition that led to the compiling of the Domesday Book.

Yet such councils were not occasions for the great declarations of law which characterized the Anglo-Saxon centuries, nor is there the slightest evidence that they were much concerned with matters affecting the wider community. They were feudal assemblies concerned with feudal problems and the consolidation of conquest. The old ringing phrases about the advice and consent of the Witan are no longer found. Sometimes, as in William's writ ordering the separation of spiritual and temporal courts, he would state that he had so ordained matters 'by the common council and counsel' (*communi concilio et consilio*) of all the prelates and 'of all the magnates' (*omnium principum*).[1] Sometimes the king might use them for political purposes, as when he summoned his councillors and all landowners (whether they were his vassals or somebody else's) from all over England to swear allegiance to him at a great gathering (described in the Peterborough Chronicle as his Witan) at Salisbury in 1086. This was a meeting intended to be an antidote to some of the aspects of feudalism that seemed potentially dangerous to the crown, and it was essentially a feudal occasion.

Sometimes, however, a Norman king might find it expedient to look a little wider, and when faced with the rebellion of his Norman barons, to make promises of good government to the English nation as a whole in return for their help. Thus the Conqueror's ill-reputed successor, William Rufus, more than once called on the native English to defend him against baronial revolts, which the English were prepared to do since they felt the exactions of the magnates more than the more distant hand of the king. The Anglo-Saxon Chronicle for 1088 records that, faced with the treachery of the barons at the start of his reign, Rufus 'sent for Englishmen and explained his need to them and asked for their help, and promised them the best law that there had ever been in this country, and forbade every unjust tax and granted people their woods and hunting rights – but it did not last

---

[1] Printed in Stubbs, *Select Charters*, p. 99; translation, *E.H.D.* Vol. II, p. 647.

any time.' The politics of Rufus's reign remained no more than baronial strife and the wider nation played no part in counselling the king.

The same is true of the much more effective king (but still more disagreeable personality) who succeeded to the throne after the mysterious death of William Rufus in the New Forest in 1100. Henry I, the second of the Conqueror's sons to rule England, began the 'charter of liberties', with which he inaugurated his reign, with the statement that he had been crowned king by the mercy of God and 'by the common counsel of the barons of the whole kingdom of England' (*communi consilio baronum totius regni Angliae*).[1] The Chronicle more realistically observed that on Rufus's death, 'the councillors who were near at hand chose his brother Henry as king.' Yet apart from a broad declaration against 'unjust' exactions, and a polite but generalized bow to the law of King Edward, almost all the liberties with which Henry's charter was concerned were feudal, and the redress that was promised related to the grievances of his barons not those of the wider nation. (One exception, perhaps, was a promise to abolish what was called the *monetagium*, a kind of sales tax, which was introduced by the Conqueror and was collected throughout the cities and counties, but which, as Henry I's charter put it, 'did not exist in King Edward's time'.) But even as a feudal document, Henry I's charter contained no hint of any bargaining between king and barons, and no guarantees. It was no more than a manifesto of Henry's willingness, for the sake of stable relations with the barons, to end his brother's abuse of the king's right to exact certain dues from feudal estates. The document was to be of importance in the mythology of English liberties because it provided a precedent for Magna Carta. But it was not the product of wide deliberation between the king and his great council, and it was witnessed by only a handful of magnates, prelates and officials. Sometimes, however, it suited the king to be able to say he had consulted his counsellors, the barons and chief men of the kingdom. He did so, for instance, both in his negotiations with Rome and over the choice of his second wife, according to Eadmer's contemporary life of Archbishop Anselm.

Yet despite his charter and efforts to improve relations with the barons, Henry's rule began with a baronial rebellion, just as Rufus's had, though this time it was put down with greater ease, again with the help of the English. Much of Henry's reign was taken up with fighting in Normandy against his brother Robert who held the duchy (while often contending with baronial unrest in England at the same time). Henry finally conquered

---

[1] Stubbs, *Select Charters*, p. 117.

Normandy and re-attached it to the English crown, which had the effect of preserving the Norman characteristics of the barons of England, and delaying their anglicization. War in Normandy also had constitutional consequences since it kept Henry out of England for much of his time, with the result that arrangements had to be made for the government to be carried on in his absence. This was done by a new 'aristocracy' of officials, the most important of whom was the justiciar who was even enabled to issue writs in his own name. The crown was withdrawing from reliance on governing through the baronage, and was developing its inner council of professional ministers in the interests of centralized government. This, however, encouraged a pent-up baronial reaction which burst out in the so-called Anarchy of the disputed succession after Henry's death.

This conflict gave a new impetus to the influence of the barons which, in more ordinary circumstances, they would have exerted through the greater council. After the loss of Henry's son and heir in the wreck of the White Ship, the king had obliged the barons, at a Christmas court of 'all the chief men, both clerics and laymen', to swear allegiance to his daughter Matilda. But the oath to obey a woman was taken only with the greatest reluctance, and when Henry I died in 1135, after thirty-five years on the English throne, the barons ignored Matilda's claim. Instead, they immediately accepted as king Count Stephen of Blois, the son of the Conqueror's daughter, and a man with considerable estates in England. So began a time of conflict between Stephen and Matilda when the barons were free to build castles and wage private warfare as they chose. Even if the chroniclers tended to generalize too freely from the many acts of terrorism which were committed, there is no doubt that the Anarchy caused a breakdown of centralized order and baronial power. It was characteristic of the time that the number of earls, which the first three Norman kings had kept small, was sharply increased. These men, from the most powerful Norman families, claimed substantial local powers and, disregarding the weakened crown, often took the law into their own hands, behaving with tyrannous cruelty and almost regal pretensions. The reign of Stephen showed that although king and barons were part of a single system, in which each recognized the place of the other, there was also a natural tension between them which, when the crown was weak, would produce a reaction against its centralizing tendency. Towards the end of Stephen's reign, a peace was negotiated between himself and Matilda's son, Henry Plantagenet of Anjou, under which the crown was to be held by Stephen for the rest of his life, and would pass thereafter to Henry. In 1154, Stephen was succeeded by Henry II.

At this stage, then, some of the seeds of future constitutional development were already set. After the subjugation of the English, and the planting of the Norman baronage, consultation might have withered to little more than the bargains struck among the striving members of the new ruling class. Either a weak king fencing with a powerful feudal nobility hard to control, as in France, or an all-powerful king using the nobility as his janissaries to rule a conquered land might conceivably have been the outcome of the Conquest. Neither happened, largely because of the Norman kings' deliberate decision to use the English institutions they had inherited, especially the sheriff and the shire court which became vehicles of the king's authority against the jurisdictional claims of independent magnates. The adoption by the Norman kings of the Anglo-Saxon writ, in which pre-Conquest rulers had tersely and succinctly communicated to the shires their decisions and instructions in the vernacular (uniquely so in Europe) buttressed the kingly authority further, albeit the post-Conquest writs were in Latin. The new kings also continued to travel the land, when they were in it, and to send their commissioners to find answers to particular questions, or to call into the shire or hundred courts those who could speak for the local community, and provide information in what was virtually a representative capacity.

Even the feudal idea played its part in the evolution of accountable government. Though both king and feudal nobility recognized their need of each other, the tensions between them were to be increasingly important in preventing the power of the crown from becoming arbitrary. For if the king could claim to stand for the nation's law against the private will and jurisdiction of individual barons, the feudal idea of a contract related to land could also tacitly imply the idea of a broader political contract between king and magnates which was ultimately breakable if the king flouted understood custom. The barons were to struggle against the crown only in the interest of their own feudal 'liberties', but the idea of liberties eventually seeped out to the wider community. Further, if the notional 'contract' between king and barons was not unconditional, and might even be dissolved on certain conditions, might not the same apply to the tacit contract between king and nation? That would be the question implicitly posed by the political struggle that led to Magna Carta and the constitutional conflicts that arose in the centuries after it.

In the Norman and Plantagenet reigns, feudal differences between king and baronage repeatedly interacted with the historic claims of the English people to law and custom. If it suited them, both king and nobles would seek to enlist the support of wider elements in the community. When kings evoked the concept of the law of the people, and made statutes for the whole realm, they reinforced an idea of law which was to become stronger than the crown itself. Likewise, when the magnates of the realm obliged the king to heed them on the grounds that they were his natural advisers, they were paving the way for an evolving society in which, well before the middle ages were over, kings would be expected to consult a wider community represented by the Commons in Parliament, and would indeed see good reason for doing so in their own interest. The reign of Edward III was to be pivotal in the king's acceptance that the Commons had a useful political voice. Successful medieval kings acted on the general assumption that to take counsel was a source of strength and not of weakness. It was usually the weaker kings who resisted it. 'I commit myself and the people of the whole kingdom of England to your counsel and to the counsel of those who ought to advise me,' wrote Henry I, on his accession, to Archbishop Anselm. Who those were who 'ought' to counsel the king was determined by custom and the politics of power at any time. Yet counsel was the heart of medieval politics and from the concept of counsel emerged the idea and practice of Parliament.[1]

III

Henry II, king of the English, Duke of Normandy, Count of Anjou and Duke of Aquitaine, ruled over a disparate collection of possessions stretching from the borders of Scotland to the Pyrenees. Nothing united the dominions of what was once misnamed the Angevin empire other than the person of the ruler to whom these territories had come by inheritance or marriage. Henry Plantagenet, who was more foreign than any king since the Conqueror himself, spent over two-thirds of his long reign out of England. Yet under his rule, the English nation began to emerge again as something like a single entity for the first time since the Conquest. The author of the *Dialogue of the Exchequer*, a contemporary account of how that institution worked in Henry's reign, observed that 'with the English and Normans dwelling together, and alternately marrying and giving in marriages, the races have become so fused that it can scarcely be discerned at the present day – I speak of freemen alone – who is English and who is Norman. I

---

[1] 'It was rather the king's privilege than his duty to receive counsel... A feudal monarch had to dread the isolation not the union of his liegemen.... It was only a weak or tyrannical king – a John or a Richard II – who neglected to ask counsel; for the ruler who acted without the advice of his great men distinctly outraged the moral feeling of his day.' Dicey, *The Privy Council* (1887) pp. 2–5.

except, however, the bondmen, who are called villeins, and are not permitted, if their lords object, to change their status.' That exception was, however, a big one. As a consequence of the Conquest many of those ceorls who had been freemen, and who perhaps might still strictly speaking be accounted free, had sunk to a position of virtual bondage and dependence on a feudal lord. The unfree may have been as much as three-quarters of the whole population, and there had probably been very little fusion at this broad base of society. What is more, the author of the *Dialogue* was probably describing what he saw in London, which was certainly not representative of the country as a whole. It was among the freemen of towns, and particularly those of London (now for the first time appearing as something like a capital city) that most fusion had taken place.

Culturally, French had almost entirely ousted English as the language spoken by anyone who wanted to rise in the social scale. The Anglo-Saxon Chronicle had ceased to be compiled (although here and there the vernacular was still being written) and French, as well as being the language of social aspiration, also had the advantage of being the common tongue throughout the Angevin possessions. Men of English and mixed descent who were ambitious, especially perhaps the better off citizens of London, needed a full command of French for public life and for successful business, whether or not it was the language of their homes, as it often must have been now that many had Norman forbears. But English remained the speech of the poorer sort of Londoners, as it did of the mass of people in the countryside, and the upper classes needed to speak it well enough to communicate with their dependants and bondsmen. The linguistic division was largely one of class, but the line was not rigidly drawn. There is evidence that some families of knightly rank spoke English in their homes; where this was so, it was presumably a consequence of their own family's origin, or perhaps of distance from an urban centre where the influence of French was strong. But when all reservations are made, and the bilingualism of large numbers of people is taken into account, French was now the language of government and of the upper classes, just as Latin was the language of the law as well as of the church. When Parliament emerged in the following century, French was to be used in its official proceedings and in the record of its business. It would be over 200 years before the English speech of the majority of the people, shorn of its ancient inflections, and having absorbed a large French vocabularly, would be heard in the king's presence in Parliament, and would go on wholly to replace French as the speech of all classes.

Henry II's ability as a ruler, and the general peace he gave to the country during his 35 years on the throne, assisted the political integration of the two language groups in England, despite his frequent absence for war in France. He was a restless man possessed of relentless energy which he knew how to put to constructive use. Impatient and ill-tempered, he was always on the move from one part of his dominions to another. Yet Henry was an efficient and businesslike ruler with an urge for good government. Determined to re-establish a law-abiding kingdom, he made sure that he was served by men of intellectual and political quality. England was of particular importance to him because, alone of his possessions, it gave him the rank of king. His first need, therefore, was to bring the country to order. After his accession to the English throne his immediate task was the dismantling of the unlicensed baronial castles built in Stephen's reign, and the reassertion of the crown's rights against baronial encroachments. He then set about augmenting the scope and power of the royal courts against the rival jurisdiction of the barons' manorial courts, putting the common law on the firm foundations of royal authority. The means he used were to have important consequences for the evolution of statute law and Parliament's future part in making it. But he was equally concerned to protect the lay law from church pretensions. As it happened, his efforts to do so provide the clearest illumination we have of the emergence of the greater council as a political body foreshadowing the main functions of the future Parliament.

Since he was so often away from England for long periods, the king could govern effectively only by delegating his authority to his ministers. Like his grandfather, Henry I, he used a justiciar to whom he gave power to act in his name, and he employed other administrators who were not necessarily from the baronage. The success with which the reformed royal government administered and taxed in the king's name was bound eventually to arouse baronial resentment, and under Henry's successors this would be expressed in the greater council which was now clearly distinguishable from the inner council of the king's executive ministers. Meanwhile, the greater baronial council, or 'the king's common council', was already moving towards becoming an occasional deliberative assembly which was anxious to be heard and concerned to see that the king should take its advice. Moreover, Henry II himself virtually encouraged the barons in his common council to think of themselves as a political gathering by consulting them and seeking their support. Sometimes he turned to the baronial council in order to obtain a basis of legitimacy for his intended actions in much the same way as Henry VIII turned to Parliament to legalize his break with Rome. The outstanding instance of this arose from the most famous of medieval disputes over ecclesiastical jurisdiction. The king's quarrel with Thomas Becket, Archbishop of Canterbury, provides us with the earliest detailed evidence to survive of the great council in session.

During the long quarrel between king and archbishop, the great baronial council, with a large attendance and the king presiding, was the scene of debate of an embryonic parliamentary character. The outstanding occasions were the councils held at Clarendon, near Salisbury, and at Northampton, both in 1164. As chancellor, Becket had been Henry's personal adherent and friend. As Archbishop of Canterbury he became a challenge to the royal authority. The seeds of the conflict had been set when William the Conqueror caused a separation of ecclesiastical from lay jurisdiction, by issuing a writ which forbade cases concerning 'the rule of souls' to be heard in the hundred courts. Instead he had reserved such cases for church courts where ecclesiastics were to try them in accordance with canon law. Churchmen then ceased attendance at both shire and hundred courts which had been former practice. At the same time, the church courts had come not only to exercise jurisdiction over both laymen and clerics (or clerks), in respect of moral, including sexual, offences. They also claimed exclusive jurisdiction over ecclesiastical persons, however serious the crimes of which they were accused, as well as over ecclesiastical causes.

During the century since the Conqueror's ordinance, the ecclesiastical courts had steadily advanced their activities at the expense of the king's courts, and the years of anarchy during Stephen's reign had particularly strengthened their position against that of ineffective lay justice. For one thing, as the church courts were often more efficient than the lay courts, and during the anarchy were certainly more just, they had sometimes attracted litigation of the kind we should call civil. A consequence of the encroachment of church courts was the loss by the royal courts of profits from fines. But it was the claim of the ecclesiastical courts to an exclusive right to judge and punish anyone in holy orders, including minor orders, which most concerned the king. This immunity protected not only priests and monks but also the many clerks who were in minor orders. The penalties imposed by the church were much less harsh than those inflicted by the state at a time when the death penalty and mutilation were common deterrents against lawlessness, and a clerk convicted of a serious crime benefited greatly from being tried in the bishop's rather than a lay court. Since the church courts could not pronounce a sentence involving the taking of blood, even clerks convicted in these courts of murder escaped the death penalty.

Convinced that the light sentences of the church courts were inadequate deterrents against breaches of the peace, Henry was determined to re-establish the jurisdiction of the royal courts, and he almost certainly had Becket made archbishop because he assumed that the worldly man who had served him so well as chancellor would help him to do this. He was wrong. Becket's obduracy and thoroughness were now brought to the defence of what he took to be church interests, just as when he was chancellor they had formerly been devoted single-mindedly to the king's service. For example, the archbishop successfully challenged the king's claim that certain revenues did not belong to the church and should go to the Exchequer. Far more important, however, was the resistance of this stubborn and uncompromising man to the king's attempt to end the abuse of clerical immunity. Henry therefore determined to bring the matter to a head.

At a council held at Westminster in the autumn of 1163, the king declared that spiritual penalties would not deter the many clerks who had committed robbery, rape or murder. He therefore demanded the agreement of Becket and the bishops to his wish that clerks found guilty in the church courts of serious offences, and who were there degraded and deprived of their orders, should be handed over to the king's court for sentence and punishment. The prelates then withdrew to discuss the king's demand, deliberating apart as they sometimes, and the Commons generally, were to do in the Parliaments of the future. In these separate deliberations, Becket persuaded the bishops that the king must be resisted. To sentence clerks in both courts would, in his view, be double punishment, and therefore unacceptable; degradation from clerical orders and loss of livelihood was punishment enough.

When the prelates returned to the great hall, Becket announced their refusal to agree to the king's demand, justifying this by canon law. Henry replied that he did not ask them to disobey the canon law but merely to observe the customs of the realm as their predecessors had done under his. In a great fury, the king went on to demand that the bishops should say whether they would swear obedience to the customs of the kingdom. After consultation, the prelates, under Becket's leadership, each answering individually, conceded that they would do so, but with the qualification 'saving their order'. That ended the council meeting. The bishops' reservation so inflamed the irascible king that he disgraced the archbishop by taking back from him honours and castles he had held since he was chancellor. But Henry II seldom allowed anger to over-master political calculation in the long run. He therefore now set about winning over the other bishops, bringing to bear on them the influence of the Pope whom he had assured that he would not introduce any new customs or require the prelates to do anything against their order. All that was at issue seemed to be the simple qualification 'saving my order', which the king wished to be dropped. Finding that the bishops were moving to the king's side, and that the Pope would not give him the backing he needed, Becket then edged towards compromise. He went to see the king at Woodstock and promised to observe the customs of the kingdom 'in good faith' and to obey the king 'in everything that is right', without other reservation.

That, however, was not enough for Henry who was as persistent as his erstwhile friend. He told the archbishop that there must be a further meeting of the council where words which would restore his honour should be spoken as publicly as the alleged injury to his royal dignity had been. To make sure that he had gained his point, he summoned a great council to meet at Clarendon, the king's hunting-lodge near Salisbury, in January 1164. But when Becket was confronted in the council with the king's demand that he should say publicly what he had already said privately, he gave an evasive response and insisted that he must consult apart with the bishops. The king was furious and two or three days of acrimonious debate followed. Threats linked with promises finally persuaded Becket to give way. Indeed, according to Becket's enemies among the prelates (he had several, including the Archbishop of York and the Bishop of London), the bishops at large were prepared to stand firm, until the archbishop himself suddenly reversed his position in the midst of their private discussions, and virtually betrayed them. But however it came about, Becket led the prelates back into the hall, and declared for himself that he would observe the customs in good faith. The rest of the bishops spoke in the same terms. Yet the king was still not satisfied. He wished to establish without ambiguity which customs were to be observed; those of the more recent years in which the church had expanded its jurisdiction, which was what Becket had in mind, or those of Henry I's reign, which were the customs Henry II wished to enforce. To leave no doubt, the king ordered his justiciar and officials to hold an inquest, or inquiry, and to draw up a formal statement of the customs of the land concerning the jurisdiction of church and state so that it should be given the assent of all the council. Such customs had never before been written down, and the 'record and recognition' that was now made of them was to represent the agreed understanding of the jurisdictional rights of both the church and the king. The council was then adjourned for about a week, after which it met to receive the document known as the *Constitutions of Clarendon*.[1]

This recorded that the 'recognition' of a number of the customs of the land had been made in the presence of the magnates, lay and spiritual, and that Becket and the other named bishops had granted and 'steadfastly promised, *viva voce*, and on their word of truth' that the customs which were

[1] Stubbs, *Select Charters* pp. 161–167 (Translated excerpts in Stephenson and Marcham, *Sources of English Constitutional History*, and *E.H.D.* Vol. II, pp. 766–770).

listed should be held and observed. Becket and the bishops were outraged. It was one thing to give a verbal acceptance of customs undefined, and quite another to agree to 16 articles in writing, which would make future negotiation and compromise almost impossible. But verbal assent to a general undefined principle meant little to a king with a passion for legal clarity and systematic justice. Henry required formal acceptance of a record of the customs which was virtually a declaration of law, and which, like traditional Anglo-Saxon law codes, was to be validated by the agreement of the great men of the land. Much of the document was unacceptable to Becket and two of its enactments were particularly offensive. The first was a provision (clause 3) that criminous clerks who had been tried, convicted and degraded in the bishop's court should no longer be under the protection of the church, but could be removed by the king's officials (who should be present at the trial in the church court) to undergo whatever punishment would be inflicted on a layman guilty of the same offence. The archbishop also strongly objected to a provision in the document that no appeal should go beyond the king's courts, or in other words to Rome. Nevertheless, he contrived to leave Clarendon without another open breach with the king. Resting on his reluctantly given verbal promise to observe the unspecified customs of the realm, Becket avoided putting his seal to a document which transmuted malleable unwritten customs into a presumably rigid written law. On this point, the bishops were with him, and the Pope himself, who had been willing to tolerate a general statement of adherence to the customs, now agreed that written concessions which would permanently diminish ecclesiastical privileges must be resisted.

The Constitutions of Clarendon are not only of significance on account of the light they throw on the conflicting jurisdictions of church and state. They are also of great historical interest because the document sets out the composition of a great council when it met for an important political purpose under Henry II. It stated that a declaration of the customs was made 'in the presence of the archbishops, bishops, and clergy, and of the earls, barons, and magnates of the realm. And these same customs were acknowledged by the archbishops, and bishops, and the earls, barons, nobles, and elders (*antiquiores*) of the realm.' The magnates present included the two archbishops, and twelve bishops, ten earls or counts, twenty-eight named barons or court officials (including the chamberlain, the steward, and the marshall) 'and many other magnates and nobles of the realm, both clerks, and laymen.' The list of names included in the Constitutions indicates that there was a deliberative assembly at Clarendon of well over fifty people at which the rival cases were argued out, often vehemently.

The assertion in the document that Becket had 'acknowledged' the customs undoubtedly stretched the truth. He had simply refrained from further protest. Moreover, he had left Clarendon in a mood of self-condemnation for having conceded so much, and had publicly begun to subject himself to penances in a manner which was a virtual criticism of the king. In the months between Clarendon and the next council, complex discussions took place between Rome and both parties to the English ecclesiastical quarrel. Becket's continued resistance to the Constitutions of Clarendon was blatant and wherever he could he tried to hinder the king's officials from putting them into practice. Henry therefore decided to destroy the archbishop's power once and for all. In October 1164 the king called another 'general council' to meet in Northampton. But the archbishop was not summoned to it individually by virtue of his rank or office, which was the normal practice for lay and spiritual magnates. Instead, he was simply ordered by a writ of the sheriff to appear in order to answer several civil charges which had originally been heard in the archbishop's court. The council, which assembled in the great hall of Northampton castle, lasted for several days, and its often heated meetings were occasions of high political drama. Becket was straightaway accused of contempt of the crown on the grounds that he failed to appear at Westminster to answer the suit of John the Marshal, one of his vassals, who claimed that he had been denied justice in the archbishop's court in a case concerning property. John had therefore appealed to the king's court under the Constitutions of Clarendon, but Becket had refused to appear. Now, therefore, he was summoned to answer the charge before the full council at Northampton. In other words, the Archbishop was to be on trial on a secular matter in the highest royal court.

In fact, John the Marshal did not come before the council, and his suit was not tried at Northampton. That did not matter. His case was an excuse for the king's action, not its cause. The business before the council in reality was not John the Marshal's suit but the archbishop's failure to appear in the king's court to answer it some weeks earlier. Becket's explanations were not accepted, and it was decided that he should be 'at the king's mercy', which meant in theory that his movable possessions were at the king's disposal and, for practical purposes, that he was to be fined. An argument then arose between the barons and bishops about who should pronounce the sentence. The barons argued that the bishops should do it as Becket was one of their order. The bishops contended that it was a secular and not an ecclesiastical judgement, and that they should not have to deliver it. Besides, as bishops, they could not judge their archbishop. Eventually, the king ordered Bishop Henry of Winchester to pronounce the sentence and Becket agreed to pay the fine. The king would have liked then to proceed with a straightforward attack on clerical immunities. But he was persuaded that this would simply unite the bishops with Becket, and he therefore determined to complete the archbishop's humiliation by different means.

First, Becket was faced with demands from the king that he should account for money which had passed through his hands when he was chancellor. This, moreover, was simply the prelude to a more serious attack, for Thomas was then required to account for the proceeds of the archbishopric while it was vacant, and for the revenues of other bishoprics vacant while he was chancellor. These were not charges on which he had been summoned before the council and he would obviously have needed time to prepare his answers. The total sum demanded by the king is not known with certainty but it was probably a large one. For two days over the weekend, Becket consulted with his fellow bishops, some of whom wished him to resign. The proceedings were then held up further because Becket was ill, probably with a stone on the kidneys. When, eventually, the archbishop appeared on the final day of the council, he did so (against advice) carrying his own cross, which would normally have been borne by his chaplain, as though his purpose was to challenge the king with his spiritual authority. 'You are holding your cross; suppose the king wears his sword. What a brave show king and archbishop will make,' observed the Bishop of London, Gilbert Foliot, who was an old opponent of Becket and the chief of the king's friends among the bishops. (When he was asked to protest against Becket's conduct, Foliot also remarked acidly that Becket had always been a fool and always would be.) The king, however, had withdrawn to an upper chamber in order to avoid personal confrontation with the archbishop. From there, often in a rage, he issued his instructions, summoning magnates and bishops to him while Becket fluently stated his case in the hall below. Eventually, the much troubled bishops were excused from judging the archbishop, and took their seats apart from the barons. But the king demanded that a judgement should be delivered by the earls and barons and, according to an eyewitness, 'certain sheriffs and barons of the second rank, men full of years, were also summoned to take part in the judgement'. Curiously, we are not told what precisely the verdict and sentence were, but only that Becket refused to stay to hear them. Making a dramatic exit to abusive shouts from some of the lay lords inside the hall, and applauded by a crowd outside, he left the council chamber declaring that they had no right to judge or sentence him. After retreating to a nearby monastery, the archbishop left it secretly by night, and made his way disguised out of the country and into exile.

Six years of bitter argument and negotiation with the king followed, and on a number of occasions the two met, fruitlessly. Becket nurtured his righteous indignation, even excommunicating some of his foes, including the justiciar whom he blamed for the Constitutions of Clarendon. The Pope, however, annulled these sentences as the English bishops wished. Eventually, in 1170, a superficial reconciliation between the king and archbishop was reached at a meeting between them in France, but on what terms is unknown. The Constitutions of Clarendon seem not to have been discussed, but the king may have supposed that Becket would now accept them, if only tacitly. The archbishop then returned to Canterbury, only to reopen his campaign from the moment of landing in England. During his absence abroad, Henry had had his young son crowned according to a continental practice of the time, in order to make the succession sure. The archbishop of York had performed the ceremony, with six other bishops assisting him. Becket's first action on his return was to pronounce sentences of suspension on those bishops who, in his absence, had infringed the prerogative of Canterbury by taking part in the crowning, and two of them were excommunicated as well. This characteristic defiance and the complaints of three of the suspended bishops (including the Archbishop of York) who had crossed the channel to lay their case before the king so inflamed Henry that he uttered the intemperate words which moved four of his knights to set out for England and murder the archbishop in his cathedral. The most politically powerful of all English martyrs had been made.[1]

Despite the enormity of the crime, Henry secured his absolution from the Pope for his unintended part in it, and in return he agreed to cancel any new 'customs' he had introduced into England concerning the church. But since he claimed that little in the 'ancestral' Constitutions of Clarendon was new, the provisions of that declaration were generally adhered to. There were, however, two important exceptions. Appeals to Rome were, after all, to be allowed (with the important reservation that no harm to the crown or kingdom should ensue) and no clerk was to be tried by a secular judge for any crime except a forest offence (an exception which was considered to be justified by the rule under which clerics were not supposed to hunt). Both of these clerical privileges survived until the reign of Henry VIII when the immunities of the clergy were destroyed as part of a parliamentary process which played a crucial part in the evolution of Parliament, and particularly of the political influence of the House of Commons. But many of the other provisions in the Consitutions of Clarendon remained operative, including

---

[1] For extracts from sources related to the king's quarrel with Becket, see *E.H.D.* Vol. II pp. 702–777. A principal collection is *Materials for the History of Thomas Becket* (ed. J. C. Robertson, published 1875–85 under the direction of the Master of the Rolls).

the king's control of elections to high church office, his right to the revenue of vacant sees and the jurisdiction of the lay courts over clerics accused of lesser offences than felony.

These remarkable and well documented events show the council to have been displaying several attributes which were later to be associated with Parliament. First, it was freely discussing an important political question brought to it by the king, who needed the support of the lay barons, and at least the acquiescence of the bishops, in order to take his action against Becket. In the second place, the use of the council to determine and promulgate the custom of the realm with regard to clerical immunities was tantamount to a declaration of law in the manner of the Witan, and it also foreshadowed the future parliamentary modification of the common law by written statute. Finally, in his wish that the council should sentence Becket, the king was using it as the highest court in the land, which was also to be an attribute of Parliament.

In all these respects, the great council of Henry II developed substantially ahead of the post-Conquest baronial councils, and in a parliamentary direction. It is true that the Norman kings may sometimes have held politically significant meetings of their baronial council which we do not know about because they were not recorded. But it is certain that William I and his sons had never consulted their greater council in as sustained a manner as Henry II did his, and that the Norman council had never been asked to assent to such declarations of law as those which were among Henry II's greatest achievements. The quarrel with Becket was not the only matter of political importance which Henry brought to his council, and the Constitutions of Clarendon were very far from being the only or most important declarations of law which he issued with the council's assent. The function of the great council was changing because feudalism itself was waning, and the power of the magnates in future would take a new form.

The state of affairs at Henry's accession might in one sense be regarded as having contained an inherent contradiction. On the one hand feudalism as a form of land-holding was becoming a diminishing force. In its purest form it was a nexus of dues, service and rights attached to land, but as society became more settled such arrangements created many practical uncertainties about ownership. Since each man held land of another, and ultimately from the king, who was the lawful possessor of land? Was it the lord from whom it was (increasingly theoretically) held, and to whom service continued to be due for it? Or was it the man who was in possession of it because his forbears had held it? By the latter part of the twelfth century, it was already becoming accepted in practice that the possession of land by inheritance from a previous feudal tenant betokened something very like an absolute right of possession, and Henry II gave this new reality legal recognition. Several of his enactments tilted the balance decisively in favour of the possessor and his heirs. His assize (or enactment) of *Novel Disseisin* enabled a man who had been arbitrarily evicted from his land to purchase a writ from the king's chancery instructing the sheriff to call together a local jury of recognition to give evidence on the question whether the plaintiff had been wrongly 'disseised' or dispossessed. By this means, a man might protect himself against an attempt by his feudal overlord to dispossess him.

Similarly, under the assize of *Mort d'ancestor* (1176), an heir could obtain possession of his father's lands if such a jury recognized that his father had died in possession of them, and that the plaintiff was, indeed, his father's rightful heir. Later, the Grand Assize (the date of which is not certain) enabled a lawful tenant whose possession was being threatened to have the question of his right determined under oath by a jury of twelve local knights (who were chosen by four other knights of the shire) in place of trial by battle, fought by paid champions, which had been the final means of settling property cases. Each of these enactments imposed a restriction on feudal property rights, in addition to which the use of the empanelled jury had fundamental implications, as we shall see, both for the future of British justice and for the idea of representation in Parliament.

So much for the sense in which the feudal idea in relation to property was decaying. On the other hand, the years of anarchy had given the feudal barons pretensions to political power which they would not have dared to claim under William I and his sons, and which were inimical to a strong crown. Moreover, Henry wished to build a kingship which was something more than the apex of feudalism. Despite its strength, the rule of Norman kings had been inextricably entwined with the feudal principle and depended heavily on the personal authority of the king. Henry wanted instead a national monarchy which would have independent political strength not unlike that of the Anglo-Saxon kingship, and which free men of all conditions would have an interest in upholding. Symbolic of his purpose was the revival of the fyrd under the Assize of Arms (1181) which laid down that all knights, freemen and burgesses must provide themselves (according to their status and means) with arms as stipulated, and must be ready to answer the sheriff's call to arms in the king's service in time of need. Furthermore, every such bearer of arms was required to swear personal fealty to Henry.[1] Thus the king was provided with military support which was not dependent on feudal obligation. The importance of the feudal host

---

[1] Stubbs, *Select Charters*, pp. 183–4; *E.H.D.*, Vol. II, p. 449–451; Stephenson and Marcham op. cit. p. 85.

was beginning to diminish. He also had a growing preference for money in place of traditional military service. The system called scutage (shield money) by which a tenant might commute his military service to the king for a cash payment had been used on occasions since the Conquest, but Henry II made it a regular practice and his successors developed it further. Scutage gave the king greater flexibility and independence in gathering together a royal army as and when he wanted it. Money provided by magnates in place of their personal service could be used to pay mercenaries fighting alongside feudal knights. But the principal buttresses of the Plantagenet national monarchy were a system of royal government which (under a vice-regal justiciar) could operate without the king when he was out of the country, and the retrieval of the administration of justice from feudal domination.

Although the feudal property nexus had become weaker, the power of the feudal nobility over justice in their localities had been increasing since the Conquest. They, or their officials, not only administered justice in their own feudal courts; their influence was often decisive in the shire and hundred courts as well. For the most part, therefore, the administration of justice was either aristocratic or in accordance with local custom. There was now little provision for the fulfilment by the king of his ancient obligation to provide equal justice for all men under a common law. To remedy this, Henry II systematically issued writs which drew cases to the royal courts. The writs either required those responsible for delivering justice to do so or to answer for it in the king's court; or they specifically instructed the sheriff to remove particular cases to the royal courts forthwith. Further, in 1166 (the year in which the Assize of Novel Disseisin put freehold property rights on to a new basis) the king began taking royal justice out to the people who were far from his court. Itinerant justices had been used by Henry I, but from now on they were employed much more comprehensively and in subsequent years, a number of circuits was established for the king's justices in eyre, or *in itinere*, who travelled the land dealing with both legal and administrative cases. Everyone who came before the king's justices was deemed to come before the king. The arrangements under which the justices were to try criminal cases were laid down by the famous Assize of Clarendon which was issued just before the general eyre of 1166.[1] In 1176, this enactment was revised and extended by the Assize of Northampton to cover more crimes and to define penalties.[2] This second enactment (unlike

[1] Stubbs, *Select Charters*, p. 170; E.H.D., Vol. II pp. 440–443.
[2] Stubbs, *Select Charters*, p. 178; E.H.D., Vol. II pp. 444–446.

the first) also specified that the jurors should be knights, or freemen if knights were not available.

The Assize of Clarendon (two years after the 'Constitutions') was made with the assent of 'the archbishops, bishops, abbots, earls, and barons of all England'. Its most important provision decreed the use of a jury of presentment in criminal cases, which was of great potential significance, politically as well as legally. Twelve of the more lawful (or responsible) men of the hundred (an administrative sub-division of the shire) and four men from every village or township were required to state, on oath, who in their locality were accused as robbers, murderers or thieves, or who were 'publicly known' as such. They must state likewise who had been harbourers of such criminals. The jury of presentment was not the invention of Henry II. An ordinance of Ethelred the Unready suggests that something like a sworn inquest of informers to provide evidence against criminals had been used in Anglo-Saxon England. But it was the Normans, following the Frankish model, who were responsible for the more general introduction of the jury in England, and Henry II systematized its use.

It was not, however, the function of such a jury to pronounce a verdict. After the jury of presentment had stated on oath whom they believed to be criminals, the accused were tried before the justices and then had to submit to the ordeal by water. The accused person was bound and immersed in consecrated water. If he did not sink, the water was deemed to have rejected him, and he was found guilty by the judgement of God. (The other method of reaching judgement used at this time was compurgation, which obliged the accused to find twelve good men willing to swear their belief in his innocence, which was no mere formality in an age when perjury was believed to imperil the immortal soul. In legal disputes over property, the ordeal by battle, introduced by the Normans, was used.)

We may well think that the discovery of guilt or innocence by so barbarous and superstitious procedure as the ordeal, which was forbidden by the Lateran Council of 1215, was a contemptibly primitive method of justice. Yet by the time an accused person was put to the ordeal, the facts of the case must often have been fairly well tested. The sworn jury of presentment, in giving collective witness to the facts as they knew them, must also have generally been registering an implicit judgement on the guilt of the accused from their knowledge. Although the jury of presentment in criminal cases existed only to establish the suspicion of guilt, not proof of it, the evidence offered from a collection of witnessing jurors on oath must have carried a flavour of informed and collectively corroborated judgement. To the extent that this was so, it paved the way for the later trial and verdict by jury as we know it. This was even more true of the jury which was required under the Grand Assize not merely to give sworn evidence in property cases, but also to determine in the light of their local knowledge who had the better right to disputed land. Such juries clearly intended to give a virtual verdict, and they foreshadowed the Petty Jury which eventually took the place of the ordeal and whose function of giving a final verdict remains at the heart of British justice.

The development of the jury under Henry II also has parliamentary significance. The part played by the jury at a local inquest was not unrelated to that of the knights who would be chosen during the next century to represent the shires at Parliament and who were expected to give evidence from their local knowledge if called upon to do so. The increasing use of knights to take responsibility in local matters was to be of fundamental importance in the development of the communities of the shires and their eventual representation in Parliament.

Taken altogether, Henry's legislative and political changes had the effect of shifting power and jurisdiction from feudal lords to the agents of a strengthened central monarchy. Where the feudal principle was waning in relation to the ownership of property, the king legislated to confirm the trend towards security of tenure. Where feudal power seemed to be growing stronger, he acted against the trend, using writs, administrative change and legislation, to shift justice from the feudal to the royal courts. As well as providing itinerant justices who could act for him throughout the land, he also made the *curia regis* itself accessible for judicial purposes, to ordinary men, as well as to the great. Five men from his court, two clerks and three laymen, were appointed to travel with the king wherever he went in order to hear complaints by free men. This arrangement anticipated the future court of common pleas, though this would not be itinerant, but (as Magna Carta was to require) would function in a fixed place which came to be Westminster.

By all these means a system of common law and common procedures gradually replaced local custom and feudal justice over the country as a whole, laying the foundations not simply for the re-emergence of the national law-declaring kingship of the Anglo-Saxons, but of a single law and uniform legal system such as they, with their wide variety of custom, English and Danish, had never known. To contemporaries, however, these changes might have seemed to flow easily from feudalism. Royal justice (which brought the crown large profits from fines as well as protecting the king's peace) could therefore be considered as arising from the feudal structure, since the king's court was also the most powerful of the feudal courts. It has even been argued that the law was becoming common because it was administered by the only feudal court with authority throughout the land.[1]

It is more to the point, however, that though the influence of the strictly feudal idea was waning, the political influence of the magnates themselves was not. It was simply taking a new form. The king, after all, had used the great baronial council to sanction his legislative changes and to approve his political actions. Nothing so close to the declarations of law by Anglo-Saxon kings, made with the assent of their council, had been seen since the Conquest. Now that society was more settled this was a natural development. Although a medieval king's rule was personal, there was a well understood distinction between the Christian obligation to act in the interest of the realm and the actions of a tyrant. The more the exigencies of conquest receded into the past, the more consent would return to government. What is more, although the success of Henry II in making the law common owed much to Norman influences, and the continental interest in Roman and canon law, it drew most heavily on the Anglo-Saxon tradition.

It is true that a great deal of Anglo-Saxon practice had not been carried forward. For instance, the old emphasis on penalties meted out according both to the gravity of the crime and to the victim's *wer* (his valuation for compensation according to his rank) had no place in the new common law. Yet the common law of Henry II was built on the Anglo-Saxon tradition that the law existed beyond and above the will of the ruler and was discoverable from immemorial custom. Above all, the effectiveness of the common law depended on the old shire courts, answerable to the king, which were an antidote to feudalism, and where locally chosen knights were already learning to play a public role in response to the king's writ summoning them to jury and other local responsibility. The knights were taking the preliminary steps towards becoming parliamentary representatives.

Authority was thus both centralized in the king's court and devolved to his non-feudal agents. At the centre, however, it was increasingly accepted that important political decisions and legislation should involve consultation with the 'community of the realm' represented by the great council of

---

[1] The point was made rather too strongly, by C. H. McIlwain, *The High Court of Parliament*, pp. 43-44, who also concluded: 'The Common Law was, in the main, the product of a court not a legislature, and its development was brought about by activities that are more accurately described as judicial than legislative.' But if the uniformity, or commonness, of the law resulted from its administration of the highest court in the feudal structure, its superiority also owed much to the assumption that the king's courts traditionally dispensed not laws invented by the king (though they often were) but ancient customs of the realm and people.

lay and spiritual magnates acting in a parliamentary way. Barons who owed their position in the council to their traditional position as tenants-in-chief increasingly adopted an attitude more aristocratic than feudal. It had never been possible for territorial magnates to challenge the English king as they did the French. That would have required compact possessions, and the Norman barons had been deliberately given scattered English fiefs at the Conquest. Nor was it part of their thinking to destroy the crown's effective power. Instead, they developed the urge collectively to influence the king and to control the machinery of its government where it impinged on their privileges. The baronial struggle to force the crown into consultation played its part in the evolution of English liberties, just as the king's promotion of the common law and centralized government did.

The strength of Henry II's system of government was well tested in the closing years of his reign, and even more so under his successors. In 1173, the king was threatened by a serious rebellion in his Angevin dominions which spread to England. A baronial uprising in the eastern counties was a foretaste of the revolt against Plantagenet methods of government under King John. Again, just before he died in 1189, Henry II was engulfed in a rebellion in France where his own sons were used by the French king as instruments to destroy Plantagenet rule there. The king died shattered by the knowledge that John, the younger son to whom he was most attached, was leagued against him. The fragility of the Angevin 'empire' and its dependence on the strength of character of its ruler had been exposed. Yet in England, once the rebellion of 1173 had failed, Plantagenet rule remained as firm as a rock, despite the absences of the king, as the reign of his absentee successor was to show.

IV

Before he inherited the English throne, Richard I had spent most of his life in Aquitaine where he had also gained all his political experience, ruling it as duke. With his brothers, he had been involved in the rebellion against his father in 1173 to 1174, which had begun in France with a feudal family quarrel and had spread to England. Even more seriously, he had joined Philip Augustus of France in the final attack on Henry II which had almost destroyed Henry's grip on his French possessions when he died. A famed soldier who had governed his difficult duchy with competence, Richard had shown himself wholly uninterested in England. When he became heir on his elder brother's death, he was offered the opportunity by his father of giving up Aquitaine to his younger brother John, and working alongside his father. That would have given Richard the experience of England which he wholly lacked. But he refused. He came to the English throne almost wholly ignorant of the country, and in ten years as king spent only six months in England. The rest of his time was passed on the third crusade, in captivity in Germany (where he was held to ransom after being taken prisoner by the Archduke of Austria on his return journey from Palestine to England) and, for the last five years of his life, fighting in France.

Yet despite his absence from the realm and the persistent treachery of John, Richard's hold on the throne was never seriously shaken. Even the heavy taxation needed to pay his ransom was accepted without resistance. The security of Richard's position can be ascribed principally to the efficient control over the government's business exercised by the professional administrators whom his father had appointed, and especially to the political stature of extremely able justiciars (starting with Ranulf Glanville, appointed by Henry II in 1180) who were empowered to rule virtually as regents in the king's absence. It has to be said for Richard himself that he was shrewd in judging the ability of the men he picked for the task. But the stability of the realm also owed much to the general disposition of the baronage not to disturb it and, at several points of crisis, even to the deliberations of the great council. The barons had an interest in stability and their passage from feudal towards aristocratic attitudes which has already been remarked had not yet gone so far as to inspire them to any coherent critique of the policies of the crown. They may not yet have thought of themselves as a collective influence in the state, as they did under King John. But the reign of Richard I again showed the great council acting as a stabilizing deliberative assembly. It was even the scene, though not the prime mover, of the removal of one minister and the installation of another.

Immediately after his coronation, Richard began preparations for the crusade, selling anything available, from manors to government offices, in order to raise money. On his departure, he left the justiciarship divided beween William Longchamp, Bishop of Ely, who was also chancellor, and the Bishop of Durham. Longchamp, who was described by a contemporary, Richard of Devizes, as 'a remarkable person who made up for the shortness of his stature by his arrogance', exploited to the full the power of his two offices. In a short time, he had managed to push the Bishop of Durham out of any share in government, and had become himself (he was also papal legate) the sole effective ruler. Neither Longchamp's efficiency, nor his loyalty to Richard was in any doubt. But his assertiveness, his ignorance of England (he was by birth pure Norman, as distinct from English-settled Norman) and the vigour of his tax-raising on Richard's behalf alienated many important and less important men. He was even criticized for not understanding the English language.[1] In opposition to him stood not only many of the magnates, but also the King's brother John, who had set up a rival court, possessed a powerful and compact fief in England, and claimed to be the champion of the baronial interest. Open strife seemed to threaten, and to deal with this Richard sent to England Walter of Coutances (an Englishman by birth, despite his name) who was Archbishop of Rouen, with full powers to mediate and act as he thought fit. He managed to negotiate an agreement between John and Longchamp. But political confusion reached a new climax of discontent when Longchamp's men seized Henry II's bastard (and loyal) son Geoffrey, who had been consecrated Archbishop of York while in France, and had just arrived in England to take over his See, having previously been exiled by Richard.

The Archbishop of Rouen had come to England with letters stating that Longchamp should not presume to act without his consent. But Longchamp had done so. He was therefore called to appear at the great council, which was summoned by John (who strictly speaking lacked authority to summon a council in the king's name) to meet at Lodden Bridge between Reading and Windsor. Instead, he fled to London, took refuge in the Tower and sought unsuccessfully to win the support of the citizens. Almost all the magnates, lay and spiritual, attended the council at Lodden Bridge. After recitals of the charges against Longchamp had been heard, the Archbishop of Rouen proposed that he should be deposed, which was agreed. The magnates then moved on to London where they gathered in the chapter house of St Paul's, with the citizens of London also present. At this point, John no doubt supposed that all power in England had fallen to him. But the Archbishop of Rouen then produced the king's sealed authority ordering that if Longchamp had acted to the detriment of the kingdom, or against the advice of the archbishop, he should be deposed and that the Archbishop of Rouen should take his place as chief justiciar. This was agreed 'by common deliberation' of the king's vassals. According to one account, it was agreed not only that the archbishop should become justiciar, but that John should be named regent. But if John did have that title it was a formality. Walter of Coutances was now the country's governor, acting with the advice of the council and John was henceforth occupied plotting to get the kingdom for himself. Longchamp, who perhaps did not deserve his fate, and suffered for being the over zealous servant of the king, was allowed to leave England.

[1] Stubbs, *Constitutional History*, Vol. I, 5th ed. pp. 588.

It would be wrong to think of this affair as some kind of constitutional development in which the barons in council had dismissed a minister who displeased them. They had got rid of Longchamp only by the proposal of the king's specially commissioned emissary and plenipotentiary. Nevertheless, Longchamp's deposition had demonstrated the importance of governing with the assent of the magnates who represented the political nation, and also the ability of the barons to express their opinion and speak for their interest in the king's larger council. Longchamp had not fulfilled the condition that a ruler must listen to advice; Walter of Coutances, in contrast, made it clear from the start that he intended to act by the counsel of the barons. One who would not listen had been replaced by one who would, because the king accepted the need for the change. The council had taken a first step towards its future claim to speak for the community of the realm.

Two other episodes of activity by, or in, the great council under Richard I are of interest in the prelude to Parliament. During the king's captivity in Austria, John was intermittently involved in plots and rebellion against him, and on Richard's return in 1194, it was at a great council at Nottingham that he called for a judgement on his brother and other rebels. (It was, nevertheless, a sign of the strength of the Plantagenet system that the rebellion had virtually been broken before Richard landed.) John was required to come within forty days or forfeit his lands and his right to succeed to the throne. He did not appear, though after Richard had left England for the last time he forgave his brother when he encountered him in France.

Before his departure, the king had placed the government of the country in the hands of an exceptionally competent justiciar and administrator, Hubert Walter, Archbishop of Canterbury. It was under Hubert Walter's government that another event occurred which indicated the growing political significance of the larger baronial council. As the Norman barons had become settled in England, they had become increasingly reluctant to discharge their feudal obligation to serve the king personally, or to provide him with knights, in campaigns overseas. The wider the king's possessions in France spread, the less the barons of England were inclined to serve him there. The king's dominions in France, they could fairly argue, belonged to him in a separate feudal relationship and had nothing to do with his English tenants. Henry II had used scutage as a means of financing his foreign wars, but since it was a customary tax the barons were reluctant to pay more than the traditional sum of one mark for each knight's fief. In 1198 at a great council at Oxford, Hubert Walter presented the barons and bishops with a demand from the king for a force of knights to serve in Normandy: each knight was to be provided with money for a year's service. This proposition met with a flat refusal from the future saint, Bishop Hugh of Lincoln. Stating that he would rather go home to his native Burgundy than agree, Bishop Hugh insisted that his lands were liable to render military service in England but not elsewhere. He was voicing the protests of knights who were church tenants. Some of them, from Bury St Edmunds, were present at Oxford and heatedly advanced their case with the bishop and their own abbot. It seems clear that the objection was not to the amount of the 'tax' (though this seems to have been exceptionally high), nor to service or scutage as such, but only to service abroad. Indeed, it has been argued that Bishop Hugh (who was supported by the Bishop of Salisbury) was not even taking his stand against *paying* for service abroad, but objected only to the enforced personal service of knights outside England. On such grounds, it has been concluded that it would be wrong to regard this incident as an early example of constitutional refusal of money to a king.[1]

Even on this interpretation of uncertain evidence, however, this was a noteworthy instance of opposition to a demand for money from the king by those who would have to pay. That was so, whether the objection was purely a legalistic appeal to feudal convention or whether it had broader political significance. (The same had been true of a successful opposition by Becket to the king's claim on the local levy at the council at Woodstock in 1163.) What is more, Bishop Hugh's resistance seems to have been successful for the time being, since the scutage was withdrawn generally, and not simply for the benefit of the two objecting bishops. Although this incident was far from being an assertion in principle that taxation needs the consent of the taxed, the king's minister found it necessary in practice to seek agreement to the tax and dared not simply impose it. In medieval conditions, money could not be raised unless those who had to pay could be persuaded to agree. Avoidance was possible simply by local non-cooperation, and gaining cooperation in tax-paying was to be a fundamental motive for the first calling of representatives of the shire communities to Parliament. They would go to Parliament to take part in the determination of how much *could* be collected, and then return to their shires with the authority to see that it *was* collected. Not long after this episode, Hubert Walter resigned as justiciar, being succeeded by Geoffrey Fitz-Peter.

The growing importance of the 'representative' knights in the shires in the performance of public duties was shown by another action of Hubert Walter in 1198, which was the last full year of Richard's reign. Again, it arose not from any sort of theory but from practical politics. The justiciar had revived what amounted to the old Danegeld under another name, the

---

[1] J. H. Round, *Feudal England* (1895); reset 1964, Allen and Unwin, p. 339.

carucage. This was a five shillings tax on each carucate (roughly one hundred acres of ploughland) and in 1198, Hubert Walter sent out officials, who operated roughly on the lines of the Domesday inquiry, to conduct a survey of the liability of each shire. In each shire court, the king's itinerant officials were to join with the sheriff to call before the county court four men of each township and two knights from every hundred to take an oath on how many carucates were liable in their district. The amount was registered on rolls; the money was collected by two knights and the bailiff of each hundred, who accounted to the sheriff. In turn, the sheriff accounted to the Exchequer. This use of local men in the shire court, both to represent the community and to act for the crown in the calculation and accounting (but not yet the granting) of taxation was, however, only one sign of the increasing importance of the knights in the shires.

They were employed not only on the juries enpannelled in the shire courts for both criminal and civil cases but also to deal with other local abuses, tax assessment and the enforcement of the military and fealty requirements of the Assize of Arms. To all this and much else, Hubert Walter added the responsibility of knights for overseeing the oaths to keep the peace which all free men were now required to take; this, perhaps, anticipated the future justices of the peace. In all this there can be seen, before Magna Carta, the conjunction of local representation in the shire courts, responsible to the king and theoretically independent of the local magnates, with centralized royal authority. What might be called the upper middle classes were already beginning to play their role as instruments of local authority in the king's name, and it was from them that the first representatives of the Commons in Parliament would be chosen in the shire court.

In the towns, meanwhile, charters were being granted for money and tallages were being levied on the citizens since the cities were deemed to be part of the king's demesne.[1] The Londoners had been granted their charter for the election of a mayor and for self government as a reward for their help in the overthrow of Longchamp. Subsequently, in 1196, there was an insurrection of Londoners against the unfair incidence of tallages. In general, the towns increasingly felt their independence, and the growth of urban self-government was also preparing the way for the eventual representation of the boroughs at Parliament.

Finally, in the great council of magnates, there was political debate, criticism of royal policies and sometimes resistance to the king's wishes, as

---

[1] Tallage was increasingly the term used to describe arbitrary taxation levied on the king's tenants in his own demesne. They were usually raised at the same time as a scutage.

well as assent to law-making. In addition to these quasi-parliamentary activities, the council also maintained its claim to approve or recognize (which word is the more correct is debatable) the succession to the throne. In 1199, Richard I died in France as a result of an arrow wound and the succession was immediately disputed. Was the new king to be Arthur, the son of Richard's late elder brother, Geoffrey? Or was it to be John, the youngest son of Henry II? The disadvantage of Arthur was that he was a boy. In Brittany (to which he was heir through his mother) Arthur was recognized, as he was in Anjou, Maine and Touraine. In Normandy, John was recognized. In England there was at first uncertainty. Hubert Walter, it was said, would have preferred Arthur but was prepared to agree to John, who had been Richard's designated successor. Even now there was no strict idea of royal primogeniture. Indeed, the concept of an elective monarchy was openly deployed by the chronicler, Matthew Paris, in his retrospective account of John's succession. The Archbishop, he tells us, publicly announced at the coronation that 'no one has a previous right to succeed another in the kingdom unless he is unanimously elected by the whole kingdom under the guidance of the Holy Spirit because of the superior merits of his character. . . .' John had been so elected. According to this account, written in the glare of hindsight, the Archbishop was moved to make these remarks because he knew by revelation that John would one day bring the kingdom into confusion, and he therefore wanted to warn him that he owed his kingdom to election and not to hereditary right. If the Archbishop was so sure of the trouble John would bring on the country, it is hard to see why he should have been willing to risk placing the responsibility on the Holy Spirit, since his hearers could hardly have read into the words which were later ascribed to him any suggestion that the election had been without due spiritual guidance.

Nevertheless, even the apocryphal anecdotes of hindsight can be instructive. Although the passage was obviously written with Magna Carta in mind and represents the writer's point of view rather than an historical account of what the Archbishop had said many years before the collapse of John's authority, it suggests that for at least some people in the thirteenth century, the reign of John could be interpreted as making the case for limited monarchy, and the claim that it had an elective element. At all events, it was clearly understood at the time of John's accession that the recognition of the new king must take place in a great council. Accordingly, the new justiciar, Geoffrey FitzPeter, summoned such a meeting to Northampton and persuaded the magnates to take an oath to John. After six weeks' delay, John landed in England in May and was crowned at Westminster.

V

Magna Carta, wrested by the barons from King John under military duress, was England's first great parliamentary document, although Parliament did not exist when it was devised. Re-issued in 1225 as a statement of law, the Great Charter also came to be regarded as the first English statute. The charter as reissued in 1225 was traditionally printed first in all early collections of the Plantagenet statutes, and parts of it remain on the statute book to this day. It was to become the document of ultimate appeal at almost all points of constitutional conflict until the end of the 17th century. Magna Carta, or the legend that arose from it, gave sacrosanct authority to an evolving concept of liberty which was inextricably woven into the development of Parliament. It was a parliamentary document in the sense that it implicitly needed the existence of Parliament to make effective the idea of government that logically underlay it, impossible though it would have been for its framers to forsee this.[1]

In 1215, however, the Great Charter was simply the authentic record, under the king's great seal, of John's grant to the clergy, barons, towns and freemen severally, of their customary 'rights' and liberties, as these were interpreted by the leaders of the barons and by the mediators who negotiated with the king's officials. It was issued by the king as the price paid for the settlement by the barons of their war with him, and for their renewal of homage. Yet although it was the consequence of a treaty, Magna Carta was not itself a treaty. Indeed, every effort was made in the charter to diminish the fact that the barons had been at war with the king. (The euphemism 'quarrel' or discord (*discordia*) was the preferred description of the military hostilities which the charter was supposed to settle.) Nor was Magna Carta designed as a new statement of law, let alone as a prescription of constitutional principle. It was conceived as an acknowledgement by the king of the custom of the realm as it was, or as the barons pretended it to be. Since feudal custom was imprecise, Magna Carta itself often lacked precision. It was, moreover, a negotiated political document designed to be acceptable to two parties at the end of a dispute (with whatever private reservations) and its authors therefore inevitably took shelter behind vagueness at points of insuperable difficulty, as always happens when such

---

[1] The original Magna Carta and the reissue under Henry III which became the basis of future confirmations are printed in a collection of early charters at the beginning of the Statutes of the Realm, Vol. I. Subsequent confirmations (eg. under Edward I) are printed as statutes.

formulae are devised. Yet whatever the imprecision of some of its prescriptions, the questions and grievances to which it was addressed were wholly specific in the manner of law and were never generalizations. Moreover, although it was not formally designed or presented in 1215 as a statement of new law in the manner of future statutes, this was what it was in reality. For the barons had included in it new things alongside old custom, and had intended that its provisions should be a permanent record of enduring rights and liberties with the force of law.

The rebellion that produced Magna Carta arose partly from the character and shortcomings of King John, but more fundamentally from the legacy his father and brother had left him. That John was treacherous, occasionally violent, and not infrequently viciously cruel and vengeful is not disputable. He was ruthless in self-protection, obsessively suspicious, and jealous of other men of standing. His feudal power over the baronage was often used harshly and unjustly. Yet he was not the phenomenally useless, vile and even subhuman monster suggested by those later chroniclers who created the traditional historical view of him. His political and administrative ability was substantial, and was not denied even by John Richard Green who took as his text the ringing denunciation of the thirteenth century chronicler, Matthew Paris: 'Foul as it is, hell itself is defiled by the fouler presence of John.'[1] Although Green's account of John set the fashion of the school text-books until comparatively recently, the Victorian historian himself conceded that despite his 'supreme wickedness' John possessed 'profound ability', and that 'in the rapidity and breadth of his political combinations, he far surpassed the statesmen of his time'. John was also acquitted of sloth and incapacity by J. R. Green who, unlike some of his cruder imitators, saw that this Angevin king 'possessed in a high degree the political ability of his race'. This is even more emphatically the view of recent historians, who have stressed his relentless energy, the remarkable development of administration and administrative record-keeping under him, his shrewdness, his cultivated tastes (he was a literate man) and his ceaseless travelling the length and breadth of England giving judgements in small as well as important cases, when he often showed considerable wisdom and sometimes (his own interest not being involved) compassion.[2]

[1] J. R. Green, *A Short History of the English People*, 1874 (Revised edition 1888).
[2] See particularly W. L. Warren, *King John* (1961) on which I have drawn heavily in assessing John's character. The definitive modern commentary on the great charter is by J. C. Holt, *Magna Carta* (1965), by which I have been generally guided in this discussion of the events leading to Magna Carta and the significance of the document. This supersedes the former standard commentary on the charter, W. S. McKechnie's *Magna Carta* (1905) which nevertheless remains of considerable historiographical interest as does Kate Norgate's *John Lackland* (1902). See also J. C. Holt's *The Northerners* (1961).

Where recent historians who have mined the records as well as having read the chroniclers differ most significantly from the traditional view is in their interpretation of what brought John down. Green thought that he perished 'in a struggle of despair against English liberties' and in a wilful attempt to promote tyranny. But it is now easier to see that John was driven to the politics of failure by the need to try to hold together an almost impossible conglomerate of dominions on both sides of the English Channel. To pay for their defence at a time of sharp inflation, he pushed to dangerous lengths financial exactions which had received their initial impetus in his father's reign. In this sense, therefore, Magna Carta was more the consequence of inherited political problems than of wanton personal behaviour. There is a certain resemblance between the failure of John and that of the inadequate Edward II who was to be even less able to cope with the inheritance left by a brilliant and ambitious father.

Yet our clearer understanding of the cause of John's behaviour should not blind us to the part played by the king's personality in shaping events. That John's character was seriously flawed, not least by his propensity to ungovernable rage, is the truth underlying his evil reputation. The probably correct suspicion that he was responsible for, and may in a fury have himself committed, the murder of his nephew Arthur, must have coloured a great deal of contemporary opinion. Angry impetuosity also marred his capacity to rule. A king of better character, confronted with the same difficulties, might well have handled them more successfully in both England and France, and could certainly have avoided being driven by them into provoking a great political conflict which put the authority of the crown at risk. The modern interpretation does not altogether overthrow but rather explains the old one by enlarging our understanding of why John acted as badly as he did. The reality is that Magna Carta, like most other great constitutional advances, did not arise solely from an unavoidable clash of interests, and owed nothing at all to any theory of government. Defects of character, accidents of personality and circumstances and the inability of a particular king to manage government in the circumstances of his time, also contributed to the production of the most fundamental of parliamentary documents.

Richard I had been struggling with rebellion in France when he died in April 1199; John was encompassed by rebellion from the first moments of his reign. At first he was successful in establishing himself as his brother's accepted heir in the northern provinces of his French dominions although he was challenged by rebels and by the French king in the name of Arthur of Brittany. However, John faced a more serious war. It was precipitated by the proud and aggressive Lusignan family of Poitou, whom John had offended by taking as his second wife Isabella of Angoulême, formerly engaged to Hugh de Lusignan. From this rebellion sprang a series of campaigns in which Philip of France assaulted and captured most of Normandy in 1203. Rouen fell to the French king in the summer of 1204. By the spring of the following year, John had lost his last strongholds in Anjou and a year later Brittany was taken by the French king. This great defeat for John, and the final severance of Normandy from the English crown were caused less by military inefficiency on the part of the king (who was often skilful and sometimes daring in action) than by the desertion of the Norman barons of the duchy. Their feudal loyalty had already been badly strained by the rule of Henry II, and to compensate for this John had relied extensively on mercenaries, which merely deepened disloyalty among the Norman nobility.

After gaining Normandy from the English crown, Philip Augustus invaded Poitou. An attempt to save it by an attack on La Rochelle failed, and in 1206 a long truce left John in possession in France only of the lands which had belonged to his family south of la Rochelle. His inability to mount a successful counter-attack can largely be explained by lack of support from the English barons, who were increasingly reluctant to give either military service or money to protect the king's lands overseas, as well as being made restive by the financial burdens placed on them by the king. At this point, John, who had returned to England when his hold on Normandy had virtually come to an end in 1203, became involved in a much more intractable dispute over the rights of the crown.

On the death in 1205 of Archbishop Hubert Walter, the monks of Canterbury, without consulting the king, elected their own prior, Reginald, as archbishop. The king's response was to order them to elect his own nominee John de Gray, which in form they proceeded to do. Reginald, however, was already in Rome where he appealed to Pope Innocent III in his own cause. It was this that threw John into conflict with the most powerful and determined Pope of the middle ages, who quashed both 'elections' and proposed his own nominee, Stephen Langton, a man outstanding far beyond either of the other candidates. The king, however, insisted that no archbishop could be elected without his licence, and he refused Langton entry to the kingdom. John also sequestrated the estates of Canterbury and expelled the monks. So began the long conflict with Pope Innocent which led to the imposition of an Interdict on England in 1208. In theory at least, religious life was brought almost entirely to a standstill. Marriage was permitted only in the church porch; the sacraments were forbidden, though eventually the Pope allowed the last sacrament for the dying. What effect the Interdict had in practice is uncertain. It lasted for over six years, but there is no evidence of public discontent. Whether this means that the Interdict was loosely applied or that people were more willing than might be supposed to manage without the ministrations of the church is not clear.

John had not been wholly obdurate before the sentence, and he continued to negotiate. He was willing to admit Stephen Langton as an exception to the rule, if the Pope would accept the rule itself and acknowledge the king's right in principle to licence the appointment of a new archbishop. But when it was clear that the Pope would make no conditions, John issued orders for the confiscation of the property of clergy unwilling to celebrate mass. This, however, was less onerous in practice than in theory. Various arrangements were made allowing many abbeys and bishoprics to manage their own property and to keep what they needed, generously assessed, for their own maintenance. In 1209, however, John was excommunicated, and he now turned much more bitterly against the church, raiding and confiscating clerical property, which was only returned to the clergy when a fine had been paid, and which they were required to administer largely for the crown's benefit. For a time, this eased the crown's financial difficulties.

Through all this religious disturbance, the barons were inactive, and only a few of the bishops felt that it was no longer proper for them to have anything to do with the king. Yet the barons were inevitably worried by the turn of events. If the king could assault the property rights of the church in this way, might he not do the same to theirs? They were already uneasy about the increase in the power of centralized royal government, and since Henry II had crushed the rebellion of 1173 they had enjoyed less responsibility, and had lost power to the administrators. What is more, royal justice under the Angevin kings was by no means always fairly applied. The royal courts could prevent the barons from acting outside the law, but were themselves capable of stretching the law in the king's interest. Sometimes the barons also had to pay heavily to avoid the king's ill-will.

Above all there were the grievances over feudal dues and taxation. Almost every year there was a scutage or an aid. Even more objectionably, the Angevins exploited the discretion they possessed over the amount of the fine which feudal custom required an heir to pay the king in order to succeed to his father's estates. Even more than his predecessors, John abused the convention that the amount of the fines was entirely a matter of what could be agreed with the king. He also interfered unduly with inheritances and with the marriage of widows, over which he had rights under feudal custom. As well as general discontent over fines and amercements, there was an accumulation of personal grievances of individual tenants-in-chief over such matters as John's plundering of estates which were under his wardship, and forcing widows into marriages convenient to him. The grievances of the barons as a class were the sum of many individual discontents against a particular king in respect of particular persons and properties.[1]

If these measures arose from John's unavoidable need to raise money to defend his lands, it was a failure of competence arising from the streak of recklessness in his character which led him to try to browbeat into submission those who were discontented instead of trying to win them over. During the period of his excommunication, he drove the hardest bargains he could with inheritance 'fines', burdening his tenants until they were forced into the grip of the exchequer and, where he was suspicious, taking hostages. In 1212 he hanged twenty-eight sons of Welsh chiefs because their fathers had broken an undertaking, and he even used threats against the invariably loyal William Marshal, the Earl of Pembroke. But probably nothing was to do more to alarm the barons than John's treatment of one William de Briouze whom he himself had raised: after William was driven into exile in 1210 for treasonable activities, his wife and son died in the king's prison, starved to death according to generally credited reports.

Meanwhile, having successfully managed expeditions into Wales, Scotland and Ireland, John next set about recovering his lost lands in France. Having made a league with Flemish princes and with the German Welfs, then at war with the Hohenstauffen who were allied with the French king, John planned a campaign for 1212 in Poitou. But in face of a Welsh revolt and baronial restiveness and suspicions of treason at home, John was forced to put the campaign off. Moreover, the Pope was now threatening to depose him and to authorize Philip Augustus to invade England. Despite a success when an English naval expedition destroyed the French invasion fleet, John saw that he must make terms with the Pope and he decided to turn this necessity to his advantage. He not only capitulated completely in the matter of the clergy, acknowledging his offences; he also surrendered England and Ireland to the Holy See, receiving it back in return for homage and an annual tribute of 700 marks for England and 300 for Ireland. It was an action for which there were precedents in Europe, and which did not seem as offensive to contemporaries as it did to later chroniclers. Politically, it was an astute decision, since it turned the Pope into the King's future supporter, as well as removing the Interdict and excommunication. But it also meant danger. The lifting of the Interdict brought to England Stephen Langton, who was to be a decisive influence in the formulation of the great

---

[1] The grievances of individual barons against John are enumerated in considerable detail by J. C. Holt, *Magna Carta*.

charter, as well as the return of a number of hostile barons who had previously left the country.

In 1213, baronial resistance again hindered an invasion of Poitou. Knights complained that they had no obligation to serve the king there unless he paid them, and when the northern English barons flatly refused to follow him abroad, John began an expedition against them which was only stopped by a threat of excommunication from Langton. It was at this stage that what has since been called the 'unknown charter of liberties' was apparently drawn up in unknown circumstances. This contained not only a list of concessions by the king, which dealt with the principal feudal grievances and which were to reappear in one form or another in Magna Carta, but also a compromise on overseas feudal service. This would have restricted the obligation to serve the king overseas to Normandy and Brittany, but when Magna Carta itself came to be formulated the clause against foreign service was not included for the simple reason that by then the English king's position in France had so collapsed as to make this seem an irrelevant safeguard.

It was, nevertheless, France which provided the final catalyst for baronial revolt. While the German and Flemish alliance was to attack the French in the north, John himself embarked on a campaign in Poitou and Anjou and achieved some initial successes. But the Poitevin barons soon withdrew their support, and at the crucial battle of Bouvines in 1214, the French decisively defeated the Imperial and Flemish forces. It is not an exaggeration to say that this single battle, in which English soldiers were scarcely involved, was a formative influence in the building of English liberties. For it precipitated the revolt which led to Magna Carta. Of all his former possessions, John was left only with Aquitaine, and he went home, humiliated, to face an intensity of baronial resentment never experienced by any former post-Conquest king. The justiciar, Peter des Roches, had already met with a flat refusal by some of the barons to pay scutage for the king's expedition, and had thereupon put distraint upon their property. The king's defeat in France now stimulated open rebellion, much of which initially came from a group of northern barons, under a leader, Eustace de Vesci of Alnwick, who was motivated by bitter personal enmity towards John. In the guise of appealing to custom, they were in reality insisting on a new immunity against both feudal service abroad and any demand for money in place of service. But John's unjust exploitation of his feudal rights at the expense of baronial estates was no less a grievance. The rebels wanted to make him concede a definition of their rights, and they were prepared to make their allegiance conditional on his doing so. Soon after his return, John was confronted with the convenient precedent of Henry I's charter of liberties which, though it had not dealt with scutage, had provided a general undertaking that the king should not unjustly exploit his feudal rights, and had also been vaguely respectful about the laws of Edward the Confessor. It was by reference to this insubstantial precedent that the barons were to build the much more concrete edifice of Magna Carta.

Although the northern barons were the first to take arms, the main force of the rebellion came ultimately from the eastern counties, and there were revolts in other regions too. The leaders of the rebellion were Robert FitzWalter, another of the king's personal foes, and his family group of barons. Many of John's opponents were disreputable and lawless men who were no less arbitrary by inclination than the king, and the committed rebels probably numbered no more than about forty. On the other hand, John himself still had the support of a group of influential magnates led by William Marshal, and although there were fewer loyalists than rebels, by far the largest number of barons (the figure has been calculated at around a hundred) was inclined to be neutral.[1] It was these moderates who were largely responsible for the constructive negotiations which prevented a fight to the finish by the acceptance of Magna Carta by both sides.

The rebellion never came to outright battle; since the neutrals would not help him John was forced to come to terms. Moreover, although the Pope was now supporting his vassal's authority, Stephen Langton was among those convinced that John must be brought to a position more acceptable to the barons. In May 1215, the rebels renounced their homage and fealty to the king. John responded with a conciliatory statement offering not to go against the rebels, or to disseise them except by the law of the land or by the judgement of their peers in the court – which was a foreshadowing of Magna Carta. Having thus tried to establish his reasonableness, the king was about to move against the rebels in force when they contrived to get into London with the help of sympathizers there. From London they appealed to the whole baronage for unity. It was in this position of stalemate that the moderates took charge, and with Langton taking a leading part in the negotiations, mediated between the two sides. A preliminary statement of what the king had conceded to the barons' emissaries, known as the Articles of the Barons, was probably agreed and sealed on June 10. It was in effect a treaty document. Magna Carta itself, however, which recorded already agreed concessions, was not a treaty but a legal instrument which was later recopied and distributed. Final agreement on the charter was reached at a full meeting at Runneymede. Magna Carta records that the king's seal was affixed to it 'in the meadow which is called Runneymede

---

[1] W. L. Warren, op. cit. pp. 228–232.

between Windsor and Staines on the fifteenth day of June. . . .' This may have been the nominal date of the charter rather than the day on which the king's seal was actually affixed to it; a few days may well have been needed for the document to be put into appropriate language by the chancery clerks, and then copied out. At all events, peace was not finally achieved until June 19 when the barons renewed their homage.[1]

In the glow of inspiration which it provided during later constitutional conflicts, Magna Carta came to be regarded as a deliberately designed declaration of political liberty. It was nothing of the sort. Like every subsequent advance in the evolution of Parliament it owed little or nothing to theory and virtually everything to the practical needs of politics in a crisis. Its object was to clear up disputes about such specific matters as scutage, wardship and inheritance, and it contained no general statements of political principle. It was a list of particular 'liberties' acknowledged by the king. As this came to be understood, historians discarded the older more idealistic view of the charter, and laid stress instead on the crude feudal self-interest of the barons and on their selfish opposition (from which posterity only accidentally benefited) to the centralizing efficiency of royal administration. Anachronistic ideas of liberty as a general philosophical concept were stripped from the historical interpretation of the charter, and emphasis was placed instead on its purely feudal and legal aspects. These were, indeed, of great importance. Yet to concentrate on Magna Carta principally as a document of feudal 'law' is not only to attribute to its statements a legal precision which they did not possess (as future disputes about their meaning were to show) but also to detract from its political significance in its own time as a document designed to settle government for the future. It was a political as well as a legal document even though it was not a document of political theory.[2]

As well as being an attempt by the barons to build bulwarks against royal acts which damaged their interest, it was also a genuine political endeavour to find a lasting solution to the problems of power in the nation. This was to be done by dealing *ad hoc* with the grievances arising from the lack of any clear statement of the limits of the king's feudal power. Magna Carta resulted from a political tension about whether certain behaviour by the king was to be tolerated and if not what was to be done about it. Moreover, although it was principally concerned with feudal grievances, it also made statements about other liberties, including those of citizens of towns and

[1] For the fullest account of these events, see J. C. Holt, op. cit. Ch. V.
[2] Magna Carta is printed in Stubbs, *Select Charters*, p. 292 (Latin), and there are translations in *E.H.D.* Vol. III. 1189–1327, Ed. by H. Rothwell, pp. 316–324; Holt, op. cit. p. 322 and elsewhere.

freemen generally, as well as those of the church. (The first clause of Magna Carta declares 'that the English church shall be free, and have its rights undiminished and its liberties unimpaired' and that the king had granted 'to all the free men of our realm for ourselves and our heirs for ever, all the liberties written below, to have and to hold. . . .')

Magna Carta also carried three most fundamental assumptions anticipating the cardinal principles on which the power of Parliament was eventually to be founded. It implied that the king was subject to the law; that he could only make law and raise taxation (other than his customary dues) with the consent of the 'community of the realm' (which then meant the great council but came to mean Parliament) and that his subjects owed him no absolute and unconditional obedience. All these ideas are to be found in various provisions of the charter but they are also generally subsumed in a clause which sanctioned the right of resistance to the king if he broke faith and disregarded the charter. Clause 61 declared that if the king, or the justiciar in the king's absence abroad, failed to correct any transgressions of the charter that had been brought to his notice, then twenty-five barons (who were to be elected by the barons generally, and empowered to see that the liberties granted by the king were preserved) should 'with the community of the whole land distrain and injure us in every way they can . . .' ('. . . *cum communia totius terrae distringent et gravabunt nos modis omnibus quibus poterint.* . . .') How this might be done, and the limits of such action were carefully defined. The barons might proceed 'by seizing (our) castles, lands, possessions, and in such other ways as they can, saving our person, and the persons of our queen and children, until in their opinion, amends have been made; and when amends have been made, they shall obey us as they did before'.

Thus into a document that was supposed to be a statement of feudal and other liberties there was formally introduced a notion of contract between ruler and kingdom which, even if it could not be finally broken, could at least be put into suspense by one party to force the other to fulfil the essential conditions. The idea of contract (homage given and homage withdrawn) had always lain behind the feudal idea, but Magna Carta made it explicit by laying down a procedure (though it proved to be unworkable) through which it was hoped to make the bargain effective. What is even more remarkable is that, for the first time, opposition to established government was made legitimate, and written down as an agreed non-treasonable procedure centuries before parliamentary practice had formalized the idea of legal opposition after the crown had been taken out of politics. Magna Carta had virtually asserted (and not by clause 61 alone) that kingship, which had always had a quasi-elective aspect in England, was limited by law. The principle of conditional monarchy was to be put into rough practice with the depositions of Edward II and Richard II, and it thereafter found its way into the subconscious thinking of the political nation, emerging as the mainspring of parliamentary action against the Stuarts in the seventeenth century. By the revolution of 1688–89 and the establishment of a monarchy conditional on a religious test, the idea of a dissoluble contract was written into the law of the land. Yet the original authors of Magna Carta unwittingly looked even farther ahead than these exercises in revolutionary action since they tried, though they failed, to devise agreed means whereby opposition could be applied without the kind of revolution which wholly destroys regimes, dynasties or particular monarchs. This was a political concept which, only gradually and reluctantly accepted, began to be put into hesitant practice in the parliamentary politics of the eighteenth century and reached its eventual fruition in the official designation of a Leader of the Opposition, paid by the state, in the twentieth.

Clause 61 was not, however, to survive when Magna Carta was re-issued, and in the early evolution of Parliament its significance lay not so much in its anticipation of the idea of legal opposition, as in its formulation of what was to be the theme of thirteenth century politics: the persistent attempt of the baronial opposition to control the king and his administration. Taken together with a number of other articles, clause 61 made the claim of the community of the realm to be consulted on matters concerning it, and that claim would be transmitted from the baronial council to Parliament. Perhaps most important, Magna Carta anticipated Parliament's principal weapon for securing the redress of grievances, its right and power to withhold the supply of money to the king if redress was not forthcoming. Clause 12 of Magna Carta declared that 'no scutage or aid is to be levied except by the common counsel of our realm' (*per commune consilium regni nostri*). A similar provision was made specifically for financial aids from the city of London. (Exception was allowed only for aids required for ransoming the king, knighting his eldest son and providing for the first marriage of his eldest daughter.) What is more, the charter even anticipated, very roughly, the manner in which future Parliaments were summoned. Clause 14 (which was later dropped) provided a precise procedure for summoning the appropriate men in order to 'obtain the common counsel of the realm' for assessing an aid or scutage. Archbishops, bishops, abbots, earls and greater barons were to be summoned individually by letters from the king. That would be the manner in which the peerage would be summoned. Other tenants-in-chief would be summoned generally through the sheriffs and bailiffs, which was the method by which, not lesser tenants-in-chiefs but the knights and burgesses would eventually be called. All letters of summons would state the reason for the summons.

It was to become a fundamental parliamentary principle that the liberties of the subject under the law should be supreme in England, and Magna Carta was the great charter of English liberties. Yet the notion of liberties it enshrined was not our modern conception of the liberty of individuals each having equal rights. To medieval men, each class of people and each 'interest' had its own recognizable liberty or privilege. The barons, freemen and townsmen (and even the villeins up to a strictly limited point) had their class rights as well as their duties. The right of a man to be 'tried by his peers' (Clause 39) was wholly in accord with medieval thinking. (A peer of the realm's right to be tried on any criminal charge by his fellows in a full assembly of the House of Lords was a late anachronistic survival of this concept. The last trial of a peer by the Lords as a House was that of Lord de Clifford in 1935 and the privilege of peers in this respect was not abolished until 1948.)[1] At the time of Magna Carta, the cruder system of the Anglo-Saxon *wergild* was a thing of the past but a medieval class or group could still stake its claim to particular rights under the law. So by the beginning of the thirteenth century many local liberties were well rooted in towns as well as shires and, the special provisions in Magna Carta for towns, boroughs and merchants, as well as freemen is a recognition of this. The barons were not now so strong that they could afford to dispense with allies in other classes of the nation. It is significant that one of the twenty five 'barons' appointed to control the king was the mayor of London.

Medieval society was a nexus of distinct and often competing communities: barons, freemen, towns, guilds and, above all, the church. In the twentieth century, when the power of Parliament is often held to be threatened by the growing influence of corporations and private interests, each of which deals separately with the executive, it is at least worth remembering that it was from a much more 'corporatist' background that the medieval Parliament arose. Concerned strictly with particular rights, Magna Carta did not make the statements of general principle about liberty which are characteristic of the founding documents of other nations (the American Declaration of Independence, for example) and which are then left to the interpretations of judges or other bodies. Yet its recognition of particular rights logically, if subconsciously, postulated a transcendental concept of the liberty of every subject as well. In this respect, the most important article in the original charter was clause 39, which declared that 'no free man shall be taken or imprisoned or disseised or outlawed or exiled

---

[1] The Criminal Justice Act, 1948. s.3.

or in any way ruined, nor will we go or send against him, except by the judgement of his peers, or by the law of the land.' In the earlier statues of Edward III, 'no free man' became simply 'no man' without any reference to an individual's social condition. By 1354, 'no man' had become 'no man of whatever estate or condition he may be', and in the same statute the vaguer expression 'the law of the land' had become 'due process of law', which meant that a man could only be proceeded against by a writ or by an indicting jury.[1] What began as a statement of respect for feudal custom came to imply that the baron should do justice in his manorial court to the villein who came before him, just as he expected it to be done to him in the king's court, and especially as the freeman could expect it in the common law courts, where eventually the villein too would have his case heard.

Nobody in 1215 supposed that clause 39 (which became clause 29 in the reissue of 1225) would come to symbolize an Englishman's right to trial by jury, but it did. Nor did clause 40 ('To no man will we sell, to no man will we deny or delay right or justice.') embody in 1215 the safeguard to personal liberty that it denoted later when it came to signify that a man must not be kept in prison for an indefinite period without trial. At the time it meant simply that the king would act justly in his own courts, and would not give tainted justice. Magna Carta was not unique as a document enumerating the liberties of barons and towns forced from a king; similar charters were extracted from rulers on the Continent in the twelfth and thirteenth centuries.[2] What made it different was that in the social conditions of England it could not be diminished by becoming simply the instrument of a feudal ambition to destroy monarchical power, which the English magnates were never strong enough to attempt. Instead, the barons used the charter and the principles underlying it as a means of trying to exercise some control constitutionally over a crown which they neither could nor wished to destroy. The struggle for the control of the king's administration was the theme of politics during the whole of the thirteenth century and beyond, and it was closely linked with the rise of Parliament.

Within three months of the issue of Magna Carta, however, the peace which it was supposed to symbolize had broken down. The imprecision of the some of the statements of the charter bred uncertainty and quarrels, neither king nor barons in practice being willing to subject their interests to them. A start was made on fulfilling the obligation to restore lands, castles and franchises to those who had been deprived of them unjustly, but the barons failed to give the king the security and loyalty he wanted. In August

---

[1] Holt, op. cit. p. 9.
[2] Holt, op. cit. p. 20 et seq.

John felt it unsafe to attend a conference with the barons at Oxford, and sought moral support from his liege lord the Pope. He also began to bring mercenary troops from the Continent. The Pope annulled the charter, but before his letter arrived in England war had broken out again. In the ensuing conflict, the king's mercenary troops ravaged the country, often committing fearful atrocities, and by the end of the year, John was in control of the north and east. Militarily weaker than the king, those barons who were at war with him (and many of the more powerful were on his side) held only London. Their only hope lay in help from outside. So throwing aside any pretence that they were simply seeking to distrain the king (as the charter allowed) they invited Louis, the son of Philip Augustus of France, to invade England and take the crown. For a time, the king had considerable successes, but by the beginning of June, 1216, Louis had entered London in triumph.

The last few months of the king's campaign were indecisive. In October John died of a fever on his way south, leaving a child as his heir. Given the disinclination of the time to accept child kings, his death might have seemed a catastrophe for his line. In fact, it probably saved the dynasty since it created the opportunity for a new beginning under a boy king governed by moderates acceptable to the baronage. The alternative was the importation of another foreign dynasty bringing adherents who would be a threat to the barons of England. Faced with these alternatives, the majority of the baronage, now cut off from their Norman roots and thoroughly settled in England, could only support the Plantagenet heir if they wished to avoid absorption in a new French empire. So the crown passed to Henry III who wore it for most of the rest of the thirteenth century. The politics of his reign were dominated by a long drawn out struggle with the baronial opposition over the charter. In the midst of this struggle Parliament was born.

CHAPTER 2

Henry III:
the Emergence of Parliament

I

HENRY III succeeded to the throne as a boy of nine and occupied it for the next 56 years. During this time, Parliament emerged by name as an organ of government, already performing intermittently the basic functions which were to be characteristic of it in the centuries ahead. It was the highest court in the land where justice was dispensed. In it, and with its assent, the king also declared law. It also began to grant, or refuse to grant, extraordinary (that is to say non-feudal and non-customary) taxation. Not least it acted on occasions as a national council, deliberating on the great affairs of the kingdom. The essential constituent of a thirteenth century Parliament was the common council of the realm in which the earls, barons and prelates met in consultation with the king and his close council. Indeed, the composition of Parliament initially was essentially that of the great council gathered together on certain occasions. To some Parliaments in Henry's reign representatives of the shires and boroughs were called for the first time. But their presence was only occasional and they would not be necessary for the proceedings of a Parliament until the second quarter of the fourteenth century. The focal point of Henry's reign is the dramatic resurgence of conflict between the king and the baronage in Henry's later years, with the barons' short-lived experiments for controlling the crown. The eye of history has been caught especially by Simon de Montfort's first summons to burgesses from the towns to sit alongside the knights of the shire. Yet it was in the earlier years of the reign that Parliament first appeared fleetingly by name, and in other ways too, the period of the king's minority had its own particular significance for the development of English political institutions.

For a year after King John's death, the struggle continued between the Plantagenet royal party and the rebellious section of the baronage led by Louis of France. In an atmosphere of some emotion and with demonstrations of loyalty, the boy king was hastily crowned at Gloucester with a plain gold circlet for lack of St Edward's crown. (The French still occupied London and the south east of the country.) The youth and innocence of the king, and his non-involvement in the strife which had raged round his father, were politically healing. The moral leadership of the royal party was immediately in the hands of the loyal and chivalrous William Marshal, earl of Pembroke, and it was this aged and experienced man who, apparently after some initial reluctance, agreed to take the title of governor of the king and kingdom (*rector regis et regni*). William Marshal, then over 70 years old, had faithfully served Henry II, Richard I and John with the loyalty of disinterested and candid advice rather than with blind obedience. He was in many respects the epitome of the medieval ideal of chivalry. For the next few years, the government was to be conducted by William, by Hubert de Burgh, the justiciar, and by Peter des Roches, Bishop of Winchester, one of John's old associates who became the young King's guardian and tutor under the Earl Marshal. These three 'ministers' (appointed with the approval of the council of the realm) appear to have governed with the aid of a small inner council of indeterminate membership and variable attendance. This was drawn from the papal legate (an important and moderating influence on the tensions between those around him) and those magnates, lay and ecclesiastical, who had been John's executors, as well as the principal officials of the royal administration. Not all its potential 'members' attended all or even most of the meetings of the inner council: attendance would have depended on the importance of the occasion and the convenience of individuals. Nevertheless, the minority of Henry III was important in the development of the executive inner council as distinct from the advisory great council of the realm.

The first important decision of policy in the new reign was taken by the magnates and royal counsellors present at a meeting at Bristol only a month after King John's death. Having sworn oaths of fealty to the new king, they re-issued Magna Carta, no longer as a document sponsored by rebels, but carefully revised and pruned to become a symbol of stability to which moderate men generally could rally. The Charter was authenticated by the seals of the Marshal and the Legate, and every important lay and ecclesiastical counsellor by whose 'advice' the Charter had been granted was listed by name in the preamble. The purpose of the reissue was partly to attract back to the royal cause the less persistent rebels, but it also represented the acknowledgement by the Earl Marshal and the moderates of the king's party that Magna Carta offered a sensible and generally acceptable basis for a new beginning. Now that John was dead, there was no longer need for loyalists to suppress this view of it, and since the final outbreak of hostilities had ostensibly been over the enforcement and ambiguities of Magna Carta rather than its principle, the Charter could be made generally acceptable by revision.

The deletions, in particular, were of great significance. The most important were the dropping of articles 12 and 14 which had restricted the power of the king in raising extraordinary non-feudal revenue, and had sought to prevent him from levying an aid or scutage without the consent of the great council of tenants-in-chief.[1] It must have seemed unnecessary to impose on a young king who had not offended in such matters the same kind of restraints as had been imposed on his offending father. What is more, article 14, which required the 'common counsel of the realm' to be obtained by summoning an assembly of *all* the tenants-in-chief, may well have seemed far too cumbersome and impractical a method of ensuring some control over taxation. In any case, the royalist magnates who issued the Charter were probably most reluctant to bind themselves so rigidly now that active responsibility for the king's government had fallen to them.

Yet the most powerful reason for the omission of these clauses may have simply been a growing realization that they were in practice no longer necessary. It must have been increasingly evident that it was hardly feasible for a king to levy taxation successfully (outside the normal feudal dues) without the consent of the taxed. Even at the height of the barons' success in opposition to Henry III towards the end of the reign, it was never felt necessary to re-state Clauses 12 and 14. Nothing resembling them was to be included in the Provisions of Oxford by which the baronial insurgents sought to restrain royal power during the great crisis of the reign. The reason was presumably that from the beginning of the reign it was always found essential for such taxation to be levied only by a grant of the great council, even though there was no provision in writing to stipulate that this must be so. Sometimes, moreover, the council refused to grant money and when this happened, it did not hesitate to state its reason in forthright terms.[2] When the council refused grants, its refusal was accepted, and no attempt was made to impose it without consent.

The reissued Charter also omitted the provisions (clause 61) which had

---

[1] A scutage was strictly feudal, being a payment in substitution for feudal service, but in the Charter of 1215, it was treated as though it was non-feudal, being associated with non-feudal 'aids' in Clauses 12 and 14.

[2] See pp. 78–9.

set up a council of 25 barons ('under-kings' was said to have been John's bitter description of them) with power to control the king and distrain him if he refused to redress grievances put to him. In place of Clause 61, the reissued Charter concluded with a statement to the effect that a number of the omitted clauses were not so much dropped as deferred for further consideration later. Such clauses (it was stated) 'which seemed important yet doubtful, namely on the assessing of scutage and aids, on the debts of the Jews and others, on freedom to leave and return to our kingdom, on forests and foresters ... the above mentioned prelates and magnates have agreed to those being deferred until we have fuller counsel, when we will most fully, in these as well as in other matters that have to be amended, do what is necessary for the common good and the peace and estate (*statum*) of ourselves and our kingdom.' It was significant, however, that Clause 61 itself, instituting the Twenty-Five, was not numbered among those deferred, and must therefore have been regarded as finally deleted. That revolutionary, clumsy and premature attempt to entrench opposition in the 'constitution' had gone for good, though its spirit lingered on.

By September 1217, Louis had been forced (after a decisive victory for the royal party in the Battle of Lincoln) to give up his struggle for the crown. Having been given favourable terms, he acknowledged Henry's title to the throne and left the country. Peace was celebrated by a second reissue of the Magna Carta in 1217. The revised version of 1216 had already incorporated a number of significant revisions of detail in the retained clauses in order to make their meaning more precise and legally effective. This process was now carried further, but the 'important and doubtful' clauses of 1216 which had been deferred in 1216 were now quietly and finally dropped. All that the Charter of 1217 had to say on the subject of taxation was that 'scutage shall be taken in future as it used to be taken in the time of Henry our grandfather', an unexceptional and conveniently imprecise statement.

Indeed, the Charter of 1217 showed a number of signs of a general reaction against baronial excesses, notably in a new provision that adulterine, or unlicensed, castles were to be destroyed. This second reissue of the Charter was, however, accompanied by a new and separate Charter of the Forest dealing with the custom and extent of the forest, deforestation and the penalties for breaking the forest law. This document dealt with abuses of the royal forest rights, reversed the afforestation of the previous two reigns and lightened penalties for breaking the forest law. The Charter of the Forest was of the greatest practical importance to very many people in a largely rural society, and its existence did much, in the years of

Parliament's early growth, to encourage demands for the confirmation of the Charters and so keep Magna Carta itself politically alive.[1]

In 1219, the old and trusted regent, William Marshal, died, and for the next nine years, politics were dominated by a struggle for influence between the justiciar, Hubert de Burgh, and Peter des Roches, the Bishop of Winchester, a Poitevin adherent of King John, who had survived politically despite the movement against 'foreigners' at the time of the Charter.[2] The Papal Legate, basing his influence partly on the theory that England was still a papal fief, acted for a time as a kind of umpire between them. The justiciar was a man of great ability, but he was also personally ambitious and was much disliked by the magnates to whose ranks he had advanced himself. Under Hubert's strong administration of the king's powers, the old tensions between crown and barons now started again in a new form.

Henry III was crowned for the second time, but now with full ceremonial, in 1220, and the barons present at the coronation swore that they would restore to the king, at his will, those royal castles they held from him. This was a matter of great importance for the royal authority. England was a sparsely populated country, with probably little more than three million people, in which villages and towns were separated by great distances of forest and uninhabited land. The maintenance of law and order depended on clear manifestations of physical power and castles were the practical strongholds of authority. Warfare was largely a struggle for their control and its skills were based on the siege, storming and defence of castles, which were also used as administrative centres for both shires and baronies. It was therefore a significant question who held a particular castle, by what right he held it and whether, indeed, the castle was really a royal or a private stronghold. In many cases, the answer had become obscure. During the civil wars, many castles, royal and private, had been placed in, or fallen into, the hands of other men than their proper owners. Many a supporter of King John now occupied castles obtained in this way and many a magnate was a great pluralist of castles. It was not that such men (some of whom were foreigners) were consciously rebellious; on the contrary, they had often occupied disputed castles as King John's men. The trouble was rather that, in medieval England, what a man held in fact could quickly be deemed his

---

[1] Holt, op. cit. p. 275. The Charter of the Forest is printed in Stubbs, *Select Charters* (pp. 344–348) (Latin) and in Stephenson and Marcham op. cit. (pp. 129–132) and *E.H.D.* Vol. III, pp. 347–349 in translation.

[2] Hubert had been chief justiciar at the end of John's reign and was a long-standing and able servant of the late king.

by prescriptive right. Such a state of affairs, if unremedied, could lead to great concentrations of local power in the hands of subjects who hankered after a degree of local independence which was bound to be a challenge to the king's rule.[1]

To secure the return of royal castles from men in possession who had begun to think of them as their own, a writ for a general inquiry *quo warranto* was issued in 1220 requiring all who held castles to prove at the Exchequer by what warrant they did so. This not only foreshadowed the *quo warranto* legislation of Edward I: it also started a process of judicial inquiry into the possession of property rights which was to play a significant part in the emergence of Parliament.[2] There is no evidence that the *quo warranto* writ at this time was acted on effectively in general.[3] But the determination of the government to resume old rights in respect of castles was real enough. In 1220 William de Forz, Count of Aumâle, a powerful Poitevin landowner, had refused to surrender the castles of Sauvey and Rockingham but royal forces had frightened the garrisons into abandoning them. Then, in 1221, Aumâle went into open rebellion having refused to surrender the castle at Bytham to one of his tenants who had opposed king John but was due to have it back. Again Aumâle was forced to capitulate, but these episodes stimulated the government's determination to take back, as and when it could, royal castles held by others in the king's name. The purpose was to redistribute them in such a way as to ensure their dependence on the crown, and the policy was pursued with much vigour between 1221 and 1224. The Pope sent letters to the king's vassals saying that the king should now have control of his own seal and castles; the justiciar undertook expeditions which forced the possessors of a number of castles to hand them over. In 1223, the king's minority was formally brought to an end (he was now sixteen), and he was given limited personal use of his seal. After some attempt at resistance, the powerful Earl of Chester (who was reluctant to push his interest to the point of disloyalty) and others who had attempted to retain castles they held, submitted. In the early months of 1224 over thirty castles were handed over to the king and the danger of baronial autonomy passed. This had not been achieved without some outbursts of rebellion, the last and worst of which was that of a Norman-born adventurer, Fawkes de Breauté (an old servant of John's), when the demand was made for the return of castles he held. Firm action by the justiciar and Archbishop Langton, culminating in the capture of de Breauté's castle at Bedford, put

[1] The best general account of this episode is in F. M. Powicke, *Henry III and the Lord Edward*, Ch. II.
[2] See pp. 134–5 and pp. 141–2.
[3] J. E. A. Joliffe, *The Constitutional History of Medieval England* (2nd edition), p. 267–8.

down this revolt. To help to pay for the cost of this military action, the prelates of the province of Canterbury had joined together in providing a carucage (a charge on land under the plough, and the direct descendent of the old Danegeld). A general carucage had also been granted in 1220, and these were the last occasions on which this type of taxation was raised in England.

The broad principle that taxation needed the assent of the common council of the realm whenever a carucage or even scutage was raised seems to have been established by William Marshal from the first years of the reign. That concept continued to be acted on after him.[1] The principle that the king had no right to raise taxation (outside his feudal dues) and should live and govern by the wealth of his own demesne had been a fundamental element in the quarrel between the barons and King John. It was also to be fundamental in the future tension between crown and Parliament. But at the beginning of the thirteenth century, the idea that taxation depended on consent also carried the broader implication that even the consent of the 'community' to a tax did not necessarily bind an individual to pay if he was unwilling. Whether a tax should or should not be paid was, on this assumption, a matter of personal and individual decision by each taxpayer. When the great council granted the carucage of 1220, some of the magnates resisted payment on the grounds that they had not been present to give their consent to it.[2] After 1225, however, any claim by an individual that he had the right to contract out of taxation was to be out of the question. In future, taxation granted by the council of the realm, or by Parliament, would be binding on every individual, and this fundamental principle of the English constitution was firmly established with the reissue, in 1225, of Magna Carta as the first Act on the Statute Book.

As usual, this constitutional development had arisen from the pressures of practical politics. In 1224, just after the declaration of Henry III's partial majority, there had been a demand from the magnates that he should now, as an adult king, confirm the charters in order to ensure their legal status. His first response had been evasive, but events forced him to agree. In 1223, Louis VIII had succeeded King Philip of France and had immediately prepared to attack Poitou and Gascony. To counter-attack, Henry required more English money than had been raised at any time since the beginning of the reign, or than could be provided by the carucages and scutages granted in the past by the council of the realm. Something new was needed, and a precedent was found in a levy by King John, in 1207, of a tax of a thirteenth

---

[1] Stubbs, *Constitutional History*, Vol. II, 4th ed. pp. 30–31.
[2] Powicke, *The Thirteenth Century* (1216–1307), p. 29.

of the value of all 'movables' – that is to say, personal property and rents. This tax, which had been raised 'by the common counsel and assent of our council at Oxford' (though the clergy had strongly objected) had drawn on precedents in ecclesiastical taxation. It had also been the method used to raise King Richard's ransom.

At the Christmas great council of 1224, therefore, the justiciar asked for a fifteenth of the value of all movables. Despite the precedents, this was a new departure leading to the system which would be the basis of English taxation for over four centuries. Responsibility for the assessment and collection of the tax was placed on 'four lawful knights' from each hundred or wapentake who were to be elected in the shire court where the sheriff was to assemble all the knights of the county. Details of all exempt goods were given in the writ for the collection. For all prelates and other men of religion, and for all earls, barons, knights, and freeholders who were not merchants, books of all kinds were exempt (which is suggestive of a wider degree of literacy in these classes than is sometimes supposed); so were the ornaments of churches and chapels, riding horses, draught horses, arms of all kinds, jewels, vases, utensils, the contents of larders and cellars and grain for supplying castles. Merchants paid the fifteenth on their merchandise and movables but were exempt from paying it on their riding horses, house utensils, and the contents of their larders and cellars. Villeins were likewise exempt from payment on utensils, meat, fish, drink, hay and fodder not for sale. Clergy, noblemen and knights and freeholders were exempt in respect of arms of all kinds, and merchants and villeins in respect of the arms 'to which they were sworn' under the Assize of Arms. Regulations for swearing to the quantity and value of taxable possessions were prescribed, and to avoid corruption and influence, it was required that knights responsible for assessing and collecting the tax should not go into the hundreds of which they were residents but into those that were adjacent.[1] This type of taxation was to be levied only four times in Henry III's reign, and on each occasion it was granted only after serious and solemn debate. But because it was to become the standard method of parliamentary taxation, the circumstances in which it was first raised are of particular interest.

The justiciar's demand for money immediately met renewed insistence that the king should grant a full reissue of the Charter, and this time it could not be evaded. Magna Carta was reissued in 1225 with no material changes of content, but with a fundamental difference in the basis of its enactment. It

---

[1] The writ for the collection of the fifteenth is printed in Stubbs, *Select Charters*, pp. 351–353. Translation: Stephenson and Marcham, *Sources of English Constitutional History*.

was no longer granted on the 'advice' of the magnates, but was given and granted by the king 'of our own spontaneous goodwill' (*spontanea et bona voluntate*) to the 'archbishops, bishops, abbots, priors, earls, barons and all our realm.' The principal purpose of the new wording was to give the Charter additional weight by establishing that it had been granted freely by the now adult king, though the phrasing could also later be invoked to support the claim of the king to make law, if he so wished, by himself alone. In terms of parliamentary history, however, it is much more significant that the charter of 1225 also made it formally clear that it was granted specifically in exchange for taxation, in much the same terms as those which operated in Edward III's Parliaments.

'In return for the grant and gift of these liberties and of other liberties contained in our charter of the forest,' the Charter concluded, 'the archbishops, bishops, abbots, priors, earls, barons, knights, freeholders *and all our realm* have given us a fifteenth part of their moveables.'[1] Thus it was made clear once and for all that the council of the realm, and later Parliament, had the power to bind all subjects, collectively and individually, to pay taxation that had been lawfully granted by the representatives of the realm. It also established that the great council (or Parliament) had some duty to provide aid for essential national needs, and in return had the right to secure from the king a solemn undertaking of specified obligation to his subjects. From this exchange between king and subjects, there developed the doctrine that taxation was granted in return for the redress of grievances. This then led to the insistence of later Parliaments that they would pay tax only when they secured from the monarch policies of which they approved. In this manner, the power of the purse was exerted politically early in the thirteenth century, and the foundation of future parliamentary strength was laid.

At the beginning of 1227, Henry declared himself to be fully of age, and assumed responsibility for the government. He was a king who has generally attracted little sympathy from historians. Henry was pious (he made a cult of Edward the Confessor and rebuilt Westminster Abbey), personally virtuous, artistic and intelligent. He was also, however, generally unsuccessful in his dealings with the barons, and although we do not know much of his real character, the record suggests that he was politically impatient, deficient in judgement, inconstant and unpersistent. Yet allowance must be made for the difficulty that would have faced any king in reaching a *modus vivendi* with the magnates as feudalism disintegrated

---

[1] My italics. The charter of this year (with facsimile) is in *Stat. R.* Vol. I, pp. 21–25. Extracts, Stubbs, *Select Charters*, pp. 349–351.

in the thirteenth century. The barons might claim with some reason that they only wanted to be consulted, which the King's inner council often failed to do, and to be protected in their rights. On the other hand the challenge represented by baronial and other private franchises was hardly less of a potential threat to the King now than it had been in previous reigns. It is not surprising, then, that Henry began his personal conduct of government by strengthening and widening the inquiry into the 'right' of all landowners who claimed to hold their land by royal grant, demanding to know their warrant, and confirming charters in exchange for financial fine.

It is not easy for us to keep firmly in mind just how much property-holding was still customary in the early thirteenth century, being dependent either on tradition or the fact of possession. Often there was no certain evidence of a man's right to hold what he held. Even in 'normal' circumstances the original possession was often shrouded in uncertainty, and the upheavals of John's reign had exacerbated this difficulty since property had often changed hands by *force majeure*. Now, however, medieval society was moving into a more literate and developed condition. A new intellectual vigour was manifest (in Oxford, for example, where Roger Bacon, the Dominican scholar, taught and wrote) and a renewed spirituality was encouraged by the dedicated work of the friars generally. It was a great age of cathedral architecture, and there was a heightened emphasis on theology. The population was increasing and new property rights were being claimed as wasteland was developed and colonized. Against such a background it was natural that there should also be interest in more advanced methods of government, and not least in the evidence of the written word to authenticate rights and obligations. Charters had once been no more than evidence of possession; they did not constitute a necessary title to property. Now, however, the stage was being reached in which the written word was to be required as a title-deed.

It is indisputable that Henry III often behaved capriciously, ineptly and suspiciously in politics, and that he failed to maintain the relations with the great men of the land which they considered to be part of the natural order of things. Although his personality and attributes have not come down to us very clearly, the contrast between his failure and his son's general success suggests that, in the last analysis, he lacked that clear but not easily definable personal quality that is necessary for a political leader to have authority and command respect. On the other hand, the effort that he and his ministers made to place the administration on a more secure and systematic basis, not least in seeking to establish the 'rights' of property and franchise on firm legality, was an advance in the skills of government, and not simply a sign of arbitrary ambition.

In 1231, Bishop Peter of Winchester, who had gone abroad several years earlier (in part because of his opposition to Hubert de Burgh's policy of taking back royal castles) returned to England and immediately resumed his place in the king's confidence. A clever, sophisticated and cosmopolitan cleric, Peter des Roches arrived back at court precisely when the king was becoming disenchanted with the justiciar's control of affairs. In 1231, Hubert was dismissed from office and charged with a catalogue of disparate and sensational offences which plainly owed much more to the imagination of his accusers, and to the personal dislike that Hubert inspired, than to any real misdeeds. At first, Hubert had good reason to fear for his life, but eventually, although he was forced to give up all the other possessions he had acquired, he was allowed to keep his personal estates and go into honourable captivity at Devizes. Hubert was the last of the old political justiciars (when the title was revived later it was for an official with purely judicial functions)[1] and in his place, Bishop Peter des Roches became Henry's chief counsellor. The king's principal administrator, however, was Peter des Rivaux, who was either the nephew or the son of the Bishop, and a man of much administrative ability. Peter des Rivaux was given custody of the treasury, the king's small (or privy) seal, and the wardrobe. Now largely a financial department of government, the wardrobe was becoming increasingly the centre of financial and political decisions in the royal household. Being directly under the king's personal control, and receiving instructions under his privy seal, the wardrobe was a sharper instrument for the king's personal authority than either the treasury or the chancery. A great but static department of state, the chancery could now, for instance, issue under the great seal its own routine writs not requiring the king's authorization.

Few ministers have been more blatantly pluralist than Peter des Rivaux. He was also given financial control of the royal household for life (the finances of the household and the government were hardly distinguishable from each other) and appointed keeper of the forests and ports. For a short time, he was the sheriff of twenty-one counties as well. The purpose of this agglomeration of offices was not, however, simply crude power-hunger or greed. The object was rather to secure authority for a notable reform of administration which he effected in his two years of office, and which was to be continued after him. He advanced the work and status of the Exchequer (new types of records and practices were introduced for instance), the

---

[1] With the loss of most of the English king's French dominions, there was now no need for a justiciar with almost vice-regal powers and discretion to act for the king in his frequent absences abroad.

sheriffs being brought under much closer supervision and turned into salaried officials instead of being financial farmers of the shires' revenues for their own profit.[1] Royal rights were vigorously inspected and claimed; private claims and rights were investigated and became the subject of adjudication. The central instrument for all this was the court of the Exchequer, acting as a *judicial* body where disputes and complaints could be heard. Even after the fall of Peter des Rivaux, enquiries into the franchise claimed by the king's vassals and tenants remained a principal concern of the king through the many years of political disputes that lay ahead, and in the judicial work of the Exchequer at Parliament-time it is possible to discern part of the origin of Parliament.[2] But the immediate outcome of the reforms carried out by Peter des Rivaux was the king's first serious quarrel with his barons. Administrative actions which enhanced the independence of the crown, and were taken with little or no reference to the magnates, were a cause of deep baronial resentment.[3]

The great men of the land were incensed by the rigour of the administration, by its effect on their own interests and by the fact that it was under the management of a group of 'foreign' officials holding a monopoly of offices with direct responsibility to the king. The magnates felt themselves to be excluded from this nexus of power. The majority of magnates and tenants-in-chief, living on their estates away from the court, had an instinctive dislike of the professional politicians who ran the government without consulting them. They felt about the king's ministers and officials much as the seventeenth century 'country party' was to feel about the court politicians who served the Stuarts. They saw themselves as the king's natural counsellors who were not adequately represented on his inner council, and although they were part of the greater council, it met only occasionally and was not, as they saw it, properly deferred to by the government. The king's personal power, exercised through a few dependants, had never previously in the reign been so unrestricted. Resistance to the new order therefore hardened around Richard Marshal, Earl of Pembroke and son of the old Marshal. Several barons took up arms and a baronial confederation was organized to get rid of the king's

---

[1] The reign of John had inaugurated the practice of record-keeping. Before that, records of government business were seldom made. Under John, financial, legal and administrative records were made for the Exchequer and then for the chancery. Extracts and copies were made on parchment membranes which were then sewn together in rolls instead of being bound in books.

[2] See below, p. 85.

[3] The indispensable guide to all aspects of medieval administration is T. F. Tout's 'Chapters in the Administrative History of Medieval England.' (1920).

objectionable advisers. Peace was only ensured by the intervention of the bishops at a great council held at Westminster in February 1234. Under the leadership of the new Archbishop of Canterbury, Edmund Rich, who was to be canonized a few years after his death, the bishops persuaded Henry to agree to think about his relationship with his ministers. After a short interval, a truce was negotiated with the rebels, and at a further meeting of the great council in April, Henry confirmed that Peter des Rivaux and other ministers were to go.

This was perhaps the first occasion when a king was forced to change his ministers at the behest of the great council. The attempts of the 'community of the realm' in council, and subsequently in Parliament, to control and approve those whom the king appointed to serve him, and the king's resistance to having his servants chosen for him, provided a persistent theme of politics in the centuries ahead. The matter would not be finally resolved until it was established at the end of the seventeenth century that the king could only govern through ministers supported by a parliamentary majority. In 1234 the dismissed ministers would probably have departed with less opprobrium than they did had it not been for the killing in Ireland of Earl Richard Marshal, a deed for which they appear to have been in some way (unjustly) blamed, and which turned the king against them. In a reconciliation at Gloucester in May 1234, the leaders of the baronial party, including Hubert de Burgh, were admitted to the king's council. The position appeared to have been recognized that the king should not act wholly without consultation with his natural counsellors, who had no wish to be in strife with him.

In 1236, shortly after the king's marriage to Eleanor of Provence, a great council held at Merton promulgated the law known as the Statute of Merton, which dealt with a number of important questions of law and justice, particularly in relation to property, and attempted to remedy a number of common grievances. It is considered by tradition to be the second statute after Magna Carta.[1] Then, quite unobtrusively and unremarked, the word 'Parliament' slid into the official vocabulary to describe a full meeting of the great council in 1237 which was apparently indistinguishable in composition from other such gatherings. It was the first such meeting, so far as we are aware, to be described in the records as a 'Parliament' and we shall come back to it in the context of the question: what was a Parliament? For the moment, it is enough to note that in 1237

---

[1] The Statute of Merton is the first statute as such in *Statutes of the Realm*, Vol. I, pp. 1–4. (Translated version in *E.H.D.*, Vol. III, pp. 351–354). The Statute is 'granted by the aforesaid archbishop, bishops, earls and barons and by the King himself and others. . . .'

Henry confirmed the great charter again in return for a tax of a thirtieth at another moment of financial difficulty and discontent. He also agreed to enlarge his inner council by the admission of three of the older baronage.

Yet tensions were not ended. The arrival of Provencals and Savoyards, relatives of the new queen, brought new discontents as the latest 'foreigners' secured offices and revenues that might have gone to Englishmen. (An uncle of the queen, Boniface of Savoy, succeeded Edmund Rich as Archbishop of Canterbury.) There was increasing anger with papal demands for money to help finance the struggle of the Pope, Gregory IX, against the Emperor, Frederick II. In particular there was objection to the system of Papal Provisions, under which the Pope could reserve benefices to the Holy See and, by paying deputies to minister in them, retain the balance of their revenue for the benefit of Rome.

In addition, the king began to make new plans to recover his lost dominions in France. For much of the reign, the truce originally made at Chinon by King John in 1214 had been in force or was renewed. Peace had been punctuated only by two campaigns between 1224 and 1227, and 1229 to 1231. In January 1242, however, at a meeting of the great council, Henry asked for an aid to assist him to seek his rights in France. It was bluntly refused and the reasons stated with no mincing of words. The report we possess of the proceedings cannot for certain be described as an official one: it is inserted in the *Chronica Majora* of Matthew Paris, the chronicler of St. Albans. Nevertheless, there are no reasons for regarding it as anything but an accurate account of what took place. The barons 'advised' the king to await the expiry of his truce with the French king. If the French king broke the truce, then they would 'willingly give their utmost consideration to giving him an aid.' They reminded him of all the earlier aids they had given him, and particularly of the thirtieth of 1237, for which he had confirmed Magna Carta. All that money (they said) had been deposited[1] in the royal castles in charge of the Earl Warenne and three other magnates 'by whose view and advice, the money should be expended for the benefit of the king and kingdom. . . .' Since the barons had not heard that the money had been spent, 'they firmly believe and are well aware that the lord king has the whole of that money intact still, and from it he can provide himself now with a great deal of aid.' Then, having remarked pointedly on the King's other resources, on the poverty of the kingdom and on Henry's failure (since they had given him the thirtieth) to observe the charter (instead, they

---

[1] The money would have been collected and stored in large quantities of silver pennies and halfpennies, the only physical unit of currency at this time.

said, he had oppressed them more than usual) 'they told the King flatly that for the present they would not give him an aid.'¹

This was described by Stubbs as the first account of a parliamentary debate.² It is not easy to quarrel with the description of this meeting of the great council of the realm as a Parliament if that title is to be allowed to other assemblies of the reign (as it was, and is) of the same composition. More to the point, the occasion bears most of the marks of a Parliament as we recognize and know it. There was, for one thing, a debate, not in the presence of the king, the conclusions of which were conveyed to Henry by nobles acting as messengers. There was a discussion of high policy (that is to say, about the expediency of war in the circumstances of the moment) and a statement of the policy for which the council might be prepared to find money. There was, not least, consideration of a request for taxation and its refusal. There is even a suggestion that the previous aid had been appropriated by the council that had granted it for purposes to be approved of by four designated magnates. The term 'Parliament' was already in fairly common use by 1240, and the gathering of 1242 had some essential parliamentary attributes, even though it was not described as a Parliament in this account of its deliberations. It is a convenient moment to pause and to examine what Parliament was under Henry III and how it arose.

II

The earliest use of the word 'Parliament' (*Parliamentum*) so far traced is in a *curia regis* roll of November 1236.³ Litigation having arisen over the advowson of Stapleford Church in Wiltshire, the Sub-Dean Adam, representing the Chapter of Salisbury Cathedral, pledged his faith that he would appear 'at the Parliament' at Westminster in January 1237. As we have already seen, this was a meeting of the King's council, attended by prelates, abbots, earls and barons, as well as by his ordinary councillors, ministers and judges. At this Parliament, there were various legislating acts

---

[1] Stubbs, *Select Charters*, pp. 359–360 (Latin); and *E.H.D.* Vol. III, pp. 355–357 (English). Evidence for Henry III's parliaments is largely derived from chronicles, notably M. Paris, *Chronica Majora* (Rolls ser. ed. H. R. Luard, 7 Vols. 1872–8; extracts, *Select Charters*, pp. 326–333.

[2] Stubbs, *Constitutional History*, Vol. II, p. 59.

[3] H. G. Richardson and G. O. Sayles, (Ch. II, p. 16) 'The Earliest Known Official Use of the Term "Parliament".' *E.H.R.* LXXXII (1967), pp. 747–50.

and an aid was granted in return for the reconfirmation of the charters,[1] in addition to which, more routine matters, such as the Stapleford advowson, were dealt with. The term 'Parliament' was, however, in more general unofficial use before then. In a metrical life of William the Marshal, written about 1226, there are several references to a 'Parliament' (also called an assembly) held at Worcester a year after the departure of Louis of France. The gathering to which this writer applied the term was one which might have been called a great council of the realm. The word was also used in a chronicle (tentatively dated 1217) to describe a meeting of barons and bishops at Staines in August 1215 which waited in vain for King John.[2] Before about 1240, however, the word 'Parliament' (*parlement*) was commonly used more on the other side of the Channel than in England. It signified originally simply a talk (even one of an informal kind) but it came to mean formal business discussions between ruling or other important people or their representatives – that is to say, 'parleys'. Slowly the English chroniclers and clerks took up the word, and in 1246, Matthew Paris used it (in place of the terms *consilium* or *colloquium*) to describe a meeting called in the official records a *colloquium*. The account of this meeting given by Matthew Paris is revealing. 'Convoked by the royal edict, all the nobility of the English Kingdom assembled in London at a most general Parliament (*ad Parliamentum generalissimum*), namely, the prelates, including bishops, abbots and priors, together with the earls and barons, in order to discuss effectively the uncertain state of the realm, as urgent necessity demanded.'[3] The significant words in this passage are 'most general'; from now on, the word 'Parliament' was in increasingly common use to signify a notably large and general gathering of the great council on a particularly important occasion, and in this sense it was used (so it seems) interchangeably with the older descriptions. In the records, the clerks sometimes used it; and sometimes they did not. But was Parliament simply a synonym for a meeting of the great council for the sort of purposes that the great council usually met? Or did it signify a meeting of the same body (perhaps somewhat modified in composition) for the performance of functions of particular significance that were in some way different or distinguishable from those with which a great council was usually concerned?

An immense amount of research has been devoted to these questions, and although it has produced few answers that are entirely undisputed, it has illuminated the essential origins of Parliament. The once-held ideas that

[1] See p. 77–8.
[2] H. G. Richardson, 'The Origins of Parliament', *Transactions Royal Historical Society*, 4th ser., XI, 1928 (pp. 137–175), which deals with the early use of the term.
[3] Stubbs, *Select Charters*, p. 328 (Latin).

Parliament was the deliberate and simple invention of Simon de Montfort (because he summoned knights and burgesses to it to assist the baronial struggle against Henry III) or that it was the creation of Edward I (because he used it so thoroughly in making statute law) have been long abandoned. Parliament evolved under the pressure of political events, and the powerful men whose actions furthered its growth had no idea that they were inventing a new institution. Nevertheless, in their actions we can see its beginning, and we now also understand much more clearly the essential nature of the earliest Parliaments.

In origin, Parliament was the king's court and council. It was the High Court of Parliament and the symbolism of the House of Lords today still recalls its original nature. The (usually empty) throne at its head tells us that (as with any other court of law) the crown is deemed to be legally always present. The Privy Councillors who, though they are not peers, are allowed to sit on the steps of the throne *as of right* also remind us that this was, originally, the king's court and council. The special position of the Lord Chancellor, who legally does not have to be a peer, and the presence of other judges, emphasize that it is, and always has been, a court of law.[1] Deriving its power from the medieval king's council (*concilium regis*), the House of Lords remains to this day the highest court of appeal from all other courts, vesting its judicial authority in the Lords of Appeal. In this capacity it performs precisely the same role as the medieval king's court, when it acted as the ultimate source of justice. The official who fulfils the function of the clerk of the Lords (analagous to the Clerk of the House of Commons) is still called the Clerk of the Parliaments because, in origin, Parliament and the 'House' of Lords were one and the same. Both evolved from the council chamber with the king, with his close councillors and his judges at the centre. The Commons were grafted later on to this basic stock.

The king's court was omnicompetent; its powers could be judicial, legislative or political, and the medieval mind drew no sharp distinction between these categories. To one school of modern scholars, however, the essential origin of Parliament is to be found in its medieval judicial function. The starting point for their later analysis and research is to be found in the *Introduction to the Memoranda de Parliamento, 1305*, by the great legal historian, F. W. Maitland.[2] The significance of the 1305 Parliament will be discussed

---

[1] See Pollard, op. cit. Ch. II; also, C. H. McIlwain, *The High Court of Parliament* (1910, reprinted 1962).

[2] F. W. Maitland, *Introduction to Memoranda de Parliamentum 1305; Records of the Parliament holden at Westminster... in the thirty third year of the reign of King Edward the First*; (first published 1893, Rolls Series); reprinted *Selected Historical Essays of F. W. Maitland* (1957) ed. H. W. Cam, and in *Historical Studies of the English Parliament* (Vol. I), ed. E. B. Fryde and Edward Miller.

in more detail later in the context of Edward I's reign. Nevertheless, it is convenient to refer briefly here to Maitland's findings since they have vastly enlarged our understanding of the way in which the medieval Parliament worked, and have also led to some more debatable theories asserting the *exclusively* judicial origin of Parliament in the reigns of both Henry III and Edward I, which can also best be examined now.

Analysing the records of the Parliament of 1305, Maitland showed that the constant component throughout its meeting was not the large general assembly of earls, barons and prelates, who were actually sent home before the official proceedings had ended, but the king's council which continued with parliamentary business after the magnates had dispersed. The only bishops, earls, barons and justices to remain were those who were members of the King's ordinary council. The principal business of this Parliament, moreover, was not general policy (though this was discussed), nor legislation (of which there was little) nor taxation (which was not asked for). By far the greatest part of parliamentary business was the hearing of individual petitions of a private nature and giving judgement on them. These were not the *common* petitions to the king for some general kind of action, which were to form the basis of legislation in future Parliaments. Still less were they petitions *to* Parliament. They were petitions to the king and council *in* Parliament (or, one might say, to the king and the council deliberating.) In Maitland's words, '. . . at present, "Parliament", or "a Parliament" is not conceived as a body that can be petitioned. A Parliament is rather an act than a body of persons. One cannot present a petition to a colloquy, to a debate. It is but slowly that this word is appropriated to colloquies of a particular kind, namely those which the king has with the estates of his realm, and still more slowly that it is transferred from the colloquy to the body of men whom the king has summoned. As yet any meeting of the king's council that has been solemnly summoned for general business seems to be a Parliament.'[1]

Parliament, therefore, was a term for a solemn occasion when the king met with his council. Often it was a gathering of the wider council of the realm for political discussion, but it was not necessarily less a Parliament when only the inner (or sworn) council was present to deal with petitions, which might, if important enough, be determined by the king himself. Such petitions did not raise the sort of questions that were appropriate for discussion in the wider assembly, and the response to them was not legislative. Sometimes a petitioner simply wanted his rights in a particular matter where he had been denied them; sometimes he wanted a favour. In

[1] Maitland, Ibid.

addition, at least by Edward I's reign (and the same was no doubt true of Henry III's) the Council in Parliament gave legal judgements in cases which seemed beyond the competence of the regular courts of justice, or determined which other court should deal with the case. In the famous words of the contemporary legal writer known as *Fleta*, there was one tribunal above all other courts, 'for the king has his court in his council in his Parliaments, in the presence of prelates, earls, barons, nobles and other learned men, where judicial doubts are determined, and new remedies are established for new wrongs, and justice is done to everyone according to his deserts'.[1]

But was Parliament, in reality, principally a court in the judicial sense? Certainly, even in 1305, it had not yet developed into the sort of legislature it was to become under Edward III, when laws were made on the basis of 'common' petitions in Parliament to the king. The statutes of Edward I, which will be discussed in the next chapter, were products of the king's will and his servants' advice, not of any parliamentary initiative. The central part in parliamentary proceedings was played by the king in council and, as in 1305, this could be concerned not with politics so much as with dealing justice to remedy the deficiences of other courts. Yet a broader examination of the political history of the reigns of Henry III and Edward I, and of the circumstances in which their Parliaments were summoned, does not substantiate the view of those historians who have argued, taking Maitland's findings much further than he did, that Parliament's essential origin was exclusively judicial. Two historians in particular, H. G. Richardson and G. O. Sayles, by analysing those assemblies that were described as Parliaments by contemporary officials and those of similar composition that were not, have drawn an uncompromisingly clear distinction between Parliaments and great councils of similar composition. They asserted in presenting their evidence 'that Parliaments are of one kind only and that, when we have stripped every non-essential away, the essence of them is the dispensing of justice by the king or by someone who in a very special sense represents the king.'[2] It was not, they insisted, the presence or

---

[1] '*Habet enim Rex curiam suam in consilio suo in parliamentis suis, praesentibus praelatis, comitibus, baronibus, proceribus, et aliis viris peritis, ubi terminatae sunt dubitationes judiciorum et novis injuriis emersis nova constituuntur remedia, et unicuique justitia, prout meruit, retribuetur ibidem.*' (Quoted, Maitland, op. cit.) Fleta was actually the name of a book on English law, not of its author. It was probably written about 1290. It is described as having been written '*in Fleta*', that is in the Fleet prison, and was probably the work of a corrupt judge or lawyer imprisoned under Edward I.

[2] H. G. Richardson and G. O. Sayles B.I.H.R. (1928), Vol. 133. The statement is reasserted and elaborated in 'Parliaments and Great Councils in Medieval England, I and II', the *Law Quarterly Review* (April and July, 1961), Vol. 77.

absence of particular persons or groups that determined whether a particular assembly was a Parliament. 'Function determined whether or not a particular session of the king's council was a Parliament and so termed.'[1] Parliament, they argued, was in these reigns an afforced meeting of the council where the community of the realm and the baronage might be present but there were other afforced meetings of the council which were not Parliaments. To contemporaries, they argued, 'Parliament' carried a technical meaning which was why the clerks, when sending writs, used it on some occasions and not others. Parliament was a special occasion because it was judicial in a sense that other meetings of the great council, called for political and administrative purposes, were not. Moreover, when Parliaments were held, it was (as with other courts of law) always at the fixed law terms, which was not necessarily the case with other sessions of the great council, which were occasional.[2]

The scholarship with which this case has been argued is impressive and has yielded much greater knowledge and understanding of the beginning of Parliament. We may well be convinced that the origin of the name lay in the growing practice of dispensing justice in the highest court in the land at the time when the magnates and others were assembled in the council of the realm for broadly political (including law-assenting reasons). No doubt, the English practice of using the term 'Parliament' was stimulated by the growth at this period of the *parlement* in France, which was primarily, though not exclusively judicial. (The French *parlement*, however became increasingly more judicial as time passed, leaving the political role to the Estates-General, while in England Parliament developed politically instead of judicially). Further, the increasing use of assemblies called 'Parliaments' as the highest court of last resort was probably seen as adding grandeur to such mixed occasions of political, judicial and law-making activity. This may well account for the growing popularity of the description 'Parliament' compared with other descriptions used for assemblies of similar composition and having largely similiar functions – *consilium, colloquium, tractatus*. It is also likely that the Parliaments of Henry III were especially important judicial occasions as a result of the large number of his subjects' petitions against the actions of the exchequer in respect of property rights, which was a particular characteristic of his reign.[3] Whereas parliamentary justice under

[1] Richardson and Sayles, 'Parliaments and Great Councils in Medieval England', *L.Q.R.* LXXVII (1961), p. 7.

[2] There were four law terms, called Michaelmas, Hilary, Easter and Trinity. They were periods in which sustained legal business was possible because they were not interrupted by any of the religious festivals or other days on which litigation was not allowed. Parliaments might be summoned to meet, for example, on the Octave of Trinity, or of St. Hilary.

[3] See pp. 74ff.

Edward I was principally to involve petitions to the king's council, which could then be referred to another appropriate court,[1] petitions at Parliament time under Henry III were often direct to the exchequer court. Indeed, it has been argued from this that Henry's Parliaments were not sessions of a single high court of the king's council, but rather the coming together of several courts at the same time, the judgements of the exchequer barons on a topic of current political importance having special weight by virtue of being delivered in the context of a Parliament. According to this analysis it was not so much a matter of justice *in* Parliament as of justice *during* Parliament. In other words, Parliament was a kind of aggregation of courts, with the growth of parliamentary jurisdiction owing much to the Crown's attack, using its lawyers, on particular franchises, and to the consequent investigation of the rival claims of the king and his subjects.[2] Gradually (according to this analysis) meetings of great councils and sessions of the court came together on 'parliamentary occasions' in the middle of the thirteenth century, but Parliament was still not a constitutional whole as it was to be under Edward I. The point has been expressed in the following terms: 'Under Henry III, as far as can be judged, Parliament is still only an occasion during which a number of courts and jurisdictions are, for convenience, acting at the same time and place.' These courts were the great council of the baronage, the king's familiar council, and the judges and the barons of the exchequer sitting in their various courts.[3] It is a salutary reminder that great institutions may have amorphous beginnings.

All this informs us of the importance of the judicial functions of thirteenth century Parliaments, and of the part they played both in the early growth of the institution and in the adoption of a word to describe it. Yet it is easy to be tempted into over-simplification by the assertion that judicial functions were the hallmark which exclusively determined that certain meetings of the afforced council in the thirteenth century were Parliaments, and that other gatherings of the same composition and with the same political functions were not Parliaments because they lacked the judicial hallmark. Indeed, the distinction and the definition may be positively misleading if what we are looking for in the thirteenth century is the true ancestry of the Parliaments of the next seven centuries, and not merely the ancestry of a word. For it was not the dispensing of justice in particular gatherings which laid Parliament's deepest roots, or which set the course of its development. There are some risks in differentiating sharply between

[1] See Ch. 3.
[2] For an analysis of this aspect of parliamentary origins, see J. E. A. Joliffe, 'Some Factors in the Beginnings of Parliament', *T.R.H.S.* 4th Ser. XXII (1940) reprinted in *Historical Studies etc.*, edited by Fryde and Miller.
[3] Joliffe, op. cit.

meetings of the same composition on the grounds that some were described as Parliaments and some were called by other names. The Commons, for instance, were not required to attend in connection with Parliament's judicial business since they were not involved in presenting the individual or special interest petitions which went through other channels. But since the Commons, like the magnates, might be at a Parliament for some weeks without being necessary for judicial business, where does this leave the theory that judicial business was the only business which defined a Parliament? What was the Commons' function? The concern of the magnates was political; the king consulted them as his natural counsellors. As for the Commons, Maitland himself observed that we can only guess at what they were doing during the three weeks they spent at the Parliament of 1305 while the king and council were dealing with the mass of petitions. All that is known for certain about their activities on that occasion was that they joined with the magnates in a petition about the exportation of wealth from the monasteries (to which the king assented though no statute followed), and that they presented two petitions of their own which were refused. Nevertheless, Maitland thought that since the king did not ask them for money, or require their consent to new law, there was probably 'no little truth' in the idea (though it might be 'pressed too far') that they were there to represent the grievances and interests of their communities.

Yet there was another and no less important side to the Commons' presence. To govern effectively, the king and his ministers needed to know what men were saying in the more distant parts of the country, what abuses needed attention there, and perhaps also what the prospects were for raising future taxation. Consultation means not only seeking advice but also obtaining information. The presence of the knights from the shires in the early Parliaments would enable the council to speak to them individually so as to discover the state of affairs in the shires, and also to give them instructions about matters (including, quite probably, appointments) affecting their communities. The representatives of the communities had, after all (again as Maitland observed) been told in the writ of summons to come to Parliament in order that they might do what had been ordained.

All this points in one way and another to the political functions of Parliament alongside the judicial. From the fourteenth century until our own time, its principal business has been the redress of grievances and obtaining information, hearing or approving legislation, granting taxes, and discussing important policy with the crown and its ministers. These characteristics are much closer to those of the political, legislating and fiscal activities of the great council or Parliament (however they are described) in the thirteenth century than they are to the idea of Parliament as the king's court acting judicially, and largely using the king's professional officials to do so. The account of particular Parliaments in the remainder of this chapter, and in the next, illustrates the early development of its political functions. Yet even on the basis of terminology used in contemporary medieval records, there is impressive evidence that those assemblies which were *called* Parliament, even if they can sometimes be distinguished by their judicial activities from non-parliamentary councils, acted more often politically than judicially in the reign of Henry III.[1]

Of forty-six occasions in the reign of Henry III to which the description 'Parliament' was applied in the chancery rolls, twelve were in a judicial or quasi-judicial context, indicating that it was found convenient to settle such matters at general assemblies of the King's Council called Parliaments, held at the customary dates of the exchequer and other courts. But the other thirty-four occasions when the chancery used the word Parliament were primarily political, not judicial; as, for instance, when the magnates forced the king to accept the great charter again in 1244, and the Provisions of Oxford in 1262, and when foreign policy was discussed (with the Welsh in 1258 or 1260), or when conflict with France was in question. In 1248, for instance, the king gave instructions that a papal order granting first fruits of all livings as a gift to the See of Canterbury was not to be enforced, 'since our magnates, in our last Parliament which was held at London, refused absolutely to consent', and the king was 'unwilling to attempt anything further in this matter until he has again held colloquy with the said magnates'. (The sentence itself is evidence of the interchangeability of terminology.) But perhaps the most impressive evidence that men working for the government in the 1240s already regarded Parliament as a political occasion is a reference in an *order by the king* himself, in the chancery rolls (1224) to the meeting of King John and his barons at Runneymede for the purpose of attesting the charter. This great occasion is retrospectively described as '*parleamentum de Rumened' quod fuit inter J. regem, patrem nostrum, et barones suos Anglie*, (the Parliament of Runneymede which was between King John, our father, and his barons of England.)[2] The historical accuracy or inaccuracy of this description of Runneymede is neither here nor there. What is significant is that a political, legal and crown-restraining colloquy between king and magnates could be described by mid-thirteenth century

---

[1] T. F. Treharne, 'The Nature of Parliament in the Reign of Henry III', *English Historical Review*, LXXIV (1959), pp. 590–610, reprinted in Fryde and Miller. The over-emphasis on the judicial functions of Parliament is also corrected in F. M. Powicke, *Henry III and the Lord Edward*, pp. 340–342. (Richardson and Sayles replied with criticisms of Trehame's method in *L.Q.R.* Vol. 77, pp. 401–426.)

[2] R. F. Treharne, op. cit.

officials as a 'Parliament'. Their notion of a Parliament was evidently that it was a great political occasion for consultation. Likewise, in 1262, the order of the King enforcing the papal condemnation of the Provisions of Oxford described the assembly which had been responsible for the Provisions as a 'Parliament', which was, indeed, how the barons themselves had seen it.

Towards the thirteenth century, Parliament was a word coming into fashion (perhaps encouraged by its French usage for a court) to describe important meetings of the council (often but not necessarily the great council of the realm) where justice was delivered and where great political questions might be discussed. There was no sharp dividing line between the great and the inner councils, but it was the inner council that gave judgements, and might well continue to do so after the magnates, the political business finished, had departed. The early use of the word Parliament was neither precise nor systematic but, if anything, it would be as accurate to say that the judicial aspects of Parliament which were prominent in the thirteenth century were grafted on to the main consultative stock of Witan and great council as to insist on Parliament's purely judicial origin. The atrophy of the great council from the fourteenth century onwards (though it was still formally alive in the 17th century as an alternative, at least in the mind of Charles I) point us to the truth. The great, or common, council had atrophied because Parliament had replaced it and inherited its political, fiscal and law-declaring, as well as its judicial, functions. The distinction between the last two functions was in any case a nice one. What, after all, does new law making by statute amount to if it is not (in *Fleta's* words) establishing 'new remedies' for 'new wrongs'? Parliament, from the beginning, was a political body.

III

It is one of the ironies of Henry III's reign that the second serious baronial outbreak against the king's authority should have arisen from the favour shown by Henry to the barons' future leader, Simon de Montfort. In 1238, Simon secretly married the king's sister, Eleanor, with Henry's full approval but with none of the usual consultation with the magnates. Simon was a Frenchman whose father of the same name, the ruthless crusader against the heretical Albigensians, had inherited the title of Earl of Leicester. The older de Montfort had never taken possession of his inheritance, but in 1231, Simon the Younger came to England to claim his title and quickly became a favourite of the king. His marriage with Henry's sister was, however, deeply offensive to the English magnates. For one thing, Simon was a newcomer, and although it would be anachronistic to make much of his 'foreignness' in relation to the French-speaking English baronage, there was a growing prejudice against the incursions of outsiders into areas of influence claimed by the indigenous upper classes. Secondly, by this marriage Eleanor was breaking a vow of chastity she had taken after her first husband's death. Above all, the marriage seemed to be one more example of the king's determination to act without the advice of his natural counsellors, and de Montfort, an intensely ambitious intruder, might well, at this stage, have seemed to be the natural successor of the disliked Poitevins (Peter des Roches, Peter des Rivaux and others) as the object of baronial resentment. The outcome was a revolt headed by the king's brother, Richard of Cornwall, which forced the king to take refuge in the Tower for a time, and then to make terms. The agreement itself has not survived but it is possible that a draft plan of reform which was inserted in a copy of Matthew Paris's *Chronicle* under the year 1244 related to the crisis of 1238.[1] This advocated a new Charter and proposed that 'four men of rank and power shall be chosen by common consent from the most discreet persons of the whole realm to be of the king's council and sworn to handle faithfully the affairs of the king and kingdom and do justice to all without respect of persons. These shall follow the king, and if not all at least two of them shall always be available to hear each one's complaints and be able to help quickly those suffering an injustice. The lord king's treasure shall be managed under their supervision and authority and money granted by them all specially and for the benefit of the lord king and the kingdom shall be expended as they think best. And they shall be conservators of liberties. And as they are elected by the assent of all, so none of them shall be removable without general consent ... No justiciar or chancellor shall be appointed in place of another, save with the assent of all in solemn assembly ...' Whatever its date of origin and purpose, this draft, which was largely written in rough note form, plainly represented the thinking of some important group or person in the middle of the reign about the need to control not only the king's conduct but even his appointment of ministers, and in this respect it was a significant augury of things to come. Indeed, the draft even proposed bluntly that 'those thus far suspect and not needed are to be removed from the lord king's side'.

[1] *E.H.D.* Vol. III, pp. 359–60; N. Denholm-Young, 'The "Paper Constitution" Attrib. to 1244', *E.H.R.* LVIII (1943); Powicke, *Henry III and the Lord Edward*, pp. 291–3; Powicke, *The Thirteenth Century*, pp. 77 and 79; B. Wilkinson, *Cons. Hist. of England* I, Ch. III, and C. R. Cheney, 'The "Paper Constitution" ... M. Paris', *E.H.R.* LXV, 1950, pp. 213–221.

Nothing came of these ideas and peace was made between Richard of Cornwall and Simon de Montfort. In the following years Henry conducted himself more warily towards the baronage. Yet tension between king and barons persisted. On the king's side, the sworn council which he used in the ordinary business of government became more professional, more select and more conspicuously set apart from the baronage.[1] It included a few barons, the chief officers of the realm and the household (which two categories were not sharply distinguishable), and clerks, secretaries and other special counsellors, among whom were friars and literate knights chosen by the king. It was not a body that held regular meetings or kept records as a modern government would; its members were employed as and when the king wished. The councillors with the most important influence on the conduct of government were clerks such as John Mansell, of whom the king wrote: 'He was trained under my wing. I have tested his ability, his character and merits since his boyhood. He has always been serviceable and loyal in my affairs and in those of the kingdom.'[2] These men were experts in administration, in raising the maximum money possible from the king's demesne, in checking and enforcing his rights and in obliging others who claimed 'liberties' of one sort and another under the crown to have their rights proved and then established once and for all by charter for which they would have to pay. Although there were many Provencals, Savoyards and Poitevins at court, the men at the heart of government and the majority of the king's counsellors, contrary to legend, were Englishmen.[3]

In their clarification of liberties, and in extracting a price for clarification, the king and his officials were moving towards a more ordered society. To the barons, however, it was objectionable that there were so many 'foreigners about the court' and especially that the great officers of state, the justiciar, chancellor and treasurer were at this time men closely connected with, or trained in, the royal household rather than men of their own sort. What was more, the sifting of claims and rights of the royal servants were often contrary to baronial interests. The barons' response to their sense of

---

[1] In a surviving counsellor's oath of 1257, counsellors swore to give faithful counsel as often as they considered it useful; that they would not reveal secrets of the royal council to any unauthorized or dangerous persons; that they would not consent to any alienation of the ancient demesne of the crown; that they would see that justice was done impartially to rich and poor; that they would receive no gift from anyone concerned with suits in the king's court; that no member of the council serving the king should obtain from him a gift himself, and if the king wished to give him anything he shall not accept it without the consent of all or a majority of the council. Such an oath may well have been exceptional, however. Powicke, *Henry III and the Lord Edward*, p. 337.

[2] Powicke, *Henry III and the Lord Edward*, p. 294.

[3] Ibid., p. 296.

separation from the king's intimate council was to withhold the supply of money from him. Although the barons would pay scutage and the conventional feudal dues when required, no extraordinary taxation was granted for twenty years following the thirtieth given to the king in 1237. The king had to manage as best he could by tallaging his own demesne, the towns, the Jews and foreign merchants. London sought to resist his demands but failed; the Jews on one occasion were collected together in a quasi-parliamentary assembly and obliged to assess themselves for tallage; the foreign merchants were forced to pay for the privilege of trading under threat of expulsion. In these years, therefore, although the king, who was a great patron of the arts and had a lavish court, was often short of money, there was no serious long-term imbalance between his revenue and expenditure. There was therefore no over-riding need for him to make new terms with the barons in order to get money. It was to take a political crisis of a much more serious kind to precipitate the open conflict which brought into question the fundamentals of the power-structure in England. When it came, this crisis was to be of the type which has repeatedly had important constitutional consequences in English history.

The refusal of money in the Parliament of 1242, with reasons unambiguously stated, has already been noted.[1] In 1244, the barons' response to a similar request by the king was even firmer. In October 1244, the great council (or Parliament) met in the refectory at Westminster, and the king explained his needs.[2] Six days of discussion followed. Although the lay magnates left the refectory so that the prelates could consider the matter separately, it was agreed that both groups should reply to the king jointly. Nothing was to be done without the agreement of the whole body, and a committee of twelve (four bishops, four earls and four barons) was elected to produce a report, demanding the reform of government, which was to be accepted by the whole body of magnates before being put to the king. In order not to appear to have yielded to compulsion, the king refused to accept the proposal, and the great council deferred the matter until

[1] See pp. 78–9. The king did not, however, easily take no for an answer in 1242. One by one he had them summoned to his private room, according to Matthew Paris, 'like a priest calling his penitents to confession. He tried to do with them singly what he could not do with them in the mass, to shake the spirit of those already affected by his harangues. He would say, "See, this abbot has already given me so much, and that so much" and would hold out a roll on which the sums promised were written, although as a matter of fact no promises had been made. By this means he carefully caught many in his net; but many stood firm by the general decision to which they had sworn.' (F. M. Powicke, *Henry III and the Lord Edward*, p. 306. [*Chronica majora iv, 182*]). It was not the first time that this technique of extorting money from reluctant barons had been used by medieval rulers. William of Normandy used it on his barons to obtain money for his invasion of England in 1066.

[2] Stubbs, *Select Charters*, pp. 326–7. (M. Paris *Chron. Maj.* IV, pp. 362ff.)

February. The lay barons dispersed though Parliament continued for other business. Henry tried to detach the bishops from the barons but they refused to budge, being exhorted by Robert Grosseteste, the great scholar and Bishop of Lincoln: 'Let us not be divided from the common council; for it is written, "If we are divided we shall all die".' In February the magnates came together again, but only to grant a feudal aid for the marriage of the king's daughter. As it happened, king, barons and bishops all by then had a common interest in resisting new financial demands from the Pope, and the question of extraordinary taxation to assist the king was dropped. But the demand (as in the plan of reform of 1238 or 1244) that the justiciar, chancellor and treasurer should be elected did not die away, and the barons and bishops continued to act together.

The efforts of the barons to secure redress of grievances and the reform of government (including the demand for the appointment of the chancellor, treasurer and justiciar by the common counsel of the realm) continued to be the theme of meetings of the great council (or Parliament) in 1248 and 1249, and there were repeated protests against papal exactions. At last, in 1253 the king (who had taken the Cross two years earlier) secured both an aid and a scutage in exchange for a solemn confirmation of the charters, and set off for Gascony. He left the kingdom in charge of the queen and Richard of Cornwall, who had now abandoned the baronial cause he had formerly supported. It was during their regency that for the first time, so far as we know for certain, knights of the shire, the representatives of the Commons or communities, were both summoned to and attended Parliament.

For the calling of knights into consultation about the king's affairs, there was, however, a certain shadowy precedent. In the reign of King John, a summons had gone out in 1213 to all sheriffs requiring them to cause 'four discreet men of your country' (*quator discretos milites de comitatu tuo*) to come to a council at Oxford (the barons were also summoned to come, unarmed) 'to consult with us about the affairs of our realm.' (*ad loquendum nobiscum de negotiis regni nostri*).[1] There is no record of the proceedings or the composition of this council; we do not even know for certain that it took place, since only the writ of summons survives. It is more likely to have been a military council than a meeting of the ordinary council of the realm for political purposes, and in that sense it provides no precedent for what was to happen in 1254. Nevertheless, Stubbs's description of King John's writ of 1213 as 'an omen of the institution of representative Parliaments' remains fundamentally accurate.[2] Whenever the king decided to consult his

---

[1] Stubbs, *Select Charters*, p. 282 (Latin).
[2] Stubbs, *Constitutional History*, Vol. I, 5th ed. p. 567.

counsellors, in whatever form and for whatever reason, the meeting was nonetheless one of the king's council. The summons to the knights in 1213 is an indication that the notion already existed that the representatives of the ancient shiremoot, itself the representative body of the local community in Anglo-Saxon custom, could be associated with the great council of the realm. This association was to be the basis of the Parliaments of the future.

For the next forty years there is no evidence of any similar summons to knights of the shire. Yet the social standing and therefore the political significance of the country gentlemen below the level of magnates was rising with the prosperity of the nation. As we have already seen, elected knights had been extensively employed on the judicial and financial business of the shires since the reign of Henry II. Moreover, John, at a moment of crisis in his relations with the barons, had presaged the future participation of burgesses in Parliament by summoning to a great council at St. Albans in 1212 representatives from the townships of the royal demesne, each of which sent its reeve and four legal men.[1] Subsequently, knights were on occasions summoned to the king's court to testify to decisions reached in the county court. In the earlier years of Henry III, they were on several occasions made responsible either for receiving the proceeds of taxation, or the assessment, made on oath, of the tax due.[2] In 1227, writs were sent to the sheriffs of 16 counties requiring the election, by the 'knights and good men' of their bailiwick, of 'four of the more lawful and discreet knights' to come before the king at Westminster to set forth 'on behalf of the whole county their quarrel with you, should they have one, regarding the articles contained in the charter of liberty that has been granted to them....'[3] Similar writs to nineteen other counties also contained additional clauses regarding the perambulation of the forests. Not until 1254, however, were knights representing all the shires summoned, along with 'the earls, barons and other magnates' to be present at a great council, or Parliament, and this time we know precisely why, and also what happened.

Towards the end of 1253, the king, who was in Gascony, sent to the regents a demand for men and money on the grounds that he was about to be attacked by the King of Castille. In January 1254, therefore, a Parliament was held in which the prelates promised an aid on their own behalf, but

---

[1] Stubbs, *Const. Hist.* Vol. I, 5th ed. pp. 566–567: 'The reeve and four men were probably called upon merely to give evidence as to the value of the royal lands; but the fact that so much besides was discussed at the time, and that some important measures touching the people at large flowed directly from the action of the council, gives to their appearance there a great significance.'

[2] Stubbs, *Select Charters*, pp. 351–359.

[3] C. Stephenson and F. G. Marcham, *Sources of English Constitutional History.*

insisted that they could make no promise on behalf of the rest of the clergy without their consent, which, they thought, would not be given unless the king abandoned the tithe already promised for the crusade he was supposed to go on. As for the barons, they promised to do their feudal duty and go to the assistance of the king in Gascony if he was attacked, but they did not think that they could commit the rest of the laity, who were not bound feudally to serve him in Gascony, to provide him with money. The regents, therefore, wrote to the king telling him that they did not think that the rest of the laity would give him an aid (and, of course, the characteristic of the non-feudal taxes on movables was that *all* the laity was liable to pay them) unless the charters were reconfirmed, and letters were written to the sheriffs commanding their observance.[1] To deal with the problem, the regents informed the king that they were going to hold a deliberation (*habituri sumus tractatum*). It was to be an enlarged meeting of the great council to be held at Westminster in April. The regents' writ instructed the sheriffs that, in addition to the magnates, they were to 'cause to come before our council at Westminster on the fifteenth day after Easter next' two 'lawful and discreet knights' (*legales et discretos milites*) from each county 'whom the said counties shall have chosen (*eligerint*) for the purpose, to represent all collectively and individually (*vice omnium et singulorum*) of the said counties'. The representative role of the summoned knights was made quite clear. They were to be elected; they were to come already empowered, by consultation in their counties, to speak for all and sundry; and before they arrived they were to 'arrange what aid they were willing to pay us in our need'. The sheriffs, moreover, were instructed in the writ of summons to set before the knights and others of the county an account of the king's needs, and to 'persuade' them to pay a sufficient aid, so that the knights summoned before the council 'shall be able to give definite answer concerning the said aid to the aforesaid council, for each of the counties'.[2] In other words, the knights were to go to Parliament carrying the wishes of their constituents. There is almost a hint of mandate in this. Yet it is also clear that, once they reached Westminster, they were to have a representative role, and were expected (having put forward the views of their counties) to reach a general decision with the other representative knights on the amount that all should pay. This decision was to be binding on all the taxpayers of all the shires. They were to be 'discreet' knights in the sense that they were to go to Westminster

---

[1] A translation of the regents' letter to the king is given in B. Wilkinson, *Constitutional History of Medieval England*, Vol. III, pp. 260–261.

[2] Stubbs, *Select Charters* (Latin), p. 365. Translations in C. Stephenson and F. G. Marcham, op. cit., p. 141, and B. Wilkinson, *Constitutional History of Medieval England*, Vol. III, pp. 302–3.

with discretion, as a modern representative does, to decide themselves how best to represent the interests of their constituents in the circumstances they found there. Moreover, it is clear that the right of choosing the summoned knights in the shire court was not restricted either to barons or other knights. Even at this early stage there is no reason to suppose that freeholders of sufficient standing (who precisely these were was of course undefined) were excluded from a part in the choice, or election, of representative knights.

In this writ then, we can see clearly stated the main functions for which medieval kings first required representatives of the Commons, or communities, to attend Parliament. They were needed because only they could say, as the men who would largely be involved in the business of collecting any money that was granted, whether it could in practice be raised. As it happened, however, such an answer was not required in 1254 since the need for financial supply suddenly disappeared. Simon de Montfort had now returned from France, and what he had to say destroyed the case for the proposed aid. In 1248, Henry had appointed de Montfort his vice-regent in Gascony, where he was required to pacify the king's last remaining French possession. Though a good and efficient soldier, and capable of attracting personal devotion, Simon was also hasty, arrogant and overbearing, and such had been the weight of complaint against his conduct in Gascony that he had been suspended and obliged to defend himself in what was virtually a trial before the king's court. Simon had then relinquished his command, and although on the surface relations with Henry remained amicable, the earl had ceased to be the king's man and moved over to the baronial side. Gascony had been the turning point. De Montfort now arrived, to tell the Parliament that, after all, the king had nothing to fear from Castille. By letter, the king had himself confirmed as much, but we may suppose that Simon de Montfort put the case against both an aid and the king's policy in Gascony with uncompromising relish. No aid was granted, and the Parliament of 1254, to which the first representative knights of the shire were sent because of a false alarm in Gascony, dispersed.

Through all these years of intermittent tension between the king and the baronage there had been no fundamental breakdown in their relationship of reciprocal toleration. The magnates could, and did, press their case for a change in the king's political and administrative behaviour; they could try to persuade him to rely less for advice on his chosen clerks and dependent officials, and turn more to men of their own sort; they could wish him to appoint a justiciar, a chancellor and a treasurer of whom they could approve, and then be guided by these great men rather than by his humbler familiars. Yet it was not in the magnates' interest, or even thinking to challenge the fundamentals of the kingly government under which they all lived and prospered. Even if the king could not be moved, there had so far been nothing sufficiently objectionable in his conduct to drive the baronage to take any more serious action against him than to refuse him extra money when he asked for it. Indeed, the impression that one has of thirteenth centuries politics generally is of men trying to find some agreed rules within which to play a hard, but still ultimately friendly power-game, and anxious to avoid any kind of conflict that would put the political structure at risk. It was not a period in which uncompromising and drastic solutions to political problems seemed easily to spring to the minds of powerful men, even when their discontent was considerable. It is a striking and revealing feature of the thirteenth century that the axe and judicial murder for political offences were largely absent from the political scene. In the fourteenth and fifteenth centuries it would be different. Three kings were then to be deposed and murdered; many great men died on the scaffold; there was to be a long dynastic war. To look down the family trees of the magnates of the fourteenth and fifteenth centuries is to be struck immediately by the considerable proportion of lives that ended in execution. Yet in the thirteenth century, that ultimate political remedy was seldom used. In part, no doubt, this was a consequence of the temper and ingrained habits of a close-knit society in which the old feudal values of personal obligations and duty were not yet quite dead. When military conflict did break out in the thirteenth century, it was usually conducted within certain rules (whatever the ferocity of the fighting itself) so that real war and its aftermath had a certain resemblance to the tournament. When strife ended it usually seemed to be assumed that some kind of settlement could be negotiated which did not wholly destroy the defeated. The barons' war against King John, and the formula for limited distraint on the king set out in Magna Carta had been a striking example of this. It is tempting to wonder whether even Simon de Montfort's life would have been forfeit had he been captured instead of killed at the battle of Evesham. Probably it would have been, for by then times and attitudes had already changed, but in Henry's earlier years conflict and rebellion usually ended in parley. Given the tensions between the royal administration and baronial claims, some credit is probably due to Henry personally for the avoidance of dangerous conflict for so long. When the breakdown did come, it had momentous consequences both for Parliament and for the idea that, in certain circumstances, opposition to a king might be pushed to the point that the crown might be placed under restraint. As with all other great constitutional changes in English history, these developments were precipitated not by theories of government, but by hard political facts and accidents. What eventually strained the relationship of the king and barons to breaking point was a gross and almost ridiculous mistake on Henry's part, and the accident of a political scheme devised far away in Rome.

For a number of years previously, Henry had been caught up in papal politics, sometimes furthering the Curia's wishes and financial exactions in England (for he was always conscious that he owed his succession to the throne partly to the protection of the Papacy) and sometimes resisting them. In 1250, Henry had committed himself to take the cross, but subsequently he allowed himself to be entangled in the Pope's policies for uprooting the Hohenstauffen Imperial dynasty from Italy. The Pope had been engaged in a long conflict with the Emperor Frederick II, the excommunicated, brilliant and ruthless infidel who had gained for himself the description *Stupor Mundi*, and who had made the kingdom of Sicily his base. After Frederick's death in 1250, the Pope had proposed that Henry III's brother, Richard of Cornwall, should become emperor, and he was, indeed, crowned in Aachen in 1257, though he was never able to establish his position as king of Germany. Henry then foolishly committed himself to accept the crown of Sicily on behalf of his younger son Edmund, the Pope commuting his crusader's vow for an expedition to take possession of Sicily. Henry was not only to send a military force, but was also to pay the papal debts, which amounted to 135,541 marks, before Michaelmas 1256: if he did not fulfil these obligations, the king would be excommunicated, and his kingdom laid under an interdict.[1] New papal taxes were levied on the clergy; loans were imposed on the great religious houses; Roman tax collectors were established in England. The clergy protested; the magnates refused to help the king find the money. The impossibility of meeting the debts incurred has been described as a nightmare comparable to the negotiations about the payment of reparations after the great war of 1914–1918.[2]

In March 1257, Henry brought Edmund, the young king-designate of Sicily, before a 'great Parliament' of magnates and prelates, explained his difficulties and asked for money.[3] 'It is necessary that we should have "treaty" with you and with other prelates and magnates concerning our great and arduous business,' ran the writ of summons to the magnates.[4] But the barons, stating in some detail their reasons for disapproving of the impracticable Sicilian enterprise, would give nothing, while the prelates offered no more than £52,000, and that sum only provided they could get

---

[1] 'He had simply turned himself and his realm into sureties for the repayment of the debts of the Curia.' F. M. Powicke, *King Henry III and the Lord Edward*, p. 372.
[2] B. Wilkinson, *Constitutional History of Medieval England 1216–1399*, Vol. III, p. 303.
[3] Stubbs, *Select Charters*, pp. 329–30.
[4] Powicke, op. cit. p. 374.

the agreement of the lower clergy. The king was already negotiating for peace with France to free his hands for the Sicilian expedition, and he now tried to get the Pope to moderate his demands. The only concession he obtained, however, was a delay until the summer of 1258 in imposing the penalties the king would suffer for not fulfilling his financial commitments. In April, 1258, another Parliament met in London and was told by the king of the Pope's insistence that the agreement must be carried out to the letter. The magnates' response was an immediate demand for reform of the administration of the kingdom in exchange for money. Seven of the most powerful barons, including the earl of Gloucester, the earl marshal of Norfolk, and the earl of Leicester (Simon de Montfort), entered into a sworn agreement to 'help each other, both ourselves and those belonging to us, against all people, doing right and taking nothing that we cannot take without doing wrong, saving faith to our lord the King of England and to the crown.'[1] A deputation of earls, barons and knights then went to the king in his palace of Westminster carrying their swords (which they politely left outside the door) and secured from Henry an undertaking that he would reform the realm. In return, and provided also that the Pope would moderate his demands, the magnates promised to try (but no more than try) to 'use their influence' to get an aid from the community of the realm, by which they clearly meant the tax-paying nation as a whole, beyond the baronage itself. The king further agreed that reform was to be devised by a joint committee made up of twelve of his council and twelve of the magnates. The committee of reform was to meet at Oxford in a month's time.

In June one of the most famous of all Parliaments met at Oxford, a place chosen perhaps in order to keep clear of the influence of the Londoners, and perhaps because Oxford was the point of muster for an expedition planned against the Welsh. The proceedings began with what became known as the Petition of the Barons, which was a statement of grievances which included complaints against the barons as well as by the barons. It covered a wide range of topics from grievances about land tenure and inheritance payments to complaints against sheriffs, the maladministration of justice, and the king's habit of taking 'prises' (compulsory purchased victuals for maintaining the royal household) which he 'scarcely ever' paid for. The barons were clearly claiming to speak for the whole community in a petition which set the themes for subsequent reforms and indeed of much future legislation. Then Lord Hugh Bigod, brother of the Earl of Norfolk and marshal, was made justiciar of England, an appointment that had previously lapsed.

[1] *E.H.D.* Vol. III, p. 361.

From an eloquent description of the proceedings written by a member of the king's court, we learn that the new justiciar swore that he would do justice to all who made complaints 'and that he would not falter in this for the lord king or the queen, or for their sons, or for any living person or for any thing, nor from hate nor love, nor prayer nor payment; and that he would accept nothing from anyone except such food and drink as are usually bought to the table of a well-to-do-man.' The committee of twenty-four first decided that the lands and castles which the impoverished king had alienated to his Poitevin brothers and others must be restored to him if his financial position was to be improved. Then the twenty-four duly presented (probably in several stages) the programme of reform which was to become known as the Provisions of Oxford. The proposals appear to represent what the king and Parliament agreed, and not simply what was presented by the twenty-four. They were, however, probably not a single, formal, carefully designed document but notes taken piecemeal of decisions as they were reached in Parliament. This is suggested by the facts that the provisions were in the spoken language of Parliament, French (other than the first clause, providing for four knights in each shire to record grievances, which alone was in the more formal Latin), that there were certain inconsistencies between clauses and that the provisions were not enrolled.

The most drastic of the Provisions was, however, immediately put into force: the election of a new permanent king's council by wholly exceptional means. It was, as required, chosen by four electors, two of whom were nominated by the king's twelve on the council of twenty-four, and the other two by the baronial twelve. (The choice was subject to the approval of the twenty-four.) The Council of Fifteen was given power under the Provisions to advise the king on all matters touching the kingdom 'and to amend and redress everything that they shall consider to need redress and amendment; and over the chief justiciar and all other persons.'[1] The justiciar, the chancellor and the treasurer were added to the Fifteen *ex officio*.

The constitutional edifice put in place by the Provisions of Oxford obliged the king to act by the permanent Council of Fifteen, which might be

---

[1] Clause 23. The most substantial collection of documents on the baronial movement after 1258 is R. F. Treharne and I. J. Sanders, *Documents of the Baronial Movement of Reform and Rebellion, 1258–1267*, (Oxford Medieval Texts) in which all the documents mentioned here (including the Provisions of Oxford), and others not mentioned, are printed in the original language, Latin or Norman French, with English translations. For that reason further detailed footnotes on this episode are not given here. A number of the documents are printed in Latin, French and old English in Stubbs, *Select Charters*, pp. 369–411. Translations of some of the documents are in Stephenson and Marcham, pp. 142–150, and in *E.H.D.*, Vol. III, pp. 361–384.

described as the first fixed council in English history (even, perhaps, to illustrate its revolutionary character, as the first Cabinet) on which the baronial party was numerically dominant. We may take as an instance of the king's subordination the fact that a number of royal castles was now given custodians who were required to surrender them to nobody but the king, and not even to him during the next twelve years unless they did so by command of the personal council. Had this 'constitution' endured, the king of England, far from being a ruler acting by the advice of his natural counsellors, would have been reduced, at best, to the status of a first among equals and obliged to taking instructions from the government's majority. The Provisions, however, did not survive, and their most lasting effect was not the attempt to put the king in leading strings held by the council, but the enhancement of the political role of the knights of the shire to promote the baronial cause.

By the arrangements to which Henry agreed at Oxford, there were to be three Parliaments a year, meeting at Michaelmas (October 6), Candlemas (February 3) and on June 1. 'To these three Parliaments shall come the elected councillors of the king, even if they be not summoned, to review the state of the realm and to deal with the common business of the realm and of the king together.' Additional Parliaments were to be summoned if necessary, but in any case the community of barons was to elect a body of twelve to represent them, who could act on legislative and other matters with the fifteen even when Parliament was not sitting. ('... the community should choose twelve sound men who shall come to the Parliaments, and at other times when need shall be, when the king and council shall summon them....' Cl. 22) This body, which might be described as a kind of standing parliamentary committee, was perhaps designed not only as an additional baronial safeguard but as saving the expense of calling full Parliaments more often than was absolutely necessary. It was further provided that the justiciar, treasurer and chancellor were to hold office for one year only, after which they were to be answerable to the king and council for what they had done during their term of office. Furthermore, the Provisions recorded the appointment of another twenty-four magnates 'to negotiate for the aid for the king', as promised, though there is no evidence that they met or that an aid was granted. For the rest, the Provisions included means for controlling sheriffs and other officials, and proposed the reform of the king's household.

But the most enduringly significant of all the things done at this time was the provision that four 'discreet and law-worthy' knights should be elected (we do not know by what procedure) in each shire to attend every meeting of the shire court, in order to hear and record every complaint of injury and trespass done by sheriffs, bailiffs and others, and to ensure that the parties concerned appeared before the justiciar and other judges, to whom the records were also submitted. The knights were also subsequently given the task of surveying local administration and inquiring into any misdeeds, and also of reporting on malpractices by Jews, usurers and merchants. The chosen four knights were also empowered to use other knights to collect information for them, and were then required to appear themselves before the council in the Michaelmas Parliament and submit their returns. It is known that knights from at least fifteen counties did so.

In terms of the practical reform of local administration (and most administration was local in the thirteenth century) and of the redress of grievances, this new responsibility for the knights of the shire was of considerable immediate importance, but its significance for the development of Parliament in the longer run was still greater. Although knights were not summoned as shire representatives (which process was to be the eventual foundation of the House of Commons) to the Oxford Parliament of 1258, nor to the Westminster Parliament in the autumn of the same year, the new responsibilities given to them under the Provisions were a recognition by the baronage both of the increased importance of the class of knights, and of their growing restiveness. The terms of the barons' agreement with the king in April, by which they had promised to try to raise a general tax, had made it clear that this would depend on the acquiescence of the taxpayers generally, who included knights and freeholders. So the question for the barons at Oxford in regard to taxation had been whether in granting it they could still answer for the whole realm, as well as for themselves, as they had done in 1225.[1] They were now obviously of the opinion that if they were to do so, the knights' goodwill was needed and was best assured by associating knights representing the shires more closely with the searching out of grievances for redress, and with the presentation of complaints and petitions to the king so that justice could be done. Another Provision made at Oxford had the same purpose; the sheriff, who was to serve for only one year, and without pay, was to be a local landowner (presumably a knight) in order that the people of the shire could be well treated and (as was stated quite bluntly) need neither fear him nor hesitate to make complaints about him. Though it was not in essentials a new development for knights to be given important duties, it was a considerable advance that they should have them on this scale and should be given the responsibility of investigating grievances and bringing their findings to Parliament. Their assignment in 1258 was a forerunner of their wider role in

[1] See pp. 72–3.

the future, and even when the Provisions of Oxford had been abandoned and the king had resumed his full powers, the local gentry did not lose their political importance. On the contrary, Edward I, learning from his experiences in his father's reign, found it useful to summon them to Parliament with a wider discretion. After 1258, it was beginning to be taken for granted that the 'gentry' were the class best able to represent the freeholders of the shires, and that the king's government would benefit by their support.

At the October Parliament in 1258, a proclamation declaring that the things that had been done were to be 'firm and lasting' was issued by the king in three languages – English, as well as the more usual Latin and French. This official use of the speech of the great majority of the people was not only a new recognition of their part in the nation; it may well also have reflected the fact that as more families from the broad mass of the English, who had lost status after the Conquest, were rising in the social scale, English was now again the home language of more of the middle sort of people.[1] A second proclamation, also in the three languages, assured the people that a start would soon be made on the redress of their wrongs; this was to be read frequently in the shire courts. A year later, in the October Parliament of 1259, a long list of administrative and legal reforms known as Provisions of Westminster, was enacted, many of them arising from the petitions of the barons in the Oxford Parliament and from the work on grievances done since then. They were of considerable legislative importance, but they were also significant because they were apparently adopted on the demand of the 'community of the bachelors of England' (*communitas bacheleriae Angliae*) a term which referred to men below baronial rank and probably covered both the lesser nobility and the knights. Before the Parliament opened, the 'community of bachelors' appealed to the king's son and heir, the Lord Edward, saying that, whereas the demands of the barons had been met, the barons had not fulfilled their promises. Edward is said to have called on the barons to honour their oath, threatening to support the community of bachelors if they did not do so. The Provisions of Westminster, made 'by the common Counsel and consent of the... king and Magnates', then followed and were duly enrolled as a statute. How far they were the result of the appeal of the 'bachelors' is not knowable.[2] Many of the reforms in the Provisions of Westminster had been foreshadowed in a separate baronial document known as the Provisions of the English Barons. But it seems likely that the 'bachelors' tipped the balance in favour of

[1] The English version of the proclamation, with a modern English translation, is printed in Stubbs, *Select Charters*, pp. 387–389.
[2] *Stat. R.* Vol. I, pp. 8–11.

Parliament's adopting the reforms against resistance from the more conservative barons. What is clear is that a number of the clauses of the Provisions of Westminster served the interest of the smaller landowners and 'mesne' tenants, while lesser people generally benefited from their administrative reforms. The shires, for instance, were given a say in the choice of the sheriffs, and four knights were appointed to record wrongs done by sheriffs. It is of interest that one of the reforms was designed for the benefit of the majority of the English people. The 'murder fine', first imposed by the Conqueror on communities where a Norman was found slain, was often now abused as a money-raising device by being applied when a 'Norman' was found dead, whether or not he had been murdered. Clause 22 therefore enacted specifically that the fine was to be incurred only for 'felonious slayings', but not for accidents. Finally, we may note that under the Provisions, unauthorized attendance at Parliament under arms was forbidden, except by writ of the king or council. (The protection of Parliament against armed intimidation was to be a common theme in the future.) Most of the Provisions of Westminster remained the law of the land, however little they were observed in practice, eventually being incorporated in the Statute of Marlborough. They were not intrinsically inconsistent with the return of personal government by the king; for the most part they simply defined and extended the common law of the land, also marking a further stage in the submission of the feudal courts to the law of the land. Politically, however, the old tensions within the community of king and barons had not been resolved at Oxford, and what might be described at the first attempt in England at a written constitution (even though what are now known as the Provisions of Oxford were not written and designed as a single document) had scarcely been devised before it was moving towards collapse.

Even during the assembly at Oxford, the king's Lusignan half-brothers,[1] who with other foreigners were a source of baronial discontent, had expressed their opposition to the Provisions, and one of them, William de Valence, earl of Pembroke, argued strongly there that the proper business of the government should rather be war against Llywelyn, who had taken the title Prince of Wales and had made himself pre-eminent in that country. Unlike the mass of the barons, the Lusignans and some of their English friends refused to take an oath to observe the agreement made with the king and William de Valence quarrelled with earl Simon. This faction then left Oxford 'without asking permission' and took refuge at Winchester, of

---

[1] Henry's widowed mother had remarried into the family into which it had been intended that she should marry, and from which King John had diverted her.

which Aymer de Lusignan was bishop elect, where they were followed by the king and the rest of the barons. Complex negotiations followed which led to the expulsion of the four Lusignans and the placing under surveillance of the king's nineteen-year-old heir Edward. To all that had been done, the king had apparently assented with good grace, but with a reluctance that must have been intensified that autumn when the Pope cancelled the grant of Sicily to Edmund, which had had such momentous and profitless consequences for the English crown. On the other hand, the barons failed to obtain papal approval for their cause, and this lack was to play some considerable part in their eventual failure. The gradual falling apart of the baronial party also had something to do with the very success of the reformers in investigating local grievances which could in practice often be as awkward for barons as for the king's officials. Besides, magnates who had been happy to push the royal government along the road of reform were reluctant, when it came to the point, to get down themselves to the detailed work of government in councils and committees. It was one thing to try to turn the king in a new direction, and quite another for the barons to involve themselves in government at the expense of their own business of managing their lands. Gradually, therefore, a gap opened up between earl Simon, with his uncompromising insistence on the Provisions, and the more moderate barons.

This could only be to the king's advantage. Henry's position was also strengthened by a peace with France which settled the long dispute between the two crowns over the French provinces which England had lost. He had started to work for an agreement before the crisis of 1258, and after the conclusion of the Westminster Parliament, he had departed for France to bring the negotiations to a conclusion. At the end of 1259 the Treaty of Paris was signed and the English king formally gave up his claim to his lost French provinces, doing homage for those that remained to him in the south to the French king, St. Louis. This treaty was to give England a long period of peace, and the abandonment of Plantagenet pretensions to Normandy and Anjou assisted the growth of English nationhood. But the immediate effect was to help Henry to throw off the shackles of the baronial party. For one thing, it gave him the French king, with his great reputation, as a new potential backer.

The weakness at the heart of the baronial cause was meanwhile becoming manifest. Though the barons had imposed rule by the fixed council in place of personal rule by the king, the structure of government was still of a monarchical kind. It continued to require the operation of a single directing will which the council as a body could not supply, and which no individual member of it possessed, except Simon de Montfort. Others, however, were quite unwilling to let Simon exert it; he had, for one thing, quarrelled with the powerful Earl of Gloucester. This lack of unity on the baronial side was Henry's opportunity, and recovering his confidence after the treaty with King Louis, he set about regaining his royal power. His first resolve was to make sure that a Parliament which was due to meet in February 1260 did not do so. In a letter from France to the justiciar, Hugh Bigod, Henry explained that he had been unavoidably detained in France, partly because the death of the French king's son had delayed the marriage of his own daughter, Beatrice, to John of Brittany. He referred to a Welsh attack on the marches, told the justiciar 'to postpone and entirely to set aside all thought of a Parliament' in order to deal first with the Welsh and then repeated: 'Make no arrangements for a Parliament and permit none to be held before our return to England, for when we arrive there, we shall arrange, with your counsel and that of the magnates, for the holding of a Parliament as may be best for us and for our realm.' It was a flat defiance of the requirement in the Provisions of Oxford for three Parliaments a year.

In February, 1260, therefore, Earl Simon began to demand the meeting of the postponed Candlemas Parliament. The king became increasingly alarmed by news of the earl's renewed opposition and especially by his friendship with Henry's son Edward. By the end of March, Henry had heard of a plan to call a Parliament despite his absence. To counter this, Henry, who had been further delayed in France by illness, sent letters across the Channel ahead of him to summon a meeting of over a hundred barons and tenants-in-chief who were to come to London ready to do military service. But the situation worsened and, amid other signs of active opposition, the king heard that Simon, with Edward's support, was about to hold a Parliament, or *colloquium* in London. In letters to the justiciar and to the mayor and people of London, the king said that he had heard that during the forthcoming Parliament 'which was meeting against the king's will' Edward was proposing to occupy the houses of the bishop of London in St Paul's Close with horses and arms, from which the citizens feared danger might arise. Therefore neither Edward nor 'anyone else of whom suspicion of evil might be entertained' was to be allowed to stay in the city. This was arranged, and a plan was also agreed between Richard of Cornwall and the justiciar with the citizens of London for closing the city gates and arming the male population. Furnished with money borrowed by King Louis, and sustained by a force of knights, the king now arrived in London. The Lord Edward, denying that he had ever intended opposition to his father, was immediately and fully reconciled to the king after his brief, impulsive association with Simon de Montfort. The king then summoned a Parliament which met in July and decided to bring de Montfort to trial before it. A small committee of inquiry was to report to the council which would then decide what amends the earl should make. A long document setting out the king's charges against the earl and the earl's answers has survived from this inquiry.

One of the charges was that de Montfort had held a Parliament (against the king's command to the justiciar) and had gone to it armed (against one of the Provisions of Oxford). A certain nonchalance, even arrogance, comes down to us from the earl's replies. To the point that the king had instructed the justiciar that there should be no Parliament before his return, it is recorded simply: 'The earl says that the king may very well have so ordered him.' To the statement that the justiciar had given the order against holding a Parliament to the earl and the rest of the council, de Montfort replied in the same offhand style. To the statement that the earl had held the Parliament at Candlemas, there was simply the reply that three Parliaments a year, one at Candlemas, had been prescribed, that therefore the earl had come with other councillors, and that when they heard that there should be no Parliament until the king returned which was to be in three weeks, 'the Parliament was adjourned from day to day for three weeks.' To the charge that he had come armed, the earl replied in terms which remind us of the need to travel protected, and the difficulty of determining how much armed force was too much. 'The earl says that he did not come there with either horses or arms, except in the usual way of travelling about the country.'

Eventually, the charges were dropped. The council, which by implication was itself included in a number of the charges, refused to condemn de Montfort and he was cleared in Parliament. But a fundamental question had been raised. Could Parliament only meet, as Henry claimed, with the king's consent, and could there be no ordinances without him? Or could Parliament meet and act, as Simon believed, without the king if necessary? This question had to be settled. For one thing, the king found that the Parliament which he had called to meet in October 1260 was more opposition-minded than the councillors; indeed, it forced him to accept a number of new, and less royalist, officials including a new justiciar, Hugh Despenser who was one of de Montfort's adherents. Yet tradition was undoubtedly on the king's side in his claim that Parliament could not be summoned against his order. So, keeping within the letter of the Provisions for the time being, Henry set about securing papal support for overthrowing what had been agreed at Oxford. In April 1261, the Pope released Henry from his sworn obligation to observe the Provisions on the grounds that this had improperly infringed royal liberty. The king then resumed full power.

Henry had already begun to disregard many of the limitations placed on him, notably those concerned with the appointment of sheriffs, the raising and spending of money, and the disposing of castles and wardships. Likewise, although he kept some of the Fifteen about him, he increasingly turned again to his familiars for counsel. The barons for the most part acquiesced in what he did: they wanted to lead their own lives and were not unwilling to let him deal with the professional business of ruling, provided he did so in an acceptable manner. Nevertheless, Henry's abandonment of the Provisions led a number of the barons, de Montfort among them, to appeal to King Louis, and when Henry denounced the Provisions, some of his opponents tried to enforce them by a rival administration. But the majority of the barons was unwilling for open conflict; Earl Simon left England and a compromise was patched up, from which Henry gradually built up his own position. By the summer of 1262, he was again fully in charge of the realm, and he then went to France, partly to negotiate with Louis over Gascon matters, partly to settle the problem of Earl Simon who had by now left England for France. In Paris, however, Henry fell seriously ill, and did not return until Christmas. Once again there was baronial unrest and in the spring of 1263 Simon was called back to England. Another Welsh war now disturbed the realm; there was disorder in the Marches and rebellious incidents disturbed the peace elsewhere. Those disappointed by the collapse of the Provisions took their cue from these events, and Simon assumed the leadership of their movement. The younger earls and barons adhered mostly to Simon; their elders stayed with the king. The barons' wars which followed were wars between barons, not between all the barons and the king.[1] Had Henry been faced by a united baronage, he could not have resisted.

In May, Simon met his chief followers at Oxford and sent demands to the king that the Provisions be observed; all who refused, save the king and his family, were to be treated as enemies of the realm. The king naturally rejected these terms, and the rebels began to harry the properties of royalists who had stood out against the king's opponents. Earl Simon took the Channel ports, cutting off the king's communications with France, and Henry himself, occupying the tower of London, was forced to surrender by the citizens' concern for their own interest. Simon and his associates occupied London and took over the government and royal castles. Alongside each sheriff they placed a new official, a warden of the peace (*custos pacis*) to deal with all administrative duties, leaving the sheriff only as a financial official. Edward, who had occupied Windsor, had to surrender it when the king was forced to assent to an attack on it by the feudal host if

---

[1] F. M. Powicke, *King Henry III and the Lord Edward*, p. 435.

necessary. Men who had been dispossessed of their land by the rebels were obliged to swear to the Provisions before they could regain possession and a Parliament, which achieved nothing, was summoned for October. But the royalists made one last effort, helped by the discontent of those who had been recently harmed by the baronial party. Once again Edward seized Windsor and Henry joined him there; Simon now held the tower of London, but found the forces against him stronger than he had supposed since some of his younger baronial supporters from the Welsh marches had returned to Edward's allegiance.

It was now agreed by both sides to refer their differences to Louis of France and to accept his verdict on the Provisions. Should the king be free to appoint his own ministers, even aliens if he wished, or should government be jointly by king and a council appointed by the baronage? In January 1264, by the judgement known as the Mise of Amiens, Louis declared in the king's favour. The king's right to choose his own ministers was upheld, and he was bound by nothing except the charters and the customs of the realm. The Pope sent a legate, Cardinal Gui (himself soon to become Pope) to restore the king to his rightful position, and the realm to peace. Far from quietening the dissidents, however, the Mise and the intended arrival of the cardinal only spurred them to resist such foreign intervention. War broke out between the king's forces and the barons who supported de Montfort. The king scored an initial victory at Northampton, but Simon controlled London and the south-east. At the Battle of Lewes in May 1264, the king was defeated and Simon was at last in charge of government. Edward and his cousin, Henry of Almain (the son of Richard of Cornwall, the nominal German king) were hostages for the fulfilment of peace terms. Yet Henry was King of England still; there was no question of deposing him, as his grandson was to be deposed, since his personal position was too strong for this to be possible even if there had been, which there was not, any will for such a drastic remedy. If Henry, who was not an unpopular king, were harmed there would be outrage in England, and the French would invade with the Pope's blessing. Agreement was therefore still necessary, and Simon set about devising yet another form of government to place the king under the control of the baronage.

A Parliament was summoned to meet on 22 June, and the important part played by the gentry, as distinct from the baronage, in the success of Simon's party was acknowledged in the writs appointing new keepers of the peace in each country, and ordering them to send knights of the shire to attend Parliament. It was not so much the summons of the knights that was significant (that was not new) as the terms in which they were summoned. The writs stated that peace had now been 'ordained and established between us and our barons' and that 'whereas in our approaching Parliament, it is necessary for us to deliberate with our prelates, magnates, and other faithful men concerning our affairs and those of our kingdom' there should be elected in the county court 'four of the more lawful and discreet knights of the same county elected for that purpose by the assent of that county.' These knights were to be sent 'to us on behalf of the entire county' and should come to London 'in order to deliberate with us on the aforesaid matters.' In other words, the representative status of the knights is made clear and so is the intention that they should *deliberate*. Although theirs was a lesser status than the barons' and although this was a partisan Parliament, it seems that the knights were required, on this occasion at least, to do more politically than simply speak for the amount of taxation that their shires would provide.[1]

Almost as soon as it met, Parliament gave its approval to a new arrangement of government (*forma regiminis*). The Bishop of Chichester and the Earls of Leicester and Gloucester were named as electors who were to appoint a new council of nine, by the advice of which the king was to rule (much as he had previously been expected to rule under the guidance of the Fifteen). Three of the nine were always to be with him, but the ultimate power in the land was with the three 'electors' who had the authority of Parliament to change the composition of the appointed council of nine if they wished. The three 'electors' themselves could only be changed by the magnates and prelates (in other words by the common council of the realm) though in fact their power rested on their military victory. These arrangements were supposed to be provisional until a final settlement had been obtained, and this depended in part on how King Louis responded to yet another appeal for arbitration that had been addressed to him following the temporary settlement, known as the Mise of Lewis, reached after the recent battle.

England, meanwhile, was under threat of invasion from France on the king's behalf, and in July the feudal host was summoned by the government. Since peace had nominally been declared, all men, whichever side they had taken in the recent struggle, were supposed to rally to it. In fact, however, sections of the baronage, particularly the lords of the Welsh Marches and the north of England, stood apart. Earl Simon's government, therefore, had to rely heavily on a special levy of knights and men from the shires, which was organized throughout the nation, the counties nearest the coast being responsible for sea defence. To these levies, the shires sent free

---

[1] Stubbs, *Select Charters*, p. 399 (Latin); C. Stephenson and F. G. Marcham, *Sources of English Constitutional History* (translation). Treharne and Sanders, op. cit., document 39.

tenants and a certain number of men from each township, as well as knights. It was a sign of the extent to which the campaign for the Provisions (which had been confirmed again under the Mise of Lewis) commanded enthusiasm in men of all ranks. This formative chapter in parliamentary history, like every other, took place in an intensely political atmosphere. Partisan political 'songs' (the Song of Lewis, extolling and vindicating Simon de Montfort, is the notable surviving example) were composed and circulated, popular feeling was aroused (not least by the cry of 'down with the aliens') and knights and freemen, citizens and burgesses, gave service and money beyond what was customary.

Indeed, the help given by the towns does much to explain the famous decision of Simon de Montfort to summon to the next Parliament for the first time 'two of the more upright and discreet citizens or burgesses' from the cities, and boroughs and four from the Cinque Ports along with the knights of the shires.[1] This Parliament, summoned to meet in January on the Octave of St. Hilary (January 21) 1265 at Westminster, was a highly partisan gathering, attended by only twenty-three barons, who were all Simon's adherents, though all the bishops, who were mostly supporters of Simon's cause, attended, together with a hundred heads of religious houses as well as the knights and burgesses. (This is the earliest Parliament for which there has survived a list of those to whom writs were sent.) The council ordered sheriffs to allow reasonable expenses to the knights because of the burden of attendance, and the writs stated that the prelates, magnates and nobles were summoned for the matter of Edward's release and other business concerning the community of the realm.[2] At this Parliament, Prince Edward was released on condition that he took an oath to the new government and remained in England for three years: he could be disinherited if he broke faith. His household was cleared of suspected persons, and some of his castles were handed over to Simon. The king and the prince swore in Westminster Hall that they would uphold the settlement, and Parliament, which lasted until the middle of February, proceeded to judicial business.

Yet the peace could not have lasted. Power was concentrated (through the group of three and council of nine) in many fewer hands than had been the case in 1258; invasion (held off partly by the danger to the royal

[1] Stubbs, *Select Charters*, pp. 403-44 (Latin); in Treharne and Sanders, op. cit., docs. 41 A-D and in Stephenson and Marcham, ibid., pp. 151-152 (translation). Powicke, *King Henry III and the Lord Edward*, pp. 487-488.

[2] R. F. Treharne; 'The Nature of Parliament in the Reign of Henry III', *E.H.R.* LXXIV (1959), pp. 590-610; reprinted in Fryde and Miller *Historical Studies of the English Parliament*, Vol. I (p. 85).

hostages) remained a threat; and the new papal legate, Cardinal Gui, who had been refused admission to England, was demanding from across the channel, under pain of excommunication, that the Provisions be renounced. There was also sporadic unrest and disorder, particularly in the Welsh Marches. Above all, Simon's government was now revealed in practice, despite its higher aspirations, as no better than a partisan regime under which political responsibility, offices and castles went to Simon's family, friends and adherents. Simon de Montfort has often been likened to Oliver Cromwell, and there is some truth in the comparison. In his own eyes, Simon was no rebel but a loyal vassal, upholding the proper spirit of government by king and baronage acting in concert, and he was willing to force this desirable state of affairs on the king if it could not be achieved otherwise. He saw himself as acting from moral imperatives, and as spurred on by necessity, in much the same way as Cromwell was to regard himself as called by a higher power to restore the constitutional balance he deemed to have existed in Elizabeth's day. Like Cromwell, Simon de Montfort possessed the idealism that is given power by a sense of destiny. Where necessity drove, each would follow at whatever cost. Each, in practice, eventually came to rely on force and on a party of personal adherents, and neither succeeded in establishing his authority on the basis of legality. The Parliament of 1265 was no 'democratic' assembly and it was not in response to any theory of representation that Simon de Montfort summoned the burgesses to attend this Parliament of his friends.

Yet this does not diminish the historical significance of the partisan Parliament of 1265 which first brought representatives of the townspeople to the periphery of government. Indeed, it was in some respects an anticipation of the Parliaments of the far distant future, in which kings and political leaders came to understand that workable government was best secured in England by obtaining a (partisan) majority of the House of Commons to support it, whether this was achieved by 'packing' Parliaments, manipulating elections or, eventually, giving political responsibility to the leaders of the party which had been honestly elected with a majority. The summons to the burgesses in 1265 was also a sign of the increased importance of the ancient borough communities which had kept a considerable control over their own affairs since pre-Conquest times. By now they had also managed to escape from a position in which they had been tallaged at the king's will, first by arguing over the amount of the tallage, and then by achieving a state of affairs in which the money they gave was deemed to be an aid that they had conceded rather than a tax imposed upon them. Prosperous, oligarchical and dominated by the guilds, the towns were already a power in the land, and it was a recognition of their wealth and status that Simon de Montfort, in the king's name, should send for their representatives to 'lend counsel' in the great matter of Edward's release.[1] It is significant that, whereas in the future, the representatives of the boroughs were summoned by writs to the sheriffs, the writs of summons (in the king's name) were addressed to 'the citizens' in January 1265, a direct appeal for support.

To describe Simon de Montfort as the 'founder' of the House of Commons is an unqualified error. What he had done when he summoned the burgesses and knights together in a political emergency was not necessarily intended to be repeated. The medieval mind did not act according to constitutional theory but as a response to necessity in particular circumstances, duly reconciled so far as possible with the spirit of custom. Even so, in calling the communities of the towns and shires to Parliament in order to bolster the baronial cause, Simon de Montfort had set an example followed by Edward I, when it suited him, to strengthen the authority of the crown. Eventually, these representatives of the communities were to succeed so well in establishing their own power over money grants that they were able to bargain for the redress of their grievances in exchange for taxation. On that foundation, foreshadowed in writing at least as early as the confirmation of Magna Carta in 1225, the presence in Parliament of the Commons would be turned to their own advantage instead of the crown's, and the foundations of the future House of Commons built.

In May, Simon de Montfort caused another Parliament to be summoned, at first to meet at Westminster and then to be diverted to Winchester so as to be nearer trouble that was already breaking out in the Welsh Marches. The burgesses were not summoned, a confirmation that no precedent was supposed to have been established by their presence in January. As it happens, we have an interesting insight into the logistics of a thirteenth century Parliament from a note of instruction to the chamberlain of London, who was ordered to obtain in the city 'one hundred tuns of wine, both by purchase and prise', which 'because the king is to hold his forthcoming Parliament at Westminster, so that he will require many wines there' was to be taken 'and placed in the king's cellar there'.[2] But this Parliament never met. Before another one assembled, Simon de Montfort was defeated and dead. His fall was precipitated by a breach with Gilbert de

---

[1] *Close Rolls of the Reign of Henry III, 1264–1268* (London, 1902–38), pp. 87, 89, 96; quoted in R. F. Treharne, 'The nature of Parliament in the reign of Henry III', *E.H.R.* LXXIV (1959), reprinted in Fryde and Miller, Vol. I; Stubbs, *Select Charters*, p. 403 (Summons to the Parliament of 1265) (Latin).

[2] Treharne and Sanders, op. cit., Doc. 43.

Clare, Earl of Gloucester, whose family could not tolerate the height to which the de Montforts had risen in the kingdom. The subjection of the king and of the Lord Edward to Simon's will was increasingly resented by those of de Montfort's equals who were not tied to his cause and were not rewarded for adherence. The reality of power was that Simon either had to be king himself (and that could not be contemplated by the great majority of magnates) or he could, for the long run, be tolerated in no higher role than that of any other great councillor. A powerless *de jure* king, ruled by a 'mayor of the palace' had served for a time in Merovingian Gaul, but it was wholly alien to the thinking of thirteenth century England, in which *de jure* and *de facto* power were seen as necessarily vested in the same man, even though he was expected to use his power according to law and custom.

The end came with a rising in the Welsh Marches and the escape of Prince Edward who, with the king, had been held in captivity by Earl Simon, first at Gloucester and then at Hereford. By a trick while out riding at the end of May, Edward escaped with Thomas of Clare, Gloucester's brother, who with Henry de Montfort, had been given the duty of watching over the prince. It had been a plot arranged with Gilbert of Clare who was ostensibly treating with Earl Simon but was actually waiting for Edward to join him. The prince, Earl Gilbert and other marcher lords met at Ludlow. Simon was now cut off by the Severn from the basis of his strength in London, and his hold over the administration began to crumble. He first moved the king and court to Monmouth, having made a treaty, with the king's formal approval, recognizing Llywelyn as prince of Wales. But the fall of Gloucester castle to Edward put Simon in great danger on the wrong side of the river. Having failed to cross the estuary of the Severn, he then took the court and his army back to Hereford and contrived to get across the river to Evesham on 3 August. There he expected his son, also called Simon, to bring him help and to be able to move towards the south-east where his support principally was. But a few days earlier, Edward had been able to surprise the younger Simon outside Kenilworth castle, capturing most of the barons and knights who were with him although the younger Simon himself escaped. Earl Simon had staked everything on his son's bringing reinforcements, and when he failed to do so, the earl was trapped. In the battle of Evesham at the beginning of August, Simon de Montfort, his son Henry and most of his closest associates were killed, and the king himself, who had been held in their midst, was wounded. The immediate consequence was the restoration of full power to Henry III, though Edward was now the active element in government. But three years of disorder followed before peace was fully restored.

The baronial party was broken, but for some time resistance was continued, principally at Kenilworth and in the Isle of Ely. In the end, this was dealt with by the government without much vindictiveness. But it can hardly be said that moderation to the vanquished was the prevailing spirit at a great council of some magnates which was hastily summoned to Winchester in September.[1] Although this was described as a Parliament in records, no prelates were present and no representatives of the communities. It seems to have been simply a meeting of those lay magnates who were the king's supporters, and it is improbable that there was much if any opportunity for the routine judicial business of Parliaments. The general principle that had been adopted was that royalists might keep whatever they had seized from the king's enemies. At this assembly it was ordained that lands belonging to the defeated party should be taken into the king's hands, some being distributed to the king's supporters. This stimulated the further resistance of the 'disinherited'. Before they were dealt with, however, London was brought to surrender and fined heavily, and a settlement was made with the Cinque Ports which had also resisted. Earl Simon's widow Eleanor, the King's sister, was allowed to go abroad with her daughter to join her two youngest sons, and the Leicester title and lands were given to the king's son Edmund. Subsequently, the younger Simon, who had taken refuge in the fens with other rebels, was forced to place himself at the king's mercy and was allowed to go abroad. But the disinherited and the rebellious still held out in woodlands and in swamps, especially in the Isle of Ely.

In the summer of 1266, Earl Simon's castle of Kenilworth, still held by the rebels, was placed under a royal siege which lasted for six months. But there was now a general wish for a settlement, towards which the king and his council were urged by the new papal legate, Cardinal Ottobuono Fieschi. In August, therefore, the king summoned a Parliament to meet at Kenilworth, and there he appointed three bishops and three barons who nominated one more bishop and five more barons to form a committee of twelve to produce a settlement. The result was the Dictum of Kenilworth, which the rebels accepted in December after many hesitations. They were then allowed to leave the castle bearing arms. It was not a negotiated settlement but an offer from the king which the rebels accepted. Politically, it revoked all that Simon de Montfort had done and removed all restraints on the crown, though it acknowledged the king's obligation to the charters and to the grants he had made freely and not under compulsion in the legal sections of the Provisions of Westminster. But the Dictum also provided an escape from the prospect of wholesale disinheritance and from the social instability that would have arisen from it. Although anyone who continued to resist would be outlawed, those who had lost their lands could redeem the

[1] *Dignity of a Peer*, Vol. I, p. 156.

greater part by the payment of fines either to the crown or the recent tenant, and arguments were to be settled in the courts. A new beginning was made possible. In February, 1267, another Parliament was held at Bury St Edmunds, from which negotiations were conducted with the rebels still holding out at Ely. Then a new emergency occurred in April when the Earl of Gloucester, discontented with the apparent supremacy of some of his rivals, marched on London and possessed it. But by June a reconciliation had taken place and the king entered the city. The rebels on Ely were forced to submit, and with only a few pockets of resistance remaining, general peace was restored.

In November, at a Parliament or great council at Marlborough, the Statute of Marlborough placed on the Statute book the majority of the legal safeguards that had been included in the Provisions of Westminster in 1259, and which were the enduring legacy of the baronial movement. This appears to have been a Parliament of magnates and prelates only, but the preamble of the Statute of Marlborough stated that it was enacted, 'the more descreet Men of the Realm being called together, as well of the higher as of the lower estate', which suggests the possibility that some knights were present.[1] Towards the end of the reign there occurred a further significant development in the evolution of taxation. Owing to the difficulty of raising taxation from the laity in the great post-civil war confusion, the king was forced at first to rely on taxing a reluctant clergy, with the Pope's assent. In dealing with the laity, even in the matter of tallaging his own demesne, he seemed to have taken considerable care. A lesson had been learned from the recent strife and discussion was protracted. But the king was making plans to go on a crusade (though in the end it was Edward and not Henry who went) and for that general taxation was needed.

In April, 1268, the mayor, bailiffs and six representatives of 27 selected cities and boroughs were summoned to have special colloquy with the king on urgent business concerning their own affairs.[2] It may have been concerned with the general settlement and the restoration of privileges after the upheaval during the previous decade. They were to bring with them authority to act for their own constituencies; an anticipation of the plenary powers which would be regular after 1290. We do not know what took place at the assembly which was presumably not a Parliament. However, it appears that some agreement in principle was given to an aid at a Parliament of magnates in the autumn of 1268. In the following October, a great assembly was called to Westminster for the translation of the bones of

[1] *Stat. R.* Vol. I, p. 19 (Henry III).
[2] G. O. Sayles, *E.H.R.* XL, pp. 580ff.

Edward the Confessor to the new Abbey church which Henry built, and which was now dedicated. Not only magnates but the more powerful men from cities and boroughs were apparently present. Taxation seems again to have been debated, and a twentieth may have been granted by some sections of the community on that occasion. It was also a matter before the lower clergy who were meeting in their own lower assembly at the same time and who were concerned to establish their right to tax themselves. Finally, a large Parliament met in April 1270, apparently attended by bishops, earls, barons, knights and freeholders, when a general tax of a twentieth on personal property was granted, the first tax of this nature since the thirtieth of 1237. This was to be the stable mode of direct taxation in the future, and it is significant that knights were called upon to assess and collect it. Unfortunately, however, we know little of the Parliaments of Henry's last years or of the discussions on taxation. Some of the evidence is confused because few records survive, in stark contrast to the remarkable abundance of evidence, from official papers and from the king's own letters during the years of strife with de Montfort and his party.

Henry died in 1272, his great new abbey church achieved and with dangerous political storms weathered. It had been as inevitable as anything can be in politics that Simon de Montfort's attempt to formalize conciliar control over the king should fail. A thirteenth century king who reigned but did not rule was a practical impossibility. The authority of the crown had been re-established and Edward had learned much from the threat to it. When his father died, he was away on the crusade, and it was two years before he returned to take up the responsibility of government. Edward was the first post-Conquest king to succeed immediately on his father's death without any discussion and without dependence on the coronation ceremony for his right to rule. His peaceful, automatic and unchallenged succession testified to the restored authority of the crown and the new political stability. Yet the baronial rebellion was of outstanding constitutional significance, foreshadowing much of the process by which the influence of Parliament would be enhanced in the future. The fundamental cause of baronial resentment had been the unresponsiveness of the crown and its officials to discontent in the political nation. The trigger of baronial opposition was the crown's need for money to pay for military adventure. In future, that need would be used increasingly by the political nation to secure the redress of its grievances by the crown. More than that, the attempt of the baronial opposition to transform Parliament from being an occasion dependent on the king's will into an institution with an automatic life of its own, had done much to plant the idea of regular Parliaments firmly in the consciousness of the English nation.

CHAPTER 3

— * —

Edward I:
King, Law and Parliament

I

THE emergence of Parliaments as significant political occasions during the long reign of Henry III had owed everything to political conflict and nothing to the king's will. Edward I, in sharp contrast, saw from the beginning of his reign the usefulness of consultation in Parliament with the politically important sections of his realm. This was often made clear by the terms in which his writs of summons were expressed. The contrast between the two kings is even sharper when Parliament is considered as an occasion for legislation. Parliament under Henry III was of comparatively minor significance in the making of general law as distinct from its judicial functions as a high court dealing with particular cases. Edward, however, repeatedly used Parliaments for the promulgation of statutes designed to make new and more effective law and to correct social conditions tending to weaken the royal government. There had been no law-making on this scale since the great law-codes of the Anglo-Saxon kings had been issued with the witness and assent of their Witan. The assizes of Henry II had concerned legal processes rather than making new law.

Edward's use of Parliaments as occasions for making law implied no concession by the king that he was restricted to legislating only in Parliament. Sometimes he issued ordinances which had the force of law from his council; sometimes a Parliament in which he legislated was, in composition, hardly distinguishable from a council. Yet Edward obviously believed that the promulgation of statutes in Parliament added something to their solemnity and effectiveness and the general precedent that he set made it difficult for his successors to declare new laws except by parliamentary enactment. By the use he made of Parliament for legislating during the first twenty-two years of his reign, Edward did more than any other medieval king to enlarge the importance of parliamentary assemblies without being under political or financial duress. Without any idea of creating a new institution, he did much to establish the concept of Parliament as a natural process of government simply because he held Parliaments regularly and transacted important business in them. Under some of his successors the regularity of Parliaments would cease and their frequency diminish, but by then Parliament had become a recognized and accepted feature of the political landscape, and one, moreover, that could be used by other interests than the king. Indeed, this development was to begin in the last thirteen troubled years of Edward's reign when there took root the idea that Parliaments could be used by political oppositions to wring concessions from a reluctant king. In these final years, Edward, who during the first two-thirds of his reign had used Parliaments as a buttress of the royal authority, experienced a taste of the way in which they could be turned against him by powerful men determined to frustrate the royal will. If, in his first twenty two years, the development of Parliament owed everything to the king's will, during his last thirteen political conflict was again the principal anvil on which parliamentary influence was forged. The years after 1294 were both to recall the challenge to his father's authority and presage the conflict that was to destroy his son.

Edward I was hard and hard-working, frugal, free from temperamental dependence on favourites and disposed towards orderly, efficient and just government. As a man, he was not the paragon of unsullied virtue that he has seemed to some historians. Though he was an affectionate husband, a loyal friend and a king with principles, he could be ruthless, harsh and unjust when his interest seemed threatened.[1] Yet he understood the importance of certainty in law, and possessed an acute, energetic and persistent political mind able both to discern in the social features of his time potential threats to the crown's authority, and to devise effective responses to them. He was determined to be master of the realm, but for the most part he tempered this resolution with an understanding that his dominance would not be best sustained by trying to drive powerful men and interests to accept what seemed to them unacceptable. In his impressive and handsome person, and with his reputation as a successful soldier, Edward seemed very much the incarnation of kingly virtues as they were understood by the age in which he lived. These personal characteristics undoubtedly helped him in the exercise of his authority, and his task was also made easier by the

[1] Matthew Paris (*Chronica Majora*, Vol. 5 p. 598) also alleges that, in his youth, Edward was guilty during a Welsh rebellion of an act of particularly wanton cruelty and mutilation.

thorough defeat, at the end of his father's reign, of a baronial party that had seriously over-reached itself. Rebellion had discredited opposition and Edward had learned much from his experience of those troubled years. By his own qualities, therefore, and assisted by circumstances, Edward I was enabled to be the strongest of our medieval kings. Yet, although his achievements were great, his campaigns in Wales, Scotland and France subjected the realm to such political and financial strains that Edward was eventually to bequeath to his incompetent son a more vulnerable inheritance than he himself had received. The latter part of Edward's reign began the process by which the growth of Parliament was nourished, not by the king's will, but by the persistent need of the later Plantagenets for money with which to pay for their military adventures. From this need came the dependence of the crown on parliamentary taxation and eventually, in the distant future, the controlling influence of Parliament over policy. Before Edward's reign ended, the claim had been unapologetically made by the magnates that taxation needed the consent of the taxed and that grievances must be redressed before taxes were granted.

When his father died, Edward I, who still was overseas, was immediately proclaimed king by hereditary right, and an assembly of lay magnates and 'four knights from each county and four persons from each city' seems to have gathered to signify their adherence to him, with the higher clergy meeting separately for the same purpose. (This assembly, which is known only through one contemporary chronicler, the Winchester annalist, could not, of course, constitute a Parliament, having been summoned in the king's absence.)[1] Edward was so confident of his position that he saw no cause to hurry home, stopping in Gascony to settle matters with those of his vassals there who were causing trouble. It was two years before he reached England in August, 1274, when he was crowned at Westminster.

Edward's first Parliament met in April 1275. To it were called both knights and burgesses, and in his summons requiring their presence, the king described the assembly as a 'general Parliament' (*generale Parliamentum*) with his prelates and magnates, which he had originally proposed should meet in February but which had been prorogued until after Easter. In his writ to the sheriffs, the king commanded them to send to this Parliament 'four knights from among those knights of your county who are more discreet and law-worthy,[2] and likewise from each of the cities, boroughs and market towns of your bailiwick, six or four citizens, burgesses or other good men....' The purpose for which these representatives were called was stated in the summons, and the precise words used are significant. The

---

[1] Stubbs, *Select Charters*, p. 421.
[2] '*discretioribus in lege*' (alternative translation, 'with knowledge of the laws', *E.H.D.*).

knights and burgesses were 'to consider, along with the magnates of our kingdom, the affairs of the said kingdom . . .' (*ad tractandum una cum magnatibus regni nostri de negotiis ejusdem regni* . . .)[1]. The terms of this summons alone suggest that, from the outset of the reign, Parliament characteristically had functions wider and less specific than the transaction of judicial business, but we also have direct evidence from the King himself of Parliament's political role. In 1275, after his first Parliament had dispersed, Edward wrote to Pope Gregory X explaining why a papal request for the payment of arrears of the annual money promised by King John had not been considered in the council of magnates in Parliament, as the king had previously said it would be. Illness, Edward wrote, had compelled him to dissolve the Parliament before it could consider this matter, and he could not give an answer without the consent of the prelates and magnates, since he was bound by his coronation oath to preserve uninjured the rights of the realm. Without such counsel, so Edward informed the Pope, he could do nothing affecting the crown of the realm.[2] The king therefore promised to deal with the matter at the next Parliament at Michaelmas, the terms of his letter also indicating his general practice of holding at least two Parliaments a year at Easter and Whitsuntide.[3]

It would be absurd to suppose from this letter that Edward regarded himself as bound in any constitutional sense to make his decisions in Parliament. It was often convenient for a medieval king confronting an awkward political situation to procrastinate by shifting the burden of responsibility in part at least on to other shoulders. But such an excuse would have carried no conviction without the general assumption of medieval society that consultation was part of the natural political order. The full personal responsibility of the king for government was taken for granted, but so was his obligation to govern under the law and take advice. This was not merely a tacit assumption. A number of medieval philosophers, including St Thomas Aquinas, had voiced it in one form or another, and the judge Henry de Bracton had stated it clearly in the remarkable account he left behind him of the laws and customs of England in Henry

---

[1] Stubbs, *Select Charters*, pp. 441–2 (Latin). Translations are in B. Wilkinson, *Constitutional History of Medieval England*, Vol. III, p. 306, and in *E.H.D.*, Vol. III, p. 396. This writ to the sheriffs (of which only that to the sheriff of Middlesex survives completely) makes no command that the representatives were to be *elected*, but it is to be presumed that the knights were elected in the shire courts on this as on previous occasions, and that the burgesses were chosen by the principal men of their towns.

[2] F. M. Powicke, *The Thirteenth Century*, p. 343. The letter is printed in *Parliamentary Writs*, i. 381.

[3] This would coincide with regular sittings of the law courts, see p. 84.

III's time. 'The king himself ought to be subject to no man, but he ought to be subject to God and the law, since law makes the king. Therefore, let the king render to the law what the law has rendered to the king, viz. dominion and power, for there is no king where will rules and not the law.'[1] What is thought to be an interpolation by a hand other than Bracton's made the even stronger statement that, as well as God and the law, the king has as his supporters his court, that is, the earls and barons, since these are his associates and 'he who has an associate has a master'. Whoever wrote these words, they provide an insight into the extent to which a medieval king could seem, to a contemporary mind, under a natural obligation to seek consent. In England Parliament was increasingly becoming the principal means by which consent was sought.

The representatives of the communities, on those occasions when they were summoned to Parliament, were at this stage almost certainly concerned largely with taxation. Whether or not it was thought that to collect taxation from the shires might be difficult if the representative knights were not present when it was levied, it is a fact that they were on almost all occasions present in Edward's reign when grants were made.[2] Further, the king's wish to obtain a new export tax was certainly his principal reason for summoning representatives of the merchant interest to the first Parliament of 1275. The most usual function of the Commons was to carry back to their communities their witness and testimony that the taxation being levied was properly and lawfully ordained and granted but some of them at least were also almost certainly consulted on the practical question of how much taxation could be raised without difficulties.

Yet important though the Commons' role already was when taxes were granted, we should go beyond the evidence if we regarded taxation as the sole and simple reason for the attendance of the representatives of the communities at Edward's earlier Parliaments. Financial aid was not sought from most of Edward's Parliaments, yet on a number of these non-taxing occasions, representatives of the communities were there just the same. What is more, if the words of the summons to his first Parliament mean what they appear to mean, it is hard to assert convincingly that the business of the knights and burgesses was wholly devoid of political implications. They were, after all, invited to 'consider', along with the magnates, the 'affairs' of the kingdom. We cannot know which of the kingdom's affairs

---

[1] Bracton: *De legibus et consuetudinibus Angliae* (ed. G. G. Woodbine, 1915–22). See *A History of Medieval Political Theory in the West*, R. W. Carlyle and A. J. Carlyle, Vol. III, Part I, Ch. IV pp. 69–72.

[2] The only exception seems to have been the fifteenth granted by the baronage in the Parliament of 1279. See p. 135.

they might in practice 'consider', nor the extent and manner of such consideration. Yet we may reasonably guess that they were expected to listen to some explanation of the expenditure needed, and of the policies to pay for which their communities were asked for money. It is not impossible that some among them might have been used to provide the king and council (perhaps in private) with information on the state of opinion in their counties when this was needed. Not least, the representatives of the communities at Edward's Parliaments sometimes had a role to play as witnesses to the promulgation of his more important statutes. It was, no doubt, a largely passive role, but it could have been important in publicizing and gaining assent for new law in the shires. Edward, it seems, had taken from Simon de Montfort the general point that there were times when the support of the communities was a valuable buttress for government. By the end of Edward's reign, we shall see clearer signs that the knights, if not the burgesses, were beginning to approach something like an identifiable political role. But even in his earlier years, we must not assume that they were never, on any occasion, able to do more than listen, voiceless, to what the council and magnates ordained about money. At the least, it is not impossible that there were individual knights and burgesses of sufficient individual stature to be asked to contribute some information or opinions which would assist the government in reaching some of its decisions.

The underlying explanation for the increasing tendency to call knights and burgesses to Parliament was their greatly rising prosperity and social influence in the remarkable economic expansion which took place in the thirteenth century. There was an unprecedented increase in population. New land that had recently been marsh or forest was brought into cultivation. Though still small, the towns and boroughs had grown into oases of comparative independence from the feudal obligations which were still the prevailing, if waning, feature of social and economic relationships in the countryside as a whole. The original characteristic of a borough was that some of those who dwelt within it held their property by 'burgage tenure', paying money rents for it instead of providing the customary work and personal services which the ordinary countryman rendered to the lord for the land he held.[1] The property of the burgesses could be freely inherited, sold or mortgaged. Burgage tenure may have originally applied

---

[1] The sum of money due to the crown in return for the town's charter was the *firma burgi*, or the farm of the borough. The inhabitants had the right to farm the borough themselves, instead of the sheriff of the county doing so and making what profit he could for his pains by raising more than was due to the crown. This *firma burgi* was apportioned among the burgesses as money rent for the houses, land or shops they owned, and together they were the community of the city, *communitas civitatis*.

to more freeholders, or at any rate to a higher proportion of a borough's population, than it did at the end of the thirteenth century. But by the reign of Edward I, the majority of towns-dwellers did not hold their property as burgesses, who were rather a privileged minority. Burgess tenure had become attached to particular tenements or property holdings, which were usually quite large, were quite often not wholly occupied by buildings or were sometimes subdivided to contain a considerable number of cottages. In addition, other areas of the borough or city which had not previously been built up were now occupied by cottages of the poorer people, adding to the number of inhabitants who did not hold their dwellings by burgage tenure. The burgesses, however, were usually merchants or craftsmen of the richer sort who enjoyed a number of privileges, trading, economic and political, for the higher rent they paid. They were a kind of citizens' aristocracy, controlling the borough court and the market. They also provided the small number of men who apparently took part in the early elections of the borough's representatives in Parliament, and burgess tenure remained one qualification for the franchise in some boroughs until the Reform Act of 1832, although other sorts of franchise developed as well.[1]

Burgage tenure, however, was exercised very much under the control of the sheriff of the county. Although the writs of summons to Simon de Montfort's Parliament of 1265 were enrolled as having been sent to 'the citizens of York, Lincoln, and to the other boroughs of England', there is no list of the 'other boroughs'. Moreover, it subsequently became the general practice simply to require the sheriffs to send two representatives from each borough and city without particular boroughs being specified. Obviously, the larger boroughs and cities would be required to send representatives; if London, York, Bristol and Lincoln had not done so questions would presumably be asked. But for the rest, it was for the sheriff (no doubt in consultation with the towns in his shire) to decide which should send representatives since there was no standard list and no definition of which towns and townships were classed as boroughs. Some might choose to negotiate with the sheriff to avoid the expense of sending representatives or to avoid the classification of 'borough' since boroughs were subject to a higher rate of tax than non-boroughs. Others, knowing that they could not avoid being classified as boroughs for tax purposes might prefer to go to Parliament in order to have some influence over whether or not tax should be granted. What seems certain is that when

---

[1] Eventually, there was a variety of different franchises in different boroughs. In some places every man with a hearth of his own, or who was a freeman, or who paid scot and lot, that is to say, who contributed to the local rates, might have the franchise. In others the right was restricted to the local corporation or to guildsmen.

representatives were sent, those who took part in choosing them were few in number.

Certainly the principal towns, of which London was the largest, with Bristol and York second and third (though with populations well under half that of the capital's) were dominated by small oligarchies, who were probably more often merchants than richer craftsmen. Such were to be the men who were now beginning to be asked to pay tax on the value of the movable goods in their shops and houses. This was a heavier tax on urban men, who had little in rents from land, than it was on countrymen. There was, however, a threshold below which no tax was paid, and below that threshold, and perhaps well above it, the ordinary freeman had little influence over his town's affairs. Nevertheless, the position of the towns outside the declining feudal structure was of great importance in the evolution of the medieval Parliament. Though some boroughs were small, and scarcely justified the description of town, their privileges attached to burgage tenure were an important beginning to civic independence. As for the largest cities and towns (which were still strictly speaking considered as within the king's demesne and under his personal jurisdiction) they enjoyed no grand independence comparable to the wealthy free cities of Italy and Germany. Yet their privileges, including the right they had established to negotiate over their payment of tallage to the king, gave them self-confidence, and their growing commercial wealth made them increasingly taxable. But if they were to be taxed effectively, their representatives would be needed alongside those of the shire communities at Parliament.[1]

The prosperity of the towns was linked to a social fluidity that affected the countryside as well. Some who were technically villeins (a class that probably accounted for at least a quarter of the population) were beginning to buy and to own freehold property in addition to the land they held through a servile relationship to their lord. Others were able to purchase their freedom or, like the men of the boroughs, to commute their work for money rents. Above all, the knights (who themselves now generally paid money rents to their lords in substitution for military service) together with the important freeholders below the rank of knight, constituted an increasingly important upper middle class in the countryside. They had already long been employed in various sorts of public service in their neighbourhood on the king's behalf. It was a natural response to their new

---

[1] For discussion of the nature of the borough and its parliamentary significance, see M. McKisack, *The Parliamentary Representation of the English Boroughs in the Middle Ages* (1932) and J. Tait, *The Medieval Borough* (1936). Of great interest in providing solid information about both urban and social life in England at this time is R. H. Hilton, *A Medieval Society, The West Midlands at the End of the Thirteenth Century*,' (1966; reissued 1983).

social and economic importance that they were increasingly required to send their representatives to Parliament.

King Edward's reasons for summoning representatives of the Commons to particular Parliaments probably varied from occasion to occasion. He did not envisage Parliament in any narrow functional terms, either fiscal or judicial, but saw it rather a general aid to his consistent purpose of enhancing the crown's authority against feudal jurisdiction and competition. Every king since Henry II had attempted the same thing, but Edward carried the policy much further. The nation's law was the common law, and traditionally that law was mostly construed pragmatically by custom and by decisions in the royal courts. Until now, it had only occasionally been supplemented or clarified by statute. Edward, however, used statute much more comprehensively than his predecessors to establish the certainty of law, to increase its scope, to curb the 'liberties' or legal powers of the barons over their tenants, and to preserve the rights of the crown. He was particularly concerned to prevent the loss of the crown's rights over its property, and to stop the break-up of estates by subinfeudation. If landholders could create new fiefs and tenancies at will, there would arise a proliferation of muddled tenurial relationships which would reduce the authority of the king. Above all, Edward was determined to ensure that sufficient funds were available for his government. The outcome of this insistence on protecting the power of the crown was the making of a new body of law, as well as the codification of existing laws, in Edward's statutes.

These began with the first Statute of Westminster, the great achievement of Edward's first Parliament. Its fifty-one clauses amounted to a legislative code which either defined or reformed the law in respect of almost every subject that the law touched. The groundwork for this statute was a great inquest which the king ordered into the state and government of the nation on his return to England. After his coronation, Edward had set out on a progress through part of his kingdom, accompanied by his judges of the King's Bench, hearing plaints and petitions. It was the custom of medieval kings on occasion to participate in giving judgements, and their justice, personally dispensed, could often be the last hope of those who felt themselves misused by inferior courts, or who had been mistreated in some other way and were unable to obtain redress. The scope for miscarriages of justice in medieval society was enormous when the king was a long way off, and particularly when he was absent from his realm, as Edward had been. His own officials were often the worst offenders, for how could an appeal be made against the injustice of the king's servants except to the person of the king himself? Sheriffs could be cruel and extortionate tyrants; barons could seize the property and usurp the rights of others; the crown's own revenue was often diminished by malpractice. Justice could never be better assured than when the king came and saw for himself, and gave his own judgements. The ideal model of a virtuous medieval king was that of Edward's uncle, St. Louis of France who would sit beneath an oak at Vincennes giving his own judgements.[1]

On Edward's first progress, what he heard about misgovernment, corruption and the infringements of property rights, especially his own, led him to appoint commissioners who were to travel throughout the land, inquiring into the loss of his property and revenues and into other abuses affecting his subjects. The commissioners took evidence on oath from juries, and the resulting returns on pieces of parchment, to which the seals of those testifying were attached, were known as the Ragman Rolls. It was the most important and thorough investigation since Domesday, and the information it provided not only led the king to dismiss a large number of offending sheriffs, but also formed the basis of much of the first Statute of Westminster. This and other subsequent inquests also paved the way for future legislation.

In drafting the first statute of Westminster, the decisive part was taken by the king's judges. Throughout Edward's reign their practical experience was applied not only to the information uncovered by the inquest, but also to general grievances revealed by individual complaints and petitions to the king in Parliament. Statute law was the outcome. Under Edward I, statutes were for the most part the government's response to general problems suggested by particular complaints. When not acting on the judges' advice to right general wrongs in the kingdom, he would sometimes be responding to pressure from the clergy (the statute *de Bigimis* of 1276 was one instance of this) and at other times to complaints of the baronage. The preambles to the statutes usually give a fair indication of the quarter from which inspiration came. Yet the initiative for statute-making was the king's, the law was written by his servants and it is highly unlikely that what they drafted was ever subject to any kind of parliamentary amendment. This does not, however, diminish the importance of the part played by the magnates and others present at Parliament when they gave their assent to statutes brought before them on the king's behalf. Whatever the importance of parliamentary judicial business in relation to the regular sittings of lesser courts, Edward's use of Parliament to make law by statute greatly enhanced its political significance. The assent and witness of the magnates, and sometimes of the Commons, to the royal enactments was seen as

---

[1] The wives of King Louis and King Henry were sisters.

confirming the validity and the binding nature of the statutes when they were published throughout the land.

The magnates were always central when they were at Parliament though they were not always called in large numbers. The Commons were still only occasionally present and were then on the periphery. Nevertheless, when the knights and burgesses attended, it seems likely that their presence was deemed to give the king's law-making an additional and useful weight of witness. It is hard to doubt that the sonorous opening words of the Statute of Westminster I were intended as an acknowledgement of the significance of the presence of the representatives of the shire and urban communities.: 'These are the Acts of King Edward, son to King Henry, made at Westminster at his first general Parliament (*Parlement general*) after his coronation . . . by his council and with the assent of the archbishops, bishops, abbots, priors, earls, barons and the community of the realm being thither summoned. . . .'[1] ('By his council' almost certainly means by the king's ordinary council of advisers, ministers, justices and officials.)

No very precise meaning can be attached to such phrases as 'general Parliament' or 'full Parliament' in Edward's reign. The same may be true of the 'community of the realm' which had hitherto been an expression used by the baronage to describe its own role. Yet the words seem to have been employed in the Statute of Westminster as though in reference to something wider than the magnates, who were mentioned separately. In other words, it seems as though 'community of the realm' and 'general Parliament' were also references to the communities of the shires and boroughs. Of course, it is possible that these expressions were little more than conventional medieval flourishes to decorate a grand occasion and a special statute. Yet the preamble of this statute has to be considered in the light not only of the remarkable comprehensiveness of the legislation itself, but also of the exceptional breadth of representation at the Parliament in which it was promulgated, and the new tax that was granted there. Perhaps even more significant is the curious manner in which the Commons were summoned. They were called as an afterthought which was no doubt prompted by the political exigencies of the moment. The original intention had been to hold this Parliament in February, with prelates and magnates only attending it. But it was postponed until April to allow time to summon the Commons as well. The writ to the sheriff ordering him to summon the knights and the burgesses prefaced these instructions with the statement: 'whereas for certain particular reasons we have prorogued our general Parliament . . . at

---

[1] *Stat.* R. Vol. I, pp. 26–39. Excerpts from the Norman-French text are in Stubbs, *Select Charters*, pp. 442–443. A translation of the full Act is in *E.H.D.* Vol. III, pp. 397–410.

London with our prelates and the other magnates'. It could perhaps be argued that the use of the term 'general Parliament' in a manner which seems also to embrace the smaller postponed assembly diminishes the directness of its reference to the eventual large size of the assembly. Yet in a special summons to the representatives of the wider nation, the description seems more likely to refer to the comprehensiveness of this Parliament as a whole than to the smaller meeting with which it was to have opened. Taking all these indications together, it seems more probable than not that the reiterated description 'general Parliament' both in the statute and in the writ was a deliberate acknowledgement of the additional significance given to the Parliament by the presence of the knights and burgesses. At the very least, it seems to express the distinction between the important political nature of this large assembly, and the smaller judicial meetings of judges and close councillors who could continue doing their parliamentary work, as in the Parliament of 1305, after the wider assembly had departed.[1]

There is one likely and one virtually certain reason for the sudden decision that the presence of the Commons was important enough to justify postponing the Parliament. The likely (and probably subsidiary) reason is that it may well have seemed desirable that the knights should take back to their shires knowledge and understanding of the changes in the law brought about by the Statute of Westminster, which would affect very many of the king's subjects. The almost certain reason, was the desirability of obtaining the assent of the Commons to taxation, and particularly the assent of the burgesses whose co-operation was essential to the type of taxation which was granted. What had probably happened was that the government was already in negotiation with the merchants for the important new tax on wool granted in this Parliament when it suddenly became clear that the best way of ensuring the general acceptance of the tax was to bring to Parliament representatives of the communities particularly affected by it. The statement that the Commons were to 'consider' the 'affairs' of the kingdom 'along with' the magnates no doubt indicated something rather less grand than the words might superficially suggest. Considering the kingdom's affairs probably meant simply hearing an explanation of why its money was needed in taxation. Even so, listening to the government's justification for its requirement of money was the thin edge of a wedge driven into the broader structure of politics.

Nor should the fact that Edward considered himself, as he did, to have a reserved right to ordain law by himself if necessary, diminish the importance of his obvious belief that the making of statutes in a witnessing

---

[1] See pp. 81–3 and pp. 166–171.

and assenting Parliament gave the law the maximum authority.[1] He recognized the political reality that consent and understanding make government strong, and from this recognition Parliament was to gain both prestige and power. In his statutes, it is true, Edward was not consciously creating a new class of law intended to be distinct from, or higher than, common law or custom. The law written in parliamentary statutes could, and still can, be extended, qualified and expounded by the judges in the light of precedent and the Common Law. Indeed, what was written in statute form was sometimes in the Middle ages deemed to be limited by pre-existing principles of Common Law. Today, Common Law and statute law still reinforce each other. Yet when all this is said, it remains true that Edward I promoted in his statutes a kind of law that was different because, being written, it existed in a much more precise form to which men could appeal and which could be promulgated throughout the land. It was a form of law which enhanced first royal, and later parliamentary authority.

The first Statute of Westminster (which, like most of the enactments of Edward's reign was written in Norman French, the language of the lawyers as well as of the upper classes)[2] covered every sort of social problem, from feudal abuses, and those of royal officials, to crime. It dealt with the lord who kept his ward forcibly unmarried for more than two years in order to retain control over her land; it defined the reasonable feudal aids that a lord could demand for the expense of making his son a knight or marrying his daughter; it prohibited powerful men from forcing monasteries to give them hospitality; it dealt with property rights and excessive tolls in town. In its criminal clauses, it gave the king the right to sue in a case of rape if nobody else did so within 40 days, and (unhistorically) it declared it to be 'the common law of England' that known felons and men of bad repute should be tried by juries. These reforms and many more were ordained by the king 'because he greatly wills and desires to set to rights the state of the kingdom in the things in which there was need of amendment'.

In two particular respects, moreover, the first Statute of Westminster can be said to have had a direct bearing (in theory if not in practice) on parliamentary elections and on the future growth of parliamentary influence. Clause V made the first clear statement in English history that elections must be free and not subject to intimidation. 'And because elections ought to be free, the king commandeth on pain of his great

[1] It has been argued that the reference in the preamble of the Statute of Westminster I to its enactment 'by' the king's council, with the assent of those summoned (rather than being enacted by the advice and consent of those present) was a deliberate reflection of the king's right to enact law himself.
[2] Previous statutes had always been written in Latin.

forfeiture that no one, great man or any other person, by force of arms, nor by malice shall disturb any from making free elections.' Secondly, the king exacted a price for redressing the grievances covered by the Statute of Westminster: the agreement of Parliament to a new tax. Thus the bargain of 1275, like the reissue of Magna Carta in return for money in 1225, provided a precedent for one of the fundamental principles of future parliamentary power, that the redress by the king of grievances should be traded for financial supply granted by Parliament.

The new tax brought the wool merchandise of England's primary trade into the fiscal net for the first time, and there is little doubt that the representatives of the towns were summoned to the first of Edward's Parliaments specifically to co-operate in granting the new tax. Their consent was given to a tax of 'half a mark for each sack of wool and half a mark for each three hundred wool-fells which make a sack, and one mark for each last of hides exported from the kingdom of England and the land of Wales. . . .'[1] This tax was granted not only to Edward but also to his heirs. With the older duty of 'tunnage' on wine imports, it was to become a vital part of the crown's permanent revenue. Whereas the king would always have to go back to Parliament to obtain a tax on personal movables, the crown was henceforth deemed (until it was challenged in the 17th century) to have an automatic right to the new custom duty without need for a further parliamentary grant. At first the duty on wool and hides was known as the 'new custom' but it was later described as the 'great and ancient custom' to distinguish it from the deeply unpopular 'maletote' imposed in 1294 and removed in response to demands in the Parliament in 1297, and from the 'new custom' or 'petty' custom of 1303.[2] It was granted by prelates, earls and barons, and by 'the communities of the said kingdom *at the suggestion and request of the merchants*'. More cities, boroughs and merchant towns appear to have been represented in this Parliament than at any other before 1500.[3]

The words that have been here italicized, taken from a writ enforcing the

---

[1] A mark was the equivalent of 13s. 4d.

[2] Stubbs, *Select Charters*, pp. 443–444; translation B. Wilkinson, *Constitutional History of England*, Vol. III, pp. 320–321. For the 'maletote', see below pp. 149 and 157. The 'new custom' of 1303 at the end of Edward's reign constituted an additional duty on top of the existing custom on wool and hides, dues on wine, cloth and wax, and an *ad valorem* duty on all other imports and exports. The general *ad valorem* duty was the model for the later subsidy of poundage; the duty on wine, was the model for 'tunnage' (levied on the tun of wine) both of which were to be of importance in future constitutional struggles.

[3] May McKisack, *The Parliamentary Representation of the English Boroughs during the Middle Ages* (p. 5).

new tax, seem evidence enough that the granting of the customs duty was the reason for the summons of the burgesses, whom it principally affected, to the first Parliament of 1275. Their absence from the second Parliament of the same year is implicit confirmation of the reason for their presence at the first. In the Michaelmas Parliament, at which only the knights of the shire were summoned in addition to the magnates, an 'aid' of a 'fifteenth' on movables was granted towards the cost of the king's crusade. For the granting of this more general tax, the presence of the burgesses no doubt seemed unnecessary, since the summons of the knights had always sufficed for this tax in the past. The composition of the representatives of the 'communities' or Commons (on the minority of occasions when they were summoned) was in no way fixed, and they were not deemed to form any necessary part of Parliament. Indeed, Parliament had no regular composition of any sort. Even a large assembly of magnates was not essential for a Parliament to exist, and a number of Parliaments, including some which published statutes, apparently consisted of little more than the king's close councillors and officials, strengthened at the king's will by the presence of a certain number of other great men as seemed convenient to him. We best understand the nature of Parliaments at a time when all government was concentrated on the king's person and in his household (both still often itinerant) if we compare it with the sort of meeting with which most business organizations in the twentieth century are familiar in the conduct of their affairs. Those who are in charge call those whom it seems useful or necessary to call in given circumstances. There are occasions when those who are not summoned feel affronted, particularly if they are in some way insecure or on the defensive. There are some who even try to force themselves on such a meeting and others who are glad not to be bothered. It is not hard to envisage Edward and his close ministers observing to each other, in the autumn of 1275, that with the new custom satisfactorily assured in the first Parliament of the year, it was not necessary to summon the townsmen's representative to the second.

The functions of the different elements of a Plantagenet Parliament are well illustrated by the terms of the summons to the knights of the shire for the October Parliament of 1275. The king informed the sheriffs that he had commanded 'the prelates and magnates of the realm' to come to Parliament 'to treat with us, both about the estate of our realm and about certain business of ours which we shall show to them there'. In 'treating' with the king about the state of the realm, the magnates clearly had some part to play in the determination of policy. Their role was what we should call political, and, as the king's natural counsellors, they were an essential ingredient of a normal Parliament, however few or many of them the king chose to summon. The function of the knights was, however, more limited. They were an optional extra, and the purpose for which they were principally wanted can be inferred from the different terms of their summons. 'And it may be expedient if two knights of the above shire, from the more discreet and law-worthy knights of that shire, should be present in the same Parliament. For the said reasons, we command that you cause the said two knights to be elected in your full county, with the assent of the same county....' These knights were to come to Westminster 'in order to treat with us and the said prelates and magnates about the said business'.[1]

Thus, whereas the magnates were to treat, or deliberate, both on the state of the realm and about certain particular business, the knights were required only to treat with the king and magnates about the *particular* business already referred to in the writ, and which the king was to reveal in his Parliament. It can hardly be doubted that this particular 'business' was the matter of the grant of a fifteenth on all movables as distinct from 'treating' about the state of the realm more widely, which was a matter for the magnates. It is also a reasonable assumption that the knights would be informed about the purpose for which the tax was needed. Some of the more influential of them may not have been altogether excluded from discussion, formal or informal, of more general matters. But it seems certain that they were primarily required to witness and assent to the grant of taxation.

For the next fifteen years, we only have evidence that the Commons attended two further Parliaments. It does not, however, necessarily follow that they were absent from every Parliament for which we lack knowledge of their presence. The survival of documentary evidence had depended much on chance. It was not until the beginning of the present century that the accidental discovery, in Westminster Abbey, of a writ to the sheriff of Middlesex revealed that both knights and burgesses had been summoned to Edward's first, and 'general' Parliament in April 1275. Until this discovery, the so-called 'model' Parliament of 1295 had seemed much more of an innovation than it really was. Likewise, it is only through the survival of a single writ, addressed to the sheriff of Kent, that the presence of the knights of the shire at the October Parliament of 1275 is known. It is therefore possible that there were other occasions when representatives of the communities may have been summoned, even though no documentary evidence has survived to prove it. On the other hand, the chances are that for most of the Parliaments between 1275 and 1290, neither knights nor burgesses were required, and this is also suggested by the clear evidence from the preambles to enactments during this period, which show that

---

[1] B. Wilkinson, *Constitutional History of England*, Vol. III, pp. 306–307.

gatherings of a much smaller kind were nevertheless regarded as proper Parliaments.

One such statute, *de bigimis*, which in 1276 dealt with bigamy, gives us an insight into the way in which law could be framed and promulgated. (Unlike the generality of Edward's statutes it was in Latin, no doubt because the subject matter closely concerned the church.) Its preamble describes it as having been 'recited and recorded' in the presence of twenty-one named men, of whom the Bishop of Rochester was the first named, and among whom ecclesiastics were heavily represented, not unnaturally since, among other things, the statute followed up a ruling by the Pope that bigamous clerks should be deprived of clergy. Thus it seems that men specially qualified to have an opinion on the matter were called, perhaps to a version of the king's close council, to consider the statute as the officials proposed and recited it, and this group gave it their approval. The preamble then goes on to say that the provisions in the enactment were 'afterwards heard and published before the lord king and his council', and that 'all those of the council, justices and others, agreed that they should be put into writing, in perpetual memory, and that they should be observed'. In other words, they became a statute because a 'full' meeting of king and council, perhaps mainly comprising justices and officials, but probably in some degree augmented, approved them. Yet the enactment was not less a statute for being promulgated in this manner, and the council (of whatever size) which made it was undoubtedly a Parliament. Its parliamentary standing is indicated in administrative records.[1] But there is also the plainest possible evidence that this gathering was a Parliament from the statute itself which concludes with the statement: 'All these Constitutions were made at Westminster in the Parliament next after the Feast of St. Michael (1276) and from that Time forth they shall take effect.'[2]

In the same Parliament the Statute of Ragman which dealt with trespassers was enacted, and this simply began quite abruptly with the

---

[1] See Richardson and Sayles: 'The Parliaments of Edward I', *BIHR*, V (1928), 110–115 (reproduced in *The English Parliament in the Middle Ages*, 1981) and especially the valuable appendix: *Table of the English Parliaments of Edward I*, which lists all Parliaments proper with a note of evidence from records and chronicles. (This paper emphasises the authors' thesis that the bulk of Parliament's work was to do with litigation and petitions, and that representation, legislation and taxation, though they were often added to Parliament, were non-essentials.) Evidence is produced to show that at least by 1290, parliamentary privilege was asserted to ensure that a member of the king's council or a clerk employed in Parliament was protected and could not be proceeded against by distraint or attachment in time of Parliament.

[2] *Stat. R.* Vol. I, pp. 42–43.

statement that it was 'accorded by our lord the king and by his council. . . .'[1] However, the council in this context may have been not the smaller council of officials, justices and ministers which dealt with the king's everyday business, but may have been enlarged by the presence of some other magnates to make it appropriate for a parliamentary occasion. The more far-reaching statutes of this period certainly seem to have been promulgated at Parliaments at which the general body of magnates was present. For example, the important statute of Gloucester enacted in the Parliament held in Gloucester at midsummer 1278, opened with the declaration that the king had summoned 'the more discreet men of his kingdom, both of the greater and the smaller sort'. The 'smaller sort' might just conceivably imply the presence of some knights of the shire (or it could refer to smaller barons) though a retrospective reference made to this statute several years later, in the Statute of Westminster II, 1285, recalls only the presence of the prelates, earls, barons and council at Gloucester.[2]

The Statute of Gloucester itself, having simply recorded that 'the more discreet people' of the realm had been summoned, declared the provisions of the statute to be 'established and by agreement ordained'. Those who had so agreed were not identified. Yet barons great and small must have been present to agree to a statute that affected their property rights as closely as this one did, since, by this Act, all who claimed to have liberties by charters from the king's predecessors, or in any other way, were required to show before the king or the justice in eyre, 'what sort of liberties they claim to have, and by what warrant. . . .'[3] (It was another product of the great inquest held four years before.) Thus was initiated the legal process of *quo warranto* by which the king sought to identify and uproot those franchises that were illegal because no written grants could be produced for them. However, such were the delays and difficulties in giving judgements on *quo warranto* writs, and so great was the discontent, particularly among those who held their land by prescriptive right, that the king was eventually forced to make a concession. The procedure was therefore later modified in the Easter Parliament of 1290 by the Statute of *Quo Warranto*, which was the result of pressure from the baronial class, under which a man who had held his land since before the time of Richard I, and could prove it in his neighbourhood, could continue to hold it, and would have his estates confirmed by letter from the king.[4]

[1] *Stat.* R. Vol. I, p. 44.
[2] *Stat* R. Vol. I, pp. 45–50. D. Pasquet, *Origins of the House of Commons*, p. 83.
[3] Extract (Norman-French) Stubbs, *Select Charters*, pp. 449–450. *Stat.* R. Vol. I, pp. 45–50 (Norman-French); *E.H.D.* Vol. III, pp. 414–419 (Translation).
[4] *Stat.* R., Vol. I, p. 107. See pp. 141–2.

The amending act of 1290 states that the king had granted it 'for the Affection that he beareth unto his Prelates, Earls and Barons, and other of his Realm.' The assent of the baronial class in Parliament must have been for practical purposes essential when an act so closely affecting property was passed, and it stands to reason also that the Statute of Mortmain, which was likewise concerned with property, required the public assent of a substantial parliamentary representation of landed men. Enacted in November 1279, 'on the advice of the prelates, earls and other faithful subjects of our realm who are of our council', the Statute of Mortmain (*de viris religiosis*) ordained that no religious or other person should buy, sell or give any lands 'whereby such lands and tenements come in any way into mortmain', that is to say, into the 'dead hand' of the church. This was an important safeguard for the crown's property rights, which could be undermined by abuse of the privilege of the church. Since it never died, the church was never required to pay the inheritance taxes to which a lay estate was subject when it passed, on an owner's death, to his heir. (Nor could such an estate in mortmain 'escheat' to the crown, thus becoming part of the royal demesne when its owner died without an heir.) The royal objection to such arrangements was not simply on the grounds that the crown lost revenue as a result of legitimate gifts to the church. The principal object of the statute was to put an end to a deeper abuse, the bestowing of lands on religious foundations for the purpose of tax avoidance. Estates were often handed over to a religious body, and then held by the donor as a fief from the foundation to which he made his bequest; in this way, the donor and his heirs could remain the effective owner, and yet avoid the payment of the proper dues to the crown.[1] In this same Parliament, the baronage granted the king a fifteenth. It was the only occasion in Edward's reign, so far as we know, when such a tax was granted without the presence of the knights representing the shires.

In September 1283, however, two knights from each shire were present at a Parliament at Shrewsbury, along with eleven earls, ninety-nine barons and nineteen judges and officials. Twenty-one of the larger towns, including London, were also required to elect two burgesses each. The

---

[1] *Stat. R.* Vol. I, p. 51; Stubbs, *Select Charters*, pp. 451–452; translated *E.H.D.* Vol. III, pp. 419–420. The Statute of Mortmain was also Edward's response to what he saw as Archbishop's Pecham's attempts to enlarge clerical jurisdiction. Edward vigorously prosecuted clergy who had drawn such questions as debts or contracts into church courts. Subsequently, however, in 1286, he made concessions in the writ *Circumspecte Agatis* (Stubbs, *Select Charters*, pp. 469–470, translated *E.H.D.* Vol. III, pp. 462–463) in which such moral offences as adultery, the neglect of churches and church yards, certain cases of defamation, tithes up to a fix proportion, wills and marriages were left to ecclesiastic jurisdictions. This writ defined the area left to the Church Courts until the Reformation. See p. 141.

principal business before this gathering was the trial 'in full Parliament' of the rebellious and now captive Welsh prince David, who had been entrusted by Edward with some responsibility after the first stage of the war of conquest in Wales, but who had subsequently risen against the king. At Shrewsbury, David was condemned by the magnates in Parliament to be hanged and quartered, and the presence at Parliament of the knights, from whom no taxation was on this occasion required, is sufficiently explained by Edward's determination to make the judgement on the Welsh prince as awe-inspiring as possible by a large representation of the nation. The trial of Prince David, however, hardly seems to account sufficiently for the more unusual decision also to summon to this assembly representatives of a number of towns, who were not, on this occasion, required for tax. The presence of the most important burgesses was, no doubt, regarded as a useful augmentation of the Parliament for David's trial. The writ sending for them stated that the king wished to have a 'deliberation' with his 'faithful men' about what should be done with the 'aforesaid David'.[1] However, the burgesses were also required (as the writ put it) to talk with the king about 'other matters' as well, and it is most probable that, even though it may have suited the king to have the representatives of the boroughs as witnesses to his terrifying justice, the real, if humdrum, reason for calling them to Shrewsbury was an enactment directly affecting their interest: the preparation and promulgation of what is sometimes called the Statute of Merchants, otherwise the Statute of Acton Burnell.

This statute was a notable instance of Edward's willingness to make law to satisfy an important section of his subjects when it seemed advisable to do so. Just as he had on another occasion responded to the pressure of the clergy with the statute *de bigimis* so he now dealt with a long-standing grievance of the merchants. The statute, which may have been prompted by a particular case in which a Flemish merchant had repeatedly failed to get his due, provided that henceforth a debtor would have to acknowledge his debt, and also the agreed date for repayment, in a bond made before the mayor of London, or of certain other cities. In the event of a default, the mayor was to have the power to order the debtors' goods to be sold to pay the debt. The statute begins abruptly, without reference to either the advice or the consent of magnates or any other body, and asserts simply: 'Forasmuch as Merchants, which heretofore have lent their goods to divers persons, be greatly impoverished because there is no speedy Law provided for them to have Recovery of their Debts at the Day of Payment assigned, the king, by himself and by his council, has ordained and established....'

[1] Stubbs, *Select Charters*, pp. 460–461.

From such wording it might appear that this was not a statute proper but an ordinance from the king and council. But it undoubtedly had the force of a statute and there was no clear distinction at that time between law declared by the king personally and law enacted in Parliament.

There is equally no doubt that the Shrewsbury assembly was a Parliament. Evidence from records establishes that.[1] At a time when the attendance of burgesses at Parliament was still unusual, it is inconceivable that their summons to Shrewsbury was unconnected with the making of a statute which concerned their interest so closely. On the other hand, the Statute of Merchants was not made at Shrewsbury itself, but was, as the conclusion of the text records, 'given at Acton Burnell', a village a few miles from Shrewsbury, which was the seat of Edward's able chancellor, Robert Burnell, who was also Bishop of Bath and Wells. But the council at Acton Burnell was also part of the Parliament; that is indicated both by the promulgation there of a statute so closely related to the Parliament's composition and by a statement in the Worcester Chronicle that Edward held a Parliament at Acton at the instance of Robert Burnell.

But it does not follow that the entire Parliament of over 200 men, with their attendants, moved from the convenience of the town of Shrewsbury to the inconvenience of a small manor and village. Reason suggests otherwise. It is clear, however, that Edward and his council stayed there; the king himself, apparently, for several weeks. The following year, the king gave Burnell a licence to build a new partly fortified manor at Acton Burnell, the ruins of which still stand. Nearby there are also two gable end-walls which indicate a building of some 157 feet by 40 feet. There is an unsubstantiated local tradition that this was the hall of the earlier Burnell manor house, and the scene of the Shrewsbury Parliament. But the earlier manor house in which Burnell entertained Edward I is thought to have been a wooden structure, and the masonry of the reputed 'hall' which stands apart from the ruins of the later fortified manor is unlikely to be earlier than Robert Burnell's own time. It seems more likely that they are the end walls of a great barn than those of a hall. But even if this building were a hall it would seem to defy logic to suppose that the Parliament as a whole, or even most of it, moved out from Shrewsbury. What is most likely is that the most important parliamentary proceedings took place in Shrewsbury itself. Certainly the town was the scene of the trial by the magnates in Parliament of the Welsh prince and his condemnation. It is also likely that during the time that the Parliament was in Shrewsbury the king and his closer councillors would have taken the opportunity of hearing the pleas and advice of the forty-one

---

[1] Richardson and Sayles, 'The English Parliaments of Edward I', *BIHR*, V (1929), p. 152.

assembled burgesses (required in the writs of summons to be of 'the wiser and fitter citizens') on the matter of mercantile debts. (That was the 'other business' for which the representatives of the cities and boroughs were no doubt required.) The king then presumably withdrew to Acton Burnell with his closer councillors, and we might guess that they possibly took with them a very few of the burgesses who were best able to advise them on this particular matter. From the chancellor's manor, but without the majority of magnates or Commons, they proceeded to promulgate the Statute of Acton Burnell, which was not less a statute for being issued in this way.

What is shown by both the manner in which the Statute of Acton Burnell was promulgated and by the composition of the Shrewsbury Parliament is the *ad hoc* and fluid nature of parliamentary gatherings. For if the presence of the burgesses was unusual, it was even more unusual, if not wholly unprecedented, for a Parliament to be held without prelates or any other ecclesiastics. But that was because the clergy were forbidden to take part in any proceedings leading to the shedding of blood, and the shedding of Prince David's blood, with a great assembly called as witnesses to his guilt, was the principal reason for summoning so large a Parliament to that particular place. The composition of the Shrewsbury Parliament, like that of any other, was determined by the purpose for which the king called it.

The statutes of the next few years were the products of Parliaments comprising (so far as we know) only the king's ordinary council augmented with prelates and magnates. In 1285, the preamble of the Statute of Westminster II referred back to the Statute of Gloucester, acknowledged that in 'certain cases' the law had 'failed' and recorded that, in consequence, 'the king in his Parliament after the feast of Easter . . . caused many Oppressions of the People and Defaults of the Laws for the Accomplishment of the said Statute of Gloucester to be recited, and therefore did provide certain statutes', which then duly followed.[1] The first clause of the Statute of Westminster II, *De Donis Conditionalibus*, became the foundation of the English system of entail by attempting to prevent the alienation or sale of property so as to ensure that it passed intact to the proper heir. Where, for example, land had been granted by one to another on condition that it should pass only to the heirs of the donee's body, then, if there were no issue, the land must revert to the donor. Although such attempts to prevent the alienation and spendthrift dissipation of estates do not appear to have been immediately successful in Edward's reign, the idea of primogeniture that they encouraged was to assist the survival of large, unbroken estates in

---

[1] *Stat.* R. Vol. I, p. 71. Translation: *E.H.D.* Vol. III, pp. 428–457. The clause *De Donis Conditionalibus* is extracted in Stubbs, *Select Charters*, p. 463.

the longer run, with important political and social consequences. But there was more to the massive Statute of Westminster II than its famous first clause, as a few other examples of its more important provisions will show. To lighten unreasonable burdens arising from jury service, it enabled civil actions to be tried in the county where they arose (the beginning of the *nisi prius* system), instead of obliging them to be called to Westminster, with local juries, from other and sometimes far distant parts of the country. It also attempted to prevent abuses of manorial jurisdiction, and to place limits on the power of sheriffs. In particular, remedies were provided against sheriffs who falsely imprisoned for felony people who had never been lawfully indicted. It also strengthened the law against rape and other crimes. To help litigants, it permitted new writs where cases were not covered by the existing form of writs in order that a plaintiff should not 'depart from the king's court without remedy'. In short, it was a new and extensive law code, and it was given weight by its promulgation in Parliament.

Yet neither this nor any statute of Edward's reign was the product of the Parliament in which it was promulgated. The decision to make a new law was taken solely by the king in council, which, in this context, meant the smaller working council, including the judges. Many different kinds of influence might lead them to decide that a new statute was necessary. The representations of magnates, the reports of sheriffs, what was learned about the state of society from cases in the courts and from individual complaints and petitions, and the findings of government inquiries all played a part. The knowledge gained by justices from litigation was no doubt particularly influential. Sometimes awareness of a particular case led to a general law. The preamble of a statute promulgated in January 1292 shows very clearly how this could come about.[1] A certain William Butler, a ward of the king, who had inherited the estate of his late brother, had impleaded, or sued, Walter de Hapeton for waste and destruction done to his land during his late brother's lifetime. The defendant had argued that he ought not to be held responsible for damage done before the present heir's time and in the lifetime of another. The justices who heard the case had not agreed to give a judgement against the defendant. But, says the statute, 'other justices, with the more part of the king's council, were in the contrary opinion'. They thought that the plaintiff William Butler ought to be heard and should be given redress against such trespass, and likewise with others in similar cases. Therefore, the king 'in his full Parliament . . . hath ordained . . . That every Heir, in whose Ward soever he be, shall have a recovery by a Writ of Waste'

[1] *Stat. R.* Vol. I, p. 109.

in respect of waste or destruction done in the time of his ancestors. We could hardly have a clearer indication of the way in which a particular case could determine the government's thinking on a general question, and of the influence of the justices on the king's close council. But Parliament was involved only when the statute was promulgated, not when it was being devised. There was no preceding parliamentary bill.

It is of course quite possible that what was learned in discussions with some of the more influential knights at Parliament time might sometimes help to shape the government's thinking. General grievances in need of redress might (as in William Butler's case) be inferred from one individual petition or from a number among the mass of individual petitions which constituted the greater part of Parliament's routine business. But new law was never under Edward I built either on petitions from the Commons in Parliament, or on individual petitions submitted through the Commons in Parliament. The reason was that individual petitions were never requests for legislation. They were requests for administrative action to put right particular wrongs of particular persons who had failed to find redress in any other way. The individual petitions which were received and tried in Edward I's Parliaments had no resemblance at all with the future '*common petitions*' which would be submitted collectively by the representatives of the communities to the king, to become the foundation of statutes later in the fourteenth century. Nor was it even particularly the business of the elected knights and burgesses in Edward I's Parliaments to deliver or submit individual petitions to Parliament. How could it have been? Individual petitions were delivered in large numbers to Edward's Parliaments as a matter of routine when no representative knights or burgesses were present. Even when the representatives of the communities were summoned, it did not follow that they would be responsible for petitions arising from within their community. Sometimes such petitions were presented by a special delegate chosen for the task instead of by the shire representative.[1]

Nor was there any parliamentary debate, as we would understand it, on a statute before promulgation. The statutes were drafted by the judges in the light of their special knowledge and in consultation with other close councillors. This law-drafting function continued to be performed by the judges until the reign of Henry VII, and they would never entertain the idea that the Parliaments in which statutes were enacted could improve or amend the text by discussion. Chief Justice Ralph Hengham put the matter

---

[1] G. L. Haskins, 'The Petitions of representatives in the Parliaments of Edward I,' *E.H.R.* LIII (1938) pp. 1–20.

succinctly in Edward's reign: 'Do not gloss the statute, for we know better than you; we made it.' In being government produced, and based not on 'parliamentary initiative' but on information from many sources, the legislation of Edward I resembled the greater part of twentieth century legislation. The extent to which the process of legislation was dependent on the king's will and his servants' work, both for its initiation and enactment was clearly indicated in the preamble to the Statute of Merchants, which was also made in 1285.[1] In this measure, which was designed to remedy inadequacies in the earlier statute of Acton Burnell, it was stated baldly that the king, at his Parliament at Westminster, 'had the aforesaid statute, made at Acton Burnell, read out, and to elucidate certain articles of his aforesaid statute, has ordained and established. . . .' At the same time, although the wording of this later statute emphasized the extent to which it was made at the king's will, it is also clear that the king was acting in response to external grievances, those of merchants, even though no representatives of their interest were apparently present.

Similarly, the Statute of Winchester, which was also promulgated in 1285, made no mention of enactment in Parliament or council.[2] Concerned with problems of law and order, its provisions and penalties were simply 'established' by the king. Even so, this statute, which sought to make every law-abiding man responsible for preventing and punishing crime, and to make local communities responsible for the crimes committed and the damages incurred among them, seems to have been enacted in a Parliament. Likewise, although the writ of the same year known as *circumspecte agatis*, which prescribed the bounds of ecclesiastical jurisdiction over moral offences, was simply a royal declaration, it undoubtedly had the effect of statute law and it remained in force until the Reformation.[3] No precise dividing line yet separated law made in Parliament and law made by the king alone, yet the general trend in the direction of law-making in Parliament is clear, particularly when the matter was important to the king's leading subjects.

The statutes *De Quo Warranto* and *Quia Emptores*, both of 1290, illustrate the point. The first of these is a concession given 'at his Parliament' by the king 'of his special favour and for the affection he bears his prelates, earls and barons and to the others of his realm.'[4] Such had been the discontent

---

[1] *Stat. R.* Vol. I, pp. 98–100; *E.H.D.*, Vol. III, pp. 457–460.
[2] *Stat. R.* Vol. I, pp. 96–98; Stubbs, *Select Charters*, pp. 464–466; *E.H.D.* Vol. III, pp. 460–462.
[3] *Stat. R.* Vol. I, pp. 101–102; Stubbs, *Select Charters*, pp. 469–470; *E.H.D.* Vol. III, pp. 462–463.
[4] *Stat. R.* Vol. I, p. 107; *E.H.D.* Vol. III, pp. 464–466.

caused by delays in giving judgements on pleas of *quo warranto* that the king granted that all who could prove their rights in their own neighbourhood would have these confirmed. But this statute also had another more far-reaching effect. To compromise with those who disliked his *quo warranto* proceedings, the king agreed not to contest the rights of holders of franchises who had exercised them since the reign of King Richard I. Thus the limit of legal memory became fixed as 3 Sept. 1189, the beginning of Richard's reign. By the statute *Quia Emptores* 'the Lord King in his Parliament at Westminster after Easter ... at the instance of the magnates of his kingdom, granted, provided and enacted' that it was lawful for a freeman to sell his land at will – but only if the purchaser became the vassal of the original overlord, and not of the vendor.[1] It is likely, however, that the king himself wanted this Act more than any magnate did, since it suited the Crown's purpose to prevent the creation of new feudal tenures by which lords could bind followers in new and spreading feudal relationships. It was also, of course, in the interests of overlords generally to preserve their rights against subinfeudation. However, the practical effect of the Statute *Quia Emptores* was somewhat different from the intention behind it. By preventing new grants of tenure by knight service (except in the case of grants by the king) it assisted the break-up of the old tenurial relationship between the lord of the manor and his man. Although the feudal relationship between the king and tenants-in-chief formally persisted, the bond between lords and lesser men tended to atrophy from now on. The general consequences of the enactment *Quia Emptores* were also somewhat contrary to those of *De Donis Conditionalibus*. Whereas *De Donis*, by protecting entail, tended to preserve blocks of land in a family by limiting a man's right to dispose freely of his estate on his death, *Quia Emptores* gave to a land-holder (if he were below the level of tenant-in-chief) the right to dispose of land in his lifetime provided, by so doing, he did not create new fiefs, which slowly encouraged the spread of free-holding.

From this brief survey of law-making in Edward's earlier years, it is clear that Parliament was important but not yet essential in the making of Statutes, and that it had as yet no 'rights' and no fixed composition. Yet its regular use for this purpose by Edward I added greatly to its weight as a national council and a political instrument. The effect of this was to become clear in the years of crisis after 1294.

With the politics of the first part of the reign, a parliamentary history need not be closely concerned. They were dominated by the conquest of

[1] *Stat. R.* Vol. I, p. 106; Stubbs, *Select Charters*, pp. 473–474; *E.H.D.* Vol. III, p. 466.

Wales after the Principality constructed by Prince Llywelyn ap Gruffydd in that fragmented land had virtually challenged Edward's supremacy. Building some of his hopes on a revival of the baronial opposition in England, Llywelyn proposed to marry Simon de Montfort's daughter Eleanor. War followed when Edward intercepted and captured the lady on her way to Wales. It was the opportunity Edward needed to put an end to the centuries-old interference of Welsh Princes in English politics by stirring up baronial rivalries whenever they could. The Welsh had been particularly active during the baronial conflicts under Henry III. Yet they themselves were incapable of real unity. They lacked the traditions and resources for political cohesion, and geography also pronounced against Welsh union under a single Prince. A glance at the map of Wales is enough to reveal the lack of any natural political centre. Communications in Wales run naturally east-west, pointing to England at almost all points, rather than north-south between the Snowdonian redoubt of Welsh independence and the half-Anglicized and Normanized south-coastal strip. The mountainous 'desert' of central Wales, separating north from south, was the ultimate foe of Welsh unity. A massive invasion by Edward quickly drove Llywelyn to submit, and by a peace treaty with Edward, he was allowed to keep only the smaller area of the north west and the nominal title of Prince of Wales under Edward's overlordship. Four years later, there was another outbreak, precipitated by Llywelyn's brother David, who had been Edward's ally in the first Welsh war. Both brothers combined against the English king, and it was another sign of the rising importance of the knights of the shire that they appear to have been present at a Parliament which Edward held at Worcester in the summer of 1281 to prepare the Welsh campaign. In the war that followed, Llywelyn was killed in battle and David captured and condemned at the Shrewsbury Parliament. This was the final defeat of the Welsh. The independent principality was obliterated and the king himself took over the west and north, his eldest son later becoming titular prince of Wales. The rest of the country was divided between marcher lords. Although English law was introduced into Wales alongside Welsh law, Wales was not fully incorporated into the English political structure until the sixteenth century. Its sense of nationhood to this day has remained inextinguishable. Yet Wales remained irretrievably absorbed politically into the English king's realm, and two rebellions in 1287 and 1294 were easily put down. The final settlement of the Welsh question was Edward's most durable success apart from his achievement as a law-maker. It was, however, quite otherwise with Scotland. The king's entanglement in the northern kingdom, together with his military engagement in France, led to a sharply deteriorating relationship with his magnates and the clergy in the final phase of the reign. The use his critics at home made of Parliament as an instrument of opposition was of great significance in the evolution of parliamentary power.

II

Between 1286 and 1289, Edward was overseas in his dukedom of Gascony. While abroad, he had been disturbed by reports of maladministration and injustice in England. Immediately on returning, he launched an attack on the corruption of judges and officials, and an investigation into complaints of delayed justice, corruption and oppression. His method was not a general inquiry, but an invitation to those with complaints to bring them to Westminster, where the king appointed a committee of trusted men (bishops and laymen), including Robert Burnell, to hear them. In consequence, judges, officials and bailiffs were dismissed and fined or imprisoned. Among those dismissed and fined was the chief justice, Ralph de Hengham, whose view of the statutes has already been quoted, and who is thought to have been the most distinguished lawyer of his time. (He was, nevertheless, reappointed chief justice in 1301.) The most sensational case of judicial wrong-doing was that of the chief justice of the bench of common pleas, Thomas Wayland, who fled to sanctuary, was starved out and imprisoned in the Tower of London. He was eventually released on condition that he abjured the realm for ever. Meanwhile, Edward had made a great progress throughout the land. In the following year, a long Parliament was held which was one of the more important of the reign.

In Edward's early years, his practice had been to hold only two Parliaments annually, one after Easter, the other after Michaelmas. After 1289, there was much greater variation. In some years one Parliament only was held; in others, though more exceptionally, three took place. No doubt the king's general intention was still to hold two Parliaments annually instead of the pattern of three in his father's reign, but in practice this was disrupted by frequent war and crisis. In January 1290, there was a Parliament of which little is known. In April another was summoned which lasted for three months until the end of July. It can be regarded as a Parliament in two stages, the first with the magnates alone, the second with the knights added. It has sometimes been described erroneously as two separate assemblies, with that of the knights as a kind of additional

'Parliament' over and above the three held at the conventional seasons of the year.[1] (There was a third in 1290 at Michaelmas.) In fact, it was a single Parliament with a change of composition during its course. Initially, Edward and his advisers evidently thought that the presence of the magnates alone would suffice for what he wanted, the granting of a traditional feudal aid. At the end of May, the king was accorded an aid for the marriage of his daughter in what was described in the Rolls of Parliament as a 'full Parliament' (*in pleno parliamento*), which makes it clear that a Parliament of prelates, magnates and of other 'leaders' could still qualify for the adjective 'full'.[2] Those who were present made the grant on behalf of themselves and the community of the realm 'as far as in them lies'. This qualification suggests that the granting of an aid or tax still did not necessarily ensure its full collection, and perhaps also that this tax in particular was thought likely to meet resistance. For whatever reasons, however, the king must then have decided the marriage aid would not suffice. Since it was not actually levied for several years, it also seems likely that the king agreed to postpone it, provided Parliament immediately conceded a more substantial general tax on movables. At all events, the magnates appear to have agreed in principle to such a tax, but only provided the knights were present. Writs were despatched to the sheriffs instructing them to send two or three knights to Westminster, and in the meantime, the Parliament of magnates only went on through the early summer with its normal business of hearing pleas and petitions and with the making of law. For example, the statute *Quia Emptores*, which was enacted at the behest of magnates, was promulgated early in July, shortly before the knights' arrival.

In his writ to the sheriffs summoning the knights, the king stated that he wished to confer and treat with the magnates 'and also with others from the shires' because he had received 'special requests on certain matters from the earls, barons and certain other magnates'. The two or three knights summoned were to be from among the more discreet and diligent. But more than that, they were to come 'with full powers on their own behalf and on behalf of the whole community of the shire to give counsel and consent, for themselves and their community, to what the earls, barons and leading men shall be led to agree' (*cum plena potestate pro se et tota communitate comitatus praedicti, ad consulendum et consentiendum pro se et communitate illa hiis quae comites, barones et proceres praedicti tunc duxerint concordanda*).[3] In one form of

[1] Pollard, *Evolution of Parliament*, p. 47 et seq.; Richardson and Sayles, 'The Early Parliaments of Edward I', *BIHR*, V (1928), pp. 134–135.
[2] *Rot. Parl.* Vol. I, p. 25 (Extract, Stubbs, *Select Charters*, p. 472).
[3] Stubbs, *Select Charters*, pp. 472–473; translation, B. Wilkinson, op. cit., III, p. 307.

words or another, and with varying degrees of imprecision, it had been made clear in a number of previous writs since 1254 (when the knights had been required to come on behalf of one and all to say what aid they would give the king) that representatives of the communities must be given power to speak and act for those communities. Sometimes, indeed, they had come with sealed letters to this effect. The formula of 1290, however, was the most explicit so far in this respect, with the possible exception of one which related not to a Parliament proper but to an irregular assembly held seven years earlier.

During his Welsh campaigns, Edward had been badly in need of money. At first he had been content with a scutage of 40 shillings and with compelling all freeholders who had an estate worth £20 a year to receive a knighthood, which obliged them, if they did not give armed service, to pay a fine in place of it. Then in the emergency after the revolt of Llywelyn and David of Wales in 1282 and 1283, Edward had chosen to raise money separately from individual shires and boroughs, and from persons individually, rather than seek a general grant in Parliament. When this did not suffice, and perhaps because it was difficult to summon a Parliament proper during his military operations in Wales, the king had tried a new way of raising money. At the beginning of 1283, he had called together two provincial councils from the ecclesiastical provinces of Canterbury and York, and asked them for financial help. Individuals, lay and clerical, were summoned; so were four knights from each shire, and two representatives each from cities, boroughs and market towns. These shire and borough representatives were ordered to come 'having full powers'. Yet in the regular Shrewsbury Parliament, nothing was said about 'full powers'. The Commons were required simply to 'talk' to the king. The difference can only be explained by the fact that the representatives at the irregular assembly were to be asked for money and those at the Shrewsbury Parliament were not. At these assemblies, called by church provinces, the lay and clerical estates met separately and behaved differently. The lay 'communities', both at the Canterbury assembly, which was held at Northampton, and also at the assembly at York, gave a thirtieth on condition that the lords did likewise. But the clergy of Canterbury refused, and those of York procrastinated. (There was a reluctance to provide money for shedding Christian blood, if not that of infidels.) These gatherings, instructed to hear and do what the king's servants would disclose to them (that is, they were required to pay money) are further evidence of the fluidity of institutions at this time. Taxation could still be raised outside Parliament, albeit with difficulty. There was also a still lingering idea that particular gatherings could commit themselves for tax, but not the nation. As for Edward, he clearly had no idea of making Parliament the sole tax-granting body in England.

But in the summer Parliament of 1290 the dependence on Parliament for general taxation, and the role of the knights in agreeing to it, was more precisely indicated than ever before. They were not excluded from giving counsel if the king asked for it, but that was not the reason for their summons. The wording of the writ of summons in June 1290 suggests that at least on this occasion, the magnates were more anxious than the king to have the Commons at Parliament, and the reason for the magnates' 'special' request for discussion is clear. The principal business discussed after the Commons had reached Westminster was the granting of a fifteenth by the magnates, prelates 'and all others' of the realm and the announcement of the king's expulsion of the Jews. The one was almost certainly in tacit exchange for the other. It was not that the banishment of the Jews was conditional on a tax, or vice versa; the decision for expulsion had been made by the council before the knights' arrival, though the Jews' safe conduct was only issued afterwards. The point was rather that the magnates themselves felt unable to commit the whole community of the shire to the tax, but believed that the presence of knights would suffice to commit and persuade the shires to pay it. They and the king also thought that these representatives could perform their persuasive role more effectively when they returned to the shires if they could take back the popular news from Parliament of the king's expulsion order as a kind of *quid pro quo*.

During the next few years, Parliaments were often concerned with little more than judicial and legal matters, and were frequently attended by few outside the king's regular council and judges. The quantitative predominance of the judicial and administrative business of pleas and petitions is indicated by the early rolls of Parliament which began to be compiled in Edward's reign. Under his father, and in the first years of Edward himself, such records had not been kept, probably because there were no regular parliamentary clerks to keep them. Parliament was looked after by officials from the courts and government departments, and its documents were simply those requiring administrative action, which went to the departments concerned. But with the increase of parliamentary business under Edward I, and its widening scope, it must have seemed sensible to make some memoranda of what had passed. This was done in the normal way on small pieces of parchment, though because of the occasional nature of parliamentary proceedings there was at first nothing systematic about it. The early surviving parliamentary rolls are concerned not with the political and fiscal proceedings of Parliament but with petitions and the decisions taken on them. Of course, memoranda to provide a basis for discussion of political subjects were made for the purposes of king and ministers. But these would presumably have concerned only the discussions of king and closer councillors with magnates. From 1290 onwards the parliamentary rolls were fuller and kept in a more orderly manner, but there was still no fundamental change in what they recorded. Occasionally, some general 'political' matters are noted: the memorandum of the marriage-aid of 1290 was one of them. But it was only gradually that what are now called the rolls of Parliament would begin to record, though at first haphazardly, parliamentary proceedings in a broader sense, as distinct from cases brought for administrative and judicial action to Parliament. It was not until the time of Edward III that the rolls of Parliament blossomed, and continued to develop through his long reign, as a detailed journal of parliamentary proceedings. Nevertheless, after 1290 we begin to see Parliament evolving as a much more significant political occasion than it had ever been before.[1]

The turning point of Edward I's relationship with his magnates, and therefore with Parliament, was a direct consequence of his need for war finance, which was eventually to be the biggest single cause of the increase of the Commons' influence. In the summer of 1290, however, the outlook appeared fair, and war did not seem to threaten. The king had returned from Gascony with his duchy in order. The Welsh had been suppressed and above all a treaty had been made with the Scots which seemed to ensure peace between the southern and northern kingdom. In 1286, the throne of Scotland had fallen vacant with the death of Alexander III. The nearest heir was his only descendant, the Norwegian princess Margaret, a child known to history as the Maid of Norway. In 1289, it was agreed that Margaret should marry Prince Edward, the heir to the English crown, though the Scottish leaders stipulated that Scotland should remain politically and judicially independent when a single king ruled both countries. It seemed to Edward that he could look forward to a period of constructive peace. Then at the end of 1290 this happy prospect suddenly disintegrated. When Edward was holding his Michaelmas Parliament at his hunting seat at Clipstone, north of Nottingham, the news reached him that the Maid of Norway had died. It now fell to Edward, as nominal Scottish overlord (a position long claimed by English kings, and accepted on this question by

---

[1] For a discussion of the complex questions relating to the parliamentary rolls and records, see Richardson and Sayles, 'The Early Records of the English Parliament,' *BIHR*, VII, pp. 129–153. An appendix gives a brief analysis of the parliamentary rolls between 1290 and 1321 (the so-called Exchequer series of parliamentary rolls) which shows their overwhelmingly judicial character. The nature of parliamentary records is also discussed in the same authors' introduction to *Rotuli Parliamentorum Anglie Hactenus Inediti* (Camden, third series Vol. LI).

the Scottish nobility) to decide between two rival claimants, John de Balliol, and Robert Bruce, both of whom were collateral descendants of the Scottish royal house. In the meantime, he received a shattering personal blow with the death near Lincoln of Queen Eleanor, to whom he was devoted and who was commemorated by the series of crosses in places where her body rested on the way to Westminster. From then onwards, under the stresses of war in Scotland and in France, more went wrong than right in the remainder of Edward's reign.

In his capacity as arbiter, Edward progressed through Scotland in 1291 and decided in favour of Balliol, a nobleman who also held lands in England, and who was expected to be the more pliant. Balliol was enthroned in December 1292. It was not long, however, before the English king's insistence on making his overlordship a more intrusive reality became too much even for his new vassal. The crisis was reached when Balliol was summoned to Westminster (he never came) to hear King Edward's judgement in a case between himself and one of his own Scottish subjects. Strife was looming when Edward also became entangled in the conflict with France which was to do more than anything else to weaken the crown he bequeathed to his son. In 1293, after a naval fight between French and Anglo-Gascon ships, the King of France made up his mind to assert his claim to the overlordship of Gascony. It was the feudal situation in Scotland reversed. Whereas in Scotland Edward claimed to be overlord, in Gascony he was vassal. Philip the Fair summoned Edward to Paris, and when the summons was refused, he declared the duchy forfeit. In 1294 the French invaded Gascony and occupied much of it. Edward then renounced his homage and the decision was taken to recover the lost territory by war. But it would not, as in Scotland and Wales, be war with a smaller enemy. The fight would be with a foe of equal or greater strength, and one helped by much closer lines of communication than those of the English. A great deal of money was needed, and Edward was driven to actions that were both harsh and arbitrary to finance the expedition. With the agreement of a great council of prelates and magnates which was hastily assembled in June (there was no time to call a Parliament) merchants' wool was seized, and only released on payment of a penal and arbitrary duty, the maletote.[1] Church money and treasures were taken and in September 1294 the alarmed clergy were summoned before the king who, apologizing for his methods, demanded an aid. The clergy, however, refused to give the half of their revenue for which the king asked, though they were willing to pay a smaller sum for one year only. To add to Edward's difficulties, the Welsh rebelled

[1] See pp. 130 and 157.

so that the king was forced to put off the big Gascon expedition he had planned in order to suppress this uprising.

Such was the political background against which Edward called a Parliament in November 1294. Two of the more diligent and discreet knights were summoned from each county to come to Westminster, again 'with full power' on behalf of themselves and the whole county. This time, however, the writ of summons contained an illuminating additional sentence explaining why. Full powers were needed 'so that the same business (about which the king wished to have a colloquy and to treat with his magnates) shall not remain unaccomplished for lack of such powers' (... *ita quod defectu potestatis huiusmodi idem negotium infectum non remaneat*). In other words, full powers were necessary because without them the communities could not be bound for certain to carry out what was ordained in Parliament. The demand for full powers was no mere rhetorical flourish. There were occasions when it was not made because there was no need for it. When 'full powers' were needed, the records provide evidence (confirmed by at least one chronicler) to identify what the need was. In the years between the irregular assemblies of 1283 (when the demand for 'full powers' is first found in Edward's reign) until 1297, 'full powers' were called for in the summons to every known Parliament except one, and there have survived some of the formal sealed documents carried to Parliament by borough representatives to show that the mayor and the whole community had given them such powers. In every Parliament to which knights (and sometimes burgesses) were required to come with full powers, taxation was granted. The one Parliament in this span of years for which 'full powers' were not stipulated had been that of September 1283 when no tax was granted because the knights were wanted principally for the trial of Prince David.

Taxation was thus the origin of the 'full powers' with which the representatives of the shires and boroughs came to Edward's Parliaments, even if it was not the sole and exclusive reason why their presence was thought desirable. The need of medieval kings to ensure that the shires and boroughs would honour the tax commitments that their representatives could be persuaded to accept on their behalf was the origin of the full powers which have been given ever since to members of Parliament to act not only on taxation but on all matters according to their own judgement as representatives, instead of coming to Parliament tied down by a precise mandate. Although a medieval king could claim to tax particular sections of his subjects where custom allowed, and could sometimes get away with the sort of pressure that Edward exerted on the clergy to grant money, he had no right to tax *all* free men unless they could be deemed to have given their consent. This was a broad principle in operation before the Conquest, and we have also seen that taxation agreed by the post-Conquest council of magnates was not always accepted by those who had not been present to give their consent as binding on them.[1] As the tax burden was spread wider, it had become still more important to have the consent and cooperation of local tax-paying communities if it was to be collected. In a country of great distances in terms of travelling time, there was no way in which a king could tax his subjects without their cooperation, short of plundering them and unleashing revolt. How, then, was consent to be registered? The answer was by representatives acting for those unable to be present.

Under Henry III the magnates had first expressed their inability to commit the whole community without the presence of representative knights.[2] Under Edward I their presence in taxing Parliaments became the general, if not the invariable, practice. In requiring knights to be chosen in the shire court, king and council were drawing on a long tradition. The shire court was already the basis of political, administrative and judicial organization in England. To it were traditionally summoned, to deal with shire business, earls and barons (in practice they probably sent their bailiffs or stewards to represent them), knights and free tenants. What was determined in the shire's own court was held to bind each individual in the shire, subject to the king. By bringing to Parliament the representatives of all the shires and boroughs, and insisting that they should come with full powers, the king was able to make sure that the money granted by the whole community would, subject to local wrangling about assessments and liability, reach the Exchequer.[3]

The November Parliament of 1294, faced with the French confiscation of Gascony, granted a tenth of all movables on behalf of all barons, knights and freemen. But as the cities and boroughs were not directly represented at it, separate arrangements were made with them under which they agreed to pay a sixth. There was as yet no firm understanding that aid could only be had through a Parliament, but if the burgesses were not asked in Parliament for their consent to tax, then it was evidently recognized that they should be approached out of it. The clergy also conceded an aid separately, from which, however, those who had already conceded a half of their revenue were exempt. But Edward's financial difficulties were still not overcome. After further delay to his plans for France as he set about quelling the last of

[1] See p. 71.
[2] See p. 94 for the writs of summons in 1254.
[3] For a full discussion of this subject see J. G. Edwards: 'The *Plena Potestas* of English Parliamentary Representatives', *Oxford Essays presented to Herbert Salter* (1934), reprinted in Fryde and Miller, Vol. I.

the Welsh rebellions, he began to build up forces for a Gascon expedition. For this more money was needed, and in November 1295 there met at Westminster that famous Parliament which countless textbooks, drawing on Bishop Stubbs' description of it, have called the 'model', often exaggerating this view of it beyond anything that a careful reading of that great scholar's own words would justify.

The so-called 'model' Parliament of the autumn was prefaced by a Parliament in June, to which Edward called archbishops, bishops, abbots, priors, earls, barons, some knights (apparently on a personal basis) and, of course, the office-holders, judges and others of his close council. There were, however, no representatives of the shires or boroughs. The business of this Parliament, apart from its routine judicial business, appears to have been political in the broader sense. An offer by the papal legate to mediate between the English and the French was debated, and questions of war were discussed. Such great affairs were not Commons' business. But though it contained the essential conciliar core of a Parliament, it was evidently not considered competent to grant taxation. It is quite possible that the magnates themselves, recognizing this, developed further the attitude they had adopted in the summer of 1290, and recommended the summons of the very full Parliament which met that November, and which was attended by the burgesses for the first time since the beginning of the reign.

It was an assembly of all the 'estates' and the summons to the prelates, headed by the Archbishop of Canterbury, expressed in the most precise form so far the fundamental principles of a representative Parliament. 'Just as a most just law, established by the careful providence of sacred princes, exhorts and decrees that what affects all should be approved by all, so also, very evidently, should common danger be met by all.' The quotation from the Code of Justinian, '*quod omnes tangit ab omnibus approbetur*', is not repeated in the other summonses, but their general drift is the same. The whole nation, it was asserted, and not merely Gascony, was threatened by the French, who proposed 'to destroy the English language altogether from the earth', a claim which was a sign of the renewed importance of the old tongue as the national form of speech, and indeed as the familiar language of very many of the better off. (The same rallying cry against the French was to be made under Edward III.) In this emergency, therefore, the prelates were to come with the magnates and 'other inhabitants' of the kingdom to consider how the threatened dangers were to be met. The archbishops were also required to see that the representatives of the clergy of their provinces also came to Westminster, meeting somewhat apart from the core of Parliament, but nevertheless considered as part of it. Likewise the lay magnates were to come so that the king could have 'consultation and treaty' with them to provide against the dangers from France. Eleven earls and fifty-three other barons received individual summonses. The sheriffs were told that as the king intended consultation with the leading men of the kingdom, they were to send two elected knights from each shire and two elected burgesses from each borough.[1]

In its composition this was neither a new model for Parliament which differed radically from what had gone before, nor a model in the sense of being a prototype for the future. The idea that it was a new departure arose because, when Stubbs wrote, the writs disclosing the presence of both knights and burgesses in the first Parliament of Edward's reign twenty years earlier had not been discovered. It therefore seemed that in 1295 Edward, drawing on the example of de Montfort's experiment for his partisan Parliament, was deliberately creating a national Parliament which was quite new, though Stubbs himself had made no such crude statement. The discovery that burgesses were present in 1275 disproved that theory. Other facts equally deny the inference that Edward was deliberately building a model for the future. Later in Edward's reign there were Parliaments to which neither knights nor burgesses were summoned. Clearly no binding precedent had been intended. It was not until after the first quarter of the fourteenth century that the Commons became an integral constituent of Parliament. Moreover, though the Parliament of 1295 was a model in the sense that knights and burgesses were to constitute the future House of Commons, its composition in one important respect was not to become permanent. In the great assembly of 1295, the lower clergy were an important part, but by the middle of the fourteenth century they had dropped out of Parliament permanently. The fact that the 'model' was not copied in this respect was of crucial importance. The very large Parliament of 1295 was in some respects a gathering of estates which was not to be characteristic of the future institution.

The English Parliament was to rest securely on the representation of local communities and summoned individuals, and not on rigid divisions by estates. The prelates were to sit in the future House of Lords more as barons than as ecclesiastics, while the lay magnates were summoned individually at the king's will and not automatically because they had the status of baron. Not all those who liked to consider themselves as part of the social order of barons were called. Although the principle of a parliamentary peerage, comprising prelates, earls and some barons, was beginning to emerge in a shadowy way under Edward I, the composition of this peerage was still not

---

[1] Stubbs, *Select Charters*, pp. 479–482. Translations of the various writs are in B. Wilkinson, op. cit., pp. 308 and 311, and in Stephenson and Marcham, op. cit., pp. 159–161.

hereditary but depended on the king's will from time to time. Later in the reign, the magnates who were called to Parliament were chosen from a list of the military host. Naturally enough, sons often followed their fathers, but there were some whom the king thought it not politic to admit. Moreover, when eventually a prescriptive right of summons created an hereditary peerage, no noble estate was created and the rest of a peer's family remained commoners in the eyes of the law.

As for the Commons, they were not a third estate but representative of a mixture of classes from town and from shire. Yet there was one important sense in which the great assembly of 1295 was a model for the future. Hitherto, the Commons had been required to come with full powers to consent to what the magnates agreed, even though the voices of the knights and burgesses had occasionally been sought and heard. This time they were to come with full powers for themselves and their communities 'to do what shall be then ordained through common counsel' (*ad faciendum quod tunc de communi consilio ordinabitur*). This was a pointer to their future standing; on those occasions when they came to Parliament the Commons would be intrinsic to its counsels. Their status was inferior to that of the individually summoned magnates, their writ did not give them the 'ordaining' function which the magnates were accorded, and they would not invariably be summoned. But when they were present, they would be recognized as part of that community of the realm which could express a common will binding on all individuals. The essential form of the writ to knights and burgesses remained unchanged from 1295 until the nineteenth century.[1]

The great Parliament of 1295 gave the king money, and it presumably considered the military policies for which it was to pay. In other words, the magnates and the council discussed the policies, and the Commons in general heard why money was needed and what they were asked to pay. It seems very probable that some of the more influential knights were consulted individually about what could be raised and what was acceptable. But this was probably not done in open Parliament and we have no way of knowing in any detail what passed. The outcome was that the barons and

---

[1] In the reign of Edward II, one word, '*consentiendum*' (consent) was added to the requirement that the Commons should have full power to 'do' (*faciendum*). The summons thereafter stated that the elected persons should come 'with full and sufficient power to do and consent to those things which then and there by common counsel ... shall be ordained, so that for want of such power ... the aforesaid affairs may in no wise remain unfinished'. The addition in 1313 of *consentiendum* must be taken as a recognition at the time that at least in some degree they had acquired some right of consent. Again I follow J. G. Edwards, op. cit. It would be not until later, however, that the right to consent was also recognized as logically carrying the right not to consent, and that would for a long time be restricted to a limited range of matters.

knights granted an eleventh of their movables, the boroughs a seventh and the clergy a tenth. Before the year ended Parliament had dispersed. But the king was still not able to get on with his business in France. Instead, he had to spend what had been given for a French campaign on war in Scotland.

By now John Balliol had virtually lost control to a council of notables who represented the rising Scottish determination to resist the intrusion of the English king in their nation's affairs. Scotland's independence was to be reasserted. Almost on the eve of the November Parliament, Balliol had therefore concluded a treaty of alliance with the King of France under which the Scots were bound to invade and harry England if Edward sent large forces against King Philip. No doubt the Franco-Scottish agreement helped Edward in his plea for money since a threat from Scotland touched the interest of the barons more closely than the declared confiscation of Gascony. Once again, Edward had to postpone the expedition with which he hoped to recover the lost greater part of his duchy. Instead he embarked on a ruthless campaign in Scotland, and by July 1296, Balliol had been forced to abdicate. Edward brought the ancient coronation stone of Scone to Westminster, assumed the Scottish kingship himself and placed an English governor over the Scots. For a brief moment, all three nations in the island of Britain seemed to be united under one ruler. Edward could at last turn to Gascony.

A year after the Parliament of November 1295, a new Parliament of precisely the same composition met in Bury St Edmunds. Again the laity gave grants, the barons and knights a twelfth, the burgesses an eighth. The clergy, however, refused any money, taking their stand on a Bull *Clericis Laicos* published earlier in the same year by Pope Boniface, which forbade the clergy to pay any taxation unless it was authorized by the Holy See. The Bull was produced in Parliament by Archbishop Winchelsey, who was permitted a delay until January 1297, when a congregation representing the whole clergy was summoned to St Paul's in London to consider the matter. Again the clergy collectively refused payment, though some individuals agreed to aid the king with a fifth, not officially as a tax but as a fine for the redemption of their seized property – a device to reconcile the payment with the papal decree. From those who paid nothing the king removed his protection: they were virtually outlawed. Their land became liable to seizure, their persons to imprisonment. A second convocation of the clergy in March altered nothing and there was no movement until the summer. It was then learned that the French bishops had petitioned the Pope to allow them to make a grant to their king, and so, at yet another convocation, the English clergy agreed to do the same for theirs. The prelates, however, refused to give way to the various actions by the king's servants, the seizure of goods and lands, and the threat to the person of the clergy, which they considered condemned by *Clericis Laicos*. They therefore decided to excommunicate those who offended against the Bull. Told of this just before he set sail for Flanders, where he planned a campaign against the French, the king refused to allow the sentence of excommunication to be pronounced, and insisted on the collection of a tax from the clergy straight away.

Meanwhile, Edward had encountered even more formidable resistance from the laity. The foundations of a crisis of fundamental significance in parliamentary evolution were being laid on all sides. At the beginning of March 1297 the king had met a Parliament of magnates at Salisbury in order to associate them with his plans to recover Gascony. In addition to the campaign being waged from the small part of the duchy remaining in English hands, Edward planned an attack on the French from the low countries, in concert with the count of Flanders and rulers of other provinces and in shaky alliance with Adolf of Nassau, King of Germany who, however, was shortly to come to terms with the French king. No representatives of the shires or boroughs were present at Salisbury. The subject for discussion was military campaigning and it was very much an occasion for the king and his nobility; a Parliament with distinctly feudal overtones. The king's design was that he should lead the expedition to Flanders, while a number of the barons should go to Gascony. But he met stubborn resistance, notably from the marshall Robert Bigod, Earl of Norfolk and the constable, Humphry Bohun, Earl of Hereford, the two most powerful noblemen then in England. Each had associations with the old baronial party; Bigod's father had been the justiciar forced on Henry III under the Provisions of Oxford and Bohun's father had fought with de Montfort at Evesham. Each now refused the order to go to Gascony. Their case rested on the old argument against the liability of English barons to serve the king in his foreign lands, but this was now revived in a new form. By their feudal tenure, they asserted, they were bound to go abroad with the king personally, whether to Flanders or Gascony, and to either place they would follow him and would lead the host. But to neither campaign would they go without the king. If, as he intended, he went to Flanders, then they would not go to Gascony. 'Without you, O king, I am not bound to go, and I will not go,' Bigod was reported to have said. 'By God, O earl,' the furious king replied in a bitter pun on the earl's surname, 'you shall either go or hang.' 'By God, O King, I will neither go nor hang,' was the earl's final word.[1] The Parliament dispersed having achieved nothing. About thirty of

---

[1] *The Chronicles of Walter of Guisborough*; ed. H. Rothwell (Camden series 1957) pp. 289–290. (Extracts dealing with the crisis of 1296–1297 in *E.H.D.*, Vol. III, pp. 224–230.) The

the magnates supported the earls in their resistance, and behind them were 1,500 armed men. No military action was attempted against the king, but during that summer the earls prevented the king's men, as far as they could, from seizing wool and collecting money through a new and arbitrary money-raising device which Edward authorized after Salisbury.

When, in 1275, a tax of half a mark on each sack of wool, and a mark on each last of hides had been granted in Parliament 'at the instance and request of the merchants', this had represented a commutation of the king's ancient customary rights and dues in royal ports, and was not strictly speaking an aid. Nor did it directly affect the whole community of the realm though, of course, any indirect tax ultimately reaches prices generally. It was therefore a moot question how far such a tax was a matter for Parliament. The arrangement of 1275, however, had plainly been a bargain struck by the king with the merchants which was then given parliamentary authorization. But in the emergency after the invasion of Gascony, Edward acted of his own will and without obtaining consent. In 1294, the duty on wool had been raised to the exorbitant figure of three marks (that is, forty shillings) and that on hides to five. This 'maltote' had been the cause of resentment enough, yet in 1297 after the Salisbury meeting, the king went still further, ordering all wool to be acquired (under the system of *prises*) and taken to the seaports, where it was weighed and valued. The wool of the greater merchants, those with more than five sacks, was then taken by the crown, with a security given for later payment. The wool of the lesser merchants was exempt, provided they paid a duty of 40 shillings, the maltote, on each sack. Attempts by the crown to tax wool beyond the 'great and ancient custom' established in 1275 were to be a source of bitter parliamentary opposition under Edward III, and it was deeply resented in 1297. But as he tried to prepare his expedition for Flanders, Edward I had more than the resentment of the merchants to contend with. The clergy was still trying to resist the king's determination to tax them, the laity as a whole was weighed down by successive taxes on movables, and the magnates were opposed, as English barons, to serving in a foreign war in a feudal dispute which was not their business. Now there was also widespread resentment at a wool tax which would indirectly affect the whole community, and to another imposition of the king's, a demand that each county should contribute stipulated quantities of wheat and oats, beef and pork.

chronicler was not close to the events he describes and was reporting from hearsay. Some doubt has been cast upon whether Hereford was at Salisbury, though he stood firmly with Norfolk on the general issue, including the later refusal to co-operate with the July minster. However, the reported incident unquestionably describes the atmosphere of the time, and the relationship between the king and the earls, who subsequently felt it necessary to obtain a royal pardon for their disobedience.

In May, the king summoned a military levy to meet in London in July. All who held land of at least £20 annual value were to come, whoever was their lord, summoned for service in foreign parts. Since it by-passed the normal feudal procedure, and harked back to the principle of the fyrd, this muster was offensive to the feudal magnates. The marshall and the constable, who had already withdrawn to the Welsh marches and called a pseudo-Parliament of marcher lords there, now refused to do their duty at the London gathering of enrolling those who were to serve. They were therefore suspended by the king. Edward now decided to appeal against them to a wider audience. On a stage erected outside Westminster Hall, he spoke passionately, and according to the chronicler, in tears, of his efforts in Gascony as in the interest of the realm, asking pardon for his exactions. Emotionally he presented his thirteen-year-old son Edward as their king if he himself did not return from the war. In this ceremony, the king was publicly reconciled with Archbishop Winchelsey, and the people were said to have been appropriately moved. The barons, however, were not. They advised the king against going to Flanders, asking for an end to the practice of taking tallages, and for the reissue of the charters, which Edward was prepared to renew in exchange for an aid of an eighth from the barons and the shires, and a fifth from the towns.

At this point, Edward took an action that flagrantly breached the convention that taxation required consent. Calling to his chamber a meeting of some of his own close councillors and officials, together with some of the friendly barons, he obtained their agreement to the collection of the eighth and the fifth. It was not a representative meeting and it could speak for neither shires nor towns. Yet this aid, granted not by any sort of Parliament, but 'by the laity standing around in his chamber',[1] was followed by writs announcing that 'the earls, barons, knights and other laity of our realm outside the cities, boroughs and demesne have granted us an eighth of all their movables',[2] and that the boroughs and towns had given a fifth. In return, Edward undertook to confirm Magna Carta and the Forest Charters. Not surprisingly, this 'unparliamentary' taxation provoked immediate resistance. Both Bigod and Bohun were gathering strength and most of the knights whom Edward had summoned to join him kept away.

As the king was preparing to sail from Winchelsea in August, with a military force far smaller than he had wanted, he was sent a remonstrance by

---

[1] Flores *Historiorum* (Rolls Series), iii, 295–296. ('... *qui mox concessus est ei a plebe in sua camera circumstante* ...')

[2] *Parliamentary writs and writs of Military summons*, ed. by F. Palgrave, Record Comm (1827–34).

the resisting earls and magnates in the name of the whole community, outlining the grievances of the realm. These included the irregularity of the king's writs, the tallages, prises and the tax on wool, the summons to Flanders of the £20 freeholders, the breaches of the Charters and the neglect of custom and public business. Not least, the remonstrance protested against the king's departure for Flanders just when rebellion loomed in Scotland. At the same time, the convocation of clergy decided to excommunicate anyone who disobeyed *Clericis Laicos*.

Edward's reply was to impose, on his own authority, a tax of a fifth on the clergy's goods. As for the magnates, his answer was simply a proclamation expressing the hope that the 'common aid' granted by the great lords in London should not be taken wrongly. He referred to certain grievances which he had caused his subjects to suffer, and of which he was very cognisant, 'such as the aids that he has frequently asked of his people'. This he had been obliged to do because of wars against him. 'He is much grieved that he has put such burdens upon them, and he begs them to be willing to excuse him as one who has inflicted these impositions not to buy lands or tenements, or castles or towns, but to defend himself and all the kingdom.' If he returned from the campaign, he would (the proclamation said) make 'real amends'.[1]

Having made these emollient statements, he persisted in his plans and set sail, leaving the country not far from civil war. Edward took with him not the great army of earls, barons, knights and men-at-arms that he had wanted but a mere hundred knights and fewer than six hundred squires.

The two earls now moved from protest to action. On the morning of the king's embarkation, Norfolk and Hereford went to the exchequer and protested against the writs to raise a tax which, they said, had never been granted by the earls, barons and knights as the writs claimed. They refused to pay. England, they declared, could not be treated as a land of serfs, to be tallaged at will, and they forbade the collection of the tax.

Hearing this news just before he set sail, Edward again gave his authority for the collection, but promised that it should not create a precedent. His young son was left as nominal regent, and the seal of absence was entrusted to the chancellor, John Langton, who had received that appointment on Burnell's death. Before sailing, the king also sent writs for a large number of barons and knights to rally to his son at Rochester, most of whom later went on to a Parliament summoned by the regent to meet in London at Michaelmas 1297. It was clearly intended to be a Parliament of royal supporters but events determined otherwise. Before it met, the news had

---

[1] *Rymers Foedera*; Vol I pp. 872–3. Wilkinson, op. cit. Vol. I, p. 219.

come of the devastating defeat of the English at Stirling Bridge by the Scottish insurgent leader, William Wallace. This immediately created a sense of English unity, bringing together in a Parliament of reconciliation the regency council and the opposition. The first individual summonses to the magnates and barons on the king's side were quickly followed by the summoning of Norfolk, Hereford and others of the baronial 'opposition'. They came with large military forces, and though reconciliation was in the air, it was only available at a price. The atmosphere was charged, and the conflict of rival powers underlying the Parliament was very clear. A fortnight before the Parliament of earls, barons, bishops, abbots and priors was to meet, further writs were despatched for the attendance of the knights of the shire, who were to reach Parliament a week after the individually summoned lay and ecclesiastical magnates. Once again there was an improvised Parliament, with its composition changed in response to political circumstances. Intended at first as a rally of the king's supporters, it was transmuted by the Scottish danger, and the impossibility of collecting taxation, into a Parliament at which the armed factions who attended it could peacefully settle their differences.

Yet it was a legitimate Parliament, as the decision to send for the knights to approve tax collection clearly showed. The writs summoning them began with the statement that the king, in consideration of the grant of an eighth, had agreed that the Charters should be confirmed and properly observed, and further that he would grant by letters patent that the levy of an eighth should not be a precedent thereafter. The knights of the shire were to come with 'full power' concerning the confirmation of the charters and the granting of the eighth, and were also empowered to receive 'what further shall be there ordained by the king and his council'.[1] They were necessary for providing the consent of the community, but were not expected to take part in the high politics of the occasion, which were to be resolved between the factions of magnates. The dominant theme of the Parliament was the insistence of the party led by the marshall and constable that the redress of grievances must precede the granting of taxation, and that the granting of taxation could only be with the consent of those representing the taxpayers. The Parliament, under the leadership of the two earls, was so determined to establish the voluntary nature of any grant that the original 'eighth', not having been properly granted, was treated as null and void. In its place, a ninth was granted, a writ being sent out to the knights, freeholders and community of each county establishing that the grant had been made in return for the confirmation of the great charter.

[1] *Calendar of the Close Rolls* (H.M.S.O.), 1296–1302, p. 129.

Thus the king's political and financial necessities, together with the Papal Bull on clerical taxation, had led to the resistance of the clergy, the refusal of the magnates to go without the king to Gascony, the successful refusal to pay a levy at the king's will, and to the understanding, once and for all, that it was in practice impossible for an English king to impose taxation without parliamentary consent. It was also now an inescapable fact that when Parliament insisted, grievances would have to be redressed, whether through the confirmation of charters, or, as in the future, by the ordaining of remedial laws, before taxation was supplied. The most extreme statement of these claims was made in the opening clause of a draft charter, known as *De Tallagio non Concedendo*, drawn up by the opposition, and submitted to the Michaelmas Parliament of 1297, which declared: 'No tallage or aid shall be imposed or levied by us or our heirs in our realm without the will and common assent of the archbishops, bishops and other prelates, earls, barons, knights, burgesses and other free men of our realm....'[1] The taking of wool, corn and other commodities without consent would also have been forbidden under these articles. It was also declared that the laity and clergy were granted their liberties and free customs, any statute contrary to these customs being invalid – which was an attempt to ensure that common law was ultimately superior to statute law.

In the preamble to the Petition of Right in 1637, the articles *De Tallagio* were to be described as a statute. In fact, they were not, and the actual confirmation of the charters, the *confirmatio cartorum*, which Edward ratified at Ghent, was a good deal less explicit in limiting what future generations would call the royal prerogative. The charters were confirmed, breaching them would incur excommunication, and acknowledgement was made of the 'fears' of some lest the aids and taxes they paid should be turned into a 'servile' obligation for them and their heirs. The king granted that there was no such precedent, and that he would henceforth on no account take aids, taxes and prises 'except by the common consent of the whole kingdom and for the common benefit of the same kingdom, saving the ancient aids and prises due and accustomed' – a somewhat less emphatic declaration than the opening clause of the draft *De Tallagio*. The heavy custom duty imposed in 1294 (the maltote) was abolished and was not to be taken without consent, but the old custom on wool, woolfells and hides was reserved to the king as previously granted. This is the form in which the statement appears in the

---

[1] '*Nullum tallagium vel auxilium per nos vel haeredes nostros de cetero in regno nostro imponatur seu levetur, sine voluntate de assensu communi archiepiscorum, episcoporum et aliorum praelatorum, comitum, baronum, militum, burgensium et aliorum liberorum hominum in regno nostro.*' The Latin text of the articles, originally found in the annals of the Chronicler Walter of Hemingburgh, is given in Stubbs, *Select Charters*, pp. 493-494; a translation is in *E.H.D.* Vol. III, pp. 486-487.

statute book; its phrasing is less peremptory than that of the draft but it was none the less an unambiguous reassertion of the principle that taxation needed a mechanism for consent, which had been included in the original Magna Carta but was then omitted to save the authority of the young Henry III.[1] It was now reasserted with the clear implication that the mechanism for consent should be Parliament. Finally as a gracenote to these proceedings, the Earls of Hereford and Norfolk, with their followers, were fully pardoned by the king, since they feared 'lest We have conceived rancour and indignation against them' for 'certain Disobediencies' for delaying of the king's commands and for certain 'Assemblies of armed people', no offence having ensued.[2]

All this had been achieved because the king's impositions had united every class with a political voice against him.[3] The ingredients of the crisis also influenced the future shape of Parliament. Had there been no Papal Bull and no clerical resistance, the clergy would not have been driven to hold separate convocations to determine their attitude, and might have continued, on the 'model' of 1295, as part of any 'general' Parliament. Parliament might then have developed rather more as an assembly of 'estates' or social classes (nobles, clerics and the third estate) on the continental pattern, instead of becoming, as it did, an assembly of magnates, lay and ecclesiastic, summoned individually, and of elected men representing, not other classes, but whole communities of shires and boroughs. The episode was a characteristic example of the way in which constitutional advance has in England been more effectively realized as an accidental consequence of particular political conflicts and individual grievances than through the deliberate schemes and theories of revolutionaries.

The *Confirmatio Cartorum* was the high water mark of constitutional advance under Edward I, but it did not put an end to the suspicion and conflict between the king and the baronial opposition. In March 1298, the king returned from Flanders to deal with Scotland. Neither knights nor burgesses were present at the first of two Parliaments held in that year, but representatives of both kinds were summoned to a Parliament (described as a *colloquium speciale*) held in York at Whitsun when the invasion of Scotland was planned. Even this occasion was clouded with mistrust. Fearing that the king might disregard the *Confirmatio* because it has been forced on him in his absence, the earls of the oppostion demanded a reconfirmation of the

---

[1] *Stat.* R. Vol. I, pp. 123–124; Stubbs, *Select Charters*, pp. 490f; translated in E.H.D. Vol. III, pp. 485–486 and Stephenson and Marcham, op. cit. pp. 164–165.

[2] *Stat* R. Vol. I, p. 124

[3] An invaluable source for the whole of this episode is *Documents Illustrating the crisis of 1297–98 in England*, edited, Michael Prestwich, Camden Fourth Series, Vol. 24, (1980).

charters as a condition of their attendance and service in Scotland. Edward promised to do what was required provided he was victorious in the coming campaign. In July he defeated the Scots at Falkirk, effectively destroying Wallace's leadership, but neither Wallace nor Robert Bruce (to whom the leadership of the Scottish cause was now passing) was captured. Nor had Falkirk given Edward control of Scotland. In none of three Parliaments held in 1299 were the representatives of the communities present, even though the question of re-confirmation was a major topic at Lent. A statute on counterfeit money was promulgated at Easter 'with the common consent of the prelates, earls and barons',[1] and the magnates also pressed the king to order a perambulation of the forests to ensure that the provisions of the Forest Charter were observed, and to deal with disputes about boundaries.

At Lent, 1300, however, a 'full' Parliament was held, to which came not only representatives of the communities but also those of the lower clergy, as in 1295. There was much discussion of grievances, and, under pressure from the magnates, the king granted new articles on the charters (*Articuli super cartas*) against infringement of the charters and various sorts of maladministration.[2] The king was granted a twentieth but seems not to have collected it, objecting to the conditions attached. At this Parliament, the knights and burgesses attended only until March 20, when they were given authority to claim 'reasonable expenses'. It is not possible, therefore, to assess their influence on the new articles. Plainly, these were the result of baronial pressure, but it would not be surprising if the magnates strengthened their hand by producing evidence that the knights could provide. At all events, we know that knights were directly involved in the political business of Parliament in the following year.

The Parliament held at Lincoln in 1301 was one of the most distinctive, as well as being one of the most dramatic of Edward's reign. To start with, because the perambulation of the forest previously ordered was again to be discussed, the sheriffs were instructed to send to Lincoln all those knights and burgesses still alive who had attended the previous Parliament. New representatives were to come only where death or incapacity had removed the old. Scholars from Oxford and Cambridge were specially summoned, apparently to discuss the king's rights in Scotland, but the lower clergy were absent. As a tactical manoeuvre in his resistance to the deforestation which would result from the perambulation, the king sent to the prelates

---

[1] *Stat. R.* Vol. I, pp. 131–135.
[2] *Stat. R.* Vol. I, pp. 136–141. The articles are also in B. Wilkinson, op. cit., Vol. III, pp. 313–314.

and magnates a 'bill' asking them to take the responsibility for what they demanded, and to assure him that, if he consented, he would not be breaking his coronation oath to maintain the crown's right. The response was 'a bill from the prelates and leaders of the realm delivered to the lord king on behalf of all the community'.[1] The outstanding feature of the Parliament was the use, for the first time, of a representative of the Commons, Henry of Keighley, who was one of the two knights for Lancashire, to present the bill of grievances putting pressure on the king. In this way it could be demonstrated that the complaints were those of the wider realm, not simply of the barons. The use of an elected knight in this political role seems to have been without precedent, and it foreshadowed the process by which, in future reigns, 'common' petitions would be presented to the king as bills which, if he assented, would become acts of Parliament. The king gave varying replies to the clauses of the bill which required charters to be observed, statutes contrary to charters to be declared null and void, and prompt deforestation to be implemented where the perambulators required it. Sometimes Edward's response was 'it expressly pleases the king', sometimes 'it tacitly pleases' (*placet tacite*). To one clause under which the king's ministers who infringed the charters would be subjected to penalties imposed by auditors approved by the magnates, the king replied: 'The lord king wishes to provide another remedy in this connection rather than through such auditors.' The penultimate clause of 'Keighley's bill' was phrased in humiliating terms. 'On condition that the aforesaid matters are carried out . . . the people of the realm grant the king a fifteenth in place of the twentieth recently granted. Yet this is done on condition that all the matters aforesaid are carried out between now and Michaelmas next; otherwise nothing is to be taken.'

The point could hardly have been rubbed home more brutally, yet this dominating king, possessing such great personal authority, felt obliged to respond simply: 'It expressly pleases.' Only on one point, the still burning question of taxing the church, did the king make a stand, and even then he had to admit for the record that he did so without the support of his natural counsellors. The clause in the bill stating that 'the prelates of holy church cannot and dare not assent to a contribution being made from their goods or from the goods of the clergy contrary to the prohibition of the Apostolic See' received the royal response: 'It does not please the king, but the community of barons has approved.' Understandably, the king was infuriated by the challenge implicit in this 'bill' and he did not forget. Five

---

[1] *Parliamentary Writs*, Vol. I, pp. 104–105, translated in *E.H.D.* Vol. III, pp. 510–512. See also, D. Pasquet, op. cit., pp. 115–117 for a discussion of this episode.

years later, Henry of Keighley was arrested on the king's orders and kept in honourable captivity in the Tower of London. It is not altogether fanciful to see in Henry of Keighley a forerunner of those members of the House of Commons under Elizabeth and the Stuarts who at some personal risk sought to challenge the crown over policy. There is no reason to doubt that, like them, he did what he did believing it right. On the other hand, unlike them, he seems essentially to have been acting as an instrument of his social superiors. In his instructions to the Treasurer for Henry of Keighley's arrest in 1306 the king acknowledges as much. 'We have ascertained on his own admission that he is the one who brought us the bill on behalf of the Archbishop of Canterbury (Robet Winchelsey) and the others who pressed us outrageously at the Lincoln Parliament. . . .'[1] The letter of instructions makes it clear that the king accepted that the archbishop (with whom he was persistently at odds) was really the prime mover, which was why he ordered that Henry of Keighley should 'be kept courteously and safely' in the Tower, without irons. The offending knight was released later on taking an oath not to offend the king or his crown. Keighley, who had also been a member of the Parliament of 1298, was one of the commissioners chosen under the *Articuli super cartas* to enforce the charter, and it was in this capacity, as well as that of a member of Parliament, that he had come to Lincoln. However much of the 'bill' was the work of the Archbishop and other great men, the episode illustrates that a knight could be of political significance, and did consort with those socially higher than himself. Indeed, it illustrates that the social divisions between the barons and gentry of England were then, as they remained, very fluid, and this fluidity was to be of fundamental importance in the development of Parliament and the mutual relationship of the future House of Commons and future House of Lords.

The king was more fortunate in the Lincoln Parliament's attitude to Scotland. The Pope had written instructing him to cease afflicting it, but in this matter the English baronage also had an interest. A declaration in the name of seven earls and ninety-seven barons, who claimed to speak for the whole community declared their intention to maintain the rights of the crown, even if the king were willing to accept the Pope's instructions. Later the king wrote to the Pope, basing his claim to Scotland on a historical survey starting with the coming to Britain of Brutus of Troy. Scotland, he claimed, was his by right as well as by possession.

Edward may have been disenchanted with Parliaments after Lincoln. At all events, there were fewer of them in the final troubled years of his reign. It

---

[1] *E.H.D.* Vol. III, p. 522.

was eighteen months before another was called, in July 1302, and then neither knights nor burgesses were summoned. There were, however, ten earls and eighty-three barons present, as well as thirty-four judges and officials, sixteen bishops and forty-three abbots. Although the only parliamentary business actually recorded concerned the hearing of petitions and giving judgements, the purpose of so considerable an assembly of great men must have been political. Again, the main recorded business of a Parliament held at Michaelmas, 1302, was pleas and petitions, but from the fact that it was a full Parliament of knights and burgesses as well as magnates (though not the lower clergy) it seems likely that politics were also involved, though there is no information about whether an aid was sought. Two more years then passed without a Parliament. The king was trying to break his dependence on taxation for which he had to make concessions of policy. Instead, he tried to manage by taxing foreign merchants in exchange for a charter, seeking unsuccessfully the agreement of the English merchants to a tax and tallaging the towns on the crown's demesne as well as collecting a scutage.

Then, in 1305, there was held the Parliament of whose proceedings there is more evidence in the parliamentary records than any other of the reign, and on the analysis of which Maitland constructed his concept of the primarily judicial function of the early fourteenth century Parliament.[1] The Scottish wars dragged on, with almost annual invasions, until 1304, but the resistance of the Scots was gradually eroded and although William Wallace was not captured until the summer of 1305, Edward seemed to be in control of Scotland again. Returning from Scotland, he issued his writs for a Parliament at Lent, and directed the appointment of receivers and auditors who were to dispose of petitions, so far as they could, before he reached Westminster. It was a large assembly of some 600 men, including the lower clergy as well as prelates, and the representatives of the communities as well as nine earls and ninety-four barons. Some 200 citizens and burgesses well outnumbered seventy-four knights of the shire. In addition, writs were sent to thirty-three members of the king's council. The whole assembly lasted for just three weeks, and on 21 March, the prelates, earls, barons, knights, and burgesses were told that they might go home but must be ready to appear again if summoned. The Parliament was not, however, considered to be at an end. Comprising the king and his councillors, it continued into April, and many of its doings were entered on the roll which Maitland edited. Yet although the names of the magnates and representatives of the communities are known, those of the council are not. All that can be said of it is that it included the thirty-three officials (such as the chancellor of the

[1] See pp. 81–3.

exchequer, the justices and chancery officials), and those magnates (many of them holding great offices of various kinds) who were members of the close council, or were required to attend for any other reason. Those who witnessed the acts of the king before the wider assembly had dispersed were largely those who were also active in the proceedings of the council after the rest had gone. Although the proclamation inviting petitions was made in the great hall at Westminster, the council assembled in the Archbishop of York's house (where the Parliament of 1293 had met) which stood on the site of the future White Hall. The petitions, which were the principal business of the council-in-Parliament, were written on small pieces of parchment, in French, with the king's reply, usually in Latin, on the back. Where possible, petitions were dealt with by another appropriate court; if not, by the king and council. The petitions were addressed to the king and his council, not to Parliament, and discussion of them was suitable to a small, not a large body.

At the centre of Parliament's routine work, therefore, was still the function of giving judgements and hearing, or redirecting, petitions. On this occasion, one of the principal cases before it was that of Nicholas Segrave, accused of treason for having absented himself from the king's army with the intention of going to the French court to fight a duel with another Englishman, which he knew Edward would have forbidden. Segrave had been captured as he had sought to make his way to France. He now appeared in 'full Parliament' before earls, barons and others, but not prelates, of the king's council, and was condemned by the council to death, the sentence being commuted by the king to an undertaking to surrender himself to prison should that ever be demanded. In so important a case affecting a baron, it seems quite possible that even though the case may have been determined by king and council, the proceedings were given greater solemnity by taking place in the presence of the wider Parliament of magnates before their departure. (The exact date of the trial is not, however, recorded.)

In what respect, then, did the role of the high court of Parliament, in its judicial capacity, differ from that of other high courts? How was it to be distinguished from the 'bench' (later the court of common pleas) and from the superior court of professional judges (later the king's bench) where cases were heard *coram rege* (before the king), and at which the king was always, as the fount of justice, deemed to be present? Like its descendant, the House of Lords,[1] the medieval high court of Parliament was often a

---

[1] Today, of course, the judicial function of the House of Lords is purely that of a court of appeal. Its vestigial role as a court of first instance ended with the abolition of the right of a peer to be tried by his peers.

court of first instance, able to look at special or important cases involving particular problems; able to provide justice in a manner not limited by the technicalities of precedent that might bind other courts; able to determine, where there had been doubt, in which other court a case should be heard, or to deal with that case itself, if this seemed appropriate. It could also provide direct administrative and other remedies for grievances and wrongs that were the subject of petitions. In short, the distinguishing feature of the medieval high court of Parliament was its omnicompetence, and its status above all other courts; its ability to provide extraordinary jurisdiction, and remedies where necessary to supplement the work of other courts (a function not dissimilar from that of the future conciliar court of Star Chamber). It was inevitable that Parliament's great and indefinite powers in providing justice should be exercised by the king's closer council. The magnates as a body, with their own responsibilities, were not qualified to give time to deal with tedious law business.

Their interest in a parliamentary occasion was political, and the rolls of Parliament, being concerned largely with recording decisions on petitions, do not provide us with a real window into these political activities.[1] We must, therefore, not assume from the preponderance of judicial and petitioning business on the Parliament roll that the political business of the magnates (or, if it comes to that, of the communities' representatives) was of secondary importance in the Lenten Parliament of 1305. The business of the magnates and the tax-granting of the Commons was always the great business of a Parliament; the judicial activities were routine and did not require their attention. We have already seen how often Parliaments had important and controversial political questions before them, which were largely the preserve of the magnates; how frequently Parliament was needed for taxation so that the presence of the communities' representatives could ensure that it would be collected, and how important Parliament was in legislation.

So far as politics was concerned, the Lenten Parliament of 1305 was no exception. Scotland, Edward believed, had now been finally subdued, even though William Wallace was still at large, and it was now necessary to decide what form of settled government it should have. The magnates and estates were summoned, therefore, to treat of 'certain matters specially

---

[1] Entries on the rolls of Parliament were not necessarily in date order, and the authority for action on any petition is not the roll of Parliament but the endorsement on the back of the petition itself. Later, in the 14th century, the recording of individual petitions on the Parliament roll was largely discontinued, and the roll came to deal with the common petitions of one or both estates of Parliament, which were often the basis of statute, and with the general proceedings of Parliament, including ministerial speeches.

touching our realm of England and the establishment of our land of Scotland'.[1] During this Parliament, Edward required the Bishop of Glasgow, the young Robert Bruce, Earl of Carrick (the future Scottish king), and John Mowbray to say how Scotland would be represented at another Parliament later in that year. Their recommendations was that ten representatives, two bishops, two abbots, two earls, two barons and two representatives elected by the community of Scotland, would suffice, and that was the Scottish representation at a later Parliament in the same year. Although the recommendation of the three Scots was not made until after the English magnates and representatives of the committees had gone home, it seems more than likely that the affairs of Scotland generally were discussed when the magnates were present. It also seems probable that business affecting Gascony may have been discussed in the fuller Parliament as well as Edward's difficulties with the clergy. There was certainly a petition by barons and Commons against the sending of money by monks to their 'mother' establishments abroad – to which Edward appears to have replied by making a statute. This, however, was apparently kept in suspension, since the roll of parliament, having noted that the king had made such a statute 'in the form that follows', contains a blank space where the details should be. Whatever happened to the statute, however, it seems likely that the political question of church revenues may have been one on which the king held discussions with the wider assembly. The statute was enacted or re-enacted two years later as the Statute of Carlisle.[2]

The political importance of the Lenten Parliament of 1305 was, then, far from negligible, but although the representatives of the communities were present it appears that no taxation was asked for. From this it might be possible to infer either that the calling of representatives of the Commons without asking for money indicated that they were now beginning to be looked upon as having a somewhat wider role – or, alternatively, that there had been some intention of asking them for money which was then not pursued. It is not altogether impossible that Edward's servants took the temperature of the assembly on the question of how an application for tax would be received and decided that it would be better, on that occasion, not to proceed with it.

That, however, is no more than guessing at possibilties. We know more about the Lenten Parliament's legislating activities, and what we know establishes that they amounted to very little. There was the suspended statute on church revenue and there was an ordinance about the

[1] *Parliamentary Writs*, Vol. I, pp. 136–138.
[2] *Stat. R.* Vol. I, p. 143.

perambulation of the forest. But the only notable enactment was that which is known as the Statute of Trailbastons, or, as the Parliament roll describes it, the *Ordinatio de trailbastons*.[1] It is a measure that may well be regarded more as a prerogative ordinance by the king than as a Statute as we understand the term and it is not printed as such, (though the distinction at that stage was a nice one). But more to the point than its categorization is the likelihood that this measure may well have pointed to an important non-judicial function of this Parliament in which the political advice of the wider assembly may have been of some account.

This was the 'year of trailbaston' as one annalist described it, when growing protection rackets by violent gangs and intimidation increasingly threatened the safety of ordinary people. The word 'trailbaston' is thought to have derived from the staves carried by the criminal 'clubmen', and the ordinance of trailbaston provided for special commissions to deal with the kind of disorder that was everywhere increasing.

> Through England people of great judgement
> Are appointed judges upon the Trailbastons.
> Some by trial are condemned to imprisonment,
> Others gone to hang about on gallows;
> Several are deprived of their property;
> Who offended least are allowed to escape by fines.
> If there were no chastisement of ribalds and rogues,
> A man would not dare to live in house.[2]

The ordinance of trailbaston was essentially an act of the Council in Parliament and might be regarded as no more than a use of the king's normal power to send out commissions of justice as he chose. Yet it is not impossible that what the Council had learned from magnates and representatives of the communities about the state of affairs in the country, and the feeling in their localities about it, may have played a part in the decisions of the king's advisers. There is nothing of greater importance in the governing of a country than the maintenance of law and order; certainly nothing mattered more to the reputation of a medieval king.

To deal with it, he needed to know the facts from those best able to convey them to him, and it is reasonable to suppose that these were the representatives of the communities. Maitland himself (whose discovery of

---

[1] The 'Statute' of Trailbaston was not, in Maitland's view a legislative act but an exercise of the king's discretionary power to send justice when and wherever he chose.

[2] From the verse chronicle of Peter Langtoft; excerpt in *E.H.D.* Vol. III, p. 258–259.

the importance of the medieval Parliament's judicial function did not tempt him to regard it as the one essential characteristic of a Parliament) suggested that while the king and councillors were dealing with petitions (some of which were presented by representatives of communities) the role of the knights and burgesses was not to act in concert but to represent individually the grievances and interests of their particular communities as and when they could. Difficulties in maintaining the law would have been among their concerns. The time had not yet come when they collectively presented bills which became the basis of statutes. Yet in Edward I's reign, their representation of their communities individual interest, and their relationship with the baronage, as demonstrated by the activities of Henry of Keighley, already foreshadowed the time when they would act together. What is more, to the extent that whatever was ordained in Parliament was deemed to bind all men, both in taxation and law, Parliament was doing more than expressing the acts and judgements of kings and officials. Its older and deeper roots were in consultation with the most important men of the land and in the crown's attempts to respond to the communities, which it was now able to do through their representatives. Edward I legislated in Parliament more than any other king had done since the Conquest. His law-making in the presence of people who could be said to represent the communities of the nation recalled the customary use made of the *ad hoc* gatherings of the Witan for the same purpose, as described in Chapter I. It is hardly an exaggeration to say that the reign of Edward I saw the revival of the Witan in an enhanced form, but with the all important addition of the representation of the communities through elected men empowered to act for them, which was a concept unknown to the Witan.

Yet for Parliament to become fully an institution as distinct from an occasion, some continuity of membership was needed to provide it with a sense of corporate identity, and to hand on from one Parliament to the next some idea of privileges gained and procedures devised. The beginning of such continuity can also be detected under Edward I. In his earlier years, it had been rare for the same representative to be returned twice to Parliaments. Although representatives were allowed their expenses, the duty to attend could be inconvenient, and at first might have seemed unwelcome. If a right is something to be husbanded, a duty is very often regarded as something best performed by someone else. Initially, the crown's summons to Parliament must have seemed a duty with little compensating benefit. Even so, there are always men anxious to be close to the seat of political power, and it cannot have been long before there were knights and burgesses sufficiently proud of their modest participation in such great occasions to be willing to put up with the accompanying inconvenience, and to be glad to attend a Parliament again, having once acquired a taste for mingling with the mighty. As they increasingly felt themselves to have a political role, their willingness to serve must have increased. They were called to Parliament to do 'what shall be ordained by common counsel' and although 'common counsel' was not specifically defined, the representatives of the Commons were increasingly recognized as having a part in it.

By the later part of Edward's reign, and during that of his son, there is evidence, albeit incomplete, to suggest that between 1290 and 1327 the re-election of 'members' to Parliament was by no means infrequent or unusual. Most of the Parliaments of this period seem to have contained a considerable proportion of representatives who had been elected on at least one previous occasion, and often on more than one. In about ten of the Parliaments of this period, a majority of the shire representatives had been at one or more previous Parliaments. It was more unusual for such men to have been in two *successive* Parliaments, and rarer still for them to have been elected to a series of more than two consecutive Parliaments. The burgesses, it seems, were rather less often re-elected than the knights; there were only six Parliaments in this period in which a majority of burgesses had been previously elected. There were some Parliaments in which those knights and burgesses who had experience of previous election were about equalled by those who had attended for the first time; others in which 'experienced members' were in a minority. Even so, the number of experienced members was seldom negligible.[1]

Circumstantial evidence suggests, moreover, that most of the knights and burgesses who were elected did actually turn up at Parliament. The fact that more of them were elected than subsequently collected their attendance expenses (according to the enrolled writs *de expensis*) was once seen as evidence that those who did not collect their expenses may not have attended. However, at least some of the boroughs and cities paid their own members. Furthermore, there are a number of occasions when it is known that an elected knight was present at Parliament, and yet claimed no expenses. A notable instance of this was Henry de Keighley himself, when he delivered the celebrated bill to Edward I at the Lincoln Parliament. If the writs *de expensis* were to be taken as conclusive evidence of attendance or non-attendance, he was not at Lincoln at all.[2] In any case, commonsense supports the idea that those elected would generally not fail to arrive.

[1] The evidence on re-election is given in J. G. Edwards, 'The Personnel of the Commons in Parliament under Edward I and Edward II', in *Essays presented to Thomas Frederick Tout*, pp. 197–214. The article is reprinted in Fryde and Miller, op. cit., Vol. I.
[2] J. G. Edwards, op. cit.

Certainly a man willing to be elected in the shire several times (which can hardly have been obligatory) cannot have been unwilling to attend, while the shire would have been most reluctant to be unrepresented on any occasion committing them to tax, and giving them an opportunity to convey their annoyances and grievances to the government. In the twentieth century, there is never a lack of parliamentary candidates anxious to become MPs, despite the great burdens and physical discomfort entailed; there is no reason to suppose that it was different in the fourteenth century, even allowing for the more arduous travel then.

The last two years of Edward's reign added little to the development of Parliament. A second Parliament in 1305, held in September, was attended by ten Scottish representatives and produced a short-lived 'settlement' for Scotland. In April 1306, the king called a Parliament of both magnates and representatives of the communities to meet at the end of May, on the occasion of the knighting of his son Edward. The writs stated that the purpose was to discuss and consent to the aid that it was appropriate to give on such an occasion. Nominally, this was a feudal aid, calculated on the sum for a knight's fees, but this method was now outmoded; in its place a normal tax on movables was granted. Edward was now a sick and failing man. Two months earlier, Robert Bruce, whom he had entrusted with responsibilities in Scotland, had killed his fellow-councillor John Comyn in a quarrel, and turned against the English. In March, Bruce was crowned king of Scots, and Edward was once again forced to prepare to fight for Scotland. As a prelude to military action, he made the Parliament for his son's knighting an occasion of great chivalric splendour. At a feast at Westminster, to which Edward had to be carried on a litter, two swans were brought in and symbolically laid on the table. Edward swore to avenge Comyn and then fight only in the Holy Land, Prince Edward took a vow not to rest more than one night in the same place before reaching Scotland. The drama of the occasion was probably intended to rivet Prince Edward, of whose weakness and unreliability the king was well aware, to his duties. At the ensuing Parliament, two Papal Bulls were published. One condemned Bruce; the other absolved the king from his oath to observe the articles of 1279. (Edward annulled the results of the perambulation of the forest in the following months.) Bruce's rebellion collapsed, and as many of the leading adherents as were captured were condemned mercilessly. Bruce, however, eluded capture, and the struggle continued.

The last Parliament of the reign was held at Carlisle, Edward having been lying sick at Lannercost Priory nearby. The Parliament, to which all the 'estates' were summoned, as in 1295, was opened by the Treasurer, Walter Langton. A principal subject was the financial exactions of the papal collector in England and the obligation of priories in England to send money to their mother houses abroad. (At one moment, according to one chronicler, a document of grievances suddenly descended, as if from heaven, on the open council meeting, presumably so that its origin should be unknown.) One outcome of this Parliament was the Statute of Carlisle (presumably based on the suspended statute of the 1305 Parliament which Edward again delayed putting into effect) forbidding English religious houses to send money abroad. At this Parliament the papal legate was present; on 12 March the king and he entered the Cathedral together and the cardinal explained that under the auspices of the Pope, an agreement had been reached between the kings of France and England. Peace was agreed between them, and so was the (ill-fated) marriage between Prince Edward and Isabella of France. The murderers of Comyn were excommunicated. Edward's understanding with the Pope had a further consequence in the suspension of Archbishop Winchelsey, a long-standing opponent of the king who blamed him for the proximity to political disaster which the realm had reached during the constitutional crisis. In May, Winchelsey had departed from England, not to return until recalled by Edward II.

Edward died at Burgh-upon-the-Sands, Solway, in July, on his way to tackle the Scottish insurgents. Peace with France had been achieved; the three 'nations' of Britain were superficially united for the first time. Yet the cost of Edward's military and political ambitions had left the realm of England, and specifically the crown, potentially weaker than he had found it. Just how serious that weakness was would be exposed by the incapacity of his son. In the scales of history the political confusion and financial indebtedness caused by the wars in France and Scotland have to be set against Edward's achievement as a ruler and law-giver. Ironically, both his successes and his failures as a king contributed in equal measure to the advance of Parliament.

CHAPTER 4

Edward II:
Parliament and Opposition

I

GOVERNMENT in the Middle Ages was personal to the king. His critics often found it convenient in a conflict to assert that he had been misled by evil advisers, but ultimately there was no way in which the king himself could avoid responsibility for what went wrong. A successful ruler was one who knew what was necessary for orderly government in the conditions of his time, and possessed the quality of leadership that would carry with him those on whose support he depended, accepting the need for some compromise between his own wishes and theirs. Edward II fell far short of the personal qualities needed for successful government, and he also started with disadvantages not of his own making. He inherited a crown the resources of which had been much weakened by the cost of his father's military enterprises in France and Scotland. In consequence of these campaigns, Edward II began with a huge debt of £200,000. Moreover, there was no end in sight to the war in Scotland, which promised only a continuing need for money-raising. Potentially more dangerous, however, was the legacy of distrust of the crown by the magnates which was the outcome of Edward I's financial exactions and of the often arbitrary methods of government in his final years.

Once the awe-inspiring personality of the old king had been removed, this lack of confidence was bound to manifest itself, diminishing the crown's authority until a new king, by his own merits, restored it. To do so was quite beyond the capacity of Edward II who quickly dissipated the atmosphere of superficial political affability with which his reign, like any other, opened. He also threw away such other potential advantages as he initially enjoyed. One of these was the magnates' lack of recognized leaders who might oppose the king. Two of the leaders of the old opposition, Bohun and Bigod, were dead, and a third, Archbishop Winchelsey, was in temporary exile, summoned to Rome to answer charges made against him by the late king, who had regarded the primate as his most formidable and persistent opponent. Edward II, however, being anxious to reverse as many of his father's policies as possible, brought Winchelsey back, thereby providing the opposition he was about to provoke with one of its principal leaders. The new king also deprived himself of an efficient servant and an adviser he could ill spare when he dismissed his father's grasping and detested but nonetheless efficient treasurer, Walter Langton, Bishop of Coventry and Lichfield, whom he imprisoned in the Tower of London. Most dangerously, instead of trying to extract what advantages he could from his family ties with the most powerful magnates (though even a competent king would probably have found that the potential dangers of these relationships outweighed any likely benefits) Edward behaved in such a way as to make these great kinsmen-subjects the source of leadership for the new opposition.

It had been Edward I's policy to make marriages where he could between his daughters and the great earls, whose estates were entailed on the issue of these marriages. He had thus added to the number of magnates whose combination of royal blood and great estates gave them power with which to threaten his son. The Earl of Gloucester was Edward II's nephew and the Earl of Hereford his brother-in-law, in addition to which, the most powerful of all, Thomas of Lancaster, was his cousin, as was the Earl of Richmond. The new king's personal failings were by then well known to the magnates, but there was naturally no reaction against him at the outset. A stronger and wiser man than Edward would have worked to overcome his initial disadvantages by consulting, and thus contenting, the magnates, at least until such time as he was strong enough to stand on an earned reputation as an effective ruler. This he might have achieved by remedying grievances, restoring the finances of the crown, removing the continued injustices in the administration of the crown's forest rights, and attempting to diminish the corruption among sheriffs and other officials which still undermined confidence in law and justice. Until his personal authority had been earned by such means, Edward needed to listen attentively to the opinions of powerful relations and other magnates who were certainly not disposed to allow him to take his advice from lesser men.

The king, however, acted in quite the opposite sense. Though not without intelligence, Edward seldom showed any signs of applying it effectively to government. When all allowance has been made for the dangers he inherited and for his youth (he was twenty three when he became king), the collapse of his authority must be attributed entirely to the shortcomings of an exceptionally weak and inadequate man. By persistent irresponsibility, he multiplied his difficulties and threw away every lifeline until his authority was wholly destroyed. It was a reign disfigured by repeated acts of violence, coups d'état and political murder on a scale not previously known in England, and it set a precedent. Henceforth, during a great part of the last two centuries which we commonly describe as medieval, death was to be the usual penalty for failure whenever political conflict culminated, as it increasingly did, in the clash of irreconcilable factions. It is one of the ironies of our constitutional history that such a period, characterized by recurrent episodes of political lawlessness and violence at home (or, in Edward III's long reign, by foreign war, an alternative medium for aristocratic ambition), should have seen the final consolidation of Parliament as an institution rather than simply a great occasion – an institution, moreover, that was henceforth to be first and foremost a political and a representative assembly.

Edward II was of regal appearance, good-looking, tall and athletic. He was also lazy, prone to lie in bed too long, procrastinating, irresolute and unable to summon up any sustained interest in the obligation of government. His interests were not such as to recommend him to his natural counsellors, since he preferred gambling, games, boating and music, and even thatching and ditching, to the martial enjoyment of the tournament or the ambitions of war. He wanted the pleasures but not the duties of kingship.[1] His besetting weakness, however, was his abject reliance on favourites. This failing was the more damaging because, being almost certainly based on a homosexual instinct, it induced in the king an emotional dependence on his friends that repeatedly impelled him to risk the interests and dignity of the crown to satisfy the demands for place and power of those with whom he was infatuated. In the eyes of the higher baronage, it was bad enough that he should be emotionally attached to men not drawn from the ranks of his natural counsellors, but it was far worse that he chose friends who, in their arrogance, abused the position to which the king raised them.

The underlying tension between the crown and its greater subjects was evident from the outset of the reign. Into the coronation oath, a new clause was inserted: 'Sire, do you agree to maintain and preserve the laws and

---

[1] The best contemporary account of the reign of Edward II and of the character of the principal political protagonists is *Vita Edwardi Secundi*, traditionally attributed to the 'Monk of Malmesbury' (because the original MS. came from the Abbey of Malmesbury). The author, however, was probably a lawyer and a West Countryman – possibly a John Walwayne. (Edited by N. Denholm-Young (Nelson) 1957.)

rightful customs which the community of your realm shall have chosen and will you defend and enforce them to the honour of God to the best of your ability?' To which the king's response was, 'I agree and promise.'[1] This was the form in which the new clause appeared in French, and it is the version which was probably used in the coronation ceremony, though there was also a Latin version in which the laws the king was to defend were those 'which the people shall have chosen'. Yet it was not so much the personal deficiencies of the young king that inspired the new clause, as the memory of the magnates' quarrel with Edward I, and, in particular, that king's refusal to adhere to the promises wrung out of him in the crises of 1297 to 1302. The principal question attaching to the meaning of the new undertaking in the coronation oath is one that is impossible to answer with certainty: what precisely was meant by his promise to keep 'the laws which the community of the realm shall have chosen', *(les leyes et les custumes droitureles les quiels la communaute de vostre roiaume aura eslu)*? Were they simply such laws as the statutes which had been enacted by the king in his Parliament, and the confirmation of charters to which the king freely agreed? Or was the new obligation to observe laws chosen by the community of the realm (or the people) intended to cover such concessions as those which Edward I had been forced to make after 1297 under duress, which he never regarded as binding, and from which he had eventually obtained papal release? If it was intended that the new clause should carry this second and wider significance, it would have been tantamount to an endeavour to transfer ultimate sovereignty from the king to the community of the realm. It is unlikely that the magnates consciously entertained any such precise idea. Yet the new clause must have been designed to insure against any attempts by the king to follow his father's precedent in subsequently renouncing any commitments made under duress. In any event, in the first great crisis of the reign, the magnates appear to have stood on the principle of this clause when they sought to drive into exile the king's powerful favourite, Piers Gaveston.

Gaveston was a Gascon knight, brave, vainglorious, intemperate, greedy and rashly puffed up by the king's favour. Edward I had exiled him because of his influence over his son. Edward II's first act as king was to bring him back and create him Earl of Cornwall, the first earldom to be given outside

---

[1] Chrimes and Brown, *Select Documents of English Constitutional History*, (1961) pp. 4-5 (French and Latin). A translation of the oath is also in *E.H.D.*, Vol. III, p. 525. For discussion of the meaning of the change, see B. Wilkinson, 'The Coronation oath of Edward II', *Historical Essays in Honour of James Tait* (1933) pp. 405-416; B. Wilkinson, 'The Coronation oath of Edward II and the Statute of York' *Speculum* 19, (1944), pp. 445-469; and P. E. Schramm, *A History of the English Coronation* (Oxford, 1937) pp. 203-211.

the royal family for nearly a hundred years, and a gift doubly offensive to the magnates because it was a bestowal of a formerly royal honour on a comparative nobody. On becoming king, Edward went to Scotland to receive the homage of such Scots lords as were still adherents of the English crown, and then virtually abandoned the Scottish campaign. Returning south, he dismissed the old ministers, and in October held a short Parliament at Northampton which included knights and burgesses, as well as barons and representatives of the lower clergy. Taxes on movables were granted by both laity and clergy. Like his father before him, Edward saw no need for instant coronation. He first crossed to France to marry the French princess Isabella, leaving Gaveston as regent to the disgust of the old baronage. In February 1308, the new king and queen were crowned and Gaveston, eccentrically arrayed in purple splendour, was given the privilege of carrying St Edward's crown. Immediately after the coronation, a Parliament assembled on 3 March. Magnates and prelates were called individually, but no summons appears to have been sent to knights or burgesses. However, the sheriffs had been instructed to invite to the coronation knights and burgesses as they saw fit, and these representatives may have stayed on for the Parliament. The king then sent messages, by his close kinsman, and future enemy, Thomas of Lancaster, and by the future favourite Hugh Despenser, asking the magnates to advise him on the state of the realm. This they undertook to do, but, already worried about the trend of events and angered by Gaveston's pretensions, they asked the king, through their spokesman Lincoln, who was the oldest earl, to confirm in writing that he would establish what they would ordain. Edward then put an end to this embarrassing exchange of messages by replying that he did not wish to trouble them further for the present. Dismissing them, he asked them to consider these matters again at his Parliament in April.

When the time for this next Parliament came, the magnates, now quite determined to get rid of Gaveston, assembled armed. No knights or burgesses were summoned. In a declaration thought to have been drawn up by the Earl of Lincoln, who, being of a generation older than most of them, was their effective leader, the magnates told the king that 'homage and the oath of allegiance are more in respect of the crown than in respect of the king's person'. If the king were not ruled by reason, they asserted, his lieges were bound by their oaths to reinstate the king in the 'dignity of the crown'; in other words, to lead him back to reason. If necessary, they said, this would have to be done by 'constraint'. 'As regards the person who is talked about,' the declaration went on in reference to Gaveston, 'the people ought to judge him as one not to be suffered because he disinherits the crown and, as far as he is able, impoverishes it. By his counsel he withdraws the king from the counsel of his realm (the recurrent claim of medieval magnates against their kings) and puts discord between the king and his people. . . .' Gaveston was a 'robber of the people' and a 'traitor' to the king and realm, yet since the king supported him, he could not be judged by an action at law. The people therefore 'rate him as a man attainted and judged and pray the king, that since he is bound by his coronation oath to keep the laws that the people shall choose, he will accept and execute the award of the people'.[1] If this declaration is authentic it indicates a clear attempt to make use of the new clause in the coronation oath to see that the king obeyed a decision of the 'people' (in effect, the community of the realm as represented by the baronage) against his own wish. It is possible also to see in the proposition that Gaveston should be condemned outside the ordinary legal processes because the 'people' willed it, a foreshadowing of impeachment by the Commons before the judgement of the Lords, and also of the sinister process of attainder by which men whose offence was political would in later generations be found guilty by a retroactive act of Parliament when a condemnation could not be obtained by the ordinary processes of law.

The magnates were adamant and the king was forced to yield. Gaveston went into exile. Yet Edward gave him in compensation the office of Lieutenant of Ireland, and though he lost Cornwall, Gaveston received other lands and continued to be addressed as earl. His departure did not, moreover, end the distrust between king and magnates, and at the next Parliament (about whose business nothing is known) the king was sufficiently concerned to issue a proclamation prohibiting those attending from coming with arms. Occasional parliamentary meetings of barons and bishops still took place without the Commons, and one such was held in February 1309. Then, in April the same year a full Parliament, including the Commons and lower clergy, was called to Westminster, taxation being required for a campaign against Robert Bruce in Scotland. Parliament seems to have met, as on some previous occasions, at York House, which stood on the site of the later Whitehall Palace. This place of assembly led to a renewal of a recurrent quarrel over status between the Archbishops of Canterbury and York. The dispute concerned the right of one to carry his cross in the territory of the other. When the archbishop of the northern

---

[1] *The Governance of Medieval England; the Conquest to Magna Carta* Edited by H. G. Richardson and G. O. Sayles (Edinburgh 1963), app. VII (French), with translation. A translation is also given in E.H.D., Vol. III, p. 523. It should be noted that Richardson and Sayles cast doubt on the authenticity of the document and suspect that it was concocted after Gaveston's death (Ibid, pp. 15–16). Even if the declaration was put together later in the reign, it is still an indication of the general position of the opposition magnates and of their conviction that, in a conflict, their will should ultimately prevail over the king's.

province appeared at York House carrying his cross, presumably on the theory that in his own house he was on his own territory, the Archbishop of Canterbury and his bishops refused to be present. The king then gave the northern archbishop leave to go home, and for some time afterwards, writs to stop one archbishop from interfering with the other accompanied summonses to Parliament.[1] At this Parliament the king was granted a twenty-fifth on movables by the laity, including the towns, but only, (as the parliamentary roll records), on condition that he accepted eleven articles for remedying grievances drawn up by the community of the realm.[2] Many of these were virtually a restatement of the Articles of the Charters of 1300; others were without precise precedent. Furthermore, the substance of ten of the eleven articles, more or less amended, was incorporated in the Ordinances which in 1311 the barons were to force on the king in the hope of bringing him under their control. The articles of 1309 included complaints against abuse of the king's right of purveyance and *prises* of foodstuff, the imports on wine, cloth and merchandise, the usurpation of power and jurisdiction by the steward and marshal of the royal household and constables of royal castles and the depreciation of the coinage. The articles also asked for the abolition of the new customs of 1303 and for receivers of petitions in Parliament to deal with petitions that had not been heard. Edward tried to secure the return of Gaveston in exchange for these concessions, but failed.

It is clear from the accounts given in contemporary chronicles and from our general knowledge of the way in which such protestations were brought forward that the articles of 1309 were presented by magnates and barons who had also probably been responsible for the form in which they were finally drawn up. Yet most of the grievances covered, notably over *prises*, were those of the Commons rather than of the baronage. It seems almost certain, therefore, that the substance of the articles was evolved by consultation between magnates and representatives of the Commons, both knights and burgesses. Indeed, the protest against the lack of receivers of petitions in Parliament is specifically stated to have come from the knights and burgesses. The vague term 'community of the realm', in whose name the petition of 1309 was presented, was clearly more than a synonym for magnates and barons; it represented a wider concept of the political nation even though it still seemed natural for the spokesmen for all classes to be

---

[1] *The House of Lords in the Middle Ages*, J. Enoch Powell and Keith Wallis, p. 271; *Dignity of a Peer*, iii, pp. 196–7.
[2] *Rot. Parl.* Vol. I, pp. 443–445. A translation is in B. Wilkinson, *Constitutional History of England*, Vol. III, pp. 362–4.

found among the baronage. What we do not know is the form of such consultation between barons and Commons, or where it took place. In part, it may have happened in Parliament but it has been suggested that there had also been preparatory consultation between earls, barons and knights who had assembled for a tournament held at Dunstable a few weeks before the Parliament. The evidence is purely circumstantial but it is impressive. About thirty-five or forty of the magnates and knights present in Parliament (including six earls) had been at Dunstable. An informal occasion, such as this tournament, provided an excellent opportunity for concerting 'opposition' tactics without suspicions being aroused. Oppositions in all periods try to agree upon their tactics privately before they have to confront the government whose mind they wish to change. In this case, moreover, it seems that the substance of the articles had already been determined at the start of the Parliament, in which case there must have been prior consultation. If, as there is some reason to think, Thomas of Lancaster was responsible for convening the Dunstable tournament, then this may be further evidence suggesting that it was the place where magnates and knights together discussed the grievances of the Commons, for Lancaster was now emerging as the principal opposition leader.[1] The political influence of the class of knights had been growing steadily, and since the conflict between the barons and Henry III, the magnates had usually shown every sign in a crisis of wishing to draw the Commons to their side. It was also in the interest of the barons to insure against disturbances in the land, caused by actions of the king's officials, that brought no advantage to the baronage.

The eleven articles presented to the king in the April Parliament were eventually accepted by him at a further Parliament at Stamford which the Commons and lower clergy did not attend.[2] Whatever might be their influence in parliamentary politics, their formal position in Parliament was still uncertain. It was not until after the king had formally accepted the articles that collection of the taxation conditionally granted in the previous Parliament was begun in August. It was clear evidence that, in practice, financial supply was already becoming dependent on the prior redress of grievances. The political tide, however, was now turning in the king's favour, and Gaveston was back in England. Edward had been manoeuvring with individual magnates to obtain their agreement to his friend's return, and had secured from the Pope the annulment of the sentence of

[1] The case for the Dunstable tournament as the setting for preparatory consultation for the eleven articles of 1309, and for Lancaster as convener of the tournament, is presented by J. R. Maddicott, *Thomas of Lancaster, 1307–1322*, Oxford University Press, 1970, pp. 95–102.
[2] The Articles of Stamford rank as a statute. *Stat. R.* Vol. I, pp. 154–156.

excommunication pronounced by Archbishop Winchelsey on the favourite, should he come back to England. The king's acceptance of the eleven articles in the Statute of Stamford was the price for the favourite's return to which such moderates as Gloucester and Lincoln had no great objection, provided the abuses that disturbed them were remedied. At Stamford, Gaveston even ventured to appear at the king's side. Nevertheless, the magnates present there were willing to agree that Gaveston should remain Earl of Cornwall for life, provided he gave up his hereditary claim. With Lancaster, who was not present at Stamford, it was different. For whatever reasons, his personal detestation of Gaveston remained undiminished and neither he nor Archbishop Winchelsey was reconciled. It was not long before those magnates who had been more or less won over by the king to accept the favourite's return began to move back to Lancaster's opinion. If they had supposed that Gaveston would mend his ways after so narrow an escape from permanent exile they were wrong. The insolence of his behaviour, particularly to the earls, quickly fractured the superficial reconciliation.

In October, the king seems to have attempted to hold a Parliament, or a great council (described by one chronicler as *parliamentum secretum*) at York, but some of the most important magnates, the Earls of Lancaster, Lincoln, Warwick and Arundel refused to come 'because of Peter'.[1] The king, therefore, put off the attempt and, after various delays and manoeuvres, a full Parliament of magnates assembled at Westminster in February 1310. Representatives of the Commons were not summoned; nor were abbots or priors. Nevertheless, the indirect influence of the communities was of fundamental importance to the decision taken in this Parliament to appoint Ordainers to reform the realm. The motive for establishing the Ordainers was not merely the magnates' resentment at Gaveston's arrogance and the gifts that the king still continued to shower on him; no less important was Edward's failure to fulfil the undertakings he had given at Stamford to remedy abuses affecting the communities, particularly those arising from the right of purveyence. The Commons did not attend the Parliament which established the Ordainers, but there can be little doubt that they were present in spirit.

Asserting that their safety was uncertain while Gaveston was at court, the barons let it be known that they would attend the Parliament armed. The king's reply was to prohibit arms to those summoned, and specifically to Lancaster and his friends. By now Edward must have recognized his cousin as the principal opposition leader, and he made the Earl of Gloucester

---

[1] *The Chronicle of Walter of Guisborough*, ed. H. Rothwell (Camden series lxxxix 1957) p. 384.

(whom he had sought to win over by favours) responsible, with three other earls, for seeing that the order prohibiting arms was obeyed. Even so, the opposition leaders defiantly appeared at Westminster under arms, and refused to leave their quarters on the grounds that they would not be safe so long as Gaveston was still with Edward. Eventually the king was forced to send Gaveston away, after which Parliament assembled.

Proceedings began with the rehearsal of grievances in a petition presented (according to one account, by Lancaster himself) to the king. Edward was accused of accepting evil and unsuitable counsel, and of so impoverishing the realm that he could not defend it, or even maintain his household, except by his ministers' extortions. In breach of Magna Carta, it was alleged, the king's servants took from church and people without payment. The king was further accused of losing Scotland, which his father had bequeathed him, with the result that money specifically granted for war, in order to diminish the need for *prises*, had been wasted. The war was not successfully pursued, and yet the burdens on the people were even heavier than before. During the course of this Parliament, the earls and barons continued to hold private meetings, organizing themselves as the opposition in a manner that presaged the behaviour of oppositions in the seventeenth century. Threatened by the withdrawal of the magnates' allegiance, the cornered king finally issued letters patent authorizing the 'prelates, earls and barons of our land to elect certain persons from the prelates, earls, barons and others, whomever they may choose, to ordain and establish the state of our realm and household according to right and reason', before Michaelmas 1311.[1] It was a design for handing over the realm to a government elected by the baronial and episcopal classes, even though the king received assurances that his promise to accept the Ordinances did not constitute a precedent and that his concessions would not prejudice his rights.

The Ordainers were elected in the great Painted Chamber in the old Norman Palace of Westminster. The occasion was the first to leave us with a political reference to the room that was to be important in the assembly of future Parliaments. It had been Henry III's bedchamber and it took its name from the murals, many of them biblical, with which it had been adorned. About eighty feet long and twenty-six feet wide, the room was now used for audiences, and had almost certainly been the chamber in which previous Parliaments had opened when Westminster was their meeting place. Their separate elements met elsewhere after the initial assembly.[2] In the reign

[1] *Rot. Parl.* Vol. I, p. 445.

[2] *King's Works* Vol. I pp. 497–507; see note above, pp. xxi–xxii, on the old Palace of Westminster and list of authorities in select bibliography.

of Edward III, the Painted Chamber was to be renovated and further decorated. Its ceiling was covered with carved and painted bosses and its floor with fine tiles. One of the more outstanding examples of medieval interior decoration, the Painted Chamber survived (though its murals were covered in whitewash and tapestries until 1800) until the great fire which destroyed the old Palace of Westminster in 1834. Even then the shell of this ancient room remained and was not beyond restoration, but in the end the decision was taken to erase it to realize Barry's design for the great new Palace of Westminster. Fortunately, however, the medieval paintings of the Painted Chamber had been uncovered in 1800 and careful copies made of them. From these, replicas were later made which hang in the present Palace of Westminster.

The election of the Ordainers was an act of massive resistance to the royal will. They were chosen by a process of indirect election, as the Council of Fifteen had been in 1258. Once again, the purpose was to achieve balance and the representation of differing shades of opinion, but the method of selection was very different. The Council of Fifteen had been elected by four who had themselves been elected by twenty-four, of whom the king had chosen one half and the barons the other. In 1310, however, the king had no part in the election process at all. The prelates elected two earls who then chose two bishops to join them. These four then elected two barons, and the six proceeded to elect fifteen others to join them, making twenty-one Ordainers in all. They comprised the Archbishop of Canterbury, eight earls, six bishops and six barons. The Ordainers stood at the head of a virtually united baronage, including those most attached to the crown (the moderate reformers Lincoln and Gloucester among them) as well as the most obdurate opposition magnates, led by Lancaster, Hereford and Warwick. Every earl, with the exceptions of Warenne, Oxford and Gaveston himself, was an Ordainer. Within weeks, six preliminary ordinances had been produced covering, among other things, the implementation of Magna Carta and the prohibition of crown gifts except with the consent of the barons. In August the king felt obliged to accept them.

During the ensuing months, Edward did all he could to regain control of events, and sought in various ways to undermine the authority of the Ordainers. To this end, he used his control of royal appointments; he endeavoured to win over individual magnates by inducements of various sorts; he attempted a desultory and ineffective campaign in Scotland during the winter of 1310–1311 (in which the Ordainers, apart from Gloucester, refused their personal co-operation); and he removed the Exchequer and the judicial benches to York, which made it harder for the Ordainers to act in London. All this amounted virtually to the establishment of a dual administration and for the best part of a year Edward remained in the north. He attempted to raise money by loans and by taking the customs, but his financial difficulties increased and a Parliament was unavoidable. For the Ordainers, it was essential that it should be held before their authority expired at Michaelmas and writs were issued summoning a Parliament in August. Edward came south to meet it (leaving Gaveston in the safety of the north) but he procrastinated until the last, even using a pilgrimage to Canterbury to delay his arrival for a few days until after the Parliament was due to meet.

Eventually, however, the king met his Parliament on 16 August, 1311. The work of the Ordainers was now ready for Edward's assent which he at first withheld on the grounds that it infringed his sovereignty. Finally, however, in this full Parliament, which was attended by knights and burgesses as well as by barons and prelates, the king was obliged to assent to forty-one New Ordinances which gravely weakened his authority. Even under this humiliation, Edward further lowered the dignity of the crown by intimating that he would accept any of the Ordinances affecting himself if only Gaveston could be spared. The barons were, however, adamant and the king was forced to accept all the Ordinances, though he did so with the reservation that they could be revoked if their consequences prejudiced the king or the crown. Gaveston was sentenced to perpetual banishment. The charge against him was that he had given the king bad counsel, drawn to himself royal power and dignity, helped himself to the royal treasure, forced the king to alienate crown lands, estranged the king's heart from his people and much more beside (Article 20). Three other aliens were also sentenced to banishment. The most noteworthy of them was the Italian banker Frescobaldi, whom the barons believed to have a stranglehold on the king and also (which was worse in their eyes) to be the means by which Edward might achieve financial independence from the community of the realm. The Ordinances virtually removed the king's powers from almost every aspect of government. He was not to leave the realm, engage in foreign war or, in the event of his agreed absence, to appoint a keeper of the realm, without 'the common assent of his baronage, and that in Parliament' (Article 9). The great officers of state and also the officials of the royal household were to be appointed only 'with the counsel and the assent of his baronage, and that in Parliament'. Those officers of state listed included the chancellor, treasurer and justices, and among the household officials were the keepers of the wardrobe and of the privy seal, through which household departments the king often acted administratively, thus by-passing the departments of state, the chancery and the exchequer (Article 14). Likewise, when the king wished to change the coinage (by which, it was said, the people always suffered greatly) it was only to be done by the common counsel of the baronage in Parliament (Article 30), and this form of words was repeated in each of the Ordinances which was designed to control the king's future political and administrative actions.

There was also an attack on financial mismanagement and the reduction of the royal demesne and revenue which had been brought about by the alienation of land to favourites. All such gifts of land, castles and other benefits (by which the crown had been 'reduced and dismembered') since the Ordainers were given their commission in March 1310, were to be revoked, and any such future gifts were forbidden until the king's debts had been paid off and his state 'sufficiently restored'. Anyone accepting such gifts would be punished 'in Parliament by the award of the baronage' (Article 7). This requirement for the resumption of royal estates was to be the key to the final break between the king and the Earl of Lancaster in the middle of the reign. Other articles provided that the customs and royal revenues were in future to go straight to the exchequer, and not through the Frescobaldi, who had been exploiting the customs. However, an allowance from the customs was to be made by the exchequer for the household expenses so that the king might in future 'live of his own without taking *prises* other than the ancient, due and rightful ones' (Article 8). That the king should live of his own without recourse to other taxes was a recurrent theme of politics for several centuries to come, and the failure of the ideal to be matched by the reality was a major stimulus to parliamentary power.

These attempts to restore the crown's revenue from accepted sources and by controllable means were balanced by provisions designed to prevent the king from raising money in other ways, with the result that it was virtually impossible for him to achieve the solvency the Ordainers themselves desired. But the over-riding object of the opposition to Edward II, like that of all medieval opposition, was to make it impossible for the king to achieve independence by money raised without consent. This was the significance of Article 10 which sought to control the abuse of the king's feudal right to acquire food and other commodities for his household at a proper price. It began by asserting that although it had been 'formerly ordained' that the king 'should live of his own without taking *prises* other than the ancient due and accustomed ones . . .' nevertheless 'undue *prises* are taken every day' contrary to the former ordinance. For this reason, all *prises* that were not rightful were now to cease. The underlying question here went far deeper than the correction of the abuse of *prises* in order to feed and maintain his household. The objection was not merely to the taking of such *prises* without payment (though that was a real enough grievance). More fundamentally, the practice that the Ordainers sought to eradicate was the expansion of this feudal right so that *prises* could be used to provision, not only the itinerant royal household, but also whole armies – leaving the peasantry to shoulder much of the cost of war, since payment was very often either much delayed or not made at all. Both Edward II and his father had taken national *prises* to support their Scottish campaigns, and the purveyors were bitterly accused of extortion and corruption. Although the baronial class represented by the Ordainers did not itself suffer from this abuse, the barons had a strong interest in seeing that the mass of the peasantry, which bore the brunt of it, were not stirred to insurrection. Article 10 of the New Ordinances stated bluntly that it was 'to be feared that the people of the land will rise on account of the *prises* and divers oppressions. . . .'

There was also, however, a constitutional implication which was still deeper than the fear of disorder. From the thirteenth to the seventeenth century, it was the perennial object of the political nation to deny the king any sources of taxation which he could levy at his own discretion, and which he could use to enable him to escape from coming to Parliament for tax grants. The first two Edwards used, or misused, *prises* precisely as King John had used reliefs and wardships, stretching customary feudal obligations beyond their original, limited and reasonable purpose so as to obtain payments in money or in kind without recourse to a grant that had to be negotiated. They were able to do so because, although the original purposes of the ancient feudal rights were clearly enough understood, they had no specified legal limits. Yet by now it was generally recognized that the king was not entitled to raise a tax on movables without a parliamentary grant and that taxation required consent. Why, then, should he be allowed to obtain the equivalent in kind of tax-money by taking wholesale *prises* without any grant or consultation? The New Ordinances therefore decreed that if any unlawful *prises* were taken without being paid for, and against the will of the seller, the pursuit of hue and cry should be raised against the offender, who was to be taken to the nearest gaol and to have 'the common law . . . applied to him as a robber or a thief, if he is convicted of that'. Thus in one more baronial document, we find implicitly enshrined one of the most fundamental of parliamentary principles.[1]

The New Ordinances, however, also made an explicit claim for the place of Parliament as a necessary and routine instrument in government. Many other particular grievances, including those arising from the forest law were covered, but in constitutional terms the most notable Ordinance (Article 29) was that which required Parliaments to be held once a year in a

---

[1] For a clear account of the constitutional and financial significance of the Ordinance against *prises*, see J. R. Maddicott, *Thomas of Lancaster, 1307–1322*, pp. 106–109.

convenient place, and twice a year if need be. In each Parliament, a committee of lords (comprising one bishop, two earls and two barons) was to be appointed to hear complaints against the king's ministers. The given reason for annual Parliaments was to enable pleas that had been held up, or cases where justices had been of differing opinions, to be determined, and likewise to enable bills that are delivered in Parliament to be determined, 'so far as law and reason required it'.[1] The judicial function was clearly stated as the reason for regular Parliaments but equally the Ordinances repeatedly required that stipulated political acts should be done only in Parliament, and with the barons' counsel.

The question that naturally follows is what part the various elements of Parliament played in the formulation and acceptance of the New Ordinances. The Ordainers who produced them consisted only of earls, barons and prelates, and the Parliament which appointed the Ordainers was an assembly of magnates in which the Commons had no part. The Parliament of 1311 which forced the king to accept the Ordinances did, however, include representatives of the communities, and although their primary role was that of witnesses rather than initiators, it would be unjustified to assume that representatives of the Commons had no part at all in influencing what was done. The Ordinances were, it is true, a baronial document both in their conception and their execution. Yet the likelihood is that knights were consulted on certain general grievances and points of detail (the question of *prises* is one obvious probability) as the broad framework of the Ordinances was prepared, just as they had almost certainly been consulted when the articles of 1309 were drawn up. The knights clearly had no active part to play in the Parliament of 1311 at the point when the Ordainers finally made their decisions and confronted the king with them. But their knowledge and opinions may well have provided useful evidence in the earlier stages of the work on some of the Ordinances. Yet the most important function of the Commons was witnessing and approving the reform of government. Their presence helped to signify the assent of the community of the realm; their witness enabled them to report to their own communities what had been lawfully done.

That the ordaining Parliament of 1311 was an important landmark for the Commons is clear. There had been seven Parliaments in the first two and a half years of Edward's reign, at only three of which the Commons were

---

[1] *Stat. R.*, Vol. I, pp. 157–167 (French); translation in *E.H.D.* Vol. III pp. 527–539. For discussion of the New Ordinances, see especially B. Wilkinson, *Studies in the Constitutional History of the Thirteenth and Fourteenth Centuries*, (1937) Ch. IX 'The Ordinances of 1311' pp. 227–264; J. Conway Davies, *The baronial opposition to Edward II* (1918) and T. F. Tout, *The Place of Edward II in English History* (1914).

represented. But from the August Parliament of 1311 at which the king was obliged to accept the Ordinances until the end of the reign in 1327, the Commons were invariably present with but two exceptions.[1] One was the York Parliament of Hilary, 1320, which Thomas of Lancaster would refuse to attend on the grounds that it was improper to hold a Parliament behind closed doors, a probable comment on the absence of the witnessing representatives of the communities. The other was the midsummer Parliament of 1325.[2] The position of the Commons was not yet formally recognized as necessary for a Parliament, but their presence was already now acknowledged as politically important as well as being necessary for tax-granting. It seems, however, to be straining logic somewhat to see any significant contrast between their political importance and their assumed constitutional non-importance.[3] The line between the political and the constitutional is always indeterminate, and if there is any over-riding lesson to be learned from the history of the English Parliament it is that the constitution of the realm is and always has been the evolving expression of its politics. In that sense we can fairly say that the politics of the Ordinances laid the foundations for the permanent place of the Commons in Parliament, and that the violent politics of the rest of Edward II's reign established it. In 1311 the Commons, like the magnates, ministers and justices, seem to have sworn to uphold the Ordinances. Their presence at Parliament was a sign of their future political weight, and in the turbulence that lay ahead both king and Parliament would find their support so worth seeking that by the end of the reign they would be firmly established as a permanent element of Parliament.[4]

The Ordinances themselves, however, had nothing to say about the composition of a Parliament, and contained nothing to suggest that the Commons had any right to be present, or that a Parliament was less a Parliament when they were absent. Even the requirement of an annual Parliament was included as much to ensure the speedy handling of the pleas and petitions which could only be dealt with in Parliament as to reinforce

---

[1] H. G. Richardson and G. O. Sayles, 'The English Parliaments of Edward II', *BIHR*, VI (1928), 71–88 (reprinted in their collection of articles *The English Parliament in the Middle Ages*).

[2] For references to the Parliaments of 1320 and 1325, see pp. 211–2 and p. 223 respectively.

[3] The conclusion that they were politically but not constitutionally important is argued by Richardson and Sayles in the article referred to above.

[4] M. V. Clarke, *Medieval Representation and Consent*, 1936, p. 161. 'It seems clear that the year 1311 may well be taken as a turning point in the history of the Commons. It is from that date that their regular summons to Parliament can be traced and, from that time, as the personal struggle for power grew more dangerous, both king and barons steadily competed for their support.'

the baronial control of the crown. Yet we can judge the thinking and intentions of the Ordainers to some extent by the attitudes subsequently struck by their party, which show the value they set by Parliament as a political instrument. Throughout the future years of his conflict with the king, Lancaster persistently demanded that important political decisions should be taken in Parliament; he saw Parliaments as the means by which the *complete* baronage could be assembled in order to make the king feel its weight. The requirement of annual Parliaments (or two a year if necessary) was also bound in practice to reinforce the idea that Parliaments were now an indestructable part of the process of governing.

The importance which the nation was required to attach to the Ordinances was demonstrated by the ceremony with which they were proclaimed in St Paul's churchyard in the presence of the great magnates of the land and the members of the king's close council. Yet no thought-out concept of constitutional change inspired the new devices for government. They were the result not of theory but of political action motivated by personal rivalries, emotions and ambitions joined with the discontent of particular groups which felt that their interest was insufficiently regarded. The barons who devised the Ordinances were driven to innovation not because they were natural innovators but because they had to deal with a king who was incapable of rising to the demands of his political role, of paying what the magnates regarded as proper regard to their political standing, or of contenting the communities. The ingredient of rage, which is so often the necessary tinder for political action, was provided by the intolerable insolence of Gaveston. After his return from his first exile, he had been more foolhardy than ever. He even took to jeering at the magnates with offensive nicknames. Warwick was the 'black dog of Arden', Lancaster a 'play actor', Pembroke, 'Joseph the Jew'. Such was the folly of the favourite who had estranged the king from his natural counsellors.[1]

As for the king who would exalt such an upstart, it was also objectionably

---

[1] Observing that Gaveston's 'arrogance was intolerable to the barons' the author of *Vita Edwardi Secundi* remarks: 'I therefore believe and firmly maintain that if Piers had borne himself prudently and humbly towards the magnates of the land, none of them would ever have opposed him.' That is probably stating the point too strongly. This contemporary writer's 'secondary cause' of the baron's hatred was probably the more important – namely 'that if an earl or baron entered the king's chamber to speak with the king, in Piers' presence, the king addressed no-one, and to none showed a friendly countenance save to Piers only'. It was Gaveston's usurpation of the position of chief counsellor and the use he made of his influence to batten on the royal finances that principally aroused the barons against him, though his manners, his foreignness and his lower status all fuelled the fires of resentment. A less arrogant or a more cunning or circumspect man might, however, have got away with the influence he was able to use with the king.

easy for him to make his policy on the advice of dependent bureaucrats rather than on that of the barons. It was through the power of such resentments rather than the force of constitutional conviction that a document of considerable significance in the evolution of Parliament was forced into law – if, indeed, it *was* law when the king's assent was given under duress. In its purported intention it was a conservative document. The Ordinances were designed to revive the tradition by which the king took advice from his natural counsellors. Yet it was a tradition that had always been applied loosely, according to the circumstances of the moment, and had never been subject to strict rules of enforcement. Consultation had depended on the commonsense of the king, not on 'constitutional' rules and provisions such as these were.

If the Ordinances had remained in force to the letter, their effect, far from being conservative, would have fundamentally altered the traditional balance of power between king and baronage, making the baronage supreme in the affairs of the nation and removing the king's discretion in government. They were therefore quite inconsistent with the medieval assumption that the king should rule personally, albeit in a way generally acceptable to his subjects. For that reason, though they could and did affect the general trend of thinking, it was hardly possible that they could endure, without a much more fundamental change in the general attitude to kingship than was possible to the medieval mind.

It was all but impossible in an age when all political initiatives and channels of administrative and political action flowed from the king, to enforce such sweeping restrictions on his personal rule. However, a further Parliament of barons, knights and burgesses in November produced additional Ordinances removing other specified individuals from the court. For a time Gaveston himself lay low, though whether he ever went abroad in obedience to his banishment is not certain. In any case, he was back openly with the king by Christmas. In January the two of them set out for the north, and Edward took the chancery and the great seal with him. This effectively kept control of such government as there was in his hands, since it was impossible to act legitimately in the middle ages without the proper authorization of a recognized seal. Nor could the magnates make him remove his officials. The king then reinstated Gaveston, proclaiming that he had been exiled against law and custom, that he had returned at the king's order, and that his lands were restored to him. Thus the Ordinance against Gaveston was specifically set aside at the king's will, and although a proclamation issued from the king's headquarters in York declared that the customs and laws of the kingdom were to be observed, it also made clear that the recent Ordinances would be observed only inasmuch as they did not damage or prejudice the king and his crown. A commission was appointed to treat with the barons for the revision of those Ordinances that did so. In his determination to disregard the Ordinances, Edward had even brought back as Treasurer his father's unpopular servant, Walter Langton, Bishop of Coventry and Lichfield, despite the Ordinance requiring that ministers should be appointed with the approval of the baronage in Parliament, or when no Parliament was in being, by the counsel of those who were nearest to hand.

The brink of civil war had been reached and Thomas of Lancaster now had no rival as leader of the growing opposition. He had become a man of immense territorial power. His father-in-law, the old Earl of Lincoln and Salisbury, had died in February 1311, before the Parliament in which the king had been forced to accept the Ordinances. Thomas now possessed five earldoms, having inherited those of Lincoln and Salisbury to add to those of Lancaster, Leicester and Derby which he had held already. He also had the prestige of royal kinship; his father had been Edmund, second son of Henry III and the nominal king of Sicily. A crude and forceful man, who was quick to resort to violence, Lancaster knew how to use his own power to destroy the king's but lacked the political capacity to devise a lasting settlement, though that would have been difficult even for the most subtle of politicians who would have had to cope with Edward's waywardness. Determined that Gaveston should not be allowed to survive in the king's favour, Lancaster and the leading magnates now formed a league to defend the Ordinances and followed the king north with their own armed forces. Edward and Gaveston were nearly seized at Newcastle by the Earls Pembroke and Warenne, but they narrowly escaped to Scarborough where the king left his friend, as he supposed, in safety, moving on himself to York.

Within a fortnight, however, Gaveston was forced to surrender for lack of supplies. He did so with a guarantee by Aymer de Valence, Earl of Pembroke, that he would be safe until a decision about his future was reached in Parliament, which it was later agreed should meet at Lincoln. On the way south in Pembroke's custody, Gaveston was seized by the Earl of Warwick with an armed party. The prisoner had been resting at a rectory guarded by the servants of Pembroke in the earl's temporary absence. Gaveston was taken as though he were a common criminal to Warwick Castle where, after some kind of arbitrary judgement which could not be described as a trial, he was condemned to death and handed over to Lancaster, Arundel and Hereford. In their presence and before a rejoicing crowd of Lancaster's vassals, he was executed on Lancaster's territory near Kenilworth. Warwick and his associates claimed that Gaveston had been justly condemned because, under the Ordinances, he was an outlaw and was without the law's protection. To Edward and his friends, however, the deed was murder since Edward had repealed the clause in the Ordinance by which Gaveston had been banished, though Warwick claimed not to have known that the king had done so. It could also be argued that Gaveston had been unjustly slain since he had not been tried by his peers. Which side had the better case in terms of strict legality hangs on the deeper question of whether the king could, by his own will alone, legally revoke Ordinances which he had only accepted under duress. What is certain, is that this was the first major act of judicial murder in the fourteenth century and it had a profound effect. The killing of a defeated man by his political foes set a precedent. The immediate consequence, however, was that far from assisting the king's opponents, the execution of the favourite effectively destroyed baronial unity. Pembroke and Warenne, who had given their word on Gaveston's safety, were so outraged that they went over to the king. Pembroke was never to forgive Lancaster. Edward, stricken with grief but sensing the need for caution, returned to London and negotiations began for a compromise.

Writs had been issued earlier for the Parliament which was to have met at Lincoln but this had been prorogued. The Parliament, consisting of knights and burgesses as well as barons and diocesan clergy, was then re-summoned to meet at Westminster towards the end of August, but was apparently adjourned, the Commons being told to go home until 30 September. When Parliament finally assembled it sat through the autumn until 16 December, as the king and his supporters negotiated with the opposition barons for a peace. Edward argued against the validity of the Ordinances and the barons conceded that the country ought to be governed by ancient laws and customs rather than by a written code. But they also asserted that the king, prelates, earls and barons had a duty to amend these laws and customs at the complaint of the people.[1] It was a clear restatement of the parliamentary idea that government should respond to those who represented the people, which the barons, as the community of the realm, claimed to do. What occupied the Commons during this Parliament is not clear; the main business was that which the magnates of the realm had with the king and his servants, and this was conducted warily between the two sides under letters of safe-conduct. Just before Christmas a peace was proclaimed. In return for a general amnesty, the barons were to submit to the king and receive his pardon in a Parliament which was to meet in March. No one was to be prosecuted for Gaveston's death. One important provision of the agreement was that in all future Parliaments and other assemblies henceforth,

---

[1] *Annales Londoniensis*, 1194–1330, p. 210–215.

men should come without force and without arms, peaceably to the honour of the king and the peace of the realm.

Lancaster and Warwick, however, were still resisting submission, and uncertainty persisted throughout 1313. In that year, three Parliaments were held, each attended by knights and burgesses as well as by prelates, abbots and barons. Lancaster, Warwick and Hereford, however, refused to come to the first two Parliaments which were held in the spring and summer, making the excuse that the form of writs they had received was not in accordance with precedence, though what the pretended flaw was is not known. Nothing of importance concerning the greater political questions took place at these Parliaments, and nothing was settled. We know little of what passed, and there are no parliamentary rolls for the Parliaments of these years. Bread-and-butter politics, however, were not altogether at a standstill despite the rivalries of great men and factions. One parliamentary enactment was an ordinance setting up the first compulsory wool staple at a place to be decided by the merchants of the staple (St. Omer was chosen) through which all English wool for Flanders, Brabant and Artois must pass. The merchants probably paid well for this concession, and as is the habit of opposition leaders in Parliament in every age, Thomas of Lancaster saw the other side of the case, subsequently taking up the cause of the alien merchants who suffered from this arrangement.[1]

Throughout the year, the country remained in considerable tension, with the government trying to prevent the barons from holding tournaments which might provide opportunities for mobilizing the forces of opposition. In September, however, after the king had paid a brief visit to France, a third Parliament was held. It was prefaced by writs to the Earls of Lancaster, Gloucester, Warwick, Arundel, Surrey and Hereford, forbidding them from going to a tournament, which they were intending to do, against the king's prohibition and despite having been summoned to Parliament on the following Sunday. However, Lancaster and his friends did come to Parliament, letters of safe conduct having been issued to them and their adherents.[2] A great reconciliation then took place in Westminster Hall, Lancaster and his associates asking and receiving the king's forgiveness. Pardons were issued and statutes were promulgated indemnifying those lords and lesser men who had been involved in Gaveston's death, and forbidding armed attendance at Parliaments.[3] A tax on movables was granted for the war in Scotland. By accepting the king's pardon, the

---

[1] May McKisack, *The Fourteenth Century, 1307–1399*, pp. 350–351.
[2] *Dignity of a Peer*, Vol. I, pp. 266–267.
[3] *Stat. R.* Vol. I, pp. 169 and 170.

Ordainers virtually conceded that the Ordinances affecting Gaveston had been null and void from the moment that the king, by his own will, had rescinded them. The implication was that if the king insisted, the same would apply to the other Ordinances as well. In this sense it was an unconditional victory for the king, achieved because Pembroke and others had been impelled to his support by Lancaster's extremism. At the end of this phase of the struggle, the king had no constraints upon his freedom of action.

Yet the very totality of Edward's victory was a source of weakness in a king who lacked the skill and subtlety to rebuild a genuine accord with the baronage. If the king could always countermand at will what he had been forced to concede under duress, and if he persisted indefinitely in unacceptable government, it would follow logically that there was no remedy in the end but to remove him. This dilemma of personal monarchy had been the real, though not yet absorbed, lesson of 1215–1216 and of the years of conflict after 1258. It was again the lesson of 1313, though the men then challenging the king shrank from its political logic. It was to be different in 1327, and again in 1399, 1649 and 1688–89, when with various degrees of reluctance the logic was accepted, and when more or less spurious forms of parliamentary proceedings were variously contrived to give deposition some appearance of lawfulness. At the heart of all politics lies an ultimate question: what is to be done when the legitimacy of government, after which all societies hanker, comes into full conflict with the consciences or interests of powerful social groups which cannot, or will not accept the actions of the legitimate authority? More deeply still, where is legitimacy of government ultimately to be found? Formulating the question is, perhaps, as near as we can get to finding the answer.

II

In the struggle for power which persisted through virtually the entire reign of Edward II, there were only the shortest of intermissions. The next act opened with the humiliating defeat of the English at Bannockburn. Since the death of Edward I, Robert Bruce had made himself master of almost all Scotland. Only a few fortresses were still held by the English king, and it was to relieve one of the most important of these that in 1314 Edward II led a substantial English army into Scotland. This emergency apart, there was reason enough for him to do so. The English north had suffered persistent and devastating Scottish raids with the purpose of extracting money from the inhabitants for temporary truces. Besides, Edward badly needed a military success to rebuild his battered prestige at home. What precipitated the decision to invade Scotland, however, was an arrangement made between the English governor of Stirling and Edward Bruce, the brother of Robert, who had besieged the castle. The Scots had temporarily raised the siege on condition that the castle would be surrendered to them on Midsummer Day unless an English relieving force had appeared within three leagues of the castle by then. It was a challenge Edward was bound to take up. A Parliament that had been due to meet at Westminster in April was cancelled, and the king prepared to lead the invasion. The earls put it to him that it would be better for all to meet beforehand in Parliament to determine what should be done, which would also, they pointed out, accord with the requirement of the Ordinances that the king should not leave the country nor engage in foreign war without the consent of the baronage in Parliament.[1] Edward, however, rejected this advice on the grounds that the need for action was urgent. Instead, he demanded military service from them. In a matter so closely affecting English honour, it was hard for the magnates to resist. A number of them accompanied the king, and although Lancaster, Warwick and Warenne obdurately refused to take part, even they sent their due quota of knights for military service.

The battle of Bannockburn appears to have been lost largely through the king's incompetence. Rejecting advice from the Earl of Gloucester that the army should be given time to rest, Edward allowed his tired soldiers to be engaged in battle with unnecessary speed and in a dangerously narrow and marshy field. Here his cavalry in the front line faced an impenetrable wall of Scottish infantrymen with massed shields and pikes. Edward's infantrymen were immobilized behind the English horse, and the arrows of the English archers, who had been placed in the rear, struck the backs of their own side. The defeat at Bannockburn on 24 June, 1314, was a deep humiliation for the king, who was forced to flee. Among many English noblemen slain or captured was the young Earl of Gloucester, whose death led to the division of his earldom between three favourite courtiers of the king, and thus contributed indirectly to the civil war which was to be the climax of the reign. With Gloucester's death, Edward also lost the counsel of an intrinsically loyal though independent magnate who, though he had felt driven to intervene against Gaveston's restoration in defiance of the Ordinances, had nevertheless been a principal mediator after the favourite's death, and was essentially a moderating influence.

[1] *Vita Edwardi Secundi*, edited by N. Denholm Young, pp. 49-50.

Bannockburn, which made Robert Bruce *de facto* king of Scotland, was disastrous for Edward II. Had he been victorious, he could have turned against Lancaster. As it was, he was obliged to go straight from his defeat to a Parliament at York where Lancaster and other magnates insisted that things had only gone so badly because the king had not observed the Ordinances as he had sworn to do. Edward therefore agreed that he would observe and execute the Ordinances. He was also obliged to change his officials, including the chancellor and the treasurer, and in the following months most of the sheriffs were also replaced by new men. Hugh Despenser, a persistently royalist baron and official who had supported Gaveston in his difficulties and had been one of the king's chief negotiators with the Ordainers after the favourite's death, was forced to retire from the court.[1]

For the next two years, Thomas of Lancaster was virtually master of the realm.[2] With Gloucester slain, and after the death of Warwick in 1315, Lancaster had no equals. As though he were some kind of second king he would give written orders to Edward's ministers, and was in ultimate control of appointments. Yet he often acted from a distance, keeping away from the council itself. Why he so absented himself is not clear. The explanation may partly lie in ill-health, for which there is some evidence. His energies were perhaps also absorbed in the management of his own estates, though if that was a major cause of his absence it is hard to see why other earls, Pembroke and Hereford in particular, found so much more time than Lancaster to give to the council. It is also possible that he was motivated by a wish to preserve his independence, and handicapped by a temperamental difficulty in working with others. He may well have found it particularly hard to cooperate with men of more or less equal social standing but of less power, who might wish to exert critical influence on his unquestioned leadership of the former opposition which was now in power. But whatever the reason, he failed to act as an effective king's minister. Lancaster was the one consistent opposition magnate during most of the reign. As others shifted ground between court and opposition, searching for compromise, he never diminished his insistence on the complete enforcement of the Ordinances. This arrogant, privately immoral and brutal magnate was something of a purist in politics and unwilling to temporize. He was not the first or the last political leader to find the

---

[1] *Vita Edwardi Secundi*, pp. 57–58.

[2] The definitive account of Lancaster's political life is J. R. Maddicott, *Thomas of Lancaster, 1302–22* (1970), one of the key studies of the politics of the reign and on which this account is greatly reliant.

dogmatic formulae of opposition and the quest for power in the name of uncompromising principle or theory more attractive than the practical management of affairs, or the constructive use of power when it came within his grasp. Whatever the reasons for it, Lancaster's disinclination to attend the council was inevitably a weakness, and his position was further undermined by a lack of friends. This was due in part to the fact that the anti-court cause had lacked a unifying stimulus since the death of Gaveston. The favourite's pretensions to influence had been vastly greater than their political reality. But his arrogance and posturing had provided a catalyst for baronial unity, illustrating very well how great political events may turn on accidents of personality. Now Gaveston was dead, what precisely was the baronial cause? Besides, Lancaster also suffered the loss of old allies either by desertion (Pembroke and Warenne) or by death (Archbishop Winchelsey, and in the following year Warwick, the closest of all his associates).

In January 1315, a Parliament met at Westminster. Like its predecessor at York and its successor at Lincoln, it was largely preoccupied with Scotland and with the defence of the ravaged north. But it also took the reorganization of government a stage further. Hugh Despenser was now removed from the king's council altogether, and 'the unnecessary members of his household, overburdensome to the king, and to the land', as it was said, were also ejected. 'By that displacement the daily expenses of the king's household were reduced by ten pounds.'[1] Still more important, a serious start was now made to implement the requirement in the Ordinances that grants of lands and castles given by the king since 1310 should be revoked. The resumption of alienated crown property caused great discontent among men now called upon to give up lands they had received for services rendered.

The Parliament also had before it more ordinary matters. There is, for instance, among the petitions one from the 'great lords of England' (*les grantz Seign' d'Engleterre*), the prelates, earls and barons, which concerns the service due from the totality of their fees, for only part of which, it appears, did they usually perform service. From this we see that, although the pleas and petitions are described on the Parliament roll as being before the king and his great council in Parliament (*coram Rege & Magno Consilio in Parliamento Regis* . . .), the magnates of the greater council could themselves be petitioners. In this case, clearly, the council which responded to them was the king's select or close council.[2] Another petition seems to refer to a

[1] *Vita Edwardi Secundi*, p. 59.
[2] *Dignity of a Peer*, Vol. I, p. 268.

problem of lawlessness which was emerging from a new economic and social catastrophe far more devastating than the power struggle between barons and king. The commonalty of England (*la communaute d'Engleterre*) submitted a petition concerning the 'conspirators who are in every city, borough, hundred and wapentake in England'.[1] It appears to refer to the breakdown of social order as a result of a great dearth and famine which now afflicted the land, and which persisted throughout the period of Lancaster's power. The north had already been rendered almost ungovernable by the Scottish depredations, on which grounds the shires granted a twentieth and the boroughs a fifteenth for military expenses.

Far more devastating, however, were the consequences of torrential rains which fell throughout the land during the autumn of 1314 and in 1315. Harvests were ruined, and floods destroyed crops and seeds, bringing famine, disease and lawlessness. Unspeakable misery ensued, sheep and cattle were ravaged with disease, and the price of wheat rose eightfold. In this Parliament, therefore, 'because merchants going about the country selling victuals charged excessively, the earls and barons, looking to the welfare of the state, appointed a remedy for this malady; they ordained a fixed price for oxen, pigs and sheep, for fowls, chickens and pigeons and for other common foods'. It was also provided and granted that the Gascons should carry their wines to English ports, and there sell it by the barrel according to the price assigned in Parliament and that Englishmen should not in future cross the sea as forestallers seeking wine. These matters were published throughout the land, and publicly proclaimed in shirecourts and boroughs. The parliamentary roll records a petition to the king and council from the archbishops, bishops, earls and barons that he would ordain certain prices for certain articles of food, and it is noted that prices were determined by the council for various commodities such as, for instance, 'the best live beef'.[2] This early attempt at what twentieth century politicians would describe as a statutory prices policy was unsuccessful, and was repealed in the next Parliament. Its only effect was to encourage the withholding of food from the market. 'For as a result of that statute little or nothing was exposed for sale in the markets, whereas formerly there had been an abundant market in goods, though they seemed dear to travellers. But it is better to buy dear than to find in case of need that there is nothing to be had. For although scarcity of corn raises the price, subsequent plenty will

---

[1] *Rot. Parl.* Vol. I, p. 268.

[2] *Vita Edwardi Secundi*, p. 59, *Rot. Parl.* Vol. I, p. 295, (*Il semble au conseil q' le meilleur boef vif*, etc.); *Foedera* II, pp. 263, 366.

The earliest surviving depiction (*c.* 1544–5) of the old palace of Westminster from the London panorama drawn by A van den Wyngaerde. (Ashmolean Museum, Oxford.) The Painted Chamber is on the left of St Stephen's Chapel, the gothic pinnacles of which were still in place when the drawing was made.

Westminster Hall, the oldest and principal building of the medieval Palace of Westminster to survive the great fire which destroyed the rest of the Palace in 1834. Built by William Rufus *c.* 1097, the great hall was reconstructed by Richard II after 1394, with new windows and the replacement of the original Norman columns by the massive hammer-beam roof which spans the whole width.

PARLIAMENT
OF EDWARD I.

The Parliament of Edward I from an engraving of a depiction by a Tudor artist, who shows accurate knowledge of the period. The archbishops, bishops and lay lords are in their appropriate places and, correctly, the Commons are not present. Alexander, King of the Scots and Llywelyn, Prince of Wales are placed on either side of the King. Each was present in one of Edward's parliaments but not on the same occasion.

'The Painted Chamber, looking into the House of Lords, 1834,' by Thomas Clark, a water colour of the ruins after the fire of that year and before the chamber was demolished. The House of Lords indicated here was not the White Chamber occupied by the Lords in the middle ages but the chamber known then as the Lesser Hall, or Court of Requests to which the Lords had moved in 1801.

Above: The Coronation of Edward the Confessor. *Below:* The battle of Judas Maccabeus with Timotheus and the Fall of Maspha. Water colour copies by Charles Stothard of the remains of the magnificent murals for which the Painted Chamber was celebrated in the 13th and 14th centuries. Copies by Stothard and by Edward Crocker are the basis of reconstructions later made by E. W. Tristram. (see Frontispiece.)

The White Chamber, the medieval House of Lords, or Parliament House, after the Lords had left it for the Lesser or Little Westminster Hall (also known as the Court of Requests in 1801. (Detail from an engraving in J. T. Smith, *Antiquities of Westminster*, 1807.) Built by Henry III for Queen Eleanor, the White Chamber was demolished in 1823. It had been the Lords' normal meeting place since the reign of Edward III. The Lords' move to the Lesser Westminster Hall (where they remained until the fire of 1834) followed the increase in their number by the incorporation of representative Irish peers and bishops under the Act of Union of 1800.

The Chapter House, Westminster Abbey, the meeting place of the Commons in the second half of the 14th century until their move to the refectory in 1395. Though heavily restored, the Chapter House still has original wall paintings and sculptures and the original tile floor.

Thirteenth-century sculptures in the Chapter House of Westminster Abbey. *Left:* The Virgin Mary. *Right:* The Archangel Gabriel.

improve the situation.'[1] This attempt at price restraint appears to have been drawn up by the king's privy council, acting in response to the petition of the magnates, in which the Commons had no part, though the writs to the sheriffs are in terms suggesting that some individuals of the community, perhaps of the Commons in Parliament, were consulted. The king, it seems, was given the ordinance (it was not a statute) to approve after the council had made it.[2]

During the whole of 1315, the condition of the country was extremely disturbed. Lancaster himself, a harsh overlord, experienced a serious revolt by tenants in his own county, which required a strong force to quell it. In dealing with this challenge to his territorial authority, Lancaster had the king's cooperation. Indeed, for a time there appeared to be a measure of superficial goodwill between them. To forget that Edward and Lancaster, despite all that divided them, were cousins and familiars is to misunderstand the social structure of the time. Lancaster was not an outsider stamping into the king's presence and threatening force but a kinsman who, before Edward had ascended the throne, had been numbered among his friends. There was substance in Thomas's claim to be considered the chief of Edward's natural counsellors, and the king had at last recognized this by formally accepting the Ordinances which were the be-all and end-all of Thomas' programme. The Ordinance by which Lancaster set most store, and which now had the most practical political consequences, was the requirement that the king should resume possession of all gifts of land made since 1310, and make no others until such time as the royal finances had been restored. Naturally, this caused deep resentment against the earl among the ousted beneficiaries of royal patronage, but it did much to assist recovery of the king's finances. Edward, however, while nominally accepting the requirement did his best to resist its application. As for the earl, he was incapable of looking beyond the letter of the Ordinances to promote lasting peace through reconciliation. The Ordinances have been interpreted as expressing 'an ideal of reformation working in men's brains rather than a new act of Parliament which it was intended to carry out',[3] and that indeed had been the attitude of the baronage in general. But Lancaster at least was determined to enforce them literally at the expense of the general spirit of orderly and consultative government which they were supposed to express. That was his weakness and ultimately the cause of his downfall.

Lancaster was at the height of his power, with no effective court party to

---
[1] *Vita Edwardi Secundi*, pp. 68–69.
[2] *Dignity of A Peer*, Vol. I, p. 269.
[3] T. F. Tout, *The Place of the Reign of Edward II in English History*, p. 29.

oppose him, when the next Parliament met at Lincoln in January 1316. It is the first Parliament of whose proceedings we have a 'full and intelligible record'[1] which was made on the parliamentary roll by the principal clerk of the chancery, William Airmyn, later Bishop of Norwich. As we have seen, the rolls of Parliament had hitherto provided little more than an unsystematic record of pleas and petitions and oddments of various sorts. At Lincoln, in contrast, Airmyn's account of the day-to-day proceedings, which was apparently specially commissioned by the king himself, provided an example that was generally, though not invariably, followed for later Parliaments by the chancery clerks who had the job of compiling the roll.[2]

As well as the magnates and prelates, knights and burgesses were summoned to Lincoln, where meetings of the Parliament took place in various buildings on different days, opening in the dean's house and continuing later in the chapter house of the cathedral and the Carmelite friary. (According to the writs for expenses, there were only burgesses from eight boroughs whereas there were knights from 32 shires. But the writs for the collection of expenses may well not be an accurate indication of the numbers attending, some of whom may have been paid by their own boroughs, or may not have collected the money due to them.) The duration of the Parliament was short though the action was dramatic. It lasted for no more than three weeks, and Edward himself provided one explanation. At the outset of the Parliament, he expressed his hope that business would be despatched as quickly as possible because 'the prelates, earls and others had come thither from great distances, and their stay, if prolonged, would be both tedious and burdensome on account of the high prices of food'.[3] The king communicated his mind in a speech opening the proceedings of Parliament, which was made by William Inge, a justice of the common

---

[1] T. F. Tout, op. cit. pp. 184–185; *Rot. Parl.* Vol. I, pp. 350–364.

[2] Richardson and Sayles, in 'The Early Records of the English Parliament', *BIHR* VI (1929), pp. 141–142, contend that this roll was not a narrative account of some of the principal stages of a Parliament, but was 'devised *ad hoc*, as a sort of protocol to record the steps leading to the agreement between the earl of Lancaster and the king not an attempt to give a full account of the proceedings'. They see it, not as a 'true journal' but as 'a later production, composed after the event from notes'. However, whether or not it was compiled after the events it records, it was done at the king's wish and presumably from notes made during the proceedings. Even if there was not, at this period, any 'deliberately devised' record of the proceedings of any Parliament as a whole, the fact seems to remain that some sort of example was set at Lincoln which later clerks, at first sporadically, later regularly, followed. Increasingly, thereafter we have a report of the politics of Parliament as distinct from petitions and pleas.

[3] *Rot. Parl.* Vol. I, p. 350.

bench. It was the first parliamentary speech to be noted on a roll. In it, Edward indicated that the principal business was to be Scotland and the state of the realm. But as the Earl of Lancaster and others had not yet arrived, the king wished to defer the special business of Parliament until they were present. In the meantime, those who had come were required to meet each day and carry on with ordinary business, including petitions. (The chancellor was instructed to receive the excuses and proxies of those who had not come, and the names of those who had neither come nor sent excuses were to be reported to the king.) Two bishops and two earls (Pembroke for one) were appointed the king's '*locum tenentes*' for this tedious part of the proceedings, to free Edward for recreation while awaiting his great adversary. The petitions before this Parliament embraced a wide range of matters from complaints against officials and the plea of a merchant, to a quarrel between Bartholomew Baddlesmere, constable of the castle at Bristol, and the citizens of that city. There was also a complaint from the younger Despenser (who was married to one of the three Gloucester co-heiresses) at the delay to his inheritance of his share of the Gloucester estates as a result of the possible pregnancy of the late earl's widow.

Lancaster chose not to arrive until about a fortnight after the Parliament was due to start, and when he did it was with a large armed force. He seems to have reached Lincoln two days before he came to Parliament, which time he may have spent in private negotiations.[1] His eventual appearance 'in full Parliament' on 12 February produced something like a second opening, when the business of the Parliament, including Scotland, was again described, and the king's wishes, both for money and for advice, were made known. The prelates and magnates then met apart in the chapter house to discuss these requests. In the meantime, the price-fixing ordinance of the last Parliament was repealed, and writs were issued stating that goods should be sold at reasonable prices, as previously. A number of statutes was promulgated and Parliament then got down to the important business of the reform of government. This was prefaced by a dramatic scene before the king and Parliament in Lincoln Cathedral, when a knight, Sir John Ros, violently denounced Hugh, the younger Despenser (son of the displaced minister, and one of the king's close friends), rushing at him with drawn sword. Despenser defended himself by striking Ros in the face and drawing blood. Both were arrested, being released later on the surety of two groups

---

[1] Richardson and Sayles, 'The Parliament of Lincoln, 1316', *BIHR*, XII (1934) which draws this conclusion from a letter from the treasurer which was written during the course of this Parliament.

of magnates. What significance this curious incident had for the politics of the moment is not explained on the Parliament roll.

By now, Lancaster's party had made known what concessions they required in return for agreeing to the king's request. These were a promise to observe the Ordinances and the king's agreement to accept Lancaster as his chief adviser. By the following Tuesday, 17 February, the king had been forced to agree, and he instructed the Bishop of Norwich to address the magnates, telling them that he wished to observe the Ordinances, and that he also wanted to make Lancaster chief of his council (*de consilio domini regis capitalis*). After a few days delay, Lancaster accepted, stating on oath that he took office on the king's council (though he made no specific reference to being its head) for the common profit of the realm and for the Ordinances (*pur le commun profit du Roialme e des Ordeignances*), and making the condition that he would not stay if his advice was disregarded.[1] By the Friday, the king had received grants for the Scottish wars, a subsidy of a fifteenth from the shires, and a levy of a foot soldier from every vil in the kingdom. Parliament then dispersed on 20 February.[2]

In theory, though not as it turned out in practice, Lancaster's appointment was a new departure. Hitherto there had been no systematic attempt to make the king subject to a council representing the baronage, despite the Ordinance requiring baronial approval of official appointments. The Ordainers had produced a scheme for the reform of the realm, but they were not themselves a permanent council nor had a fixed council of the sort forced on Henry III been appointed. The king's close council had continued in more or less the old way, favourites had returned, and although Edward had been forced to change some officials after Bannockburn, there had been no effort to institute a permanent baronial council before 1316. But at the Lincoln Parliament there was an attempt to do so. In addition to the appointment of Lancaster as chief councillor, it was proposed that a number of prelates, earls and barons should act as a council and that the king should do nothing important without their advice.[3] Moreover, Lancaster made his acceptance of his new office conditional on the understanding that he could

---

[1] *Rot. Parl.* Vol. I, p. 351.

[2] The account of this Parliament is printed in *Rot. Parl.* Vol. I, pp. 350–364. For the sequence of events I have followed Hilda Johnstone, 'The Parliament of Lincoln in 1316', *E.H.R.* XXXVI (1921). This convincingly rejects a theory (T. F. Tout, op. cit. p. 104) that the Commons departed after their grant of money and before the political business. For this Parliament, see also J. Conway Davies, 'The Baronial Opposition to Edward II', and A. Hughes, 'The Parliament of Lincoln, 1316', *T.R.H.S.* n.s.X (1896) pp. 41–58.

[3] *Rot. Parl.* Vol. I, p. 351; J. F. Baldwin, *The King's Council in the Middle Ages*, quoting Malmesbury.

resign without incurring the king's ill-will if Edward did not follow his advice. By his oath on assuming office, Lancaster undertook to amend whatever needed reform in the realm or in the royal household, and it was agreed that any member of the council who gave bad advice might be removed in the following Parliament, where, of course, Lancaster could be sure of getting his own way. Finally, a committee consisting of the archbishop, two bishops, the Earls of Hereford, Pembroke and Richmond, together with an influential baron, Batholomew de Baddlesmere, was appointed to reform the king's household. Lancaster's primacy on the council was matched by a corresponding decline in the influence of Pembroke, who, since Gaveston's death, had been Edward's principal adviser and who during the previous year had led an unsuccessful expedition against the Scots.

Lancaster's appointment was a curious foreshadowing of the future discretion and power of a Prime Minister, except that it was based not on a parliamentary majority but on territorial power. Even so, it was not irrelevant to the developing role of Parliament. Because of his power and leadership of the baronage he could be sure of mustering the support he needed in Parliament, which was no doubt why he persistently made assent in Parliament the test of legitimacy in government. So far as the great affairs of the kingdom were concerned, Parliament was still one of magnates, not of estates. Nevertheless, Lancaster's politics promoted the idea of Parliament, and when he finally lost power it was because he had ceased to have the support of the baronage which dominated Parliament. In fact, the attempt at something recognizably like what we call Cabinet government came to nothing. No particular group of barons was sworn in to deal with public affairs generally, as distinct from the committee to reform the household, and Lancaster's grip on public affairs hardly extended beyond a short-lived attempt to enforce the Ordinances. He failed to produce an effective plan for dealing with Scotland, being, indeed, suspected of a secret understanding with Robert Bruce. He was also at risk from the royalists who were being excluded from court and deprived of their estates, and his difficulties, like those of the king, were exacerbated by the appalling economic and social conditions of 1316.

The famine was at its peak: the contemporary writer of *Vita Edwardi Secundi* had heard that in Northumbria 'dogs and horses and other unclean animals were eaten'. There was pestilence, social unrest and violence. Serious revolts took place in Bristol and Wales. The crown was exploiting its feudal rights beyond tolerable limits in order to collect men and commodities for a campaign against the Scots who incessantly attacked the north. Bad government and corruption were rife. By the middle of 1316,

Lancaster's relations with the king, who at heart had never forgiven Gaveston's death, were tense. 'What pleases the lord king, the earl's servants try to upset, and whatever pleases the earl, the king's servants call treachery,' observed the writer of the *Vita*.

In April that year, Lancaster had left the council, apparently in the belief that he might be in danger at court. He never returned, and his absence helped the king to bring back his own chosen officials. It also precipitated a change in the political disposition of the council. Pembroke gradually again became the most influential lay magnate among the councillors, and the scene was set for the eventual emergence of a new party of moderate earls and barons supporting the king, who were to enlist the acquiescence of some of the courtiers in a new attempt to reach a settlement with Lancaster. In the meantime, relations between the king and the earl continued to deteriorate. The two quarrelled bitterly at York in August apparently because of the king's resistance to the Ordinances. During the course of the winter, Pembroke set out on an embassy to the Pope at Avignon, accompanied by Bartholomew Baddlesmere, who had been attached to the interest of the late earl of Gloucester. The overt objects of the embassy were to obtain papal support against the Scots, more favourable terms for the repayment of an earlier papal loan to Edward, permission to delay the fulfilment of a crusading oath previously taken by the king, and approval for a grant of clerical taxation. According to the writer of the *Vita* the embassy also sought the Pope's absolution of the king's oath to observe the Ordinances.[1] However, there is no evidence that the king was freed from his oath, though the postponement of the crusade and the clerical loan were granted, and the Pope declared a truce between the English and Scots, which was ignored.

Pembroke's willingness to present the king's case at Avignon indicates that he was also acting fundamentally in the king's interest when he later promoted a new moderate party to reach a settlement with Lancaster, though he also seems to have wanted a genuine agreement. Perhaps for lack of good advice, the king's relations with Lancaster became still worse during Pembroke's absence at Avignon. In January 1317, Lancaster did not attend a special meeting of the larger council, a *colloquium* of certain magnates and prelates with officials and justices which met at Clarendon to discuss the danger from Scotland. The earl's detestation of the court was deepened in the following spring when his wife was abducted by the disreputable Warenne, not for adultery but to spite him. Probably correctly, Lancaster suspected it was done with the king's connivance. (The

---

[1] *Vita Edwardi Secundi*, pp. 78–79.

abduction of the unhappy childless countess apparently had her consent; she was deserting Lancaster for a squire she later married.) Shortly after the abduction, another *colloquium* of magnates was summoned to Westminster. Not unnaturally Lancaster again kept away though two knights were sent specially to summon him. He was therefore declared an enemy of the king, though no action was attempted against him. It is an interesting example of the looseness of contemporary terminology that the contemporary writer of the *Vita Edwardi Secundi* refers, apparently in reference either to the Clarendon or the Westminster gathering as summoning 'the nobles to Parliament' (*proceres ad Parliamentum*) in order that 'according to the tenor of the Ordinances, they should deliberate in common Parliament . . .' (*. . . in communi Parliamento deliberaretur . . .*).[1] To Lancaster, however, such gatherings were not Parliaments for the (to him) all important reason that they were not complete assemblies of the baronage.

In July, Lancaster was summoned to a meeting of the great council at Nottingham, together with the Archbishop of Canterbury, the Bishops of Winchester (chancellor), Ely (treasurer), and Norwich, the Earls of Norfolk, Pembroke, Surrey, and Hereford, three barons (the older and younger Despenser and Bartholomew Baddlesmere) and ten judges and officials. Again Lancaster absented himself, and his letter of explanation to the king is of considerable interest in the history of Parliament.[2]

In it he denied allegations apparently made by the king that he had disturbed the realm by illicit gatherings of many men, asserting that he only retained men to help uphold the king's peace. He promised to bring his men to Newcastle in August, but said that he could not go to Nottingham at that time as he was unwell. The rest of the letter, however, made clear that this was not the substantial reason for his absence. He alleged that the recommendations of the committee appointed at Lincoln to reform the royal household had not been observed and that the king held dearer than ever before those who should have been removed. The king (he said) had not kept the Ordinances and should not be surprised that the earl refused to come to Nottingham since the matters to be discussed there (by the special council that the king had summoned) 'ought to be discussed in full Parliament and in the presence of the peers of the land' (*dussent estre tretez en plein parliament et en presence des peeres de la terre*). This reference to 'the peers of the land' (or as in a surviving Latin precis of the French text '*pares Terrae*') is the earliest use that has come down to us of the term 'peers of the realm' in

---

[1] *Vita Edwardi Secundi*, p. 79.

[2] *Adae Murimuth Continuatio Chronicarum*, ed. E. M. Thompson (Rolls Series, 1889) pp. 271ff; *Gesta Edwardi de Carnavon Auctore Canonico Bridlingtoniensi* (Rolls Series 1882–3) pp. 50ff. (Latin précis).

this sense, and it denotes a concept of fundamental importance to the future of Parliament.

Hitherto, the term 'peers' had denoted, in England, the status of the tenants of any lord (whether of the king or of someone below the king) as the equals of one another, and it had referred specifically to a tenant's right to be judged by his peers before he was subjected to penalties imposed by his lord. The new usage, however, copied the French idea that particular great vassals of the king were 'peers of France' in the sense that they constituted a definite social order of 'peers of the realm'. The changing usage in England clearly implied that the order of earls and barons who considered that they constituted the 'peerage' also thought that they had a right to be a part of Parliament by virtue of their tenure, and not simply at the king's personal discretion. In Lancaster's letter we have clear evidence that from the turmoil of repeated political crises the body that would in future be called the House of Lords had already been born, and that the barons increasingly claimed that their collective assent was necessary to legitimize important acts of government. Furthermore, they considered that it was the presence of the *whole* baronage that made a Parliament; a chosen few were not enough. There had already been some signs that this claim had taken root. In 1313, the dissident barons had declared that they would not come to Parliament without a safe-conduct, and further, that Parliament could not be held without them ('*Parliamentum . . . non potest fieri sine eis*').[1] Lancaster and the Ordainers would not, of course, have made any comparable claim that the presence of the Commons was an essential condition for an assembly to be a Parliament, but they would almost certainly have recognized that a grant by the Commons (who were almost always now summoned) was necessary for a tax on movables to be levied.

The near breakdown of government caused by disastrous social conditions and by the tension between the king and Lancaster over Edward's evasion of the requirement that he should take back alienated land now almost erupted into open conflict in the summer of 1317. The earl gathered his armed forces together both to frustrate the king's efforts to campaign against the Scots and to harass the courtiers whom the king had favoured. On the grounds that as Steward of England he ought to have been informed if the king wished to take up arms against an enemy, Lancaster prevented Edward from moving troops in the north by blocking bridges. The earl was also engaged in a private war with Warenne. As well as controlling a large part of Warenne's northern estates, Lancaster seized

---

[1] J. R. Maddicott *Thomas of Lancaster, 1307–1322*, pp. 192 and 200–202, for a discussion of Lancaster's letter, the Latin text of which is printed in *Select Documents of English Constitutional History, 1307–1485*, ed. Chrimes and Brown (A. and C. Black, 1961), pp. 23–25.

castles given to courtiers which the king had failed to take back into his possession. At one point Edward mounted a display of force before the earl's castle at Pontefract and was only narrowly dissuaded by Pembroke from attempting to attack his mighty cousin. The king and earl were on the brink of civil war when a new political grouping succeeded for a time in breaking the paralysis of government brought about by the earl's negative use of his power and the king's incompetence. This was an alliance between some of the higher nobility who were increasingly disenchanted with Lancaster's disruptive impact on government and a new group of powerful courtiers who had been advanced by the king.

The new alliance has been called by historical custom the Middle Party. It would, however, be more precisely defined as a coalition of different interests, leaning decisively towards the king and the cause of the crown, but recognizing the need for conciliation and for some kind of agreed settlement with Lancaster and the cause of the Ordainers. Five men close to the king constituted the principal courtiers in the new grouping. They were the two Despensers, father and son, together with Roger d'Amory, William Montague and Hugh Audley. The Despensers were an established baronial family; the others were king's knights promoted by Edward's favour to a higher status. All had long been associated with the court but what had given the three of them particular advancement was their benefit from the estates of the Earl of Gloucester, who had died at Bannockburn without a male heir, and whose estates were divided between his three sisters. One had been married for several years to the young Despenser. The other two were married to d'Amory and Audley who were thus virtually raised to the status of magnates. All in the courtiers' group had profited in one way or another by the king's rash and foolish munificence, and Edward's gifts to them are evidence in support of Lancaster's claims that, despite the heavy burden of taxation on the land, royal estates were being alienated and their revenue lost to the crown, in defiance of the Ordinances. That the courtiers may even have thought of themselves as in some sense a 'party' is perhaps indicated by the fact that each of the five bound himself to each of the others for £6,000, except that the two Despensers were not bound by such a contract to one another.

However, much more important than the courtiers to the success of the new so-called Middle Party, or moderate grouping, was the leadership of a group of royalist nobles, Aymer de Valence, Earl of Pembroke, Humphrey de Bohun, Earl of Hereford and the Baron Bartholomew de Baddlesmere. Of these Pembroke was the prime mover. Like most of the earls, he had for two years in 1310–1312 joined the Ordainers, being fired like everyone else by resentment at Gaveston's arrogance after his return from banishment.

Yet Pembroke was fundamentally a royalist and loyalist, and although he had associated himself with the fashionable cure for the political ills of the time, if he had been faced with an ultimate choice between the Ordinances and his duty to the person of the king he would probably have chosen the latter. Like Lancaster, he had kinship to the king, his father having been Henry III's Poitevin half-brother. He was largely of French extraction, being descended from the Lusignan family and from Isabella of Angoulême, King John's widow. Pembroke was a great landowner in France as well as an English magnate. Since Lancaster's insult to his honour in the matter of Gaveston's death, Pembroke had been firmly with the king. His influence had waned after Bannockburn, but with the withdrawal of Lancaster from the court, he had again become influential and on his return from the Avignon embassy in July 1317 he took charge of the moderating coalition with the new courtiers' group to seek an accommodation with Lancaster.[1]

For Lancaster, enforcement of the Ordinances and especially the resumption of alienated royal lands remained the issue, which was resisted by the courtiers who regarded such gifts as their due reward for service. Pembroke and his party (they were aided by two meditating cardinals from Avignon) therefore had to persuade the courtiers to go some way to meet Lancaster on the matter. In November 1317 Pembroke and Baddlesmere sealed a bond with d'Amory, a close favourite of the king's, under which d'Amory was to persuade the king to accept the advice of the three of them, and to refrain from making any grant of land worth more than £20 without their agreement. But if this represented a step in Lancaster's direction by the court, there was no reciprocity from Lancaster. Indeed, a Parliament that was to have met at Lincoln at the beginning of the year was postponed until March because of the danger that it might bring open war between the earl's followers and the king, after which it was again postponed until June, when it was finally cancelled. Meanwhile, in April 1318, the mediators felt obliged (such was the danger in the north) to make a tentative agreement that was quite unacceptable at court. The Ordinances were to be enforced in full, all land alienated by gift was to be taken back, all evil councillors were to be dismissed, and Lancaster was to be admitted to the king's peace. The courtiers' reply was that it was Lancaster's refusal to co-operate that was bringing disaster from the Scots. Eventually, however, prolonged negotiations produced the so-called Treaty of Leake[2] in August by which the

---

[1] The most valuable study of his place in politics is J. R. S. Phillips, *Aymer de Valence, Earl of Pembroke, 1307–1324*.

[2] The treaty is printed in *Rot. Parl.*, Vol. I, pp. 453–454, and Chrimes and Brown, op. cit., pp. 25–27.

Ordinances were to be observed but with some important revisions. There was to be a formal council including the four earls, Pembroke, Hereford, Richmond and Arundel. Lancaster, however, was not to be a member of the council but was to nominate as his representative on it a banneret (a comparatively recent term for a knight who was higher in military rank than a knight bachelor). Two bishops, an earl, a baron and Lancaster's banneret were always to be with the king and their assent would be needed for him to do whatever the Ordinances allowed to be done without Parliament's authority. This was the compromise on evil councillors. On the matter of resumptions there was vagueness. Lancaster and his supporters were pardoned and the earl and the once more humiliated king met to exchange the kiss of peace.

Yet Lancaster had achieved nothing substantial. He was still not himself present at court, and nothing significant was done about the evil counsel of officials, though at the subsequent Parliament at York which ratified the Treaty of Leake in October, a committee was set up to reform the household. Baddlesmere became the steward of the household, against which Lancaster bitterly complained on the grounds that as hereditary Steward of England he had the right to nominate the household steward. As for the resumption of alienated land, it seems to have been accepted by Lancaster at this Parliament that individual grants should be considered on their own merits, which enabled the courtiers to retain much of their recent possessions. A precarious political peace was maintained for the better part of two years, and the king was now free to move against the Scots. After a Parliament at York in May 1319, at which the magnates and shires gave an eighteenth of movables and the burgesses a twelfth, the king began his campaign, for which Lancaster sent forces. But it was with no good result.

The first objective was to recapture Berwick which had fallen to the Scots. While the English were besieging it, Robert Bruce sent a diversionary raid into England, ravaging the dales and making for York, from which Queen Isabella had to flee. The Scots then moved on to invest Lancaster's castle at Pontefract. Anxious to protect their own lands, and infuriated by promises that Edward had made to the courtiers over spoils, Lancaster and other northern lords withdrew their forces and went home. With the English divided, the siege of Berwick failed and Edward suffered the further humiliation of having to conclude a two year truce with the Scots. The court party and Lancaster's each blamed the other and once again the earl began to withdraw into isolation.

In January 1320, there was another Parliament at York. For the first time in ten years, no representatives of the Commons were summoned, perhaps because of the difficulty of travelling both in midwinter and in particularly disordered times. Or perhaps it was felt that since high politics rather than tax-granting was the imperative they were not needed. At all events, it was to this Parliament that Lancaster refused to come on the grounds that it was 'not fitting that a Parliament should be held behind closed doors (*in cameris*); for the king and his associates (*collaterales*) were suspect by him and he had openly proclaimed them his enemies'.[1] The probability is that by these delphic words he was making an excuse of some sort because he feared for his life, particularly since he was suspected of being in treasonable correspondence with the Scots. On the other hand, it seems at least possible that he was in part referring to the lack of the witness of the Commons at a Parliament which was likely to be dominated by courtiers and to be especially closed. But whether or not this was what he intended to be understood, it was probably a pretext, particularly since he was also absent from the next Parliament at Westminster in October, though he sent excuses.

The king's long struggle with Lancaster now entered its final phase, as a result of the rapacity of the younger Despenser, whose foolish abuse of the king's confidence was to break the moderate party. Despenser, who held the post of chamberlain, was not content with the share of the Gloucester inheritance he had received through his wife. He wished to obtain the whole of the late earl's property, and the title as well. Despenser had already secured some property from his neighbours, including from Audley who had one third of the Gloucester lands, but he also wished to obtain the Gower property of William de Braose who, needing money, was prepared to sell it. De Braose, however, died in 1320, and his son-in-law took over the property, on which Despenser persuaded the king to agree that Gower had escheated to the crown. This was not the custom in the Welsh marches, and the marcher lords, including his former court friends d'Amory and Audley, as well as the Earl of Hereford and the Mortimers combined against him. Pembroke's counsel of moderation was lacking as he was out of the country. By the spring of 1321 war had begun in the marches and within a very short time Despenser had been defeated and Edward had to agree that he should be judged in the next Parliament.

In the meantime, the former political picture of an alliance of courtiers with the moderates against Lancaster had fragmented. There was now a split between the Despensers, the Pembroke moderates who were in this matter unaligned, and the courtiers Audley, d'Amory and their friends, including Baddlesmere, who were now Despenser's enemies but were hindered by past quarrels from effective cooperation with Lancaster. In May, Lancaster called to Pontefract an assembly of magnates in the north

[1] *Vita Edwardi Secundi*, p. 104.

who took oaths to defend each others' lands, perhaps mainly from the Scots but also no doubt with Despenser in mind. At a second and larger assembly at Sherburn-in-Elmet in June, attended by knights as well as barons and prelates, and including men from the south, among them Hereford and Mortimer, a spokesman for Lancaster opened the proceedings with a recital of the causes of summons, which included the ill conduct of the king's ministers, unjust forfeiture and the like. This imitation of what was now the usual parliamentary procedure, and the parliamentary style of the writs of summons, have raised the question whether Lancaster was deliberately calling an opposition Parliament. That may have been his intention, but it was not the effect since there was now no longer unity in the baronage behind his leadership. He had alienated the moderates and the barons of the most northern counties were repelled by his dealings with the Scots. Nevertheless, the barons at this meeting pledged themselves to Despenser's downfall, and that was the mood with which the majority of the baronage came to a Parliament which the king had meanwhile called to Westminster in July.

The magnates now set off for Westminster, some, including Hereford, with substantial forces, though Lancaster himself stayed away. Before their arrival they had prepared a tract on ancient customs which may have been a paper, which has survived, arguing that the Steward of England had the duty to put the realm in order if the king would not. Their overriding concern was to get rid of the Despensers, and although an official record of this Parliament is lacking, it is known that the reluctant king was warned, even by Pembroke, that he would lose his kingdom if he would not agree.[1] Both Despensers, father and son, were then condemned for encroaching on the royal authority and of advising the king to act against Magna Carta, for which they were sentenced to banishment, the sentence being by 'the Peers of the Land, Earls and Barons . . .' the first time that this description was *officially* used of the baronage.[2] However, although the father went into exile, the son did not, but waited on board a ship in the channel, biding his time, and leading a life of piracy. Some months later the king's chance came. It happened that, travelling in Kent, Queen Isabella was refused hospitality at Leeds Castle by the wife of its absent owner, Bartholomew Baddlesmere, the former loyalist who was now in opposition to Despenser. Edward, displaying unwonted energy, successfully besieged the castle to avenge the insult to his wife, with the support of Pembroke and other magnates. Some of Baddlesmere's allies prepared to go to his aid but they were too late and Lancaster, still hugging his old resentment, failed to move.

[1] *Vita Edwardi Secundi* p. 112; *Dignity of a Peer*, Vol. I, p. 281.
[2] *Stat.* R. Vol. I, pp. 181–184.

The opposition was now completely divided. Some, like the Mortimers, submitted to the king. Others, including Hereford, marched to join Lancaster, who summoned his supporters to him. The king followed them to the north and proclaimed Lancaster a rebel. Hereford and Lancaster decided to draw back to the border, presumably to join with the Scots with whom they were now allied. But at Boroughbridge, north-west of York, they were intercepted by a force under the command of Sir Andrew Harclay, the sheriff of Cumberland, subsequently Earl of Carlisle.[1] Hereford was killed in the fighting on the bridge as were many more. Lancaster and d'Amory were captured. Lancaster was brought before Edward in Pontefract Castle, where, in the presence of the king, his treasonable activities were recited to those earls and barons present as known and notorious. Lancaster was condemned to die as a traitor and he was led out to execution on 22 March. With the death of as persistent an enemy as any king had ever faced, and the crumbling of the opposition, Edward had a remarkable opportunity to make a new start. But with amazing abandon he threw it away, proved himself incorrigible and doomed his own kingship.

III

The king's triumph was so complete and unconditional that, handled with competence and political sensitivity, it could have restored the royal authority and ended once and for all the baronial attempts to constrain the crown. In fact, the practice of trying to enforce written constitutions did now go out of fashion, but this was not because Edward used his new power to make them unnecessary. The reason was that his own conduct of government, when free of restraint, was to make it clear that in the end there was no safeguard against a wholly insufficient king except to remove him. Such an outcome after his triumph at Boroughbridge would, however, have seemed inconceivable. The royalist victory over a disunited baronage was such that it might have led either to a more autocratic monarchy, or at best to a strong kingship free from baronial challenge and governing effectively with the broader support of the estates of the realm consulted in

[1] An account of the events before, during and after Boroughbridge, is in the Chronicle of Lanercost, which is translated and extracted in E.H.D. Vol. III pp. 274–282. A complimentary account is in *Vita Edwardi Secundi* also extracted in E.H.D. Vol. III, pp. 282–287. The best analysis of politics between Leake and Boroughbridge is by J. R. Maddicott, op. cit.

Parliament. There is some reason to suppose that the latter is what Edward wanted. He was not unintelligent nor was he by disposition a tyrant. He seems to have seen what was necessary and how it might be done. But he lacked the will to achieve his own ends or to free himself from emotional dependency on favourites who sought their own aggrandizement at the expense of the nation's well-being. It is in this final chapter of his reign, when all the advantages were with Edward, that it becomes easiest to understand Lancaster's impatient contempt for his effete cousin who knew no better how to handle his authority than to hand it to men to whom he was emotionally captive.

Nevertheless, Edward's first resolve, prompted perhaps by the Despensers, was sensible. It was to kill the Ordinances not simply by the success of arms at Boroughbridge but by the full weight of legal enactment expressed in Parliament. Two months after Lancaster's execution, a Parliament met at York, and the king made his wishes known well beforehand in instructions to his council. The parliamentary writs were issued two days before Boroughbridge and at about the same time Edward issued notably clear and decisive instructions about how the council should prepare for Parliament. His memorandum shows a confidence in victory which no doubt reflected his awareness of the baronial disarray which had reduced Lancaster's coalition to no more than himself and the marcher lords.

There were two principal items on Edward's memorandum for the agenda. 'Remember the following: first the statute about the repeal of the Ordinances; second, to embody the good parts of them in a statute.'[1] The memorandum continues by listing such subjects for discussion as the chattels of felons, and weights and measures, and it concludes with the king's wish that every wise man of his council (*'chescun sage de son conseil'*) should think about these points and how to amend the law, by statute or otherwise, for the profit of the king and the people. Edward also stated that he wished the council to draw up their proposals for his consideration before the Parliament.

The Statute of York was brief and to the point.[2] It first enacted that 'all the things ordained by the said Ordainers ... shall henceforth and forever cease' because 'the royal power ... of the king was restrained in divers things, contrary to what ought to be, to the blemishing of his royal

---

[1] '*Fait a remembrer des choses souzescrites: A de primes de l' estatut sur le repeal des Ordenances: Item de mettres les bons pointz en estatut. Item: de remedier contre faus retours des bailiffs des franchises ... etc*'. The text of the king's memorandum is printed in Conway Davies, *The Baronial Opposition to Edward II*, Appendix No. 93 (1918), and J. F. Baldwin, *The King's Council*, (1913) p. 472.

[2] *Revocacio Novarum Ordinationum, Stat.* R. Vol. I, p. 189–190, 15 Edw. II.

sovereignty and against the estate of the crown'. This, it stated, had been the finding of the magnates and 'the commonalty of his realm' assembled at the Parliament at York, among whom (the statute recorded with a certain irony) were the greater part of the said Ordainers then living. Statutes made by the king and his ancestors were to remain in force. But henceforth, all ordinances and provisions 'made under any authority or commission whatsoever, by the subjects of our lord the king or his heirs, concerning the royal power . . . shall be null and of no validity or force'.

The king's first purpose, then, was to use a parliamentary enactment to make it impossible for the baronage ever again to force constitutional change upon the crown. The outlawing of any provisions by subjects affecting the royal power might have been taken as a simple declaration of authoritarian intentions, had it not been for the concluding and most significant passage in the statute. As a reassurance that there would be no grounds or pretexts for any such further baronial attempts to constrain the royal power, the Statute of York also recognized that government required properly constituted consultation. Its most significant clause concluded that 'things which are to be established for the estate of the king . . . and the estate of the realm and the people shall be treated, accorded and established in Parliament by our lord the king and with the consent of the prelates, earls and barons and of the commonalty of the realm as has been hitherto accustomed'. Thus, although the king was not to be constrained in his *power*, decisions on matters affecting his and the realm's *estate* must be made in Parliament with the commonalty as well as the lords assenting. In other words, in such matters he would rule through consultation and with consent.

By some earlier historians this was taken as confirming that all important law-making should be in Parliament, of which the Commons (or 'commonalty') would be a part. But the king cannot have intended to diminish his discretionary power to ordain law outside Parliament, if necessary. Nor can the reference to the part the commonalty in Parliaments should have in assenting to matters concerning the estate of the king, the kingdom and the people have implied a positive role for the Commons in legislation. For they had not yet attained their future status of a corporate petitioning body bringing forward bills leading to statutes.

They were not yet initiators, least of all in great matters affecting the royal 'estate', though their petitions could stimulate the government to law-making. Nevertheless, the presence of the Commons in Parliament as assenting witnesses had increasingly been recognized by kings, and initially at least by the Ordainers, as politically useful. It was partly this that the final clause of the Statute of York recognized. At York, Edward went so far as to widen their representation. For the first time (and the last until the reign of Henry VIII, apart from a probably abortive summons of Welshmen to the Parliament which deposed Edward II) twenty-four discreet and lawful men were called from north Wales, and the same number from the south. The writ of summons records that the king was moved to do this by the loyalty of the people of that country, and because he desired their counsel and assent on the state of the kingdom.[1] It is evidence of the value of the Commons as individuals who could give advice if asked, and who were able to testify to their constituents as to the legality of what they had agreed to and witnessed in Parliament. But what the Commons could contribute depended on the nature of the business before Parliament. The statute did not mean that all law declarations must be in Parliament, or even that the Commons must always be present. What it seems to indicate is that certain important law-making affecting the estate of the realm and the king, but not his power, should only take place in Parliament, and that on such occasions the Commons should be present, as from the end of Edward's reign they always were.

So what were the important matters which were to be settled in Parliament, and what was the difference between the king's power and his estate? Some have argued that because Edward probably considered that Parliaments with the Commons present were less dangerous than baronial assemblies, he had come to the conclusion that the best way of protecting the crown from the barons was to commit all general legislation to a Parliament of estates.[2] Yet he cannot have intended to give up the king's right to declare laws and ordinances on his own authority if necessary. Nor, given the general temper of his reign, is it likely that he had any intention of advancing the role of Parliament at the Crown's expense. Other historians have argued that far from giving Parliament, including the Commons, any exclusive right in general legislative matters, the intention in the Statute of York was to prescribe a strictly limited parliamentary role for special purposes. Much discussion has gone into attempts to define the distinction between the king's power, with which no subject should interfere, and the matters concerning the 'estate of the king ... and realm' which were to be dealt with in Parliament. No conclusive answers are possible. The probability, however, is that by royal power was meant that authority

[1] *Dignity of a Peer*, Vol. I, p. 282.
[2] An argument advanced by M. V. Clarke, *Medieval Representation and Consent*. The most valuable of many discussions on this subject are G. Lapsley 'The Commons and the Statute of York' *E.H.R.* XXVIII (1913), and also 'The Interpretation of the Statute of York', Pts I & II, *E.H.R.* Vol. LVI (1941). See also B. Wilkinson, *Constitutional History of England*, Vol. II, 1307–1399, pp. 134–156, including related documents.

which was reserved to the king, at the final point of decision, to enable him to respond as he thought fit to the needs and circumstances of the moment, and also his right freely to control the institutions and ministers through which his power was exercised. But the 'estate' (which could mean the condition, or well-being) of the king and the kingdom probably referred to matters of administration, finance and taxation, and to the general grievances of the people. These, the Statute of York enacted, could and should be discussed in Parliament. A restatement of the crown's right to its due power untrammelled was coupled with an assurance that the king intended to act in consultation with a properly constituted Parliament in ordinary matters of government.

It was a particular purpose of the Statute of York to put an end to the sort of control which the barons had tried to force on the monarchy since the time of Henry III, and to reassert the king's fundamental power, while making this acceptable with an assurance that whatever could properly be done by consultation would be so done. But consultation on matters concerning the estate and well-being of the king and people must be in a lawful Parliament free of baronial pressures, and with the king at its head acting free from duress. Efforts to restrain the royal power were to be unlawful whether they were made by powerful subjects outside Parliament or intimidation within parliamentary formalities. The Statute of York was an attempt to free the king from being forced to make changes by subjects, even when, as in the case of the Ordainers, he had been forced formally to give them authority. It also struck at the magnates' use of their power to coerce a Parliament, as had happened when Lancaster and Hereford had insisted on the banishment of the Despensers by Parliament. Not least, the prohibition by the Statute of York of actions by subjects relative to the royal power could be also taken as outlawing once and for all any idea that it was tolerable for a magnate to call his own pseudo-Parliament as Lancaster had done.

When he was at the height of his power, Lancaster had lost interest in the frequent Parliaments which had been a central demand of the Ordainers; only one Parliament had been summoned between January 1316 when Lancaster achieved his greatest influence, and August 1318 when he finally lost it, and even this had been twice prorogued and then cancelled. Now, it was the king and the Despensers who saw the value of Parliaments. Indeed, it may be that Edward and his advisers had grasped the point much earlier, since it was from the Lent Parliament of 1313, when the Lancastrian party was on the defensive after Gaveston's death, and was trying to avoid coming to Parliament that the Commons were first summoned by writ to 'consent' as well as 'to do' what was 'ordained by common counsel'.[1] The claims of the Commons had been growing through Edward II's reign. They had asked in 1310 for a properly constituted arrangement for receiving their petitions, and in 1315 they even ventured to appeal against legal commissions which the magnates were using against lesser men. There was every reason for the king to see in the Commons a potential political counterbalance against the pressure of the barons. Although Edward and the Despensers were to destroy themselves by subsequent folly, the decision of the victorious royal party in 1322 to vindicate and bolster themselves by emphasizing the importance of a representative Parliament was an acknowledgement of the political importance of the Commons in Parliament. The distinction made in the Statute of York between the magnates and the commonalty also amounted to an acknowledgement that it was now the Commons rather than the magnates who represented the community of the realm.

Evidence of the quickening growth of the Commons' importance in Parliament is also provided by a contemporary document describing the method of holding a Parliament. The famous treatise *Modus Tenendi Parliamentum* was almost certainly written between 1316 and 1324, though the only surviving manuscripts are from the late fourteenth and early fifteenth centuries. The *Modus*, which may have been roughly contemporary with the York Parliament, purports to give an account of the composition, procedure, and conduct of a Parliament. The surviving copies are generally in collections of legal treatises and statutes, and were probably used for the training of lawyers rather than as a weapon in contemporary political controversy. The *Modus*, however, contains statements which are not descriptive of facts. It purports, for instance, to describe the manner in which Parliaments were held by Edward the Confessor and which was handed on through William the Conqueror. That historical solecism, however, may simply indicate that the author was a practical lawyer with no knowledge of history. Other aspects of the *Modus* also seem to have emerged from some of the current political ideas of the time, especially those of the baronial party. They may represent what the author thought should have been, or might become, the practice. Thus, he advances the

---

[1] The formula of 1290 had required the Commons to have power to counsel and consent for themselves and their community, to what the magnates should be led to agree on. In 1295, they were to have power to do what was ordained by common counsel, to which formula the words 'and to consent' were added in 1313. See J. G. Edwards, 'The *Plena Potestas* of English Parliamentary Representatives' in Fryde and Miller, Vol. I, and J. E. A. Joliffe, *Const. Hist. of Med. England*, pp. 369-370.

idea that when there was discord between king and magnates, the steward, the constable, and the marshal should elect twenty-five men from the various estates of the realm who could choose twelve from among themselves, after which the twelve could reduce themselves to six, then to three, and if the king approved, even to one, who would act as a final arbiter. This smacks of the kind of baronial constitution-making which had been fashionable since the reign of Henry III. Indeed, the document, which is blatantly unhistorical in much that it purports to describe, so clearly corresponds to many of Lancaster's ideas that it may have been devised as a Lancastrian political manifesto.

Nevertheless, much else in the *Modus* corresponds closely with well confirmed facts about Parliament, including the manner in which it was summoned, the recital of the causes of summons, the seating of the gathering, the work of the clerks and petitions. But the principal interest of the *Modus* is what it says about the Commons. It describes accurately the circumstances in which the king could request an aid, notes the necessity for all the peers to consent to it and adds that 'two knights who come to Parliament for the shire, have a greater voice in granting and denying [an aid] than the greatest earl of England'. The king, it is stated, could hold Parliament with the community of the kingdom, even if the magnates did not come, provided they have been summoned. But if the Commons were summoned and did not come 'there would be no Parliament at all'. If the writer were making such an observation in general terms it would plainly be false. But it was made under the heading 'concerning aids to the king', and it was by now undoubtedly accepted that no aid could be taken without the assent of the Commons. The writer concludes correctly that it was the knights, the burgesses and the proctors of the clergy who represent the whole community of England, and not the magnates, each of whom was at Parliament 'for his own individual person and for no one else'.

The general idea of representation as embodied in the *Modus* does not go beyond the new facts of politics at the end of the reign of Edward II. The document can therefore alternatively be explained as the work of a chancery or exchequer clerk who let his enthusiasm for constitution-making run away with him. The author may have been the same William Airmyn who compiled the record of the Lincoln Parliament. It was certainly an accurate indicator of the rising status of Parliament. In the future there would be no Parliaments without the Commons, though there would be great councils where the magnates alone might be present. The *Modus* also correctly described Parliament as an occasion for the settling of matters of common concern to king, magnates and commonalty; in other words as a political assembly as well as a court of last resort. That, clearly, was how Edward II regarded it in the Statute of York. Within that Parliament the Commons had already almost reached a position of near indispensability which they had not held when Edward became king.[1]

In their manner of repealing the Ordinances, the king and the Despensers showed commonsense. By re-enacting the principal statutes since Magna Carta, including those concerning the rights of the church, the forest law, purveyance, and the king's peace, they both confirmed the popular and acceptable parts of the Ordinances, and also sought to demonstrate that these had been unnecessary.[2] The other principal business at York was the reversal of the banishment of the Despensers. This was revoked on the grounds that the Despensers had not been called to answer the charges, that the judgement was made without the consent of the prelates who were peers of Parliament and that the magnates had determined the sentence before they came, armed, to Parliament. It was not, however, the restoration of the Despensers which damaged the king but the irresponsible way with which they used their power and the vindictiveness with which the king treated his defeated enemies. The execution of Lancaster was not unreasonable. He had persistently hounded the king, and the contempt he felt for the character of his cousin's weakness resounds between the lines of the historical evidence. Lancaster could also be judged objectively to be a traitor on account of his treasonable correspondence with Robert Bruce. On the other hand, the arbitrary manner of his trial, at which no evidence was required other than the assertion of the king's knowledge of his notorious wrong-doing, was an ill omen for the future. Still worse was the king's treatment of the others who had been driven into rebellion, many of whom had previously been supporters of the king. The lands of d'Amory, who had died, and who would have been hanged otherwise, were declared forfeit. Baddlesmere was hanged as were more than twenty others, many of whom had been former loyalists. Audley and the two Mortimers were imprisoned.

The Despensers on the other hand were lavishly rewarded, the elder becoming the Earl of Winchester, and both received massive grants of lands a the expense of the dispossessed. They were now dominant in south Wales. When Pembroke died in 1324 there was no one left to restrain the king from acquiescing in their greed and arrogance. As administrators they were efficient, improving the procedures of government and increasing the

[1] The path-finding study of the *Modus* is M. V. Clarke, *Medieval Representation and Consent* (1936) which includes the text. The most recent presentation of the text with translation and analysis is *Parliamentary Texts of the Later Middle Ages* by Nicholas Pronay and John Taylor, (1980). This stresses the document as a legal treatise. For a discussion of the *Modus* as a Lancastrian political manifesto, see J. R. Maddicott, op. cit., pp. 289–292.

[2] *Rot. Parl.* Vol. I, pp. 456–457.

revenues by better methods of accounting. Partly as a result of these reforms Edward was well enough off financially, in the latter part of his reign, in addition to which he was free from the cost of campaigns in Scotland and benefitted from the revenue of forfeited lands after Boroughbridge. But the country as a whole suffered from increased lawlessness, resentment against the Despensers became intense, and their unpopularity spread to less culpable ministers, including the Chancellor, Robert Baldock, and the Treasurer, Bishop Stapledon of Exeter. The greed of the Despensers seemed to have no limits, and whatever their merits as administrators they were catastrophically without political good sense. The king also made enemies of several dangerous clerics, among them Henry Burghersh of Lincoln, a relative of Baddlesmere, and Adam Orleton of Hereford, who had been given his See by the Pope against the king's wishes, and who, as a marcher bishop, was an ally of the Mortimers. Another enemy was the new Bishop of Winchester, Robert Stratford, who had been sent by the king to Rome to obtain that See for Robert Baldock but contrived to get it for himself, though Edward for a short time managed to exclude him from its temporalities. Not all the faults were Edward's in his dealings with prelates whose ambition and political involvement outweighed their spiritual capacity. But these men were to be crucial in hardening public opinion against him in the final crisis of the reign.

Edward's final decline began with the failure of another expedition into Scotland. The truce which had been agreed at the end of 1319 expired in 1322, after which the north of England was persistently raided by the Scots. In November 1322, another Parliament was held at York, at which a tenth was provided by the barons and the shires, and a sixth by the boroughs and towns, for an attack on Scotland. In the meantime Edward had invaded Scotland but the Scots avoided battle, forcing him to withdraw, pursued by Robert Bruce. The Scots then made an incursion into Yorkshire and at one point almost captured the English king. Despairing of any action to restore peaceful living conditions for the people of the ravaged north, Andrew Harclay, the loyalist victor of Boroughbridge who was now Earl of Carlisle, felt moved to negotiate with the Scottish king in the hope of making an arranged peace. But news of these dealings reached the king. Harclay was arrested and executed as a traitor. One more loyalist had been driven to treason out of despair at the king's incapacity to rule. When, in May, a truce was agreed with the Scots for thirteen years, it was a clear defeat for the English. Nevertheless it gave peace to the northern counties for the first time since Bannockburn.

But at this point a new foreign quarrel arose, this time with the French, which provided the occasion for the king's overthrow. The new dispute with France arose from the burning by the Gascons of a French fortified town at St Sardos. In 1324 the French king Charles IV announced the confiscation of Gascony, and efforts to reach a settlement met no success. At home the country was increasingly lawless and uneasy. During the next confused year, the king held a number of councils and *ad hoc* assemblies which achieved nothing. A Parliament with Commons present met in February 1324 but another in June 1325 consisted only of prelates, magnates and representatives of the Cinque Ports. Government had almost broken down. But, political disasters are often propelled by personal animosities, and in Edward's case it was not only the inimical bishops and magnates he had to fear but also his queen. She appears to have begun to turn against him at the time of the Despensers' restoration. When there seemed to be a danger of invasion from France, her estates were sequestrated as a precaution.

In March 1325, nevertheless, she was allowed to go to France to negotiate a peace with her brother the French king, with whom she managed to reach an agreement. One requirement of this was that Edward should do homage for his French possessions. But the two Despensers, knowing their safety depended on the presence of the king, prevailed upon Edward not to leave his kingdom. It was then agreed that Prince Edward should go in his place. By now the discontented queen was herself the centre of a new and much more determined opposition party gathering in France, which included Bishops Burghersh of Lincoln, Orleton of Hereford and Stratford of Winchester (one of the king's ambassadors), as well as the king's half brother the Earl of Kent. But at the heart of the movement was Roger Mortimer who had escaped from the Tower of London in August 1324. In France, Isabella became his mistress.

Once Prince Edward was in her hands, Isabella let the king know that neither she nor their son would return as long as the Despensers remained at court. The king and the Despensers now began to prepare for an expected invasion from France and in November and December the king held the last Parliament of his freedom. But since Charles IV would not help his sister, Isabella removed to the Low Countries, where she arranged the betrothal of her son to Philippa, the daughter of the Count of Hainault, from whom she received a small force of Hainaulters. With this she set sail, landing in Suffolk in September 1326 and meeting no resistance. As she progressed towards London, she was joined by the noblemen and gentry of East Anglia, while in London the citizens declared for the queen and Prince Edward. Bishop Stapledon of Exeter, Edward's minister, was brutally murdered in the street by a mob. London remained tumultuous until, under authorization from the queen, a new mayor was elected, who was a supporter of Mortimer. Meanwhile, the queen and Mortimer were pursuing the king and the Despensers as they retreated to the west. The citizens of Bristol forced the elder Despenser to surrender the town, on which he was condemned and executed for treason, being denied any right of answer on the grounds that it had been denied by him to others. In Glamorgan the king himself and the younger Despenser were captured. Despenser was condemned to death for accroaching royal power, for the death of Lancaster and much more beside, and was executed with the worst excesses of the horrible penalties for treason. Edward was despatched as a prisoner first to Monmouth and then to Kenilworth castle.

The queen and Mortimer had resolved well before they landed in England that Edward should be deprived of the Crown. Now that he was in their hands the only question was how it should be done with the greatest semblance of legality and the least damage to the reputation of the crown as well as with the greatest possible safety for the insurgents. The first thing to be done was to summon Parliament so that all sections of the community could be associated with their revolution. Prince Edward had already been 'elected' as 'guardian' (*custos*) of the realm by a partisan gathering at Bristol which included the Archbishop of Dublin, several earls, (among them the king's half brothers, the Earls of Norfolk and Kent, and also Thomas of Lancaster's brother Henry) and a number of barons and knights. The election of the prince to govern the kingdom was made 'with the assent of the whole community of the realm there present' and in the presence of the queen and the prince on the pretext of the king's absence. Subsequently, orders of government had been issued under Prince Edward's own seal, which was used to summon a Parliament to Westminster for 14 December, the king allegedly being out of the kingdom. But once the king was captured, the inimical Bishop Orleton of Hereford was sent to Monmouth to take the Great Seal from him. The seal was then used to prorogue the intended Parliament and to summon it for 7 January, 1327.[1]

Thus the Parliament which was to effect the king's deposition was given formal legality by a summons in his own name. Writs were sent to bishops and abbots but only to seven earls and forty-seven barons. Those who might prove the king's friends were for the most part excluded. As well as representatives of the English shires, cities, boroughs and the Cinque Ports, twenty-four representatives from north Wales were summoned to Parliament in order to 'consent' to what had to be done and for the peace and tranquility of the nation. The writ sending for them was despatched to Richard d'Amory, a baron of the queen's party who was also personally

---

[1] *Dignity of a Peer*, Vol. I, pp. 287–288; Vol. III, pp. 369–371.

summoned, and it is virtually certain that this was in order that those chosen would be politically sympathetic to the queen's cause. The writ was issued late and there is no evidence that the Welsh representatives came to Westminster, but there can be little doubt that in general the knights and burgesses sent to this Parliament were chosen because they would go with the prevailing wind. That is particularly true of the political complexion of the representatives of London, which was wholly committed to the queen's cause not least because of the murder by Londoners of Bishop Stapleton. It was both a large and a generally committed Parliament.

There is no official record of the Parliament. But from chroniclers using well informed sources and documentary evidence the course of events is clear, though with some chronological uncertainties. Parliament assembled in Westminster Hall on 7 January, the day after Epiphany, and it seems that part of the London mob was allowed to crowd into the premises. But since Mortimer's men and those of Henry of Lancaster surrounded the premises the citizens were well under control. The king's enemy, Bishop Orleton of Hereford, then addressed Parliament, stating, according to one account, that the king was absent because the queen was afraid of him.[1] On the other hand, another account suggests a different reason for Edward's absence.[2] This chronicle describes how the Archbishop of Canterbury, Walter Reynolds, addressed Parliament a week later, speaking 'by the common consent of all', which presumably means in the name of all, and explaining how the conclusion had been reached that Edward should be deposed. The archbishop spoke of the king's misgovernment, his acceptance of bad counsel and the damage done to the happy realm he had inherited. It had therefore been agreed 'by absolutely all' that Edward ought no longer to reign and should be succeeded by the prince. To justify this decision, the archbishop recounted how the Bishops of Hereford and London had borne witness that when they had been sent to the king at Kenilworth 'on behalf of the community of the land, to request him to come to the Parliament . . . he was as cruel and malevolent as before'. Thus after the Parliament had been sitting for a week the claim that the queen feared Edward's presence had been dropped for the allegation that he had been asked to come, but would not, though there is some ambiguity about when this is supposed to have happened. Another account states even more positively that the bishops had gone to the king to ask him to come, but that he cursed them and refused to go among his enemies.[3] There seems little doubt that the Parliament was given the impression that Edward had been asked to come

---

[1] M. V. Clarke, *Representation and Consent*, op. cit., p. 178.
[2] *The Pipewell Chronicle*, extract in M. V. Clarke, op. cit., and *E.H.D.* Vol. III, pp. 287–288.
[3] *Lanercost Chronicle*, p. 257.

during the Parliament, but had refused. It was clearly on account of this that, as the Pipewell Chronicle explains, it was decided that Edward 'should no longer reign' and that such 'great folk' as prelates, earls, barons, knights, justices and others were sent to him to renounce homage 'on behalf of the whole land'.[1]

Which of these explanations of the king's absence was true? Was he kept away because the queen feared his presence, or did the leaders of the Parliament send for him only to be refused? The likelihood is that he was prevented from coming lest there might be a reaction in his favour from those in the Parliament who would not consent to his deposition. They were a minority, but they were not negligible, particularly among the prelates. The clue to the probable truth is in a private letter written before the Parliament to the Archbishop of Canterbury by his friend and adviser, Henry Eastry, Prior of Christ Church Canterbury, and a man over eighty years old. In this, Eastry said that two bishops had lately been sent to the king to ask him to come to the Parliament which was 'about to meet in London to ordain and dispose of certain arduous business' and that the king had refused. This must have been the visit to Kenilworth to which the archbishop referred a week later as the Parliament neared its end. Prior Eastry's letter shows that the impression given that the king was invited to go to Parliament while it was sitting was false; the visit had occurred before Parliament met. In any case, there would probably not have been time for the bishops to have gone to Kenilworth and back while Parliament was sitting and before the archbishop's deposition speech.

What may well have happened is that when the king was asked, before Parliament met, to go to it, he refused in order not to give validity to an assembly called in his name, but against his will, by being present. But this does not mean that he would have refused a chance to go later, had he been given it, once he realized that an appeal to potential supporters at Parliament was his only chance of restoring his position. But Prior Eastry's letter does not only tell us when the visit of the two bishops to Kenilworth took place. Even more interesting is what it reveals of the thinking of the king's opponents when they later determined the membership of the deputation sent to demand his abdication. In his letter Eastry went on to suggest that the king should again be requested to attend Parliament by an embassy of two earls, two barons, four citizens and burgesses and four knights 'specially elected to represent the whole community of the realm'. His reasoning is illuminating. 'This ought to be done in order not only that the prelates, but the magnates, nobles and chief persons of every estate and condition in the realm may be involved in the business. All this should be

[1] *The Pipewell Chronicle*, extracted (French, with translation) in M. V. Clarke, op. cit., pp. 123–124 and 193–195, and also (translation) in *E.H.D.* Vol. III, pp. 187–188.

done formally before proceeding any further. *Valete*. (A postcript exhorts the archbishop: 'Let no other eye see this letter.'[1]

This was, in the event, precisely the motive for the composition of the delegation which did eventually go to the king. But its purpose was not to give him another chance to come to London but to tell him that he must abdicate or destroy his dynasty, and to involve representatives of every estate in that demand. The truth of the matter was probably that once the Parliament was in session the queen's party were frightened at the prospect of the king's presence and kept him imprisoned. Who knows what might have happened had Edward in person been present to exert the old magic of the right of a legitimate and anointed king to the loyalty which was so potent a part of the spirit of the age? There was still a party for him, headed by the Archbishop of York; might Edward not have used it successfully to obtain one last chance, in exchange for promises? At a Parliament called in his name, where could he have been seated save at its head, and how could he have been removed from that place? The likelihood is that an earlier impulsive refusal was used as a pretext to keep him away by force.

Yet this still left the party of Mortimer and the queen with a difficulty. As has been pointed out in one of the clearest short analyses of these confused events, the medieval idea of a fair trial and verdict rested not on proof (since arraignment was taken as a presumption of guilt unless the accused could escape on a point of law) but on the presence of the accused at the trial and his chance to answer the charges.[2] Edward was not formally on trial, yet since in reality he faced a 'sentence' of deposition, the proceedings would have had something like the character of a trial. How then could he be deposed in his absence? Indeed, what procedure existed for a deposition? The answer was that there was none. Parliament was not a court in this sense, and to the extent that it was the king's court of last resort for certain kinds of cases, the king himself was its supreme judge; how then could he be tried there himself? It is true that the magnates had begun to claim the right to try accused men of their own order, as they were to do when Mortimer in turn was overthrown. But the king was a man apart.

Most of the time between Parliament's first meeting on 7 January, and the despatch of the delegation to Kenilworth a week later was therefore probably spent in trying to persuade the resisters who were placed under heavy pressure (one prelate was hustled and threatened with death) to accept deposition. At the same time, demonstrations were staged in the city of London so as make the king's deposition inevitable.

On 12 January, the mayor (Roger of Bethune, who had helped Mortimer escape from the tower), the aldermen and the commonalty of London,

[1] M. V. Clarke, op. cit., pp. 177–178.
[2] Ibid. Chapter IX.

whose citizens had been in league with Isabella and Mortimer since their landing, asked the magnates to make an agreement with them, swearing to maintain the cause of the queen and the prince, to depose Edward II and to crown his son. On the 13th, the prelates and magnates therefore rode to the Guildhall where the accusation against Edward which had been put to Parliament was read out by John Stratford, the Bishop of Winchester who was later to be Edward III's minister and adversary. The essential charge was that the king was incompetent to govern in person. More specifically it was asserted that throughout his reign he had been controlled and governed by others who gave him evil counsel, that he had refused to listen to good counsel, had lost Scotland and Gascony through misgovernment, that he had 'destroyed the holy church', that he had put noble men to a shameful death and had disinherited them, that he had broken his coronation oath by not doing justice for the sake of his own greed and that of his evil counsellors, and that he had 'stripped' and ruined his realm.[1] At the same time, Edward's old foe, Bishop Orleton of Hereford, preached fervently against him, arousing the crowd to shout their repudiation of the king. Archbishop Reynolds, who owed his advancement to Edward, announced the deposition, taking as his text *'vox populi, vox dei'*. At another meeting later the same day organized by Mortimer and the archbishop, Stratford too preached against the king, and the prelates and magnates swore an oath to uphold the queen and the prince, and to defend the city. But it was not only they who did so. Oath-taking continued for several days by 'representatives' of all the estates of the realm, from fourteen prelates (including the Archbishop of Canterbury), four earls and twenty-four barons to knights who were followers of the oath-taking noblemen, and burgesses from Bury St Edmunds and St Albans. But although the oath-takers were men who could be said to stand for all the estates, they were not representing Parliament as such; indeed, of the fifty-four secular magnates summoned only twenty-eight took the oath, and in Parliament deposition was still, it seems, resisted even though by a minority. What the oath-taking signified was the determination of the partisans of Isabella and Mortimer to associate men from all sections of the community with their cause.

These exercises in public propaganda in the city helped to bring matters to a head in Parliament. It was not to be the last time that mass demonstrations outside Parliament were arranged to further the cause of a ruthless party within it. (The technique was conspicuously used by the Long Parliament in its attacks on Charles I.) On 13 January, the archbishop

[1] 'Articles of Accusation against Edward II', printed (French) Chrimes and Brown, *Select Documents, 1304–1485*, pp. 37–38 and (English) B. Wilkinson, *Constitutional History of Med. England*, 1216–1399, Vol. II, pp. 170–171 (translation).

made the speech already referred to stating that it had been agreed that Edward should be deposed, both on account of his ill deeds and because of the two bishops' alleged report of his continued ill intent when he refused to come to Parliament. But though he was for practical purposes deposed on 13 January, in, if not by, Parliament, the difficulty remained that there was no legal precedent for deposition. The king must therefore be persuaded to abdicate, and it was decided, 'nobody daring to object' as one of the best-informed of the chroniclers put it, to send a deputation to Kenilworth to do so.[1] It consisted of about thirty men, three bishops (including Orleton and Stratford and also the Bishop of Lincoln), two earls (Henry of Lancaster and Warenne), two abbots, four barons, and a number of representatives of the Commons, probably four knights of shires, the London burgesses and perhaps a few others as well.

This parliamentary deputation reached Kenilworth on 20 January. Two of the bishops, Winchester and Lincoln, appear to have gone on ahead to persuade Edward to abdicate in favour of his son with a promise that he would be treated with royal dignity if he did so and a threat that if he did not his dynasty would be set aside and a new king, not of the blood royal, would be chosen who might, of course, well have been Mortimer. The king at last agreed, and was then led, dressed in a black cloak and from an inner room, to the royal chamber where the Bishop of Hereford had arranged the rest of the delegation in order of their dignity. Hereford then repeated the demand and the threat in harsh tones, and Edward in tears expressed his grief that the people should have repudiated him and his willingness to abdicate provided his son succeeded him. The ceremony of repudiation took place the next day. At it, the principal figure was not one of the bishops or magnates who had brought their pressure to bear on the king but a knight, William Trussell, who had been appointed spokesman for the renunciation of hommage. Trussell was a supporter of Lancaster and a justice who had delivered sentence of death on the younger Despenser. He was not an elected member of Parliament. For this errand, Trussell was given the description 'procurator of all in the land of England and of the whole Parliament'. Standing before the king and describing himself as procurator for the prelates, counts, barons and others named in his procuracy, having 'full and sufficient power' to do so, he formally renounced allegiance on behalf of the whole kingdom.[2] The steward broke his staff, declaring that

---

[1] Chronicle of Geoffrey le Baker; extract (Latin) in Chrimes and Brown, op. cit. The chronicler obtained some material from Sir Thomas de la More, later an elected knight of the shire, who accompanied Stratford to Kenilworth.

[2] Trussell's declaration is reprinted in Chrimes and Brown, op. cit., p. 38, reprinted from *Rot. Parl. Anglie Hactenus Inediti*, ed. Richardson and Sayles. Camden Soc. 3rd series. LI, 1935, p. 101.

the royal household was dissolved and the business was done. The new reign was determined as beginning on 25 January, after the formality of abdication rather than with the reality of earlier deposition. The deputation brought its news to Parliament on the 24th, and it was announced that the king had abdicated in favour of his son 'of his free will' and 'by the common counsel and assent of the prelates, earls, barons and other nobles and of the whole community of the realm'.[1] Whether or not the deputation to Kenilworth was a parliamentary deputation proper, the presence of the representatives of the Commons on it was crucial to the purpose, which was as Eastry's letter recommended, to associate all sections of the realm with what was to be done. There was safety in numbers, especially for Mortimer, Isabella and their party. The delegation spoke for the estates in Parliament, of which the Commons were now recognized as being a politically essential part.

Thus a characteristic English compromise was achieved which disguised a revolution with the camouflage of historical continuity. The king had been deposed before he had abdicated, but abdication put the record straight. The renunciation was much more than a withdrawal of feudal homage. Implicit in it was the idea of a contract between king and people which could be broken if the king could not do his job. Edward, as the articles of accusation against him had concluded, had 'shown himself incorrigible and without hope of amendment'. Yet he was not so much accused of taking too much on himself as of taking too little and handing his authority to those unfit to wield it. The abdication did not strike at the powers of monarchy as such; indeed, a notable feature of the settlement was the avoidance of any of the paper constitutions formally constraining the monarchy which had been fashionable for so long, and which had proved unworkable. Why, indeed, should such power be denounced by Edward's supplanters when they hoped to exercise it themselves? The settlement expressed the reality of the age which was that a king was expected to govern personally, that he would continue to have a great deal of latitude, but that if he governed intolerably the only solution would be his overthrow. Politically, it was as though the slate had been wiped clean of the conflicts during the past three reigns between king and his would-be natural advisers. It would now be for a new king to find a *modus vivendi* with his barons, and the warlike son of an unwarlike father was to discover this in the shared adventure of foreign war.

[1] The formal announcement of abdication is printed in B. Wilkinson, op. cit., p. 172, which contains a useful selection of printed extracts (pp. 157–175) relating to the deposition of Edward II.

CHAPTER 5

Edward III:
The Rise and Influence of the Commons

I

JUDGED in the light of subsequent history, the deposition of Edward II profoundly affected the collective mind of the English political nation. Hitherto, as the original version of Magna Carta had specifically allowed, it had not been outside the bounds of political propriety for the barons to make war against an unsatisfactory king so as to coerce him into mending his ways. But it had always appeared to be implicit in such action that the king's own person and title were sacrosanct. War had been made against John and Henry III but their possession of the Crown had not seemed at risk. Edward II, however, had been removed under compulsion and openly, not because he was evil or mad but because he was an intolerably incapable king. The political fiction that it was an abdication could have deceived nobody. What is more, though it had been done by force, Parliament, including the Commons, had been involved in legitimatizing the change, and some of the Communities which sent representatives to the Parliament of 1327, most notably the citizens of London, had given practical help to the rebellion by withdrawing their support from the king. A new precedent had been set. After Edward II, English monarchs were deposed, murdered or exiled more freely than in any other comparable European nation, and Parliament usually had a hand in giving legitimacy to the change. Richard II's enforced abdication was announced in an assembly which had been summoned in his name as a Parliament, and Parliament was used to validate the usurpation of Richard III, as well as to confirm, if only indirectly, the other dynastic changes during the conflicts between York and Lancaster. Finally, in the revolutions against the Stuarts, it was to be Parliament which made war against

Charles I and Parliament which effected a change of constitution and dynasty after James II had been driven into exile by the action of the political magnates. It is one of the more remarkable paradoxes of English political history that the one great European monarchy which has survived into the 20th century has repeatedly been called harshly to account in ways not experienced by comparable monarchies before their final fall. Historical fictions, including the notion of abdication rather than deposition, have repeatedly been used (except in 1649) to preserve the appearance of political continuity at times when one monarch has been forcibly removed to make way for another, or when the character of the monarchy itself has been radically altered. The reign of Edward II appears, in retrospect, as a kind of watershed in political behaviour, after which the tacit contract of a king's acceptance by his people could more easily be broken, especially if a Parliament (which was thereby assisted towards a new sense of its corporate importance) could be brought to have a hand in the change.

The rebellion which removed Edward II was a national rather than a factional movement, but factional government was its immediate though short-lived outcome. The new king was only fourteen, and for nearly four years after his father's deposition, the effective governor of England was Roger Mortimer, in association with Isabella, purporting to act for Edward III. Yet though Mortimer's rule had some of the arbitrary features characteristic of usurpations, Parliament continued to be an active and convenient element in the ordinary business of government, and for securing sufficient consent by petitioning for the redress of grievances. For instance, at the beginning of the rule of Mortimer and Isabella statutes obviously intended to have a popular appeal were enacted to ameliorate the forest law. The first statute of the new reign (which, in the manner of the time, was a compendium of unrelated enactments on a wide variety of matters) included safeguards for offenders against the forest law when proceedings were taken against them.[1] The second statute of Edward III enacted that the future boundaries of the forest should be those established by the perambulations made under Edward I; where there had been no perambulations, it was ordered that they should take place immediately so as to establish boundaries.[2] By thus encouraging disafforestation and relaxing the severity of the forest law, the new government was responding to the long-standing grievance that the spread of the forest encouraged lawbreakers and poachers, and was a hindrance to law-enforcement. A quasi-

---

[1] *Stat. R.*, Vol. I, 1 Edw. III St. 1. c. VIII., p. 254

[2] Ibid St. 2 c. I. Both statutes also dealt with other matters, including the misdeeds of the Despensers and indemnity for those who had supported the queen.

usurper had even more incentive than a properly established ruler to win popular support, and Parliament was to become an increasingly valuable implement for securing public support for new kings and dynasties which had taken possession of the throne. But the Commons now had a wider political importance than petitioning for the redress of grievances; wider, too, than assenting to taxation and informing their communities what taxes had been granted and what new laws had been enacted.

Parliament's political function had been greatly enhanced not only by its part in the process of abdication but also by the use made of it by first one and then another of the contending factions during the long years of turbulence. The Commons in particular were now accustomed to being summoned to attend the council of the realm on important political occasions. Both Edward II and the magnates had found it convenient to further their causes with the communities of the shires and towns by making political use of the knights and burgesses summoned to Parliament. In the great political and dynastic conflicts of the middle ages, the role of the Commons remained more or less limited to validating the decisions reached by the most powerful party of the magnates by means of victory in battle, *coup d'état* or sometimes simply show of strength. But the knights and burgesses were useful agents for conditioning public opinion to accept political change, and it followed naturally from their part on the margin of these great events that the representative Commons had now assumed a corporate identity as representing an estate of the realm. They had become a necessary part of Parliament which, after 1325, was never again summoned without them. In the thirteenth century, it had invariably been the barons who represented themselves as speaking for the 'community of the realm' in their dealings with the king, a claim which was given some colour by the degree of popular support they sometimes received, or were able to exact. By the reign of Edward III, it had come to be recognized that it was the elected representatives in Parliament who spoke for the 'community'. There was as yet no way of changing government except by force, which in the medieval period could be exerted only by the magnates, and that would remain so for nearly another four centuries. But in the everyday business of any government, consent is imperative and the Commons were increasingly the channel for expressing it.

The position of the knights and burgesses in Parliament as representing the 'community' had been clearly indicated in the declaration of Edward II's abdication, which recorded that he had resigned by his own good will and by 'the common counsel and assent of prelates, earls, barons, and other nobles, and all the community of the realm', (... *de sa bone volunte et de commun conseil et assent des prelatz, countes, et barons, et autres nobles, et tote la communalte du roialme* . . .) and the same is shown in the series of petitions presented in the Parliament of 1327 by the 'community of the land'.[1] It did not follow, of course, that the idea of the Commons as representatives of the community of the realm as yet evoked much general enthusiasm or understanding. In the chronicles, there had earlier been criticism of Parliaments which authorized too heavy taxes while doing too little to promote the redress of grievances. Later, in 1339, the author of a political poem, unimpressed by the representative utility of Parliament, commented (no doubt unfairly) that those who granted taxation paid nothing themselves and that only the needy were charged.[2] (There is a certain similarity to criticism of increases in the pay of MPs in the twentieth century, especially at times when the public is being exhorted to be restrained about wages.) The increasing tendency in the towns for burgesses to be elected by the wealthy may be one explanation for this scepticism, while in the shires, where election was in the larger county court, resentment at the cost of sending men to Parliament tended to exceed conviction that they could do their constituents much good.[3] The powerful magnates had no doubt seemed more impressive representatives of the wider community when they had chosen to assume that role. But earls and barons now regarded themselves as an estate apart – and they no longer claimed to speak for the community as a whole, or to concern themselves so specifically with its grievances. The feudal link which had implied that role was now vestigial. In the future, the business of magnates and barons was increasingly to be war overseas. It was the Commons, with the knights and burgesses sitting together, and apart from the magnates, who were now to become the principal agents of the general community in its claims in its complaints against government. How they did so is the principal political interest of the reign.

On 1 February, 1327 Edward III was crowned, taking the same coronation oath as his father. Later the same day, he went on to open a second session of the Parliament which had been instrumental in his father's overthrow. It assembled again without a re-summons and remained in being for several weeks. In response to a series of petitions, the second statute of the reign dealt, among other matters, with complaints by the Commons about military service, and particularly abuse of the requirement to serve outside the shire, specifically in Gascony and Scotland. The statute

---

[1] *Select Docs. of English Constitutional History, 1307–1485* (1961), edited Chrimes and Brown, p. 38. See also M. Prestwich, 'Parliament and Community of the realm in fourteenth century England', a paper contributed to *Parliament and Community*, edited by Art Cosgrove and J. I. McGuire, 1983.

[2] M. Prestwich, op. cit., p. 16.

[3] M. Prestwich, op. cit., pp. 16–20.

conceded the general point that requirement of military service should be as it had been in the time of the king's ancestors, and that there should be no obligation to go outside a man's shire except when there was necessity as a result of the sudden coming of foreign enemies into the kingdom (*si noun par cause de necessite de sodeyne venue des estraunges enemys en roialme* . . .).[1] The preamble to the statute itself clearly indicates that it had been initiated by the petition of the Commons, and enacted by the authority of the king and the magnates.[2] In the royal response to the petition which led to this statute, the form of words used was that 'it pleased the king and his council' to make the enactment, a reference to the council of Regency that had been set up with Henry of Lancaster at its head. (Some other responses to petitions were in the name of the council as such: '*il semble au conseil* . . .'). Mortimer himself took no place on this body, being content with the reality as distinct from the formality of power. Instead, he acted through his principal representatives on the council, Bishop Hotham of Ely, the chancellor, Bishop Orleton of Hereford, the treasurer and two other councillors, Sir Oliver Ingham and Sir Simon Bereford.

The first item of business in this first Parliament, however, was the petition of Henry of Lancaster for the reversal of the sentence on his brother. The grounds were that Thomas had not been enabled to answer the charges against him, and that he should have been tried by his peers not on the king's record of his offences. The case was admitted and Henry was reinstated as Earl of Lancaster, most of his landed inheritance also being restored to him. Mortimer too obtained the restoration of his father's property and subsequently procured for himself a huge grant of forfeited lands that had belonged to the Despensers and others. In the following year he arrogantly took the challenging title of Earl of March, with its obvious assertion of his power in the Welsh marches. He had embarked on the life of self-aggrandizement and greed which with his unpopular conduct of public affairs was to be the cause of his undoing.

In the spring of 1327, it became clear that the truce with Scotland would not endure. Bruce had moved troops to the border, in defiance of the new

---

[1] Petitions by the Commons, and the king's response: *Rot. Parl.* Vol. II pp. 8–12; *Stat R.* Vol. I, 1 Edward III, st. 2, c. 5., p. 255. Also S. B. Chrimes and A. L. Brown, *Sel. Docs. of English Const. Hist.* (1961), p. 39.

[2] '. . . to the redress of the oppressions of the people, King Edward . . . at his Parliament held at Westminster . . . at the request of the community of his realm (*a la requeste de la commune de son roialme*) by their petition made before him and his council in the Parliament, by the assent of the prelates, earls, barons and other great men assembled at the said Parliament, has granted for him and his heirs for ever these articles . . .' *Stat. R.* Vol. I, p. 255.

English king, and the English embarked on a campaign. It began badly when strife with bloodshed broke out in York between the mercenaries from Hainault in the English army and the citizens. In the subsequent campaign (though it hardly warranted that description) the harrying Scots repeatedly eluded and outwitted the English, and finally in August withdrew in triumph to their own land. It was the time of the year when the period of feudal service customarily ended, the soldiers being needed to bring in the harvest. The failure of this expedition, which was a great personal humiliation to the young king who took part in it, precipitated the long resisted recognition by the English of Robert Bruce as King of the Scots. On 7 February 1328, the third Parliament of the reign (a second had met at Lincoln the previous September) assembled in York. Before it opened, the king was married in York Minster to Philippa of Hainault whom he had gone south to meet, though the new queen was not crowned for another two years, perhaps because Isabella was reluctant to concede her that precedence. The business of this Parliament was a settlement with Scotland and to it came a delegation of a hundred Scottish knights. The terms eventually agreed represented a clear victory for the Scots. Both the old border and Bruce's independent title, free of any limitation of homage to the English king, were recognized, and a marriage was arranged between the Scottish king's heir David, who was four years old, and Edward's sister Joan, who was seven. It was a final triumph for Bruce who was dying; all the English got out of it was a war indemnity of £20,000 from the Scots. The terms of the agreement were drawn up at Holyrood abbey and were ratified in another Parliament which met in Northampton in April, from which town the treaty, otherwise known as the Shameful Peace (*turpis pax*) took its formal name. In that Parliament a statute was promulgated containing a number of enactments dealing principally with the maintenance of law and justice, including the misuse of pardons of felonies. But interestingly, it also made an early declaration of free trade, declaring that 'the Staples beyond the Sea and on this Side, ordained by Kings in Times past, and the Pains thereby provided, shall cease'.[1] Again we have a political bid by Mortimer's government for popularity, in this case to those merchants outside the Staple who disliked it. But this legislation in favour of a more free market did not endure.

In the meantime, Mortimer had continued to build up the case against himself by the most shocking of all his offences. To greed and ostentatious living, to seizure of land and money (including at least part of the Scottish indemnity) to the insolent familiarity with which he treated the young king,

[1] *Stat.* R. Vol. I, p. 259.

was now added the secret murder of Edward of Carnarvon. The former king had been moved in April from Kenilworth to Berkeley Castle where there were two attempts to rescue him, one of which nearly succeeded. On hearing of the second plot, Mortimer determined on Edward's death. It was said later that attempts were made to bring about his end through 'natural' causes by subjecting him to cold, damp and filthy conditions, but that his strong constitution resisted these assaults. Mortimer therefore had him put to a horrifying death. In September 1327, while Edward III was still engaged on the Scottish campaign, it was announced that Edward of Carnarvon had died; there was no apparent sign of violence. He was buried in a magnificent tomb in Gloucester Abbey which became the place of a popular cult. Whatever had happened, it must have been very difficult for anyone at all concerned with public affairs not to suspect immediately that he had been murdered, and for many suspicion must have hardened into virtual certainty as the passing months gave time for rumour and reports of the details of the crime to spread. Mortimer was by now generally detested, and it was presumably because he knew he lived at risk that he went to the Parliament which met in Salisbury in October 1328, with a large armed force. Later, when he was charged with Edward II's murder and other crimes, it was alleged that he had burst with this force into 'a house where the prelates were assembled to debate the affairs of state and threatened in life and limb' any who defied him.[1] The most potent sign of Mortimer's danger was the refusal of Henry of Lancaster, who had hitherto acquiesced in Mortimer's supremacy, to attend the Parliament on the grounds that the council of regency was for all practical purposes supplanted, and that the king had not enough to live of his own. Lancaster remained at Winchester where other discontented notables joined him. Civil war again seemed to threaten, and after the Salisbury Parliament had been adjourned until February, Mortimer did indeed invade Lancaster's earldom and force him to a peace. These crude demonstrations of power politics are a reminder that real though the influence of the Commons was with regard to law, taxation and everyday grievances, the last word on great dynastic matters or on changes of government remained still with those magnates (or, as in the coming downfall of Mortimer, with the king) who possessed sufficient strength or cunning to bring about change when they had become convinced that it was essential.

After his difficulties with Lancaster, Mortimer was more than ever determined to eliminate his enemies. One whom he judged to be such was Edmund of Kent, the late king's half-brother, a weak man who felt remorse

[1] *Rot. Parl.* Vol. II, p. 52.

about his part in his brother's downfall. To trap him, Mortimer had it put about that Edward of Carnarvon was still alive at Corfe Castle, and on receiving reports that a man was detained there who was being treated with the respect due to royal distinction, Kent despatched a sealed letter to the supposed prisoner. On 11 March, 1330 when Parliament was meeting at Wincester, Kent was arrested. He admitted writing the letter and in his fear confessed also to more than was known for certain, implicating others who were enemies to Mortimer and loyal to the late king as having discussed with him the possibility of Edward's rescue. Kent was hurriedly tried by his peers, found guilty, sentenced and executed. This judicial murder finally made up the king's mind that Mortimer must be brought down. For this purpose, he employed two friends he could trust completely, Sir William Montagu, his personal equerry, and Richard Bury, the Keeper of his Privy Seal, and his former tutor. While taking part in a mission to Avignon, Montagu obtained a private interview with the Pope to explain the king's plight. It was agreed that some kind of secret sign would be sent to the Pope so that he should know when a communication had come from Edward personally. When Montagu had returned to England, Bury sent a letter to Avignon, containing a sample of Edward's handwriting (the oldest autograph of an English king known to have survived) and stating that the words '*sancte pater*' in any communication under the privy seal would show that it was genuinely from the king. Edward proceeded to inform the Pope that only Bury and Montagu knew of his intention to deal with Mortimer. A plot was now hatched which seems to have been largely Montagu's work.

At the beginning of September Mortimer summoned a great council (which had the composition of a Parliament without the Commons) to meet in Nottingham in the following month, the summons being couched in terms threatening to those who stayed away. Mortimer, well guarded by his troops in the town and castle, may have suspected that there would be some move against him. At all events, he excluded all other notables from the castle except himself, the king, and the queen mother, and he required that Lancaster should remain a mile away. These precautions, however, helped the plotters, making it possible for the king's friends to prepare their action away from the castle. On 19 October, after a Council meeting, the lords left the castle, but late at night a party led by Montagu returned through a secret passage, burst into Mortimer's chamber, killed two bodyguards, seized Mortimer and hurried him through the passage and out of the castle without his soldiers knowing what had happened and despite pleas from Isabella that they should have mercy on him. The next day, the king announced that Mortimer and his associates had been arrested for malpractices and that henceforth Edward would govern for himself, with the advice of the great men of the kingdom. As he journeyed from Nottingham, Edward summoned Parliament to meet a month later at Westminster, with virtually the same composition as the Nottingham council, but with the addition of the Commons. On the first day, Mortimer was found guilty of treason and condemned to death by the 'earls, barons and peers as judges of Parliament'. They also tried and sentenced his associate Simon Bereford, protesting however that since he was not their peer they were not obliged to do so, but consented to act as 'judges of Parliament' only because the offence was so grave. Both cases were tried simply by the king's recording his personal knowledge of the accused men's crimes, it being assumed that the charges were so evident that there was no need for the accused to defend themselves. It was a precedent that had been set in the condemnation of Thomas of Lancaster and it would be followed many times in the future when there were charges of treason, a crime as yet undefined by statute. It is clear from these proceedings that the peers of the realm were acting as a distinct and separate body, at least as judges of Parliament, and also that both earls and barons were equally peers.[1]

Edward's task was to restore the badly damaged authority of the throne. He wisely began with clemency towards Mortimer's adherents. Apart from Bereford, only Sir John Daverill, the governor of Corfe was condemned. Mortimer's friends among the bishops were pardoned; so was Sir Oliver Ingham who became a useful servant for Edward. Isabella was also treated leniently, even though her greed, not to speak of her position as Mortimer's mistress, had itself been a matter of great scandal. To avoid embarrassment, no charge was directed against Mortimer with regard to Isabella, other than that he had sown discord between her and the late king. She went into a modified kind of retirement on a restricted income, but gradually began to appear more often at court, and before she died took the habit of the Poor Clares. The king also took care to restore good relations with the Lancaster family. Earl Henry (who retired from public life because he was going blind) had approved Mortimer's overthrow, and his son Henry de Grosmont was in 1337 made Earl of Derby. Naturally, the king's own supporters were also rewarded. His closest personal friend, William Montagu, was summoned to Parliament as Lord Montagu in 1331, and was to be created Earl of Salisbury in 1337. Richard Bury was later to become chancellor and Bishop of Durham. In one way and another, the young, popular and apparently extrovert king made certain that the old factions were no more.

Edward's character is in some respects harder for us to interpret than

[1] *Dignity of a Peer*, Vol. I, p. 299.

those of other medieval kings about whom, superficially, we may seem to have less solid information. Renowned among his contemporaries for his bravery and chivalry, the king who inaugurated the hundred years' war with France is more likely to strike the twentieth century mind as one who spent too much of his country's substance on useless bloodshed for ambition's sake. The founder of that great Order of Chivalry, the Garter, was also a self-indulgent man and even some of his own contemporaries noted his weakness for sins of the flesh which were eventually to undermine his capacity for governing. Yet Edward was always capable of gaining and keeping the loyalty of his nobility, who were to be heavily involved in his war for the French crown and beneficiaries from the spoils of battle, and he did not harbour grudges. He was a brilliant soldier and a great leader of men, who also attracted the loyalty of his people, associating them with his brilliant victories in the French war which helped to create a stronger sense of English nationhood than had existed before. A skilful political tactician, Edward undoubtedly acted with wisdom in his clemency towards Mortimer's friends and adherents. Yet a certain chilliness in his convivial personality seems to come down to us between the lines of the historical evidence. Even the apparent ease with which he could make terms with those who had destroyed his father is in some of its manifestations a little disconcerting; for instance one of those who had allegedly been implicated directly in regicide was eventually pardoned. Edward possessed a pragmatic temperament governing his actions by convenience. He was inspired by no great urge to improve the law or the processes of government, or even to devote himself to defending the prerogatives of the Crown in the manner of his forefathers; what he wanted most was victory in France and for this he seemed always ready for political compromises at home. It was from these that Parliament, during his long reign, was to make the biggest advance so far, as the king proved willing to provide the redress of grievances to ensure that grants of money were forthcoming from the Commons. Strong in his war policy, for the sake of which he was often yielding at home, Edward III unwittingly assisted the House of Commons to discover and use the principal source of its future power. Once again constitutional advance was to flow from the exigencies of practical politics.

Whatever may have been Edward's thinking about France at the outset of his rule, his first intention was to expunge the humiliation of Mortimer's treaty with the Scots, and to deprive the French of an effective ally north of the border. Robert Bruce was now dead and the Earl of Murray was regent for the infant Scottish king. Almost certainly with Edward's connivance, but with no formal support from him, a group of dispossessed Scottish noblemen known as the Disinherited revived Edward Balliol's claim to the

Scottish crown and prepared an invasion from English soil. Anxious not to incur penalties for breaking the Treaty of Northampton, Edward formally kept his distance from Balliol and his followers. But Balliol and his force nevertheless sailed from Ravenspur, landed in the Firth of Forth in August and defeated the Scots. Balliol was crowned at Scone as Edward I of Scotland, and subsequently declared his allegiance to Edward III to whom he proposed to cede territory on the Border.

Three parliaments were held in 1332. The first, in March, provides a new insight into proceedings.[1] At it, the king's intention of going on a crusade was explained and proposals were drawn up for dealing with breaches of the peace. The Commons were then dismissed early leaving the magnates and council in session. As the people's petitions had not been dealt with, it was announced that another parliament would be held soon. This met in September and was primarily concerned with Scotland and an appeal for help from Balliol. The crisis was discussed by 'the said prelates by themselves; and the said earls, barons and other lords by themselves; and also the knights of the shire by themselves....' It is conspicuously not stated that the citizens and burgesses played a part in this political deliberation, but those who did so advised the king to remain in England and go to the north in case the Scots invaded. Knights and burgesses almost certainly used the same chamber when they deliberated apart, but as a consequence of the burgesses' inferior social status, it may well have been assumed that their opinion need not to be actively canvassed on a strictly military matter. Yet if there was still any such notion it was already rapidly changing, as the next Parliament was to show, and by the end of the decade it was clearly recognized that knights and burgesses were conjoined as a single unit in one house. When it came to money, moreover, there was already no doubt about the importance of the burgesses. For the parliamentary roll for 1332 went on to record that the lords and 'the knights of the shire and all the Commons' (*tote la commune*) granted taxation of a fifteenth of moveable goods in the shires and a tenth in the towns of their free will' to enable Edward to deal with Scotland. This, they said, was so that the king 'could live of his own (that is to say, from his demesne revenues) and pay his expenses without burdening his people with outrageous prises or otherwise'.[2]

The king then dissolved the Parliament and moved his government to York which, for all practical purposes, became England's capital city for the next five years. A new Parliament was hastily summoned to meet there in

---

[1] *Rot. Parl.* Vol. II, pp. 64–66. See below, pp. 264ff.
[2] *Rot. Parl.* Vol. II, p. 66.

December, when Edward sought the approval of the baronage for a Scottish war. The question of what the king should do about Scotland was put in full Parliament by the chief justice, Geoffrey Scrope, and was considered by the prelates and clergy, by the earls and barons, and by 'the knights and people of the shires, and people of the community', each of these three groupings sitting 'by themselves' and deliberating for a week. But there was considerable unease at the prospect of renewed involvement in Scotland, and at the end of the week each group asked in full Parliament for an adjournment on the grounds that only five prelates had arrived, though this may have been an excuse. Parliament was then prorogued until 20 January 1333.[1]

During the recess, the situation changed radically and the Scots drove Balliol from their country. When Parliament reassembled, the chief justice, speaking in 'full Parliament' on the king's behalf, asked 'all the prelates, earls, barons and other magnates who were there, and also the knights of the shire' what should be done. Again the familiar three groups of prelates with clergy, lay magnates, and Commons were required to deliberate separately, but on this occasion an extra committee was also appointed to do so. Six prelates led by the Archbishop of York, two earls and four barons were appointed to meet as a committee separately from all the other elements of Parliament; their function was presumably to offer the king specific proposals for dealing with the Scottish problem. But there was no greater parliamentary enthusiasm for war in Scotland now than there had been before Christmas, and no agreement could be found on what the king should do. Edward therefore announced that he would consult the Pope and the French king, and dissolved the Parliament. He then prepared for war and went on to besiege Berwick, defeating the Scots nearby at Halidon Hill in July 1333. Bannockburn had been avenged, and Edward set out on a triumphant tour to the English south, returning to the north to summon another Parliament to York in February 1334. By midsummer, the boy king David Bruce, with his wife Joan, who was Edward's sister, had been driven to take refuge at the French court. Balliol did homage to Edward, who pragmatically abandoned his old English feudal claim to appellate jurisdiction in Scotland, being more interested in the land Balliol was willing to cede. Scotland, however, was not pacified. Within two months, Balliol was driven out and another English expedition was prepared. The next three years brought further campaigns, but Scotland was not subdued.

In September, 1334, another Parliament met at Westminster, making a further grant of a fifteenth and tenth.[2] It was an occasion of particular

[1] *Rot. Parl.* Vol. II, pp. 67–9.
[2] Ibid. p. 447.

significance in the development of the medieval tax system. For this time, at the behest of Parliament, new arrangements were made for the collection of the tax which resulted in a total yield of about £38,000 which thereafter became the standard figure of assessment. The change arose from allegations of corrupt practices in 1332. To prevent a recurrence, it was provided in 1334 that two commissioners, one layman, one ecclesiastic, should treat with the communities of town and shire, and agree with them the sum to be paid to the king by each shire and vil for the tenth and fifteenth. If the local people did not agree to terms, the head taxers and collectors were to make an assessment. In theory, this agreed assessment constituted the sum that each taxable unit in the community was to pay in future. Thus in 1336, and continually thereafter, the commissioners were instructed to take from each city borough and township the amount levied in 1334. So, although the taxes were still called tenths and fifteenths, the terms were meaningless and without arithmetical significance. The fact that the total amount for a community was fixed meant that there also tended to be a fixed apportionment of tax liability among its sub-divisions, and down to individuals. When either a community, one of its sub-divisions or an individual was unable to pay the due amount as a result of some kind of economic disaster or loss of means, there could be an appeal for reassessment. If the appellants secured it and their circumstances improved they naturally tried, usually without success, to keep to the more favourable figure. As a result of such appeals, however, there were small variations in the yield of the tax each year, and sometimes there had to be significant adjustments. For example, because of the Black Death, the king on three occasions reduced the amount payable but also managed to ensure that his government's revenue was not equivalently reduced. Thus in 1349, when there was a fixed legal maximum for wages, it was ordered that any wages above this limit should be subject to a levy, the proceeds of which were offset against the subsidy due from the locality; it was an early version of the twentieth century theory of incomes policy which suggests that excess wages should be taxed away. In 1352, fines under the Statute of Labourers, to reinforce wage limitation, were also allocated to reduce the general tax burden, so that while the government received the desired subsidy, the taxes paid in some districts were lowered by the amount of the penalties.[1]

In November 1334 Edward again invaded Scotland and restored Balliol to his throne, and in the May of 1335 he summoned a Parliament to York

---

[1] J. F. Willard, 'The Taxes on Movables of the Reign of Edward III', *E.H.R.* Vol. XXX, 1915, p. 69–74. More generally, see J. F. Willard, *Parliamentary Taxes on Personal Property, 1290–1334* (1934) and G. L. Harriss, *King, Parliament and Public Finance in Medieval England to 1369* (1975).

before leading the largest invasion so far into the northern kingdom. The regent Moray was taken prisoner and the Scots were left leaderless. In August, a peace was declared at Perth, but the Scottish tactics of avoiding pitched battle and launching surprise attacks on English garrisons continued. Edward therefore led yet another invasion in 1336, a year in which there were two Parliaments, one in March at Westminster, the other in September at Nottingham. Each granted a fifteenth and tenth. It was proving to be an expensive war, but Edward had shown himself to be a good soldier and although Scotland was not really subdued, it was by now weakened enough for Edward to be able to turn his attention from it towards his principal enemy, France.

The origin of the long-standing quarrels between the French and English crowns lay in the anomalous position of the English king as Duke of Aquitaine, or Gascony. As overlord of Gascony, the French monarch claimed by custom the right to intervene in jurisdiction in the duchy, and this claim had been the principal source of past conflict. The reluctance of English kings to pay homage for Gascony was another source of tension, but Edward III did in fact do so on two occasions, in a simple form in 1329 and (to remove misunderstanding) more elaborately and in writing in 1331. After the second homage, he even visited his feudal overlord to try to settle their differences, travelling to France in disguise so as not to lose prestige with his subjects. Subsequently, some efforts were made, without great success, to settle the complex disputes relating to boundaries and trade, and so long as he was embroiled with Scotland, Edward had done his best to mollify Philip VI of France. Hostilities on two fronts were to be avoided. But after the arrival in France of David Bruce in 1334, Philip informed Edward's ambassadors that David, and the Scots generally, must be included in any peace between England and France. This heartened the Scottish resistance as much as it disconcerted Edward, who was now faced either with abandoning his claims in Scotland or facing a French attack. Philip's espousal of David Bruce's cause was perhaps the most decisive proximate cause of the Anglo-French war. A short truce, arranged under papal auspices came to nothing. French aid for the Scots increased, English shipping was attacked by the Scots operating from French bases, and most ominously, Philip transferred a fleet intended for a crusade from Marseilles to Normandy, apparently in preparation for an invasion of England. Edward was meanwhile seeking allies among the rulers of the Netherlands, where he had family connections, including those of his wife Philippa of Hainault. He also exerted commercial pressure on the cloth-makers of Flanders, whose count was a supporter of the French king, by placing an embargo on the export of English wool to Flanders, thus depriving the

Flemish weavers of their staple commodity. But instead of yielding to the pressure, the count simply seized English goods and arrested English merchants. In May 1337, however, Edward sent an embassy to Hainault offering money which secured as his allies the rulers of Hainault, Gelderland, Brabant and Limburg and others. Edward even purchased an alliance with the Emperor Ludwig IV, with whom he had a ceremonial meeting at Coblenz. The French and the English kings were now at the brink of war. Since 1327, English possession of Gascony had been reduced to a coastal strip pending the payment to the French crown of stipulated sums of money to redeem the duchy. The symbol of the breakdown of peace was a declaration by King Philip in May 1337 that Gascony (which Edward had already put in a state of military preparedness) was confiscated because of the English king's disobedience. Even now, thanks to papal mediation, there was a short delay before war became certain, but in October Edward took the final step by making the claim to the French crown which became the prime English motive in the struggle which was to last intermittently for a hundred years. It was not a new claim, and it was not the basic cause of the war. Nor did Edward immediately adopt the title King of France for everyday use. He was waiting to see how the struggle developed. But it was a claim which raised Edward's cause above that of a vassal simply rebelling against his overlord, and it was not altogether without justification.

On the death of Charles IV of France in 1328, there had been no direct male heir of the House of Capet. If the throne could be passed to a woman it would have descended to Isabella of England, sister of the late king and daughter of Philip IV. If it could be passed not to, but through, a woman, Edward III would be the heir. But given French custom, it could be passed neither to nor through a woman, and the nearest heir was Philip of Valois whose claim descended from Philip III, that is to say from one generation earlier of the Capetian dynasty. He had been crowned as Philip VI. The precedent that a woman could not succeed to the throne had been established on the deaths of Louis X in 1316 and of Philip V in 1321, both of whom left only daughters. The separate question whether the French crown could pass *through* a woman had, however, not been tested, though logic hardly supported the argument that it could. Even if a woman could transmit the claim, it was obviously not practical politics for it to be transmitted to an heir who was king of England. In 1328, when Edward was still a minor, a claim had formally been registered on his behalf, but he was in no position to pursue it and had so far shown no apparent wish to do so. Indeed, his double homage to Philip could be taken as a sign that the claim was waived. Now, at the outset of the war it furnished no more than a justification of convenience for a war which had had other origins. Yet the claim was to become the prime cause which would sustain the war from reign to reign and which was to bring one of Edward's successors to a brief tenure of the French throne and a crowning at Rheims. By 1337, hostilities had already begun in Gascony, and in the following year Edward embarked on his first expedition against the French, armed with the fiscal and moral support of Parliament, but also crucially dependent on Parliament for money. It is a convenient moment at which to stand back and inspect the characteristics of Parliament as they appear in Edward's first decade, and before the rapid development of parliamentary influence during the remainder of his long reign.

II

England in the early decades of Edward III's rule was a land still largely covered with forest, but the area under cultivation had steadily increased and most of the villages of today's landscape were already in existence. Roads were extensive and good enough to link up all its regions, and men who were summoned or sent to what had now become regular Parliaments were able to make long journeys from their own towns and shires to whatever distant place the king had ordained for the assembly. Travel was, nevertheless, potentially perilous, for there was much lawlessness, and it was necessary to be sufficiently armed not only to deal with the occasional robber but also to fend off the criminal bands which roamed the woodlands. The forest was a magnet for wrong-doers, and its proximity to the villages and cultivated land provided a refuge for law-breakers and poachers. But the greatest danger was from the well-organized gangs which terrorized some localities, a few of which were even led by men with the rank of knight. For the magnates and barons, there was no cause for worry, since they habitually travelled with large bodies of armed retainers. Even in ordinary circumstances they might journey with two hundred or more knights, esquires, men-at-arms, serving men and pages. Indeed, the armed forces accompanying a magnate were sometimes so large as clearly to be intended more as a demonstration of his power, and to reinforce his political wishes when Parliament was in session, than simply to ensure a safe journey. As we have seen in the reign of Edward II, magnates of the importance of the earls of Lancaster or the marcher lords would be accompanied by many hundreds of armed men as a demonstration of their local power. Such shows of strength were a threat to political stability and some attempts were made to prohibit armed appearances at Parliament. Little notice was taken of them; perhaps the need for self-protection on the journey provided some sort of excuse. The wealthier knights were also no doubt accompanied by a retinue; the writs for the Parliament at Northampton in 1328 forbade the attendance of members with a multitude of armed retainers.[1] How lesser representative knights and, in particular, burgesses travelled to Parliament can only be surmised. But it seems a reasonable assumption that they must often have put themselves under the protection of the most available local magnate, baron or well-protected knight; at any rate, it hardly seems likely that they went unaccompanied or even with two or three supporters. Common sense suggests that men making their way to Parliament, including the ecclesiastics, must generally have joined together in arrangements for their collective security.

Yet despite the lawlessness, which had been worsened by the political troubles and the economic consequences of the great famine in the late reign, England was a land of increasing prosperity and population. The number of its inhabitants cannot be known with any certainty but it was probably between four and six million, or well over twice, perhaps more than three times, the population after the Norman Conquest. It was a rural society whose prosperity was based on agriculture and wool; more land than ever before had been taken from woodland for cultivation. In the previous century, large landowners who had once regarded their estates primarily as the means of sustaining themselves and their followers (moving frequently from one part of their scattered properties to another and consuming the produce of each as they went) had increasingly put their land under intensive farming so as to produce and sell more in the market. By improved farming methods, yields had been raised, and detailed production targets for a manor were often set for the amount or weight required of each commodity, grain, wool or dairy produce. Careful accounts were kept and sometimes bailiffs might even be required to pay for shortfalls themselves, though they could also prosper beyond the calculation when targets were exceeded. Such changed attitudes had been seeping down the social scale to knights and to peasant farmers, even including the theoretically unfree villeins who, when they prospered, increasingly bought land free of obligation to work, in addition to that which they held in bond for service.

By custom, cottars and villeins held their land under an obligation to perform work-service for their lord, both 'week-work' (a given number of days unpaid work on their lords' land each week) and 'boon-work' (extra

---

[1] Stubbs, *Constitutional Hist.* Vol. III, (5th ed.) p. 411.

days at the busy seasons of harvesting and ploughing). Now, however, the movement to a money economy was well established. Rents became an objective at every rung of the social ladder, and work-service was increasingly commuted in whole or in part for money payments. From this development there would emerge a new class of villeins, holding the franchise of their land, who were known as copy-holders, and whose title-deed was a copy of the entry in the manor court-roll of the bargain they had made with their lord. (On inheriting or purchasing such land, the copy-holder would appeal in the manorial court, take an oath of loyalty to his lord and pay a fine, usually two years' rent. On the death of a tenant, the lord would be due to have his 'best beast'.) It naturally followed from this sort of change that the distinction between the free and the unfree had become much less sharp. The old system of feudal obligation was, however, by no means dead; in some places it was retained extensively, in others there was still an option to demand work in payment for land. Nevertheless, society had become both more fluid and more prosperous, and although most classes derived some benefit from this, the landowners at the top of the social and economic pyramid had gained most.

In the twelfth century there had been much subinfeudation; to acquire supporters the heirs to the great estates redistributed at the Norman Conquest had let out more of their land in exchange for military service. Then, in the thirteenth century, military service had come to be increasingly paid for by money instead of by land, while land was leased for money-rent. Since, at the same time, there were substantial rises in both population and in agricultural production, aristocratic revenues had grown to an unprecedented extent by the early years of the fourteenth century. Improved living standards testified to aristocratic wealth, whether in the more comfortable conditions of magnates' dwellings, where new rooms were added on to their old halls (which were now also divided and protected against draughts by wooden screens) or in general ostentation of dress.

By the time of Edward III's succession, however, this improvement in agricultural performance had halted. The pressure to raise farm yields had gone as far as it could (perhaps too far for good farming) and the market had suffered distortions in the wake of the great famine. Rising rents and wages were now, therefore, being accompanied by falls in the price of produce and consequently in farming incomes. But this only assisted the aristocratic accumulation of wealth; in a falling or sluggish market for farm commodities, landlords were even more interested in obtaining money incomes from leasing land instead of letting out land for work-service which only produced more from their own estates for a smaller real return. Thus the general diminution of agricultural prosperity only acted as an incentive to commutation of work service for rent, a change which was to be further encouraged by the need for money to meet Edward's war taxation in the years ahead. A predominantly money economy based largely on agriculture was being established, and the nobility, followed by the better off members of the class of knights, was the first of its beneficiaries.

One increasing source of rural prosperity was the movement of cloth-weaving from the towns to the countryside with the discovery of the economic benefits of using water-mills for fulling, a process which town weavers had hitherto carried out by hand or foot. This mechanization, resisted by town weavers as modern technology has been by trades unions, required the natural running water of hill districts. The various stages of cloth-manufacture were now being organized by entrepreneurs, and at the same time merchant wholesalers increasingly undertook the business of collecting and marketing wool from a number of small producers. Such businessmen were the initiators of English capitalism and the founders of those rich families who, making their money from dealing in wool or cloth manufacture and export, would build fine homes and magnificent churches in the wool-producing countryside. The prosperity of the nation as a whole came to rest more and more on the export of woollen cloth, as well as of wool, the making of woollens being assisted by encouragement to Flemish and other foreign weavers to settle here, and by the exclusion of foreign cloth and foreign exporters. The requirement that wool must only be exported through the Staple, which was set up first in England, then in Flanders and eventually at Calais, after its capture, had advantages both for the merchants and the king. Its monopolistic arrangements suited the merchants, and the king benefited from the facility by which the wool could be taxed collectively, the tax collection being farmed out to the merchants who were also a source of loans to the government. Wool merchants were important among the men represented by the burgesses in Parliament. But even more important for the development of the Commons was the king's attempt, and its failure, to make successful direct tax bargains with the wool merchants outside Parliament. Had he succeeded it would have slowed down the development of the influence of the Commons which was built on general grants of taxation in exchange for the redress of grievances.

In their apperance, England's towns and cities had not greatly changed. Even London which, with some 35,000 people, was by far the largest, remained distinctly rural, and townsmen would work in nearby fields as well as at their urban trades. Houses were still made of timber frames, lathes and plaster, and streets were narrow, ill-paved and often filthy. Yet there was a new urban prosperity, and a widening gap between the condition of the wealthy citizens and that of the rest. Gilds were no longer simply small fraternities of master craftsmen and their journeymen. There was now a sharper division between the masters, who were entrepreneurs providing and selling the goods, and the journeymen who were beginning to have their own fraternities. Craft gilds had been long established, but there were now also coming into existence merchant gilds of grocers, fishmongers, tailors and the like, possessing wealth which gave the prosperous burgesses increasing civic importance. As well as requiring the king to pay attention to their complaints in exchange for the grant of taxation, they were in a position to make or withhold loans to him, and as moneylenders they were in an independent position never enjoyed by their predecessors the Jews who, before their expulsion, had been entirely in the king's hands. Thus the liberties and the claims to self-regulation of the cities grew with prosperity, and increasingly the selection of parlimentary representatives rested with the better-off citizens. Such was the nature of the society represented in the Parliaments of the first half of the fourteenth century.

There was in England no clearly defined class or caste of noblemen, legally recognized and privileged by birth, such as existed on the continent of Europe. The only distinction that could remotely be described as resembling one of caste was that between freemen and villeins, or serfs. But it had always been possible for a serf to become free given certain conditions, and the distinction between serf and free man was becoming even more blurred as some prospering serfs bought freehold land and some freemen went down in the world. A freeman could be anyone from an impoverished and landless labourer to a rich merchant or a well-off franklin who might have as much land as a knight. Correspondingly, there was no sharp class distinction between knights and barons. Of course, the older established baronial families jealously guarded their position, and medieval history is riddled with cases of the magnates' dislike and resentment of upstarts, particularly when the influence of new men intervened between themselves and the king. But in general terms, what gave a man the status of a baron was not any clear-cut or inherited social distinction setting him apart from the generality of knights but rather the wealth of his estates. Barons proper were tenants-in-chief, holding their land directly from the king, and paying an inheritance tax for it, though there also existed a second rank of barons who held land from the larger tenants-in-chief. Baronial courts had certain rights of jurisdiction, (sometimes including the right to hang a thief caught red-handed), but these did not compare with the extensive juridical rights of the French nobility. Landlords also had considerable customary powers over their tenants in enforcing their due rents and services, and manorial courts exercised a simple police jurisdiction in the locality. But all else was reserved to the king's courts, and the power of the baron was exerted largely by his social pre-eminence in the areas where he held land (since the Conquest the lands of the baronial class had been well scattered over many counties) and through the part he expected to play in counselling the king, particularly in Parliament. The survival of the Anglo-Saxon shire courts, with their judicial and administrative responsibility directly to the king, was crucial to development of a parliamentary system unweakened by any quasi-independent feudal characteristics.

As a result of the division and agglomeration of estates over generations, the baronial class included men of greatly varying wealth. Throughout the thirteenth century, and well into the fourteenth, the selection of those barons who were to come to Parliament was determined not by any list of nobility but by their power, their personal influence and their usefulness as counsellors. Whereas the communities were required to send elected representatives, the summonses to those barons who were the predecessors of the House of Lords were addressed personally to individuals. The list of the chosen had normally been the same as that which the king would use in summoning magnates to arms, and under Edward I the summons of those under the rank of earl had been haphazard. In the past, moreover, some of those summoned had not even held land by baronial tenure, that is to say, with an obligation to pay inheritance duty to the king, and a few were not tenants-in-chief. But under Edward II the basic list from which lay barons were chosen for Parliament (the ecclesiastics are discussed separately) had increasingly become fixed. The list of magnates summoned to the early Parliaments of Edward II was essentially that used by his father, with some omissions and additions. The custom was already growing of summoning the heirs of deceased attenders, and this was the germ of the later hereditary peerage. Subsequently during the reign of Edward II the number of those individually summoned fluctuated with the ebbs and flows of power in the political conflict. It had fallen particularly sharply during the ascendancy of the Ordainers, and was then substantially enlarged at and after the king's reconciliation with Lancaster. Between 1314 until after the outbreak of civil war in 1321, the list was little changed, except for deaths and successions. But after the war had begun, a fresh list was made out for the Parliament of July 1321 and this (apart from the removal of Lancaster's dead or forfeited supporters after Boroughbridge) remained the basic list for individual summons to the baronage until after Edward's capture. The last Parliament summoned by Edward II personally in 1325 included thirty-eight barons. But of these only twenty-six were among the forty-six summoned by his opponents to the Parliament which deposed him. Yet most of the new men added in 1327 had received writs to some previous Parliaments, and for the next five years the list of 1327 continued to be used with few changes. Despite changes in those actually summoned as political fortunes altered, it is clear that the basic list was more or less stable after 1312. Pragmatically, the idea had taken root that certain barons and their heirs, holding certain estates, were entitled by prescriptive right to be summoned to Parliament by individual writs as 'the peers of the realm' or 'peers of the land'.[1]

The weakness of the monarchy under Edward II had assisted this development and it was taken further by Edward III's deliberate policy of using his nobility for support. For instance, he increased the number of earls by six in the Parliament of March 1337, shortly before hostilities with France. The charters granting to the new earls the third penny of their counties (standardized at £20) made the king's reasons quite clear. Edward considered it to be the chief among 'the marks of royalty' that 'through a due distribution of positions, dignities and offices, it is buttressed by wise counsels and fortified by might powers'. Therefore, because the number of hereditary ranks had declined, and 'to raise the might of our royal sceptre and direct more wisely and powerfully the business of our realm' the king had resolved 'at the request of the prelates and magnates and the community of our realm in our present Parliament . . . to increase the number of earldoms and illustrious personages in our realm'.[2]

Substantial grants of land were also made to enable them to sustain their dignity, and Edward III went further when he created the first dukedom in England, that of Cornwall, for his young son. By his magnification of the peerage, he created allies and supporters for himself, but he had also helped to make a source of trouble for his successors. Towards the middle of the fourteenth century there were something over eighty temporal peers who joined with twenty-one bishops and thirty-one abbots to constitute what we should call the House of Lords. Such evidence as there is, however, suggests that the magnates were often poor attenders at Parliament, and certainly worse than the Commons on whom the king's officials could more easily exert pressure. In any case, it was easier for the king to see his lords at court on other occasions, and also at those assemblies which we can most conveniently, though it was not a precise contemporary term, call great councils.[3]

Exalted though the peerage was becoming, there was no sharp social dividing line between peers and the knights whose representative role was the foundation of the House of Commons and who were the origin of that

---

[1] This account follows J. E. Powell & E. Wallis, *The House of Lords in the Middle Ages*, pp. 309–315.

[2] Ibid., p. 326.

[3] See below, pp. 276–7.

class later known as the gentry. Knighthood had evolved into a term signifying something much more substantial and complex than simply the description of Norman equestrian soldiers owing sworn duty in return for an hereditary land-holding known as a knight's fee. It was now a social distinction shared by kings, princes and earls as the hallmark of chivalry. Edward II accentuated its prestige by knighting his own son and younger lords while on military service, and also by his tournaments and the foundation of the Order of the Garter. In every shire there were now established knightly families from which dubbed knights were drawn, though not every man in such families would in practice be dubbed. The wealthiest of these knightly families enjoyed a standing and estates which hardly distinguished them from the less wealthy barons. Correspondingly, the social and economic position of the richer knightly families had become sharply differentiated from that of the poorer knights who, if they had been obliged to dispose of land, might often have a level of prosperity not greatly above that of a well-to-do freeman-peasant. It was usually from the better off knightly families that men were chosen for the administrative, jury, tax-assessing and tax-collecting functions. In addition, there were the king's household knights, some of them from the great families of England, who were rewarded with land for service at court. In short, the order of knighthood generally had come to be the mark of a kind of minor aristocracy, much occupied with administration, and the general status of the elected 'knights of the shire' had assisted the standing of the House of Commons within Parliament.

Yet paradoxically the 'knights' at Parliament were far from being drawn exclusively from the wealthiest of that order. Some were of comparatively modest estate; others were not in fact knights at all. During the previous century many men who would previously have been knighted had become poorer, partly as a result of the splitting and redistribution of estates, and they were often resistant to accepting knighthood, with the financial and administrative burdens it entailed. There had developed a shortage of knights available for the traditional duties to be performed by the knights in the shires, quite apart from the loss of money and service due to the crown. Both Henry III and Edward I had issued writs for the distraint of knighthood, requiring any man (including wealthy tenants-in-chief) who held land in knight's fee worth at least the traditional £20 to be knighted and to provide the due service or money. Since the shortage had persisted, Edward I had instituted a further change by relating the obligation to become a knight to the value of land held rather than to the notion of the knight's fee. The property qualification for obligation to knighthood varied from time to time, but it had settled at £40 annually.

These remedies, however, had not produced a sufficiency of knights, and it had become accepted in practice that men who were not actually 'belted' and girt with the knight's sword might still be chosen to represent the shires in Parliament. Towards the end of his reign, Edward II had been obliged to receive esquires as the representatives from several counties, and in 1325 only twenty-seven of the knights in Parliament had been belted. In the first years of Edward III, several attempts had therefore been made to ensure the return of 'belted' knights, but in 1350 the writ for Parliament in the following year recognized that ordinary country gentlemen would have to do instead, and simply required that those chosen should not be maintainers of quarrels, but men of worth and good faith, and lovers of the public good.[1] Even so, efforts were continued to ensure that only real knights were sent to Parliament in order to keep up the standing and quality of the Commons, and for the same reason an ordinance in 1372 disqualified lawyers from membership of the Commons on the ground that they exploited this position to advance the causes of their clients, to the neglect of the public business. The same statute also disallowed sheriffs (some of whom returned themselves to represent their shires) from being members of the Commons.[2] Yet none of these efforts succeeded in reserving the representation of the shires to 'belted' knights, and during the reign of Edward III those who went to Parliament in the category of knights could be anything from members of noble or knightly families, duly dubbed, to prosperous freemen without knightly forbears.

Yet the presence in the Commons of some knights of important family had considerable significance for Parliament. The blurred social distinction between the aristocracy, which formed the future House of Lords, and the knights who were socially the more important element among the Commons, meant that there was always a certain amount of common social ground between the two 'Houses', a term not, however in use in the fourteenth century. Had all the Commons possessed a status no higher than that of burgesses, wealthy but without the dignity which martial rather than commercial attributes bestowed, they might have seemed a lesser body. But as things were, the younger sons or other relations of peers would not, in the future, scorn a seat in the Commons, while members of the lower House could aspire to the upper. Enhanced by the social status of the knights, the fourteenth century Commons were already more than the equivalent of a continental third estate.

There were, therefore, conditions in both 'Houses' of Parliament making for unity rather than for class division between estates. The fact that the

---

[1] Stubbs *Const. Hist.* Vol. III, (5th ed.) pp. 411–413.
[2] *Rot. Parl.* Vol. II, p. 310: *Stat. R.* Vol. I, p. 394.

peers had only gradually become a separate order as a result of being summoned individually to Parliament, instead of being summoned to Parliament because they were a separate order, must have acted as some constraint on any inclination of the House of Lords to see itself as an exclusive estate. In the shires, moreover, when a lay magnate was in residence at his castle or manor, the more substantial local knights, who might also be in Parliaments, were his natural company, though he was chief among them. Likewise, in the Commons where knights might be of noble family or yeomen, and burgesses might be merchants or knights, there was no rooted sense of low status. So flexible a class structure within Parliament profoundly affected its development. For all the arguments between the two Houses from time to time, it is their basic unity rather than their occasional discord which resounds through their history.

But who in practice chose the parliamentary knights? The suitors of the county courts by whom the knights were elected would, in full session, have included theoretically prelates and abbots, earls and barons, as well as knights and freeholders, the reeve and four men from each vil or township and twelve from each borough. Historically, the county court was the descendant of the old English folk-moot, a kind of local Parliament, and it was here that the king's travelling justices gave their judgements, that the shire's military business, and its assessment and collection of taxation were dealt with, and that the pursuit of criminals was proclaimed. The county court sat as a matter of routine once a month, and on such ordinary occasions it was normally only attended by those who had special business before it. The prelates and barons were free of obligation to attend for the election of representative knights, though if they were not present their bailiffs probably were. Ordinary knights could also seek exemption, freemen could be represented by proxy, and the borough representatives do not seem to have been obliged to be present except when the king's justices were at the shire court. For a full assembly a special summons was issued by the sheriff who presided over the court and directed its proceedings. The sheriff himself was a royal appointment though periodic efforts had been made to secure his election by the county itself, and in 1338 Edward III gave an order conceding that the sheriff should be elected. But in 1340 this was abandoned when complaints about the sheriff's office were dealt with by an order that no man should hold the office for more than a year and that the officers of the exchequer should be responsible for his appointment.

The precise procedure by which the knights of the thirty-seven shires were elected is not known. It is likely, however, that their election did, in practice, generally take place in a full county court, as the writs indicated it should. But how full a 'full court' was depended in practice both on the extent to which exemption from attendance was obtained and on the feasibility of holding a full court in particular circumstances. The method by which the knights were chosen could also depend on the conditions in which a particular election took place. The writs summoning the knights normally allowed about forty days notice of Parliament's opening, but sometimes, particularly in a crisis, less notice was given. Sometimes, the interval between the despatch of the summons from the king's court and the due date of Parliament's assembly could hardly have been enough for the full county court to be called, the election to take place and the knights to arrive at Parliament in time for its opening. Sometimes, therefore, the sheriff may have had to make do with a small routine monthly shire court; sometimes, in response to an urgent summons to see to the election of knights, he might call a special meeting of the court even though one had recently been held; sometimes he might have to nominate and despatch the knights himself. Often, some of the knights, especially those from the distant shires, arrived late. But the evidence is against nomination by the sheriff without the consent of the court in any other than rare circumstances, or through deliberate malpractice. That sheriffs did sometimes take it on themselves to choose their friends as the knights, without the county's consent, is indicated by various instances of complaints against the practice.[1] Later in his reign, a petition submitted to Edward II specifically asked that the knights should be elected by common choice of the best men of the county and not certified by the sheriff alone without due election. The king's ruling was that they should be elected by the common consent of the whole county.[2] But what did election mean; how free was it?

The reality is that the Norman French *eslire* or the Latin *eligere* would be better translated not by the word 'elect', with its modern connotation of head-counting, but by 'choose', or 'select'. There is clear evidence, however, that elections were intended to be free of undue interference by the great. The first Statute of Westminster of Edward I in 1275 (ch.5) had stated: 'And because elections ought to be free, the king commandeth upon great forfeiture, that no man by force of arms, nor by malice, or menacing, shall disturb any to make free elections.' It was a requirement which must often have been breached, and the bailiffs of local magnates were generally a

---

[1] A number of instances is cited by J. R. Maddicott, in 'Parliament and the Constituencies, 1272–1377' (*The English Parliament in the Middle Ages*. edit. R. G. Davies and J. H. Denton).
[2] *Rot. Parl.* Vol. II, p. 355. (1376) '*Et que les Chivalers des Countees pur celles Parlementz soient esluz par commune Election de les meillours Gentz des ditz Countees: Et nemye certifiez par le Viscont soul saunz due election . . .*' This request, preceded by a renewed request for annual Parliaments, received the royal reply: '*Et quant a l'article de l'Election des Chivalers qi vendront a Parlement, le Roi voet q'ils soient esluz par commune assent de tout le Contee.*'

powerful and often no doubt a decisive influence on choice. Even so, the shire courts meeting for parliamentary elections in the fourteenth century were large gatherings attended by knights, village reeves and many ordinary villagers.[1] The probability is that the representative knights were chosen by the same sort of process through which a large modern committee reaches its conclusions, in which the propositions of those who carry special weight for whatever reason are heard with special attention, and a pervasive majority opinion gradually emerges, in face of which any potential dissent gives way. Almost certainly the process of election did not reach a decision by the counting of heads but by shouts of assent or acclamation, the equivalent, perhaps, of a proposition approved by calls equivalent to 'hear, hear'. If there was disagreement on a proposition it seems quite likely (though it can only be guessed) that the balance of opinion may have been registered by something equivalent to the current parliamentary practice of shouting 'Aye' or 'No'. In their own house, the medieval Commons reached their decisions not by a poll but by assessing the volume of voices crying for or against.[2] The idea that a majority should be counted numerically is a comparatively recent one and it would be far more in accord with medieval thinking that agreement should be reached without formal division and in a manner which, by not quantifying dissent, would more easily be seen as binding all. Further, if there were occasions when dissent was registered vocally, or when the return of a particular candidate was disputed, it was not because elections were contested in the modern sense. That would not happen for several centuries to come.

Although there was no open competition for election, men were obviously anxious to be parliamentary representatives in the thirteenth century just as they are in the twentieth, and many no doubt did not hesitate to put themselves forward. Whatever the burdens of representation, the growing practice of re-election (already discussed earlier) suggests that they were outweighed by the satisfaction from participating in the great affairs of the kingdom, especially since wages and expenses were paid under authorizing writs at the end of each Parliament. As always, the characters and personalities of the knights who assembled in Parliaments represented their communities in both their better and in some of their worse aspects, but in the middle ages the worse could be a great deal more heinous than would be tolerated today. Many had experience of service as sheriff or deputy sheriff, as commissioners of array and of taxes, or as justices of the

---

[1] J. R. Maddicott, 'The county community and the making of public opinion in fourteenth century England,' *Trans. R. Hist. Soc.*, 5th ser., xxviii (1978), pp. 27–43.
[2] J. G. (Sir Goronwy) Edwards, *The Second Century of the English Parliament*, pp. 71–79.

peace or coroners. Some were very large landowners; some in the troubled reign of Edward II had been strong partisans either of the king, or of Lancaster or Mortimer. One representative knight from Bedfordshire who was a friend of Edward II had so many enemies that the king gave him permission to ride always armed. The knights represented the disorder of their society as well as its striving for order. Some were convicted debtors, some had been found guilty of financial irregularities or corruption. Some had been accused and acquitted, and some had been accused and found guilty of breaches of the peace and of various acts of violence. One turbulent Bedfordshire knight at Parliament had been imprisoned for killing a coroner. Another had even been accused three times of house-breaking and had served on financial commissions in respect of which he had been found guilty of irregularities. None of this, however, had prevented him from being seven times a member of the Commons. A medieval 'Member of Parliament' was not disqualified by his personal record in the manner of his twentieth century counterpart.[1]

The writ to the sheriff which summoned the knights was also the authority for the election of two citizens from the cities and two burgesses from the towns in his shire. How the sheriff decided which towns should choose representatives is not altogether clear; a town might be regarded as a borough because it had an historical claim to be one, because it had a charter, because it was taxed higher than the county, or because it had a merchant gild. The scope for anomalies was obviously considerable and there was no fixed list of parliamentary boroughs. About 140 different cities and boroughs returned members at various times between 1294 and 1337 but only something over half this number seem to have been required to return members at any particular Parliament. On average it has been calculated that perhaps seventy-five towns may have returned burgesses in the reign of Edward III; that is to say there were some 150 burgesses in Parliament compared with seventy-four knights, but in the Parliament of 1362 there were as many as 174. There seems to have been no general procedure for the election of burgesses, but it took place in the towns themselves and the choice seems to have been made by a small group of the wealthier merchants in each borough. The number of men involved in the election of burgesses was very much smaller than that for the election of knights, and the method of election in the towns was to remain disparate and irrational right up to the first reform bill of 1832. It is probable that the

---

[1] T. F. T. Plucknett, 'Parliament' (Willard and Morris, *The English Government at Work*) reprinted in Fryde and Miller, Vol. I. pp. 215–216 which gives references to sources of information on the personal records of parliamentary knights.

choice of representatives, who were usually from among the most important merchants, was made in the town oligarchy, after which the names of the chosen persons were returned to the sheriff for formal ratification in the county court.[1] It had been taxation, and in particular the subsidy levied on wool, which had first brought the English government to deal with the merchants. Their consent was sought first outside Parliament and then by summoning them to Parliament. This then led to the insistence of the community as a whole that such consent could be given only in Parliament since the ultimate burden of such indirect taxation was passed on in prices to the whole community. So far as the merchants themselves were concerned, however, attendance at Parliament was also an invaluable opportunity to be used for the defence of the privileges and charters which were the mainstay of their corporate existence. What is more, although in general the social status of knights was higher than that of burgesses, there is every reason to think that the wealthier merchants wielded as much influence, particularly in the financial exigencies of war. Some important merchant families under Edward III, most conspicuously the de la Poles with their eventual royal connections, were in the future to join the nobility.

Such, then, were the representative lay members of Parliament who in obedience to the king's writ made their way from near and distant shires and towns to Parliaments which were henceforth usually held at Westminster. There they joined those individually summoned barons, prelates and abbots who constituted the origin of the House of Lords in what was already, very roughly, a bicameral assembly. There remains to be described, however, one further element of the early medieval Parliament, the elected representatives of the clergy as a whole, They have been left until last in this account for the good reason that they were now to drop out of Parliament, a fact of great significance in its history. Had they remained, the English Parliament might have developed significantly different characteristics from those it assumed. As it was, only the prelates and some abbots remained as a permanent parliamentary element.

Whether the twenty-one archbishops and bishops and the thirty-one abbots summoned to Parliament were present principally in their spiritual capacity or as baronial tenants-in-chief is debatable. The probability is that both criteria applied, the one or the other assuming more or less importance in different circumstances. There seems to have been no very precise general principle by which these high clerics were chosen, and the number of abbots and priors summoned was smaller after the middle of Edward II's

---

[1] For this subject generally, see M. McKisack, *The Parliamentary Representation of the English Boroughs during the Middle Ages*. Also Plucknett, op. cit., pp. 217–218.

reign than in the reign of Edward I. Moreover, whereas the prelates and some of the abbots asserted their position as peers of Parliament, other abbots and priors who were the heads of smaller religious foundations actively resisted the status of peer on the grounds that it would involve them in paying tax at a higher level than would be the case if they were taxed through their own convocation. The question of clerical liability came sharply into focus after the lay and temporal peers in the Parliament of 1340 had granted tax of a ninth for two years, and each convocation of the clergy had granted only a tenth. Some attempt was apparently made to oblige certain abbots to pay both the ninth and the tenth, after which, in, 1341, the magnates gave their opinion that those foundations which held their lands by barony should pay at the higher rate and those which held nothing by barony, and were not accustomed to being summoned to Parliament, should only pay a tenth. This was accepted by the crown in respect of certain monasteries, which led others to make a similar claim for exemption from parliamentary summons. (The abbot of St. Augustine's, Bristol, considered that through being 'arbitrarily' summoned he had been 'unduly vexed in many ways'.) Such claims for exemption were always based on the grounds that the monastic land was not held by barony, but they were usually reinforced with appeals to precedent. In many instances the claim was accepted but in some it was refused, and the king still formally adopted the position that granting exemption did not bind him and his heirs for the future if necessity required otherwise. Even so, from the 1340s onward the list of abbots, like that of the prelates, was virtually fixed, and precedent was to be decisive for the future summons of ecclesiastical lords.[1]

Whatever principles of selection were applied to particular prelates and abbots, however, those of them who were present in Parliament were there as individual dignitaries, not as representatives. It was different with the lower diocesan clergy. From the reign of Edward I to the earlier years of Edward III, persistent efforts had been made and resisted to bring deans, archdeacons and clerical proctors to Parliament, not as individuals but as representatives of the lower clergy. They were to represent their clerical communities in much the same way as the knights and burgesses represented the lay communities. Their presence was required because the clergy (other than the bishops, whose lands were regarded as temporalities and taxable in Parliament) was recognized as a separate order which could only be taxed by its own consent, but whose fiscal contribution was by now established as crucial to the crown's finances.

Since the reign of Henry III, English kings had acknowledged the Pope's

---

[1] Powell and Wallis, op. cit., pp. 344-346, and *Dignity of a Peer*, iv pp. 534-536.

right to tax the clergy and had been rewarded with part of the proceeds. On the other hand, when the Pope had attempted to forbid the clergy to pay secular taxes without his consent (by the bull *Clericis Laicos*) he had been forced by Edward I to accept that this did not apply when the realm was in a state of emergency, which could be said to exist whenever the crown needed taxation. But it was accepted that, as a separate order, the clergy must consent to their own taxation. The question still unresolved in the first quarter of the century was whether consent should be given in their own convocations or in Parliament.

Repeated attempts had been made by the crown to convene tax-granting clerical assemblies, alongside or as part of Parliament. In the later years of Edward II it must have seemed likely that clerical meetings would take place regularly in answer to parliamentary summons, which was in the form of a clause in the writ to the bishops known as the *praemunientes* clause. This required them to see that the dean and archdeacons attended, and that one proctor should be elected by the chapter of the cathedral and two by the rest of the diocesan clergy. The instruction, however, was increasingly ignored by the clergy, and it had latterly been reinforced by a writ to the archbishop of each province requiring him to order the lower clergy to attend, which was last attempted in 1340. But still the clergy resisted on the grounds that they could not be forced to attend a lay assembly and the bishops connived at the disobedience.

As a compromise, however, the archbishops were willing to call the provincial convocations instead. Thus in 1331, when 140 representatives of the lower clergy were summoned under the *praemunientes* clause, the southern convocation was called by the archbishop to appear before him in St Paul's to treat of the affairs of Parliament. At this assembly (not attended by the northern clergy) the clergy apparently taxed themselves and reported the same to Parliament. It was not always possible to distinguish between purely clerical meetings and meetings of the clergy in Parliament, and some proctors appear to have attended Parliament even after convocation had clearly separated from it for tax-granting purposes. Nevertheless the proctors had ceased to be an estate of the realm by 1337 when the king, urgently needing money for his Scottish war, recognized that the quickest way to get it from the clergy was through their own assembly. By 1341, Archbishop Stratford had formally secured the concession that the clergy were not bound to attend Parliament and did not have to pay taxes levied in Parliament but should make their contribution of tax through their convocations. The clergy had established their separate status. As petitioners and tax-granters, they had been an important part of the political assembly of the nation, and the success of what one historian has called 'the clerical commons'[1] in detaching themselves from Parliament was to be a source of future clerical weakness. But by far the greater consequence was that the English Parliament did not develop according to the continental pattern of three rigid estates of which the clergy was one. Just as the combination of composition and history of the Lords and Commons was such as to prevent the hardening of an immutable class division between them, so the withdrawal of the bulk of the clergy into its own assembly, leaving prelates and some abbots in the secular politics of the upper house, prevented a rigid division between laiety and clergy. But the withdrawal of the representative clergy had another consequence as well. By ceasing to play a part in the Parliament of the nation, the representative clergy weakened the ability of the Church to withstand anti-clericalism. Its departure from Parliament probably made the Erastian revolution of Henry VIII easier to achieve, and that revolution in turn greatly increased the potential power and self-confidence of Parliament, the instrument by which the reformation was brought about.

III

'In addition, it is agreed that Parliament be held once each year, or more if it be necessary.' (*Ensement est accorde qe parlement soit tenu chescun an, unefoitz, ou plus si mestier soit.*)[2] In this brief and almost casual manner, the first provision for annual Parliaments was given the royal assent at Westminster in the fourth year of Edward III. It appeared as no more than a small item towards the end of the statute of 1330 which included a wide variety of subjects, probably because contemporaries saw no special significance in recording that Parliaments should be annual. Three centuries later the Long Parliament forced Charles I to accept the revolutionary Triennial Act which laid down arrangements for Parliament to be called automatically every three years should he himself fail to summon it. That Act began with an appeal to the laws and statutes of the realm by which 'Parliament ought to be holden at least once every year for the redress of grievances'. It was a

---

[1] J. H. Denton, 'The Clergy and Parliament in the Thirteenth and Fourteenth Centuries', (in *The English Parliament in the Middle Ages*). See also M. V. Clarke, *Medieval Representation and Consent*, Ch. VII; and T. F. T. Plucknett, 'Parliament' (in Fryde and Miller Vol. I.)

[2] *Stat. R.*, Vol. I, p. 265.

revolutionary statute because it virtually destroyed the king's ancient prerogative of summoning Parliament at his own discretion, imposing on King Charles a series of alternative mechanisms for issuing the necessary writs if he withheld them. Yet the appeal to the past in this seventeenth century Act was far from being an antiquarian contrivance. Annual and regular Parliaments were a persistent concept through much of the middle ages and were by no means regarded by medieval kings as against their interest. The Ordinances of 1311 had required Parliaments to be held once or if need be twice a year, but this had already been the practice in the years immediately before the Ordinances, and indeed was a general notion long before that. The Ordinances prescribed annual Parliaments specifically so that they could deal with delayed pleas and petitions. But their provision that a committee of lords should be appointed in each Parliament to hear complaints against the king's ministers indicates that they also intended Parliament to be used for the redress of grievances in a political as well as an administrative sense.

The idea of annual Parliaments did not die with the Ordinances. In 1327 the mayor and citizens of London, perhaps emboldened by their intervention on the winning side against Edward II, petitioned the new king that, until he was of age, he should hold annual Parliaments at Westminster.[1] (It was now clearly assumed that this was the appropriate fixed place to hold them.) More specifically, the Londoners requested that counsellors acting in the king's name should automatically be removed at the beginning of each Parliament, and that anyone with reason to complain against them should be heard, and could thus complain without fear. However, since the petition was only one on a roll of forty-four, most of which were concerned with matters narrowly concerning London, the request for annual Parliaments was probably more the expression of a routine current idea than an insistent revolutionary demand. At all events, no response is recorded, and no statute flowed from it. Subsequently, however, the 1330 statute for annual Parliaments was re-enacted in 1362, and again in 1376, in response to petitions.[2]

We do not know what, if any, petition led to the statute of 1330, or its purpose. The lack of Parliaments can hardly have been a grievance since they had been held frequently. Perhaps the enactment was simply a gesture of goodwill on the part of the king to show his wish to rule and consult in the traditional manner. Perhaps it was seen as comparable to the

---

[1] *Rot. Parl. Anglie hactenus inediti*, ed. Richardson and Sayles, p. 134.
[2] See pp. 325–6 and p. 338.

confirmation of charters, which also appeared in the same statute. At all events, though no king wished to be bound, the holding of regular Parliaments was seen by most medieval kings as at least as much a convenience to themselves as to their subjects. That was certainly the attitude of Edward III. In the hundred years from 1340 about ninety Parliaments were held, almost one annually, though each was of short duration. More than half of the Parliaments during this time lasted less than six weeks, and the great majority had only one session.

So almost every year the citizens of London and Westminster could expect to see a multitude of men of every degree flocking into their streets and needing accommodation at Parliament time. As well as the magnates, who probably had their own dwellings, and the knights and burgesses, there were lawyers and petitioners with parliamentary business to transact. Somehow the retainers of the great men (*les grantz*, as they were habitually described in the parliamentary rolls) had also to be accommodated, and food must be found for the large influx. No doubt Parliament brought many social difficulties for Londoners, but it also drew wealth into the city and gave what was now the undisputed capital of England a new sense of its own importance as it witnessed the assembly of the men of power in their magnificence. With so large a flood of men into the City and Westminster (many of whom came from the wilder parts of the country) disorder was an obvious danger and at the beginning of a Parliament a proclamation against the bearing of offensive weapons was read before the king and magnates and then 'cried' in Westminster Hall, and also in the city of London. Because of past quarrels, riots and brawls at times of Parliament, it was forbidden for anyone, whatever his degree (under penalty of forfeiting whatever he could forfeit) to be equipped with any of the arms listed, which included sword, long knives, armour, or even the padded jerkin worn under mail called an acton (aketon). None of these could be carried 'in the City of London, nor in the suburbs, nor in other places between the said City and the Palace of Westminster, nor in any part of the palace, nor by land or water (river)' ... (*en la Citee de Loundres, n'en les Suburbes, n'en les autres lieux entre la dite Citee & le Paleys de Westmr', ne nul part en le Paleys, par terre ne par ewe* . . .). (One wonders where a baronial retinue kept the arms with which it must have travelled; perhaps in encampments outside the City and its suburbs.) A proviso was added, however, that it was not the king's intention to forbid earls or barons to have their swords carried with them, except before the king or in the council. Another proclamation at the outset of Parliament forbade children to play at 'bar' (a game in which two sides are separated by a bar marked on the ground) or at other games, or to snatch at people's hoods under pain of imprisonment nor to otherwise hinder anyone from going about his business.[1]

The parliamentary proceedings proper then began with a meeting at which the king and the Lords and the Commons were all present in one place, the Painted Chamber. Precedence was given to the spiritual lords. The Archbishop of Canterbury sat at the king's right hand and next to him were the Archbishop of York and the Bishops of London, Winchester and Salisbury, below whom were the rest of the bishops in order of seniority as determined by their dates of consecration. Then came the abbots and priors. The temporal magnates sat on the king's left side. Closest to him were the dukes (after the creation of the order in 1337) next to whom came the earls (the title marquis did not appear until 1385 and after then only rarely) and then the barons without territorial titles, whose right of summons was even now not absolutely fixed. Judges and counsellors were also present. Finally, for this first session, the knights and burgesses also assembled in the lowest position. A basic record of Parliament's business was kept on the rolls of Parliament, which however seem initially to have been more the product of the enterprise of the clerks for their convenience than formally required documents. On the parliamentary rolls are recorded proclamations, the addresses to Parliament by the king's ministers, the subsequent proceedings of the various elements of Parliaments and petitions to the king and council with the responses to them. The parliamentary rolls are, however, erratic in what they cover and not a complete record.

There was only one item of business at this first general meeting, the delivery of a statement by one of the king's ministers (the chancellor or chief justice, or sometimes an archbishop) giving the 'causes of summons', that is to say the business Parliament was required to consider. The minister would then declare that the king was willing to receive and answer petitions for the redress of subjects' individual and common grievances. The first task of the Commons as well as of the Lords, therefore, was to find answers to the points put to them, which involved a complex process of consultation within and between the component elements of Parliament. This took place elsewhere, away from the king and the lords, as did the formulation and

---

[1] *Rot. Parl.* Vol. II, p. 64. The proclamation in this Parliament against carrying arms records that it is based on the Statute of Northampton (c. 3). The proclamation against children's unruly behaviour declares that '*nul enfaunt ne autres ne jue en ul lieu du Paleys de Westmr', durant le Parliament q'y est somons, a bares ne as autres jues, ne a ouster chaperouns des gentz ne autres empechemnt faire par qoi chescun ne puisse peysiblement sure ses busoignes.*' Similar proclamations were repeated in later Parliaments.

presentation of petitions. Eventually, all the component parts of a Parliament would reassemble in a single gathering before the dissolution. But they did not all meet again in the Painted Chamber itself.

After the first general meeting, the king and lords went off to a room known originally as the White Chamber. Later it was called the Parliament Chamber and it continued to be used by the Lords until 1801. The Commons had different meeting places at different times. In the early years of Edward III they appear to have remained behind in the Painted Chamber where they held their meeting after the departure of the king and lords. It was a suitably large room for the most numerous element in Parliament, and the arrangement was the one requiring the least movement of men from place to place. The Commons are recorded as having met in the Painted Chamber in 1343, 1365, 1366 and 1373. In 1352, however, having held their initial separate meeting in the Painted Chamber, they are said in the Rolls of Parliament to have moved to the Chapter House of Westminster Abbey because the Painted Chamber was needed for another meeting. The Chapter House is also specifically given as their meeting place on six occasions from 1352 to 1395. But in 1395, the Parliament roll also recorded that, after the initial general gathering in the Painted Chamber, the Commons were to meet in the Refectory of Westminster Abbey. The Chapter House is never again recorded as their meeting place; instead, on five occasions from 1397 to 1416, the Refectory is recorded as the place of their separate deliberations.

Thus the Commons had at least three different meeting places during the medieval period. What caused their move to the Refectory at the end of the fourteenth century is not known. But their departure from the Painted Chamber from time to time at an earlier stage, so as to make that room available for another meeting, was occasioned by a procedure which was of great importance in the fourteenth century Parliament. The Painted Chamber was often needed for separate consultations between Lords and some members of Commons, the purpose of which was to enable the two 'Houses' to agree on answers to the points which had been put to them by the king's minister and spokesman, especially on taxation. The rolls of Parliament refer to these consultations by the Norman-French word *entrecommuner*, to intercommune or to consult. The mechanics of 'intercommuning' may have varied from time to time, but details on the Parliament roll of 1352 of how it worked on that occasion are probably a fair general guide to the kind of procedure adopted. Having stated the causes of summons, the Lord Chief Justice told the Commons to assemble in the Painted Chamber at sunrise on the next day to discuss the points put to them. But their first and immediate task was to choose twenty-four or thirty of their number to confer with a number of Lords whom the king would send to the Painted Chamber.

The next morning, after they had all met together at dawn, the majority of the Commons would go off to the Chapter House leaving the chosen committee behind in the Painted Chamber to 'intercommune' with the committee of Lords. In due course, the committee of Commons would then report what they had agreed with the Lords to their own majority in the Chapter House, where it would then be more generally discussed. When all the Commons had reached an accord, the committee of twenty-four or thirty would report what they had decided to the king and lords in the White Chamber. They generally made their report, not en masse, but by means of a delegation, most of whom were probably the same men who had served on the intercommuning committee with the Lords. At this period, the delegates seem always to have been knights, the higher order in the Commons, even when the answers concerned tax which the burgesses and their electors would pay. Such conferences remained a regular feature of Parliaments until well into the Lancastrian period, but with some later variations of practice. For instance the Commons would sometimes suggest the names of those Lords with whom they would like to consult, and the fact that their suggestions were usually accepted was a sign of their increased power, particularly over taxation. Even by the end of Edward's reign, the Commons would on occasions take the initiative in suggesting conferences with the Lords, after some discussion among themselves. 'Intercommuning' could be complicated and involve a number of meetings over several days as the committee of the Commons reported back on a number of occasions to their full assembly. The king did not get the taxation he wanted as a matter of course.[1]

The business of Parliament was in part judicial as it always had been. Some criminal cases came within its jurisdiction, particularly those of peers accused of treason. These could be dealt with by the process in which, as at Mortimer's trial, the king recorded his knowledge of the accused man's notorious treason, on which the peers simply proceeded to judgement. Parliament could also be an occasion for settling points of difficulty referred to it by lower courts or, more often, dealing with cases arising out of feudal law, franchises, royal grants and administration. Though cases of this sort came nominally to Parliament, they seem in reality to have been settled by

[1] In this account of the arrangements for parliamentary gatherings, I have largely followed J. G. (Sir Goronwy) Edwards, '*The Second Century of the English Parliament*' (Ford lectures, Lecture I), and his '*The Commons in Medieval English Parliaments*' (Creighton Lecture in History for 1957). See also Plucknett, op. cit. and W. N. Bryant, 'Some earlier examples of intercommuning in Parliament, 1340–1348', E.H.R. (1970).

the council in Parliament's name. In the fourteenth century Parliament was nominally rather than actually the apex of the judicial system; the rise of the present supreme appellate powers of the House of Lords dates mainly from post-medieval times[1] In the fourteenth century, it was legislation and taxation which were at the heart of parliamentary activity, and the connecting link between the legislative and the judicial aspect was the petition addressed to the king and council, a device which had been inextricably linked with Parliament's origin.

The petitioners, for the most part, were not the Commons but outside persons and bodies, who were seeking the justice or remedy for their particular case which was not otherwise available. Such 'singular' or private petitions, which related to some individual or private interest, were handed to receivers. The Clerk of the Parliament acted as receiver for English petitioners and various chancery clerks for those from Wales, Gascony and other lands of the crown. The receivers endorsed the 'singular' petitions and passed them on to be tried by a panel of auditors or triers, consisting of barons, prelates and justices. (A few cases were reserved for the king himself to try.) The triers then sent the petitions, with their own findings, to chancery so that the appropriate department could take the necessary action. The Commons, however, were not normally involved in receiving or presenting singular petitions. Their business was with what we may call parliamentary petitions, that is to say with those dealing with grievances regarded as being of common interest. These had begun under Edward II, and by the early years of Edward III the concept, if not yet the name, of the common petition was a well used procedure which could lead to legislation.

Occasional petitions to the king claiming to deal with grievances in the community at large already had quite a long history. These, however, had been direct petitions by subjects to their king in which the Commons had no part. But by the beginning of the reign of Edward III, the Commons themselves were established as an actual petitioning body, putting forward what came to be called 'common petitions'. These were so described, however, not because they emanated from the Commons in Parliament but because, as it was expressed in a petition of 1346, they were petitions made 'for the common profit'.[2] Some of these petitions may have been inspired by interested bodies or people outside Parliament, but their essential characteristic was their request to the king for action on a matter which was said to

---

[1] Plucknett, op. cit., (in Fryde and Miller, Vol. I, p. 226).

[2] *Rot. Parl.* Vol. II, p. 160: '*A no're Seignur le Roi & a son Conseil prient les Gentz de ses Communes, pur commune profit que . . .*' See also H. M. Cam, 'The Legislators of Medieval England' (in Fryde and Miller, Vol. I.) p. 181.

affect the general interest of the community. Such petitions often began with the words *'prient les communes'* (the Commons pray . . .). By now, 'common interest' petitions were recognized as a category separate from 'singular' petitions and were being gathered on a single roll, which by the end of the fourteenth century was often headed with the title 'common petitions'. The term may, for convenience, also be used to describe the important petitions of this sort in the earlier years of Edward III's reign.

Parliament was already by then increasingly absorbed with legislation, and some of it originated with common petitions, or bills, which secured the king's agreement and were then made the basis of statutes. In other words, early in the fourteenth century, some law was being made in response to a direct initiative of the Commons, whereas the statutes of Edward I had arisen from the king's initiative after he had been convinced through one non-parliamentary channel or another that there were grievances he should remedy in Parliament. The preambles to Edward I's statutes often explained how he had arrived at his decisions, with such statements as 'Because our lord the King greatly desires to redress the state of the realm where it needs amendment . . .' or 'to make good the oppressions and defects of former statutes . . .' or 'understanding by the public and frequent complaint of the middling folk . . . we have decreed in Parliament for the common welfare. . . .'[1] Edward I's decision to legislate must sometimes have been prompted by direct petitions, but probably more often arose from the advice of judges and counsellors. Although the presence of the Commons at Parliament no doubt had some influence on the actions of his government, they had no direct part in any relationship between petitions and Edward I's law making. Indeed, petitions had often been handed in when no Commons came to Parliament. By the accession of Edward III, however, the common petition leading to legislation was a recognized and duly recorded procedure, which was the origin of the process from parliamentary bill to Act of Parliament in our own time.

The practice was for such petitions to be handed to the clerk of the Parliament for submission to king and council. Any that had the Commons' endorsement or 'avowal' would be more likely to be accepted as the basis of a new statute. However, a petition favourably received would only provide the rough basis for the ensuing statute, which would be drafted by the

---

[1] An illuminating sample of such preambles is assembled in H. M. Cam, 'The Legislators of Medieval England' (in Fryde and Miller, Vol. I, p. 180) with the comment that they seem to show 'a benevolent and order-loving legislator passing from concern for a complete and coherent system of law to a growing consciousness of personal and class grievances calling for redress'.

council and its officials, with the judges' help. Moreover, many petitions were never enacted, and in the first decade of Edward III many statutes were not based on petitions but simply arose from decisions of government. How many statutes flowed from petitions in the early years of the reign is not clear, since relevant documents have only survived erratically, and in particular no parliamentary rolls, on which petitions were recorded, survive for the years between 1334 and 1339. Nevertheless, seven statutes based on petitions have survived from the first ten years of the reign, beginning with one in Edward III's first Parliament. In 1327, a parliamentary roll collates forty-one petitions with the king's responses, (or, it might be said, contains a petition of forty-one items) of which sixteen were embodied in the first statute of the reign.[1] The roll begins with a petition from 'the good people of the Community' (*la bone Gent de la Comune*) placing it on record that since the Despensers had been exiled as traitors by the common agreement of the king and the 'baronage', and 'in full Parliament' (*et ceo en plein Parlement*), the approval of Parliament should have been obtained before they were recalled. The roll then records petitions on a wide variety of questions, from a request that the Pope should be approached about the canonization of the late Earl of Lancaster and Archbishop of Canterbury to the complaints about military service already discussed,[2] unfairly assessed aids, the perambulation of the forest and much else. One of the petitions embodied a protest by the Commons against the practice of putting forward in their name bills which they had not endorsed or 'avowed'. The point was made that only bills in the form of an indenture, that is to say, with serrated edges which attested their authenticity, should be taken as having the authority of the Commons.

In other words, although it was accepted practice for some bills and petitions which had originated from outside the Commons (sometimes from the council or magnates; sometimes from private interests) to be put forward in the Commons' name, the Commons nevertheless insisted that such bills must have their formal endorsement. Yet there does not seem to have been any systematic method by which the Commons considered the bills they 'avowed', nor does the majority appear to have been involved in approving them. It is possible that the decision to avow petitions was taken in small groups. At all events, petitions were sent from the Commons in the form of bills which were endorsed with the responses. (A bill was thus the official written form of petitions which might originally have been submitted either in writing or orally.) The gist was recorded by the clerk on

---

[1] *Rot. Parl.* Vol. II, pp. 7–12 and *Stat. R.* Vol. I, p. 255.
[2] See above p. 235.

the parliamentary roll. Those bills which were accepted by the king were then redrafted as statutes and duly written on the statute rolls. Such statutes were sometimes enacted in virtually the same sense as the petition and response, but often they were modified, sometimes significantly. In the case of the petitions of Edward III's first Parliament in 1327, sixteen of them were enacted as statutes, or more precisely were collected as the first statute of the reign, which specifically acknowledged its origins. It stated that the king, 'at the request of the commonalty of his realm, by their petition made before him and his council in the Parliament, by assent of the Prelates, Earls, Barons and other great men assembled at the said Parliament', had granted for himself and his heirs the enactments which followed. There were seventeen of them, of which only one did not flow from the petitions, and this was probably based on a petition of the clergy.[1] (The case of the Despensers was dealt with separately in the first statute of the reign, which provided indemnity for those who had supported Isabella and Mortimer, and which also declared void the repeal of the Despensers' exile.)

The complaint relating to military service which has already been referred to is an example of a petition modified to make a significantly different statute. The petition asked that men should not be forced to go to war against their will in lands (*en les Terres*) where they had no holdings, or in lands where they had holdings except in accordance with the terms of their tenancy. Further, it was requested that the people of the community should not be forced to arm themselves at their own cost, or go outside their counties except at the cost of the king. The response, however, had simply conceded that men should not be required to arm themselves other than as they had done in the time of the king's ancestors or go outside their counties except in case of a foreign invasion. The statute is almost in the same words as the response and gave the king more latitude than the words of the petition would have done. As for the petitions which did not find their way into statute form, some of these were dealt with in other ways, and few were rejected outright.[2]

Just as not all petitions evolved into statutes, so not all statutes arose from common petitions. In the first decade of Edward III probably most statutes did not come about in this way. No other comprehensive petition modelled on that of 1327 is recorded on the surviving Parliament rolls until 1339, though there is other evidence of two petitions in 1333 and 1337.

[1] *Stat. R.* Vol. I, pp. 255–257.
[2] For a detailed discussion of the petitions and statute of 1327 see H. L. Gray, *The Influence of the Commons on Early Legislation*, pp. 215–225 (1932). Richardson and Sayles, 'The Parliaments of Edward III, Pt. II', *B.I.H.R.* IX (1931). App. II gives a description of the history of this Parliament roll.

Other statutes may have been based on common petitions, but the nature of the legislation in the first ten years of Edward III, suggests that a great part of it was on the initiative of the government, reflecting its own assessment of what was needed, rather than that of the Commons.

In the first ten years of the reign, legislation had already become, together with politics and taxation, Parliament's most important business, and it covered a wide variety of subjects. These included matters affecting the royal prerogative, of which the request for annual Parliaments, already discussed, was one example. Another was purveyance, the right to take food for the provisioning of the royal household, or to requisition the use of horses and carts, in exchange for a promise to pay at fixed and low prices. This ancient feudal right, as we have already seen, had become a serious grievance under Edward II, both because the price fixed was unjust and because the money was often never paid at all. In 1330, it was enacted among other things that the value of goods taken by purveyance (which should be allowable only for the king, the queen and their children) must be assessed by impartial valuers, and taken only by authorized purveyors who showed their warrants as valuers, and that cartage should be voluntary.[1] This did not suffice and the next year the statute was strengthened in various ways, one of which was that any purveyor who was found guilty of breaching the lawful methods prescribed should be treated as a thief and suffer the common law penalty for larceny, hanging.[2] The abuse continued, however, even after a further statute in 1336.[3] One of the most striking features of medieval legislation was the need repeatedly to re-enact the same measure. The enthusiasm for making law in the interest of an orderly society was a characteristic of the time, but it was a great deal harder to enforce the law than to write it.

Another aspect of the royal prerogative on which there was repeated legislation in the first decade of the reign was the use and misuse of the royal pardon. Charters of pardon could be used beneficially where the law was too crude. For instance, there was no legal distinction between the felonies of homicide by accident, or in self-defence, and murder. The operation of the law could therefore be made fairer by the royal pardon. But criminals could also be encouraged by the ease with which pardons could be obtained for various kinds of violent crimes, and it was therefore enacted in 1328 that charters of pardon should not be granted except for homicide in self-defence or misadventure.[4] Though this went too far in the other direction, it

---

[1] *Stat.* R. Vol. I, pp. 262–263.
[2] Ibid., p. 266.
[3] Ibid., p. 276.
[4] Ibid., p. 257.

was re-enacted in 1330[1] and again 1336,[2] when quite unworkable conditions were attached to it. Eventually, a statute of 1390 was to provide a more satisfactory solution by simply enacting that there should be no pardons for wilful murder. Other functions of government were also subject to reforming legislation in the earlier years of the reign. These included the machinery of justice; for example, justices of the peace were given powers of trial as well as powers of enquiry, and the commissions of assizes were strengthened by restricting them to men 'who know the law'. Other changes were designed to make more effective the courts' handling of prisoners accused of criminal offences. Some attempt was also made to improve the highly ineffective arrangements for appeals against the verdicts of lower courts by extending the scope of the only available remedy, which took the form of a request to a jury of twenty-four to convict the original jury of perjury. These and many other statutes show the advance in legislative activity in Parliament well before the Hundred Years war.

Social and economic problems were also tackled by statute, and in ways which in some respects anticipated remedies attempted in our own time. In 1335, the king's government legislated to prevent foreigners from counterfeiting sterling and of endeavouring 'to send into England their weak Money, in deceit of us, and Damage and Oppression of our People if Remedy be not provided'. The melting of sterling and the export of gold and silver, in money or in plate, were prohibited, and provisions were also made for the exchanges to be regulated. So that these could be effective, it was provided that 'the Tables of Exchange shall be at Dover . . .' and that 'no Pilgrim shall pass out of our Realm to the parts beyond the Sea, but only to Dover, upon pain of a Year's Imprisonment'. Searchers were commissioned, innkeepers were sworn to search their guests and rewards were offered to informers.[3]

Another manifestation of medieval protectionism was to be seen in the remarkable sumptuary statute of 1336 which sought to control the overeating of the rich, both for the sake of their own bodies and, as it specifically stated, their souls, and also to prevent the impoverishment of the realm through the bad example set by the excesses of the rich 'to the lesser People who only endeavour to imitate the great ones in such sort of (costly) Meats' and are thereby 'much impoverished'. As a result, they were 'not able to aid themselves nor their liege Lord in time of need, as they ought'. The number of courses at meals was limited to two (except on feast days when three were permitted) and even the number of ingredients of sauces was limited by this

[1] *Stat. R.* Vol. I, p. 264.
[2] Ibid., p. 275.
[3] Ibid., pp. 273–274.

statute.[1] Other economic legislation included the abolition in 1328 of all the monopolistic staples.[2] But this did not impede informal monopoly arrangements by which merchants in the ports prevented foreign importers from selling foreign wines and foods to anyone except themselves, thus forcing up prices. To put a stop to this, a statute made at York in 1335 enacted that foreign merchants must be allowed to sell to anyone, and that any town which attempted to thwart this freedom of trade would lose its franchise.[3] The legislative importance already achieved by Parliament in Edward III's initial decade is clear, but the nature of many of the statutes mentioned here, the sumptuary laws and exchange controls, for instance, suggests much more that they were devised by the government for its own purposes than that they resulted from any genuine parliamentary initiative. It was not until 1343 that a series of long enrolled comprehensive common petitions began, and it was only after 1352 that a large number of statutes was clearly derived directly from surviving petitions.[4]

Taxation at this stage was less important than it became as the demands of expenditure for war made the king's government increasingly dependent on money granted by Parliament. Only five Parliaments of the twenty-one in Edward III's first decade granted supply whereas in the last forty years of his reign, during which time there were thirty Parliaments, only five did not grant taxation. (Usually, but not invariably, a tenth was required from the towns and only a fifteenth from the counties.) The taxes needed by the crown to meet the costs of the Hundred Years War were one of the most important formative influences on the development of the medieval Parliament.

IV

The war with France began badly, with nothing gained abroad and political crisis the first consequence at home. Having made what he supposed to be adequate arrangements for covering the cost of his campaign, King Edward

---

[1] *Stat. R.* Vol. I, pp. 278–279.

[2] See above p. 236.

[3] *Stat. R.* Vol. I, pp. 269–271.

[4] An analysis of the remarkable comprehensiveness of the legislation in the first ten years of Edward III is in Plucknett op. cit., (in Fryde and Miller Vol. I) pp. 228–239. The evolution of the common petitions at this period is analysed by D. Rayner, 'Forms and machinery of the Commune Petition in the Fourteenth Century,' *E.H.R.* LVI 1941. Bills and petitions are discussed by J. G. Edwards, op. cit., and H. Cam, op. cit.

crossed to the Low Countries in July 1338. He passed the rest of that year and the earlier part of the next in diplomatic negotiations, filling in time with jousting, and then led an allied invasion into France in 1339. It was wasted effort. At one point the enemy armies were drawn up facing each other but neither attacked. Eventually Edward was obliged to withdraw because he could not afford to pay more subsidies to his allies. Indeed, uncertainty caused by lack of money was the principal cause of his hesitations and apparent lack of clear direction when he first arrived in Brabant. From the moment he left England it had become increasingly clear that the financial support he thought he had secured would be nothing like adequate.

Although the financial resources of the crown had risen since the beginning of the century, largely through the yield of the customs tax, the king had been in no position to wage a campaign of the sort he intended without extra help. For this, he had turned partly to Parliament, and especially to the Commons who had become far more influential and powerful, not to say better off, than they had been at the time of his grandfather's French war. To begin with, Edward did everything possible to ensure that all sections of the community were committed to his cause by repeatedly consulting Parliament. Several years afterwards, when the king's minister and diplomatist, Bartholomew Burgersh, was asking the Lords and Commons, in 1343, to debate separately whether negotiations for peace should be started, he stated that the king wished to seek their consent for this because 'this war had been undertaken by the common assent of the prelates, magnates and Commons' of his realm.[1] We can be fairly certain when this consent was obtained. According to Archbishop Stratford, when he was defending his administration from the king's attack in 1341, the parliamentary decision in favour of war was taken in the Parliament held in March 1337 at Westminster, and although we have no surviving record of the occasion, circumstantial indications confirm that this was so.[2] It is also virtually certain that the Commons as well as the magnates were asked to give their opinion as to the French war, as they had been in connection with the Scottish. No doubt the question put to them expected an affirmative answer, and the Commons probably felt that once the decision for war had been taken by the king and the magnates it would be unbecoming for them to question it. Even so, the fact that they were asked indicates the growing importance to the king of the Commons' goodwill.

The Parliament of March 1337 was clearly intended to be symbolically decisive in binding the representatives of the nation to Edward's cause.

---

[1] *Rot. Parl.* Vol. II, p. 136.
[2] G. L. Harriss, *King, Parliament and Finance in Medieval England to 1369*, p. 234.

Originally summoned to meet at York in January, it was twice prorogued and was eventually redirected to Westminster in order to be nearer the source of the kingdom's peril, as the writs record. (The Exchequer had also been brought back from the temporary capital in the north.) This was also the Parliament in which, as we have already seen, Edward made his young son Duke of Cornwall, created six new earldoms and gave lavish gifts of lands to the new earls and other magnates. A month later, an embassy led by Bishop Henry Burgersh of Lincoln was sent to the Netherlands in search of allies, which the king asserted was done on the advice of Lords and Commons. It concluded treaties which determined the conduct of the first phase of the war until 1340, and also the king's financial commitments to his allies. The embassy also had instructions for further negotiations with the French king 'according to a form agreed upon in Parliament'.[1]

Yet Parliament was not the only mechanism for gaining consent or money. During this early stage of the war, Edward was also given to calling great councils to discuss his plans. Two had already been summoned in 1336 to discuss the negotiations with the French king, at the first of which only magnates and prelates were present. But the second, held at Nottingham, was also attended by knights and burgesses. Here again we come up against the question: what precisely was the distinction between a great council, at which knights and burgesses might or might not be present, and a meeting of Parliament of which representatives of the Commons were now invariably a part? With the judicial aspect of a Parliament now clearly much less important than its political, fiscal and legislative functions, it hardly seems a satisfactory answer to say simply that the distinguishing mark of a Parliament at this stage of its history was the dispensing of justice. On the other hand, Parliament did meet during the regular law terms and had judicial functions.

The formal distinction between Parliaments and great councils, even at this stage is not easily defined. There were some assemblies which can only be regarded as tantamount to Parliaments, even though they were described as councils in the writs of summons.[2] There were also a few special occasions when representatives of the Commons attended an assembly which was not a Parliament but a great council. It may be most accurate to conclude that whereas a Parliament was a greater occasion at which justice to individuals and groups could be delivered and which was now, by custom, necessary for making statute law and for grants of *general* taxation, a

[1] E. B. Fryde: 'Parliament and the French War, 1336-40' (in Fryde and Miller, Vol. I, p. 245).

[2] The Parliament, or great council, of September 1337, which granted three fifteenths and tenths spread over three years is a notable example. See p. 270.

great council was a more limited assembly called largely for some immediate and urgent political purpose, and lacking any judicial role. A great council, like a Parliament, was historically an extension of the king's general and omnicompetent council, but in practice had a narrower function and was a less formal occasion than a Parliament. It is perhaps safe to say (to the extent that it is safe to say anything on this abstruse and controversial subject) that a great council was a more purely advisory occasion than a Parliament. It was therefore natural that it should generally be attended by lay magnates and prelates alone without the presence of representatives of the Commons. For, after all, it was the magnates who were still for general purposes the king's natural councillors, as Edward III made clear by the care he took to make them his associates. With this rough and ready distinction between a Parliament and a great council we may, for the purpose of this account, leave a vexed historical question on which a great superstructure of scholarly disputation has been erected with little prospect of producing a generally accepted and wholly satisfactory answer.[1]

The king tended to summon great councils for specific and practical purposes. This can, for example, be inferred from the fact that the Nottingham council of magnates and prelates in the September of 1336 met alongside an assembly of nominated wool merchants especially summoned to give the king financial help based on their own trade. Acting on behalf of the 'merchants of the realm', this assembly gave the king an additional subsidy (the maletote) of 20s. a sack of wool over and above the normal custom of 6s. 8d., together with a 20s. loan, which, altogether, might bring in about £70,000. This maletote of 40s. was made by the merchants acting separately, yet it hardly seems likely that the discussions of the great council

---

[1] For those who wish to pursue the matter, reference should be made, inter alia, to the many articles written over a period of decades by H. G. Richardson and G. O. Sayles, which have been collected and reprinted in *The English Parliament in the Middle Ages*, especially to 'Parliaments and Great Councils in Medieval England' (from *Law Quarterly Review*, LXXVII, 1961); and to Plucknett, op. cit., to R. F. Treharne 'The Nature of Parliament in the Reign of Henry III' (*E.H.R.* LXXIV and Fryde and Miller Vol. I) and to J. F. Baldwin, *The King's Council in the Middle Ages*, Ch. V. The core of Richardson and Sayle's argument is that 'Parliaments are of one kind only and ... when we have stripped every non-essential away, the essence of them is dispensing justice by the king or by someone who in a very special sense represents the king'. On the other hand, Richardson and Sayles also conceded that at other afforced sessions of the king's council, 'indistinguishable in constitution', which are not Parliaments (i.e. at great councils) there might be performed 'any, or perhaps all of the functions performed in Parliament'. This is because there was no limitation on the powers of the king in council ('Parliaments and Great Councils'). If this is so, it is not clear how much remains of the argument that justice alone is the distinguishing and exclusive hallmark of a Parliament.

about policy towards France were unconnected with the merchants' grant. Certainly two further great councils of some prelates and magnates in the following summer were closely concerned in a scheme for exploiting the wool trade to the king's advantage which was crucial to his financial calculations, though its failure was to bring about his first serious political crisis.

The king was now negotiating directly with the wool interest for taxation almost as though it were a separate estate of the realm. For the wool merchants the return benefit from their direct grants was in the system of wool staples which gave them (particulary the greater ones) something approaching a monopoly in exports. At Stamford in May and June of 1337, just after the French king had declared Gascony forfeit, a great council of prelates and magnates discussed and agreed a preliminary plan made with the merchants for establishing an English wool company for the purpose of financing the war by means of an export monopoly, and in July another similar great council at Westminster confirmed the scheme and listened to the report from the Bishop of Lincoln's embassy. A monopoly of wool for export was granted to a group of leading wool merchants for their own and the king's benefit. Conditions for a successful monopoly had already been created in August 1336 when wool exports had been forbidden, partly in the hope (which was not realized) that depriving the Flemish weavers of wool would put pressure on the Count of Flanders to forsake the French king and become Edward's ally. But the embargo on exports was also significant financially. For while it made wool in England abundant and cheap, the price would be raised in the market overseas. To take advantage of this, the merchants were to buy 30,000 sacks at fixed prices from the growers, who were to allow them credit until they had re-sold it. The wool was then to be sold at a big profit to the starved Flemish market, half the profit going to the king. Against these expectations he was also to have a loan of £200,000.

Everything had been done by consultation of some sort, and the success of the export wool monopoly was crucial to Edward's finances. Even so, it was not enough, and in September a Parliament (sometimes described as a great council) met at Westminster to approve arrangements for the defence of the realm while the king was overseas and to receive his request for money.[1] Parliament's enthusiasm for the king's enterprise (it must have been aware of his expected income from wool) can be judged by the

---

[1] This assembly has occasionally been referred to as a 'great council' (its designation in the writs of summons) although it was attended by the Commons. But for all practical purposes it was a Parliament (not least in its tax granting) and it was described as such on the writs '*de expensis*' through which the Commons secured their pay, though it is of course arguable that this was a clerk's mistake.

remarkable grant of a tenth and a fifteenth for three successive years. Good harvests made the giving easier, and it was no doubt encouraged by the activity of the king's commissioners in the shires who held meetings to promote his fund-raising. Nevertheless, it was a wholly unprecedented act of generosity, and the purpose of the forward grant was to enable Edward to borrow against his expectations. He now had some £87,000 a year from ordinary sources, of which £57,000 came from parliamentary grants (£38,000 from the laity; £19,000 from the clergy) with £30,000 from his own demesne and customary aids. But since he was already due to pay his allies £124,000, quite apart from the cost of the campaign to come, the success of the wool enterprise was crucial. Besides, the Commons seem to have assumed that their three-year grant was a once-and-for-all offering which would enable the king to make a quick and successful push to victory. These hopes were to be disappointed, and the wool deal ended in a fiasco, the king's need for money creating the first great parliamentary crisis in English history. Of course, it was not the first time that a king had fallen foul of his Parliament over money. Edward I had done so as a result of his war needs. But whereas he had been opposed by the magnates, it was the Commons who were now to use his grandson's financial difficulties to demand reforms and changes in the king's government. The political struggle that was looming was the first to be waged almost entirely in Parliament.

In October 1337, shortly after the Commons had left Westminster, the king made his formal claim to the French throne and began to use the title in dealing with his allies, though it was not used formally in England until 1340. (Archbishop Stratford, however, was later to assert that the claim to the French crown was only made after discussion at a Parliament, or *'magnum consilium'* as it was actually described, in Northampton in July 1338.) His campaign was planned for early in the next year. But in December a Papal commission of two cardinals arrived in London seeking a truce. They were told in the king's presence that since his subjects had already undertaken to defend his kingdom and pursue his rights, he and his councillors dare not agree to a truce of any length without again consulting the magnates and Commons. The king then wrote formally to the cardinals telling them that a Parliament would be summoned for February 1338, and explaining that the need to refer matters of such importance to Parliament was a laudable custom of the realm. Meanwhile, there would be a short truce until 1 March.[1] It was not to be the last time that a medieval king would use the need to consult Parliament as a means of gaining time for political ends.

[1] E. B. Fryde, 'Parliament and the French War, 1336–40' (Fryde and Miller, Vol I, pp. 245–246).

In this case, Edward needed time to consult his representatives overseas from whom he learned that a prolonged truce would simply destroy the alliance against France. He accepted this advice.

We do not know how far the February Parliament, when it met, felt free to debate the question of peace or war, or whether it was consulted largely as a matter of form after the real decisions had been taken by the king and the most important magnates. But it was probably taken for granted that there was no need for much discussion as long as things were going well. It was when they began to go ill, and particularly when further good money was sought to throw after money that had been spent ineffectively that Parliaments tended to abandon acquiescence for active criticism. That was to be a regular pattern of parliamentary behaviour in the centuries to come. But, in February 1338, the outlook still seemed fair enough and Parliament maintained its support for war, even granting the king half the nation's wool (on condition his subjects were free to dispose of the other half) which was estimated at 20,000 sacks. (In return, the king gave up a claim he had made to scutage and a planned inquisition into dues from the chattels of felons, to which there had been objections.) On the strength of this Edward went ahead with his plans for war, borrowing more money from the Italian bankers against his expected profit from wool. In the event the shipments to Brabant were to run out to be no more than 2,500 instead of the promised 20,000 sacks.

This, however, was by no means the worst of it. More serious was the lack of success of the merchants' monopoly in collecting their wool for export, which was to be shipped to Dordrecht in Brabant, whose duke was Edward's ally. They managed to collect little more than a third of the intended 30,000 sacks and could offer the king's officials only some £66,000 instead of the expected advance of £200,000. The merchants were also anxious to sell the wool as soon as possible when it reached Dordrecht at the end of 1337, whereas the king's officials wished to delay to allow time for the market price to rise further. Eventually, the officials exercised a right given to the king in the original agreement which allowed him to buy in the wool if necessary, and to dispose of it. Although the merchants were nominally paid a fair price, they had to take it not in cash but in promissory notes to be cashed later against future export duties. (Most of these so-called Dordrecht bonds were later sold at a discount.) Thus in the early part of 1338, the king had lost the confidence of the merchants and still lacked the money he needed. These events had important consequences for Parliament. The collapse of the wool monopoly scheme presaged the end of the idea of an 'estate' of merchants with whom the king could deal separately. At the same time, the maletote was passed on in prices to consumers which stiffened parliamentary resolve that what affected people throughout the realm should only be done by parliamentary consent and not simply by agreement with the merchants.

Before the king sailed for Brabant in July, a council of his supporters was established to govern the kingdom, nominally under his infant son, the future Black Prince. But this council was left with little discretion to act. Just before he sailed for Brabant, the king issued ordinances from Walton-on-the-Naze to make sure that he would personally retain control of affairs, conveying his orders home by letters under the privy seal, which was in the hand of a long-standing clerk of his household, William Kilsby. The privy seal would virtually control the chancery and the exchequer, and its warrant would be necessary to sanction all payments by the government. The object was speed and singleness of purpose in paying for the war, to which every other consideration was to be subordinated. But this long-distance control made it harder for the ministers in England, who also had to cope with domestic difficulties and defence in Scotland, to act decisively in response to Edward's needs. There was particular public resentment at the cancellation under the Walton ordinances of all customary exemptions from tax and of former arrangements whereby debts to the crown could be paid by instalments. One aspect of the new post-1334 arrangements for a fixed sum yield of the tax on movables was also a cause of discontent. Poor people with possessions below a given threshold had lost their exemption from paying tax. In 1337, the Commons therefore had petitioned for the tax to be lightened. All these matters were discussed critically at a great council of magnates in Northampton soon after Edward's departure.

Meanwhile, Edward was again borrowing heavily in the Low Countries. Demands for more money from England produced no results and in February 1339 he was even driven to pawn his crown to the Archbishop of Trier. In July, nevertheless, he embarked on his abortive campaign in Picardy, trying, by brutal devastation of the countryside, to provoke Philip to attack him, in the knowledge that the advantage would lie with the defender. It was a risk the French king declined to take. After the brief confrontation of the two forces in battle array, both Edward's allies and the French king withdrew and Edward was forced to return to Antwerp to face his lack of money. He had already made changes in the government before leaving England and had replaced his Treasurer in the previous year. Now he decided to send to England as his chief counsellor John Stratford, Archbishop of Canterbury, the old adherent of the Lancaster family who had played a part in the events leading to the deposition of Edward II, but who was now a long-standing and trusted servant of Edward III. Stratford, who was something of a scholar as well as an ambitious cleric and politician, had already twice been chancellor, a post held after him by his brother, now the Bishop of Chichester.

A grumbling Parliament in February had given no supply. Now Stratford and other ministers presented the king's case to a Michaelmas Parliament willing in principle to help but only on conditions.[1] Three reasons for the summoning of Parliament were given to both magnates and Commons, assembled together. The first was that everyone, great and small, should consider the best means of preserving peace in the kingdom. The other questions were the defence of the Scottish border and guarding the sea against invasion. Parliament was told that Edward was near St Quentin with a great host and prospects of victory, but that he also had obligations to his allies of £300,000 sterling, or more, and must have money. Everyone then agreed that he should be aided by a very large sum in this necessity, or he would otherwise be shamed and dishonoured (... *qu'il soit aidez d'une tres graunte soume en ceste Necessite, ou autrement il serroit honiz & deshonhurez* ...). There was then a discussion about how he could be aided with 'the least cost and grievance to his people' and to his own best advantage, and 'having regard to the great shortage of money in the land' (*eant regard a la graunte defaute de Monoie qui est en la terre*). For Stratford and the council were faced with the fact that there was now an economic recession, with food prices falling, as a result of the lack of money. This was correctly supposed to be the result of too heavy taxation. Some members of the council therefore suggested that the king might be best helped by an aid in kind; namely, that for two years, every man in the kingdom should give a tenth of all his sheaves of grain, wool and lambs, in the manner of the church tithe (*en la manere quele il les donent a Seinte Eglise* ...).

After this discussion, the magnates gave the tenth sheaf from their demesne lands (excluding the lands of their bondsmen) and the tenth fleece and lamb. But they also asked that the maletote should be abolished, and that there should be a return to the ancient custom on wool (6s. 8d. a sack), as well as a guarantee by charter that their present grant would not be a customary burden. The Commons, however, were much less amenable. They lauded the king's enterprise, acknowledged that he must be helped, and asserted their own disposition to help him. But they also stated that since the aid must be large, they did not dare assent ('*ils n'osoront assentir*') until they had advised and consulted their communities ('*les Communes de lour pais*'). They therefore asked for another Parliament to be summoned, and in the meantime undertook, with all due loyalty, to return each to his own community in order to do the utmost possible to obtain a suitable aid

[1] *Rot. Parl.* Vol. II, pp. 103–106.

for the king. As though to make sure that the Commons should not include men in the king's interest, they added that the writs for the knights of the shire should state that none of them should be either a sheriff or any other official (*Ministre*). But it was also made quite clear that despite their promise of loyal endeavours on the king's behalf, the supply of money would be conditional on the redress of certain grievances, which were then set out in two bills. The first was to do with the defence of the Scottish border and of the coast. The second enumerated proposed remedies for domestic complaints.

Some of these would mean virtually abandoning much in the Walton ordinances. The bill asked, for example, for the exemption of penalties in respect of chattels for old felonies and trespasses of the forest, as well as for exemption from the feudal aids for knighting the king's son and marrying his daughter and from scutages. The Commons also requested the arrest, as breakers of the peace, of any purveyors who took goods without giving immediate payment. There was a crescendo of public protest against purveyance at this time, and it was probably in this Parliament (but arguably in that of March, 1337) that an undated petition was submitted against arbitrary seizure and assessment of goods under purveyance. It justified the plea on the grounds that supplies should only be contributed by free will 'because no free man ought to be assessed or taxed without common consent of Parliament', (*nul frank homme ne deit estre assis ne taxe saunz commun assent de parlement*).[1] The parliamentary roll also records the demand for the arrest of Sir William Wallingford, the clerk of the household, who had been in charge of purveyance, and who was imprisoned and replaced.[2]

Not least, the Commons joined with the magnates in requesting the abolition of the maletote. The knights of the shire represented the wool producers who could only lose from the king's monopolistic deals with the wool merchants, and the Commons as a whole represented consumers. The Commons, therefore, demanded the end of the maletote in much stronger terms than the Lords, adding in justification that it should go because it had been imposed, so they understood, without the assent of the Commons or the magnates (*saunz l'Assent de la Commune ou des Graunds, sicome nous entendoms*). Taken together the positions adopted by the Commons in respect of both kinds of taxation represented an unprecedented assertion of their rights. Tax grants had never been automatic but the haggling was usually over the amount, rather than about whether there should be a grant at all.

---

[1] *Rot. Parl. Hactenus Inediti*, p. 269; E. B. Fryde 'Parliament and the French War' (in Fryde and Miller, Vol. I, p. 251); G. L. Harriss, op. cit., p. 249.
[2] *Rot. Parl.* Vol. II, p. 105.

The evidence of the Michaelmas Parliament of 1339 is the clearest so far that the Commons now felt strong enough to refuse the king help if they chose and to make their giving openly conditional on the redress of grievances. By insisting on going back to their constituents before making a grant, they demonstrated where the ultimate power over taxation lay. Under the rough and ready fiscal arrangements of the middle ages, local resistance to tax collecting could always undermine the efficacy of a parliamentary grant, and the goodwill of taxpayers was important. In view of the heavy tax burdens already placed on their constituents, the Commons had good political reasons, at the end of 1339, for returning to their shires and boroughs to persuade public opinion, if they could, before agreeing to further impositions. This unusual episode, however, also carries another significance. Although the Commons were then, as they are now, representatives required to act on their own discretion, and not mandated delegates, there has always been a flavour of the mandate in English parliamentary representation. It was discernible long before the invention of the political party manifesto, or the idea that at an election politicians seek a mandate for their programme. In the fourteenth century, it was the business of members of the Commons to know what their constituents would, and would not, tolerate, and also what they wished to have from the king, conveying the information to him. It was a two way process of information and we see it in unusually visible operation in this exceptional reference back to the constituencies.

On the other hand, it would be wrong to infer from this that it would have been within the political realities of the age for the Commons, when face to face with the king, to persist indefinitely in a blank refusal of any help. Their role was rather one of bargaining, and when the next Parliament came, any resistance they may have found in their constituencies proved no obstacle to their making a grant when they were confronted with Edward's personal importunity. Indeed, it seems highly likely that the principal, but not the only reason for their insistence, in the Michaelmas Parliament, on consulting their constituencies was to use delaying tactics so as to extract from the king as much as they could in exchange for the further tax grant which they probably foresaw they would eventually have to make. In stating their conditions and waiting for another Parliament before the matter was settled they seemed to be deliberately leaving the king time to absorb his dependence on them and to accept the price he must pay for their help. They clearly intended that the next Parliament should be one of standing since it was stipulated that the knights sent to the next must be 'girt with swords' (*ceynt des espes*). As though to rub in that the king had no option but to accept this request, the record of the Parliament concludes by recording the decision that a new one was to be summoned for the Octave of St Hilary: '*ITEM, Fait a remembrer de somoundre le Parlement as oytrave de Seint Hill' susdit.*'

Accordingly, another Parliament was summoned for January 1340.[1] Because of bad weather many of the lords, prelates, knights and burgesses were late in their arrival and so the Parliament was postponed from day to day until the following Monday. The first thing to be done was to set out to the Commons the cause of summons: namely, that they should make a good response concerning their promise to give suitable aid. The Commons replied that they wished to talk among themselves and discuss the matter. They then delayed giving their answer until the Saturday when they offered the king 30,000 sacks of wool on certain conditions, which were to be drawn up in indentures. But since these conditions intimately affected the king's 'state' (that is, his prerogative) the council decided to refer them, with its advice, to the king personally and his privy council ('*son Counseil Secrez*') at Antwerp. However, on the same day the Lords themselves granted for themselves and for all who held their land by barony the tenth sheaf, fleece and lamb from all their demesne lands. The Lords seem to have been much more seized of the danger than the Commons, whom they reminded that money was urgently needed for a fleet and for defending the coast. What, asked the Lords, were the Commons prepared to do about this, so as to provide for their own safety?

The Commons replied 'after a long discussion between them' (*apres long tretiz ent eu*), which presumably means by the usual processes of intercommuning between magnates and Commons, that they would give the king 2,500 sacks of wool which would be counted as part of the 30,000 sacks if he obtained them by fulfilling the necessary conditions. If he did not, the king would simply have the 2,500 as a gift.

With this hard bargaining, and some ordinances on smaller matters, the Hilary Parliament came to an end, having declined to give the king what he needed except on terms he wished to resist. Having just incurred new debts, Edward now had no alternative but to come home and seek to persuade or overawe Parliament into giving more help than had been forthcoming. He arrived in February and issued writs for a Parliament which assembled in March.[2] After the routine proclamations against disorder and the appointment of receivers of petitions, the causes of summons were declared, first to the magnate specially (*en especialte*), and then again to the magnates and Commons together (*en generalte*). Was this, perhaps, a move on Edward's part to put the Commons in their place by putting more distance between

[1] *Rot. Parl.* Vol. II, pp. 107–111.
[1] Ibid., pp. 112–116.

them and the Lords? At all events, the impression given by the Parliament roll is that whereas on the previous occasion the causes of summons had been put to both 'Houses' together, this time the king personally was sharing his thoughts with his magnates first.

Again the case was made that the king would be dishonoured for ever if money were not found and that he would have to return to the Low Countries and live there as a prisoner until his debts were paid. No doubt this dramatic appeal had some effect since two days later the Commons as well as the Lords had agreed to pay a ninth sheaf, fleece and lamb and a ninth of the movable goods of citizens and burgesses for two years, 1340 and 1341. For the Lords, the grant superseded that made by themselves alone in the previous Parliament. (Merchants not living in cities or boroughs, and people dwelling in forests and waste, or who did not live by 'gain' or store of cattle were to be taxed at a fifteenth.) But it can hardly be doubted that the money was ultimately forthcoming not so much in response to Edward's presence as to an understanding that he would accept the principal conditions set out in the Commons' schedule in the previous Parliament. A series of petitions was placed before the king and his council, and this was referred to a special committee which, significantly, included twelve knights and six citizens as well as lords and officials, charged with turning the petitions into statutes (*de le mettre en Estatut*). It was a further acceptance of a parliamentary initiative in statute-making.[1]

Four statutes dealing with grievances were the outcome and they concluded a remarkable episode of parliamentary bargaining.[2] In the first, which implemented the demands of 1339, the maletote was abolished, though its continuance for a further fourteen months was authorized. The king also pardoned all old fines of chattels of felons and fugitives, old trespasses of the forest and old debts to himself and the Exchequer. The people were also pardoned (that is, exempted from) aids for knighting the king's son and marrying his daughter 'for all our time'. Thus those parts of the Walton ordinances which had disallowed exemptions and respites of debts and dues to the king were virtually cast aside. One of the most important grievances to be redressed was that against sheriffs who contrived to stay in office for a long time and were thus 'encouraged to do many Oppressions to the People, and evil service to the King . . .' The wicked sheriff of Robin Hood legend was often a reality at this time, and to prevent such misdeeds, the statute provided that 'no Sheriff shall tarry in his Bailiwick over one Year, and then another convenient shall be ordained in

[1] G. L. Harriss, 'The Commons Petition of 1340', *E.H.R.* LXXVIII (1963), pp. 625–654, is a useful account of this subject.
[2] *Stat.* R. Vol. I, pp. 281–294 (14 Edw. III, Sts. 1–4).

his place' by the exchequer annually. Not the least interesting of the reforms was the abolition of the Presentment of Englishry, the old law by which a community could be fined when a Norman was found killed within its boundaries by some unknown hand. Since the two peoples were now wholly indistinguishable by race, even though two languages were still used, it was a wholly anachronistic law, but also one which was deliberately abused in some areas. Commissioners were also appointed to hear complaints about delays in courts of justice. Among the other reforms in this long statute were a provision for single and standard weights and measures, the keeping of gaols, and, inevitably, safeguards against the misuse of purveyance. Finally, the statute enacted the grant of the ninth sheaf, fleece and lamb in terms which virtually acknowledged that they had been given only on condition of the king's willingness to agree to the reforms provided.

Yet it is the second statute which was the more significant for the long run. After returning to the grant of the ninth, it went on to provide an indemnity that this should not be an example for the future. It then made an important statement of general principle. There was to be no further aid or charge 'if it be not by the common assent of the Prelates, Earls, Barons and other great men, and Commons ... and that in the Parliament'. Among the aids thus ended was tallage, the ancient and much resented feudal charge which the crown could levy on demesne land and towns. Furthermore, all profits from the aid and from marriages, wards, and customs must be spent exclusively on supporting the realm and the wars and nowhere else. It was an unmistakable indication of Parliament's early interest in the appropriation of supply. In conclusion, in allowing the continuance of the maltote for a short stipulated period, after which the wool tax would return to the conventional figure, the statute stated that no additional cusom should be levied in future without the assent of Parliament. The third statute was denoted entirely to reassuring the English people that they would never be subject to Edward, or to his heirs, in their capacity as kings of France. The fourth statute redressed grievances of the clergy.

For the first time there had been revealed the full extent of the crown's dependence on the Commons for money in a crisis, and the determination of the Commons to exploit this to their advantage. But these events had also demonstrated the willingness of this particular king to sacrfice the finer points of his prerogative for the sake of the glory of his war. In such ways, constitutional change habitually follows the accidents of extraneous events and of the personalities who are brought by chance to power.

The statutes, however, were not the only price Edward had to pay for the financial aid he had received. It was also politically necessary for him to accept the appointment to his council not only of Stratford but of the Earls Lancaster, Huntingdon and Warenne, and to give the council in England (despite the Walton ordinances) full power to exercise the royal authority in his absence. However, there seems no reason to suppose that he was yet distrustful of Stratford, whom he appointed chancellor in April in addition to his presidency of the council. Edward now prepared to return to the Low Countries. Hearing that a great French fleet, with mercenary Genoese allies, was assembled at Sluys, which was probably intending to intercept him, the king decided to attack it first. Stratford, however, sought to disuade him from going overseas again. The chief councillor had grown increasingly apprehensive about the financial and political consequences of the war. Edward was already incurring new debts on the strength of the grant he had just received, but the money was slow in coming; for one thing much of it had to come from selling the ninths of wool and corn which could not be before the shearing and the harvest. No doubt Stratford was beginning to see more serious trouble ahead. But Edward refused to heed the Archbishop, rebuking him for being fearful without reason. Thereupon Stratford resigned the seal and his councillorship (though not his place in the regency) on the eve of the king's departure, apparently on the plea of ill health. Edward still did not seem to be hostile, however, since he gave the seal to Stratford's brother Robert, the Bishop of Chichester.

The king then set sail and attacked the much larger French fleet which was dangerously huddled in the mouth of the river at Sluys with no room for manoeuvre. Ramming the enemy ships with his own, Edward achieved a great victory by hand-to-hand fighting under cover of archers' fire. The French fleet was virtually destroyed, over 200 ships being captured by the English. It was a momentous victory since it gave England the control of the Channel and freed the English coast from the damaging French attacks of the previous two years. But once on land, Edward again achieved nothing. A siege of Tournai was a failure and in September Edward had to agree at Espléchin to nearly a year's truce. There was disunity among the allies, pressure from creditors and a lack of money from England owing to great resistance to paying the ninth. Edward again had no option but to return home. This time, however, he came in a very different frame of mind. He had now been persuaded that the fault lay principally with Stratford, and his mind seems to have been turned with great anger against the Archbishop by some of his close councillors, probably the clerk of the privy seal, William Kilsby, among them.

Edward had been at Ghent with his followers, and it was supposed that he intended to celebrate Christmas there. But in November, without even telling most of his intimates, he slipped away secretly with only a handful of his followers, pretending (according to the chronicler Adam Murimuth) that he wanted to take a walk. He went immediately to Sluys, embarked, and spent three days and nights crossing the Channel and sailing up the Thames. In the darkness, almost at cock-crow, the furious king disembarked at the Water Gate of the Tower of London. With him were the queen and his younger children, whom it seemed unsafe to leave in Brabant, and about eight close supporters including the Earl of Northampton, Walter Manny, one of his celebrated commanders, and his clerk of the privy seal, William Kilsby. Edward was still further enraged to find the constable of the Tower absent and his other children inadequately guarded. Immediately at cock-crow, he sent for his principal ministers and chief justices. Robert Stratford, the Bishop of Chichester, was instantly removed from his position as chancellor, and the Bishop of Coventry and Lichfield from the Treasurership. So angry was Edward that he contemplated sending them to Flanders or locking them in the Tower, but when the Bishop of Chichester pointed out the consequences in canon law for imprisoning a bishop, he let them go. But the constable of the Tower was arrested and imprisoned, so was a number of the justices and merchants (including William de la Pole) and some of the greater chancery and exchequer clerks.

Swearing that he would never again appoint clergy to high office, but only such as could, if convicted of treason, be 'drawn, hanged and beheaded', Edward gave the vacant great offices of state to two younger laymen. Sir Robert Bourchier became chancellor, the first layman to hold the office. The treasureship was given to Robert Sadington, who however was quickly replaced by another layman, Robert Parning. Writs were issued for the trial of judges and ministers and a commission of magnates was set up to investigate the conduct of ministers and justices towards the king and the people since the beginning of the reign. Commissions of trailbaston (the common term for commissions with special powers) were also appointed to look into the misdoings of lesser officials throughout the country. There was to be an enquiry in every parish into the true value of the ninth, and into the collection of parliamentary grants and wool. So much might have been popular; what was not were attempts to enforce payment of long-standing dues and fines.

There then followed a remarkable conflict of will and propaganda between Edward and Stratford, who had withdrawn to Canterbury.[1] The

[1] For an account of Edward III's conflict with Archbishop Stratford see especially Gaillard Lapsley, 'Archbishop Stratford and the Parliamentary Crisis of 1341', Pts. 1 and 2, *E.H.R.* Vol. XXX (1915), pp. 6–18, and pp. 193–215, Powell and Wallis op. cit., pp. 335–342, Stubbs' *Constitutional History*, Vol. II, Ch. 5, B. Wilkinson *Const. Hist. of Med. Eng., 1216–1399*, Vol. II, Ch. 5. In the last of these, extracts from a number of the basic sources are

king summoned the archbishop to London, but Stratford assumed a Becket-like posture, preaching a sermon on the Feast of St. Thomas the Martyr, 29 December, in which he blamed himself for his concern with secular at the expense of holy matters. He followed this with a political speech in English dealing with alleged infringements of Magna Carta, and finally excommunicated anyone who so offended, excepting the king and his family, but not presumably the king's officials. Stratford rebuked Edward by letter, reminding him of the danger to kings who were misled by evil counsellors. He bluntly illustrated this by a reference to the king's own father, who by evil counsel had seized peers and other men, putting some to death and confiscating the property of others. 'And what happened to him for that cause, you sire do know.' Stratford also accused the king of breaking his coronation oath by his actions. He then asked for the prelates and magnates, the peers of the land, to be assembled for inquiry into the responsibility for the financial difficulties, so that he and others accused could safely go to them. Stratford (who had also forbidden his clergy to pay the ninth as well as the clerical tenth granted the previous year) was now under arrest at Canterbury and was again summoned to London. He refused to go, even under safe conduct. He was willing to go to a Parliament but not to a council. The king replied that there were good reasons for not summoning a Parliament just then.

The propaganda war then became even more intense. In February, the king issued what became known (it seems to have been Stratford's description) as the 'infamous tract' (*libellus famosus*). Formally addressed to the archbishop and distributed to a number of bishops and deans, it was actually an appeal to public opinion. It accused Stratford, with much personal abuse, of criminal negligence in his ministerial responsibility to the king and of failing to see that the king received the funds promised in the last Parliament. He was therefore answerable for the failure of the king's expedition owing to the lack of money. He was said to have taken bribes, and was accused of treason. (The tract, which was read out in public by Kilsby, the keeper of the privy seal, himself in minor clerical orders, at the market cross at Canterbury may have been written by Bishop Orleton of Exeter, an old personal foe of Stratford's, who denied it, or by Kilsby himself.) The government ordered the tract to be published from pulpits, and Stratford had it read and answered point by point in his cathedral. He

printed. See also Wilkinson's *The Protest of the Earls of Arundel and Surrey in the Crisis of 1341*. The basic narrative sources are: *Vitae Archiepiscoporum Cantuariensium* (ed. H. Wharton, Anglia Sacra, attributed to Birchington); the *French Chronicle of London*, ed. G. J. Angier (Camden Soc. 1844), & Adam Murimuth, *Continuatio Chronicarum*, ed. E. M. Thompson (Rolls Series, 1889).

also sent and issued his own reply to the king. As well as describing the clergy as 'fathers and masters' of kings, princes and all the faithful, he produced a constitutional theory that ministers are only responsible to the king collectively, and when their policy, framed in council and authorized by Parliament, had been properly adhered to. These conditions, he asserted, had not been met in this case. As well as answering the charges against him point by point, and disclaiming responsibility for the king's problems, he asked to be allowed to clear himself before the peers of the realm, and repudiated the jurisdiction of any secular judge.

This remarkably modern doctrine of ministerial responsibility, however, did not fit the realities of the time. It was irrelevant in a period when the king was expected to be a personal ruler. How could he fulfil that role if he were obliged to accept ministerial advice which he felt to be wrong? That was the continuing problem in the middle ages. A wise king took counsel and accepted good advice but in the end, when he considered advice not to be good, he must have the last word or become a cipher, which nobody wanted. If, on the other hand, the king persistently rejected good advice in favour of bad decisions because his judgement was faulty and if his last word went consistently against the magnates, their only solution was to use some sort of force against him. But no such real dilemma underlay Edward's conflict with Stratford. Both his policy of war with France, and the consequent money-raising, had been agreed in Parliament with his natural counsellors. This was not a dispute genuinely affecting the constitution. It was rather a personal quarrel in which an angry king blamed his former minister for administrative failings for which his own policies, agreed in Parliament, were ultimately responsible, and in which a clever, scholarly and indignant cleric pursued his personal quarrel with the king by inventing theoretical arguments which were largely irrelevant.

But in one crucial respect, Stratford's argument was highly relevant. As well as acquitting himself of blame for the war and for the king's financial troubles, he claimed, as a peer of the realm, to be heard by his fellow peers, and he repudiated any secular judge's right to try him. In pointing out the danger to all peers if a precedent were established by which he was condemned unheard, he touched the interest of all other magnates, and it was this that was to make the crisis of 1341 important constitutionally. (The 'peers of the land' were also, perhaps, not unsympathetic to a reference he made to councillors, by which he meant the king's privy councillors, whom he described as 'tyrants' in the land.) But what is most remarkable about this episode is the unprecedented political campaigning from both sides in order to win over public opinion. That tells us something of significance about the reign and the relationship of the king to the secular and spiritual magnates. It also illuminates the king's pragmatism, despite his anger, and the political temper of the time. It is hardly possible to imagine that an archbishop could have behaved in this way during the century to come without losing his head. Angry though his magnates and Commons often were at the cost of Edward's policies, they were in basic agreement with them and the hallmark of the reign was the care the king had taken to ensure that they should be and his willingness to pay the price necessary for their support.

Needing money, Edward decided to summon Parliament, despite his earlier resistance. It assembled on Monday 23 April 1341, the appointed day, but as too few magnates had arrived, no business was done until the Thursday. Meanwhile, on the Tuesday, Stratford arrived at Westminster with his brother and nephew, the bishops of Chichester and London, and accompanied by a large number of clerics and esquires. At the entrance of the great hall, the normal way in to the chambers of the palace in which Parliament met, his way was barred by the king's steward, Lord Stafford, and the chamberlain, Sir John Darcy. He was instructed that he must first go to the exchequer, which was in another building just by Westminster Hall, for the purpose of answering to some kind of small financial matter. Under protest he did so, and then went to the Painted Chamber to join the few bishops who had so far arrived, explaining his case to them. The next day, he was again stopped at the entrance to the Hall by Darcy and other household ministers. Again they tried to direct him to the exchequer, but this time he refused and again went to the Painted Chamber with other bishops. The king did not appear. On the following day, Parliament began its business[1] and when Stratford, accompanied by his episcopal relatives, arrived again, he was told by the sergeant at arms that the king was holding his Parliament. Stratford, who was carrying his own cross (like Becket), declared that he was summoned by writ and asked for admittance, refusing to go away without the king's own command. Some of the king's close councillors then appeared, including the chamberlain, Sir John Darcy, who asked him angrily what he was doing. The archbishop again stated his claim to enter and his intention to remain there. 'May you stay there for ever, and never depart,' said Darcy. When Stratford, in the role of potential martyr, offered his body for torment and his soul to his Maker, Darcy replied: 'No such thing; you are not so worthy nor we so foolish.' The angry exchange between the archbishop and the king's ministers continued until the latter departed.

[1] *Rot. Parl.* Vol. II, pp. 126–131. In the narrative sources (see footnote, p. 290) there are points of ambiguity and conflict about the day on which Stratford was escorted to the Painted Chamber by the earls, and about the precise sequence and dating of events.

Some of the magnates then decided that it was time to intervene. The Earls of Northampton and Salisbury came out to see the archbishop, agreed to take a message to the king and led the Stratfords to the small Westminster hall, where they found some other bishops. Then, when the king had withdrawn, the prelates went with the two earls to the Painted Chamber, where there was argument about what should happen. The king did not return, but at some stage, Earl Warenne came to the king in Parliament where he found Kilsby, Darcy and other councillors who 'ought not properly to sit in Parliament'. Earl Warenne then observed to the king that 'those who ought to lead are excluded and others are here in Parliament who ought never to be in such a council where only the peers of the land can support you, my lord king, in your great need'. Darcy then got up and withdrew, followed by Kilsby and others. (One of those who appear to have left the chamber after he had been named by Warenne was Lord Stafford who did in fact have a barony, and whose father had been summoned, though he himself had only been summoned since 1337.)[1] The episode directs attention to an important development that was slowly taking place in Parliament. It had grown from the king's council, at which all sorts of councillors, both magnates who advised the king, and officials who served him, sat together. The council was still notionally at the centre of Parliament, but the magnates had now come to feel that as the king's natural counsellors summoned with writs, they sat in Parliament as an estate of which his officials, who were not so summoned, were no proper part. Gradually such officials would cease to attend regularly though they would still be present as required.

There was now clearly a movement of parliamentary opinion towards Stratford. It was based principally on the peers' wish to preserve the right of any one of them to be heard only by his fellows. After the councillors who were not peers of the land had left, the Earl of Arundel pleaded with the king to let Stratford come before him, and if he could not defend himself, the rest of them would deal with him. The king agreed and for the first time since his return met the archbishop. The first step towards reconciliation had been taken. Over the weekend Darcy and Kilsby held meetings with the mayor and aldermen of London to turn them against the archbishop by reading out articles against him, which seem to have been repeated to the 'community in Parliament' in the ensuing week. Stratford again offered to clear his name in Parliament but the essence of the argument was no longer between himself and the king but between the peers and the king. On 3 May a bill concerning the privileges of peers was put before the king, which was

---

[1] Powell and Wallis, op. cit., pp. 337-338.

to provide that peers, whether officials or not, could only answer charges in Parliament. Since the king thought that this 'would be improper and contrary to his estate', the magnates asked that the matter should be put to a committee of twelve peers, which contained a number of Stratford's supporters including his brother and nephew. On 7 May, the committee reported that peers ought not to be charged 'save in Parliament and by the peers of the land' and 'whereas it had recently been questioned' whether a peer who had been chancellor or some other office holder had this privilege, it was the 'view of the peers of the land' that he had.

The archbishop then formally made his submission (*se humilia a nostre Seignur le Roi* . . .) and was received into the king's grace. Edward agreed to his request to be arraigned in full Parliament, but on condition that other business was dispatched first. A small commission was established to consider Stratford's case, but the whole matter remained in suspense until 1343 when the king had the charges altogether quashed. In fact, the Stratford affair was no longer important. Its significance was that it had led both 'Houses' to bring forward petitions, all more or less relating to matters touched by the controversy, to the following effect. The Lords asked for a statute confirming the privilege of peers to be tried before their peers in Parliament. The Commons asked that the Charters should be observed and that chancellors, treasurers, barons of the exchequer, the keeper of the privy seal and other ministers should swear, on taking office, to maintain the law of the land, the Charters and the statutes. Both Lords and Commons petitioned together that the accounts of those who had received wool, or other aids, for the king should be audited, that expenditure at home or overseas should be enrolled in Parliament; and that, because of many evils arising from 'bad councillors and ministers', the king should appoint 'in Parliament' the chancellor, the chief justice, the treasurer, the chief baron and chancellor of the exchequer, the steward, a 'clerk fit to keep his privy seal' and other ministers, all of whom should be sworn to obey the law. This meant that, by designating and announcing ministerial appointments in Parliament, the king would virtually have to obtain Parliament's approval for them, which was potentially by far the most serious infringement of his prerogative.

The king was resistant, and the Lords and Commons considered that his first responses 'were not so full or sufficient as was proper'. Edward then referred the petitions to a committee of magnates and eventually the king responded in terms which conceded all the main points. On the matter of the office-holders, he made two concessions. First, if one of the great office-holders was removed by death or some other cause, the king would obtain the agreement of such magnates as were most easily available to the appointment of the new office-holder, who would be sworn at the next

Parliament. Secondly, he agreed that at every Parliament these appointments should be taken into the king's hands so that officials could answer complaints against them in Parliament. The parliamentary roll records that the chancellor, treasurer and certain judges would not assent to all this on the ground that it might be contrary to the laws and usages of the realm. Nevertheless, the petitions were turned into statutes, as was a grant of 30,000 sacks of wool in place of the second year's ninth of sheaf, lamb and fleece.[1]

All this, it must have seemed, put the king very much in the magnates' hands. To get control of the crown's ministerial appointments was an old baronial aim. But the triumph did not endure. Six months later, the king notified the sheriffs that after consultation with the magnates and other counsellors, he had decided to annul the 'pretended statutes', to which he had never willingly agreed, because they infringed his prerogative. His annulment, subsequently enrolled as a statute, was expressed in terms of remarkable candour.[2] It began by declaring that '. . . certain Articles expressly contrary to the Laws and Customs of our Realm . . . and Prerogatives . . . were pretended to be granted by Us by the manner of a Statute'. But being bound by oath to defend the law and prerogative, and being 'providently willing to revoke such things . . . which be so improvidently done' the king had consulted 'the Earls, Barons and other wise Men of our said realm'. (That is to say, he had sought advice outside Parliament.) He had 'never consented to the making of the said Statute, but as then it behoved us' he had 'dissimuled in the Premisses of the said statute . . . to eschew the dangers which by the denying of the same We feared to come, forasmuch as the said Parliament otherwise had been, without despatching anything, in discord dissolved, and so our earnest business had likely been ruinated'. In other words, if he had not agreed, he would have failed to get the required supply of money from Parliament, to the ruin of his war effort; a clear indication that Edward at least took seriously the possibility that parliamentary supply might be refused outright. The statute went on to record that he had consequently permitted the 'pretended Statute' to be sealed. It therefore seemed to 'the said Earls, Barons and other wise Men that sithence the said Statute did not of our free Will proceed, the same be void, and ought not to have the name nor strength of a Statute . . .' Therefore the king had declared the said statute to be void and annulled. It was not the first time that Edward and his forbears had annulled statutes.[3]

---

[1] *Rot. Parl.* Vol. II, pp. 126–131; *Stat. R.*, Vol. I, pp. 295–296.
[2] *Stat. R.* Vol. I, p. 297. 15 Edw. III st 2.
[3] Sayles and Richardson, 'The Early Statutes' *Law Quarterly Review*, L (1954), reprinted in *The English Parliament in the Middle Ages*, XXV 27.

But it was perhaps the frankest explanation offered for so doing. Yet nobody seems to have objected, not even Stratford, who was henceforth again to be Edward's loyal supporter in his war.

We can only conclude that nobody was seriously shocked by supposing that some great point of principle had been breached. The king's making of a new statute outside Parliament is a reminder that even in the mid-fourteenth century, statutes were enacted not by Parliament but by the king on Parliament's advice, and that it might still sometimes be politically feasible for him to make law on other advice. After the Stratford case, no further Parliament was summoned until 1343 when the offending and annulled statute was formally repealed, and Edward's declaration of annulment was formally approved as a new statute, which also provided that certain parts of the old statute which accorded with the law should be re-enacted. Significantly, the Lords registered no objection. Only the Commons petitioned that the king should keep the laws of the land, to which Edward replied by declaring that the statute he had annulled was contrary to his coronation oath and the law of the land, and a blemish on his crown. He asserted that 'the king may make such ministers as he pleases and as he and his ancestors have done in all time past'.[1] Perhaps the most enduring legacy from the episode was the confirmation that a prelate who might be charged with an offence was as fully a peer, and as much entitled to trial by his fellows, as any lay lord. The application of this privilege only to peers summoned by writ also implicitly registered the fact that the privileges of peerage belonged only to an individual, and not to his family who, however noble, were in matters of justice on an equality with any other commoner. But in constitutional terms, the ease with which Edward could ignore what had been temporarily forced on him registered the reality of contemporary politics: the king could only be coerced on basic constitutional matters by the magnates, who were themselves far too deeply involved in his war policy, and its potential spoils, to fall out with him. This was particularly so in the early 1340s when new prospects of success were opening up in France.

To the question how it came about that Edward III could place on the nation far heavier burdens than his ancestors and yet get away with it, there can also be only one answer: the magnates were fundamentally on his side. Edward's true parliamentary critics were the Commons. But they could not unmake or challenge a king's policies as such if the magnates were with him. What they could do was to refuse him money which was a real, if limited, power and one which would continue to be used to extract remedies for the

---

[1] *Rot. Parl.* Vol. II, pp. 139–140.

wrongs that most concerned them. The power of the Commons to influence statute-making increased during the next thirty years, but Edward faced no new parliamentary crisis until he was in his dotage. He had learned some lessons about money, and though his demands were constant, they were not again quite so exorbitant as they had been during the years when he was seeking to purchase allies. In any case, the political conditions for parliamentary crisis were lacking once the victories in France were being marked up in the years ahead. National pride was to be built on these successes, and a new sense of Englishness was encouraged which was to be manifest in the coming triumph of the English language over French. Edward III had made some grave errors in his early years, but he had the knack of inspiring political trust which is essential for successful leadership. Both the magnates and the Commons had come to understand that, for all his faults, he was not a king whom they need fear, nor one whom they must resist because he threatened their liberties.

V

After 1341, the war with France took a new direction in which a series of outstanding military victories relieved the king of serious difficulties with his Parliaments. This did not mean an end to discontent with the cost of the war. On the contrary, the Commons continued to complain, sometimes strongly, and to associate their tax grants with demands for the redress of grievances. At times, the supply of money was explicitly made dependent on the legislative action. But there was no new crisis of the kind which had confronted Edward in the first years of the war, and for this there were two reasons. First, costly though the war still was, it no longer drained the country to the same extent as before, largely because Edward's war policies ceased to be dependent on the purchase of allies. Secondly, the campaign in France erupted into a series of brilliant successes in battle which made the Commons and the nation shareholders in the king's glory. It is one of the sadder paradoxes of English history that the new sense of pride and unity in nationhood which characterized the fourteenth century was associated with a type of war which, beneath its chivalric veneer, was even more systematically and persistently squalid and cruel than most medieval conflicts. The war was the more popular because it was cheap, and it was cheap because of its very ruthlessness.

The attempt to defeat the French with bought allies had now all but collapsed. Edward's title of Imperial Vicar-General had been revoked by the German Emperor, and the English king was rapidly losing his hold over his Flemish allies. Contemporaries believed that one, if not the principal, reason for Edward's claiming the French crown had originally been his wish to give a flavour of legitimacy to his case sufficient to encourage the Flemish to do homage to him. That homage was now meaningless, though by an historical irony the claim to the French crown survived to shape English foreign policy for more than a century. As it happened, however, a new dynastic accident now enabled Edward to turn against his Adversary of France, as Philip VI was customarily described in Parliament, from a new direction. The death of Duke John of Brittany without children provided Edward with his opportunity. Two of the late duke's relations were rival claimants to the duchy. His niece, married to Philip VI's nephew Charles de Blois, had the support of the French. The late duke's half-brother, John de Montfort, who also held the title Earl of Richmond, was the natural candidate for English support. Both Philip and Edward were taking positions which were flatly opposite to those they had adopted in the matter of the French succession. Philip supported the female line, Edward the male. Self-interest naturally triumphed over consistency. For Edward, Brittany provided a base from which he hoped to drive a wedge into France, and where he could also expect some support from the Breton people with their resentment of French domination. In the early stages of the fighting between the two claimants, however, John de Montfort had become a prisoner of the French. His cause was maintained by his duchess Joan, but Charles de Blois had taken over most of the duchy, and throughout the winter of 1341 she was besieged in Hennebont near Lorient.

In March 1342, therefore, Edward sent a small expedition to Brittany under his brilliant captain from Hainault, Walter Manny, by whom Hennebont was relieved. The next month the king summoned a great council of over 100 magnates and a small number of prelates to meet at Westminster in order to secure their adherence to his plans. Another, and larger, force was sent to Brittany in the summer under the Earl of Northampton, and this also began successful operations against the French. In the autumn, the king himself crossed with a larger army, and without meeting the French in pitched battle, which both sides wished and managed to avoid, he took control of much of the duchy by a campaign of sieges, raids and skirmishes. By these means, he got as far as Vannes, where he was within a few miles of Philip's army. Again, neither chose to attack, and in this situation of mid-winter stalemate, with little achieved, a truce was proposed by papal emissaries, and was agreed at Malestroit, near Nantes, in January 1343. The king sailed home in a violent storm, landing at the beginning of March.

A Parliament was then summoned for April, at which the Lords and Commons were told by the chancellor that 'the sovereign and principal cause (of summons) is to treat and counsel with the magnates and Commons of the realm (*les Grantz & Communes du Roialme*) about what is best to be done' concerning the truce.[1] Then, Bartholomew de Burghersh, who (as it was explained) had been in Brittany with the king when the truce was arranged and knew how things had been going there, was put forward to explain how matters stood. He first reviewed the campaign, reported on the king's achievements and spoke of the successful *chevauchée* by which Edward had taken towns and castles until he had reached Vannes. The kind of campaigning described to the, no doubt, admiring Lords and Commons by the term *chevauchée* was to be characteristic of the next phase of the war. To *chevaucher* was to make a fast moving mounted raid or expedition in which a ravaging army covered large distances, living off the land, plundering and terrorizing the countryside, slaying civilians, and thus disrupting the government of the enemy and breaking down good order and law. This technique was, no doubt, used with more restraint in Brittany, where the English were hoping for Breton support, than it was to be in France proper. But as the conflict progressed in France the *chevauchée* was developed to a systematic money-saving instrument of policy. While the war between combatants, particularly those of a higher rank, was conducted with elaborate displays of courtesy and honour, the code of chivalry did nothing to protect the common people. A cruel war, which was continued on the flimsiest of justifications, and waged frivolously for loot and glory, was thus made even more immoral by the savage manner of campaigning. Yet precisely because it enabled soldiers to live off the countryside, and so to be in large measure self-supporting (apart from pay), it called for much less support by the tax-payers at home. Beneath the glittering veneer of chivalry, the truth was morally ugly, but nobody would have thought so at the time. Humanity has a great capacity to defend its self-interest by turning a blind eye to convenient evil. To the magnates, the French war brought wealth from ransoms and spoils. For many a captain it provided the means for founding a new family of substance at home, and for the ordinary soldier, too, it gave prosperity from plunder. As for the people at home, who were consistently informed about the war and its achievements

---

[1] *Rot. Parl.* Vol. II, p. 136.

through Parliament and from the pulpits, they enjoyed a new pride in Englishness and a unifying hatred of the French. For the Commons the war was that much more acceptable because financial burdens were not what they had been.

So, having described the king's exploits, Burghersh told Parliament how Edward had reached Vannes and had accepted the Pope's plea for a truce, perceiving that the 'form of this truce was honourable and profitable to him'. There would be discussions for a peace which the king would agree to if it were 'honourable for him'. If not, he would 'pursue the quarrel as before'. Nevertheless, de Burghersh continued, 'since the war had been undertaken and begun by common consent of the said prelates, magnates, and Commons, the king did not wish a treaty of peace to be made nor peace to be undertaken, without their common assent' (. . . *sanz lour commune Assent*). The prelates and magnates were then told to meet in the White Chamber 'by themselves' to treat, counsel and assent together whether an embassy should be sent to Rome explaining the king's rights. The Commons were charged to assemble in the Painted Chamber likewise to treat, counsel and assent among themselves on the same business. When they had done so, they were 'to report their response and their assent'.

Accordingly, the prelates and magnates reported in the White Chamber that they found the truce honourable, and said that 'every Christian' must wish that the war should be brought to a good and suitable end. They therefore agreed to the truce being maintained, and to an embassy to the Pope, not as a judge or arbitrator (*compromessair*) but as a common friend (which was the formula by which Burghersh had referred to the Holy Father). 'And then came the knights of the Shires and the Commons, and replied by Master William Trussell in the said White Chamber . . . (and) in the presence of our Lord the King and of the said Prelates and magnates.' They, too, agreed that the truce should be kept in preparation for an honourable peace, and to solemn messages to the Pope setting out the king's case. But if an honourable peace was not possible, the Commons would 'aid him to maintain his quarrel with all their power' (*lui eider a meyntenir sa querele ove tote lour poair*). Once again Edward had wooed Parliament to his will, and the William Trussel who reported the Commons' conclusions may have been the son of the man of the same name who sixteen years before, as 'proctor for the whole Parliament', had renounced allegiance on behalf of the kingdom to Edward II. The Trussell of 1343 (like his earlier namesake) seems not to have been an elected member of the Commons and may have been a counsellor. Nevertheless, he was clearly acting in the role of the later Speakers (a description not yet in use), in presenting the Commons' advice to the king, though there is no evidence at this stage that whoever acted as Speaker in this 'spokesman's' role also presided over the Commons' private deliberations.[1]

The account of the 1343 Parliament in the parliamentary rolls is the earliest clear description that we have of the meeting of the two parts of Parliament in their separate 'houses', but there is little doubt that they had done the same for a number of years before that. Once the question of the war had been dealt with, the king came again with the Lords and Commons to the White Chamber. The chancellor then explained that the king, on his return from Brittany, had heard of various oppressions and grievances of the people, and that the law had not been maintained as it should be. He wished it to be applied equally to 'the poor and rich' and he therefore required the Lords and Commons to go and consider, each by themselves, and to 'report their advice'. The next day, the Lords and the Commons produced a long and discursive account of their thinking on such matters as the administration of justice, foreign merchants, the export of good money and the bringing in of bad, and needless to say, wool. The Commons submitted a petition of thirty five articles under the heading '*Les Petitions des Communes*'. These were petitions concerning matters of common interest, but it does not follow that the Commons necessarily formulated all of them. In some cases they may have done; in others not.[2] Nevertheless, it was the fact that the Commons adopted and presented common petitions which gave them their importance in the eyes of the king and the government. In 1343, the king merely replied to most of them, using various forms of words, to the effect either that the existing law would suffice or that he would take advice or think about the matter, which was simply a delaying tactic, often couched in words which anticipated the later standard form for a royal veto of a parliamentary bill: for example '*Le Roi se avisera . . .*'. The petitions of this Parliament, as was very usual, included a protest against the maletote, and still more strongly one against the unpopular claim of the Papacy to appoint its own nominees to English ecclesiastical benefices in certain circumstances.

This parliamentary complaint against the papacy had first been heard in 1307, but now it was voiced much more strongly. By tradition, the popes had claimed, under canon law, to have the right to appoint, or 'provide' a new incumbent to a vacant benefice in certain circumstances, including the death of the previous holder while he was at the Papal court. But during the fourteenth century popes had much increased the use of their right, also

---

[1] *Rot. Parl.* Vol. II, pp. 135–136.
[2] D. Rayner, 'The Forms and Machinery of the "Commune Petition" in the Fourteenth Century,' Pts. I and II, *E.H.R.* Vol. LVI (1941), p. 570.

claiming, for instance, the right to provide the new incumbent in cases where the vacancy had arisen because the Pope had appointed the former holder to a higher position. As well as being offensive to the ordinary patron of the benefice, the papal claim aroused particular resentment when foreigners were preferred to Englishmen, and especially when the result was the drainage of the income from the livings to France. The fact that the Papal court was now at Avignon intensified anti-papal feeling. There could be no doubt in 1343 that Pope Clement VI was pro-French, and that he was more than happy that Avignon should remain the permanent home of the papacy. The lay protest in the Parliament of 1343 was, therefore, particularly strong. However, it had no support from the prelates and the king himself connived at papal provisions, partly because they could sometimes be useful as a means of arranging benefices for his own ministers. Nothing therefore came of this protest.

Only one new statute, which was concerned with the regulation of money, emerged from the Parliament.[1] Of considerably greater interest is the formal repeal of a previous statute already quashed on the king's sole authority. This was the statute which had been forced on him as a result of the quarrel with Stratford. In their petitions in 1343, the Commons included a strong protest against the king's annulment of this statute which he had only accepted under duress. But the complaint was rejected. With the Lords acquiescing, it was recorded that '... it is granted and agreed that the statute made at Westminster ... in the fifteenth year of the reign (1341) shall be entirely repealed and annulled and shall lose the name of statute as being prejudicial and contrary to the laws and usages of the realm and to the rights and prerogatives of our lord the king ...'.[2] But it was also agreed that some articles of the statute, which accorded with 'law and reason', should be made into another statute by the advice of the justices and wise men. This statute of repeal was formally considered to date from 1341, the year of Edward's declaration of annulment, not from 1343, thus reserving the king's right still to make law on his own if necessary. Yet the importance attached to the parliamentary declaration in reinforcing the king's declaration of repeal is no less clear. In general terms, however, it may be said that this was a Parliament in which the Commons expressed strong views with little result. But then it was also a Parliament at which the king did not ask for money, and those two facts are almost certainly not unconnected.

The truce did not lead to peace. The probability is that neither side

[1] *Stat. R.* Vol. I, p. 299.
[2] *Rot. Parl.* Vol. II, p. 139.

supposed that it would. Before the year was out, a number of important Breton nobles had been seized by the French and executed on Philip VI's orders. This increased Breton resentment and it was later to provide an excuse for the resumption of hostilities. But for the moment Edward took no action. At the beginning of 1344 he held a great tournament at Windsor which was designed as a symbolic embodiment of the chivalric ideal which he was making his personal theme and by which he grappled the English aristocracy to his enterprise in France. Robed, wearing his crown and accompanied by his magnates, the king ceremonially swore at the tournament to found a Round Table of 300 knights in the manner of King Arthur. Work began on building both a massive Round Table and a tower to house it in, but the project was discontinued, probably for lack of money. Instead, the foundation of the Order of the Garter four years later, after Crécy, was to express his concept of chivalry in a different and more economical form. Meanwhile, though negotiations for a peace were taking place under papal auspices Edward had already begun to prepare the mind of the political nation for the resumption of the war. At Easter he held a great council at which it was agreed (as the parliamentary roll for the subsequent Parliament records) that there was very great business concerning the realm to be dealt with, which could not be discharged 'without Parliament'. Accordingly Edward summoned a Parliament to meet in June.[1] During part of the time of Parliament's meeting, the Archbishop of Canterbury was presiding over a Convocation of the clergy of his Province in St Paul's Cathedral, which was summoned for the same purpose as Parliament: the provision of money. (This Convocation, which was not part of Parliament, agreed to give the king a tenth for two years, as did the Province of York.) But apart from Archbishop Stratford himself, only the other two Stratfords, the Bishops of London and Chichester, and one bishop-elect were present when the Convocation was due to open. The parliamentary roll records that when the king had heard this he marvelled greatly (*il se marveill trop'*) at it, as he also did at the failure of most of the lay magnates to arrive on the day of summons. On both scores he 'held himself little satisfied'. Once again, too few magnates had turned up for business to begin on time, and the weather hardly provided an excuse in midsummer. Parliament was adjourned until the next day. But still they had not arrived, and it was ordered that the names of the lords who were summoned were to be read before the king in Parliament to see who had come and who had not. The names of those who had not come were to be sent to the king 'who shall order such punishment as he sees fit'. We do not know what, if any,

---

[1] *Rot. Parl.* Vol. II, pp. 146–148.

penalties were imposed. There were probably none, and the magnates' lack of punctuality continued to be a problem in the years to come. The king, after all, was dependent on the support of the magnates and there must have been a limit to the extent to which he could express his annoyance. So we must envisage the angry king waiting from day to day until these great men deigned to arrive; it was not until four days after the due date that there was a full enough attendance for business to begin. The interval was used for such routine matters as the cry against armed attendance (even though most of the magnates had not arrived to hear it) and the appointment of receivers and triers of petitions.

Eventually, when business proper began, the chancellor, Sir Robert Sadington, addressed the magnates and Commons. He informed them of the terms of the truce and spoke of the offences against it: the seizure and villainous execution of the Breton lords, and the seizure of land by the king's Adversary. Furthermore (and there is a certain irony in the recording of the frightening news in the formal language of Norman French) the king and the council had heard 'for certain' that Philip VI was determined 'to destroy the English language and to occupy England, which God forbid, if a remedy be not provided against his malice by force' (*a destruire la Lange Engleys, & de occuper la terre d'Engleterre, que Dieu defend, si remeide ne soit mys contre sa malice par force*). Then, after a reference to the Scottish raids, the magnates and Commons were asked to consider all this and give aid and counsel. They went off to deliberate until Monday, which proved to be not long enough; their meetings were prolonged until Wednesday but what they were discussing (presumably by inter-communing) can only be guessed at. Perhaps they were considering the amount they would pay; perhaps they were keeping the king in suspense. At all events, when Lords and Commons reassembled in the White Chamber they told the king that considering the perils from his Adversary's malice, and the heavy charges suffered by the magnates and Commons for the war, which (it was pointedly remarked) had been prolonged by means of the pretended truce, they wanted an end to the war or to have a truce that was genuine. Each magnate speaking for himself (*chescune singulier Persone des Grantz a par lui*) asked the king to put an end to the war either by battle or, if possible, by a suitable peace, and not to be put off by prayers from the Pope. The king fully assented. The prelates and clergy then granted a tenth for three years, and on the Saturday the Commons granted two-fifteenths from the community of the land (which they, not the peers, now represented) and two-tenths from the cities and boroughs 'according to conditions set out in a schedule'.

In this the king was told that this sum was a heavier charge on his poor people (*plus chargeant a vostre poure Poeple*) than the four fifteenths were previously. It is stated without any ambiguity that the grant was made on certain conditions (*cestrui Grante Vous fait vostre dite Commune sure tiele conditions*), which then followed. First, the whole of the grant was to be spent on the business indicated to this Parliament by the magnates' advice (presumably conveyed through inter-communing), another early attempt at the appropriation of supply. Secondly, the petitions put to Parliament should be granted. Thirdly, the aid from the north should be spent on the defence of the north. Then the Commons, bluntly wielding the power of the purse, granted another fifteenth on condition that the king personally went abroad to 'put an end to the said Business'. There followed a list of petitions upon the customary grievances, to which the king and, it should be noted, also the magnates replied in a manner suggesting the shadowy beginning of a formal assent by the Lords to the passage of the Commons' bills.[1] Many of these were incorporated in the second statute of this Parliament, which recorded the threats to the nation ('even to the tongue of England') to prevent which the counties had granted two-fifteenths and the cities and towns two-tenths for two years. The conditions in respect of the use and appropriation of the funds contained in the original Commons' response were duly recorded in the same statute. This also enacted, among other remedies for which the Commons had petitioned, that the unpopular commissions of the new inquiries (the general eyres) were repealed with certain exceptions, and that instead Keepers of the Peace ('men of the best reputation') should be appointed in each county. (Whereas the crown wished, by the general eyres, to extend the activities of the king's bench in the country, the Commons wanted loyal men in each county to do the work.) The statute also dealt with purveyance, weights and measures, the coinage, and the pay of soldiers.[2] The first statute of the Parliament concerned wool; the third provided remedies required by the clergy in exchange for their grant. It was two years before Parliament met again.

For a time the negotiations at Avignon continued under papal auspices. They broke down because the English insisted that Gascony at least should be held in full sovereignty while Philip VI insisted that it should again be a fief of the French crown. In May 1345 Edward declared the truce to be at an end, and forces were again sent to Flanders, Gascony and Brittany. Edward himself went on a fleeting expedition to Flanders. But his ally, the aggressive and dictatorial populist Flemish leader, Jacob van Artevelde, was assassinated. The attempt to concert an attack from Flanders was now at an end, and Edward returned to England. Meanwhile, in Gascony the

[1] *Rot. Parl.* Vol. II, pp. 148–151.
[2] *Stat. R.* Vol. I, pp. 300–301.

campaign under the leadership of Henry, Earl of Derby, was very successful, and important towns and districts were taken by the English. On the other hand, in Brittany an expedition had achieved little and the death of John de Montfort had left only an infant heir as the weak English-supported claimant to that duchy. In any case, Edward now had a different object in mind; an assault on Normandy. At the beginning of 1346 he set sail with a vast expedition from Southampton, his destination unrevealed. It was generally supposed that he might be going to the assistance of the English force in Gascony which was now under some pressure from the French king's son, John Duke of Normandy. In fact, the destination was Normandy itself, which Edward saw had the advantage of enabling him both to launch an attack into France itself in the direction of Paris and to draw French forces away from Gascony.

Accompanied by the Prince of Wales, who was now nearly sixteen, and most of the great men of England, Edward landed at St Vaast-la-Hougue. One of his first acts was to knight Prince Edward, which by tradition qualified the king for a feudal aid. Shadowed by their fleet, the English next marched to capture Caen where a documented plan for the invasion of England was discovered, to the great benefit of Edward's propaganda. It related to a previous time, but the government was able to represent it to Parliament as a current menace. It was sent home by the navy, together with vast amounts of spoil which the English had taken in the pillaging of Normandy, even though Edward had made some effort to stop this at the understandable request of his Norman ally, Godfrey de Harcourt, a claimant to that duchy. But as Edward launched a merciless, fast and devastating *chevauchée* into France proper, there was no such restraint. In an extremely daring operation, Edward marched north-east towards his Flemish allies, with his army looting, raping and living off the land and (perhaps the most useful effect of this kind of exercise) disrupting ordinary life and the processes of government. Near Rouen, the king was threatened by Philip at the head of a much larger army. At one point it was a question of whether Edward should make a dash for Paris; instead, he contrived to get across the Seine by repairing a broken bridge at Poissy, while the French were distracted by raids on the outskirts of Paris. He then led his army to the Somme, with Philip on his tail. After the Somme had been crossed at a ford, the English had to fight at Crécy, but in conditions of their choosing. A tremendous victory was achieved as a result of the French king's mistake in attacking with the cavalry which formed the overwhelming proportion of his army. The French attack was destroyed by the English archers placed in a strongly defensive position. French casualties were massive.

The dead included the blind king John of Bohemia (whose ostrich feathers were taken by the Prince of Wales for his insignia), the French king's brother the Duke d'Alençon, and his nephew Guy de Blois, among over 1,500 men of noble and good birth. Philip managed to escape in the darkness. It was the end of August, too late for Edward with his weary army to attack Paris, and it was pointless to advance to the Flemings. In need of a good port, he besieged Calais for nearly a year, with Flemish support, until the town surrendered in 1347 after which it was planted by English colonists. It remained in English occupation until the reign of Mary I. Meanwhile, the English had achieved further successes in Gascony, and a Scottish invasion of England had been heavily defeated at Neville's Cross, the Scottish king, David Bruce, being taken prisoner. In June 1347, the English inflicted a further defeat on the French in Brittany, capturing Charles de Blois, the French claimant to that duchy. In the autumn, with the English in a state of triumph, a new truce was agreed at Calais.

In the meantime, another Parliament had been held in September 1346 at which the victory at Crécy less than a month before was fully reported.[1] In the absence of the king, it was held at the command of the Prince Lionel, who was then eight, and Archbishop Stratford who had been left as chief counsellor in England. It was a Parliament dominated by prelates, as indeed was the government itself since Edward had now resumed the practice of appointing clergy as his ministers, which since they could be rewarded by benefices, was cheaper than lay appointments. John Offord, dean of Lincoln was now chancellor, and the treasurer was William Edington, bishop of Winchester who became chancellor a decade later. Only three lay barons were present in Parliament, the great majority of magnates being with the king in France. But a number of laymen was summoned as councillors and judges, as well as the prelates, abbots and Commons. A final day was set for the submission of petitions, and receivers and triers were appointed. There was then an adjournment and Parliament awaited the arrival of Bartholomew de Burghersh, John Darcy the chamberlain, and John de Thorseby the clerk of the Privy Seal who, it had been learned, were on their way bearing news of the king's victories. When the king's emissaries came into Parliament, letters of credence from the king were read, and Burghersh made his report. He described the king's achievements from la Hougues and Caen to Crécy and Calais, stating that after his great victories the king did not wish to return to England before he had put an end to the war. He therefore wanted the Lords and Commons to consider what aid and remedy they could provide to enable him to finish the matter that had been begun with their consent. The captured draft French invasion

[1] *Rot. Parl.* Vol. II, pp. 157–163.

plan, which, Parliament was told, was intended to secure the destruction of the whole English nation and the English language was then read out. It is copied in the parliamentary roll. Having heard this, they 'all thanked God for the victory he had granted to their liege lord' (*touz mercierent a Dieu de l'Exploit qu'il avoit donez a lour Seign' lige* ...) and said that all the aid they had given him had been well spent. They would now, they said, aid him further but first they wanted time to consider what they could manage to provide.

Eventually the Commons replied that they would give two fifteenths, though the king was required to agree that if the war was over in the first year, the subsidy should be remitted for the second. They also produced an indentured schedule of their complaints, a principal one of which was a strong protest against the king's practice, without the assent of Parliament, of using commissioners to oblige landowners to find men-at-arms and archers, or to make a composition payment according to the value of their lands. The government's reply indicated that this was an emergency measure which constituted an informal grant by the Lords, and that the king did not intend it to be a precedent. Likewise there were complaints about a subsidy on wool exports which the prelates had arranged with the merchants, to which the answer was that it could not be repealed except by the assent of the king and magnates. Finally, after the petitions had been dealt with, a letter was produced from the bishop of Durham and other magnates who were with Edward notifying as witnesses that the king had knighted his eldest son and stating that he should have the due forty shillings aid for every knight's fee. This seems then to have been granted by the prelates and lay peers without reference to the Commons. Thus it both breached the limit of 20 shillings laid down under Edward I and the right of the Commons to assent to taxation, quite apart from the king's promises in 1340 to cease levying this feudal aid. The magnates' support of the king aroused the anger of the Commons, who nevertheless waited for a later opportunity to complain in the following Parliament.

Meanwhile, it was clear that although the king's ministers were faced with a revival of complaints against misgovernment and the methods of military recruitment, these were less of a difficulty than on previous occasions because of the triumphs in France. Crécy had been taken as a visible sign that Providence, if not the Pope, was on the side of the English in what Edward described as his 'just quarrel'. English pride responded accordingly. The nobility had not only glory and vast profits from war but also the hope of French lands. Men from backgrounds sometimes no higher than freemen, and whose forbears may have been even humbler, advanced themselves as captains to the ranks of the gentry. Ordinary soldiers, paid by indentures of war, or contracts between the king and the captains who recruited them, prospered from good pay and loot. Though some men were conscripted forcibly, for the most part it was an army of patriotic mercenaries. At the same time, the king was less pressed for money than previously and the collapse of the banking houses of Bardi and Peruzzi, to which his own indebtedness had contributed, freed him from the need to repay these old loans.

Nevertheless, the king's need for money was still enough to cause discontent. At a great council in March 1347, attended by comparatively few notables, a forced loan of 20,000 sacks of wool was obtained from the merchants, which added to the resentment over taxes imposed without the Commons' consent. When the next Parliament met in January 1348, after the king's return, Edward found himself facing distinct signs of protest and disenchantment.[1] At this Parliament, for the first time, some of the king's great captains were raised to the peerage, Walter Manny among them.[2] The causes of summons were declared to be to advise the king about the war and the maintenance of the peace within England. On the matter of war, the Commons professed themselves, perhaps with some acidity, too 'unknowledgeable and simple' to be able to offer advice, and they therefore wished to be excused.[3] They had grasped the point that when Edward asked for advice, his real purpose was simply to commit them to the war so that he could say afterwards that what they had advised they should pay for. But while declining to comment on foreign policy, they were forthright on the matter of the peace at home, delivering a very long list of petitions asking for remedies, which they wished to be endorsed, concerning the law of the land. They complained against the taxes imposed in the last Parliament without their assent on wine and wool, the monopolies on wool and tin; the commissions of array which forced landowners with a given value of land to provide a specified number of soldiers (agreed to by the magnates because it was not possible for the besieging army of Calais to live off the land in the manner of a *chevauchée*) and against the taking of victuals. To none of these were there satisfactory answers. The Commons also petitioned against a new custom on drapery, only to receive the reply that it pleased the king, the prelates, the earls and other magnates that this should remain in force. With the triumphant nobility at his elbow, Edward had no difficulty in resisting most of the complaints, and the fact that no money appears to have been asked for in this Parliament made the Commons' demands that much more resistable.

[1] *Rot. Parl.* Vol. II, pp. 164–174.
[2] Powell and Wallis, op. cit., p. 355.
[3] *Rot. Parl.* Vol. II, p. 165.

Two months later, however, on the last day of March 1348, the king called another Parliament when he did ask for an aid.[1] The causes of the summons invited Parliament's advice on the future of peace or war abroad, in view of the uncertainty of the truce and the Adversary's infringements of it. The Commons were told to withdraw together and take good counsel on how to withstand the malice of the enemy, and how the king could be aided to his best advantage and the least burdening of his people. This time, having deliberated on their own, the Commons contrived even more sharply to avoid taking any responsibility for the continuing war, and they made very clear the burdens it laid upon them. It appeared, they said, that because of the latest news the king was asking 'a too heavy charge of his poor Commons', and they asked him to hear of all the burdens and charges they had already endured. There was the aid for knighting the Black Prince taken without the Commons' consent at twice the old rate, the subsidies, the commissions of array, the subsidy on wool, the forced loan of 20,000 sacks and more besides. They were prepared to make a grant, but only on certain conditions. These were the end of all judicial eyres, that the merchants should make no separate grant to the king, that the 20,000 sacks compulsorily borrowed should be returned to the community, and even that the king of Scots (who had been lodged in the tower of London since his capture at Neville's Cross) and other Scottish prisoners should not be released without consultation with the Commons. Their last condition was a clear instrusion into the king's traditional control of foreign policy. They also wanted an undertaking that the king would claim no aid for the marriage of his daughter, that no imposition should be levied by the '*Prive Conseil*' (the king's close council) without their grant and assent in Parliament and that all the conditions should be recorded on the Parliament roll as a 'thing of record', so that they should 'have a remedy if anything was attempted to the contrary in time to come'. On these conditions, though it would be 'to their own excessive hurt' they would grant a fifteenth and a tenth for three years. The conditions were stringent and the use of the money was firmly designated. Nothing more than the due fifteenth should be levied in each of the three years (in equal portions at Michaelmas and Easter) and should be 'assigned and kept solely for the war'. It was not to be used to pay old debts. The king accepted the grant and most of the petitions; although no statute emerged from them this could be taken as meaning that he accepted that they did in fact constitute law as it was. For example, general eyres had been covered by the statute of 1344, but probably little had been done. In the middle ages it was easier to make law than to secure its

[1] *Rot. Parl.* Vol. II, pp. 200–204.

observance, which is why the same subjects so persistently recur in legislation.

This Parliament also represents something of a development in the constitutional and procedural evolution of the Commons. The parliamentary roll records that the Commons were instructed that all individual petitions should be presented to the chancellor (the rolls record these separately from the petitions presented from the Commons collectively) but that petitions touching the Commons in general should be presented to the clerk of the Parliaments. By prescribing a separate procedure for the common petitions (though there had already been indications of this from at least the 1339 Parliament) the king and his council now clearly acknowledged the importance of the Commons' new corporate role in petitioning on matters of general and national rather than local concern. Even more interesting is that the announcement of the new procedure for petitions in 1348 gave the Commons the chance to pursue their attempt to ensure that petitions agreed to for legislation should (in the manner of future parliamentary bills) be firmly enacted in the form in which they were originally agreed. In practice, this was often not the case. Sometimes, for instance, clauses of a petition were omitted from the ensuing statute; at other times, provisions were added to the statute which negated or diminished what was supposed to have been granted.

So, after noting the special procedure stipulated for common petitions, the parliamentary roll for the second Parliament of 1348 went on to record the Commons' request that the petitions presented in the last Parliament, and granted by the king, the prelates and the lords of the land, should be observed. Furthermore they asked 'that, by no bill presented in this Parliament in the name of the Commons, or of anyone else, shall the responses already granted be changed: for the Commons acknowledge no such bill as may be presented by anyone to effect the contrary'. The king's answer was evasive. He had, he said, already, with the advice of the lords, answered the Commons' petitions about the law of the land by saying that the laws and customs of the land could not be changed except by making a new statute, 'to do which the king could not then and cannot see his way'. But as soon as he could, he would with the advice of the 'skilled men' of his council ordain such articles that involved amending the law 'so that right and equity (*reson & equite*) shall be enforced for all and each of his lieges and subjects'.[1]

This was the last Parliament before the Black Death struck England. It was brought to Dorset by ships from Gascony in the summer of 1348, and

---
[1] *Rot. Parl.* Vol. II, p. 203.

reached its peak in the summer of 1349. Estimates of its impact vary, but it is likely that as much as a third of the population of between the five and six million people in England at the time perished. In the early stages, the plague was spread by black rats and their parasitic fleas; at a later stage it appears to have been passed from human being to human being in a pneumonic form. The Black Death went through England with amazing speed; victims died quickly and horribly. By the winter of 1348–49 it had reached London and the king put off a Parliament he had intended to call. The disease struck with varied intensity. For lack of hygiene, towns suffered worse than the countryside but some villages were virtually depopulated, whole families being wiped out and houses falling into ruin. On account of their better conditions the rich suffered less than the poor, at least in the first outbreak. One of the king's daughters died of the disease, but otherwise his family did not suffer, and few of the magnates died, though they were afflicted more in the second outbreak of 1361. The disease was endemic and recurrent throughout the middle ages and beyond, so that the population did not recover. To many people the plague appeared as a visitation in punishment of licence and frivolity, and it plunged the people into a condition of life which could hardly be in greater contrast to the trimphant gaiety which had seized the prosperous and the upward moving classes who had done well out of the war in the aftermath of the triumphs of Crécy and Calais. Socially, the plague made the preservation of order even more difficult. Economically, the immediate consequence was a sharp fall in the prices for all goods and produce, and an extreme shortage of labour as a consequence of depopulation. In places the land ceased to be cultivated. To remedy this the king issued the Ordinance of Labourers in 1349[1] which was designed to hold wages to their lower level of before the plague. That was subsequently to be re-enacted as a statute. The precise difference between a statute and an ordinance remains difficult to define. Whereas a statute might now most often arise from petitions of the Commons, an ordinance was more usually an act of government. Yet both had the force of law. Equally, an ordinance might often be, but by no means always was, devised as temporary legislation. In their first form, the regulations on wages and prices could only be in the form of an ordinance, since they were issued in an emergency when no Parliament was in being. Whether or not the Ordinance of Labourers was originally intended to be temporary is unknown, but its subsequent enactment as a statute was plainly intended to make it durable. It remained the king's prerogative to issue ordinances when he thought fit, or when it could not be done in a statutory form, but a

[1] The Ordinance is printed in *Stat. R.* Vol. I, pp. 307–309.

statute was the higher and more permanent way of law making. The statute of 1351 which followed the ordinance 'established' as well as 'ordained' what was enacted.[1]

The Parliament which met in February, 1351 was opened by the king's son Lionel in his father's absence.[2] Little had changed in the war, though Edward had won a naval battle against a Spanish fleet off the South Coast and the English had captured the castle at Guines. When the opening formalities had been completed, the assembled magnates and Commons (at the initial assembly only, the knights were mentioned in the parliamentary roll as being present with the lords in the White Chamber) were told in the causes of summons of the king's wish to redress what was wrong. As a result of the pestilence and the war it had not been possible to hold a Parliament earlier, but the king had now been told that peace within the kingdom was ill kept, that there was much wrong-doing and that servants and labourers would not work as they should. There was a shortage of money because wealth was going abroad. The king openly recognized his subjects' restiveness and invited all who wished to 'petition in common or individually' to do so and he would right wrongs. He also expressed his gratitude for the great aids and subsidies he had received and all the duties and charges that his people had endured, in body and belongings, to maintain the war and defend the kingdom.

In reply, the Commons described the distress of the country, the high price of corn, the non-cultivation of land, and the use of commissions to take corn and other produce by purveyance. Such charges, they said, should not be levied without parliamentary assent. They also protested against the forty shilling charge on wool exports as a burden on all the people, even though the merchants paid it. Not least there were strong protests against the increase of papal provisions, or appointments, to English benefices, which led to the export of wealth. The Statute of Provisors made in this Parliament was one outcome.[3] This enacted that bishops and other dignitaries of the church should be freely elected and that patrons of livings should be able to exercise the right of presentation. If they were hindered from doing so by the Pope, the king himself would present a cleric to the benefice or office. Any papal provisor or his agent would be arrested, if found, and imprisoned until he renounced his provision. If he could not be found he would be outlawed. The statute was not effective since the king

---

[1] For a general discussion of the relationship between statutes and ordinances see Richardson and Sayles, 'The Early Statutes', reprinted in *The English Parliament in the Middle Ages*.
[2] *Rot. Parl.* Vol. II, pp. 225–235.
[3] *Stat. R.* Vol. I, pp. 316–318, 25 Edw. III, St. 4.

did not choose to enforce it; for one thing, it was useful in bargaining with the Pope, and, for another, papal provision could sometimes enable the king to have his own nominees appointed by the Pope, which was a cheap way of paying his ministers and servants with clerical positions.

The second important statute of this Parliament confirmed and enlarged the Ordinance of Labourers of 1349, which had attempted to deal with 'the great scarcity of servants', and the refusal of many to serve without 'excessive wages'. It had obliged labourers to take wages no higher than those customarily given in their districts in 1346, under pain of imprisonment. The ordinance had also tried to put a stop to the social upheaval caused by the mobility of workers in the aftermath of the plague. Throughout the country the great need for workers had stimulated labourers to move wherever they could get the highest pay. To give lords the first claim on the services of their men, therefore, labourers had been forbidden to depart from the personal service of their lord. Employers would be fined for paying more than the approved rates, and at the same time an attempt had been made to control prices by requiring foodstuffs to be sold for 'a reasonable price'. Anybody exceeding this would pay double the amount they had so received. But this attempt to deal with the great economic and social problems of the time in very general terms had proved ineffective.

In 1351, therefore, much more precise regulation was attempted. The Statute of Labourers began by referring to the ordinance which had attempted to deal with the 'Malice of Servants ... not willing to serve after the Pestilence without taking excessive wages'. It recorded the king's understanding from 'the Petition of the Commonalty' that servants had shown 'no regard' for the ordinance, and had refused to serve without double or treble the wages they had formerly received. The statute went on to prescribe in detail the wage rates and terms of service for particular jobs; mowers, reapers, threshers, carpenters, masons, tilers, and so on. Likewise, prices charged for manufactured goods by cordwainers, shoemakers, sadlers, tailors, and other craftsmen were to be kept to the level of 1346. It was the first prices and incomes legislation in England, and it was no more successful than comparable legislation in later centuries, including our own. Subsequently, between 1352 and 1359 special and salaried commissioners were appointed in each county to enforce the Act, after which it became the responsibility of the justices of the peace.[1] Ultimately, however, the urge of employers to compete for labour by offering higher pay, and the determination of workers to exploit the market shortage of labour,

[1] *Stat. R.* Vol. I, pp. 311–313, 25 Edw. III, St. 2.

destroyed this legislation. Labour became more mobile, and by the end of the century wages had about doubled. Despite the country's fall into poverty, the Parliament of 1351 granted the forty shilling wool export custom, which it said should not be granted by the merchants alone, and clerical subsidies were given by the two convocations of Canterbury and York.

For a time the plague in both countries had brought hostilities between England and France to a stop, but in the new decade they continued in an inconclusive way, especially in Brittany most of which was now dominated by the English. In January 1352, another Parliament assembled, at which the Chief Justice William de Shareshill announced the causes of summons.[1] Having stated that the king had learned that the peace of the realm was not being kept, nor the statutes observed, he quickly came to the matter uppermost in Edward's mind by once more going through the ritual recapitulation of the king's grievances, his claims to France, and the resistance of his new Adversary, King John, who had succeeded Philip VI. Edward's tactics of placing upon Parliament the responsibility for what were really his own policies could hardly be better illustrated than they were by the form of words used. Parliament was told that when, at the outset, the king had consulted the magnates and Commons, they had said that 'they knew not how otherwise to counsel him than that he should purchase allies . . .'[2] Now, Shareshill went on, the new Adversary had broken the truce in Gascony, in Brittany and at sea. The chief justice then came to the point; the king was grateful for past aids, and he once again asked the Commons to give their advice (which meant money), and to state their grievances. The parliamentary roll then records for the first time the process of intercommuning already discussed.[3] It was put to the Commons that 'to shorten their stay in the town' (could this have been a reference to a possible recurrence of the plague or to the cost of living in London?) and to hasten the business, they should elect twenty-four or thirty of their number to negotiate in the Painted Chamber with 'some magnates sent to them by the king'. The rest were to go to the Chapter House where the committee elected would report to them what had been said with the Lords. There seems to have been some resistance to this scheme, although the Parliament roll is not altogether clear on the matter.

At all events, it appears that all the Commons came to the Lords in the

---

[1] *Rot. Parl.* Vol. II, pp. 236–245. The parliamentary roll spells the name of the Chief Justice 'Shareshull'.
[2] *Rot. Parl.* Vol. II. p. 237.
[3] For intercommuning, see above, pp. 266ff.

White Chamber, where they heard again from Bartholomew de Burghersh of the Adversary's misdeeds, and were asked to give advice and submit petitions on their grievances. Then, after long deliberation among themselves, 'and with the advice of those magnates sent to them by the king', the Commons presented a roll to the king which stated the aid they agreed to, and the petitions to which they wished to have an early answer. Aids of three tenths and three fifteenths were given, but only on condition that all the reasonable petitions should be granted, confirmed and sealed before the Parliament departed. The inclusion of the grievances and the grant on the same roll was an obvious attempt to associate supply with the redress of grievances. Among the conditions made were that no tallage or aid should be levied in future; that nobody should be forced to make loans against his will; that nobody should be obliged to find soldiers without parliamentary consent; that any reasonable aids for knighting the king's eldest son or marrying his eldest daughter should be at the old rate of twenty shillings. The king agreed and statutes were made along the lines of the petitions. Another important achievement of the Commons in this Parliament was the statute already referred to, which provided that fines imposed under the Statute of Labourers should be applied to offset the subsidy granted by this Parliament.[1] However, the most important statute of 1352 was that which provided a remedy for the judges' practice of condemning as traitors ordinary criminals brought before them for a wide variety of offences which had nothing to do with any reasonable definition of treason. The motive behind this abuse was the benefit to the king, to whom the goods of a convicted traitor, unlike those of an ordinary felon, were forfeit. The Commons therefore petitioned the king to 'declare the points of treason in this present Parliament'.[2] Accordingly, the statute defined treason as a specific crime, which covered encompassing the death of the king, his chancellors or judges, violating his wife or eldest daughter or making war against the king in his own kingdom. On the other hand, robbery, kidnapping and other crimes were to be felonies or trespass. It was the Commons rather than the magnates who were responsible for this important reform. In the same statute, an attempt was made to correct the abuse of purveyance by requiring that goods so taken should be taken only at the true value.[3]

More than two years passed before the king called a new Parliament. He had found the Commons much more difficult in the Parliament of 1352 than

---

[1] *Stat. R.* Vol. I, pp. 327–328. See above, p. 243.
[2] *Rot. Parl.* Vol. II, p. 239.
[3] *Stat. R.* Vol. I, pp. 319–324.

in any other for a decade and had been forced to yield on many important points. In the meantime, despite the formal truce between the two nations, hostilities between the French and English continued in an inconclusive manner. In 1350, on the death of Philip VI, the throne of France had passed to his son King John the Good, whose reputation, such as it was, for virtue was certainly not matched by ability as a political or military leader. He made forays against the English occupied areas of France, which infringed the truce but with little success. In Brittany, the new John de Montfort, claimant of the duchy, inflicted a devastating defeat on an invading French army in which many of the Knights of the Star, the new French order which was created in rivalry to the Order of the Garter, were killed. In France, King Charles the Bad of Navarre, who, as well as his kingdom in the south, also held territories in the north of France and who, like Edward had a claim to the French throne through the female line, was making overtures to Edward. Against this background Innocent VI had launched a new attempt at a peace, and a conference began at Guines. At home the country was recovering from the plague and prospering again, and in 1352 and 1353 the king called two great councils. In August 1352 one knight from each county, and representatives from a small number of boroughs, who were summoned directly by writs to town officials, were called to a great council.

In this first council, grants of money were discussed but nothing was done which could be seen as challenging Parliament's right over taxation. In the second council of the following year, however, there was an experiment in obtaining money and devising legislation through a less formal type of consultative mechanism than Parliament. This great council, which was so described (*un Grant Counseil*) in the parliamentary roll recording its proceedings was summoned by the king in September, 1353.[1] Commons as well as lords and prelates were present, though it appears that only one knight was summoned from each county and two citizens came from each of the thirty-seven towns and cities with a strong merchant interest. The latter were called by writs sent directly to the officials of the boroughs and not, as was usually the case, to the sheriffs. It was a clearly recorded example of a great council summoned principally, though not exclusively, for one over-riding purpose: in this case to deliberate and authorize a new arrangement for the wool staples. It had long been an objection to the citing of the staples abroad that they could only be operated by comparatively small syndicates of the larger merchants. This suited the king because he could more easily borrow money from the monopoly which he so authorized, but it led to high profits and prices, as well as

---

[1] *Rot. Parl.* Vol. II, pp. 246–253.

excluding the larger number of merchants. In response to the wishes of the Commons, the Bruges staple had been ended in 1344, and free trade was allowed in England. It seems clear that the Commons who attended the great council of 1353 played a considerable part in framing the Ordinance of the Staple which was the principal product of this assembly.

The roll of Parliament records that the king, Lords, and Commons gathered in the White Chamber where Chief Justice Shareshill explained the causes of the summons in a parliamentary manner. The king had heard, said Shareshill, that because 'the staple of the wools of England, which are the sovereign merchandise and jewel of his kingdom of England' (*l'estaple des Leines d'Engleterre, qui sont la Sovereine Marchandise de son Roialme d'Engleterre* . . .) were held abroad, foreigners were enriched to the country's loss. A draft of what was proposed on the advice of the magnates, was read out to Lords and Commons who were told that if they had anything 'to add or amend' they should produce it in writing (*monstrer en escript*). The Commons (they were described as such, even though it was a great council) then asked for a copy of the points, which was given them. 'After great deliberation' the Commons gave their advice 'in writing' which was read and debated by the magnates – after which the Ordinance of the Staple was made in a form set out in the parliamentary roll. The embryonic parliamentary method of one 'house' reading and debating what the other had put forward was clearly used, even though this was no Parliament. A number of home staples was established in England, home merchants were prohibited from exporting, and wool for export was to be bought in the English staples to give the producers a better price. Yet though this great council might seem to have been usurping the functions of Parliament, the Commons who were present were so careful to preserve parliamentary rights over permanent as distinct from emergency legislation, that they petitioned that, to the extent that the Ordinances made in the great council were not a matter of record, they should be recited in the next Parliament and entered on the roll 'as if they had been made by the Common Parliament'.[1] The king agreed that they should be so rehearsed and recorded on the roll 'for greater certainty'. In this great council there is the hint of a wish on the part of the king to act outside the constraints of a formal Parliament and also the wish of the Commons that he should not do so.

Yet in many respects this great council did act as a Parliament. It petitioned the king on general matters, and it also granted a wool subsidy for three years. It was told how the king had sent his emissaries to discuss peace at Guines. It also produced what became the Statute of Praemunire

---

[1] *Rot. Parl.* Vol. II, p. 253.

which prohibited appeals to Rome in cases where the crown claimed to have jurisdiction.[1] There was still an overlap between what a Parliament and a great council could do. In the next few years there was an increase in the number of councils of variable composition, and correspondingly fewer of the Parliaments which so systematically insisted on associating taxation with law making, to the king's annoyance.

In April 1354, however, the king called a Parliament at which the chief justice announced as the first cause of summons the new English staples for wool, leather and lead to be governed by given regulations, which had been prepared by *'les Sages de son Conseil'*, the wise men of his (great) council of the previous September. The ordinance had been proclaimed throughout the kingdom, and now the king had summoned Parliament in which the ordinance might be made a 'perpetual statute'. The knights of the Commons should apply for a copy of the ordinances and put in writing any ammendments and additions. Having considered the ordinances, the Commons approved them and desired that they should be made a statute which was done with some amendments.[2] The point had clearly been made that while the king in council might issue an administrative regulation with the force of law, a statute was essential for permanent law making.

But from the king's point of view, a second cause of summons was more pressing. Parliament was informed that the great council had been notified of the peace negotiations at Guines, about which Parliament would be told more before its departure. There then followed other comparatively minor business, including the annulment of the proceedings against the late Roger Mortimer and the forfeiture imposed upon him, in the interest of his heir who had served Edward well. A large number of petitions on familiar subjects was then submitted, and after the responses had been given, the parliamentary roll records an episode of great interest.

Explaining in greater detail the negotiations undertaken by the king's emissaries at Guines, Bartholomew de Burghersh, who was now the chamberlain, told the Parliament that there was a good hope of peace. But the king did not wish to bring the matter to an issue without the assent of the magnates and Commons. The chamberlain then asked the Lords and Commons if they would assent to a peace, provided one could be had by negotiation and agreement. To this the Commons, 'with one assent and with one accord' replied that whatever decision it pleased the king and magnates to take 'was agreeable to them'. Burghersh then put the specific

---

[1] *Stat*. R. Vol. I, pp. 329–31, 27 Edw. III.
[2] Ordinance in *Stat*. R. Vol. I, pp. 332–344, 27 Edw. III, St. 2, confirmed in *Stat*. R. Vol. I, pp. 348ff, 28 Edw. III, Art. 13.

question: '*Donqes, Vous Voillez assentir au Tretee du Pees perpetuele si homme la puisse avoir?*' ('So, you will agree to a permanent treaty of peace, if it can be obtained?). '*Et les dites Communes responderent entierement & uniement, Oil, oil.*' So, for the first time the roll records the Commons making their decision in precisely the same manner as they do today when there is sufficient agreement to make a division unnecessary: 'And the said Commons replied wholly and with one voice, Aye, aye.'[1] There is no reason to doubt that this was the manner in which they voiced their decisions in their various separate deliberations, as well as when they answered before the king and magnates.

The country was war weary, and the Commons, the only channel through which public opinion could be expressed, voiced this. The terms proposed at Guines were the clearest possible testimony to Edward's astonishing achievement. He would renounce his claim to the French throne in return for recognition of his full sovereignty over Gascony, Poitou, Anjou, Maines, Touraine, and Calais; in other words he would be king of half of France. A draft treaty was drawn up but never ratified. Despite all that it would have given him, Edward was eager to bring the war to a total victory since he now supposed himself to have as his ally Charles of Navarre, who had quarrelled bitterly with King John. (In the event, however, Charles was shortly afterwards reconciled to the French king, who then, in 1356, seized and imprisoned him, on which his brother went over to the English.) Plans were therefore made for a new English advance on several fronts, though the most notable achievement in 1355 was a highly lucrative *chevauchée* of quite extraordinay ferocity and horror, led by the Black Prince as far as the Mediterranean coast.

In November of 1355 a Parliament met at Westminster,[2] and to forestall any criticism by the tax-granting Commons of the likely cost to them of the breakdown in the peace negotiations, none other than the soldier Walter Manny was nominated to declare the cause of summons as one who had 'full knowledge' of these matters, and especially of the overtures for an alliance that had been made by Charles of Navarre, and of how Charles had then broken the subsequent agreement. But little of real consequence passed at this Parliament other than the gift of the usual subsidy on wool and the submission of petitions under the forthright heading '*Les Grevances de la Commune d'Engleterre*'. But this Parliament does provide an instance of a decision by the king himself to deal with a singular (that is to say an individual) petition, that of Lady Blanche de Wake against the bishop of Ely. Having heard the petition, Edward declared publicly; 'I will take the quarrel into my hands' (*Jeo prenk la querele en ma main*).

[1] *Rot. Parl.* Vol. II, p. 262.
[2] Ibid., pp. 264–267.

There was no Parliament in 1356, the most successful military year since Crécy. In September, while Lancaster launched a *chevauchée* from Normandy to the south, the Black Prince advanced northwards from Gascony, with the intention that the two forces should meet. Lancaster, however, was forced to retreat and the prince, finding it impossible to cross the Loire, also had to fall back. As he did so, his army laden with booty, he found that he had been overtaken and by-passed by the French king and his army, who barred the southwards withdrawal of the English force near Poitiers. Forced to fight outnumbered, the English achieved a great victory. The Black Prince placed his archers at the front and his knights, dismounted, at the rear. When the French cavalry charged, they were largely destroyed by the English archers. The rest of the French knights then advanced on foot but, lacking archers to support them, were also overwhelmed. The magnitude of the victory is to be measured, however, not by the casualties, as at Crécy, but by the number and importance of the prisoners taken, who brought great profits from ransom to the English. They included King John himself, who was captured in the final mêlée, treated with elaborate courtesy by the prince and taken to Bordeaux where a two year truce was arranged. The prince then set sail with his royal captive for London where again John was treated with great dignity, entering the English capital in great state on a white charger. The king received and embraced his French Adversary in Westminster Hall and took him and other noble French captives to dinner. In due course, John took up residence in the Savoy, Henry of Lancaster's grand new London dwelling between Westminster and the city, where he lived in state with a large French household, enjoying frequent recreation, notably hunting and tournaments, in the company of Edward, the Black Prince and other members of the English royal family. The two year truce was confirmed and Edward prepared the ground for a peace satisfactory to himself by the affability of his relationship with the Adversary. In the meantime, the subjects of the English king were as buoyed up by the grandeur of the victory and its consequences as those of King John were ravaged and distraught. Massive profits from ransoms began to flow in to the great benefit of the crown, since it was the practice for every soldier to pay a proportion of his profits to his captain, who in turn paid a third of these profits and of his own to the crown. Furthermore, the ransom of royal prisoners or commanders was reserved to the crown, although the captor was well rewarded.

In April 1357 a Parliament was held, but unfortunately no parliamentary roll exists to record its no doubt excited pleasure at the great victory of Poitiers and the prospect that the English taxpayers would be more free of the cost of war. A comprehensive statute was enacted covering a wide range of matters, including grievances concerning the wool trade, extortionate fines (that is to say, charges) taken by bishops' officers for the probate of testaments, and amendments to the Statute of Labourers. The statute also provided the king with a subsidy of a fifteenth in exchange for this legislation against grievances. The contrast between the orderly amelioration of grievances in the peaceful conditions of England, and the confused misery in France could hardly have been more stark.

After the wholly unexpected defeat at Poitiers and the king's capture, government in France had broken down. While John enjoyed the edible fruits of chivalry in London, its poisoned fruits were the lot of his people. The first consequences of Poitiers were an attempt by the French Estates General to wring reform out of what was left of the royal government, followed by a communal revolt in Paris where, until he eventually escaped, the nineteen year old Dauphin was held virtually as a prisoner by the controlling faction of the city burgesses. Their leaders also assisted the escape from prison of Charles the Bad of Navarre, whom they were using in their attempts to force concessions from the Dauphin and the captured king. Outside Paris, France was convulsed by the ferocious peasant rising known as the Jacquerie which began in the region of Beauvais, and was eventually put down with ruthlessness. Disorder was everywhere and despite the truce that had been arranged, English 'free companies' of marauding soldiers, nominally operating under the banner of Charles of Navarre, ravaged the land, seizing castles from which they dominated the surrounding countryside. But by the late summer of 1358, the Dauphin, who despite an unsoldierly mien and character was a far more competent politician than his soldierly father, had outmanoeuvred his enemies and was firmly in charge of the capital though not of ravaged France outside.

In the meantime, Edward made no attempt to give a *coup de grâce* to the disordered French state, and appeared happy to settle for an agreement making him full sovereign of that western half of it which had once been the full extent of the Angevins' possessions. By 1359, King John was persuaded under much heavy pressure to agree to a peace which would have given him freedom in exchange for four million gold crowns (over £600,000), the equivalent of many parliamentary subsidies, and for his acceptance that the English king should have virtually half of France in full sovereignty. In return, Edward would resign his claim to the French crown. But such terms were unacceptable to the French, and ratification was refused by the Dauphin and the French council. Edward therefore determined on another campaign, starting in the autumn of 1359, and this time aimed at final conquest. It failed. The strategy was to march from Calais to Rheims where Edward hoped to be crowned King of France in the traditional coronation city. But Rheims did not admit him and he was forced to blockade it.

Reluctant to take by assault the city in which he hoped to be solemnly anointed France's rightful king, he withdrew in the direction of Paris, but shortage of supplies made any successful action against the French capital out of the question. Progress was clearly impossible.

In May 1360, therefore, negotiations for peace began at Brétigny, near Chartres. A truce was concluded and with it a draft treaty was agreed by the Black Prince and the Dauphin, which was to be confirmed later by both kings. King John's ransom was fixed at £500,000, still a huge sum but less that that which had originally been demanded. The first instalment was to be paid at Calais within four months and hostages were to be given as security for the payment of the balance by instalments over six years. The French king himself was to be released after the first instalment. (In fact, he was, nevertheless, to die in honourable captivity, since though he was released in return for hostages, who included some of his sons, he felt it his duty to return to captivity when one of them broke a parole given to Edward and fled. John died in 1364 in London to be succeeded by the much more competent Dauphin as Charles V). In addition, the Treaty of Brétigny gave Edward III full sovereignty both of Gascony, and neighbouring lands of Poitou, Quercy and the Limousin, as well as parts of northern France, including Calais, Ponthieu and Guines, but not Normandy. In return, Edward was to renounce his claim to France and to restore French fortresses. The treaty was ratified at Calais in October. But the clauses dealing with the renunciation of titles and the ceding of land were to be incorporated in a separate treaty which was not completed, so that John never formally renounced Gascony nor Edward his title to the French crown.

Nevertheless, Edward ceased to call himself King of France for nearly a decade. Though the claim was to be raised again, Edward wanted no early return to war because he sensed that his people had had enough. It is virtually certain that the known attitude of the Commons in Parliament was crucial to his decision to make and take the still advantageous terms that were available. He had managed to wage his victorious war since 1341 without inordinate demands on the Commons, thanks to the spoils of battle and ransoms. Even so, the Commons had grumbled. Edward must have known in 1360 that the money needed for a campaign to bring complete victory would not be forthcoming without great difficulty and perhaps considerable political risk to himself. His wars had brought profit and glory, and bound to him the nobility which had destroyed his father. Why should he risk losing all that had been gained? The Treaty of Brétigny, which produced peace for nine years, can reasonably be seen in large measure as the outcome of Edward's intelligent anticipation of the reactions of his Parliaments had he attempted to continue the war.

VI

England now settled down to a triumphant peace under a king who had freed himself from the French overlordship which had irked his ancestors. Edward's court clothed itself in magnificence; the king's rebuilding of Windsor Castle which had been his birthplace symbolized a prosperity which in some degree seeped down through the social ranks of a society which was undergoing a new mobility in the aftermath of the plague and the spoils of war. Some of his subjects were getting ideas of luxury above their station, which was to provoke restraining legislation. The king himself, who had made his eldest son Prince and ruler of Aquitaine continued to build up the grand fiefs for all his sons which were to be a source of rebellion and civil war in the following century. The most important of these was that of John of Gaunt, who had been married to Blanche, daughter of Henry of Lancaster. In 1362, the plague struck again, this time hitting the upper classes much more heavily, and Lancaster was one who perished. John of Gaunt, father of the usurper who was to dethrone King Edward's grandson, thus became possessed of the great Lancastrian estate.

Parliament continued to grant taxes but also to insist on remedies for grievances. The king was given a tenth and a fifteenth in 1360; and subsidies on wool for three successive years in 1362 and in 1365, for two years in 1368, and again for three years in 1368, from the following Michaelmas. Yet the Commons' vigilance over their control of supply did not diminish. In 1362, the king felt obliged to concede by statute what he had so often resisted in practice, that henceforth there should be no tax or charge on wool, whether by agreement with the merchants or any others, without the consent of Parliament. For the rest of the reign all wool taxes did indeed have parliamentary assent.[1] Parliament now also gave practical expression to the idea of English nationhood which, during the war, had been encouraged by skilful propaganda through the Commons as well as from pulpits and by proclamation. In 1362 a statute (which contained much besides) enacted that all pleas in the law courts should henceforth be dealt with 'in the English tongue', though they were still to be enrolled in Latin. The reason given was that French was 'much unknown' in the realm, in consequence of which people had 'no Knowledge nor Understanding of that which is said for or against them'.[2] By now the upper classes were generally at ease in

[1] *Stat. R.* Vol. I, p. 374, 36 Edw. III, St. I. c. 11.
[2] Ibid., p. 375, 36 Edw. III, St. I. c. 15.

English, partly perhaps because in war it was now necessary to use that language to communicate with captains and others who had little French. Langland was writing Piers Plowman and the Canterbury Tales were to follow two decades later. It was still the fashion for the upper classes to be taught good French. Yet, since even Henry of Lancaster admitted, no doubt over-modestly, that as an Englishman he was not greatly skilled in French, the average English-speaking knight from the shires and burgess from the towns must have been much less so. It was almost certainly for their convenience that a year after English had become the language of the courts it also became the language of Parliament.

On the due day for the opening of the Parliament of 1363, the Chief Justice, Sir Henry Green, 'said in English' that the king was ready to begin his Parliament, but announced its postponement until enough of the Lords and Commons had arrived. When proceedings began, the parliamentary roll notes (though still in French which remained its language of record for some time to come) that 'the causes of summons were shown in English by the Bishop of Ely'. The Commons were invited to submit petitions for the righting of wrongs, and the mood of the time was well exemplified by the rhetorical flourish with which they began the submission of their requests. 'Sire ... the Commons thank their liege lord as much as they know and can for the graces, pardons and good will shown to them ... and from their hearts entirely thank God who has given them such a lord and governor, who has delivered them from servitude to other lands and from the charges suffered by them in times past.'[1]

In beseeching the king to continue his grace to them, however, the Commons at this period continued to leave no doubt of the strength of their complaints, particularly in respect of the old social grievances. Thus in 1362, in response to petitions, it was enacted by statute that because of abuses by the purveyors of victuals for the royal households, the 'heinous name of purveyor' be changed to 'buyer'. The buyers were forbidden to take produce with 'menaces', and were required only to take victuals where they were plentiful, and then only for payment in ready money. Likewise there were to be safeguards against unfair measurement, and buyers were forbidden to take bribes. The statute purported to come from the king's own will but it was the money-providing Commons whose wishes underlay it. In response to another of their petitions, the same statute also contained a provision that, to ensure the maintenance of statutes and for the 'Redress of divers Mischiefs and Grievances which daily happen' a Parliament should

[1] *Rot. Parl.* Vol. II, p. 276.

be held each year, as it had been previously ordained by statute.[1]

Some legislation, however, was obviously the product of the king and his council rather than of the Commons' wishes. Sumptuary legislation enacted in the Parliament of 1363, which attempted to regulate both what people could wear and how much they should eat according to their station in life, was a notable example. It was an attempt to counteract excesses which were the symptoms of a period of social mobility and upheaval after plague and war had improved the fortunes of many survivors. The Parliament roll records that, after Parliament had dealt with various matters arising from both petitions of the Commons and individual petitions, as well as the king's business, the chancellor, speaking in the White Chamber in the king's presence, told the magnates and the Commons that the king's will was to hold and keep the ordinance that had just been made to regulate apparel. By this he presumably meant that it was to be a permanent rather than a temporary measure. Both Lords and Commons were enjoined to keep the ordinance, and the Commons were told that on going back to the country, they should explain it to the people in order that every man should so conduct himself that he and his servants obeyed it. Here again is an example of the use of the Commons as conveyors of information to their constituents. Both magnates and Commons were told that what had been agreed was new and had not been seen before this time. Parliament was then asked whether it wished to have the things thus agreed done by ordinance or statute, and the terms of the answer explain clearly what the distinction between the two kinds of measure was understood to be. The government was told that 'it would be good to implement these things by way of ordinance, and not by statute, in order that if anything needed amendment, it could be amended in the next Parliament. 'And so it was done.'[2] Although the measure was enrolled in the Statute roll[3] it is self-described as an ordinance in the text and can be so regarded. A curious enactment, coming from the government of a king whose court wallowed in luxury, it was as bound to fail as were the attempts to impose prices and wages control, to which it also made additions. (One clause of the ordinance on diet and apparel laid down maximum prices for all kinds of poultry because of the 'great dearth'.) For every class from lords and knights to yeomen and workers with goods worth less than forty shillings, the statute prescribed permitted limits of expense and luxury for dress and meals because of 'the Outrageous and Excessive Apparel of divers People against their Estate and

---

[1] *Stat. R.* Vol. I, pp. 371–376, 36 Edw. III, St. I.
[2] *Rot. Parl.* Vol. II, p. 280.
[3] *Stat. R.* Vol. I, p. 380, 37 Edw. III cc. 8–15.

Degree, to the great Destruction and Impoverishment of all the Land'.

On one matter, however, the instincts of court and Commons were at one: preventing the encroachment of foreign clerical power. The anti-clerical mood in the nation was illustrated in *Piers Plowman*. There were friars who 'preched þe peple for profit of hem-seluen' and explained the gospel as they liked and who 'for couetise of copis construed it as þei wolde'. Worse still were the pardoners with their bulls to whom ignorant men 'geuen here golde glotones to kepe'. Nor were bishops, however high, blameless, least of all the bishop whose pardons were for sale:

Were þe bischop yblissed and worth both his eres
His seel shulde nouȝt be sent to deceyue þe peple.

The reference was to the Bishop of Rome. In the Parliament of 1363-4 a statute was passed against the jurisdiction of the Papal courts.[1] Papal encroachments were also much in the minds of the politicians at the next Parliament which met in January. (The parliamentary roll on this occasion conveys something of the atmosphere of an assembling Parliament by recording that a 'cry' was made in Westminster Hall on the first day instructing those summoned to go to their hostelries and to gather in the Painted Chamber the following morning.) Early in the proceedings the question of papal encroachments was specially put to the magnates in the White Chamber, while the Commons remained in the Painted Chamber. During that year, the Pope also tried to insist on the renewal of the tribute which had been conceded by King John and which theoretically involved an annual payment of 1,000 marks which had always been resisted and of which no payment had been made for a very long time. The burden of papal tribute was therefore formally renounced in the Parliament of 1366, the matter of the tribute being specially and separately put to the spiritual and lay lords for their advice. Their finding was that neither King John nor anyone else could place the realm in subjection without the magnates' consent. With this opinion the Commons subsequently agreed.[2]

Meanwhile, in France the precarious peace was gradually crumbling. The transfer of territories between the two powers, unpopular with the inhabitants, was slow; English 'free companies' which were officially

---

[1] *Stat. R.* Vol. I, pp. 385-387, 38 Edw. III St. 2. The friars 'preached to the people for their own profit', and 'for greed of copes construed it (the gospel) as they chose'. Ignorant men 'gave their gold (to pardoners) to keep gluttons'. As for the Pope: 'If the bishop were blessed and worth both his ears, his seal would not be sent to deceive the people.' *Piers the Plowman*, ed. R. W. Skeat, lines 77-8.

[2] *Rot. Parl.* Vol. II, pp. 289-290.

disowned but were nevertheless unrestrained continued to terrorize parts of France. In 1364 war had broken out between the two claimants to Brittany, and English soldiers helped de Montfort to victory. His rival Charles de Blois was killed in battle, which left the French no option but to accept de Montfort, the only other claimant, as Duke of Brittany. That, however, presented them with no problem. Earlier the same year, King John of France had died in captivity in London, to which he had chivalrously returned when his son, the Duke of Anjou, who had been a hostage for the king's ransom, had broken parole. The new French king, Charles V, was a great deal wiser and shrewder than either of his predecessors. Sensing the increasing weakness of the English position in France, he was preparing for a resumption of hostilities and was quite happy to deprive Edward of an ally by recognizing de Montfort as Duke of Brittany in exchange for the homage to which he was entitled under the treaty of Calais. In the end, the train of events which led to the collapse of the English position in France was set off by the participation of the English and French on opposite sides in a civil war in Castille. The English supported Pedro the Cruel, the French his half-brother Henry of Trastamara, and for both the principal objective was to secure the support of the Castillian navy.

In 1367, the Black Prince led an English army into Castille and won a famous victory at Najera, but at a disproportionate price. The prince was soon forced to withdraw, his army ravaged by sickness and his own health ruined by contracting the illness which was eventually to kill him. Despite the success of the English in battle, their candidate Pedro the Cruel was not the victor in the war, and was later defeated, murdered, and replaced on the Castillian throne by his rival. The English effort was not, however, merely abortive in Castille, whose navy now became a tool for the French. It also led to unrest in Gascony which the French were able to use as the catalyst for the dissolution of the uneasy peace with the English crown. Even before the expedition to Castille, the Black Prince had aroused discontent in his duchy by levying heavy taxation and by an unwise tendency to give important posts there to English men in preference to Gascons. This resentment was greatly intensified after the Spanish campaign when the prince tried to make his Gascon people pay the wages of the soldiers who had gone to Castille. The French king naturally stood ready to exploit the unrest in his old opponent's duchy. Peace was already approaching a breakdown when Edward summoned Parliament in 1368 which was, perhaps principally noteworthy for an episode indicating both the social rise of the Commons and a new claim they were making to influence over the conduct of the king's officials.

On the last day of the Parliament, May 21, after the Commons' petitions and the king's answers to them had been read, the king thanked both Lords and Commons for their attendance and for a further grant of a wool subsidy. The parliamentary roll then records that 'all the Lords and several of the Commons stayed and ate with the king that day'. This dinner is clear evidence of the social status of an important section of the Commons which was crucial to the general advancement of their position in Parliament. The roll then states that after dinner, 'the prelates, dukes, earls, barons and some of the Commons came to the White Chamber' to which the former steward of the household, Sir John de la Lee, was brought in order to answer various points brought against him by the Parliament, and declared by the chief justice at the command of the Lords. The charges, which were concened with abuses of his position, were duly recorded. Being unable to reply or clear himself, he was committed to the Tower, to remain there until he paid a fine at the king's pleasure.[1] This early instance of the Lords acting as a court to try a household official who was not one of their own peers, at the instance of parliamentary petitions, was a forerunner of the process of impeachment, which was to emerge more clearly in the turbulent Parliament of 1376.

A year later another Parliament met, in June 1369. By then the situation in France was much worse. Two Gascon lords had appealed to Charles V against the Black Prince's taxation, and the French king, claiming the right to hear their case, had summoned the Black Prince to come before the *parlement* of Paris to answer it. Inevitably that demand was refused. Instead, the French king's misdeeds were once more rehearsed to the English Parliament, and the summons to Paris was held to be in breach of Edward's acknowledged sovereignty in the ceded French territories, in exchange for which he had resigned his title to the crown of France. Edward's claim to the French crown was referred to the archbishop and prelates in Parliament, who advised the king that he could resume the title 'by right and in good conscience'. The lay lords and Commons then agreed with this 'in full Parliament.'[2] The king was granted increased customs, and on June 11, he resumed the title of king of France. Peace was at an end but the new war was to be quite unlike the old. Instead of bringing glory, it was to sour Edward's final years with the most serious political crisis of his reign. The French had deliberately provoked the war in the belief that the advantage now lay with them, in which judgement they were correct. The English were generally unready for the war, for which the French had been preparing, and were further weakened by the discontent of the Gascons. When the fighting

---

[1] *Rot. Parl.* Vol. II, pp. 297-298.
[2] Ibid., pp. 299-300.

began, the English also found that the old tactics of the *chevauchée* no longer worked since the French refused to join battle with the English raiders, and either remained in their own fortified towns or attacked English bases weakened by the absence of raiders. Gradually the French began to erode the English position in the new enlarged Gascony. At home too, Edward III was beginning to lose his grip on public affairs, and to fall into premature senility, which was by some contemporaries ascribed to his long overindulgence in fleshly pleasures. Queen Philippa, a much respected consort, had died in 1369, since when the king was increasingly seen as under the influence of his mistress Alice Perrers, who had formerly been attached, it seems, to the queen's bedchamber. She was probably more guilty of flaunting her position tactlessly than of abusing it politically; nevertheless, she was widely suspected of exerting a malign influence over Edward, even by witchcraft. Undue power was also thought to be exercised by several unpopular courtiers for their own ends, and there was no member of the royal family who seemed capable of restoring confidence. The Black Prince was back in England, but he was sick. Lionel, Duke of Clarence had recently died, and John of Gaunt was either involved unsuccessfully with the French war or preoccupied with his claim to be king of Castille, having married the daughter of Pedro the Cruel after the death in the plague of his first wife, Blanche of Lancaster. It was in this disturbed atmosphere that the first major attack on the royal authority took place in the Parliament summoned in 1371.

Parliament met in February, the opening taking place as usual in the Painted Chamber with the king himself present. It assembled in a mood of deepening anti-clericalism which was not only the consequence of the Pope's financial demands but was also inspired by theological questioning of the justification of ecclesiastical wealth, to which the commitment of the Franciscans to poverty had constituted a challenge. During the course of this Parliament, two Austin friars were brought in to argue the case for taking over some church lands for the use of the state, and the Oxford theologian, John Wyclif, who had not yet developed his doctrines to their heretical extreme, was present to hear them. He may have been brought there by the young Earl of Pembroke, a leading figure among the anti-clericals. Subsequently, Wycliff himself was publicly involved in arguing the case for some disendowment, and his espousal of the rights of the state against those of the church prompted John of Gaunt to make use of him after a much more serious parliamentary crisis six years later. It was not, however, the theological disputation about church property but the place of churchmen in politics which was the principal matter under question in the Parliament of 1371.

The chancellor, William of Wykeham, Bishop of Winchester, began the proceedings with an account of the vast preparations being made for war by the King of France to oust Edward from his French possesions, and of the enemy's naval preparations to destroy the English fleet and invade England. He asked for the advice and the support of Parliament in order to safeguard the English navy and prevent invasion. Once again the need was for money. The response, however, was not what was expected. Resentment of the cost of a failed war combined with the prevailing anti-clerical feeling to express itself in an attack on the king's employment of clerical ministers. By a curious irony the critics argued their case by precisely the same reasoning as that used by Edward when he had sworn thirty years earlier to have no clerics as ministers after Stratford. With the young Earl of Pembroke a leading figure among them, the outraged earls, barons and Commons joined together to petition the king to choose laymen instead of clerics as his ministers on the grounds that churchmen could not be brought to justice when blameworthy, as laymen could. The Commons petitioned that henceforth only laymen should hold such offices as those of chancellor, treasurer, clerk of the privy seal, and barons of the Exchequer.[1] William of Wykeham, the founder of New College Oxford, and of Winchester College, was in any case personally unpopular. He had risen from humble beginnings to be the king's clerk and then surveyor of the king's rebuilding of Windsor castle. Though he was a talented administrator he was also a great pluralist, and his was the kind of rapid advancement that always bred resentment. Thus the failures of the war were blamed on the ministers rather than on the king himself who, for all the criticism of his unpopular and greedy mistress, was still protected by his past reputation. In his immediate reply, the king would say no more than that he would act as he thought best on the advice of his council, but at the end of March, William of Wykeham was replaced as chancellor by a layman, Robert Thorpe, the chief justice, who in turn was soon succeeded by another lawyer Sir John Knyvett. The Bishop of Exeter was likewise deprived of the treasureship which was given to a baron, Richard Scrope of Bolton, one of Lancaster's supporters. These ministrial dismissals were Parliament's price for a grant, and afterwards one was given in an unusual form. £50,000 was granted as a lay levy on all the English parishes, each of which was to pay 22s. 3d., but this was conditional on a similar and separate contribution from the clergy. A large number of Commons' petitions was then dealt with, and a statute

---

[1] *Rot. Parl.* Vol. II, p. 304. It was said against the clerical members that they *'ne sont mye justiciables en touz cas'* and that the king should appoint only *'lays gentz'*.

was passed which included a re-statement of the enactment of 1362 that wool should not be taxed without parliamentary assent.

The Commons' requirement that the clergy should match their own parish levy placed the clergy under exceptionally heavy financial pressure. In January of the previous year they had already been pressed into giving three tenths for three successive years, and a month after the dissolution of the Parliament of 1371 they were called from their convocation in St Paul's to John of Gaunt's palace of the Savoy to be asked for £50,000 to match the parliamentary grant. The clergy was more or less forced to give the money, which was to be paid in two instalments. Under the weight of both lay and clerical taxation, the mood of the nation was increasingly sour. In June, the king summoned a great council consisting of magnates, and of one knight and one burgess from those who had represented the cities and boroughs at the previous Parliament. This council seems to have been called principally because it had been found that there were fewer parishes in England than had been supposed, and that the levy on each must, therefore, be increased five times to produce the required sum. This was approved by the council, which also dealt with outstanding petitions.

The following year, 1372, was one of continued disaster for Edward. An English fleet, under the Earl of Pembroke, attempted to relieve Aquitaine by taking the port of La Rochelle and failed disastrously, the English ships being destroyed by the Castillian fleet. The French also gradually took control of much of the enlarged Aquitaine acquired by Edward before 1360, until he was left with little more than the areas around Bordeaux and Bayonne. After the failure to relieve La Rochelle the king, who was now sixty, made a last abortive attempt to take a personal part in the war. Appointing the Black Prince's five year old son Richard to be guardian of the realm, Edward, accompanied by the Black Prince, Lancaster, and his younger son Edmund of Cambridge, embarked at Sandwich to try to regain the lost territory. But adverse gales frustrated his purpose and after about six weeks on board ship the king abandoned the attempt in October. Cancelling the writs for a Parliament which was to have met under his grandson, he summoned another for November. It is noteworthy that after the Commons had departed on the first day, the king, the prince, 'dukes, earls, barons and bannerets' discussed the particular problems of the Black Prince in Gascony, particularly in respect of inadequate funds for governing the principality and waging the war. Gascony, which the prince had now surrendered back to his father, may have been considered to be aristocratic rather than Commons business. Nevertheless, the Commons, or some of them, were present on the next day to hear the causes of summons, in which the reverses of war were described and advice was sought in the usual manner. A wool subsidy was granted but perhaps the most notable action in a comparatively tranquil Parliament was an ordinance prohibiting the election to Parliament of sheriffs, and of lawyers with business in the king's court. The case against the lawyers was that they brought to Parliament petitions 'in the name of the Commons, which do not at all concern them, but concern only the private persons' who were their clients. Sheriffs, it was said, should remain in their shires to do their common duty to everyone by the king. But at least a subsidiary reason for the dislike of sheriffs in Parliament may have been a concern lest the Commons should be packed with the king's officials.[1] This petition was granted by the king. It is also notable that after the knights had been told to obtain their writs for expenses and depart, the citizens and burgesses were required to stay behind and to assemble before the king, the prince and other magnates in a room near the White Chamber. There they granted a special year's renewal of the custom of tunnage (the duty on wine), and of poundage on merchandise. This flouted the general principle, supposed to have been established with the wool tax, that taxation should only be granted by Parliament as a whole, and not simply by the interest directly concerned with paying it.

The year 1373 brought one of the great fiascos of the war. In August, John of Gaunt set off from Calais with an expeditionary force to cross France, make for Bordeaux, and recover the lost regions of Gascony, taking plunder on the way. It was hoped that the English army would eventually cross into Castille and take that kingdom's throne for Lancaster. Instead of making for Bordeaux direct, however, this *chevauchée* set off first towards Champagne and Burgundy. The French, however, refused to engage with the English, taking refuge in towns which could not be stormed. Forced to cross the *massif* of Auvergne in a vicious winter, Lancaster lost half his army and nearly all his horses, being harassed by enemy raids under the direction of the brilliant French captain du Guesclin. In January 1374, Lancaster was forced to accept a truce. Great injury was done to French people by the expedition, and much plunder was taken, but nothing was gained for the English cause to justify Lancaster's huge loss of men.

The Parliament of 1373 met in November, before the full scale of John of Gaunt's failure was grasped in England, which was just as well for the government.[2] The causes of summons were declared in the Painted Chamber by the Chancellor, Sir John Knyvett. He described the great cost of Lancaster's expedition, stated that advice and aid were essential and that particular petitions must wait 'in suspense' until the greater and urgent

---

[1] *Rot. Parl.* Vol. II, p. 310.
[2] Ibid., pp. 316–320.

business was dealt with. Further, the Commons were ordered to depart and think about these matters, and to come back the next day to the Painted Chamber (instead of their more customary recent meeting place, the Chapter House of Westminster Abbey), so as to be near the Lords in the White Chamber in case their advice should be needed. It was perhaps resentment at the peremptory manner in which money was asked for and petitions were shelved which prompted the Commons to take the convention of 'intercommuning' a stage further by themselves requiring discussion with a committee of the Lords, asking specifically for the Bishops of London, Winchester and Bath, the Earls of Arundel, March and Salisbury and Guy Brian, and Henry le Scrope. This request was granted, and several days of consultation followed in 'the chamberlain's room near the Painted Chamber'. It was there agreed that the Commons would grant a fifteenth for two years, if the war lasted so long. Tunnage and poundage were also given for two years, but only on the same condition. The grants for 1374 were unconditional; those for 1375 would be annulled if the war ceased in the second year. The Commons also stipulated that the money should be spent only on the war, and that members of Parliament should not be collectors of the tax. These conditions are set out in a schedule recorded in the Parliament roll under the heading: *La Fourme & Manere du Grant fait au Roi en cest Parlement*.[1] Among the petitions on the roll were complaints against papal provisions to benefices because of the loss of money to the realm, and the control over the church exerted by aliens. It was even suggested that alien clergy revealed the secrets of the kingdom and sent them to the enemy abroad. These burdens, in addition to the cost of the war, were, it was said, too much for the Commons to endure. The council, however, was able to reply: 'The king has sent his honourable envoys to the court of Rome about the grievances contained in this petition.'[2]

This embassy had been despatched because the king had as much reason as the Commons to resist new financial demands by the Pope which underlay much of the anti-clerical feeling. Gregory XI, politically active as well as high-minded, was the last Pope to reign from Avignon. He had set his mind on returning to Rome and on maintaining the papacy's temporal power. This involved him in war in Italy, to pay for which he was driven to borrow, and also to tax the clergy elsewhere in Europe. A demand was sent in 1372 to the English archbishops for either a mandatory tenth (worth 120,000 florins) or a charitable subsidy (100,000 florins) to be paid by the clergy, and this was later reinforced by the threat of excommunication. The

[1] *Rot. Parl.* Vol. II, p. 317.
[2] Ibid., p. 320.

clergy were thus ground between the demands of the Pope and those of the king. The more the Pope took from their revenues, the less was available for the king. That mattered not only to the government itself but to the Commons since the less the clergy contributed the more the Commons would be asked for. As for the king, the more he must ask of the Commons the more parliamentary difficulties would face him. Resentment was also aroused by the Pope's efforts to increase the supply of money from annates paid by the lower benefices, and particularly by the activities of the special tax collector he sent to England for the purpose. Accordingly, shortly before the Parliament of 1373, the embassy of which the king informed the Commons had been despatched to Avignon with the demand that the Pope should ask no more financial aid from the English clergy so long as the war continued. The emissaries also protested against papal interference with royal patronage in clerical appointments and in the election of bishops and abbots, and complained about the number of benefices given to aliens. But the Pope refused to give up any of his powers, though be promised to use them moderately, nor would he give way over annates. As for the subsidy he was demanding, his only concession was a deferment until Easter 1374.[1] Meanwhile, a Convocation of the English clergy at St Paul's which followed the Parliament of 1373 was extremely resistant to Crown taxation, despite a visitation by lay lords from the council. Under pressure, however, the grant of a tenth was made to accompany the parliamentary grant, though it was not payable until the following June.

It was over two years before another Parliament was held, and it was to be the most remarkable of Edward's reign. In the meantime, the English position in France continued to deteriorate, and anti-court and anti-clerical sentiment intensified. The king had hoped to retake Brittany whose duke, John de Montfort, had now deserted the French and was a refugee in England. But in 1375 that intention had virtually to be abandoned. After the Avignon embassy, the Pope, who had long been trying to negotiate a peace between the English and the French to further his own return to Rome, persuaded Edward III to agree to meet the Pope's representative in 1374 at Bruges, where one of the English envoys was John Wyclif, the Oxford theologian and future heretic. Nothing immediately came of this, but three-cornered negotiations followed the next year between the Pope, the English king and his 'Adversary of France'. By then the English court was anxious for a peace. Various plans for the future of Gascony were discussed,

---

[1] George Holmes, *The Good Parliament* (1975), Chapter 1. This study, to which I am much indebted in what follows, is a valuable account of the questions of foreign, defence and financial policy underlying the challenge to royal authority in the Good Parliament.

including one by which the Duke of Lancaster might hold it, or some of it, from the French crown, and another for Edward to have it in full sovereignty. But the English refused to surrender any part of the territory completely to the French, and while the Bruges conference was taking place, an English expedition was launched into Brittany to relieve pockets of English resistance there, and presumably also with the hope of influencing the Bruges negotiations to the English advantage. But it was too late to make any difference, and by May agreement had nearly been reached on a year's truce, which was to be followed by discussions for a permanent peace based on a settlement in Aquitaine. In the same month a great council of prelates and magnates was summoned to London and when the terms of the proposed truce were received, Lancaster was given the power to implement it, with the advice and consent of the great council.[1] On such a purely political occasion, when an urgent question of foreign policy, but no taxation, was involved, the great council still had its place. As well as the truce with France, the English made a *concordat* with the Pope. Edward's council agreed not to obstruct a clerical subsidy for the Pope which was, however, reduced to 60,000 florins (about £9,000). In return, papal bulls were issued in September making some small concessions in favour of royal nominees to English benefices. The Pope also agreed that Simon Sudbury, bishop of London, should become Archbishop of Canterbury; to the crown it was always important that the primate should be favourable to its interests.

The English council and ministers (the king himself, who may have suffered from a series of strokes, no longer had any personal grip on affairs) had been driven to accept peace by the crown's financial difficulties. Lacking any military successes, the English government needed a peace as quickly as possible, but not so soon as to disqualify it from receiving the second year's taxation for 1375, which had been granted in 1373 only on condition that the war had not ceased. So the truce was concluded on 27 June, just after the qualifying date for the parliamentary lay subsidy. It still theoretically put at risk half the second year's tunnage and poundage, and the whole of the second year's wool subsidy, but this money (unlike the conventional tenths and fifteenths which needed co-operation of the knights of the shire) could be raised at the ports without parliamentary authority. Peace was needed by the English government both to ease its financial difficulties with the laity and to make the papal taxes tolerable and so avoid a quarrel with the Pope. The agreement with the French and that with the Pope were interlinked, and both were unpopular because they were

---

[1] Holmes, op. cit., p. 44.

seen as humiliating. After so many years of wasted money, Edward's conquests had vanished. Even so, his government was still not free from the need to appeal to Parliament for money. There was a new threat from the Castillian navy which possibly portended a renewed French-Castillian attack. It was to prepare for this that the first summonses to what became known as the Good Parliament were issued on 18 December, 1375 for 12 February. On 20 January the meeting was postponed to 28 April to allow time for the envoys at Bruges to return.

The Good Parliament assembled in the third week after Easter and lasted for ten weeks until 11 July.[1] 'No Parliament had ever met for so long before', as the *Anonimalle Chronicle* noted. The general mood was instantly and deeply critical of the political and financial conduct of the king's ministers. They were held responsible for the failures of war and corruption and embezzlement were suspected. The principal targets of attack were Lord Latimer, the chamberlain, Lord Neville, the steward of the king's household, and a group of London financiers and merchants, especially one Richard Lyons. Latimer was a long-standing companion of the king and was a knight of the Garter who had been at Crécy. On the first day the Parliament met in the king's chamber, but no business was done as a number of Lords and Commons had not yet arrived, and the king was advised to wait until the following day. The proceedings then began, as usual, in the Painted Chamber, where the prelates, the lay magnates, Commons, justices, and Sergeants at law all assembled with the king present. The Chancellor, Sir John Knyvett explained the causes of summons. The first and foremost was the internal peace of the kingdom; the second was the safety and defence of the realm by land and by sea, and the third the best means of prosecuting the king's quarrel. The chancellor then besought the Lords and Commons, each 'by themselves' to take 'diligent counsel' and make 'a good response' as soon as possible for the sake of prompt action by Parliament. Certain prelates and lords were named as triers of bills and clerks as receivers. The Commons were then ordered on behalf of the king to retire to their 'ancient' (or 'former') place (*lour aunciene Place*) in the Chapter House of Westminster

---

[1] The two most important sources for the Good Parliament are *Rot. Parl.* Vol. II, pp. 321–360, and the *Anonimalle Chronicle*, 1333–1381, ed. V. H. Galbraith, 1927, pp. 79–94. Substantial extracts (in French) from the *Anonimalle Chronicle* and the parliamentary rolls are given in Chrimes and Brown, op. cit., pp. 93–110. A translation of some of the more significant passages of the former are in *E.H.D.* Vol. IV, pp. 117–121. An often illuminating account of the Good Parliament, the part played by Speaker de la Mare, and the impeachment of the courtiers is also given by Thomas Walsingham in the *Chronicon Angliae* though this is excessively biased against John of Gaunt. See also B. Wilkinson, *Constitutional History*, Vol. II, pp. 204–226; J. G. Edwards, *The Commons in Medieval English Parliaments*, (1957).

Abbey to discuss these matters. (The requirement of 1373 that they should occupy the Painted Chamber to be near the Lords was not repeated; it was probably anticipated that it would be needed for intercommuning, and it is also possible that the Commons disliked meeting there because it gave them insufficient privacy.) The lay lords and prelates were likewise to hold a discussion, which took place in the White Chamber. Both Lords and Commons were told that 'report should be made from one group to the other concerning the acts and intentions of each'. When they eventually returned it was with a reply very much to the crown's disliking.

What particularly exercised the minds and emotions of the Commons was that, despite the failure of the war, the chancellor had asked for the usual subsidies, a fifteenth from the laity, a tenth from the clergy (who were to meet in Convocation) and the prolongation of the customs. But even apart from this the Commons had met in a mood of high tension. This is evident from the hundred and forty six petitions which complained against the royal household, the church, foreign merchants, abuses in local government and the malice and disorderliness of labourers and beggars. Annual Parliaments were asked for, which was presumably a complaint about the lack of Parliaments in the previous two years, and it was requested that the election of knights and sheriffs should be 'by the common choice of the better people of the shire'. The depth of the laity's resentment (which was also shared by a part of the clergy) against papal exactions was indicated by the detail and length of the petitions submitted against them. The first petition, described as a *'Bille encontre le Pape et les Cardynaux'* (Bill against the Pope and Cardinals), referred back to the good old days when benefices went to the people most worthy of holding them, and the kingdom was therefore prosperous and the clerks and clergy loyal. It observed that, since the sin of covetouseness and simony had prevailed, there had been 'wars and pestilences, famine, murrain of beasts and other grievances, by which it (the realm) is so impoverished and destroyed that there is not a third part of the people or of other things that there used to be'. (The Pope's exactions, it would seem, were even held responsible for the Black Death.)[1] Other clauses of the ecclesiastical petitions attacked papal appointments of foreigners, pluralism, papal demands for money and especially the activities of the papal tax collector who had set up 'a great house in London', where he had clerks and officers as though he were a prince or duke and (allegedly) sent to Rome 20,000 marks a year.[2] Moreover, or so the petition asserted, the papal demands were furthered by the crown and by some of the

---

[1] *Rot. Parl.* Vol. II, p. 337.
[2] Ibid., p. 339, cl. 105.

magnates. When the Pope wanted subsidies for his wars in Lombardy, the prelates dared not refuse it, and the lay lords took no care to save the church from being destroyed and 'the money of the realm wickedly being taken away'.[1] The anti-clerical mood of the Commons, as expressed in these petitions, does much to explain the vigour with which they pursued their case against the court in this Parliament.[2]

The greatest grievance, however, was the threat of still more lay taxation after so much money had already been given for a war which had ended in failure. This was the matter on which the meeting of the Commons concentrated when it began in the Chapter House on the second day of the Parliament. The *Anonimalle Chronicle*, written at St. Mary's Abbey, York, provides us with the first account, in remarkable detail, of a debate in the 'House' of Commons based on information that had originally come from an eyewitness. It is almost the only description that we have of proceedings of the Commons in their separate discussions before their Journals began in 1547, and like the same chronicle's account of the Peasant's Revolt, the report of the Good Parliament was almost certainly taken from a London writer, and interpolated in the *Anonimalle Chronicle*. The manuscript also gives an account of the debates in full Parliament, including what the Speaker, Sir Peter de la Mare, and John of Gaunt said to each other, which is even more precise and dramatic than its report of the Commons' separate discussions. The vivid detail of the proceedings in full Parliament is such as to suggest that the report was originally written by someone who had either been present or had been directly informed by an eyewitness, and on all essential points the chronicle's account of what passed in the Parliament itself is corroborated in dryer form by the rolls of Parliament. The account of the proceedings in the Chapter House by comparison seems somewhat more distant; it does not give the names of those who spoke (with one notable exception) and what they said does not greatly expand on the report of their conclusions subsequently given in full Parliament. Nevertheless, there can be no reasonable doubt that its origin was in an informed account passed on by someone who had been in the Chapter House and was familiar with the Commons' method of going about their business.

All the knights 'sat down in a circle, each one next to the other' and began by unanimously agreeing 'that it would be well at the beginning to be sworn each to the other to keep secret what was discussed and agreed amongst them and to treat and ordain loyally for the profit of the realm without concealment'. They then took an oath to be loyal to one another, obviously

---

[1] *Rot. Parl.* Vol. II, p. 339, cl. 107.
[2] The petitions concerning Pope and church are in ibid. pp. 339–340.

regarding secrecy as the only available safeguard of their freedom of speech. A debate was begun when one said that 'if anyone of us knows anything to say for the profit of the king and the realm, it would be well for him to show his knowledge among us, and afterwards, one after another to show what is on his mind'. After this 'a south country knight (*une chivaler de south pais*) arose and went to the lectern in the middle of the Chapter House, so that all could hear, and leaning on the lectern, began to speak'. (The Commons in session in the fourteenth century more nearly resembled the half-circle of a continental assembly today than the post-sixteenth century two-sided House of Commons.) Beginning with a Latin blessing, this knight spoke of the king's 'disturbing' request for taxation. 'It seems to me,' he said, 'that this is too great to grant, for the Commons are so weakened and impoverished by various tallages and taxes already paid that they cannot bear such a charge at this time, and on the other hand, all that we have granted for war for a long time we have lost by malversion because it has been badly wasted and falsely spent.' The question to be considered, therefore, was how the king could govern the realm and maintain the war with his own revenues, and without demanding money from his loyal subjects. The south country knight went on to say that, as he had heard, 'there are various people who have a great store of gold and silver belonging to our lord the king without his knowledge, which they have falsely concealed.' He then returned to his seat.

Other knights spoke of the wasting of resources, especially in connection with the removal of the wool staple at Calais, to the profit of the Chamberlain, Lord Latimer, Richard Lyon and others. (The essential charge was that Latimer and Lyons had arranged for licences to be issued, at 11s. a sack, to allow exporters to avoid the Calais staple. As a result, Calais had lost revenue essential for its defence, leaving the king, or, in practice the taxpayers, to make good the loss.) One knight then suggested that the king should be asked to assign certain bishops, earls and barons 'such as we shall name' to talk to the Commons, and this proposal for intercommuning was agreed. When the knights who had spoken had all returned to their seats, they 'deliberated with one another' how best to proceed, which presumably means that they spoke together informally in their seats. Then one of them took an initiative which led to his designation as the first recognized Speaker of the Commons to be formally appointed to represent the Commons. Sir Peter de la Mare, a knight of the Welsh marches and the Steward of the Earl of March spoke as follows. 'Gentlemen, you have heard the speeches and advice of our companions and how they have shown their purpose, and it seems to me that they have spoken loyally and profitably.' The writer of the Chronicle then states that Sir Peter 'repeated, word for word, all the points which they had made, wisely and in good form. Moreover, he advised them on various points and articles as will appear more fully later; and so ended the second day.' From this and what followed, it appears that Sir Peter's role was more than simply that of a *rapporteur* with a duty to sum up the sense of the meeting, secure its approval for his summary and report this to the full Parliament. Nor was he a non-participating chairman, which is the role of the non-political modern Speaker, but rather an active chairman steering the meeting towards an eventual consensus which he himself did much to determine by the manner in which he interpreted the discussions. He also extemporized when representing the Commons before the Lords, using his discretion. He was, that is to say, a political Speaker who was much more than a passive mouthpiece when he acted as the Commons's spokesman. His position was also radically different, as we shall see, from that of those who had spoken for the Commons in previous Parliaments. In the history of Parliament, he is a figure of as much political as constitutional interest.

Sir Peter de la Mare was one of the two knights returned for Herefordshire.[1] His leadership among the Commons is the more remarkable since this was the first time that he had been a member of Parliament, though he was to represent that county in five future Parliaments, those of October 1377; January and November, 1380, May and October, 1382, and February 1383. He was, however, only to be Speaker once more, in the October 1377 Parliament, the first of Richard II's reign. He held manors in Herefordshire, one of which he held from the Mortimers, Earls of March, an aristocratic connection which was of considerable relevance to his parliamentary activities. When he came as a knight of the shire to the Good Parliament, Sir Peter was already steward to Edmund Earl of March, who was a critic of the king's councillors. Furthermore, March was also hostile to John of Gaunt, to whom Sir Peter de la Mare was to appear as an infuriating adversary when the Speaker returned to give the Commons' reply to the government's demands for money. For it fell to John of Gaunt to preside over the Good Parliament since the king, who was incapable of doing so, himself retired immediately after the opening, and the Black Prince was too ill to take his place. The brusque encounter between John of Gaunt and Sir Peter de la Mare set the tone of the events that followed. Had the Black Prince been in charge, matters would presumably have gone differently since the Commons knew that he was sympathetic to their case

---

[1] For a biographical account, see J. S. Roskell, 'Sir Peter de la Mare' *Nottingham Medieval Studies* Vol. II (191158) pp. 24–37. See also the same author's *The Commons and their Speakers in the English Parliament, 1376–1523* (1965).

and distrustful of his father's ministers. As it was, the Black Prince died in June while the Good Parliament was still sitting, leaving his young son Richard of Bordeaux as the king's heir.

The underlying tension in Parliament was thus increased by fears of what might happen if Richard were not to survive, a serious possibility in an age when a child's life was fragile and recurrent plague a constant menace. In the event of Richard's death, the next in strict line of succession was not the Duke of Lancaster, who was the king's fourth son, and now the unpopular head of the government. If the rule of succession were observed, the crown would pass to King Edward's great-grandson, the infant Roger Mortimer, who was descended from the king's third son, the late Lionel, Duke of Clarence. This claim was transmitted through Lionel's daughter, Philippa, who had married Edmund Mortimer, Earl of March, to their son, Roger Mortimer. (It was the Mortimer claim, subsequently passed by marriage to the Dukes of York, which was to be the Yorkists' justification in the Wars of the Roses.) But if after King Edward's lifetime, the death of one child simply passed the claim to the crown to another, especially to one so far removed from King Edward, it was inevitably feared that the throne might be usurped by Lancaster. Indeed, might not the disliked Lancaster usurp the throne from Richard in any case? As events were to prove, that suspicion misjudged Lancaster, but in the meantime, he had motive enough to be resentful of March's interest in the order of succession, and he undoubtedly looked upon the Commons' attack on the court party as being in reality directed at himself. March, on the other hand, was sympathetic to the case of the Commons, as well as hostile to Lancaster. Since Peter de la Mare was both March's man and the active leader of the Commons, the rebellion of the Commons in this Parliament has sometimes been suspected of being largely instigated by a party of the lords which was led by March.

That the conflict in the Good Parliament over the conduct of the government was given force and enthusiasm by clashes of personality and of personal ambitions among the powerful poltical leaders of the time can be taken for granted. It is hard to think of a political conflict in any age where this has not been so. The Commons' determination was no doubt strengthened by the knowledge that they had allies among the Lords, and their willingness to be guided by Sir Peter possibly owed as much to their knowledge that this would assure them of the Earl of March's valuable support as it did to Sir Peter's eloquence. Nevertheless, the weight of evidence, from the chronicles and from the nature of the petitions in this Parliament, indicates that this was genuinely a protest of the Commons which some of the lords and bishops (including William of Wykeham) espoused and strengthened. So it came about that after various knights (nothing is said of burgesses) had spent about ten days debating and denouncing the government's misdeeds, Sir Peter summarised the case and advised his colleagues so well that they asked him to 'take charge for them' and speak on their behalf in full Parliament before the lords. On Friday 9 May the king sent a messenger asking for their answer; he was, according to the *Anonimalle Chronicle*, 'impatient for them to grant his petition' and wished them to release the Parliament as soon as possible as 'he wished to be elsewhere for his pleasure'. (Though Edward was not an active participant, it no doubt seemed necessary for him to remain at Westminster when he would doubtless have preferred to be at Sheen or another of his favourite dwellings away from London.)

So when all had agreed what de la Mare should say, the Commons set out for the 'Parliament house' (*al huse de parlement*), the first time this expression seems to have been used. (The terms House of Commons and House of Lords were still not employed.) When the Commons arrived, 'some of them got in, but others were pushed back and shut out'. Then Lancaster, who is described as being 'very ill at ease', no doubt because reports of the Commons' deliberations had reached him, asked: 'Which of you is the spokesman of what has been agreed among you?' (*Quel de vous avera la parlaunce et pronunciation de ceo qu vous avez ordine parentre vous?*) Sir Peter replied that 'by common assent he would speak that day (*par commun assent il averoit les paroles a la iourne*)'. This exchange was presumably the customary formula, since the Commons always gave their replies through a spokesman. Usually, however, it was a fairly casual assignment and a Speaker appointed for one day may not necessarily have been the one designated on the next occasion. Nor do previous spokesmen seem to have had the political role which de la Mare had clearly assumed. Perhaps, therefore, Lancaster assumed that he had before him simply a mouthpiece, able only to repeat parrot-fashion what the Commons had agreed formally. But when invited to speak, de la Mare reminded the duke that the Commons had all been summoned to Parliament by the king's writ, and that 'what one of us says, all say and assent to'. He therefore required to know why some were kept outside, and concluded by saying: 'I shall not proceed to any other matter until they are all present.' The duke then replied, as the chronicler records, 'There is no need for so many of the Commons to come in to give a reply, but two or three at a time are enough as has been the custom previously.' De la Mare insisted, however, that he would speak 'no word' until all were present, and Lancaster gave way. Two hours were then spent finding all the Commons who had not been admitted.

When they were all gathered de la Mare spoke, but offered nothing for the government's comfort. The king, he said, had asked the Commons to 'treat and ordain' for his estate and the realm; they had found many matters needing amendment for the king's benefit but the Commons were 'so simple of wit and wealth' that they needed the counsel of wiser men to redress such matters. They therefore asked for a committee of twelve Lords (four bishops, four earls and four barons or bannerets) to be associated with the Commons, and 'to hear and witness what we say'.[1] The Lords debated this and agreed. The Earl of March and others of his party were among those nominated by the Commons to the committee. In noting the names of the lords who were assigned 'to go to the said Commons and be of aid to them, joining with them and discussing the said matters . . .' the Parliament roll itself neither mentions de la Mare by name, nor does it use the term Speaker.[2] No doubt the clerk still felt himself primarily responsible to the king (or, in this case, to his deputy, the Duke of Lancaster) and would have sensed that there would be no eagerness on the part of the government to magnify the role of the knight who was so clearly challenging the royal authority on the Commons's behalf.

Intercommuning took place over the weekend and on Monday, 12 May, de la Mare and the Commons reappeared before the Lords. Lancaster asked who would speak for them and de la Mare replied in what seems very much like a deliberately impertinent if not disrespectful manner: 'Sir, as I said three days ago, it was ordered by common assent that I should have the speakership (*la parlaunce*) at this time.' If Lancaster had expected a different Speaker he was being told that de la Mare would hold that role throughout the Parliament. De la Mare then added the protestation which was to be a model for his successors: if he 'mis-said' anything on any point he submitted himself to the correction and amendment of his colleagues (*compaignouns*). In thus establishing the position that the Commons could amend what he said if they disagreed, but that unamended it was the position of them all, de la Mare prepared the way for the Commons' attack on the king's ministers. Although that attack would be pursued through one man's voice, it was the action of the Commons collectively, who could not be punished for it as individuals might have been.

The Speaker then returned to the matters which had been the subject of the weekend's intercommuning. He reported the Commons' opinion that the demand for new taxes was unreasonable, that if the king's money had

---

[1] By this time, 'banneret' had become a description of a social rank, or estate, and a banneret could be individually summoned to Parliament as a kind of lesser baron in the peerage, the summons often continuing in the same family. For a general discussion of the term with reference to individual cases, see Powell and Wallis, op. cit.

[2] *Rot. Parl.* Vol. II, p. 322; The *Anonimalle Chronicle* and the parliamentary roll differ in respect of two of the men on the committee.

been spent wisely and without waste taxation would have been unnecessary, and that the king had certain councillors and ministers who were not loyal and who had deceived him. The parliamentary roll confirms and amplifies the chronicler's account at this point, recording that the Commons, having reminded Parliament of the grants they had made in the past Parliament, asked the king to excuse them this time from granting any further subsidies. They said that they had been so destroyed by the past payments, by 'pestilence of servants', murrain on animals, and failed harvests that they could pay no more at present. The roll also records the Commons' protestation that, although they were as willing as ever to help the king with their bodies and belongings, it seemed to them that the king would be very rich 'if he always had loyal councillors and good officers around him'. If only he had such loyal councillors, they said acutely, he would have no need to lay burdens on the Commons, considering the great ransoms he had received from the kings of France and Scotland, and from other prisoners.[1] Surprised by the attack on the unnamed ministers, the Duke of Lancaster asked who they were, and de la Mare spoke of Lord Latimer and Richard Lyons, and of the evasion of the Calais staple which deprived the king of a prosperous community able to pay for its own defence out of the profits from the customs. Lord Latimer then intervened to say that it had been done by the king and council. According to the *Anonimalle* chronicler, de la Mare replied that this was against the law of England, and produced documentary evidence to show that the Staple had been unalterably fixed at Calais. (If such evidence was produced, however, it cannot have been in the form of a statute, as the *Anonimalle Chronicle* describes it, since no such statute is known, but it is possible that the Speaker produced royal orders establishing the Staple.) Sir Peter de la Mare then went on to accuse the ministers of raising unnecessary loans for the king on extortionate terms, details of which were given, to the advantage of the lenders who included Latimer and Lyons. Yet, said the Speaker, there was no need for this loan at all since an offer of a loan without any premium had been made to the king by certain citizens of London on condition that no further licences were issued for the evasion of the Staple. The Speaker then called for evidence from Richard Scrope, who had been the treasurer at the time, and also from the treasurer before him, Bishop Brantingham of Exeter. Lord Scrope undertook to give evidence if the king put him on oath.

Latimer and Lyons were also charged with buying some of the king's

[1] *Rot. Parl.* Vol. II, pp. 322–323, cls. 9 & 15. The sequence of the parliamentary rolls is not altogether in accord with that of the account in the *Anonimalle Chronicle* and places the appointment of a nominated council (see below) at this point, earlier in the proceedings than it seems to have happened.

debts at below half their value for their own profit. Finally, Alice Perrers was accused of peculation and bribery, and of taking £2,000 to £3,000 a year from the king. 'It would be a great profit to the kingdom to remove that lady from the company of the king,' he said, 'so that the king's treasure could be applied to the war, and wardships not lightly frittered away.' Having delivered this unprecedented attack on the king's authority, the Speaker and the Commons departed. Parliament was then adjourned for several days during which the government agreed that the treasurers should state what they knew; in the meantime, there was further intercommuning between the Commons and the Lords' committee.

It may have been after his second encounter with de la Mare that the outraged Lancaster spoke privately to his followers in something like the terms attributed to him by the hostile chronicler, Thomas of Walsingham. Who, the duke allegedly asked, did these 'degenerate knights' think they were? Did they think they were princes in the land? Where had they got their pride and arrogance? They were ignorant of his power and he would so terrify them that nobody like them in the future would dare provoke him. According to this account the duke was then warned by one of his followers to recognize how strongly the knights were supported: 'They are not common people as you have said, but men powerful and strenuous in arms.' Whatever may be the truth of the chronicler's jaundiced account of John of Gaunt's rage, the warning he was allegedly given about the knights' social standing carries the ring of historical truth. They were not common people, but men of standing having connections with nobles. It was precisely because they were men of position as well as representatives of the communities of the shires that they carried weight. Their superior status among the Commons also placed them in a better position than the merchants to complain about grievances which probably affected the merchants more closely than the knights themselves. For the knights, the over-riding issue was the general waste of taxation, but the specific charges of corruption, for which the burgesses and merchants could provide the evidence, were an invaluable lever to exert against the king's unsuccessful ministers.

Whether or not he had at first contemplated some such show of royal ducal strength, Lancaster showed not harshness but conciliation when he next encountered the Commons. A sermon highly critical of the court and of Alice Perrers, which had been preached by the Bishop of Rochester on the Sunday before Gaunt's next meeting with the Commons, may have shown him that he must bend to the wind. Even according to Walsingham, John of Gaunt told the Speaker and the Commons, when they next appeared in Parliament on 19 May, that he realized that they spoke only for the good of the realm. When they asked for an answer to their petition, the duke enquired whether the Commons had further articles to present, to which the Speaker replied that they did not wish to say anything more until the truth was known in connection with the points they had already made, and redress had been given by those guilty of corruption. Again the points were repeated concerning the Calais staple, the unnecessary loans and Alice Perrers. The circumstances of the loan were then investigated by Lancaster and the Lords, with Scrope providing information that Latimer and Lyons had in fact lent money to the king for their own advantage. After that the Commons called out for the incrimination of Latimer and Lyons and the arrest of the latter. There then seem to have followed four days in which the Lords in their Parliament House and the Commons in the Chapter House treated from day to day about what was to be done, until the Commons were again sent for to come into Parliament.

Then, on 24 May, Peter de la Mare complained that though the Commons had explained what was 'grieving their hearts', and had declared various wrongs to the Lords and council, they had had no redress. Instead, the king had about him people who mocked and scoffed and worked for their own profit instead of giving good counsel. Therefore, he said, the Commons would say nothing further, that is to say, they would do nothing about the provision of funds, until the king had removed his evil counsellors and had replaced the chancellor and treasurer, for they were useless (*quare ils ne sount pas profitablez*), and until Dame Alice Perrers had been entirely removed. They also wanted the king's council to be afforced by a new nominated continual council 'up to the number ten or twelve' (according to the parliamentary rolls) without whose assent no great business should be dealt with. At least four or six of this body were to be continually present at the king's council.[1] This was agreed to and a council of nine (the number asked for by the Commons according to the *Anonimalle Chronicle*) was appointed composed equally of bishops, earls and barons, a number of whom had also been on the intercommuning committee. The new councillors (whose names are given in the Chronicle but not on the official record) were the Archbishop of Canterbury, Bishops Courtney of London and Wykeham of Winchester, the Earls of Arundel, March and Stafford, and Barons Henry Percy, Guy Brian and Roger Beauchamp. At the same time, Lord Latimer, his son-in-law, Lord Neville of Raby, who was the steward of the household, and Alice Perrers were removed from court.

When the new council of nine appeared in Parliament, the Speaker and Commons resumed their attack, this time also accusing Latimer of

[1] *Rot. Parl.* Vol. II, p. 322. cl. 10.

responsibility for the loss of the strongholds of Becherel and St Sauveur in Brittany. The court capitulated and the parliamentary roll records in some detail the cases and judgements against Latimer, Lyons and others impeached with them. Latimer was accused not only of evading the Calais Staple and of the unnecessary and usurious loans to the king but of losing Becherel and St Sauveur, extortion in Brittany, brokerage of the royal debts, and releasing spies from prison. But he seems only to have been 'found guilty in full Parliament' of the first two charges. He was sentenced to be imprisoned at the king's will, on which the Commons petitioned that he should be removed forever from offices of the king, which was granted. However, Lord Latimer found securities for the duration of the Parliament, and the marshal, the Earl of March, allowed him to be at large. Richard Lyons, who was brought into Parliament, was charged with involvement in evading the Staple, of the extortionate loans, and of brokerage of the royal debts. He was imprisoned. Among others impeached was a John Peche, accused of exploiting a monopoly in the sale of sweet wines in London, and William Elys who was said to be guilty of extortion at Yarmouh where he was Lyons's deputy farmer of the poundage customs. Lord Neville, who was accused of pillaging the people of Hampshire on his way with an expedition to Brittany, was removed from all offices under the king on a plea of the Commons. All were to be fined, and Elys and Peche were to be imprisoned. Adam Bury, a former mayor of Calais and a citizen of London, was 'impeached by clamour of the Commons' of various corrupt practices in his former office. As he did not appear, his goods and chattels were put under arrest. Alice Perrers was to be permanently banished from the court. The accusations generally were motivated by the grievances of commercial and other interests, especially in London, which had suffered in one way or another by such actions as the evasion of the Staple and the loans. But the deeper reasons for the determination with which the charges were pursued were the lay and clerical discontent with a corrupt court which controlled the king instead of being controlled by him, and resentment at the policies which Lancaster had been forced to pursue in making terms with the French and the rapacious Papacy.[1] The commercial grievances were an invaluable weapon because the merchants and burgesses could provide firm evidence

---

[1] A very detailed account of the complex financial and other accusations against the impeached men, and of the interests behind the charges is given in G. Holmes, op. cit., Ch. 5. On impeachment see: T. F. T. Plucknett, 'The Origin of Impeachment', *T.R.H.S.* 4th series, (1942), M. V. Clarke, 'The origin of impeachment', in *Fourteenth Century Studies* (ed. L. S. Sutherland and M. McKisack) (1937), and B. Wilkinson, 'The Good Parliament' (*Const. Hist. of Engl.* Vol. II, Ch. 6, which includes a selection of extracts from sources in translation).

for them. But they were probably more the means than the root cause of the impeachments.

The essence of the procedure used was the making of charges by the Commons acting as one, who were therefore not vulnerable to a countercharge of false accusation as an individual might have been. It was a long and detailed business. The parliamentary roll records 'that much was said and argued' in respect of Latimer and that there were 'many examinations' both in full Parliament and before the prelates and Lords alone. In this process, the Commons were the accusers and the Lords were the judges. The Commons' use of impeachment might be regarded as bringing into Parliament the common law idea of a jury of presentment. Or impeachment can be seen as transplanting the concept of 'notoriety' from the common law (as the crown had already done to secure the judgement of the Lords against 'notorious' traitors) and applying it to an accusation by the Commons collectively by means of bills of impeachment. Latimer and Lyons were accused of 'notoriously accroaching royal power', and, as the parliamentary roll records, the impeachment of Latimer and Bury was 'by clamour of the Commons'. A process of political trial had been devised which was to be used ruthlessly in the future as a means of getting rid of politicians who could be removed in no other way, though it could equally be used against any other of the king's subjects.[1]

Impeachment was bound up with a fundamental change in the relationship of Parliament to the crown during the reign of Edward III. At the beginning of the reign, it could still be said that the council was at the centre of Parliament, which for political purposes was a body called by the king to assent, or conceivably not to assent, to what the king put before it. During Edward III's reign Parliament had evolved a new life of its own, and it had done so through the accidents of war and politics. Parliament was still formally a single chamber assembly, with the Commons outside it when they deliberated privately. This is shown repeatedly by the terminology of the *Anonimalle Chronicle* with its repeated references to the Commons going into Parliament whenever they came before the council and the Lords. Nevertheless, the reality was already different. The Commons had

---

[1] The word impeachment (*empeschement*) originally meant a hindrance or embarrassment, and was not at first a description of a new legal process, but was rather a term used by an accused person to describe an action to him which he regarded as having malice in it. In 1376 it became a method of proceeding against officials whom it would not be practicable to prosecute in the common law courts. Petitions had previously been used by the Commons to lay information against an individual which then became the basis of an official indictment (e.g. the case of Sir John de la Lee in 1368). But in 1376, the petition itself was the indictment.

established their political claims through the control of money, winning a certain power of initiation by means of petition and impeachment. In the Good Parliament, Lords and Commons acted together as allies to bring the council and the king's ministers to book. Parliament was no longer simply the extended council; it had become a separate institution of Lords and Commons working together and using political, fiscal and judicial power to establish that the king's ministers had, in the last analysis, some sort of responsibility to Parliament. Impeachment made Parliament a High Court in a sense very different from that in which the expression has been used to define the distinguishing features of Parliament in the thirteenth century.

The new parliamentary challenge to executive power by means of impeachment came about from a combination of accidents of personalities and politics: the non-functioning king and the corruption of his court, the dying Prince, the unpopularity of the Duke of Lancaster who was seen as representing the failure of the crown's war policy, the financial demands of the Pope, the collapse of a costly and useless war, the Commons' ever increasing sense of their financial power over the crown, the dynastic suspicion between Gaunt and Mortimer, the general grievances of the knights against taxation and the specific complaints and evidence of merchants in Parliament (though they are largely silent in the records) against the court officials.

The death of the Black Prince on 8 June must have distracted the mind of the court from the difficulties facing it. But it also deprived the Commons of a supporter and, eventually, made it easier for John of Gaunt to undo the politics of the Good Parliament, though not its institutional importance. After Prince Edward's death, the Parliament still had a month to run; there was an exceptionally large number of petitions to deal with, and it seems that some particular charges against the accused courtiers (who in general may have been less culpable than their accusers made out), were still being looked into. The suspicion and dislike of John of Gaunt now became open when the Commons (as the parliamentary roll records) prayed 'that it would please their lord the king, to the great comfort of the realm, to cause the noble child Richard of Bordeaux to come before Parliament . . . so that the Lords and Commons of the realm can see and honour Richard there, as true heir apparent of the realm'. Parliament could hardly have made its fear of a usurpation more obvious. 'Which request was granted; and so Richard came before all the Prelates, Lords and Commons in Parliament, the Thursday, the day after the feast of St John the Baptist.' After the Archbishop of Canterbury had spoken movingly of the 'exact image or true likeness' of the young prince to his departed father, the Commons asked that Richard should have his father's title of Prince of Wales, and the lords and prelates promised to make urgent representations about this to the king.[1]

In respect of the government of the moment, the Commons remained wary. Although they made a grant of the customs for three years, they gave the king no tax on movable goods in return for the crown's acceptance of the Commons' impeachments. On July 10, the Parliament dissolved. The parliamentary roll records that, the king having gone to his manor at Eltham because of the 'disease of his body' (it seems likely that Edward III suffered from a succession of strokes), the prelates, Lords and Commons went to him there to hear the responses to their petitions, to hear the ordinances that had been made and the judgement on individuals, and 'make an end to the Parliament'. There was a forewarning of Lancaster's intentions in the refusal of petitions which asked for the sentences on the impeached to be carried out, and for a commitment that the judgements of the Good Parliament would not be reversed. It seems improbable that King Edward himself was much aware of what was going on. There was, however, a more appropriate end to the Good Parliament in London. As the Lords were preparing to depart from Westminster, Sir Peter de la Mare and the knights of the shire gave a great feast for various lay and spiritual lords, including the king's two younger sons (one of the complaints of the critics of the court was that they ought to be more prominent there), a number of bishops, various earls (including March) and barons, and also the mayor and citizens of London and other burgesses. The king gave them two tuns of red wine and eight deer; other lords gave them a great sum of gold and much wine. There could have been no more fitting demonstration that the Commons were not simple plebians, or an estate apart, than the company they kept.

Immediately the Good Parliament had dispersed, John of Gaunt, the effective head of the government, set about reversing what had been done. It was not difficult. Although Latimer and Neville had gone from court, the principal officers of state, including the chancellor and treasurer, remained unchanged. The continual council of nine quickly faded out, and no section of the nobility wished to cause trouble. Nor had any one of the great number of petitions in the Good Parliament become a statute. Besides, once a medieval Parliament was dissolved, and magnates and knights had dispersed to their estates, its power had largely gone, especially if there were no grants of money to be collected. On the other hand, the financial crisis remained without remedy, and John of Gaunt's unpopularity was deeper than ever. In the autumn of 1376, a great council met at Westminster at

---

[1] *Rot. Parl.* Vol. II, p. 330 (translated in *E.H.D.* Vol. IV p. 122).

which William of Wykeham, who been on the Commons' side in the Good Parliament, was accused for actions he had taken as chancellor years previously. He was deprived of his temporalities and forbidden to come within twenty miles of the court. Peter de la Mare was imprisoned at Nottingham, Latimer was restored to favour, and became close to Gaunt, and March ceased to be Earl Marshal. The others punished during the Good Parliament were pardoned and even Alice Perrers came back to court. In January 1377 a new Parliament (sometimes called the Bad Parliament) met and lasted until April. It proved to be remarkably pliant to the court's wishes. The new Speaker, Sir Thomas Hungerford, a knight of the shire for Wiltshire, was Gaunt's steward and familiar. The point had been taken that if the crown was to have any degree of influence over the Commons it must have control of the Speaker. Lancaster also managed to pack the Commons to some extent, though even so some of the knights tried, but without success, to secure the release of Sir Peter de la Mare.

Lancaster had set about trying to overcome his own unpopularity with some adroitness. Prince Richard, who was ten, had been created Prince of Wales, and was now made formal head of the Parliament in the king's absence. The duke also appealed to the anti-papal feeling. Just before Parliament met, Lancaster tightened his grip on affairs by appointing a new chancellor and treasurer, the Bishops of St. David's and of Worcester, which gave him the advantage of new ministers who were beholden to him. Parliament was opened with an address by the new chancellor, which is recorded in detail in the parliamentary roll.[1] It was a long and flowery salute to the king, the royal family and above all acclaimed the great fortune of the nation in the young Prince Richard. The king had been so ill, said the bishop, that his life had been in danger, but now he was much better. Reminding Parliament that it was the year of the king's jubilee he spoke of the blessings the king had had in his wife and his sons, and of the way in which the realm had been enriched and reformed. Now, he continued, Parliament had the king's grandson and heir to preside over it, and the prelate illuminated that great mercy by scriptural references to God's sending his Son into the world. The chancellor then exhorted the nation to unity and obedience in appreciation of these benefits, and told them of the need for money to prepare for the resumption of war with France, to repel seaborne invasion, when the truce between the two countries ended.

In exchange for an aid, the government had an appealing announcement to make, which could not be by the lips of the episcopal chancellor. After the Bishop of St David's had spoken, the chamberlain, Sir Robert Ashton

---

[1] *Rot. Parl.* Vol. II, pp. 361-364.

announced that he had something to say from the king which was for 'the profit of the kingdom' but which it was inappropriate for 'the prelate' to speak of since it concerned the Pope. The king, he said, fully recognized the Pope's rights, but 'many usurpations have long been done in the kingdom by the See of Rome' and the king was determined to resist them.[1] Encouraged by this promise, the Commons then went off to the Chapter House, and a committee of lords was appointed for intercommuning. After deliberation, Parliament conceded a poll tax of 4d. payable for every person over fourteen years of age, the first use of an inequitable and much resented tax which was to have devastating consequences in the coming reign. But the Commons also required that two earls and two barons should be appointed as 'guardians and treasurers' for the subsidy, which was to be spent 'entirely for the war'. The 'high treasurer of England' was to take none of it, not 'meddle' with it in any way. It was a much more accommodating Parliament, the Commons even petitioning, successfully of course, for the reversal of the judgement against Latimer and others. Yet the communities' representatives still had a mind of their own on what touched them most closely: taxation.

In return for the poll tax there was a general pardon of all offences to commemorate the king's jubilee. Wykeham, however, was excluded from this until the Convocation of Canterbury made it clear that they would pay nothing until he was allowed to join them, when they too conceded a poll tax. In the meantime, the clergy had had a revenge by making charges against the theologian John Wycliff, who had been brought from Oxford to London by John of Gaunt to preach against the church's endowments. Wycliff had still not yet fully developed his doctrines, and it is less likely that Lancaster was an active sympathiser than that he found Wyclif useful. Nevertheless, Lancaster appointed doctors of divinity to defend Wyclif, attended the theologian's trial with the new marshall, Sir Henry Percy, and a body of armed retainers, and finally brought the proceedings to an end in a furious quarrel between himself and Bishop Courtney of London. Despite the prevailing anti-clericalism and the unpopularity of the financial exactions of a wealthy church, the London citizens turned against John of Gaunt and in favour of their bishop, who seems to have been popular with them. The citizens of London were already at odds with Gaunt and they may have interpreted his armed presence at and around St Paul's as an infringement of their liberties. Uproar followed. The citizens besieged Gaunt's palace of the Savoy, accused him of treason (symbolically inverting his arms in the city of London), mockingly questioned the legitimacy of his

---

[1] *Rot. Parl.* Vol. II, p. 363.

birth by alleging that he was the son of a Flemish butcher of Ghent, and drove the duke to escape by river and take refuge with the Black Prince's widow at Kennington. Eventually a peace was made, the mayor was removed, apologies were offered to Lancaster, and a parliamentary deputation to the king at Sheen received his general pardon just before Parliament was dissolved. Gaunt was no more popular but he had managed to reverse what had been done against the government's will in the Good Parliament.

Edward III died on 21 June, 1377. His fifty years as king had been the most formative period of the English medieval Parliament, and on the whole they were also a time of remarkable harmony between king and subjects. To a considerable extent, this was because Edward's reign was also a distraction from the ordinary realities of English medieval domestic power politics. His predecessors and successors were beset by challenges from powerful magnates whose claims and ambitions were a threat to the authority of the crown, and therefore to political stability. Edward III was free of such threats from his magnates because he engaged their energies with him in his French enterprise. With the minds of the king and magnates occupied elsewhere, except when they needed taxation, the Commons had also been free to develop politically through the conditions they had attached to their financial support of the king's war. Their control over taxation had been firmly established and was never seriously threatened thereafter in medieval politics. The foundations of their future part in legislation had also been laid. When, after Edward's death, aristocratic power politics returned to England, the Commons were more actively involved than they had been at any time before the Good Parliament, though always in a secondary role. In the later fifteenth century, as the political order disintegrated into dynastic struggle, the Commons never lost what they had gained. They took the opportunity to tighten their grip on legislative and fiscal politics, and to extend their privileges, while the great questions of which king or dynasty should rule were settled by a self-destructive aristocracy on the battlefield.

CHAPTER 6

——— * ———

Richard II:
Parliament and the Crown's Authority

I

THE reign of Richard II brought to an explosive end the old ambiguous relationship between crown and magnates which had been a characteristic of the thirteenth and fourteenth centuries. Since Magna Carta, English domestic politics had persistently expressed an inner contradiction in the way men looked at government and sought to practice it. The king was expected to rule personally, accepting the ultimate responsibility for policy and its execution. In the social conditions of the age, no government would have been workable which was not rooted in a strong, central, individual and legitimate authority. The king embodied this authority and his hereditary right to rule constituted its legitimacy. Yet he was expected to accept the guidance and advice of the higher nobility who had shown themselves willing to engage against him if he persistently refused to heed them or preferred to take advice exclusively from professional ministers or personal friends. It was largely as a result of this tension between king and magnates that Parliament, which had begun as an instrument of the king's will, had also become a vehicle for political opposition. During the successful years of Edward III's profitable French enterprise, the tension between king and magnates had temporarily ceased as both united in a common interest. Instead the Commons used their control over the supply of money needed for the war to build up their own influence in Parliament. They had become well placed to be valuable and assertive allies of the Lords when aristocratic discontent reasserted itself after the collapse of the English position in France towards the end of Edward's reign. Lords and Commons continued, for the most part, to be allies under Richard II.

This alliance was to frustrate Richard's attempts to make personal kingship work at a time of exceptional social, financial and political difficulty. The claims of the aristocracy had become much more demanding as a consequence of Edward III's policy of encouraging the aggrandizement of aristocratic houses and the hunger for power of junior branches of the royal family. In trying to resist their challenge, and in the hope of breaking out once and for all from a position in which he always felt his independence at risk, Richard was eventually tempted to excesses of royal authoritarianism which destroyed him. In the catastrophe which ended his reign, the old forbearance snapped. No attempts were made to reconcile royal authority and conciliar influence by means of formal constitutional devices, and the king was removed to make way for a successor who could make no legitimate claim to the throne. Richard's deposition by a usurping rival was to take place in a spirit significantly different from that in which Edward II had been forced to abdicate in favour of his legitimate successor. The overthrow of Richard II was to reduce the monarchy for much of the fifteenth century to the leadership of whichever faction was victorious in battle, powerful though it remained as an instrument of government.

Richard's attempts to give the crown a new authority were not ignoble. He had high standards of kingship, and he was goaded beyond his endurance by the pretensions and ambitions of angry kinsmen and magnates. The arrangements made for the management of his minority equipped him badly to cope with the difficulties which were to confront him. Neither he nor the realm was given the benefit of a wise governor capable of exercising the royal authority effectively while Richard was too young to do so and of bringing him up in the ways of government. Instead, authority was diffused among rival groups, and Richard was at first involved too early in the events of government, and subsequently held back from constructive responsibility in a manner which built up impatience and frustration within him. It is impossible not to have some sympathy with his wish to break free from domineering and patronizing magnates and with some of his political intentions. Yet if he had succeeded in establishing the royal authority as he wished in his last two years, the direction of English history would almost certainly have changed towards a more powerful and less responsive throne, somewhat in the French manner, and a much less influential Parliament.

At the coronation of the ten year old king on 16 July, a month after King Edward's death, the principle of legitimate succession was given particular emphasis. This was John of Gaunt's doing. His overriding concern was to allay the unjust suspicion fostered by his opponents that he had designs on the throne for himself, or that he at least intended to dominate the realm during the king's minority. As he was to say later, he had too much to lose from any such attempt. The throne he had set his mind on was that of Castille. Accordingly, the new reign began with gestures of reconciliation, which included the release from prison of, among others, Peter de la Mare who, according to the St Albans chronicler, was given a reception by the Londoners reminiscent of that enjoyed by Thomas Becket on his return from exile. Gaunt was also publicly reconciled in the king's presence with the Londoners and with William of Wykeham.

Richard's coronation was of exceptional splendour. John of Gaunt, who, as Steward of England, was in charge of the ceremony, walked ahead of the king from the palace of Westminster to the Abbey bearing a great sword, the other royal kinsmen preceding him. The importance of strict legitimacy of succession was clearly implied through a change in the coronation ceremonial. Previously, the recognition of the king by the people had preceded the king's coronation oath, which might convey some suggestion of an element of election to kingship. This time, however, the coronation oath was taken before the archbishop put to the people the question 'whether they wished to have and obey him as king and liege lord', to which they unanimously gave their assent. The intention was to make it clear that he was already the rightful and sworn king before the people's recognition of him, and to dispel any lingering notion of election. Even the oath itself enhanced the royal authority since the king was required to swear not simply to keep the laws 'which the people shall have chosen' (the oath devised for Edward II) but to keep and maintain the laws which 'the people shall *justly and reasonably* have chosen'.[1] The ceremonies of anointing with holy oil and vesting with robes, symbols that the king's power came from God, together with the adulation to which he listened when he presided over Parliament, must have helped to encourage in an impressionable child that dangerous sense of the uniqueness of his person which was to influence Richard's future conduct. Before the coronation banquet, four earls were created among whom was Edward III's youngest son, Thomas of Woodstock, Earl of Buckingham, whose malignant opposition was to pave the way to Richard's destruction.

Despite the king's boyhood, no regency was established. This again was almost certainly Gaunt's deliberate decision. Because of his seniority in the royal family there could have been no other regent than himself, and his unpopularity with a section of the nobility, the Londoners and the clergy

[1] *E.H.D.* Vol. IV, pp. 403–405.

would have made it politically risky for him to assume the regency. For the first few weeks he and an *ad hoc* council carried on the government but immediately after the coronation a great council of magnates appointed a new continual council to govern the realm. It was for all practical purposes a council of regency, but in theory it was Richard himself who ruled. He had his own great seal, privy seal and signet, and what the council did was done in his name. John of Gaunt was not a member of the continual council, though he sometimes attended it for special purposes, nor were the other royal uncles, the Earl of Cambridge, later Duke of York, and the Earl of Buckingham, later Duke of Gloucester. (In any case, Gaunt was away on the Scottish border during the early months of the reign dealing with the situation arising from the expiry of the truce with Scotland.) Gaunt did, however, have at least two supporters, Lord Latimer and the Bishop of Salisbury, on the council which consisted of two bishops, two earls, two barons and two bannerets, the model indicated by the abortive continual council of the Good Parliament.

The letters patent appointing the council to deal with the estate of the realm, and to 'aid' the chancellor and treasurer, expressly stated that their most urgent task was to raise money for the resumed war with France.[1] The councillors were empowered to borrow by whatever possible means, 'by prest, engagement or obligation' and from any persons, 'whatever sums of money' they could because of 'certain great and pressing demands touching the safety and necessary defence of our realm . . .' The danger from France was indeed pressing, and Bordeaux and Calais were threatened. During Edward III's last months the worst raids for many years had been inflicted on the south coast. There had been attacks on Portsmouth, Plymouth and Dartmouth, the Isle of Wight (which had been occupied for a time), Winchelsea and Hastings. Raiding had also increased from Scotland where only a few bases, including Berwick and Roxburgh, remained in English hands. The country had already been subject to forced loans, and the injunction to the council to borrow was followed up by a loan of £15,000 raised from the city and particularly from two wealthy Londoners, John Philipot and William Walworth, who were to play a significant part in the Commons' attempt to control the government's spending. But loans were not enough. The government's dependence on taxation was more clear than ever, and the king's ordinary revenues from his estates and customary dues at this time provided only about a fifth of the crown's total income. Such was the disillusion in the land that, despite the grandeur of the coronation,

---

[1] Rymer *Foedera* III, iii, p. 64 and *E.H.D.* Vol. IV, pp. 122–123.

Richard II's first four years were more like a dispiriting coda to the old reign than an optimistic start to the new. It was in this mood that Richard's first Parliament assembled at Westminster on 13 October, 1377.[1]

In the otherwise dreary years of Richard's minority, the independent political claims of the Commons were the most striking characteristic of Parliament. They exhibited an unabashed wish to influence the politics of power, making political terms in exchange for their money, demanding investigations into the conduct of government, and even obtaining the dismissal of council and ministers, and for the most part they acted independently of the Lords. In the late fourteenth century, the Commons were more than the followers of aristocratic faction, and there is little evidence that their 'House' was systematically packed either by magnates or by the government. Even the Parliament of 1377, in which Gaunt had managed to reverse the work of the Good Parliament, does not seem to have been decisively packed, though there were nearly two dozen men in the Commons who were in some way connected with him. The same is true of most of Richard's Parliaments, though eventually the king made some attempts to influence elections. The truth of the matter is that there was a natural tendency for the magnates and Commons to share the same grievances, especially when a government was both unsuccessful and begging for money. Many in the Commons would also have had local connections with some magnates in the ordinary course of events, and both social deference and shared interest would often incline the Commons majority to sway with the prevailing wind from the Lords. It is probable that skilled management of the Commons, rather than packing, was the Lords' way of dealing with them.[2] Management had been the function of Peter de la Mare for the opposition in the Good Parliament, and it was subsequently the function of Thomas Hungerford for Gaunt. Understanding this, Richard II was eventually to attempt unsuccessfully to control the Commons by making the Speaker his servant.

Richard's first Parliament was opened with a speech by Archbishop Sudbury of Canterbury, which was part sermon and part political exhortation. Proclaiming with reference to biblical texts that the king came to the throne 'not by an election or by any such similar way' (*nemye par election ne par autre tielle collaterale voie*) but only by 'right succession of inheritance' Sudbury extolled Richard as the nation's solace in its adversities and as the upholder of its laws, liberties and customs, and went on to ask for counsel on how to meet the government's great expenditure on

[1] *Rot. Parl.* Vol. III, pp. 3–31.
[2] J. G. Edwards, '*The Commons in Medieval English Parliaments*' (Creighton Lecture, 1957).

the defence of the realm.[1] Later on the Commons asked to have a meeting with a committee of the Lords whom they named (it included both Gaunt and March) to discuss money. At this point Gaunt rose to make a dramatic gesture to disarm criticism of himself. Kneeling before the king he asked to be heard on 'a weighty matter touching his own person'. He could not, he said, be a member of the Committee to consult with the Commons unless he had been excused (that is, acquitted) of 'those things which had been evilly spoken of him'. However unworthy, he was a king's son and was 'one of the greatest lords in the land after the king'. Yet he had virtually been accused of plain treason. None of his ancestors on either side had been traitors and it would, he said, be 'strange indeed if he were to stray from their path' since he had 'more to lose than any man in the realm', which was clearly the truth. If anyone dared to charge him with treason, he would defend himself with his body 'as though he were the poorest bachelor in the realm'. This intervention had exactly the effect desired. All the prelates and lords arose, according to the official account, and asked the duke to cease such speech since no one would say such things about him. The Commons likewise exclaimed that he was free from all blame and dishonour, and that they had chosen him as 'their principal aid, comforter and counsellor in this Parliament'. How precisely the Commons expressed these sentiments is not stated in the parliamentary roll, on which the event was recorded, no doubt at Gaunt's behest. Since they normally only spoke through the Speaker, and since it was obviously not possible to withdraw and give him their instructions we must assume either that their support of Gaunt was given in improvised clamour or by the Speaker hastily canvassing the views of as many as possible of those who were present (not, we can assume, the whole body) on the spot. But since it is an official record, we can probably take it as an accurate account of the Commons' reaction. Gaunt then replied that those who accused him were the traitors, and the Commons got down to the business which most closely concerned them.

Once again Peter de la Mare came forward as Speaker. It is impossible to say to what extent the challenging mood of the Commons in this Parliament was the result of his leadership and how far he was chosen Speaker because the Commons were in a much more oppositionist frame of mind than in the last Parliament. The Speaker began by making the first Protestation to be recorded on the official roll, declaring that what he had to say was not on his personal behalf 'but by the initiative, assent and express wish of all the Commons'. If he offended, or said anything which did not have the common assent of his colleagues (*compaignons*) or which offended them in

[1] *Rot. Parl.* Vol. III, pp. 3–4.

anything, it would be withdrawn by them and amended. Sir Peter then put a number of radical proposals to king and council. The first was for the reconstitution of the council by the appointment of eight 'fit persons of various estates to remain continually in council with the king's officials on the needs of the king and the kingdom'. This was accepted by the king, on the advice of the lords, with the proviso that the chancellor and other principal ministers should be free to carry out their duties without reference to the council. It was also decided that there should be nine councillors, but significantly, Gaunt's supporter Latimer was no longer included, his omission being in response to a petition that those impeached in the Good Parliament should be ineligible. The new council was to serve for a year, its members being ineligible for membership for another two years. It was an understandable precaution against the exploitation of the king's minority by over-ambitious councillors, but it was also a mistake since continuity of government was thereby undermined.

The Commons' second request was that those about the king should be appointed in Parliament, and that the expenses of the king and his household should be met entirely from the crown's ordinary revenues, with grants of taxation by the Commons being allocated to pay for the war only. But the 'Lords of Parliament' replied that the first request was too severe and burdensome, and that anyone placed near the king should be pleasing to him. The Lords would concede only that those about the king should not be allowed to sue for lands, offices or wardships for themselves while Richard was of 'tender age'. Nor would the Lords agree to the restriction of household spending to that which could be covered by ordinary crown revenue. They would only undertake to discuss the matter with the household officials to see whether the Commons' proposal was feasible. It is clear that the Lords were determined to stand firmly against any breach of the royal prerogative. They did, however, think it 'reasonable' to grant the third request that the common law and statutes should be kept, and that 'whatever was ordained in this Parliament should not be repealed without Parliament's assent'.

All these answers were given after the Commons had withdrawn to consider other business, leaving the prelates and lay lords to determine their responses, which the Commons returned to hear. They were satisfied enough to give a generous grant of two fifteenths and two tenths, but only on condition that two of their number, John Philipot and William Walworth (who had recently lent money to the government and were representatives of London in Parliament) should be appointed treasurers for the tax receipts to ensure that these were spent only on the war, and to account for the money. The Commons' challenging frame of mind was also indicated by a further petition against Alice Perrers. She was brought into Parliament to have her case rehearsed again before the Lords, and was forced to submit to the sentence of 1376. The case against her was, however, conducted by the steward of the household, with the Commons playing no part in it, which may have represented an attempt to secure control of impeachments by the government. The Commons' close interest in political reform is further indicated by the nature of some of their petitions. Of seventy petitions submitted, fourteen were closely related to the Ordinances of 1311, in words and content. There had been little reference to the Ordinances in the intervening seventy-six years, and most of the Commons may not have been aware of their similarity to the petitions. But whoever drafted the petitions must have had the text of the Ordinances in front of him (or them) and have thought these ideas worth reviving, even though only as requests. There were, however, significant modifications. Thus a request for councillors and eleven leading ministers to be appointed in Parliament would apply only until the king was of full age. To this it was conceded only that while Richard was of tender age the continual councillors and four chief ministers only should be chosen in Parliament, other ministers being appointed by the councillors. Likewise, it was requested that no grant of royal land should be made without the consent of councillors, or made to any of the councillors, which was conceded, but only during the royal minority.[1] Even so, the harking back to the reign of Edward II seems with hindsight like an ill omen of Richard's unhappy future, and these innocent attempts to exert parliamentary control over the king's continual council and over ministerial appointments because he was a minor perhaps helped to influence the thinking which led to the attempts to control Richard's advisers when he was adult. It was a further step in Parliament's attempts to secure influence in areas not traditionally its concern. One further petition of this Parliament worth notice alleged that villeins in parts of the country had combined in efforts to withdraw their services and had collected money and documentation, such as exemplifications from the Domesday Book, to support their cause. The landed classes, it seems, were already aware of the kind of discontent which was to erupt in the Peasant's Revolt.[2]

Richard's first Parliament was dissolved in December but the government's difficulties did not abate. There were renewed attacks on the English coast and Gaunt led a disastrous attack on St Malo, near Cherbourg, the

[1] J. G. Edwards, 'Some Common Petitions in Richard II's First Parliament', *B.I.H.R.* XXVI (1953), pp. 200–213.
[2] *Rot. Parl.* Vol. III, p. 21, cl. 88.

failure of which did nothing to rescue his standing, especially with those who had financed the campaign. But what harmed his reputation more was an abuse of sanctuary at Westminster Abbey by the Constable of the Tower, Sir Alan Buxhill, which was widely believed to have been Gaunt's responsibility. In fact, since he was in Brittany at the time, blame more probably rests with the government, which had its own interest in the matter. The incident had arisen from a characteristic episode in fourteenth century chivalry. Two squires, Robert Hawley and John Shackell, had taken a Spanish nobleman prisoner at the battle of Najera. He was set free, leaving his son hostage for the due ransom. When the money was available, the government (which had agreed its own terms) tried to take possession of the hostage but Hawley and Shackell refused to give him up for which they were imprisoned in the Tower. They then escaped to sanctuary in Westminster Abbey. The constable of the Tower thereupon pursued them to the abbey, recapturing Hawley, killing Shackell and fatally wounding a sacristan during the affray, all during High Mass. Such was the general outrage that the king and council had to agree to found a chantry for the dead men's souls. Eventually, Hawley was released on giving up his hostage, but Gaunt made matters worse needlessly. When Bishop Courtney excommunicated all who had violated sanctuary but made a pointed exception for the king, the Princess of Wales and Gaunt (which was a way of hinting at some sort of official complicity) Gaunt promptly attacked the bishop. So by the time the next Parliament met Gaunt found himself again defending an unpopular case in which the Londoners were once more against him. It was for this reason, so his contemporary critics believed, that the decision was taken to summon the next Parliament to Gloucester. They were probably right, though there may have been other reasons as well, including an impending agreement with the Hanse merchants which was unpopular in the city. At all events, it was to escape the possible threats from the easily manipulated London mob that the second Parliament of the reign met on 20 October, 1378, in the abbey of St Peter at Gloucester, the first Parliament to be held away from Westminster since that held in York in 1335.[1]

The hall, or nave of the abbey church, was used as the Parliament house (*commune Parliamentum*), where Parliament met as a whole, and which took the place of the Painted Chamber at Westminster. The chamber of the hospice was assigned for the private deliberation of the magnates, that is, as the equivalent of the White Chamber. The Commons deliberated apart in the chapter house of the abbey at Gloucester as they did in that of

---

[1] *Rot. Parl.* Vol. III, pp. 32–54.

Westminster.[1] The monks of St Peters, it seems, had to eat outside because the refectory was used for 'matters concerning the law of arms', or as a court of chivalry presided over by the constable of England, then the Earl of Buckingham, and by the marshal, which dealt with military matters, the bearing of arms and heraldry.[2] The court of chivalry was to be concerned with the ransom arrangement in the Shackell case. It may have been with this in mind that, in his opening speech at Gloucester, the chancellor took the opportunity to say that the law of the land and the law of arms ought to reinforce each other.

The Gloucester Parliament is of exceptional interest because of the Commons' stubborn resistance to the government's demands for more money, and for the self-confidence with which they stood their ground and repeatedly came back to argue their case, point by point, with the government's spokesman. As usual, the opening was delayed to await late comers. The prelates and lords were therefore commanded to go to their hostels and take their ease and return the next day, the same 'cry' being made 'to the Commons outside'. Proceedings then began when the king, 'with his uncles of Spain (Gaunt was habitually referred to in the rolls as *Monsr d'Espagne*), Cambridge and Buckingham, and the two Archbishops of Canterbury and York, the Earl of March and almost all the bishops and earls of England who were fit to travel (*qi poient travailler*), and numerous abbots, priors, barons, bannerets, judges and sergeants ... assembled in the great hall (nave) of the abbey, which was appointed, furnished and adorned for holding Parliaments therein'. The reference to the earls who were 'able' to come is a reminder that the parliamentary attendance of magnates was to say the least fitful. Most Parliaments were held up because some were late; others were excused attendance (sometimes for life) on grounds of infirmity; others simply failed to turn up. The level of attendance seems to have depended on the importance of the business and the lords' interest in it. On some occasions at the end of the fourteenth century, when many more magnates were members of the ordinary council, a meeting of the Lords may not have seemed much larger than an enlarged gathering of that council.[3] At all events, the attendance on this occasion seems to have been fairly high, and on the first day of the proceedings, the Commons ('who were very near') were called in to hear the chancellor, the Bishop of St Davids, give an account of the cause of summons.

---

[1] *Historia et Cartularium Monasterii Sancti Petri Gloucestriae*, ed. W. H. Hart, Rolls Ser. (1863–7) Vol. I, p. 53.

[2] Powell and Wallis, op. cit., p. 383.

[3] J. S. Roskell, 'The Problem of the Attendance of the Lords in Medieval Parliaments', B.I.H.R. XXIX, pp. 153–204 (1956).

The first was the king's concern for the laws and good government of the realm. Secondly, said the bishop, Parliament was summoned in response to the desire expressed in the past for annual Parliaments, a reference to that old statute which was rarely volunteered by a king's spokesman. Not least, of course, was the danger from France and from Scotland. The chancellor's address, which expressed the Parliament's good fortune to be meeting in so holy a place, also contained a curious passage which was prompted by the discontent with the government and adverse rumours which were being spread about the great, presumably including the council and Gaunt. There was, said the chancellor, a 'great mischief' in the realm in need of amendment, namely that in many parts of it, 'bad people' (*les malvoys gentz*) were guilty of spreading 'false, horrible and dangerous lies about the Lords, great officers and the good people of the realm' (*fauxes, horribles, & perilouses Mensonges des Seigneurs & autres grantz Officiers & bones gentz del Roialme*) so that it was a wonder there was not discord and riots. Those responsible for these inventions, 'who were called backbiters, were like dogs who ate raw flesh' (*qi sont appellez Bacbyters, sont auxi come chiens qi mangeont les chars crues*). These false 'bacbiters' attacked good people behind their backs with allegations they dare not make in front of them. Perhaps, the chancellor added, it would please the lords and gentlemen to include among their other petitions to the king a request for an ordinance to deal with this. This fascinating passage, with its solitary English colloquialism to describe a commonly understood kind of behaviour, was evidence of the government's concern about the troubled state of the nation.[1]

The next day, Friday, Richard le Scrope, who a few days later was to replace the Bishop of St Davids as chancellor, addressed Lords and Commons. Scrope asked for money and remarked defensively that in case any of those present were wondering where and how the previous grants and wool subsidy had been spent, he could vouch for the fact that the money had all been used solely for the war by the hands of the treasurers John Philipot and William Walworth. The new Speaker, Sir James Pickering, a knight from Westmorland, then made the usual Protestation, but in an even more careful form. As usual, the Speaker protected himself by declaring that he was merely the mouthpiece of the Commons, and safeguarded the Commons by stating that they could disown and put right anything he said amiss. But he also allowed for any offence to the king and Lords in anything he rightly reported as the mind of the Commons by offering an apology for it, and asking that it should be considered as not said. Pickering then went on to speak in terms which could well have been considered offensive by the

---

[1] *Rot. Parl.* Vol. III, p. 33.

government. He expressed the Commons' astonishment at the crown's poverty in view of the previous large subsidies and all the other revenues including those from the Black Prince's lands, alien priories, and wardships. The king should therefore have no need of more money, and the Commons asked to be excused because 'to say the truth' they could give no more because of their poverty. That, however, did not end the matter. Scrope continued to argue his case, saying that every bit of the money had been properly spent and that 'William and John' would vouch for it. The Commons then had a short discussion, and asked to be shown 'how and in what manner' the great sums of money given for the war had been spent. They also voiced their concern about who was controlling the young king, asking to be informed who were his councillors and 'the governors of his person'. What is more they requested that the king's councillors and great officers should be named in Parliament while he was of tender age. Faced with the Commons' open determination to exert political influence on the government, Scrope then said that the king, of his own volition but not through any coercion on account of this request, agreed that Walworth and others of the council should show to the Commons the receipts and expenditure in writing. He again asked them to give advice as quickly as possible about how the war was to be carried on.

The Commons then asked to see a copy of the enrollment of the last Parliament's subsidy, which request was granted again on the king's own volition. After this, the Commons asked that five or six of the Lords should come to them to discuss the demands for money, and at this point they received an unexpected rebuff. The Lords replied 'that they ought not to do so nor would they'. This method, they said, had only been recently employed and the normal custom was for the Lords to choose a small number of themselves, 'say six or ten', and for the Commons to do likewise. These commissioners from Lords and Commons 'should consult informally, without murmur, shouting or noise, (*sanz murmur, crye, & noise*), so that they could the sooner agree on proposals and report back to their respective bodies. This method and no other were the Lords now willing to adopt.' It is clear that the Lords' committees which had recently been nominated by the Commons, had been expected to negotiate with the Commons as a whole, and had to do so in an atmosphere of clamour and interruption. They did not like it, and would put up with it no longer. The Commons were therefore obliged to agree to the election of a small number of themselves and the Lords to talk together in the old manner.[1] But still nothing of value to the government came of it.

[1] *Rot. Parl.* Vol. III, p. 36.

After examining the enrollment, the receipts and the expenses, the Commons returned to Parliament and agreed that the money had been spent honestly. But they could not see why money should be spent at all on Gascony, Brest, and Cherbourg and other places abroad which did not belong to the kingdom. The government's reply was that such places 'were barbicans of the realm of England' which therefore had to be guarded as a kind of front line of defence. But the Commons remained unpersuaded, and observed that the king must be very rich 'with the possessions of his noble grandfather, whom God assoil, which were all in his hands'. The Parliament roll describing these encounters reads like a long debate between the government and the stubborn Commons, who in the end, granted no more than a slight increase in the wool tax for a few months. In return it was agreed that the names of the new councillors should be reported to Parliament as soon as they were appointed. But this was not done, as Parliament had to be ended quicker than expected because of difficulties of accommodation in Gloucester with the onset of winter, and the discomfort which was being inflicted on the monks.

It had been an altogether unhappy Parliament for the government, and not only because of the Commons' refusal to provide money. The archbishop and prelates had reasserted their protest against the violation of the Westminster sanctuary and certain doctors of theology, Wyclif among them, were therefore brought by Gaunt into Parliament to argue against the prelates' case. Nothing conclusive seems to have followed, the principal effect being that Gaunt further damaged his own cause. Parliament would hardly have been much impressed by Wyclif's assertion before the Commons that 'the king and his Council could safely and with a good conscience drag esquires out of holy church for debt or for treason, and that even God could not dispense for debt', though the king and the council were said to have been greatly heartened by such speeches.[1] In the longer run, the most far reaching decision taken during the Gloucester Parliament was a declaration of English support for the Roman Pope, Urban VI, against the Avignon Pope, Clement VII, which solidified the division of Europe between two papal allegiances and prolonged the Great Schism. The statute records that the king had produced a letter from rebel cardinals against Urban, and that, after deliberation, the bishops had declared Urban to be the true bishop of Rome, the Lords and Commons assenting.[2] That decision was virtually inevitable since the repudiation of Urban had arisen from the wish of the predominantly French college of cardinals to return to

---

[1] *The Anonimalle Chronicle*, ed. V. H. Galbraith, p. 123; E.H.D. Vol. IV, pp. 124–125.
[2] *Stat. R.* Vol. II, 2 Ric. II, Stat. I, c. vii, p. 11.

Avignon, and the English naturally took the opposite side. The decision on the papacy, however, was only part of the single statute enacted at Gloucester. It also contained measures concerning commercial dealings and alien merchants, and it confirmed the unpopular statute of labourers, which was one of the causes of the general discontent among the peasants underlying the revolt three years later. It is not a minor point that the statute also dealt with the chancellor's complaints about 'backbiters', penalties being provided against 'devisors of false news and of horrible and false lies about prelates, dukes, earls, barons, and other nobles and great men of the realm' and about the chancellor, the treasurer and other of the king's ministers.[1] The government was serious in its misgivings about public discontent, and with good reason.

The financial crisis continued. At a great council in February, the magnates authorized new loans, more or less forced, which raised so little that a new Parliament had to be called for Easter 1379 at Westminster.[2] At the beginning of its proceedings the chancellor, Richard le Scrope, apologized for the short interval of six months since the Gloucester Parliament and adopted a much more conciliatory approach. He informed them that because of 'the sudden departure' from Gloucester, the king had not completed appointing his continual council but that this had now been done. Now in desperate need of money, the chancellor announced that the treasurers were 'ready and prepared, at whatever hour pleases you (*prestz & apparaillez, a quelle heure qui vous plest*), to show you clearly and in writing their receipts and expenses made since the last Parliament'.[3] The Commons were also given the appointment of a committee of prelates and lords (including the Archbishop of Canterbury and the Earl of March), to examine 'the estate of the king', look into the revenues from the wool tax since Michaelmas, and supervise the revenues of the realm generally, and also wages and annuities paid. The committee was also to see what had become of the late king's 'movables' (*de surveer les Moebles*), to see what remained in the king's hands and 'what has happened to the rest'.[4] There was virtually no area of royal finances which was not under scrutiny, and what is more all this was offered formally on the government's own volition in a long and conciliatory statement by the chancellor in the causes of summons at the outset of proceedings, before any formal representations by the Commons could be made. But it was nonetheless the Commons' doing. A more stringent form of accounting, in theory at least, would be hard to

[1] *Stat. R.* Vol. III, 2 Ric. II, Stat I, cl. v, p. 9.
[2] *Rot. Parl.* Vol. III, pp. 55–68.
[3] Ibid., p. 56.
[4] Ibid., p. 57.

imagine, and in return the Commons granted a graduated poll tax, setting out the tax liability for each man according to his degree, starting with Lancaster (ten marks), the earls (£4 each) down to 4d. which was to be paid by each married man for himself and his wife, and by each single man, except for those who were 'veritable beggars'. But the yield of the tax, an augury of the future idea of graduating tax to wealth or income, raised too little. Still more borrowing was necessary and crown jewels had to be sold.

When the next Parliament met at Westminster in January 1380 the government's situation was as bad as ever.[1] A military expedition led by Sir John Arundel had ended in shipwreck and the chancellor had to report that the proceeds of the graduated poll tax had gone uselessly on the abortive expedition, that the king could not repay his loans, and in short that the treasury was once more empty. The reaction of the Commons was now more forthright than ever. It was now no longer enough to enquire how money had been spent. Instead, the new Speaker, Sir John Gildesborough, a retainer of the king's uncle Thomas of Woodstock, demanded on behalf of the Commons that all members of the continual council should be dismissed, and that since the king was of 'good discretion and fine stature' no others should be appointed. Richard, who was now 13, was, they said, almost the same age as his grandfather had been at his coronation. The Commons considered that the officers of state, who should be nominated in Parliament, would be enough to advise him. The desperate government gave way and there were no more continual councils. Scrope resigned, and was replaced by Archbishop Sudbury of Canterbury, an inexperienced and amiable cleric who was an unsuitable choice and whose appointment was his sentence of death at the hands of a peasant mob in the following year. The government also conceded the Commons' request for a complete enquiry into the royal finance and household, for which a new committee was appointed. This, like its predecessor, seems never to have met. In return, the Commons generously granted a tenth and a half and a fifteenth and half, with another year's subsidy on wool, all of which was to be spent on the war in Brittany. The Commons asked that no Parliament should be held to burden them with tax before Michaelmas 1381. They were disappointed.

The political problem was not, as they supposed, one of political corruption, but rather one of insufficient resources for an ill conducted and difficult war. Another fruitless expedition to France, led by Buckingham, and more trouble on the Scottish borders, resulted in the summons of another Parliament in November. This time it was held at Northampton,

---

[1] *Rot. Parl.* Vol. III, pp. 71–87.

apparently because relations with London were again bad, and also, according to the monk Walsingham, because there was a case to be examined in Parliament which might well have aroused the fury of the Londoners had it been dealt with at Westminster. A London mercer, John Kirkby, was alleged to have murdered a Genoese merchant with diplomatic protection. He was examined by Parliament, and condemned and executed for treason, which could be done without risk of trouble at Northampton, but might have aroused the London mob had the Parliament been held at Westminster.

Parliament met in the priory of St Andrews. The Lords assembled in a chamber assigned to the king's council, another chamber was allotted for the meetings of Parliament as a whole, and the Commons were given the 'new dormitory' for their own meetings.[1] Northampton was an inconvenient place for a Parliament, especially in winter, and accommodation and fuel were scarce. This was also a singularly ill attended Parliament. The opening was delayed for several days to await the arrival of Lords and Commons delayed because of the dangerous roads (*perilouses chemyns*). 'Outrageous floods of water' had been caused by 'great and continual rains and storms'. Even when proceedings began, the 'Lords Temporal' (the first use of this term on a parliamentary roll) were 'very few in number' (*moelt petite nombre*) because *Monsr d'Espagne* and a great part of the earls and barons were absent with him on the Scottish border, from where he arrived at Northampton during the course of the Parliament, having secured the agreement of a year's truce.

Seldom has more damage been done in a Parliament than was done at Northampton, where the non-graduated poll tax which precipitated the Peasant's Revolt was granted. The government's plight was desperate and its coffers were empty. The chancellor, Archbishop Sudbury, opened the proceedings with an account of financial woe which exceeded even that to which Parliament was accustomed. He spoke of the need for money, the arrears of wages due to the soldiers in Calais and elsewhere, the fact that the king was 'outrageously in debt' and that his jewels (many had already been sold) 'were about to be lost' (*le Roi est issint outrageousement endettez, et ses Joialx en point d'etre perduz*), and that Buckingham and his company must be paid for the failed expedition to Brittany. The Commons were asked to go off and intercommune on the matter before them, and when they returned, the Speaker, Sir John Gildesborough, asked for a 'clear declaration' of the sum the government needed. On being presented with a schedule of various sums necessary, which amounted to £160,000, the Commons declared this

---

[1] *Rot. Parl.* Vol. III, pp. 88–97.

sum to be 'very outrageous and utterly intolerable' (*moelt outrageous & oultrement importable*). They asked, not for a Lords' committee to consult with, but for all the Lords as a body to advise them by what means the money could be raised. The alternatives put to them were another poll tax on every male and female, the strong aiding the weak (*le fort aidant al feable*), or if that did not please them, a tax on the sale of merchandise, or a subsidy of tenths and fifteenths. The Lords expressed their clear preference for the poll tax and the Commons chose it. Spread over the whole people, it was the method which would fall least heavily on the smaller landowners they represented. It was a disastrous decision which was the immediate cause of the Peasants' Revolt, and the Commons were responsible for making it. Yet the greater fault was that of the Lords for their recommendation. Had Scottish affairs and bad weather not kept so many great lords of influence away from Nottingham, it is possible that more sensible advice might have been given to the Commons and the catastrophe of the following year avoided.

As it was, a tax of three groats (a silver coin worth 4d.) a head was to be levied ungraduated on the whole population. Having dismissed the originally demanded figure of £160,000, the Commons would only accept £100,000 as necessary, of which they would provide two-thirds, about £66,000, from the poll tax if the clergy produced the rest. (The clergy would not give a formal undertaking in Parliament but indicated that they would contribute.) The calculation was that the three groat poll tax on everyone over fifteen, three times the rate of the previous flat levy, would produce that sum. Despite a vague proviso that the rich should help the poor, no means of ensuring that they did so were devised, and the tax fell most heavily on the poorest. Each district was assessed to produce a given sum calculated at the flat rate per head for each liable tax payer, and it was left for the inhabitants to allot the incidence on individuals as best they could to fulfil the wish that the rich should help the poor. But this redistributionist ideal was severely restricted by the provision in the grant that the most wealthy should not pay more than 60 groats (20 shillings) for himself and his wife and that the poorest should not pay less than a groat, 4d., which was a high proportion of their wages. Only 'veritable beggars' were exempted from the tax. In making the grant the Commons stipulated that the grant was only for 'the sustenance of the earl of Buckingham and the other lords and men in his company in parts of Brittany, and for the defence of the realm and the safeguard of the sea'.[1]

Quite apart from the restriction on the extent to which the rich could help

---

[1] *Rot. Parl.* Vol. III, pp. 89–90.

the poor, there were districts where there were no rich men to do so, and a poor peasant might have to pay two shillings for himself and for his wife. A tax on people instead of the old tax on property suited the landowning Commons, but to the poor peasantry it was an incitement to resistance. Some of the better off had the wit to see the danger, and the *Anonimalle Chronicle* recorded that various lords and commons thought the tax unfairly levied from the poor, and also that the collectors had retained most of the yield.[1] There was much evasion, and even more resentment at the inquiries into personal circumstances which followed. It had at first been intended to collect the tax in two instalments, but the money began to come in so slowly that an attempt was made to collect the tax all at once, and rumours spread that this was being done without parliamentary sanction. The Commons had failed in their duty as representatives capable of supplying the government with accurate information about how their communities would react to taxation and the chances of collecting it without difficulty.

The poll tax of 1380 was the fuse which lit the Peasants' Revolt, but much of the dynamite was already in place. The existence of peasant unrest had already been acknowledged by the property owning classes and the breakdown of the old manorial system with its ties of mutual obligation had led to new hopes and a new sort of relationship between master and man. Peasants wanted freedom from work service and from such feudal obligations as the requirement to give up their best beasts on inheritance of land, or pay a fine on the marriage of their daughters. Their obligations were the more disliked now that many villeins owned property which they had bought with money gained from the commutation of work service for wages. There were also more landless labourers who expected to be reasonably paid. The Black Death, with the consequent shortage of labour, had transformed rapid social change into an upheaval; labour was in short supply and Parliament had tried to restrict wages by repeatedly re-enacting the Statute of Labourers, which had again been confirmed only a year before. Much bitterness was caused by the attempt to restrict wages by law with harsh penalties which the Commons repeatedly demanded should be enforced. There was a growing resentment at the contrast between the opulence of the upper classes who still enjoyed the previous spoils of the French war and the poverty of the peasants who now had to pay for its useless continuance. The wealth of the church was also increasingly contrasted with the Christian doctrine of the holiness of poverty. A number of lower clergy were to be involved in the coming revolt, and one of them, John Ball, has taken his place in history for preaching a kind of primitive

---

[1] *Anonimalle Chronicle*, ed. V. H. Galbraith, p. 134; *E.H.D.* Vol. IV, p. 127.

communism. As so often happens in revolutionary movements, the naked ambition of a less than balanced demagogue struck a chord with the grievances and aspirations of many. To peasants long used to hearing poverty extolled and the selfishness of riches attacked from the pulpit, the ground was already tilled to receive the seed of revolutionary propaganda, but there was little coherent theory in it.

The immediate impulse for the Peasants' Revolt appears to have been the result of the way in which the commissioner appointed to deal with the poll tax in Essex performed his duties. The resistance of a group of villages quickly turned into a general rising in the county against the collectors, and manors and the houses of better-off people were sacked. The peasants of Kent also embarked on a general revolt, took the castle at Rochester, marched to Maidstone and chose as their leader a certain Wat Tyler. The rebels then marched to Canterbury, entered the Cathedral and proclaimed that one of the monks should be elected archbishop since Archbishop Sudbury was a traitor who would soon be beheaded. The vagabond priest John Ball, who was in the archbishop's prison, was released and joined Wat Tyler who led the Kentishmen to Blackheath outside London. There Ball preached his famous egalitarian sermon on the text:

Whan Adam dalf, and Eve span,
Wo was thanne a gentilman?

a text which was already a familiar one in fourteenth century sermons and which normally carried no revolutionary significance. In the meantime, the peasants from Essex had marched, burning and looting, to Mile End where they encamped. Messengers sent from the king to Blackheath were told that the peasants wished to save the king from traitors and to speak with him. Nothing was done by the magnates to defend London for fear of arousing the mob within it, but the king took refuge in the Tower. On 13 June, the men from Kent entered the city across London Bridge with the help of sympathizers, and those from Essex through Aldgate. John of Gaunt's palace of the Savoy and its rich furnishings and plate were systematically destroyed by fire or by being thrown into the Thames. Looting was forbidden on the grounds that this was a punitive not a self-seeking operation; one looter who took a piece of John of Gaunt's silver was, indeed, thrust into the flames for doing so. But the self-discipline of the rebels quickly broke down; there was much arson and sacking of houses, prisons were opened and the lawyers' books and documents were burned at the Temple. In this crisis the young king, who was now fourteen, took the initiative. He first set out fom the Tower by boat, accompanied by the chancellor, treasurer and other councillors, apparently in the hope of negotiating with the rebels. But seeing the mass of people, they turned back at the behest of the councillors who did not wish to endanger the king, though he was apparently willing to continue. Richard then addressed the mob outside the Tower from one of the turrets and promised a charter of pardon, which the rebels scorned. So he sent messages that he would go to Mile End to meet the peasants. This they accepted. It was apparently the king's hope that it would give Archbishop Sudbury the chance to escape from London. On 14 June, with remarkable courage, Richard, accompanied by a few Lords and knights and by the Mayor of London, William Walworth, rode to Mile End, where the rebels fell on their knees and one of their spokesmen proclaimed that they wanted no other than he to be their king. They demanded that traitors, including Sudbury and other councillors, should be handed over to them, the abolition of serfdom, free labour contracts, and the right to land at 4d. an acre. The king accepted all this except the rebels' demand to punish traitors, saying only that they might seize any they thought were traitors and bring them to him for trial and justice. In the meantime, other rebels had exacted their own injustice at the Tower which, despite the garrison, they managed to enter, seizing Archbishop Sudbury, Sir Robert Hales, the treasurer and other councillors whom they beheaded. The king took refuge at the Wardrobe in Baynard Castle near Blackfriars where he was joined by his mother.

The disorder continued, Flemings were massacred, and on 15 June the king met Tyler and some of the rebels at Smithfield where the final and familiar act of this extraordinary drama took place. Tyler rode out in front of his men and made the same demands as those that had been made at Mile End, and others still more radical which included the abolition of all lordship save that of the king, the equality of all men, the confiscation of church property, and the abolition of all bishoprics except one, which was no doubt reserved for John Ball. 'To this,' according to the *Anonimalle Chronicle* 'the king gave an easy answer, and said that he (Tyler) should have all that could fairly be granted saving to himself the regality of the crown.' Wat Tyler, who had already treated Richard with rough familiarity, calling him brother and taking him by the hand, now demanded a flagon of water because of the heat, and on getting it 'rinsed his mouth out in a rude and disgusting manner before the king'. He then called for a flagon of ale which he drained in an insolent fashion. One of the king's yeomen from Kent accused Tyler of being a robber and thief, the upshot being that Tyler threatened the yeoman and was struck from his horse and wounded by William Walworth, who may have thought that the king was in danger. The rebels' leader was then run through by one of the king's squires.

In this moment of peril the king, with astonishing courage, rode forward to the mob which was about to advance on him calling out: 'Sirs, will you shoot your king? I will be your leader, follow me,'[1] and they were by now so well used to follow that they did so. Richard refused to allow violence to the rebels when Walworth returned with forces, and pardoned them. The rebellion in London was over, and William Walworth, Mayor of London, and John Philipot, the two former members of Parliament who had been the Commons' treasurers overseeing the grants, were knighted for their loyalty and help to the king. So was another rich Londoner, Nicholas Brembre, who was to be involved with the king in much unhappier circumstances later.

Outside London, the rebellion had spread, but it was largely confined to the south east. The worst disorder was at St Albans, Suffolk, Essex, Cambridge, and in Norfolk where a certain Geoffrey Lister was crowned 'king of the Commons'. Within a month, order had been restored, and apart from the execution of the leaders, including Lister and Ball, there were no general reprisals, though there was harsh brutality in places.[2] By the advice of his council the king had revoked his concessions to the peasants, including manumission. The Peasants' Revolt achieved no sharp social reform. Yet it finally undermined villeinage and hastened its replacement by paid labour. The uprising was also a warning to the governing classes which to some extent conditioned their future behaviour. A similar poll tax was not tried again.

II

In 1381 Richard became king in something more than name. His bravery in front of the rebels and his ability to take an initiative in an emergency had given him a certain personal authority despite his age, and the performance of the ministers and councillors of his minority had not been such as to encourage any conscious wish, so far, to hold the king back now that he was

---

[1] There are differing accounts of Richard's words, which are not quoted directly in the *Anonimalle Chronicle*.

[2] One of the most vivid and full contemporary accounts of the Peasants' Revolt is that of the *Anonimalle Chronicle*, ed. by V. H. Galbraith, the relevant extract of which is translated in *E.H.D.* Vol. IV, pp. 127–140; other accounts are in *Chronicon Angliae*, pp. 285ff and Westminster monk, printed as an appendix to Ranulph Higden *Polychronicon*, Rolls Ser. Vol. IX, pp. 1–9, and Walsingham *Historia Anglicana* II, pp. 1ff. For a synthesis of the chroniclers' accounts see B. Wilkinson, 'The Peasants' Revolt of 1381', *Speculum* 15, 1940.

approaching adulthood. For a short time too, the king's personal authority may have been enhanced by the gap left in the government by the murder of the chancellor and treasurer. At all events he had ceased to be a wholly passive element in the government and he was quickly to show that he had his own ideas about how he wished it to be conducted. That Richard himself seems to have favoured the policy of freeing the serfs is perhaps evidence of a certain independence of thought. It is impossible, however, to know to what extent he took his thinking from some of those about him in his court. It is only certain that such ideas were quite unacceptable to the land-owning aristocracy and gentry.

Richard's sense of the mystical power of his kingship had come to him dangerously early. He had presided over Parliament and listened to the adulation of his person which was the fashion of the age since he was ten years old, and had done so even in his grandfather's time. It would have needed quite extraordinary political sensitivity in a boy of his age to distinguish between style and substance, appearance and reality. He had been crowned in a manner that emphasized the divinity hedging a king, and his authority with the peasants probably encouraged him to precocious self-confidence. Watching the humiliation of his councillors year after year as they besought Parliament for money, he must have found it easy to believe that he could have managed things better. He was not a lazy and incompetent king like Edward II. His flaw was rather that a fitful temperament and the wrong kind of upbringing had combined to give him an idea of the authority of a king which made it hard for him to understand the reality of opposition and how to deal with it. So it was that he was already convinced that it was his right to take advice and give friendship where he chose without taking account of the need for the political support of the powerful. He had been brought up by three tutors, knights appointed by the Black Prince, of whom the most important was Simon Burley, a man of chivalry and loyalty who was acting chamberlain. But the most powerful of influences on the king was his friend the hereditary chamberlain, Robert de Vere, Earl of Oxford, who was only five years older than the king himself. Though his was the oldest earldom in England in the direct male line, it was also the poorest, and neither de Vere's personality nor his means impressed the more powerful noblemen who thought themselves the king's natural counsellors. They were as affronted when the king began to shower gifts of lands on his aristocratic but impoverished friend, as their forbears had been when Edward II had lavished gifts on the upstart Gaveston. They also recognized in de Vere an irresponsible man who, instead of inculcating a sense of realism in the king, encouraged him to over-estimate his personal power. Nevertheless, after the peasants' uprising, it was still Gaunt who was the principal power in the land. Though the rebellion had demonstrated more clearly than ever the general hatred of him, his reputation had been enhanced by the truce with Scotland, and to those without prejudice he should have been recognizable as the most loyal of the king's mighty subjects. Around the throne prowled men much more dangerous, of whom the king's other uncle Buckingham and the Earl of Arundel would eventually be the most menacing of all.

The first Parliament after the Peasants' Rising met on 4 November, 1381.[1] The atmosphere was troubled by social instability and soured by a bitter quarrel between Gaunt and the Earl of Northumberland over their conflicting interests in the north. Both magnates brought to London 'a large force of men at arms and archers in battle order' as the parliamentary rolls record, and 'the lords of the kingdom were very greatly occupied with appeasing them'.[2] The business of Parliament was delayed for a week until Northumberland apologized to Gaunt. The new chancellor, William Courtney, former Bishop of London and now Archbishop of Canterbury elect, then opened proceedings with a good sermon in English on a biblical text (*une bone collacion en Engleys*), after which the new treasurer, Hugh Seagrave, announced the causes of summons. They were the peace of the kingdom after the insurrection, enquiry into its causes and the chastisement of the guilty, and especially the question of emancipating the serfs. The king, as Parliament was told, had been 'constrained to grant' letters of liberty and manumission to the serfs of the kingdom under the great seal to put a stop to their malice. But, said the treasurer, this had disinherited lords and prelates and was consequently unlawful. The king had therefore revoked them as being made under compulsion and against reason, and now wished to know from prelates, Lords and Commons 'if it seems to you that by this repeal he has done well and to your pleasure, or not'.[3] 'If,' Seagrave went on, 'you wish to enfranchise and manumit the said serfs by your common assent, as he has heard some of you desire, the king will assent to your prayer.' The treasurer then instructed the Commons to go to their place in the abbey and respond to these matters diligently, adding that the king was greatly in debt for the maintenance of his estate and household, and that officers of the household would be sent to them to explain the king's great need.

Two days later the Commons returned. The Speaker, Sir Richard Waldegrave, having made the conventional protestation, explained that the Commons were in part 'at variance' among themselves about the charge

[1] *Rot. Parl.* Vol. III, pp. 98–121.
[2] Ibid., p. 98.
[3] Ibid., p. 99.

given to them, and asked 'his royal Majesty' (a new mode of address in the parliamentary rolls) to repeat it once more so that they could understand more clearly. It is possible that they did not really believe that manumission was a serious option, though for Richard personally it may have been. It is even conceivable that this was their way of indicating that they could not believe their ears; the question may have subtly implied rebuke. The king then asked Richard le Scrope, who had just become chancellor in place of the archbishop, to explain the matter again, and the repeal of the charter of manumission. When he had done so, 'prelates and temporal lords as well as the knights, citizens, and burgesses replied with one voice that this repeal had been well done; adding that such grant of manumission or enfranchisement of serfs could not be made without the assent of those who had the greatest interest. And to this they had never assented of their free will, nor would they ever have done so except to live and die the same day', in other words, under duress. They therefore asked that the manumission made 'by coercion' should be 'quashed and annulled by authority of this Parliament', which was done.

The Parliament was thus at one with the wish of the government (even if it was not entirely shared by the king personally) to resist social change. But the Commons went on to criticize the misgovernment which they regarded as responsible for the peasants' uprising, regardless of their own responsibility for it in granting the poll tax of 1380. Once the matter of manumission was settled, they asked for a committee of lords to intercommune with them on the 'charge' put to them, including financial supply, and a committee was named which included Lancaster, Buckingham and Arundel. This seems to have returned to the practice of discussing the 'charge' with the Commons as a whole, and not with a Commons' committee. The Commons also made one curious request which was quite out of line with anything that had gone before or that came after. They requested that the prelates, great temporal lords, the knights, justices, each separately, 'and all the other estates separately' should be asked to treat about the charge given them and their advice be reported to the Commons so that a good remedy could be reached. But it was replied that the ancient custom was for the Commons to report their opinion on the matter submitted to them to the king and the Lords of the Parliament, and the opinion of the Lords was then to be declared. This was to continue.[1]

When the Commons came back into full Parliament with their answer to the 'charge', the Speaker said that if the government of the realm were not quickly reformed the kingdom itself would be 'entirely lost and destroyed

---

[1] *Rot. Parl.* Vol. III, p. 100.

for all time'. He then attacked the royal household and its expenses in terms which probably indicated that there was already uneasiness about Richard's tendency to give wealth away. Criticizing the faults of those about the king, he protested on the Commons' behalf against 'the outrageous number of familiars in the household', and the abuse of purveyance to maintain it. They complained also about the maladministration of government and the failure to defend the realm against the enemy and his ships, despite the funds that had been granted. They finished with a request that bad officials and councillors should be dismissed and replaced by better.

The upshot was that the king, on the advice of the lords and council, conceded that a committee of prelates, lords and others should 'survey and examine' the estate and governance of the king's person as well as that of his household, and should report to the king their proposals for reform. 'The lords in Parliament then declared that it seemed to them that, if reform of government was to be made throughout the kingdom, attention should begin with the principal member, who was the king himself (... *au Principal Membre q'est le Roi mesmes*) ... and then pass from person to person, from the highest to the lowest degree, sparing no one.' There could hardly be a clearer statement of misgivings about the way in which the young king was already beginning to assert himself; it was the first of many personal humiliations for Richard which were to replace the adulation to which he had become used. The appointed committee included many of the most important men in the land. It was headed by Gaunt and included both archbishops, the Earl of Arundel, various noblemen and bannerets and 'others' who may have been members of the Commons, but no members of the household. To leave no doubt about what they wanted, the Commons then specifically asked Lancaster and his committee to appoint good and worthy men around the king, and to see that the size of the household was such that the king could live honestly of his own (*que nostre dit Seigneur puisse vivre honestement de son propre* . . .), that is from his own ordinary revenue without recourse to taxation, debt or the abuse of purveyance.[1] Such was the attention to detail that the Commons specifically petitioned for, and obtained, the removal from the household of Thomas Rusbrook, Richard's confessor, a friar who was regarded as a bad influence on the king and who was now only to be allowed at court at the four great annual religious festivals. (He was later, however, to become a bishop in Wales.) Although reports of some of the committee's recommendations were given during the course of the Parliament, and an ordinance for the management of the household seems to have been drafted, no text survives and, as had

[1] *Rot. Parl.* Vol. III, p. 101.

happened before, the committee apparently ceased to function when Parliament was dissolved.

Among the other requests of the Commons was that a wise and discreet man should be appointed as chancellor (similar requests were made about other offices) and it was presumably to satisfy the wishes of Parliament that Courtney gave up the great seal and was replaced by le Scrope, a banneret who had been connected with Lancaster. Another decision which indicated the political mood of this Parliament was the appointment of Arundel and Michael de la Pole as advisers and governors of the king's person.[1] With the king thus hedged in and placed under discipline, or so it was hoped, Parliament was then adjourned for Christmas and for the arrival, marriage and coronation of the new queen, Anne of Bohemia, in January 1382. Before it adjourned, general pardons for the uprising were issued, but with a long list of exceptions which were recorded in the Parliament rolls.

When Parliament reassembled, Lancaster, who now had new plans for taking possession of the throne of Castille, asked for the Commons to guarantee a loan of £60,000. His brother the Earl of Cambridge was already in Portugal with a small following hoping to gain Portuguese support for an allied attack on Castille in which Lancaster would lead the main assault from the north. Money was needed but there was much reluctance to grant it. The Lords were divided, and the parliamentary roll records a great argument (*grant disputison & altercacion*) among them.[2] After the recent disturbances, many lords were reluctant for Lancaster to leave the kingdom, and nothing was settled. Nor dared the Commons grant more taxation after the peasants' uprising and in the troubled state of the realm. All that the government obtained, after much discussion, was the continuance of the wool subsidy, and on 25 February the Parliament was dissolved after a life of over three months.

Richard was now fifteen, a married man and only a year younger than his father had been at Crécy. He had shown himself capable of action in a crisis and yet he was, or seemed to be, still under a kind of tutelage. His apparent willingness to make concessions over serfdom, and the gifts he was making to members of his household were equally out of key with the thinking of the established landed aristocracy. But in fact the tutelage was more apparent than real and the gifts seem to have been motivated more by political design than by a wish to enrich favourites for the sake of doing so. Richard's two new governors were wholly ineffective as such. Michael de la Pole, a loyal and honest man of considerable ability, had been a former

[1] *Rot. Parl.* Vol. III, p. 104.
[2] Ibid., p. 114.

supporter of Gaunt in Parliament, and may well have been chosen to guide the king by Gaunt, who understood that Richard must quickly grow up into the use of power. De la Pole, however, was soon drawn into the king's interest and became the leader of the court party. Although he was a banneret, de la Pole was disliked by the old nobility because of the speed with which he was rising beyond his family's mercantile origin. Arundel was a rough, aggressive, quarrelsome and jealous military man, and an instinctive opponent of royal authority. He had no inclination to win the liking of a king who, despite his personal courage, was not cut out by temperament and perhaps not by physical build to emulate the prowess of his warrior father on the battlefield.[1] Indeed, one of Richard's shortcomings in the eyes of the aristocracy was to be his preference for a peace policy which would have undoubtedly been the rational course in the wake of the collapse of Edward III's attempt to take the French throne. Arundel therefore quickly dropped out of any effective rôle at court. A greater and worse influence on the king was that of his two half-brothers, Thomas and John Holland, the sons of Joan, Princess of Wales, by an earlier marriage, both of them aggressive and arrogant men lacking political sensitivity.

Before the year was out there was evidence from the court to confirm parliamentary misgivings about the household. Richard was already beginning to build up his household as an instrument of government to the exclusion of the influence of the older nobility. There was no continual council to guide him, and there were no effective 'governors' to influence him in the way that the aristocracy thought he should go. Instead, Richard increasingly used the organization of the chamber, the king's private office within his household, as the instrument of his wishes, by-passing the normal channels of government. At first under the acting chamberlain Burley, and then under the hereditary chamberlain de Vere (after he came of age), the number of knights, esquires and yeomen of the chamber increased and they and others of the king's servants were lavishly rewarded with grants of lands and the custody of castles. They were employed on diplomacy abroad as well as government at home and the king used his private signet to give direct instruction to the chancellor who held the great seal, by-passing the privy seal which was the normal channel. To support all this, the finances of the chamber were enlarged and eventually the king's chapel also became an active secretariat. The baronage had always objected to what they regarded as the profligate alienation of estates and lands to

---

[1] The view that Richard, though not a coward, was probably a 'physical weakling' was advanced by his biographer, Anthony Steel, *Richard II* (1941) who devoted considerable attention to an attempt to analyse the king's psychological complexity.

courtiers, and the king was already indulging in the practice. But it was perhaps even more objectionable to the old aristocracy that he did so as part of a systematic attempt to build up the independent royal authority for the future. The clearer it became that Richard was establishing a new courtier nobility wholly dependent on himself, with de Vere and de la Pole its leading figures, the more the magnates and the baronage were put out. Once more they felt that they had lost the king's ear. The Commons too resented the use made of the power of patronage and the application of the king's revenue to pay adherents instead of to reduce debts. A further sign of Richard's self-emancipation came as early as July 1382, within months of the last Parliament's dissolution, when he dismissed le Scrope after a dispute about patronage, replacing him with the king's secretary, Robert Braybrook, who also became Bishop of London.[1]

Another short Parliament met between 7 May and 22 May 1382 at which the principal subject was money for Gaunt's Castillian enterprise.[2] He had already put forward to a great council in March a plan for an expedition to Gascony which the king would personally lead, and which could eventually be switched to Castille. The May Parliament was asked for financial support, and at the suggestion of the knights the question of raising the money was put to a group of merchants, whose names were listed in the rolls of Parliament, as being a matter particularly appertaining to them. But their conclusion was that the money could not be found to finance the expedition, and all that was granted was tunnage and poundage to protect the coast. Two provisions of political interest are contained in the statutes passed in this Parliament. The first was an enactment that every individual or representative of a community summoned to Parliament, whatever his rank from archbishop or duke downwards, who absented himself unexcused would be amerced or otherwise punished. The second was an act against those 'evil people' who were going from place to place simulating holiness but preaching heresy to 'the great peril of the realm'. They were to be arrested and forced to justify themselves 'according to the law and reason of Holy Church'.[3] This was the first English statute against heretics, but in the October Parliament of the same year it was repealed in response to a petition of the Commons on the grounds that it had been passed without their consent *(laquiel ne fuist unques assentu ne grante par les Communes, aves ce quo fuist parle de ce, fuist sanz assent de lour . . .)*. The petition and the king's assent

---

[1] For an account of Richard's policy of building up the household as an instrument of policy see Anthony Tuck, *Richard II and the English Nobility* (1973), especially Ch. 3.
[2] *Rot. Parl.* Vol. III, pp. 122–125.
[3] *Stat. R.* Vol. II, 5 Rich. II, st. 2 cls IV & V, pp. 25–26.

to the repeal is recorded on the Parliament roll but is not entered among the statutes.[1]

Gaunt's proposal for an expedition was again brought forward in a Parliament held in October of the same year.[2] In a speech by the Bishop of Hereford, on behalf of the king, it was now presented as a religious matter concerning the Great Schism. Two possibilities had been put by God before the nation, said the bishop. One was for a general crusade against the supporters of the 'Antipope' Clement, wherever they were. This would be led by Henry Despenser, the Bishop of Norwich, a military ecclesiastic who had energetically and ruthlessly put down the peasants' rising in East Anglia. The other possibility was an expedition against Castille, which would also count as a crusade because the incumbent king of that country, whom Gaunt sought to displace, was a supporter of Clement VII. In either case, Pope Urban had promised plenary remission of sins. Lords and Commons were asked to declare their wish on the two options, but were divided. The Commons favoured an expedition to Flanders where they had commercial interests, and where the Flemish people would be on their side against the French Clementists. The Lords, and apparently the king, favoured Lancaster's wish to go against Castille. The Commons this time gave a tenth and a fifteenth for the defence of the realm and left it to be applied as the king and the council saw fit. In this Parliament also a statute was enacted which marked the successful culmination of a campaign by the mayor of London against the unpopular fishmongers' monopoly which was accused of forcing up prices. The campaign was the work of the smaller gilds, under the leadership of the mayor, John of Northampton. The petitions of this Parliament included a 'bill against the fishmongers' and the resulting statute gave freedom of trade to outside fishmongers and excluded the London fishmongers.[3] One of the fishmongers, Walter Sybille, entered a protest in Parliament and was accused of complicity in the rebellion of 1381 and cleared. A year later there was a reaction against John of Northampton and his place was taken by Nicholas Brembre, a grocer, who was to become a supporter of the king and lose his life for it. Alongside the great questions of finance and politics, bread-and-butter decisions affecting the ordinary people continued to be an important part of the business of Parliament.

The Commons' grant in the Parliament of October 1382 would probably have been applied to an expedition to Spain if Cambridge's venture had not foundered in the meantime. Besides, a French army had defeated the

---

[1] *Rot. Parl.* Vol. III, p. 141.
[2] *Rot. Parl.* Vol. III, pp. 132–143.
[3] Ibid., p. 143; *Stat. R.* Vol. II, 6 Rich II st. I, cl. XI, pp. 28–29.

Flemings and killed the leader of the men of Ghent, Philip van Artevelt. The Burgundians had captured Bruges, and the English wool trade was threatened. Everything therefore now pointed to an English 'crusade' in Flanders which would also have the advantage from the Commons' point of view that it could largely be financed by the alms of the people without great cost to the government and taxpayers. But who should lead it: the king or the bishop? At a Parliament held in February 1383, the advice of the Commons, through their Speaker who was again Sir James Pickering, was that the bishop should lead it. They said that they were reluctant for the king or his royal uncles to leave the country in its still troubled social state and in view of renewed danger from Scotland.[1] In this they were again at odds with the Lords, who would have preferred Gaunt to lead the expedition. Besides, the Lords were not easy about sending an army to enforce the rights of the church against the king's French subjects, which might set an unfortunate precedent. Two of the bishop's supporters were his nephews, Philip and Peter Courtney, sons of the Earl of Devon, the first of whom at least was present in this Parliament as a knight of the shire. Norwich's case was won and Gaunt is said to have withdrawn from Parliament out of frustration.[2]

In this Parliament the Commons again returned to the matter of the household, now having much more cause for concern. They asked the king to so order it that he lived within his own resources, and to surround himself with honourable, wise and discreet men. But Richard now felt a great deal more independent. His household was proving an effective instrument of his will, he was sixteen, and in this Parliament the Commons lacked the support of the Lords, the two 'estates' being at odds over foreign and military policy.[3] Richard's reply to the Commons smacks of haughtiness. He would, he said, place around his persons sufficient people, 'Lords and others, as seems best to him, for his honour and profit. And as for the rule and government of his household, the king will, with the advice of the Lords and others of his council, make such good provision (*ordinance*) for it as shall seem best to him to do, saving his honour.'[4]

The crusade which Despenser led to Flanders in May was an utter disaster. It was seen on its way with superstitious enthusiasm as people bought indulgences to remit their sins and those of the dead, to the indignation of John Wyclif. But after a few initial successes, the campaign ended with a humiliating retreat before the advance of the French armies. Despenser was driven back to Gravellines and was forced to give the town

---

[1] *Rot. Parl.* Vol. III, p. 145.
[2] Westminster monk, printed as appendix to *Polychronicon Ranulph Higden*, IX, p. 18.
[3] *Rot. Parl.* Vol. III, p. 147.
[4] Ibid., p. 147.

up, sacking it first, before retreating to England. The English position in respect of its wool trade was worse than ever, and the 'crusade' was discredited by the brutal behaviour of ill-disciplined troops. In a Parliament which met in the autumn of 1383, the pressure from the Commons to impeach Despenser was such that de la Pole, whom Richard had now made chancellor, undertook the matter himself, the Commons playing no part in it.[1] This was a further attempt to wrest the process of impeachment from them, and the trial was virtually a dialogue between the accused and the accuser. Despenser lost his temporalities (though they were restored after two years) and some of his captains were also impeached and imprisoned for a short time. Despenser was given two trials, complaining after the first that he had been interrupted so often that he had omitted or had forgotten what he was going to say in his defence. The result, however, was the same and Despenser was told by the chancellor that the king could, if he chose, judge him as a temporal subject, seeing that he had behaved as such by waging war, but out of consideration of his estate would spare his person at present. The next impeachment would be that of de la Pole himself.

Politically, however, the more important feature of the Parliament which met in October 1383 was that the Lords had ceased to be at odds with the Commons about military policy, and now themselves attacked the Court.[2] It was a signpost to the future hostility of the aristocracy which was to be Richard's undoing. The king and chancellor were not only blamed for the failure of the expedition, though they had not initiated it. The Lords also asked the king to take personal responsibility for government (another hit at the household) while at the same time wanting him to take their advice, to which the king is said to have replied that he would take advice wherever he chose.[3] The Lords were also critical of de la Pole's policy of seeking peace, but as taxpayers the Commons found it more to their liking. The rumblings of a decaying foreign war policy were continuing when the next Parliament met at Salisbury, in the Bishop's Palace, in April 1384.[4] According to the Westminster chronicler this was the scene of a furious quarrel between the king and Arundel. The earl, who now as always took no trouble to conceal his contempt for Richard, told the king that the whole realm was in danger of destruction for lack of prudent government, and that unless it was succoured by appropriate remedies it would fall to pieces. It was virtually an accusation against the king personally, and on hearing it Richard 'burned' with anger and turned with fury to the earl. His face contorted, Richard said

[1] *Rot. Parl.* Vol. III, pp. 153–156.
[2] Ibid., pp. 149–165.
[3] Westminster monk (Higden) p. 26.
[4] *Rot. Parl.* Vol. III, pp. 166–174.

that Arundel lied in accusing him of bad government in the kingdom and concluded: 'Go to the devil!' (*vadas ad diabolum*). It was a manifestation of Richard's tendency to uncontrolled outbursts of rage which was one of his worst defects, and it fell to the duke of Lancaster to calm the two of them down by reinterpreting the earl's words more favourably.[1]

On the Parliament roll, a drama of a different sort is recorded. For at this Parliament de la Pole was himself impeached, being accused by a certain John Cavendish, a fishmonger, of corruption. The complaint was made first to the Commons, at a time when the Lords' committee was present, and the accusation was then repeated before all the prelates and Lords. De la Pole defended himself, was declared innocent and the fishmonger was imprisoned until he paid damages.[2] Despite the government's unpopularity, the Commons made a grant of half a tenth and half a fifteenth. But the Parliament ended in some haste, apparently as a result of another political scandal and quarrel. A Carmelite friar alleged to the king that Lancaster was plotting Richard's murder, and on the advice of the Lords the king committed the friar to prison while the charge was investigated. On the way to prison, the friar was intercepted by some nobles and knights, John Holland and also various Lancastrians among them, taken off and tortured to death. What underlay this episode is a mystery but it seems very probable that the hand behind it was de Vere's, who may have been making use of the old enmity between Gaunt and the friars. At all events, the matter precipitated a second outburst against Richard by one of his future enemies. His uncle Thomas of Woodstock, Earl of Buckingham, burst into the king's room in fury saying that he would kill anyone who accused his brother Lancaster of treason, with nobody excepted, not even the king himself.[3] Such was the atmosphere in which this sensational but inconsequential Parliament was hastily dissolved.

Relations between the king and Gaunt were now at their worst. Richard seems to have genuinely but wrongly suspected his uncle of plotting against him, and the king was thought to have been aware of a plot against Lancaster in the spring of 1385. For a time Gaunt withdrew to his own possessions in the north. In the political nation generally there was growing concern about Richard's character and court. His fitfulness and preoccupation with his grandeur did not encourage loyalty, nor did his urge from time to time to inflict verbal humiliation on those great men who displeased him. The nation itself also felt humiliated at the hands of the French and Scots. The general wish of the nobility was that Richard himself would now lead

---
[1] Westminster monk (Higden), op. cit., p. 33.
[2] *Rot. Parl.* Vol. III, pp. 168–170.
[3] St Albans Chronicle: Walsingham, *Historia Anglicana*, Vol. II, pp. 114–115.

an army against the French or the Scots and a Parliament which met in November 1384 was persuaded to make a generous grant of two fifteenths and two tenths on the understanding that 'the lord king intends to fight his enemies in person', this being 'his first expedition'. (Half was unconditional and the other half dependent on the war being prolonged.) In the event, it was to Scotland, not, as Parliament expected, to France that Richard set out at the head of a large force, the justification being that the French were again activating their Scottish alliance. On the way, a new cause of dissension arose when the violent John Holland, to the king's dismay and fury, killed the young heir of the Earl of Stafford in a quarrel and was forced to flee. Richard was accompanied on this expedition by his uncles and as soon as they were across the border he conferred the dukedom of Gloucester on Thomas of Woodstock, Earl of Buckingham, and the dukedom of York on the Earl of Cambridge. At the same time, the young Earl of March was recognized as heir presumptive, thus invalidating any idea of a Lancastrian succession. To the distaste of the old aristocracy, Richard also conferred the vacant earldom of Suffolk on de la Pole, who had already received much of the territory of the last earl.

The English successfully swept through the south of Scotland, sacking several abbeys on the way on the grounds that they were Clementist. Although a Scottish army had by-passed the invaders, making for England, Gaunt wished to continue the English raid northward in the manner of his old *chevauchées*. Richard, however, would not do so, perhaps because he had no taste for fighting and bloodshed, perhaps because he had more humanitarian instincts than most noblemen of the time, but quite probably also because he saw more clearly that such a raid would put the English army at risk for no solid purpose. Announcing his decision he characteristically said that Gaunt could go on if he wished but he himself was leading his army homeward. In fact, both of them returned to England, and shortly afterwards a great Portuguese victory over the Castillians, achieved with the help of a small force of English bowmen, prompted the disillusioned duke once more to revive his proposition that the best way of moving against the king of France was 'by way of Portugal'.

This plan was put to a Parliament which met at Westminster in October 1385. The idea was that if the English army could secure Castille, the pressure on the French king would force him to make a satisfactory peace. Parliament accepted this and granted a tenth and a half and a fifteenth and a half, partly to be used for Gaunt's campaign. But the reality was that domestic concerns loomed larger than foreign in the eyes of this Parliament. Once again there were complaints about the household and its cost, and a petition, or bill, of the Commons asked for an inquiry. They wished it to investigate royal extravagance, the misuse of patronage, and the misapplication of the king's ordinary revenues. Control over royal officials was also sought. The king felt obliged to agree to a committee of nine to survey his estate and to inquire into his revenue; this did not include the royal uncles or any of Richard's major critics but it did, presumably to his discomfiture, include a number of former officials, including le Scrope, who knew from practical experience what was happening. But all this only made the king more determined than ever to resist control and he was capable of doing so. The parliamentary ordinance setting up the committee was ignored and it never met.[1] Richard dealt with the matter in the spirit of the reply he gave to one of the Commons' petitions asking for an annual review into the royal household by the chancellor and treasurer: 'The king will do as he pleases' (*le Roi voet faire quant lui plerra*).[2]

This Parliament (for which the Parliament roll oddly reverts to Latin, except for the schedule attached to the Commons grant, which, like the petitions, is in French) was also marked by the great ceremony of confirming the new royal dukedoms. The king personally girded each duke and put on his head the cap and coronet, and also girded Suffolk. He then affronted the old nobility once more by conferring on de Vere the rank of Marquis of Dublin, the first use in England of this title which gave him precedence over all other earls. With it went a grant of all royal lands in Ireland, where he would virtually be a viceroy. This was the first Parliament to which Richard's eventual supplanter was called; Gaunt's son Henry Bolingbroke was summoned as Earl of Derby, one of his father's titles.

In the following summer of 1386, Gaunt set out for Portugal. He did not return until 1389, after the first great crisis of his nephew's reign. No doubt it was with relief that the suspicious king saw him go, yet if he had remained in England that crisis might have been prevented. Gaunt's departure was mistimed in another sense too, for it coincided with the gathering of a great French army at Sluys which was expected to invade Britain, though the attempt was never made. The fear of invasion gave power to Richard's opponents, above all to Thomas of Woodstock who had been freed by his brother's departure to take the lead against the king. Thomas had many grievances, not only about the manner of the king's government through a court nobility instead of with due regard to the old nobility, but also arising from what he felt to be his lack of land commensurate with his dignity, and his reliance on annuities. The territorial gifts to de Vere and Suffolk had

---

[1] *Rot. Parl.* Vol. III, pp. 213–214; Anthony Tuck, *Richard II and the English Nobility* (1973) pp. 99–101. J. J. N. Palmer, 'The Impeachment of Michael de la Pole in 1386,' *B.I.H.R.* XLIII (1970), p. 100ff.

[2] *Rot Parl.* Vol. III, p. 213.

intensified his resentment and he had begun to woo the Commons to his cause against the king.[1]

Richard now stood on the brink of a political explosion, the power of which he cannot have foreseen when a Parliament next met on 1 October.[2] Even so, the extent to which he was being criticized for his attitude to military matters was revealed in Suffolk's opening statement. It began with a reference to the king's decision, by 'his own volition and courage' to cross the sea 'personally with royal power' (*en propre personne, ove Roiale poair*). He had called a great council at Oxford to discuss this, but, said the chancellor, the council dared not assent without Parliament. It would be better to defend the realm abroad than at home, Suffolk continued, and yet some had been saying that the king did not wish 'to go in his own person' (*travailler en propre personne*). The king was determined 'to avoid that slander' (*eschuire tielle esclandre*), and therefore an aid was needed. All grievances would be redressed. What exactly happened in Parliament after Suffolk's opening speech is unclear. The business of the next two weeks is not officially recorded, and it may be that pressure was being put on the king in the private deliberations of the peers in the White Chamber, of which the rolls usually had nothing to say. The Commons, presumably, simply waited. Argument between the king and the magnates may well have been directed at the amount of money wanted, rumoured to be very large, as well as at the insistence of the opposition Lords that something must be done about the king's ministers and household. What is certain is that the magnates were aroused to intense anger when, on 13 October, Richard raised de Vere to a dukedom, a rank hitherto reserved to members of the royal family, save for the ill-fated precedent of Gaveston. De Vere had only a little distant royal blood on his mother's side, but Richard chose to describe him as his kinsman. The royal dukes were among those who witnessed the charter of his appointment, but the parliamentary roll records no ceremony in Parliament. Soon afterwards, Richard withdrew to Eltham and stayed there for much of the Parliament. The reason is not recorded, but it may well have been an ill-judged attempt to resist the attack which he knew was to be made on Suffolk. Richard might, of course, have dissolved Parliament, but financial need and fear of invasion presumably prevented him. His departure was a final slight which aroused the magnates of the realm to furious defiance.

For what happened next we are largely reliant on the best informed

[1] For an account of Thomas of Woodstock's financial and other grievances, see A. Tuck, op. cit., pp. 101–104.
[2] *Rot. Parl.* Vol. III, pp. 215–224.

chronicler of these events.[1] The magnates and Commons sent to the king to say that chancellor and treasurer should be removed from office and that the chancellor in particular must go as they had 'such business to do with Michael de la Pole' that they could not transact with him so long as he remained in the chancellor's office: in other words they intended to impeach him, and presumably at this stage saw some difficulty in doing so as long as he was one of the king's ministers. The furious king told them to say no more and go on with the business of Parliament, adding that he would not remove the meanest scullion from his kitchen at their request. But the Lords and Commons sent back the reply that they would proceed with no business in Parliament, 'nor speed forward the smallest point' until the king showed himself in Parliament and removed Suffolk from office. Richard then ordered them to send him forty of the most experienced knights from the Commons to explain to him what was wanted, but this was refused, allegedly for fear of a plot which would endanger their lives. Instead, they sent to Eltham Thomas of Woodstock, Duke of Gloucester, and Thomas Arundel, Bishop of Ely and brother of the earl, 'on behalf of Lords and Commons'. They carried with them a most extraordinary message.

After wishing the king success against the enemy and a 'most worthy bond of peace' with his subjects, they told him, on his subjects' behalf, that there was 'an old law and a praiseworthy and approved custom... that our king is to call the lords and magnates of the realm and the commons once a year to his Parliament, as to the highest court of the whole realm', to do justice to all, reform the errors of the kingdom and take wise counsel. But there was also another old law which said that if the king unnecessarily, and by 'his uncontrolled whim', absented himself for forty days, they could all lawfully return to their own homes without permission. Richard was then said to have told them that it seemed that the people and commons intended to rise up against him, 'and in view of such an attack it does not seem that we can do better than call on our cousin the king of France, to ask his counsel and aid against the plotters, and submit ourselves to him rather than surrender to our own subjects'. On the face of it this is likely to have been a piece of deliberate misinformation from the opposition magnates. Nevertheless, it has to be taken into account that the draft of a treaty Richard made with the French in 1396 did contain a provision for French assistance against any who owed him obedience, though this probably referred to any rebellions in Gascony or another peasants' uprising.[2] If, indeed, Richard said anything of this sort to Gloucester and Thomas Arundel it is hard to

[1] *Chronicon Henrici Knighton*, II, pp. 215ff. Extracts of the ultimatum are printed in translation in *E.H.D.*, Vol. IV, pp. 150–152.
[2] See p. 423.

overstate its folly. For the King of England openly to threaten to call in the hereditary enemy who occupied the French throne to which he himself laid claim was to invite repudiation. Indeed, the two emissaries are said to have replied that this was 'no sane plan' since the French king would despoil rather than help him. Then after reminding him of the struggles of his grandfather and father against the French, and of the treasure poured out by the Commons for the war to their own impoverishment they issued a startling threat.

'There remains one thing more for us to show to you on behalf of your people. It is permitted by another ancient law – and one put into practice not long ago, unfortunately – that if the king by malignant counsel or foolish contumacy or contempt or wanton will or for any other improper reason, should alienate himself from his people, and should be unwilling to be governed and guided by the laws and statutes and laudable ordinances with the wholesome counsel of the lords and magnates of the realm, but rashly in his insane counsels exercise his own peculiar desire, then it is lawful for them, with the common consent of the people of the realm to pluck down the king from his royal throne, and to raise to the throne in his stead some very near kinsman of the royal house . . .' Whether or not Richard had provoked it as this account alleged, there can be little doubt that the threat of deposition and the grisly reminder of the fate of Richard's great-grandfather Edward II was made. Not the least extraordinary is that it should have been uttered by his own uncle, who thus struck such at blow at the theory of the legitimacy of kinship that it echoed through the remainder of our medieval history. The effect, as the chronicler put it, was to recall the king from anger. Richard promised to come to Parliament in three days and when he did, Suffolk was deprived of the chancellorship and Thomas Arundel was appointed in his place. The Bishop of Durham was replaced as treasurer by the Bishop of Hereford.

At this point the Parliament roll begins to record the proceedings. 'The Commons, together and with one accord assembled, came before the king, prelates and lords in the Parliament chamber (the first time that the Painted Chamber is so described) with grave complaints against Michael de la Pole, earl of Suffolk . . . and accused him by word of mouth on certain charges . . .'[1] Some of them, which related to the conduct of the war and supplies, were eventually dropped, and the main attack was on Suffolk's use of his powers as chancellor. In fact there was no real case against him; he argued well in his own defence and le Scrope, himself an opponent of royal extravagance, and Suffolk's brother-in-law, spoke of his past service to the realm. In the end, he was found guilty only of technical charges of fraud in

[1] *Rot. Parl.* Vol. III, p. 216.

relation to grants and maladministration. He was sentenced to forfeiture of estates granted to him, and to be imprisoned at the king's pleasure. But Suffolk retained his earldom. The Parliament then resumed the attack on the royal household, appointing a continual council to govern for a year. This included Gloucester, the two Arundels, and a number of moderates, among whom were the ageing William of Wykeham and le Scrope. The council was to control the great and privy seals, and the exchequer; to reform the government; put an end to Richard's reliance on the officials of his household; and deal with the enemy. A grant of a tenth and a fifteenth was made dependent on the appointment of this council, which would have been virtually in the position of a council of regency, had it functioned. But the king's determination not to co-operate with it was made clear just before the dissolution on 28 November, when Richard declared in full Parliament 'by his own mouth' that nothing that had been done in this Parliament should prejudice himself or the crown and that his prerogative and the liberties of the crown were reserved.[1]

It is impossible to think clearly about the reign of Richard II without constantly reminding oneself of his age. The king was still not quite twenty at the time of his humiliation in the Parliament of 1386, and when all allowance is made for the earlier maturity of the men and women of his time, the fact remains that the impulsiveness and inexperience of youth must very largely have been responsible for the way in which he had damaged his own cause, and had played into his opponents' hands. That he still intended to go his own way was quickly evident. He remitted Suffolk's fine and brought him to Windsor for Christmas. During the 1386 Parliament, Richard had given an undertaking to choose a new steward of the household by the new council's advice, but he now appointed one of the knights of his household, Sir John Beauchamp of Holt, on his own responsibility. In the following October Beauchamp was the recipient of the first of a new type of peerage. A patent issued by the king made him a 'peer and baron' of the realm for his past and future services, with the title Lord Beauchamp, Baron of Kidderminster, which was to descend to his male heirs. In the past a baronage denoted that its holder already held lands as a tenant-in-chief, in consequence of which he might be summoned to Parliament, creating a prescriptive right to a peerage for his descendants. Richard had now made a baronage a dignity in itself, as a dukedom or earldom was. The title was unrelated to a grant or possession of land, and it gave the recipient and his male descendants the right to a place in Parliament.

In February, Richard left Windsor, accompanied by de la Pole, de Vere, Burley, Beauchamp, and the chief justice of the king's bench, Sir Robert

---

[1] *Rot. Parl.* Vol. III, p. 224.

Tresilian, and others of his court, staying away from the capital for nearly a year. The courtiers who went with him were tantamount to a rival council to the one that had been established in Parliament. Yet Richard continued to send some instructions to the privy seal, authenticated by his signet, to be transmitted to the chancellor, and these were obeyed. The administration still had some need of the king to function properly. In March an English fleet with Arundel as admiral achieved a magnificent and popular victory in the channel over a combined French, Spanish and Flemish force, after which the English had some successes in raiding and plundering France. But Richard and his court still stayed away from Westminster, spending much of the summer in the midlands and Welsh marches. They were busy building up a party of adherents (they won over Archbishop Neville of York when visiting that city), seeking the agreement of sheriffs to raise forces in their shire if necessary, and trying to encourage them to influence the elections to the next Parliament in Richard's interest, apparently without success since the king was said to have been told that the 'Commons favoured the Lords'.

Yet on the theory of his rights, Richard was able to obtain weighty reassurance. At meetings held at Shrewsbury and then at Nottingham a group of judges, including the chief justice, Tresilian, was asked for their opinion about the legality of the commission that had been given to the new council in the previous Parliament. At Nottingham, five of them found that the council had been given an unlawful commission, which was contrary to the prerogative, and that those who had been responsible for some of the acts in question deserved punishment as traitors. It was also their opinion that the direction of proceedings in Parliament was for the king, and that Lords and Commons had no legal right to insist on discussion of their own business, (that is, their grievances) before dealing with the king's business (that is, granting him money). They further said that the Lords and Commons had no right to remove his servants, or impeach them without his consent. Finally, they found that some who had allegedly raised the 'statute' of Edward II's deposition (there was, in fact, no such statute) were traitors, and that the sentence against Suffolk was wrong and revocable. The archbishop of York and Richard's other supporters attested this manifesto.

When they were later brought to trial by the king's enemies, the judges were to plead that they had acted under duress. In fact, there is no evidence or likelihood of this, and Richard was in no position to coerce the judges. Their findings were in essentials a correct statement of the constitution as it was formally understood, and they had given a true opinion to questions of law which Richard was entitled to ask. The prerogative had indeed been damaged by the appointment of the council of 1386–87; it had always been the right of the king to summon and dissolve Parliaments and to order their business, and impeachment was still a questionable procedure. Successive kings had also managed to maintain their right, against parliamentary encroachment, to choose their councillors, who were also responsible to them. The judges' least convincing finding was that grants of money by the Commons should precede redress of grievances. The history of Parliament for the previous hundred years shows that taxation grants were not automatic and could in practice be conditional, though not always in form. The judges' answers were an important legal statement by high judicial authority. Politically, however, it was dangerous to make public at this moment so uncompromising an assertion of royal power. It was particularly inadvisable to reintroduce into politics the concept of treason, with its hideous penalties, after this had been so successfully kept out of the politics of the preceding thirty years. Wisely Richard decided to keep the judges' legal findings secret for the time being.[1]

On 10 November, Richard returned to London where he was given an enthusiastic reception by the mayor and the Londoners. The year's life of the council which had been forced on him was over. Both Gloucester and Arundel had, however, refused to meet him on the grounds that their enemies were all about him. Instead, they raised their own army which was gathered at Harringay Park, to the north of London, from where they moved to Waltham Cross. Their supporters also put about all kinds of unconvincing stories about Richard's intentions, of which one of the more implausible was that he had it in mind to sell Calais to the French in exchange for help against his own subjects. The judges' answers had been betrayed to Gloucester and his associates, who were determined to destroy the court party.

A number of the commissioners of 1386 then went to Waltham Cross in search of a settlement, which both they and Richard desired. There Gloucester, Arundel and the earl of Warwick, who had now joined forces with them, formally and in writing 'appealed' (that is, accused) the archbishop of York, de Vere, Suffolk, Tresilian and the merchant knight, Sir Nicholas Brembre, of the crime of 'lese-majesty'. The charge was presumably expressed in this form because the offences with which they intended to accuse these five 'lords of straw' (as the account of the contemporary Thomas Favent describes them) could not be covered by the law of treason as restricted by the statute of 1352. The three appellants then accepted an invitation to come to Westminster to meet the king, who

[1] The questions to and answers by the judges are printed in *Rot. Parl.* Vol. III, p. 233, and also in Higden, Vol. IX, pp. 98–102. See especially: S. B. Chrimes, 'Richard II's Questions to the Judges, 1387', *Law Quar. Review* lxxii (1956), pp. 365–90.

sought a peaceful agreement principally to save his friends. The lords appellant were received with much formal courtesy by the king in Westminster Hall on 17 November, and their fears were explained in a speech by le Scrope, acting as a mediator. They demanded that those they accused should be arrested and tried by common law, if a procedure could be found, in the next Parliament.

To gain time, Richard agreed to the summons of a Parliament eleven weeks later, on 3 February, and to the trial of the accused men before it. The king's hope was either that he would have re-established his power by then or that his friends and supporters would have escaped. The 'appellants' also needed time to prepare their case and so the arrangement was accepted. The encounter ended in ostensible good humour, and the appellant lords went to drink with the king in his room. But immediately afterwards, the archbishop fled disguised as a priest to his archdiocese, de Vere got away to the north west, and Suffolk escaped to France twice, having been sent back on the first occasion by the governor of Calais. Tresilian hid at Westminster and only Brembre was arrested. Unable to bring out London on his behalf, Richard issued writs on 17 December summoning Parliament. This time an extra qualification was required in those elected. They were to be 'indifferent to recent disputes', a stipulation reflecting the king's fear that his opponents would pack the Commons.[1] Later Richard was forced to issue new writs without this provision. In the meantime, de Vere was gathering an army in the north with which he marched on London. Some of the magnates are said to have spoken of deposing the king but Warwick would not hear of it. Instead, the appellants, who now included Henry Bolingbroke, son of the absent Gaunt, and Thomas Mowbray, Earl of Nottingham, a former friend of the king, mustered their forces against de Vere. He was intercepted and trapped at Radcot Bridge near Oxford in December, with Derby in front of him and Gloucester in the rear. The situation was hopeless and the Duke of Ireland fled in the concealment of a fog, subsequently escaping abroad. His army disintegrated and Richard took shelter in the Tower. He was at the mercy of his enemies who marched to London with their forces after Christmas and set about winning the Londoners over by propaganda. The appellants then entered the Tower with 500 men, and are said to have threatened Richard with deposition and replacement by his heir, who was now of full age. They forced him to agree to the arrest of others of his supporters including Simon Burley, the steward Sir John Beauchamp and the judges. The royal household was forcibly purged and several were arrested.

On 3 February, 1388 the Parliament appropriately known to history as

[1] *Dignity of a Peer*, Vol. IV, p. 725.

the Merciless assembled in the White Hall at Westminster. The magnates went with a large force, and the course of the proceedings was dictated by the fact that the king was an isolated figure acting under duress. To the king's right were the prelates, on his left the lay lords, with Bishop Arundel on the woolsack in front of the throne. Every corner of the hall was crowded. It was an unusually well attended Parliament but there is no evidence of systematic packing, which was probably unnecessary since the majority of knights shared the same attitudes as the magnates. The scene is described by an eyewitness, Thomas Favent, who was probably a clerk.[1] The five appellants 'with a numerous throng', entered the hall together, 'arm in arm, wearing cloth of gold, and after staring at the king, bent the knee to him in salutation'. The chancellor opened the proceedings with a general statement of the causes of summons, of which the most important was how the great dissension in the realm resulting from the 'lack of good government' should be brought to an end.[2] The parliamentary roll also records that Gloucester denied rumours that he had sought to depose the king, and usurp the throne, which was presumably a reference to whatever threats had been directed at Richard in the Tower. This denial was accepted by the king, and Gloucester, according to Favent, with his associates, thanked him 'bending his knees low'. The clerk of the crown, one Geoffrey Martin, then stood and read the articles of appeal which lasted for two hours; these (as Favent sensationally put it) contained so many 'horrible' revelations that the faces of many were 'swollen with tears'.

It was then proclaimed that the accused should appear, and when they did not, the appellants demanded judgement by default. The king now withdrew with other lords and justices to consider, not the judgement, but whether the appeal was legal. The common lawyers' advice was that the appeal was invalid under common and civil law. The appellants replied that in so high a crime, touching the person of the king and the estate of the realm, perpetrated by peers and others, 'the process shall not be taken anywhere except in Parliament, nor by any other law except the law and course of Parliament'. Judgement was a matter for the Lords with the assent of the king, and lower courts existed 'only to execute the ancient laws and customs of the realm and the ordinances and establishment of Parliament'.[3] With these ringing words, a group of conservatives who had adopted revolutionary methods, and who were about to inflict monumental

---

[1] T. Favent, *Historia . . . Mirabilis Parliamenti*, ed. M. McKisack (Camden Miscellany Vol. XIV). Extracts are given in (Latin) Chrimes and Brown, op. cit., pp. 140–143, and (English) *EHD*. Vol. IV, pp. 161–163.
[2] *Rot. Parl.* Vol. III, p. 228.
[3] Ibid., p. 236.

injustice on largely innocent men, manipulated to their purpose the respectable doctrine of parliamentary supremacy as the fount of law-making. An incidental effect was that the law of 1352 on treason was utterly flouted.

The clergy now withdrew because they would not be present at a process leading to a judgement of blood, the Commons busied themselves in their chapter house, and the Lords spent ten days investigating the charges, the essence of which was contained in the first of them, namely that the accused had exploited the youth of the king in order to accroach royal power and that they had made the king follow their counsel. Among other charges against them were alleged corrupt practices, persuading the king to establish a large retinue, trying to keep the king from attending Parliament, seeking the appointment of sheriffs who would pack Parliament, plots against the appellants, neglect of the defence of the realm and de Vere's recourse to military operations. Tresilian was charged on account of the answers, printed in the parliamentary roll, which the judges had given to the king's questions. Suffolk, de Vere, the Archbishop of York, and Tresilian were all found guilty of treason and, except for the archbishop, were condemned to its full penalties, but none of them was present. Only Sir Nicholas Brembre was available to deny guilt, and he offered as a knight to defend himself by battle, which was refused him. At this point the Commons seem to have intervened to state that they themselves would have accused Brembre, presumably by impeachment, if the appellants had not already acted. But the king was still trying to save Brembre, and appears to have intervened in his defence, which aroused the appellants to fury. At one point they and all the lords, with many knights and squires, are said to have 'thrown down their gloves before the king in full Parliament . . . to the number of 305 gloves', wagering that Brembre was a traitor.

A committee of twelve peers, including the duke of York, then examined Brembre's case and found him not guilty of anything deserving death. At this point, the former chief justice Tresilian was discovered in hiding at Westminster, and was dragged on a hurdle to a horrifying death at Tyburn. To make sure that Brembre suffered likewise, the appellants then brought external pressure to bear on the moderate lords. They first called on representatives of the gilds to give an opinion on Brembre's guilt, but this did not produce the answer wanted. So they then put the question to the mayor, aldermen and recorder of the city, who said they thought Brembre was more likely than not to be guilty, the recorder adding that anyone who concealed treason deserved death. This seems to have swayed the Lords who thereupon found Brembre guilty and sentenced him to death. An account of this appalling way of reaching a verdict, however, is omitted from the parlimentary roll, which is a partisan document adapted to suit the interest of the victorious party, but the events are described by Favent and the Westminster chronicler. Brembre followed Tresilian to Tyburn.

That, however, was not the end of it. A number of smaller offenders was impeached and executed. So in March were four of the knights of Richard's chamber, Burley, the recently enobled Beauchamp, Berners and Salisbury. All were accused of exploiting the king's youth and turning him against his natural counsellors. Additional charges against Burley included helping de Vere to escape and encouraging Richard's relationship with de Vere. Burley was an honourable and an honoured man, a knight of the garter with a great reputation for chivalry. Richard tried to save them and at his request the queen went on her knees to beseech Gloucester to spare Burley. The Duke of York also intervened on his behalf, and even Derby and Nottingham did so. But Gloucester, Arundel, Warwick and the Commons were obdurate. The only concession made was that Burley, Beauchamp and Berners were beheaded instead of being subjected to the full penalties for treason. Salisbury, accused of conducting the alleged treasonable negotiations with France, which almost certainly never took place, suffered in full. The remaining judges were also found guilty but were pardoned on the petition of the prelates, after they had pleaded guilty but claimed to have acted under compulsion. The Pope was persuaded to move the Archbishop of York to St Andrews, a 'Clementist' See and therefore a purely nominal appointment.

So one of the most discreditable and vindictive Parliaments in English history moved towards its end. The Commons demonstrated their pliancy to the prevailing power by granting £20,000 to the appellants for their great expenses in the business of rescuing the realm. Provisions were made for the king to have a nominated council, for the offices of state to be investigated and for Bohemians to be dismissed from the queen's household. Finally, in response to a Commons' petition, it was enacted that any persons seeking to reverse the 'appeals, prosecutions, accusations, process, judgements and execution' of this Parliament were to be judged and executed as traitors. Yet, it was also petitioned that these processes and judgements were not to be held as examples or as a precedent for the future. Henceforth, the treason act of 1352 was to stand. Thus Parliament made a mockery of its own position as guardian of law, by inventing a 'law' of treason, and a process for implementing it, which were valid for one Parliament only. (It has, however, to be recognized that there was an unusual flexibility about the act of 1352 which provided that, since cases might arise of an unforeseeable sort, that might or might not be treason, judgement should be stayed until the matter was referred to the king in Parliament to determine whether it was treason or not. This is the only known case of a Parliament reserving power to interpret a statute.)

The case has been argued that the appellants were not simply vindictive and unjust men lacking any real plan, principle or constitutional logic.[1] Instead, it has been claimed for them that what they did in the Merciless Parliament was the logical continuance of their intentions in 1386, and that the appellants were now answering Richard's attempts at personal governent with a clearly envisaged notion of parliamentary supremacy. On this analysis, they intended to elevate Parliament to the high court of the realm, and were searching for a new law of Parliament, with the Lords acting as the judges of high crimes affecting the king and the realm. As Professor Wilkinson saw it, even though Brembre was executed for political reasons and 'without absolute justice', he did have a formal trial, charges and witnesses were heard and there was a committee of investigation. Therefore, although his trial did not follow the forms of common law, it followed the law and procedure of Parliament, according to which Brembre got justice in the high court of the realm. All this has been construed from the appellants' declaration of the supreme right of Parliament to make and administer law over all lower courts. The conclusion drawn is that the appellants simply anticipated the theory of the unqualified sovereignty of Parliament.

There can be no ultimate determination of what was in the minds of Gloucester and his associates and historians will continue to debate the matter. It may well be that the appellants envisaged a sovereign Parliament as their instrument against a personal monarchy which they had despaired of controlling in any other way. Yet in reality they used Parliament to impose the will of a dominant party by overriding existing laws and forms of law to secure their ends. Behind their actions lay the sanction of force, that of their soldiers outside. It is hard to believe that this was justice, or that the injustice suffered by those condemned for crimes they had not committed can be justified by the right of a sovereign and omnicompetent Parliament to improvise its legal processes and its law to suit its wish to condemn political opponents. In any case, the enactment in the Merciless Parliament that its legal processes and judgements set no precedents undermines the assertion that Gloucester, Arundel and their friends had a clear idea of establishing a new law of Parliament, one which enabled the

---

[1] The case for the lords appellant as having a coherent political plan, and a concept of the supremacy of Parliament is most strongly argued by B. Wilkinson, *Constitutional History of Medieval England, 1216–1399*, Vol. II, Ch. 8. See also T. F. Tout, *Chapters in Administrative History*, Vol. III, Ch. 10.

Lords to act as a court of law in such cases without recourse to anything like the future bills of attainder. Moreover, according to evidence from several chronicles, the appellants seem at first to have intended that the accusations should be dealt with under civil law in the court of chivalry, presided over by the Constable of England, who was none other than Gloucester himself, and the Marshal. If this was so, it hardly supports the suggestion that they had begun with a wish to use the case to demonstrate parliamentary sovereignty. The difficulty was that although the process of appeal which they had adopted was one known only to the court of chivalry and not to the common law, the crimes alleged were not within the court of chivalry's jurisdiction, but were actionable under the common law.

It was on these grounds that when the new judges (who had taken the place of those now on trial) and other lawyers were asked at the outset to advise 'the Lords of Parliament' how to proceed, they answered that the appeal was not made according to either the civil or common law. The appellants were then quick to turn this finding to their advantage and 'the Lords of Parliament' (in effect the appellants and their party) promptly made their declaration that England never was, or should be, ruled by civil law, that the common law courts were there simply to execute the common law and that of Parliament, and that the process of appeal was 'good and effectual according to the laws and course of Parliament'. Historically it was nothing of the sort; the appellants simply improvised a process in Parliament which would secure the end they wanted. Indeed, there is evidence from some of the chronicles that it was Richard himself who had originally proposed Parliament for Suffolk's trial.[1]

The question of the appellants' thinking is not one which is likely to be answerable, but it is certainly far from clear that they had originally planned the demonstration of the sovereignty of Parliament they found it convenient to proclaim. That the lords appellant saw Parliament as an instrument for controlling the crown in their interest is clear enough. In a somewhat twisted sense they anticipated the latter idea of the sovereignty of Parliament. They were fighting against personal kingship and for the old idea of consultation with their own group. Yet they were willing for Parliament to act in their interest as capriciously as any absolute monarch unfettered by law. In this they were out of tune with the better spirit and tradition of parliamentary sovereignty, which is that Parliament (of which the sovereign is a part) must abide by its own law. The Merciless Parliament acted as a revolutionary tribunal. It is a reminder that the most valuable of

---

[1] See especially M. V. Clarke, 'Forfeitures and Treason in 1388', in *Fourteenth Century Studies* (1937).

institutions can be perverted to injustice. These events, and the three men most responsible for them, Gloucester, Arundel and Warwick, had also sown seeds of a terrible future. A king who, for all his faults of immaturity and wilfulness, had been neither brutal nor unjust, and whose disposition was to be loyal to his friends, was obliged to watch helplessly the destruction of those whose only real crime had been loyalty to him. Before it dispersed Richard entertained the Parliament at Kennington and after high mass at Westminster Abbey on 3 June, the Lords and Commons renewed their oaths to him, and he promised to be 'a good lord and king in future'. But who can doubt or wonder that he bided his time in the hope of vengeance?[1]

III

Like the Ordainers, the Lords Appellant were better fitted to take power by force than to make constructive use of it. They were simply revolutionary conservatives who had engineered a *coup d'état* to overthrow the party in power with no other object in mind than to force the king to take their advice and to destroy the influence of his own adherents. They did not even possess a constitutional document to provide them with terms of reference. Their motives were instinctive and personal rather than systematic. It was disagreeable to be subject to the wilfulness of a boy who often seemed incapable of controlling his emotions and who rated his own grandeur highly while disregarding theirs. They had also become unused to having to deal with an active king. For the fifteen years of Edward III's senility and Richard's minority, the royal power had been in roving commission, oscillating between this or that competing group, and subject to the checks and balances of political rivalries. As Richard had built up his personal power, however, governing through councillors and officials of his own choice, the magnates and barons had found themselves confronted with the

---

[1] The principal sources for the Merciless Parliament are *Rot. Parl.* Vol. III, pp. 228–252; *Stat. R.* Vol. II, 11 Ric 2, pp. 43–55 (the statute passed to cover the proceedings of this Parliament); Thomas Favent, ed. M. McKisack, Camd. Misc. XIV, 1926; The Monk of Westminster (Higden), *Polychronicon*, Vol. IX; and Thomas Walsingham, *Chronica Monasterii*, the last of which is prejudiced for the appellants. Useful selections from these sources are in Chrimes and Brown, *Select Documents*, pp. 139–151; *E.H.D.* Vol. IV pp. 154–163, (trans.); and B. Wilkinson, *Const. Hist. 1216–1399*, Vol. II, Ch. 8. For short accounts see M. McKisack, *The Fourteenth Century*, pp. 454–461, and A. Steel, op. cit., Ch. VI and A. Tuck, op. cit., Ch. 5.

prospect of a new centralized personal monarchy in which there was little room for their political influence, though their territorial power was greater than ever.

Their immediate end was satisfied when they managed, by the rope, the block, and wholesale dismissals, to root up the former court party and take its place on the king's council. Gloucester himself was a member of it and at first he probably provided such direction of policy as there was. Arundel also sat on the council when he was at hand, but for the most part he was engaged in naval activities against the French, and especially in organizing a raid on La Rochelle. Thomas Arundel, now Archbishop of York, remained chancellor, the office he had held since Suffolk's dismissal. Warwick, as well as sitting on the council, was a member of a small committee, including Richard le Scrope, which was set up to advise and govern the king. But there was little change of policy because there was little agreement among the appellants themselves about what needed to be done.

At first there was some attempt to pursue a more active campaign against France, but the appellants were soon drawn towards a policy of seeking negotiations for a peace, although this had been one of the principal charges for which they had condemned Suffolk and their other fallen predecessors. A principal reason for their change of attitude was the worsening of the threat from Scotland. The appellants' policy towards that country was feeble. They had neither persuaded the Scots to renew the truce which expired in the summer of 1388 nor had they made proper preparations to defend the border. The result was a startling defeat at Otterburn in August, when a raiding Scottish army took prisoner the younger Henry Percy, one of the most active defenders of the northern border. Such was the danger that there was every incentive to seek terms with France. For many years ahead, the north remained unsafe, but at the end of 1388 a short truce was arranged with France which was periodically renewed throughout the reign until a truce for twenty-eight years was agreed in 1396. War with France ceased to be an instrument of policy under Richard II.

The appellants were neither the first nor the last victorious party in politics to continue the policies for which it had condemned and brought down its predecessors. Nevertheless, their conduct both of foreign and domestic affairs disposes of any claim that they were political innovators. A Parliament which met at Cambridge in the autumn of 1388, the only one during their period of power, showed how lacking the new administration was in initiatives and constructive political thinking. It also provides evidence that the Commons were already discontented with the appellants' use of their power. Differences were revealed between the Commons and Lords which showed that their unity in the Merciless Parliament had been dissolved. This gave Richard the chance to take a certain initiative as arbiter, and to adopt an independent position. The Cambridge Parliament must have revealed to him much more clearly the opportunities that were gathering for him to resume power, and how to go about it.

The Parliament met on 7 October at Barnwell Priory. Richard presided over it as he had done, formally, over council meetings since the destruction of his former friends. He seemed acquiescent in all that had happened. There was no other posture he could adopt. All his friends were dead or in exile: Burley, the man he had relied on since childhood; de Vere, his closest friend; Suffolk, his trusted and able chief minister. His household and administration had been purged of the men of his choice. Emotionally shattered and isolated, he could only dissemble and wait for the wind to change. Though he could not act against the appellants, they could not harm him so long as he was cautious. He possessed one enormous advantage; the presumption of the Merciless Parliament that there was no criticism of him personally. If Gloucester had done anything during the Merciless Parliament to encourage the opinion that he sought to take the crown from Richard, the appellants' cause would have been broken. Every effort had therefore been devoted to making good the claim that the attack on Richard's servants was not an attack on the king himself. The essence of the charges against his servants had been that they had exploited his youth and that he was the innocent victim of bad councillors. Since he was now twenty-one, that claim was becoming increasingly unconvincing, but the more reasonably the king now behaved, the more unreasonable it would seem that an innocent king of full age could be kept under tutelage. All that was needed was a little time in which Richard could demonstrate his responsibility. It would then be impossible to resist his resumption of power when the moment came. For the time, therefore, he showed no resentment, taking part in court festivities and hunting as the occasion required, which was later to be construed by his enemies as a sign of callousness.

There is no official record of the Cambridge Parliament, the roll having been lost. The work of the Parliament has, however, been reconstructed by relating a detailed account of the Commons' petitions which is provided by the chronicle of the Monk of Westminster, with the enrolled statute of Cambridge containing the enactments of the Parliament. Many of the enactments are based on the petitions, but not all the petitions were accepted. On the other hand, some of the enactments do not appear in the petitions, having emanated from the Lords, or from the council itself. A detailed record has survived of the expenses of four representatives of London at this Parliament, showing how much preparation was necessary for those attending. Among much else is included 'timber and carpentry, tilers, and daubers, in preparing the house for their lodging, as well the chambers as the hall, buttery, kitchen, and stables for the horses; and for making stools and forms throughout, and for carting out the rubbish, such house being quite ruinous: as also, for payment made to the good man of the house, for the said lodging – £6.9s.' With table linen, draperies, utensils, fuel, the cost of the journey (including transporting wine from London) and the provision of food and servants in Cambridge, the whole came to the not inconsiderable sum of £112.7s, to be defrayed by the representatives' constituents.[1]

The Cambridge Parliament met in fulfilment of a petition in the Merciless Parliament requesting that one should be summoned for Michaelmas.[2] Among the 248 members of the Commons who gathered at Cambridge, 52 had been at the Merciless Parliament, a high proportion of re-elected members for this period. Yet the new Parliament was critical of the way in which the appellants had in the meantime conducted the affairs of the kingdom. More had been expected in the way of reform than had been done (even the royal household was no less expensive), and it had been hoped that less taxation would be required, bearing in mind the revenue enjoyed by the government from the forfeited estates of those condemned in the Merciless Parliament. Yet the Commons were once more asked for money, and they granted a tenth and a fifteenth, which may have been less than the government had asked for. But the question of forfeitures was raised, and discontent was voiced about the management of the French wars, the cost and conduct of Arundel's expedition and the devastation of the north by the Scots. What concerned the Commons even more, however, was the deterioration of law and order at home as a result of the abuse of one of the most fundamental social practices of the middle ages, maintenance and livery for which the great lords were responsible.

Neither retaining followers nor identifying the members of a retinue by the lord's livery, or heraldic device, was new. A medieval lord's standing had always been reflected by the number of his household and retinue – knights and squires, pages, men-at-arms, grooms and others, many of whom he would bring to Parliament as the symbol of his power. At the

[1] *E.H.D.* Vol. IV, pp. 451–452.

[2] The account given here of the proceedings in this Parliament is largely drawn from the reconstruction by J. A. Tuck, 'The Cambridge Parliament, 1388' (1969), *E.H.R.* LXXXIV, pp. 225–243. The primary sources are: (a) *Stat.* R. Vol. II, pp. 55–60, 12 Ric. II. (b) Westminster Monk (Higden), op. cit., pp. 189–198, (c) Chron. Hen. Knighton ii, (ed. J. R. Lumby, Rolls ser., 1895.), pp. 298–308.

centre of a magnate's affairs, there were also officials and an administrative council to run his estates, in a manner not unlike the king's household. The household retinues of lords were not, however, the principal cause of grievance. The cause for concern was the spread of livery beyond the household retinue and its misuse for the purpose of intimidation, and the corruption of justice by the practice of maintenance.

As the fourteenth century had progressed, more and more knights, squires and lesser men were tied to the service of lords by sealed contracts, or indentures, under which they could be bound for life to be available for his service in peace and war in return for an annual payment. Among those so bound to magnates were men from the lesser gentry of the shires, the class from which sheriffs, justices and other officials and, of course, parliamentary knights were chosen. This gave great scope for malpractice. Through such connections a lord could use his influence in the courts to maintain, or uphold, cases in which he, or others of his dependents, or faction, had an interest. A man at issue with a great lord, or with one of that lord's following, was not likely to get much justice when those who tried his case were retained by the other side, and when juries could either be picked or intimidated. Nor was it safe to complain of malpractice when the officials charged with the administration of the law were themselves corrupted. Even justices, jurymen and officials who were not so tied could be intimidated. For underpropping the perversion of justice by corrupted officials were the private armies of liveried adherents, extending well beyond the lord's household, who could both intimidate resisters and menace the peace of the realm as they pursued their private feuds. The military retainers of the baronage could be used constructively for defence and the maintenance of order, particularly on the Scottish border, and for the purposes of war more generally. But retaining and the related vice of maintenance had been dangerously encouraged by the use of indentured service in the French wars, and the return home of men from the marauding free companies gave a stimulus to private armies at home. English society under Richard II had a high price to pay for what had been done in France under Edward III, and complaints in Parliaments had been increasing. Retaining and patronage underlay the power of Gloucester, Arundel and of every other great lord. Their castles and households were power bases in rivalry even to those of the king. Livery, maintenance and faction were a canker growing in late medieval society which, together with the political bitterness created by the events of 1386–1388, was to lead to the disintegration of the old order in the Wars of the Roses. The danger ahead was already scented by sensible men, and it was expressed in the Cambridge Parliament.

To put a stop to the misdeeds of bands of liveried retainers, the Commons petitioned for the abolition of all liveries which had been assumed since the first year of Edward III, including those of the king as well as of other lords. Another petition was directed specifically at maintenance, asking for justices of the peace and of assize to be given the power to investigate and try cases where maintenance was alleged. What exactly constituted maintenance, however, was debatable, and the Commons therefore attempted a comprehensive definition which covered most forms of corruption and intimidation of juries by threats, gifts or promises. Penalties for those guilty of wearing livery and of the practice of maintenance were asked for. The degree of suppression requested probably went beyond what the Commons either expected or wanted to obtain, and was perhaps a bargaining counter to obtain lesser concessions. The petition for the prohibition of all liveries assumed since 1327 was politically unrealistic since it would have covered the whole of a lord's retinue, including his household and his ordinary administrative, serving and military retainers. The ordinary retinues of lords were part of the social system in which many of the Commons themselves were probably personally involved. The offenders were those paid liveried retainers, often outside the household, who were reponsible for intimidation and disorder.

The Commons' petition on livery and maintenance naturally aroused strong opposition from the Lords. They promised to punish all offenders, if they could be found, as a warning to others, but this did not satisfy the Commons who again stated that the restoration of law and order required the abolition of liveries assumed since the first year of Edward III. The king himself then intervened, offering to set an example by abolishing his own livery. It was the first initiative he had taken since the Merciless Parliament, and it was a significant step towards his recovery of influence. The Lords, however, refused to accept his offer and attacked the Commons for presuming to raise the matter. With the Lords and Commons at odds, the king again intervened to avoid dissension, and persuaded both sides to accept a compromise by which he and his council would seek a satisfactory solution, though nothing was to be done until the next Parliament. When the next Parliament met in 1390 the king himself was to raise the matter and a statute was enacted forbidding maintenance altogether and restricting livery to household servants and to knights and esquires retained under written indenture. But neither this nor subsequent legislation against this abuse was to restrain the magnates, nor was it strictly enforced. The Commons' initiative at Cambridge, therefore, is significant not for what it achieved but because it was the start of the king's personal commitment to this reform and because of the opportunity it gave him to begin the recovery of his influence by offering to reconcile the Lords and Commons now they were at odds with each other instead of with him.

The second controversial social matter tackled by this Parliament at Cambridge was labour and wages. On this, however, the Lords and Commons were more or less at one. Thirteen petitions on the subject were presented by the Commons, largely it seems on their own initiative since the smaller landowners were worst affected by high wages and had the strongest interest in restricting the pay of migratory workers and in controlling the movement of labour. The initiative of the Commons had also been behind the labour legislation of Edward III, but their part then had been limited to making the general complaint, after which they left the council to draw up the details of legislation. At Cambridge, however, the Commons themselves suggested the detailed content of the law they proposed, including wage-scales and machinery for restraining the mobility of labour and enforcing the labour laws. Accordingly, the statute enacted that no servant or labourer should leave his hundred, rape or wapentake to live elsewhere without 'a letter patent containing the cause of his going and the time of his return, if he ought to return, under the king's seal'. Any labourer 'wandering' without such letter would be put in the stocks (a pair of which were to be kept in every town for the purpose) until he found a surety to return to his proper service or to service in the town whence he came. A servant could depart to serve elsewhere only if 'he be in certainty with whom' and provided he carried the necessary letter. The servants of lords, however, when travelling on their masters' business, were exempt from carrying such a letter, an amendment almost certainly introduced into the statute on the Lords' insistence. In addition to this system of work passes, the statute also set out the wages for different categories of labour in a detailed exercise of what, in twentieth century economic jargon, would be called wage-evaluation. The annual pay of each kind of worker from a carter to ploughman was given, and we have some idea of the supposed value of the job from the fact that whereas a shepherd had 10s., oxherds were allowed 6s. 8d. and swineherds only 6s. This statute also anticipated the twentieth century idea of a counter-inflation penalty by taxation. Both 'givers' and 'takers' of wages above a prescribed maximum were supposed to be fined the value of the excess, and twice and treble the value on the second and third offences.[1]

Another petition of the Commons at Cambridge, which also seems to have been inspired by the fear of social unrest, asked for the suppression of all gilds and fraternities apart from chanteries and ecclesiastical founda-

---

[1] *Stat.* R. Vol. II, pp. 57–58, 12 Ric. II, cl. 4–9.

tions. This curious request may have reflected a fear after the Peasants' Revolt that the rapid spread of parish gilds might in some cases have more to do with fomenting discontent than with religion. Another reason may have been financial; the petition wanted the goods and chattels of the suppressed gilds to be used as revenue for the war. But no legislation followed, although there was later an administrative inquiry into the constitution, property, finances and objects of such gilds, on which no action was taken.[1] Nor was a petition accepted by which the Commons sought to extend to the free tenants of peers the liability for contributing to the wages of knights of the shire. A peer and his villein-tenant were exempt on the grounds that they were represented by the peer in Parliament, and the question was whether the increasing number of men of villein status who were employed for pay without land tenure were also exempt. The statute simply confirmed the existing position, stating that if a peer bought land which was liable to contribute, then he assumed that liability.

The statute of Cambridge includes much that is revealing of the life of the time. One clause forbade servants to carry swords and daggers but positively instructed them to have bows and arrows, and what is more 'to use the same on Sundays and Holydays' and leave playing at tennis (*pelotes*), football and other games. There were also penalties against able-bodied beggars and any persons who defamed peers. But the clause which reveals the conditions of medieval life most vividly to us is one which attempted to deal with the filth of the streets. The conditions described in the statute as needing remedy were appalling, and it may not be altogether fanciful to see the king's own hand in this attempt at social legislation. A fastidious and sensitive man, and the first English king known to have carried the pocket handkerchief, Richard was a patron of arts and inclined by disposition towards being an improver. The foul conditions of a medieval habitation must have been disagreeable to such a man, and Richard had perhaps had a closer acquaintance than most medieval kings with the state of streets unprepared for a royal passer-by. On his return from Mile End at the height of the Peasants' Revolt he had wandered for hours through the streets of London and its suburbs when disorder was at its worst, before he eventually took refuge in the Great Wardrobe at Blackfriars. Quite probably, however, it was the specially insanitary condition of Cambridge itself, of which there is other evidence from the same year, that immediately prompted the enactment which ran as follows. 'For that so much dung and filth of the garbage and entrails as well of beasts killed, as of other

---

[1] A. Tuck, op. cit., p. 237.

corruptions, be cast and put in ditches, rivers, and other waters, and also within many other places, within, about, and nigh unto divers cities, boroughs, and towns of the realm, and the suburbs of them, that the air there is greatly corrupt and infect, and many maladies and other intolerable diseases do daily happen', both to the inhabitants and those travelling to these places, to their great annoyance and peril, proclamation was to be made throughout the realm, 'where needful' that anyone responsible for polluting 'ditches, rivers, water, and other places aforesaid' with ordure, entrails and garbage should cause them 'utterly to be removed, avoided, and carried away' before the following Michaelmas on pain of forfeiting £20 to the king. Mayors and bailiffs were to enforce this, and anyone who felt aggrieved because it was not done could appeal to chancery.[1] Whether this attempt at enforcing public hygiene had much general effect may be doubted. On the other hand at a time when some of the conditions of living were improving this first English sanitation act may have had some influence in reinforcing the by-laws which already existed in many towns against the pollution of streets and water.

Politically, however, the interest of this busy if short Parliament lies in the evidence that the appellants had dissipated much of their influence in Parliament for lack of any serious reforms. Six months later they lost their power, which they had held less than a year, and it was done easily and without resistance. At a council held in Westminster Palace on 3 May, 1389, Richard suddenly announced that as he was now over twenty-one he was entitled to the rights which the meanest heir in his kingdom would acquire on reaching his majority. Both the wording of the subsequent proclamation and the chroniclers' descriptions of the episode suggest that the declaration was made to a great or enlarged council of magnates rather than to the small everyday council dominated by the appellants where it could have been more easily resisted. The magnates then assured him that he had both the right and duty to take on the responsibilities of ruling, to which Richard replied in some such words as the following: 'You know well that for the twelve years of my reign, I and my realm have been ruled by others, and my people oppressed year by year with grievous taxes. Henceforth, with God's help, I shall labour assiduously to bring my realm to greater peace and prosperity. Up to now, I have been allowed to do nothing without my protectors. Now I will remove all these men from my council, summon to advise me whomsoever I will, and transact my own business myself. I therefore, order, as a first step, that the chancellor shall surrender the seal to

---

[1] *Stat.* R. Vol. II, 12 Ric. II, cl. 13, pp. 59–60.

me.'[1] There was no resistance and Archbishop Arundel immediately resigned the seal to the king.[2] According to Walsingham, Richard put it in a fold of his dress, left the room, and returned shortly to hand the seal to William of Wykeham. Richard may indeed have left the room carrying the seal, but it was on the next day that the elderly Bishop of Winchester was appointed chancellor, when the office of treasurer also changed hands, and Bishop Brantingham of Exeter replaced the Bishop of Hereford. Among other changes, Gloucester and Warwick were dismissed from the council and the Earl of Arundel ceased to be admiral. There were many changes of judges and officials, and a proclamation on 8 May informed the realm that, on the advice of the magnates, the king had assumed the entire government, and hoped to rule more prosperously than before. Nevertheless, all the pardons safeguarding those responsible for the actions of the Merciless Parliament were confirmed and as an earnest of his good intentions, Richard, acting on his own decision and without advice, as it was carefully pointed out, postponed the collection of part of the previous subsidy. He did this in acknowledgement of the weight of taxation, and in the hope of peace with France.

Truces with both France and Scotland followed and the kingdom entered into a period of unwonted peace. In October, John of Gaunt returned to England at the king's command, having given up his claim to Castille in exchange for a pension and the marriage of one of his daughters to the king of that country. Gaunt was warmly received by Richard and his presence furthered reconciliation since his influence was, as before, used on Richard's behalf. Thomas Mowbray, Earl of Nottingham, the friend of Richard's earlier years, was returned to the king's favour and he and his fellow appellant, Gaunt's son Henry Bolingbroke, Earl of Derby, were restored to the council. So, more remarkably, were Gloucester and Arundel, and when Bishops William of Wykeham and Brantingham resigned their places, the latter after a few months, the former in 1391, it was the appellant chancellor and treasurer who were reappointed. Richard was content to have as the principal administrative vehicle of his own will Edmund Stafford, brother of the first Earl of Stafford, and himself a banneret who had served the Black Prince. Stafford, who was to become bishop of Exeter, was appointed keeper of the privy seal and retained that position until 1395 when he became chancellor, for the rest of the reign.

---

[1] These words are a reconstruction by T. F. Tout of the statement attributed to Richard in various versions by the chroniclers. *Chapters in the Administrative History of Medieval England*, Vol. III, p. 454. A description of the episode by Walsingham, *Historia Anglicana* II, p. 181, is given (trans.) in *E.H.D.* Vol. IV, pp. 164–165.

[2] Tout's naming of the chancellor who resigned as Neville is an error.

The first Parliament after Richard's resumption of power met on 12 January 1390.[1] It began with a declaration of the causes of summons by William of Wykeham. The principal cause, expressed in terms which make rather odd reading, was that 'the king had been for a great time of tender age, and is now of such an age, thank God, that he is of greater understanding and discretion than he was before'. The king had long wished to govern his realm in quiet, peace, tranquillity and justice, said the bishop, and was now of greater and better will, and of firm purpose, to govern the people and the land well. This statement, which almost seems an admission that it had taken Richard longer than most kings to reach an age of discretion, was presumably intended to establish that Richard disclaimed all responsibility for anything done at any time in the past. After making the customary declaration of the king's wish that all traditional liberties should be enjoyed, the chancellor went on to describe the way in which the country was surrounded by enemies, the efforts being made for peace, and the king's need for money for these endeavours. The king also wished to be informed how the laws of the land and statutes were being kept, whether there were disturbances and (harking back to the Cambridge Parliament) about those who undertook and 'maintained' quarrels and disputes. How were such ills to be redressed?

There then followed a singular charade designed to produce a show of parliamentary confidence in the king's ministers while reserving his right to dispose of them at will. The chancellor, treasurer and 'all the lords of the great council', except, significantly, the keeper of the privy seal, Stafford, resigned, asking the king to consider the great labour and expense they had put into their office, and to discharge them, appointing good and sufficient persons in their place. They were then all dismissed, on which they prayed that anyone who had any complaints about them should declare them in Parliament. The next day, the Commons gave their answer to Lancaster who was representing the king. After 'diligent discussion' they said that they had no complaints to make, adding that the ministers deserved to be thanked in full Parliament for their good services. The Lords concurred, and all the ministers and councillors were restored to their offices and places. It was at this point that Gloucester was added to the council, together with Lancaster. All this was a grand gesture intended to convey the king's concern to listen to Parliament without implying that he had any obligation to heed it. For the king then stated that what had been done was not to be made a precedent, and that he wished to be free to remove and appoint his officers and councillors at his pleasure.[2]

[1] *Rot. Parl.* Vol. III, pp. 257–273.
[2] Ibid., p. 258.

Parliament then granted a subsidy on wool and merchandise, but two treasurers of war were appointed to collect and account for the tax. John of Gaunt was given the rule of Aquitaine with the new title of Duke of Guienne for life with full powers. The Parliament also produced two important enactments. First, a new statute of Provisors re-enacted the statute of 1351, but went further with additional safeguards against Roman pretensions. The right of free election to bishoprics and other benefices, and the rights of the king and lords as patrons, were reasserted against the Pope's growing practice of granting benefices to aliens as if he were patron. Stern penalties were prescribed for anyone, whether layman or cleric, who helped a member of the clergy to obtain a favour from Rome. It was also forbidden to introduce into England any retaliatory sentence of excommunication pronounced by the Pope, though a petition from the Commons to exclude the unpopular papal tax collectors was not accepted.[1]

The wording of the statute of Provisors sought to make it clear that it was a response to the Commons and the same was undoubtedly true of the second important enactment of this Parliament, the statute against livery and maintenance. This referred to the Commons' complaints at Cambridge, which they had repeated at Westminster, about the oppression of the people by maintainers and 'embracers of quarrels' many of whom were 'bold' in their evil deeds 'because that they be of the retinue of Lords and others', receiving payment and wearing 'Liveries of Company'. It was therefore ordained that no liveries were to be given by any lord to knights or esquires not retained by him for life, for peace and war, by indenture, or to anyone not a 'domestic and familiar residing in the household'. Lords were to 'utterly oust' all maintainers and embracers of quarrels from their service and livery, and no other lord was to receive them. No lord was to undertake or maintain any quarrel (that is legal or other dispute) other than his own. All who wore such livery were to leave it off within ten days of the proclamation by sheriffs.[2]

By raising the abuse of maintenance himself, through the chancellor, Richard demonstrated his personal interest in this social grievance. It was one among several signs that he was now embracing the Commons' causes in search of their support. Another was an enactment in the first statute of the Parliament which responded to the Commons' 'grievous complaint' that the court of chivalry, presided over by the constable and marshall, was encroaching on contracts, covenants, trespasses and other actions which should be pleaded at common law. The king declared 'by the advice and

---

[1] *Stat. R.* Vol. II, pp. 69–74, 13 Ric. II, st. 2.
[2] Ibid., pp. 74–75, 13 Ric. II, st. 3.

assent of the lords spiritual and temporal' that the power of the constable was to be limited to cases of contracts touching deeds of arms outside the common law. The enactment is not only interesting in the light of the attempt the appellants had made to use the constable's court for their purpose. It also illustrates the Commons' persistent concern to defend the common law. This made them wary of having cases of the abuse of maintenance drawn to the king's council, which was Richard's principal remedy. It was also largely in response to the Commons' influence that restraint was put on the granting of pardons for murder, rape and treason which had been abused; henceforth they were to be given only under the privy seal and after proper enquiry.

This Parliament reaffirmed the Cambridge statute of Labourers, but with an amendment to mitigate its harshness. Because it was impossible to know for certain what the price of corn and other victuals would be, it was now left to the justices of the peace, using their discretion, to proclam how much each type of worker should earn, 'according to the dearth of victuals'. The statutes of the first Parliament after Richard's self-emancipation also touched on a number of other matters which throw light on the social attitudes of the time. Two examples must suffice. The first statute recorded complaints that numbers of labourers, servants, artisans and grooms were keeping greyhounds and other dogs with which they went hunting 'when good Christian people be at church', to the destruction of parks and warrens. What was more, such persons were said to be using these expeditions to make 'assemblies and conspiracies' against their 'allegiance'. It was therefore enacted that no layman with land worth less than 40s. a year (or clerk worth less than £10) should keep such dogs nor use ferrets or any other means to take deer, rabbits, 'nor other gentlemen's game'. The Parliament ended on 2 March.

Richard had entered on his happiest years. He was deeply devoted to his wife, Anne of Bohemia, he presided over a brilliant court and he had friends and supporters once more whom he could trust. He was at peace with the magnates, and governed in consultation with his council, often accepting advice against his own wishes; thus he would have liked to bring de Vere and Neville back home (Suffolk had died in 1389) but refrained in face of the council's resistance. He had a policy for peace abroad and sought to bring about a more orderly society by restraining maintenance and livery. In this he must have known that he would face the obstruction of those lords who were the guilty parties in the matter, but he seems to have hoped that the Commons would support him. The trouble was that the Commons were split-minded. Many of them were involved in the abuse of maintenance themselves, quite apart from their persistent suspicion of the civil law procedures Richard was prepared to employ in bringing cases of maintenance to the jurisdiction of his council. In the Parliament of 1391, they specifically complained against calling men to the king's council when they should have been dealt with at common law.

The reality was that the odds were against the king in his efforts to control the abuse of maintenance. This is clear from the outcome of a case in 1392 when the Earl of Devon was accused of intimidating the justices of the peace and the jury who were to hear an indictment of murder against one of his retainers. The case was brought to the council, yet the earl was still able to attend an afforced meeting of the council while the case was pending, and despite admitting his guilt, he was pardoned by the king at the insistence of the Lords. The king would get no support in this matter from the Lords and in the last resort the Commons themselves were ineffectual allies.[1] His failure to enforce the law against maintenance by statute, or in his council, largely explains his eventual conclusion that the armed power of the aristocracy could be held in check only if he built up the military side of his own household. It was about this time that Richard adopted as his livery the badge of the white hart which was worn not only by knights and others in his own household but by retainers throughout the shires, especially in his lands in Cheshire. They formed an increasingly large royal army in reserve which could be called on through the sheriffs to restrain maintenance, or if necessary, to defend the king.

For the moment, however, the condition of politics was comparatively bland. The peace policy diminished the need for taxation and none was levied in a Parliament held in the autumn of 1390.[2] The Parliament which met from 12 November until 3 December was principally concerned with the peace negotiations with France and Scotland, and the chancellor's opening statement described what was being attempted. During this Parliament the Dukes of York and Gloucester submitted a petition asking the king to provide that their income in relation to the dukedoms he had bestowed on them should be made clearly hereditary. The king's agreement is an indication of his intention at this stage to preserve good relations with his dangerous as well as with his friendly uncle. In the autumn of 1391 Gloucester began to prepare for a crusade with the Teutonic Knights in Prussia, where Derby had had notable military success a year earlier. In late October, Gloucester set out across the North Sea but was forced home by bad weather before Christmas.

In the meantime, the peace negotiations with France continued and the

---

[1] A. Tuck, *Richard II and the English Nobility*, pp. 146–152.
[2] *Rot. Parl.* Vol. III, pp. 277–283.

three year truce of 1389 was renewed in 1392, 1393 and 1394. On the face of things, the idea of peace and less taxation was popular. Yet a final peace was difficult to achieve. In the first place, the French were seeking the return of Calais, something quite outside the realm of practical politics in England. Secondly, there was the future of Aquitaine. The solution proposed by Gaunt, and apparently acceptable to the king, was that as Duke of Guienne he should establish his own hereditary duchy there, to be held directly from the French king. A break with the English crown, however, was unacceptable to the Gascons who valued their English connection for the independence it gave them. They stood firm for the tradition that the English king should only alienate the duchy to his own eldest son and heir. Even in England peace was not unambiguously welcomed. Though the Commons would benefit from lower taxation, they disliked the idea that Guienne should become simply another French duchy under the house of Lancaster. For one thing, the knights did not altogether welcome the loss of the opportunities for war which had brought prosperity to so many of their class. Even the burgesses would lose money if there were no more contracts for the supplies of war. The truth of the matter was that war had become something of an addiction to English society and was hard to give up.

At the opening of the Parliament which met from 3 November to 2 December 1391, the chancellor, who was now once more Thomas Arundel, Archbishop of York, announced four causes of summons.[1] The first was to determine how to uphold the peace and quiet of the land, which was much disturbed by maintenance, a further manifestation of Richard's preoccupation with this menace to stability. Second, the price of wool had fallen 'beyond measure' and Parliament was to consider how it could be raised. Third, if the war had to be renewed, how was it to be paid for? Finally, said the archbishop, quoting the text *Render unto Caesar*, there was the Pope's opposition to the statute of Provisors; how could the Holy Father have his due and also the king his? Since Gloucester, who had adopted a highly critical view of the negotiations for a peace with France, had just departed on his abortive crusade, he was not available to stir up the Commons and they were willing to leave the question of France to the king's discretion, granting half a tenth and half a fifteenth, albeit on certain conditions (*sur certaine forme & condicions*) which were set out in a schedule providing for another full tenth and fifteenth if the king actually went to war. The Commons also stated 'in full Parliament' their opinion that if negotiations for a truce or peace were to take place, the Duke of Guienne should be in charge of them since he was 'the most sufficient person in the realm,' to

[1] *Rot. Parl.* Vol. III, pp. 284–296.

which the king agreed. We cannot know whether this was a spontaneous opinion of the Commons or one to which they were inspired by the king or Lancaster. Assuming, however, that it was arranged by the government, which is the more likely, it is significant that the Commons were now considered of such political importance that their declared support was thought desirable in a matter which not long before would have been regarded as none of their business. The same is true of an even more highly charged declaration made by the Commons made just before this Parliament ended.

On 2 December, the Commons 'prayed openly in full Parliament, that our lord the king should be and was as free in his regality, liberty and royal dignity in his time as any of his noble progenitors, former kings of England, were in their time; notwithstanding any statute or ordinance made to the contrary before these times, and even in the time of King Edward II'. If any statute was made in Edward's time in derogation of the liberty of the crown, they said, it should be annulled. All the prelates and temporal lords then spoke likewise and the king assented, thanking them all for their concern for the safety of his honour and estate.[1] This was undoubtedly carefully staged propaganda, arranged through the government's friends among the Commons. Nevertheless, it was a measure of Richard's temporary recovery that it could be staged at all, and the fact that it was thought worthwhile indicates the king's understanding of the importance of the Commons' support. It also reveals the extent to which Richard was haunted by the fate of Edward II whose canonization he had already begun to seek, personally visiting Gloucester where Edward was buried to collect evidence of claims of miracles, and pressing the case for canonization with the papal curia. As for the Pope's campaign against the Act of Provisors, it was decided that this should not be repealed, the Commons leaving it to the king, with the advice to act as he thought right. It is worth noting that there was a complaint against calling men to the king's council in cases when they should be dealt with at common law since this once more indicates the sort of objection which the Commons had to the methods Richard was using to suppress maintenance. Finally, Richard rejected a Commons' petition that villeins should not be allowed to acquire lands or to send their children to schools 'to advance them by means of clergy' for fear that this would increase the power of the clergy at the expense of the rights of the Lords.[2] In many social matters, he was less conservative than many of his subjects.

On the face of things, Richard was well in control of events. The

[1] *Rot. Parl.* Vol. III, p. 286.
[2] Ibid., p. 294.

negotiations for peace continued and, unpressed for money, he called no Parliament during 1392. At this time, he was making more use of large councils than of Parliaments. For example, a great council attended by knights of the shire as well as by magnates and officials met to discuss the question of war and peace at Stamford where policy was debated between the Duke of Gelderland, who wished to continue the war, and Lancaster, who favoured peace. The peace policy was accepted. Similar great councils which met in June and July were concerned with a quarrel between the king and citizens of London over money. At the same time, the ordinary council was on occasions enlarged by the presence of magnates, and as such it exercised a considerable degree of influence over policy, the king frequently deferring to its opinion when it was contrary to his. In fact, the line between a great or enlarged council and a privy council attended only by the officers of state and a few chamber knights was blurred. The writs, records and procedure for both were the same.[1] Faced with the power of the augmented council, Richard remained wary, as when in 1392 he was contemplating bringing back de Vere and Neville. A record exists giving day by day proceedings of the council at this time, and it tells us that in February 1392 the three royal uncles, the prelates and other lords guaranteed Richard's power, promising to be the king's loyal subjects and undertaking to do nothing in private or openly against him or any other lord or against the people in any way contrary to the law. But in return the king promised, 'of his own will' and on the word of a king, that he intended no harm to any lord and that 'it was not his intention to restore any person' of those who had been condemned 'in full Parliament'.[2] That these undertakings should have been felt necessary was an indication of the continuing distrust beneath the surface of affability. Meanwhile, Richard was building up a new court party of noblemen and officials. The latter included several chamber knights of considerable efficiency, notably Edward Dalyngryg, William Scrope and Richard Stury. Among the noblemen influential at court were the two Holland brothers, and also the Earl of Salisbury and York's son, the Earl of Rutland.

The next Parliament met on 20 January, 1393.[3] Its place of assembly was Winchester, instead of Westminster, apparently because of the king's bad relations with the Londoners at the time. The two principal causes of summons were, first, meeting the cost of the negotiations for peace or a truce, second, to respond to the trouble being made by the Pope over the

[1] J. F. Baldwin, *The King's Council*, p. 134.
[2] J. F. Baldwin, *The King's Council*, p. 495. (The journal of a clerk of the council is printed as an appendix).
[3] *Rot. Parl.* Vol. III, pp. 300–308.

statute of Provisors. The Pope's reply to the statute of 1390, including its ban on bringing any sentence of excommunication into England, had been to annul all such legislation by the English Parliament. The result was the promulgation at Winchester of a new statute of Praemunire, reinforcing the law against papal provision to English benefices and once more forbidding anyone to take to the papal courts any cases concerning patronage which were for the king's courts. The statute begins by describing the Commons as 'grievously complaining' against the Pope's encroachment of the right to sue in the king's court to recover presentments to benefices, and the enactment itself was said to be made by the king 'at the request of . . . his Commons'. So far as papal provisions were concerned, the statute made little difference. Neither side wished to push the matter to extremes, and the same Parliament also gave the king full discretion to negotiate on the matter as he thought fit, virtually authorizing him to try to make terms with the Pope.[1] The real target of the statute was the Pope's threats of excommunication of clerks presented to benefices by laymen, and in this respect the Pope took notice, influenced perhaps by the possibility of an English transfer of allegiance to Avignon, which was not altogether lacking credibility in the light of the peace negotiations with the French. Parliament once again granted one and a half tenths and fifteenths.

A few months later an insurrection in Cheshire provided new evidence of the underlying instability of Richard's reign. It was principally directed at the Dukes of Gloucester and Lancaster because of their involvement in the peace negotiations with France. It had been the king's intention in the spring of 1392 to send Gloucester to Ireland to try to restore the authority of the English government there which, under the pressure from resurgent Irish chiefs, had ceased to function outside the Pale. Preparations for the expedition had been well advanced when the king had suddenly cancelled his uncle's appointment. Instead, Gloucester had gone to Calais with Lancaster to negotiate for a peace or truce with the French, though he was instinctively hostile to the policy. In their absence the men of Cheshire rebelled, principally, it seems, because of the alleged surrender of the king's rights in France. Cheshire was traditionally an area which provided soldiers and from which a number of the prominent captains in the French wars had come. Soldiering was a staple occupation for many Cheshiremen. There also appear to have been grievances against Gloucester, whose appointment for life as justice of Chester and North Wales had already caused unrest. Disturbances in Yorkshire affecting Gaunt's estates occurred at the same time. Both dukes therefore returned from France to deal with the rebels,

---

[1] *Rot. Parl.* Vol. III, p. 301.

which they did leniently and with minimum force. It is again indicative of the general atmosphere of suspicion that at the height of the disturbances Richard thought it desirable, in view of his close connection with Cheshire, to proclaim that his men there could expect no support from him against the magnates whose nobility 'sustained the crown'. Afterwards, however, he made Nottingham justice of Cheshire in place of Gloucester to placate the Cheshiremen, and although the leader of the revolt, Sir Thomas Talbot, was imprisoned for a time, proceedings against him were suspended and he was eventually allowed to escape.

It might have been expected that the Earl of Arundel, the one lord appellant who had remained brooding and angrily apart from the current settlement between king and magnates, would have helped put down the revolt. He would have been particularly well placed to do so from his castle on the Dee. Yet he did nothing. His inactivity was no doubt partly his own protest against the peace negotiations of which he deeply disapproved. But it was also a mark of his unwillingness to help Lancaster.

Arundel's jealousy and dislike of Lancaster manifested itself in an astonishing outburst in the next Parliament which was in session between 27 January and 6 March 1394, at Westminster.[1] The causes of summons were to 'ordain' the peace and quiet of the realm, to provide remedies against the dangers without, to rehearse the matters to do with the negotiations for peace and to consider questions touching the 'extremities' of the realm, Guienne, Calais, Ireland and Scotland. The Commons then presented 'as their common Speaker' (*pur lour commune Parlour*) Sir John Bussy, the first Speaker to be named in the rolls for a decade and one who was to come to unenviable prominence as one of the king's close adherents. Bussy, who was immortalized as one of Shakespeare's trio, Bushy, Bagot and Greene, was a knight of the shire for Lincolnshire. He had sat in six consecutive Parliaments, and was a retainer both of the king and of Lancaster. He was retained for life as a 'king's knight' for forty marks annually, and was chief steward of Lancaster's estates north of the Trent. Richard had grasped the value of being able to persuade the Commons through their Speaker and he and Lancaster may well have exerted their influence to have him chosen. Yet the Commons' choice of Bussy probably also reflected a genuine willingness to support the king and Lancaster at this stage.

Soon after the beginning of the Parliament, the storm broke and the official roll vividly records the details of Arundel's vicious and public onslaught.[2] In the presence of the archbishops, Gloucester and various

[1] *Rot. Parl.* Vol. III, pp. 309–323.
[2] Ibid., pp. 313–314.

magnates, he blurted out that there were certain matters 'which lay so close to his heart' that he could not in conscience conceal them. It was, he said, against Richard's honour that his uncle the Duke of Lancaster 'often went hand in arm with the king' (*alast sovent en mayne & brace du Roi*), and he then went on to list his other charges. Item: the king wore the livery and colour of the duke. Item: the duke often in council and Parliament 'spoke words so harsh and rough that the said earl and others dare not fully say their meaning' (*parle si grosses paroles & aspres, que le dit Count & autres n'oserent sovent dire pleinement lour entente*). Item: that it was against the king's interest that he had made Lancaster Duke of Guienne. Item: that Lancaster had been given so much money for his Spanish expedition and, item, that he had had his debts remitted. Finally, Arundel criticized Lancaster's conduct of the negotiations for peace.

Richard defended his uncle against these accusations one by one. He pointed out that he also went hand in arm with his other uncles. He wore Lancaster's livery as a sign of goodwill, as he did that of his other uncles, he said. As for the words that dare not be spoken (and here the king's ironic tone can be sensed in the clerk's record) the earl and anyone else 'could speak fully' their understanding of anything they had heard the duke say in Parliament and council. Richard then recalled that the duchy and the money grants had been given with the assent of Parliament. Finally with regard to the peace treaty, the king said that Lancaster had done nothing other than that which he had been charged to do by the council, of which Arundel was a member. Arundel's complaints and the king's replies were then considered by the Lords who said that the complaints were without substance and that there was nothing with which the duke should be reproached. They asked Arundel if he wished to say anything else touching the duke, to which he replied, 'No.' Then, on the advice of the king and the Lords, the bitter earl apologized and the parliamentary roll slips briefly into English to record the grudging manner in which he did so. 'Sire, sith that hit semeth to the Kyng and to the other Lordes, and eke that yhe ben so mychel greved and displeisid be my wordes, Hit forthynketh me, and byseche yowe of your gode Lordship to remyt me your mau-talent.' An apology which was only offered 'since' it seemed to the king and lords that he had offended Lancaster, reads like a foreshadowing of the kind of apology sometimes forced by Speakers from reluctant members of the modern House of Commons who have used unparliamentary words of other members and who only apologize 'if' what they said is out of order, leaving no doubt that they are far from regretting it.

To persuade Parliament to accept the peace negotiations, the chancellor had observed in his opening speech that Parliament had assented to the war in the first place and would have to continue financing it if there was no peace, a reminder that if they wished to be free of war taxation they should not obstruct the peace treaty. Nevertheless, Lords and Commons disliked the treaty and especially the intention to detach Gascony from the crown and give it to Lancaster, and according to the Westminster monk, they at first sought to impede it. However, the Parliament roll records their eventual agreement, with some reservations of detail. Tunnage and poundage was continued at the full rate, and the second part of the previous subsidy was granted.

In retrospect, the year 1394 seems to have been the turning point in Richard's fortunes. So far all had gone remarkably well. Parliament had accepted the peace policy, if reluctantly, and even Gloucester had done so. There was peace at home. Yet many symptoms indicated danger. The episode of Arundel's protest against the familiarity of Gaunt and the policy of peace, the Commons' and Lords' suspicions of the policy for ending the war which had been part of everybody's lives for so long, the resistance to restraints on maintenance, and the jealousies and feuding of magnates give the impression of a cauldron which the king was vainly trying to damp down. Finally, the king was struck by personal tragedy. In June the queen died at Sheen leaving Richard for a time distraught. Whether or not Anne of Bohemia had acted as a restraining influence on him, there was no question of his devotion to her nor of the general regard in which she was held, despite hostility which had been shown to the Bohemians she had brought with her. Richard was so deeply affected that it would not be surprising if his personal judgement suffered from the blow, given the other stresses he was under. The depth of his feelings was revealed by his furious reaction to another exhibition of Arundel's intolerably boorish behaviour at the queen's funeral. The earl did not join the funeral procession to Westminster Abbey, and 'when he arrived late, he straight away asked the king for leave to withdraw on account of certain matters that were pressing him'.[1] Richard was so outraged that 'he grasped his rod and struck him with such force on the head, that he fell at his feet and shed his blood profusely on the stone floor. He would have killed him in the church if it had been allowed'.[2] For a time Arundel was lodged in the Tower, and eventually had to appear before the king and take an oath on his future behaviour, with his brother the

---

[1] Walsingham, printed in Johannis de Torkelowe, *Chronica et Annales; Annales Ricardi Secundi* p. 424. '... *cum tardius advenisset, primus omnium petiit a Rege licentiam recedendi, propter certas causas quae eum urgebant.*'

[2] Ibid '... *accepta lictoris canna, percussit eum violenter in capite, tanto nisu, ut caderet ad pedes ejus, et sanguis decurreret largiter in pavimentum; voluitque occidisse eum in ecclesia, si permissus fuisset.*' See also ibid., pp. 168–169.

archbishop and a number of magnates acting as his sureties pledging £40,000.

Before the queen's death, Richard had already planned to lead an expedition to Ireland to restore the royal authority which had all but collapsed since the death of Edmund, Earl of March, who had been the king's lieutenant there. At the end of September, therefore, he set out accompanied by a substantial force and a large part of the nobility. Most of them were younger members who were closely associated with the court, notably the Earl of Rutland (York's son), the Earl of March (the most important landowner in Ireland), the Earls of Nottingham and Huntingdon (John Holland) and many barons and household knights. An exception from the older generation was Gloucester, who accompanied Richard, while the Duke of York remained in England as keeper of the realm. The expedition was a notable though temporary success, and the Irish insurgents were outmanoeuvred and brought to submission with few battles and comparatively little bloodshed, the English archers easily overcoming men equipped mainly with axes. Richard's policy was one of constructive pacification. The Irish chiefs, many of whom came to Dublin to submit to him personally, were given full legal status under the English crown, and some were knighted. In return they recognized the English over-lordship. Some grants of land were made to English lords but the emphasis was on conciliation. However, money was needed, and Ireland was the principal matter before a Parliament which met in January 1395.[1] The chancellor, Thomas Arundel 'rehearsed the manner of the king's passage to Ireland and the great zeal he had shown for the conquest of the rebels in those parts, and how honourably, with God's help, he had acquitted himself'. Gloucester had been sent home to ask for money and with some reluctance the Commons granted a tenth and a fifteenth. But their hearts were not in the Irish venture; they were more worried by troubles nearer home and the lords of the council sent a letter from this Parliament congratulating the king but asking him, now that he had 'probably' conquered most of Ireland, to speed his return to deal with other matters. They were particularly worried by threats from the Scots to break their truce.[2] It was not, however, until May that Richard returned from Ireland, before which time the uneasy settlement in that unruly land had already begun to break down.

The matter of the French peace was now to be settled and a rebellion of the Gascons forced the English to abandon the idea of holding the duchy

---

[1] *Rot. Parl.* Vol. III, pp. 329–336.
[2] E. Curtis, *Richard II in Ireland*, pp. 137–140.

from the French crown. In March 1396 a treaty was signed agreeing to a twenty-eight years' truce, which was almost as good as a peace but got round the difficulty for both sides in respect of Calais and Aquitaine. The English, however, gave up their temporary occupation of Brest and the virtual peace was to be accompanied by the marriage of Richard to Isabella, the daughter of Charles VI. Since she was only seven, this meant that the prospect of an heir to the English throne would be put off for nearly a decade, and although Richard was not yet thirty the lack of an heir apparent did not ease the tensions in English politics. For Gloucester, the nature of the treaty was unsatisfactory since it meant the permanent return to English political life of Gaunt, and his heir, Henry Bolingbroke. Since Gaunt would remain the king's firm upholder, Gloucester's freedom of action was bound to be impeded. Nor can Gloucester have been altogether easy about a stipulation in the king's instructions to his negotiating ambassadors, the Earls of Rutland and Nottingham, and William Scrope. They were told to bring the negotiations to a conclusion, and to assist them the English demand for a money payment was reduced. But the king made it a condition that his new relations, the French royal Family, 'should be allied with him against all manner of men who ought to obey him in any way, and also that they should aid and sustain him with all their power against any of his subjects'.[1] This uneasy echo of the threat Richard had allegedly made to Gloucester in 1386 to appeal if necessary for French help might give a potential dissident cause for concern, though the fact that the uncles themselves were to join in the guarantee hardly suggests that Richard intended it to be directed at one of them. The probability is that it was meant to refer to any wider revolt of his subjects. Naturally the understanding did not appear in the treaty proper. In November the new queen made her entry into London, and her coronation followed at the beginning of 1397.

At the end of January, 1397 a Parliament met at Westminster.[2] None had been called during the previous year since the government had had no great need of money. Now, however, Richard required funds, both to help to pay for the heavy expenses of the celebration of his marriage and because of the rising cost of his household which he had been steadily extending. He had also undertaken to assist the French king in support of the Duke of Burgundy against the Visconti of Milan. Very few peers had arrived to hear the new chancellor, Edmund Stafford, the Bishop of Exeter, announce the causes of summons. (Richard had consented to Arundel's translation to Canterbury the year before, and was presumably not sorry to be able to

[1] Rymera, *Foedera*, III, iv, III (translated extract, *E.H.D.*, Vol. IV, p. 167).
[2] *Rot. Parl.* Vol. III, pp. 337–346.

replace him by one of his own adherents, the former keeper of his privy seal.) The causes of summons were given in very general terms: good government, observation of the laws, and peace at home and abroad. Then, after the Speaker, John Bussy, had delivered his protestation, the chancellor spoke to the Commons of the causes of summons, and said that the officers would give them a detailed account the next morning at 8 o'clock. He also instructed the Lords to be at Parliament each morning at nine o'clock, none to be absent without the king's personal licence. The next morning, the chancellor, treasurer, clerk of the privy seal and other councillors 'declared to the Commons in the Refectory at Westminster, in detail, the intent of the king and the causes of summons'. Clearly, the Commons were not happy with the request for money since later that day, they went to the king and Lords in Parliament to ask that all the Lords who were absent should be sent for. They evidently wanted the Lords' support. The king replied, through the chancellor, that this would make for too long a delay. Nevertheless, he agreed to send for those Lords who were 'quite near'. It was a mark of the standing the Commons had attained that the high officers of state should go to them to negotiate, and that the Commons should feel free to request that the Lords be sent for. Despite the attempt to win them over, the Commons were not persuaded to underwrite policies they disliked. They firmly though courteously declined to help financially with the expedition to Italy. Richard argued his case with them, 'with his own mouth' but in the end gave up the idea. Then there emanated from among them a still greater challenge to the king's authority.

On Friday after Candlemas, Richard called the Lords to him after dinner, saying that he had heard that on Thursday they had been with the Commons who had raised various matters contrary to his regality and royal liberty. He commanded the chancellor to tell him about the matters raised. Three of the Commons' complaints concerned the appointment as sheriffs of men with insufficient income who were continued in office for more than a year, the failure to protect the Scottish border, and the grant of liveries to yeomen outside lords' households and the abuses of maintenance. None of these, however, gave great cause for royal offence. What did was a fourth complaint, a petition that 'the great and excessive charge of the king's household be amended and diminished'. This bill, which complained of the 'multitude of bishops' advanced at court and of the number of ladies and their attendants dwelling in the household, had been submitted by a certain Thomas Haxey.[1] The revival of the old attacks on the independence of the royal household and its extravagance aroused the king to fury. That there

---

[1] Haxey's bill and the subsequent Lords' judgement are printed in *Rot. Parl.* Vol. III, p. 407-408.

Left: Edward III, effigy from the tomb in Westminster Abbey.

Right: Richard II, the earliest portrait of an English king known to have been made in his lifetime. It is in Westminster Abbey.

The ruins of the magnificent gothic St Stephen's Chapel in the old Palace of Westminster after the fire of 1834 (water colour by R. W. Billing). Begun by Edward I, continued by Edward II and completed by Edward III, the chapel was later used as the post-Reformation House of Commons, with the walls panelled and a ceiling inserted.

THE COMMONS ARE CONSULTED ON NEGOTIATIONS FOR A PEACE TREATY

The parliament roll for April 1354 provides the earliest clear description of putting a question on policy to the Commons collectively. (see pp. 319–20) Informing Lords and Commons that there was a 'good hope' of a negotiated peace, the chamberlain, Sir Bartholomew de Burgersh, said that the king did not wish to accept it without their assent. Asked whether they would 'assent and accord' to such a peace, the Commons replied that whatever action the king and magnates pleased to take was agreeable to them.

To associate the Commons more positively with the prospective treaty, the chamberlain then (lines 9–10) asked: *Donqes, vous voillez assentir au tretee du pees ppetuele si bōme la puisse avoir.* (So, you wish to assent to a treaty of perpetual peace if it can be had.) *Et les dites coēs (communes) responderent entierement & uniement, Oil, Oil.* (And the said Commons replied wholly and unanimously, 'Aye, Aye.') The decision was then made a 'public instrument.'

(PRO doc. C65/18)

The interior of the medieval Painted Chamber (looking east) painted by William Capon in 1799 and as it was before the fire of 1834. Beneath the tapestries and covered by whitewash were concealed the wall paintings from the reigns of Henry III and Edward I.

A RELUCTANT PARLIAMENTARY APOLOGY

In the Parliament of 1394, Richard Earl of Arundel bitterly attacked John of Gaunt, Duke of Guyenne and of Lancaster and uncle of Richard II, saying that he could not conceal certain matters which lay 'close to his heart'. He asserted that Gaunt had been over-familiar with the king and had been shown too much favour. (see pp. 419–20.) The king defended his uncle from all the charges and the parliamentary roll records that, after the Lords had considered Arundel's accusations, it was declared that they had no substance (*ne furent de null force ne d'effect*). (9 lines from top) Asked whether he wished to say anything more, Arundel said that he did not.

With the advice of the Lords, the king then required the earl to speak the following words (*q̃ le dit Count deveroit dire a dit Duc illoeqes les poles q'ensuent*) at which point the narrative records the apology in English: 'Sire, sith that hit semeth to the Kyng and to the other Lordes and eke that yhe ben so mychel greved and displeisid be my wordes, Hit forthynketh me, and byseche yowe of your gode lordship to remyt me your mau-talent.' (lines 12–14 from top). The roll then records in French that the earl spoke these words to the duke in the presence of the king and the lords in parliament. (PRO doc. C65/54)

Left: Effigy of Henry IV from the tomb in Canterbury Cathedral.

Right: Henry V, from a portrait in the National Portrait Gallery by an unknown artist.

The Jewel Tower, a surviving part of the medieval Palace of Westminster, built for Edward III in 1365–6, on land belonging to Westminster Abbey, as the wardrobe to house the king's personal treasure and plate. It was later used for over two centuries to store parliamentary records which are today in the Victoria Tower.

Left: Henry VI from a portrait in the collection of H.M. the Queen.

Right: Edward IV from a portrait in the collection of H.M. the Queen.

was something in the complaints is clear. Richard kept a sumptuous court and was a great patron of the arts; at this very time, great expenditure was being devoted to the reconstruction of Westminster Hall, with its hammer-beam roof, in the form in which we know it. The French influence at his court had probably also encouraged his expenditure and it is not impossible that his visit to France and his contact with the French court had inclined him to seek more autocratic solutions to his endemic political problems; Bishop Stubbs thought it even possible 'that the sight of continental royalty . . . wrought in him . . . an irresistible craving for absolute power'.

There were significant differences between the court party of 1397 and that which had been uprooted a decade earlier. The new court was more aristocratic than the old, so that it was harder to complain of the patronage to new men and in any case the king's grants were more cautious. Yet the Commons' anxiety about both the cost and power of the court, from which Gloucester and Arundel felt excluded, had been aroused again, perhaps in part through Gloucester's influence, and perhaps with more reason since the court party was politically more self-assured and powerful than it had been under Suffolk. Besides, Richard's enlargement of his household was even more startling on the military than on the administrative side. He had recruited to his liveried retinue large numbers of men, especially archers, who bore his device of the white hart throughout the land, and they were particularly numerous in Cheshire. Despite the fact that their Speaker was Richard's retainer it seemed that enough of the Commons were concerned to have allowed Haxey's bill to go forward.

When he had heard the chancellor's account of the Commons' submissions, the king expressed 'his will' to the Lords, declaring that 'by the gift of God he was by line and right of inheritance king and inheritor of the realm of England and wished to have his regality and royal estate and liberty'. He then went on to indicate that on some of the matters raised which did not infringe his regalities, he was prepared to listen or to give a reasoned reply. On the matter of the sheriffs, he thought that men would do the work of sheriffs better if they had time to gain experience. As for the border, he would be glad if the Lords considered a remedy. But on his household he was adamant. There were innumerable small signs that his view of his prerogative was now higher than ever. For example, he had recently legitimatized the Beauforts, John of Gaunt's children born to Catherine Swynford before his marriage to her, and he informed this Parliament that he had done so as 'entire emperor of his realm', *entier emperour de son roialme*.[1] The Commons' questioning of his household was

---

[1] *Rot. Parl.* Vol. III, p. 343.

therefore quite unacceptable and, as the Parliament roll records, he declared it a great 'grief and offence' to him that they should 'presume' to take it on themselves the ordering or governance of the king's person or household. It was an offence 'against his regality and Royal Majesty and the liberty of both himself and his honourable progenitors'. Richard then commanded the Lords that they should, on the Saturday morning, convey his 'will' to the Commons. 'Furthermore, when the king had heard how the Commons had been moved and instigated by a bill presented to them . . .' he commanded Lancaster to charge 'Sir John Bussy, Speaker of the House of Commons, on his allegiance, to reveal and declare the name of the man who had presented the bill to the Commons'.

The Lords accordingly 'were with the Commons' (or presumably a committee of Lords was) on the Saturday and declared the king's will. The Commons then delivered up the bill with the name of the man who had presented it, namely Sir Thomas Haxey, who for fifteen years had been a clerk of the court of common pleas and was also a connection of the Earl of Nottingham. (Nottingham himself was, as events were to show, an uncertain friend but Richard does not seem to have suspected him of being implicated since in the next Parliament he made him Duke of Norfolk.) The king then ordered the Commons to come before him 'in Parliament' where 'with all the humility and obedience of which they were capable, they expressed deep sorrow, as appeared from their demeanour, that the king was so displeased with them'. They humbly apologized, declaring that it was never their intention to say or do anything to displease the king's royal majesty, whether concerning his person, his household or the ladies and gentlemen of his entourage. They understood very well, they said, that such matters 'did not pertain to them at all, but solely to the king himself'. If this had become political convention, and if the household had been established as the centre of administration, the core of government would have been removed from any sort of parliamentary influence. Through the chancellor, Richard fully accepted their apologies and then he spoke himself, saying that the Commons were bound to him in many ways, especially because, for their ease and quiet, he had refrained from asking them for tenths and fifteenths.[1] The Commons then granted tunnage and poundage for three years and the subsidy on wool and leather for five.

Despite the Commons' apology, the king still insisted that the author of the petition be brought before him. Haxey was produced and condemned for treason but was pardoned at the behest of the Archbishop of Canterbury

---

[1] A detailed record of this episode is given in *Rot. Parl.* Vol. III, p. 338–339. Extracts (trans.) are in *E.H.D.* Vol. IV, pp. 167–169.

because of his cloth. As well as convicting him, the Lords declared, on behalf of the king, 'that if anyone, of whatsoever estate or condition, shall move or excite the Commons of Parliament or any other person to make remedy of any matter which touches our person or our government or our regality, he shall be held a traitor'.[1] This ruling would have built an impregnable fence around the royal prerogative against parliamentary influence and fear of an accusation of treason would have inhibited the political scope of petitions submitted through the Commons. It is hard to say whether the episode of Haxey's bill is more remarkable for the initial signs of the Commons' continued independence of thought or for their final capitulation to the king's will.

IV

During or soon after the first Parliament of 1397, Richard seems to have come to the conclusion that he faced a serious threat to the royal authority he was now determined to have. Whether or not there was such a threat, and if so what its nature was, can only be subjects for discussion. All that is certain is that during the summer he reached the conclusion that he was now strong enough to make a pre-emptive strike against those he feared would sooner or later move to destroy him. His advantages were many. He had peace abroad. The lightly taxed Commons should be his friends; their Speaker was his retainer and the king had stood against the practice of maintenance by a dangerously powerful nobility. He enjoyed Lancaster's solid support, and he was bolstered by a strong court party, by officers of state and councillors of his own choosing and by the invaluable and efficient knights of the household, including Sir Henry Green and Sir William Bagot, as well as Bussy. (All these three had been involved with the appellants' party in 1388 but had been fully pardoned.) Above all, the king had in reserve his private army of retainers with which to resist the retinues of the over-mighty subjects who were his target. He seems to have seen in Haxey's bill a plot which awoke fears of a return to the humiliation of 1386–8 and this time, perhaps, of an actual rather than a threatened deposition.

Richard cannot have had definite knowledge of a plot since the charges which were eventually made against Gloucester and Arundel related only to their wrong-doing between 1386 and 1388. Yet it does not follow that

[1] *Rot. Parl.* Vol. III, p. 408.

because he lacked proof of any connection between them and Haxey's bill they had had nothing to do with it.[1] He had experience enough of their ruthlessness to give him cause to fear that they were again conniving with a party in the Commons to achieve his subjection, and it is possible that information hard to substantiate may have reached him. Moreover, their behaviour during the following months was such as to give credibility to his suspicion. Both Gloucester and Arundel angered the king by absenting themselves from meetings of the council. Moreover, at a banquet at Westminster in the early summer, Gloucester openly criticized the decision to surrender Brest to the French, despite the fact that it had been held only as a short-term pledge for a money payment and had now been redeemed. The two embittered and arrogant noblemen may also have resented tentative if highly unrealistic overtures that were said to have been made for the election of Richard as king of the Romans. Richard was aware of Gloucester's and Arundel's contemptuous opinion of him as a peace-seeking king who had no sympathy with their military adventurism. He knew that they resented still more deeply his determination to exalt his regality far above their nobility.

According to a French chronicle there was a plot about this time which involved not only Gloucester, Arundel and Warwick but the Earls of Derby and Nottingham, the last of whom allegedly betrayed it to the king and so precipitated Richard's decision to act. The details of the alleged plot are not credible, especially the involvement of Nottingham and Derby in view of their elevation to dukedoms soon afterwards.[2] There may well have been confusion with the later alleged plot which was the cause of the quarrel between them for which both were banished. Yet a movement of some sort against the king may have been in the making. During the summer of 1397, Richard had embarked on the unpopular course of raising loans under pressure, which led to one of the charges against him in the articles of deposition.[3] The loans were not, in the proper sense of the term, forced, and there was a high refusal rate. Contemporary complaints about them probably had to do more with the efficiency of the commissioners who raised them than with actual duress. The loans were admittedly not

---

[1] J. A. Tuck, op. cit., p. 182, finds it hard to believe that noblemen would have used Haxey to criticize the king when they could have done so direct. But there are numerous other instances of the Commons being put up by the king (for instance, in the matter of the petition on the prerogative in 1391) or by the Lords (for instance, in the Merciless Parliament) to take positions helpful to them.

[2] The plot is duscussed in Steel, op. cit., pp. 230–232 and J. A. Tuck, op. cit., p. 184–185.

[3] The so-called forced loans are discussed by C. Barron, 'The Tyranny of Richard II', B.I.H.R., Vol. XLI, No. 103, May 1968.

profitable to the lenders; it would have been deemed wrong to take advantage of a king's need by charging a high rate of interest. But they were not unconstitutional. Similar loans were raised by the Lancastrian kings and the articles of deposition carefully avoided any suggestion that they were illegal. Richard was simply accused of raising money to be repaid on certain terms and then failing to repay it. Yet even the failure to repay cannot have been a serious cause for complaint as early as the summer of 1397. The more general grounds for grumbling were probably that the loans were inevitably accompanied by some degree of pressure which was hard to resist. Those who shared Gloucester's and Arundel's thinking may have been more worried by the fear that the loans indicated Richard's determination to lessen his financial dependence on Parliament.

Plot or no plot Richard determined to strike and he did so swiftly. He invited Gloucester, Arundel and Warwick to a banquet with the intention of arresting them. Gloucester declined on grounds of ill-health, which seems to have been genuine. Arundel simply stayed away in his castle at Reigate, suspicious of the king's intentions. Only Warwick accepted, and having been received in a friendly manner was arrested immediately after the banquet and taken off to the Tower. Arundel was shortly afterwards persuaded by his brother, the archbishop, to give himself up on an undertaking that he would come to no harm, but he was promptly despatched as a prisoner to Carisbrooke Castle in the Isle of Wight. Richard decided to give himself the pleasure of arresting Gloucester and rode through the night to the duke's castle at Pleshey in Essex, accompanied by the Earls of Rutland, Nottingham and Kent, and with armed Londoners and men of his household. When they arrived in the morning Gloucester came out to meet them at the head of a procession of monks and clerks from a collegiate church he had founded. As his uncle bent the knee to him, Richard put his hand on his arm and arrested him personally.[1] Richard then returned with most of his forces to London, despatching Gloucester to Calais in charge of the Earl of Nottingham. To fend off criticism of the arrests it was put about that the arrests were in relation to a new plot, not to old offences, and the king ordered the arrest of anyone who protested.

At a council meeting in Nottingham, it was arranged that eight lords, Rutland, Kent, Huntingdon, Somerset (Gaunt's son, John Beaufort), Nottingham, Salisbury, Despenser and Scrope, should lay a bill of appeal against the three arrested noblemen. This was then referred by the king to a Parliament which was summoned to meet on 17 September at Westminster.

---

[1] The most detailed account of the arrests of the accused men is in Walsingham *Annales Ricardi Secundi*, (Rolls Series), pp. 201ff.

The king had been heavily recruiting archers in Cheshire since the summer and a large muster of his retinue was summoned to meet at Kingston-on-Thames two days before the opening of Parliament. Accompanied by this force and by the new appellant lords, the king rode to the opening of his Parliament of revenge. It had two sessions. The first lasted from 17 to 29 September, when it was prorogued. It then met for a second and important session at Shrewsbury on 29 January though this lasted for only three days.[1]

It assembled in a temporary open-sided structure at Westminster. The Painted Chamber was evidently considered not large or imposing enough, and Westminster Hall, being under reconstruction, was presumably not available. The king's archers were assembled around the building and because of its open structure were visible to the eyes of those present. Richard sat on a throne of exceptional height and splendour. 'One king shall be king over all' (Ezekiel, ch. xxxvii, v. 22) was the text on which the chancellor opened the proceedings. No kingdom, he said, could be governed except by the power of one king, and good government depended on the king's power to govern, on ensuring that the laws were justly kept and executed, and that the subjects should obey the king and the laws. Kings have privileges and prerogatives so that they can govern and these could not be alienated. The king had therefore summoned 'the estates of Parliament' to be informed if any rights of his crown were being 'subtracted or diminished' so that by their advice remedies could be provided to give the king the same liberty and power as his ancestors, and so that 'there shall be one king for all and he shall govern all'. A king's government began with the laws, and 'as a father teaches his son how to abstain from vices and evil' by placing him under threats, so the king 'like a good father to all his people' taught the people how to behave towards him by laws reinforced with penalties. Without good laws, no man would have his property. Then, having made this general statement of the divine right of kings, the chancellor made an announcement.

The king, he said, had considered the various misdeeds committed by the people before this time against their allegiance, as a result of which they stood in peril of the law, and he wished to show grace to them so that they had courage to do better in future. He therefore 'wished and granted to be made' a general pardon with the exception of fifty people.[2] The names of the fifty excluded persons were not, however, published and the pardon was not actually proclaimed during the first session of Parliament. Richard was thus able to create a sense of insecurity among those who felt vulnerable to

---

[1] *Rot. Parl.* Vol. III, pp. 347–385.
[2] Ibid., p. 347.

suspicion, and who were uncertain whether or not they had been pardoned. By this means, he also prepared the ground for such people to sue for individual charters of pardon, which some of them began to do later that autumn, thus implicitly confessing their guilt. It was to be one of the charges against Richard in the articles of deposition that he had forced men to sue and pay for pardons, and sometimes to pay twice, a charge which appears justified.[1]

Richard's principal purposes, however, were to establish the unlawfulness of the commission which had been set up in 1386 to control his household and to invalidate the proceedings leading up to and in the Merciless Parliament. The next step, therefore, was a specific declaration that the commission of 1386 to control the household had been invalid. Sir John Bussy, once again Speaker, 'showed' the king how in 1386 Gloucester and Arundel, who were two traitors, had, by 'false imagining', created the commission by statute in order to have the government of the king's household. The offending statute was then rehearsed, and written into the parliamentary roll. 'Which commission ... seemed to the Commons to be prejudicial to the king and his crown, and a usurpation of his dignity and royal power. Moreover, the Duke of Gloucester and Earl of Arundel sent a great person, a peer of the realm, as messenger to our lord the king to tell him that unless he would grant and assent to the said commission and statute he would be in great peril of his life.' The Commons therefore prayed the king that the statute of 1386, made under compulsion, should be repealed as having been made traitorously against the king's regality. It was duly repealed by the king, with the assent of the Lords and Commons and it was enacted that anyone who tried to procure such a commission in the future was a traitor.[2]

The next step was to revoke the pardons that were supposed to protect the former Lords Appellant for their doings in 1387–88. First the Commons 'showed' the king how Gloucester and Arundel had traitorously recruited Warwick, raised a great number of men at Harringay, forced the king to call a Parliament and made him accept acts done there under compulsion. They asked for the repeal of the general pardon of 1388 which was supposed to protect the Lords Appellant and the king assented. They then petitioned for the repeal of the individual pardon granted to Arundel in 1394 on the grounds that it had been conceded under duress which, of course, had not been the case. This repeal was also enacted by the king. Subsequently,

---

[1] The question of pardons is discussed in C. Barron, op. cit.

[2] *Rot. Parl.* Vol. III, p. 350. It will be noted that the threat as stated here did not involve deposition, which was no doubt something the king preferred not to mention, nor did it refer to Gloucester's own visit to Eltham.

however, the other members of the commission of 1386 were exempted from the revocation of the pardons as being innocent of malice, and the Commons specifically petitioned the king on behalf of two of the appellants of 1388, Nottingham and Derby, on the grounds of their later help to the king against Gloucester and Arundel. Saying that these things were 'better known to him than any other', the king granted them his pardon. It is one of the more curious aspects of this Parliament that these two of the former Lords Appellant, Mowbray of Nottingham and Bolingbroke of Derby, now stood in the posture of judges on their former leaders. Their own quarrel and banishment was later to be the immediate cause of Richard's overthrow and of Bolingbroke's usurpation.

The Parliament then turned to the trial and punishment of the accused men.[1] These now also included Archbishop Thomas Arundel, who had only been arrested after the Parliament had begun. He had been present at the opening ceremony and had indeed been named as one of the triers of petitions. The decision to arrest him may have been taken because he had resisted the revocation of the pardons.[2] Another possibility is that he may have opposed the proposal that the prelates and clergy should nominate a lay proctor when they withdrew on the usual grounds that they must not participate in a judgement of blood.[3] On the second day of the Parliament, the Commons had 'shown' the king, through the mouth of their Speaker John Bussy, how in the past various judgements and ordinances under his predecessors had been repealed because the estate of the clergy had not been present as peers of Parliament to sanction them. This was a reference to the attack in 1322 on the judgement against the Despensers on the grounds that it had been invalid because of the prelate's absence. At the Commons request, therefore, a proctor, Sir Thomas Percy, was appointed to act for the clergy. Archbishop Arundel, who had already withdrawn from Parliament by order of the king, was then impeached by Bussy, on behalf of the Commons, for his actions between 1386 and 1388. The archbishop was not allowed to answer the charges on the grounds that the facts were notorious, and on September 25 he was sentenced to lose his temporalities and to banishment. His archbishopric eventually went to the treasurer, Roger Walden, Arundel being translated by the Pope to a See obedient to the anti-Pope. He eventually returned to England with Henry Bolingbroke.

The process against the principal accused magnates now began. In

---

[1] The charges etc. are in *Rot. Parl.* Vol. III, pp. 374–385. Chronicle sources include notably Walsingham, *Annales Ricardi Secundi*, p. 210ff and *Chronicon Adae de Usk*, ed. E. M. Thompson, 1904.
[2] *Annales Ricardi Secundi*, pp. 211–213.
[3] M. McKisack, *The Fourteenth Century*, p. 480.

deliberate imitation of the events of 1386, the eight new Lords Appellant appeared dressed in robes of red silk, with white borders and embroidered with gold. They appealed against Gloucester, Arundel and Warwick on grounds of their treason, asking for them to be brought into Parliament. Lancaster presided over the trial as lord steward of England. Arundel was the first to appear and was said to have been told by Lancaster that, according to his own idea of law, he deserved to be condemned without being allowed to answer. Arundel pleaded the pardons he had received only to be told they had been revoked because they had been given under constraint ('at a time when you were king', as one account puts it). While Arundel was still arguing that to grant pardons was the king's prerogative, Bussy and the Commons interrupted to demand that Arundel be condemned as a traitor. According to Thomas of Walsingham, whose account at most practical points confirms the parliamentary rolls but whose descriptions are heavily biased by enmity to Richard and the court, Arundel rebutted the charge by saying that it was not the faithful Commons who were making the demand but Bussy. According to another account, when Bussy asserted that the charters had been revoked by king, Lords and faithful Commons, Arundel replied scornfully: 'The faithful Commons are not here,' which was probably an accusation that the king and his council had packed the 'lower house' with their friends. The charge that Richard had influenced the elections to his purpose was made in the deposition articles[1] and there is no doubt that he had built up a party there which determined the attitudes of the Commons. There were rather more new members than usual and as well as Bussy, both Bagot and Green and various members of the household were elected to Parliament.[2] The king's men in the Commons may not have been dominant numerically but there was a cadre of his friends who were able to manage the Commons. There is no evidence, however, that they owed their election to intimidation by sheriffs. There were other ways of building up a party to steer Parliament.

Arundel's trial proceeded swiftly. The appellants threw down their gloves and Arundel still took his stand on the pardons, flatly denying the charges and refusing to say more. He was condemned to a traitor's death but the king immediately reduced the sentence to one of beheading on account of the earl's 'worthy blood'. The same day, Arundel was taken through the city and executed on Tower Hill. His death was unpopular and, almost inevitably, the chroniclers opposed to the court wrote of his body as a source of miracles. The only other defendant to stand trial was Warwick,

[1] *Rot. Parl.* Vol. III, p. 420.
[2] N. B. Lewis 'Re-election to Parliament in the Reign of Richard II', *E.H.R.* XLVIII (1933), p. 366.

who broke down, confessed his guilt and implicated Gloucester and others. Well satisfied to have this confession, Richard commuted the sentence to one of perpetual exile to the Isle of Man and forfeiture of his estates. It has been suggested, though there is no evidence for it, that Warwick's confession may have provided some proof of a recent conspiracy which was later removed from the roll.[1]

Before Warwick came before Parliament, however, Gloucester's case had already been dealt with. When he was formally summoned to appear, it was announced by the earl marshall that the duke had died in prison at Calais. The general consensus of historical opinion is that he had been murdered on the king's orders and with the complicity of Nottingham, who was captain of Calais. However, in view of evidence that he had been genuinely ill at the time of his arrest it is not impossible that Gloucester had died of natural causes; indeed, the sea journey and the conditions of prison life could have speeded his end. If Gloucester was murdered, it was possibly to avoid popular protest but perhaps more probably to spare Lancaster from having to face the capital trial of his own brother in Parliament.[2] For Parliament the question was now the forfeiture of Gloucester's property. To ensure this the appellants prayed that he should be declared a traitor on the grounds that he had waged war against the king's person. The Commons reinforced the charge by stressing his notorious appearance arrayed for war at Harringay. Once again we see the Commons, under Bussy's leadership, highly active in the politics of the moment.

On the following day, a full confession of guilt which was said to have been made by Gloucester at Calais was read out by a justice, William Rickhill, who said that he had obtained it the day before Gloucester's death. The confession, in English, is printed in the Parliament roll.[3] The duke admitted to being 'on wyth steryng of other men to assente to the makyng of a Commission; In the which Commission I amonges other restreyned my Lord of his fredom, and toke upon me amonge other Power Reall, trewly naght knowyng ne wytyng that tyme that I dede azeyns (against) his Estate ne his Realte, as I dede after, and do now'. Afterwards, however, he had submitted to the king 'and cryed hym mercy and grace'. He confessed too that he had come armed into the king's presence, 'howsoever that I dede it for drede of my lyf, I knowleche for certain that I dede evyll . . .' So the Lords found Gloucester to have been guilty and sentenced him to forfeiture. No other magnates were appealed, but a certain Sir Thomas

---

[1] Steel, op. cit., p. 236.

[2] Questions have been raised about the date of Gloucester's death and these are summarised by Steel, op. cit., p. 238f.

[3] *Rot. Parl.* Vol. III, p. 379.

Mortimer was impeached by the Commons in his absence and ordered to present himself in three months, and Lord Cobham, one of the commission who had condemned Burley was impeached and sentenced to exile in Guernsey.

Whatever may be said of the proceedings against those who were accused in this Parliament, it is hardly controvertible that they had at least been guilty of a travesty of justice in 1388, as those who now condemned them in 1397 were not. It is equally undeniable that Richard, despite his determination to secure and register his ascendancy, was a great deal less cruel and vindictive than the condemned Lords Appellant had been. There was no persecution. He had also taken great care to use legal procedures, admitting the Lords' right to try their peers and making no claim, as Edward II had done, to have the accused condemned on the king's record of their notorious guilt. He used the procedure of impeachment by the Commons but took control of it, Speaker Bussy formally asking the king's leave to make the charges before doing so. In all this, it has to be remembered that Richard had the support of the Dukes of Lancaster and York, and had he used his new authority calmly he could have survived.

The king now rewarded those who had supported him. Five of them were given dukedoms; Henry Bolingbroke received Hereford, and Mowbray of Nottingham became Duke of Norfolk. The dukedoms of Exeter, Surrey and Aumale went respectively to the king's half-brother, John Holland, his nephew, Thomas Holland, and his cousin, Edward of Rutland. It was an exceptionally liberal bestowal of the highest order of the peerage, and Walsingham scoffingly described the new dukes as *duketti*. In addition, Richard created John Beaufort Marquis of Dorset, and distributed four earldoms. Thomas Despenser became Earl of Gloucester, Lord Neville became Earl of Westmorland, Thomas Percy Earl of Worcester and William Scrope Earl of Wiltshire. At the same time the forfeited estates were redistributed in such a way as to break them up as units. The king also made Cheshire a principality attached to the crown, enlarging it with some adjacent lands that had belonged to Arundel. On 30 September, Parliament was prorogued, to meet again at Shrewsbury in 27 January, 1398. Before the prorogation, mass was celebrated in Westminster Abbey and a number of the lords, the clergy's lay proctor and the knights of Parliament swore to maintain all that the Parliament had done.

Shrewsbury was perhaps chosen for the reassembly of Parliament because it was near the king's power base of Cheshire. The session lasted only four days but its acts were the point at which Richard's fortunes finally turned downwards.[1] At the opening of the session the chancellor asked for

[1] *Rot. Parl.* Vol. III, pp. 356–373.

money for the defence of the realm and the king's possessions overseas. Then 'at the instance of the Commons' (as the parliamentary roll puts it) the Earl of March, who had not been present at the first session, swore to uphold the acts already done by the Parliament at Westminster. In fact, this great landowner, who was heir presumptive to the crown, had been specially summoned by Richard from Ireland, where he was the king's lieutenant, so that he might be bound in loyalty by oath. This is another instance of the use Richard had learned to make of Commons' petitions as a means of associating the Commons with his own intentions. Seven of the eight appellants of the last Parliament (Thomas Mowbray of Norfolk was absent) then petitioned that all the judgements and acts of the Merciless Parliament should be annulled and repealed as having been 'done without authority and against the will and liberty of the king and the right of his Crown', which was duly agreed. Next came the rehabilitation of the judges' answers of 1387; these were rehearsed in Parliament and the sergeants-at-law gave their opinion that the judges had advised the king correctly. Although the men of law pointed out that, under the Statute of Treasons of 1351, Parliament could define treasons not defined previously, the chief justice added that his own opinion was that of the judges in 1387. The past was further reversed with the restoration of the earldom of Suffolk to the heirs of Michael de la Pole.

After this, the Speaker replied to the chancellor's request for money by saying that, although the Commons were 'in great poverty' they were ready as loyal subjects to do all in their power, but asked the king to grant the general grace and pardon to all the people which he had offered in the previous session. To this the chancellor replied that the king wished first to know 'what they would do, on their side, for him' (*coment ils voillent faire de lour part a luy*). It is clear that, although the Commons sought to bargain their grant for a pardon, the king was even more determined to make the pardon conditional on the grant.[1] The Commons then took the political initiative when Bussy, 'rehearsing' how acts and ordinances of various Parliaments had been reversed in times past, asked for it to be established, in the interest of the safety of the king and kingdom, that the acts of this Parliament should in no way be reversed, under penalty of treason. The king's response was to charge 'all the estates of Parliament' to advise him on the matter, to which the 'Lords spiritual and temporal' replied that they had sworn to uphold the acts of this Parliament with all their power. The king then asked the judges if they saw any sure way of guarding these acts and judgements 'perpetually', to which the judges replied with what might be

[1] *Rot. Parl.* Vol. III, p. 359.

taken as a classic statement of the theory of the sovereignty of the king in Parliament, however much it was breached in the observance. 'The greatest surety there could be,' they said, 'is that which is established ordained and affirmed in Parliament' (*que le pluis greindre seuretee qui poet estre, est ceo q'est establiz, ordeinez, & affermez par Parlement*). Oaths of loyalty were then taken on the cross of Canterbury by various lords, the proctor of the clergy, and the knights. During the year ahead, Richard was to make increasing use of oath-taking in the community at large for his own security.[1] The Commons, with the assent of the Lords Spiritual and Temporal, then granted Richard the customs on wool and leather for the whole of his life, an unprecedented gift which could be expected to diminish his need for frequent Parliaments. (It was stipulated, however, that this was not to be a precedent for his successors.) In addition, he received one and a half tenths and fifteenths in the usual manner for a year and a half. Richard's promised general pardon for all who had 'ridden in arms and risen forcibly against the king' in 1387 was then announced. But the declaration specifically stated that this was given 'in consideration of the grant they had made at this time out of their good will, which was more than for any of his ancestors' (*pur consideration del Graunte q'ils ont fait a ceste foitz de lour bon volunte pluis q'ils ont fait as ascuns de ses progenitours...*). The pardon promised at Westminster had been deliberately delayed so that it could be made conditional on the exceptional grant. To leave no doubt about this, immediately after the formal pardon had been read, the king himself made a verbal statement (*par son bouche*) that if Lords or Commons in future Parliaments placed any impediment on the grant of the customs for life, 'the grace and pardon would be quite void and wholly annulled' (*la dite Grace & Pardon soit tout voide, & tout outrement adnulle*).[2] In this last Parliament of Richard II, the Commons were at the forefront of the political action on the king's behalf, though not because the king had packed them. It was rather a remarkable early example of the management of the Commons by a king's councillor who was one of their number, in a manner not unlike Tudor practice. In 1397, however, that councillor was also the Commons' Speaker.

The Shrewsbury Parliament thus seemed to register Richard's total triumph, not least because it had given him a degree of financial independence none of his predecessors had enjoyed. Yet the most dramatic scene in it presaged his downfall. On 30 September, the day before the dissolution, Henry Bolingbroke, Duke of Hereford, came into Parliament and on the instruction of the king, 'not by malice or emnity', told what had

---

[1] *Rot. Parl.* Vol. III, p. 359.
[2] Ibid., pp. 368–369.

passed between himself and the new Duke of Norfolk, Thomas Mowbray, whose absence was thus explained.[1] In December, said Hereford, the Duke of Norfolk had approached him on a journey and had warned him that both were about to be destroyed (*Nouse sumes en point d'estre dissaitz*). Why? Hereford had asked. 'Because of Radcot Bridge,' was the reply. How could this be so, said Hereford, when the king had given them his grace and they had been loyal to him? Norfolk had answered that it was 'a strange world and false' and that he knew Hereford and Lancaster would be taken and put to death when they went to Windsor after the Parliament. The parliamentary roll records all this and more of their conversation. The core of it was Norfolk's allegation that the king had not forgiven them, that the Duke of Surrey and the Earls of Wiltshire, Salisbury and Gloucester were plotting their destruction while the king was trying to draw the Earl of March and others into their plot. There are several different accounts by chroniclers of the episode, but it seems that Hereford had confided in his father who had advised him to tell the king of Norfolk's treachery. The king had then instructed him to write an account of the conversation and bring it to Parliament. Yet Richard had no wish for this delicate matter to be settled in open Parliament. Instead, a committee of eighteen, headed by the Dukes of Lancaster and York, and other magnates and six knights, among whom were Bussy and Green, was appointed to 'terminate and finally discuss' the quarrel between the two dukes.

Inspired by the government, the Commons also petitioned for a committee of Lords and others to deal with the 'divers petitions, as well for individual persons as others, which had been neither read nor answered' owing to 'shortness of time'. The same committee was to deal with these petitions as with the Hereford-Norfolk quarrel, but there were to be different arrangements for a quorum. During the next year the committee met on various occasions and in the articles of accusation against Richard at the time of his deposition, he was said to 'have subtly procured and caused it to be granted' that 'the power of Parliament to decide certain petitions . . . should devolve upon certain persons' in order to 'oppress his people'.[2] Earlier historians took the parliamentary committee to be a sign of Richard's unconstitutional intention to do away with Parliament, and Stubbs described the Shrewsbury Parliament which authorized it as a 'suicidal Parliament'.[3] In fact, the parliamentary committee of 1398 was no

[1] *Rot. Parl.* Vol. III, p. 360. (Extracts from Hereford's testimony and the subsequent parliamentary record of his case against Norfolk are in *E.H.D.* Vol. IV, pp. 175–177.)

[2] Ibid., p. 418. (Trans. Stephenson and Marcham, p. 252, and *E.H.D.* Vol. IV, pp. 407–414).

[3] Stubbs, *Constitutional History* II, p. 522 (4th edit.).

innovation. A similar committee had been set up to deal with outstanding petitions at the end of the Merciless Parliament and there had been earlier precedents too. The parliamentary committee also bore a resemblance to the much earlier practice whereby the council, acting as Parliament, dealt with petitions after the larger Parliament had dispersed.

Nor is it likely that Richard had caused the parliamentary committee to be set up in order to dispense with Parliaments in the future.[1] Yet eventually he did use it improperly and he, or his ministers, also caused the parliamentary record to be falsified to give the misuse an appearance of justification. Three separate manuscript copies of the parliamentary roll describing the Shrewsbury Parliament survive. The two earlier ones simply state the Committee's terms of reference as being to settle the quarrel between Hereford and Norfolk and to deal with outstanding petitions. The later manuscript, however, which is wholly written in a new hand, adds that the committee was to deal with 'several other matters' which also could not be dealt with for lack of time. It is this later version which is printed in the collected Rolls of Parliament and it includes another interesting addition to the original account. The record states that, following the parliamentary oaths to maintain for ever the judgements of the Shrewsbury Parliament, 'all the people' were asked by proclamation whether they agreed with this 'way of safety', in other words, with oath-taking. 'Raising their right hands,' it was said, 'they cried their assent with loud voices.'[2] This interpolation is also obviously intended to give weight to Richard's case.

Yet the fact that the record had to be falsified shows that the Parliament at Shrewsbury did not have suicide in its mind when it set up the committee. Likewise, Richard would have had no reason to falsify the parliamentary record, which could only be for the benefit of future Parliaments, if he had intended to murder Parliament as an institution. This is also confirmed by the general use he made of the parliamentary committee. It met, so far as it is known, on five occasions. On 19 March, 1398, it sat with the king at Bristol, and its proceedings were recorded. This meeting dealt with five petitions of minor significance, as Parliament had intended. A characteristic example was a complaint that, contrary to the statute of 1390, already mentioned, shoemakers were continuing to tan leather as well as to make shoes. The responses to these petitions then became statutes. One of the parliamentary committee's statutes might perhaps seem to exceed the powers of the committee in that it declared anyone attempting to secure the repeal of its

[1] The documentary evidence for what follows is examined by J. G. Edwards, 'The Parliamentary Committee of 1398,' E.H.R. XL (1925), pp. 321–333, reprinted in Fryde and Miller, op. cit., Vol. I, pp. 316–328.
[2] Rot. Parl. Vol. III, p. 360.

statutes to be a traitor. Yet this did no more than reaffirm what the full Parliament, from which it had delegated if limited powers, had already enacted in respect of its law-making. At the same meeting, the committee also tried to get to grips with the quarrel between Hereford and Norfolk as it was required to do, and decided that if sufficient proof could not be found, the dispute should be settled by trial of battle.[1]

On 29 April, the two dukes again appeared before the parliamentary committee at Windsor. Peers and 'the chivalry of England' were also present 'in great number' which presumably turned the occasion into something like a great council. With their assent, and that of those who 'had the authority of Parliament' the king decided that the two magnates' quarrel should be settled by battle.[2] The fact that Richard chose to invoke the 'authority of Parliament' (the first time this expression seems to have been used) hardly suggests that he intended to do away with Parliaments, however much he intended to manipulate them and free himself from dependence on their money grants. There was, however, to be a long delay until September before the fight between the two magnates, which was presumably because Richard still hoped for some other more satisfactory way of dealing with the affair.

By now, he must have thoroughly distrusted Norfolk. Yet could he afford to trust to the victory of Hereford, that other former appellant who would soon inherit estates which would make him the greatest power in England beside the king? Hereford was by no means as close to the court as Norfolk had become, and he had been less active than Norfolk in Gloucester's overthrow. It is also not impossible that some sort of precautionary action had really been planned at court against the Lancastrian interest, as Norfolk had alleged, since there were other rumours to this effect. Indeed, a possible explanation of the curious episode of the two dukes is that Hereford had actually believed, perhaps with reason, what Norfolk had told him, and had decided to relay it to the king as a means of conveying to Richard that he was warned of what was contemplated while purporting to disbelieve it. If this was indeed the explanation Richard would have reason to fear the victory of either duke and to seek some other outcome.

At all events, no escape from the dilemma could be found and on 16 September at Coventry, with the parliamentary committee assembled, Hereford and Norfolk met to do battle on the occasion immortalized by Shakespeare.[3] The king, however, palpably uncertain about which if either

[1] *Rot. Parl.* Vol. III, p. 383.
[2] Ibid., p. 383.
[3] Ibid., p. 383.

magnate could be trusted, stopped the fight. No doubt he had a rational scepticism about whether battle would necessarily uncover the wrongdoer. Norfolk was banished for life and Hereford for ten years, which was later reduced to six. Richard's action in putting a stop to what was to have been a magnificent and spectacular demonstration of chivalry is not likely to have enhanced his popularity with the noble and knightly classes.

Richard was now so undermined by a sense of political insecurity as to be driven to one unwise and impulsive act after another. In February 1399 John of Gaunt died. We do not know whether he had disapproved of his son's banishment, or whether he had any fear that Henry Bolingbroke would again, as in 1387, forsake Gaunt's own principle of loyalty to the crown. He is certainly not known to have protested against the sentence on his son. But with Gaunt's death Richard had lost his strongest support, and came to the conclusion that he dare not allow Henry Bolingbroke to return home to his vast inheritance and perhaps to use it against the authority of the crown. Accordingly, the parliamentary committee was summoned for its fourth meeting at Westminster on 18 March, where it revoked the letters patent which had been granted, allegedly by 'inadvertence', to Hereford and Norfolk, allowing them to receive any inheritances falling to them.[1] Again it was done by the king and the committee which had its power 'by virtue and authority of Parliament'. Hereford's banishment was extended for life, and his lands were taken into the king's hands. They were redistributed later among Richard's supporters. This was the act which finally brought Richard down.

Strictly speaking, the banishment was within the committee's original terms of reference which included settling the magnates' quarrel. But another action taken at this meeting was not. The parliamentary committee, by virtue of the powers it now claimed to have to deal with 'other matters', posthumously condemned for treason a former chief baron of the exchequer, Sir Robert Plessyngton, who had supported the appellants in 1388. The purpose was to obtain the forfeiture of his property. It was at this point that the decision was taken to change the record to enlarge the committee's powers to cover 'other matters' than petitions and that a fresh copy of the altered parliamentary roll was made. The committee's last known meeting was in April 1399, when it condemned for treason a clerk named Henry Bowet who had helped Hereford draw up a petition in respect of his property. But he was abroad, out of harm's way, with Hereford, and later became Archbishop of York.

The evidence does not suggest that the parliamentary committee had

---

[1] *Rot. Parl.* Vol. III, p. 372.

been invented to supersede Parliament but merely that, under the drive of political need, the king had improvised new powers for it. If there was a plot against Parliament it was one designed to reverse the process by which it had become an instrument of opposition and to make it once again an instrument of regal power. This, after all, was the way in which Edward I had used it, and it was also the idea in the minds of those responsible for drafting the Statute of York, who had envisaged a king ruling benignly by seeking the advice of the Lords and Commons but on all essentials having the last word. Richard's concept of kingship might perhaps be described as a kind of consultative absolution, and by the nature of things it did not work. The question was still who was to have the last word on policy in a crisis; king or Parliament. That would not be settled until after 1689 when the convention took root that the crown governs only with the advice of ministers acceptable to the parliamentary majority. In 1399 Richard's management of Parliament gave many of his subjects cause for concern and the number of his subjects who were to flock to Lancaster's support was the mark of Richard's unpopularity.

Yet the trigger for the action which destroyed him was not so much Richard's designs for Parliament as the danger he seemed to present to property and liberty. Magnates and gentry became convinced that the political power they derived from land could not survive the kind of authority the king intended the crown to have. Property and propriety were much the same thing in the middle ages. The sense of the morality of property was so strong that, alongside the most barbarous penalties inflicted on individuals, fairly scrupulous efforts were usually made not to dispossess men and their families from their property by arbitrary action. But if the Duke of Lancaster could be dispossessed, whose property was safe? It was this gnawing insecurity which turned against Richard lesser men as well the great. Richard's greatest mistake was to try to use his subjects' insecurity as a weapon against them. After Shrewsbury, he had continued to employ the giving and withholding of pardon as a threat. After first requiring individuals who had been in any way implicated in the business of 1387 to seal letters submitting to his goodwill, he returned these and instead caused proctors to be appointed who had to deliver sealed letters of submission on behalf of all the people of London and sixteen counties. These documents became known as 'blank charters'. These were so called not because they were blank but because they gave the king *carte blanche* over the persons and property of these areas as a precaution against any misdoing. The 'blank charters' were virtually all destroyed under Henry IV, when Richard was accused of using them to extract money. Little is known about them, but although they may have been accompanied by a fine their real purpose seems to have been to force individuals and communities to pledge their persons and property as securities for loyal behaviour. Richard also tried to bolster himself by continuing to demand from his subjects oaths of loyalty and of adherence to the acts done by the Parliament of Westminster and Shrewsbury.[1] But durable loyalty is never founded on fear and the oaths were worth little.

The question why Richard acted in so foolhardy a way has been answered by one of his biographers with the opinion that he had become mentally ill and was now in a condition of advanced neurosis.[2] Hostile chroniclers also cast doubt on his mental stability, describing him as descending into megalomania. He was said to have exalted himself on a high throne, where he sat requiring obeisance. Yet his policy-making, his clear concept of the monarchical system he wanted and his ability to choose highly talented ministers hardly support the conclusion that he was out of his mind. The impression left by his reign is rather that of a king trying to hold down the lid on a cauldron of aristocratic power which was at boiling point; a man unable to live with the magnates, attempting a new system of kingship and temperamentally a gambler, with a gambler's mixture of patience and rashness. He could sometimes wait, plan and calculate. He had, for instance, been shrewd enough to break up and redistribute Gloucester's and Arundel's estates in order to give a number of beneficiaries an interest in what he had done. In sequestrating the Lancastrian inheritance he had taken care not to disturb any of its lesser beneficiaries and pensioners. Yet he would also risk all on a few throws, and this is what he did in his final year, raising the stakes and losing everything. He persistently over-estimated the power he derived from his anointed kingship, and also the support among the Commons for his notion of an orderly society based on the power of the crown against that of his mightier subjects. With great recklessness, therefore, he offended vested interests which could in return damage him.

Richard wholly failed to understand how to work with the political grain of the time and the importance of securing the consent of those with the power to destroy him. Incapable of understanding the type of men who threatened him, he was still less interested in diverting the energies of the powerful into war. Like all politicians who go impatiently against the grain, he was almost bound to fail. Yet he had an understanding of what needed to be done which was in many ways correct, and his attempt to build a stronger monarchy bore some resemblance to what was done with greater skill by Edward IV and the Tudors. He was in some ways in advance of his time. He

---

[1] Richard's oaths and blank charters are discussed by C. M. Barron, op. cit.
[2] A. Steel, op. cit.

had reached the conclusion that effective monarchical government over an orderly society was not compatible with the power the magnates exerted, and that he must hack out a new pathway for kingship through the forest of old quasi-feudal ideas. He therefore set about exalting the mystique of the throne and buttressing it with supporters and retainers who could outmatch those of the magnates. His attempts to break up consolidated landholdings, and to control the abuse of maintenance were aspects of the same design. That his methods of governing would have led to some degree of absolutism is likely; that he consciously intended despotism is not. His general reaction to others was too soft to qualify him for tyranny. He was a man with some virtues for government. Yet for all the artistic sensitivity which distinguished his court, he was a man singularly lacking in sensitivity for politics; a king incapable of understanding the reactions of the aristocracy of which he was the head. After his deposition, aristocratic ambition erupted into a prolonged period of political instability, the climax of which was the Wars of the Roses.

For the most part Richard had stayed away from London after the Shrewsbury Parliament, as he had done in 1387, moving from place to place accompanied by his Cheshire archers. Early in 1399 he came back to Westminster to face a new challenge. In the previous July, the Earl of March, who had returned to Ireland after the Shrewsbury Parliament, had been ambushed and killed by the Irish, leaving a child, Edmund Mortimer, as the next heir to the throne in strict line. The Irish peace settlement which Richard had made in 1394 had broken down; Ireland was now again in rebellion and Richard determined on an expedition to reduce it. To leave England at this time seems, especially with hindsight, to have been the height of folly. The danger from Hereford was obvious and Richard had further increased his unpopularity by continuing to raise loans under pressure. But he seems to have assumed that by his oaths and his bonds he had sorted out friends from foes and that he was safeguarded by his own supporters and retainers throughout the English shires. He was apparently oblivious to the discontent in the political nation and he may have been too remote in his regality for his councillors to feel comfortable about telling him of his unpopularity, if they themselves were aware of it. At all events, he sailed from Milford Haven for Ireland at the end of May with an expedition which included most of his aristocratic friends. For his own safety, he took with him the sons of Hereford and Thomas of Woodstock. The realm was again left in the keeping of Edmund of York, with the government managed by Stafford the chancellor, Wiltshire the treasurer and the trusted councillors Bussy, Bagot and Green. Once Richard had gone, all kind of rumours were spread, one of which was that he intended to rule from Dublin, subjecting his English subjects to tyranny.

Little more than a month later, early in July, Henry Bolingbroke Earl of Hereford accompanied by Archbishop Arundel and a small band of friends and retainers landed at Ravenspur on the Humber and made for the old Lancastrian seat at Pontefract. The decisive factor in his success was the decision of the two northern marcher earls, Percy of Northumberland and Neville of Westmorland, to declare for him. They too had their grievances against Richard: Northumberland, in particular, because Richard had shown signs of wanting to dilute the influence of the ambitious Percys in the north. They possessed large forces which were used to guard the border and these were decisive in the early stages of the Lancastrian usurpation. The position Henry formally adopted was that he had come simply to claim his Lancastrian inheritance, not to dethrone Richard, and the Percys were later to justify their adherence to him on the grounds that these were what they had understood his aims to be. Yet it is hard to believe that they did not know or suspect the direction in which Henry Bolingbroke was going. Even at the outset, as though he were a king, he had issued a commission, under his seal of Lancaster, appointing Northumberland warden of the West March of Scotland (of which he had been deprived by Richard) as well as the East March. Then, after gathering his forces, Henry marched south gathering adherents all the way.

Richard was slow in returning from Ireland. Aumale, York's son, had advised him to divide his forces, send an advance force to north Wales under Salisbury and follow himself later. This probably crucial delay may have been deliberate treachery by Aumale, who was soon to desert the king. In the meantime, York himself was wholly ineffective in defending Richard's interest. He first moved the administration from London (whose citizens he feared) to St Albans and began raising troops too late. The councillors then moved to the west hoping to join Richard but whereas Wiltshire, Bagot and Green went to Bristol as a centre of resistance, York and the rest of the council occupied Berkeley castle. Bolingbroke might have been expected to go to London but this would have left Richard free to gather support in the rest of the country. Instead, therefore, Bolingbroke also turned to the south west. When he came to Berkeley, the Duke of York submitted to him and was forced to order the surrender of Bristol. The Earl of Wiltshire, Bussy, and Green were taken and beheaded; Bagot escaped.

Almost at the same time Richard left Ireland and landed at Haverfordwest. There he seems to have been advised by Aumale, again perhaps treacherously, to disband much of the force he had with him and to go to join the men he had sent under Salisbury to north Wales. But Salisbury's men were also beginning to desert, and both Aumale and Thomas Percy, Earl of Worcester, now abandoned the king. Richard was left to make the slow journey northwards along the Welsh coast to Conway, where he would be near his Cheshire base. But Bolingbroke was able to make a parallel journey inland with much greater speed, arriving with his forces at Chester. Isolated in Conway castle, and cut off from Cheshire and from his support in the rest of England, Richard was now deceived and betrayed into surrender by false promises. For what happened we rely on the mutually confirming accounts of several chronicles. The parliamentary rolls, when they take up the story give what is now known as being a falsified account of Richard's surrender and abdication.[1]

In Lancastrian historical fiction, Richard wandered slowly and aimlessly along the Welsh coast in isolated despair, realizing that all was over and ready to surrender. According to the Lancastrian chronicler, Thomas of Walsingham, he 'lost heart for fighting'. At Conway, therefore, he was said to have sought a meeting with Thomas Arundel and with the Earl of Northumberland. He allegedly told them he would yield the kingdom if he were guaranteed security of life and honourable living conditions. Subsequently, after a brief meeting with Bolingbroke, Richard travelled to London with his cousin and the Lancastrian army and was lodged in the Tower. The rolls of Parliament which later gave an account of the process of abdication and deposition, state that Richard, 'while still at liberty' at Conway, had promised the Earl of Northumberland that he was 'willing to renounce the Crown.' When Richard was reminded of this in the Tower by Northumberland he is said to have undertaken to fulfil that promise. Then after some negotiations, the king 'willingly . . . and with a joyful countenance' (*ac hillari vultu*) took the schedule of abdication in his hand, said he wanted to read it and 'signed it with his own hand', the first recorded information we have, incidentally, of a king's signing as distinct from sealing a document. Then, according to the parliamentary roll, he said that 'if it were in his power', Lancaster should succeed him, and gave his cousin his signet as a token.[2]

This account is inherently improbable and has been shown to be false by the analysis made by M. V. Clarke and V. H. Galbraith of the work of a group of minor chroniclers who had not been fed with the official version as the Lancastrian chroniclers were. The truth is that Richard had made as much haste as he could to Conway, only to find himself without any forces

---

[1] The definitive reconstruction of these events is by M. V. Clarke and V. H. Galbraith, 'The deposition of Richard II', reprinted in *Fourteenth Century Studies* (M. V. Clarke) which shows the account in the rolls of Paliament and in Walsingham to be false. A selection of related documents (translated) is in B. Wilkinson, *Const. Hist. of Med. England, 1216–1399*, Vol. II, pp. 284–327. See also B. Wilkinson 'The Deposition of Richard II and the Accession of Henry IV', *E.H.R.* LIV (1939), pp. 215–239, reprinted in Fryde and Miller, Vol. I, Ch. 13.

[2] *Rot. Parl.* Vol. III, p. 416–417.

and cut off from contact with his supporters. There he was visited by Northumberland who promised that Richard should keep the crown if he would restore Hereford's estates, refer to Parliament his claim to be hereditary steward and allow five councillors to be tried. After some consultation the king agreed, allegedly with the mental reservation that he would have his revenge if he could. Northumberland then 'took oath upon the body of our Lord' to stand by his word, and Richard set off with Arundel and Percy to meet his cousin. Northumberland had gone separately. On the way they were ambushed by Lancastrians, possibly with Northumberland's connivance, though his alleged treachery has been contested. Richard was then taken to Chester not willingly but as a prisoner. From there writs were sent out in his name for a Parliament to meet on 30 September and Richard was brought by Lancaster as a prisoner to the Tower of London.

The question now was how to proceed with his dethronement and Lancaster's succession. Richard almost certainly asked to be heard by Parliament but as with Edward II that was refused. In fact he was obliged to abdicate before a Parliament met. Those who had been summoned to Parliament by his writ met in Westminster Hall on 30 September, but because he had ceased to wear the crown, they were not a Parliament. Care had been taken to extract Richard's abdication from him the day before the assembly of those summoned by his writ so that they should not be a Parliament. Instead, this gathering, which was probably augmented by Londoners, was classified as a gathering of the estates of the realm. There were probably several reasons for this procedure. For one thing, since the king was central to Parliament, it was hardly credible that Parliament, in its capacity as a high court, could be used to depose him. It had no life without him. Furthermore, if an attempt had been made to depose Richard by the high court of Parliament, he would almost certainly have had to appear before it, which could have destroyed Henry's enterprise. It had been easier to depose Edward II because the throne passed immediately to his uncontested legitimate successor. There were undoubtedly those who opposed Richard's deposition, as there had been a party opposed to that of Edward II, and it has been strongly argued that the Percys were at the centre of this resistance. On this reading of events Northumberland had not been privy to Richard's capture after he had given his word as to the king's safety, and even the Percys had opposed the deposition to the last.[1] But whether or not Northumberland was innocent of breaking his word to Richard, it is certainly likely that political opposition was even more of a difficulty for

[1] B. Wilkinson 'The Deposition of Richard II and the Accession of Henry IV', *E.H.R.* Vol. LIV (1939) (reprinted Fryde and Miller, op. cit., Vol. I).

Bolingbroke than constitutional propriety, which was another reason for avoiding the formality of a Parliament and preferring a vaguely constituted assembly of 'estates and people' (as it was described) as the instrument of deposition. Besides, it would not have been comfortable for the incoming king to have to meet regularly the body which, having formally deposed his successor, could therefore, in theory, depose him. It was desirable that the deposition should be by an extraordinary assembly, though it was also preferable, in the recent tradition of parliamentary trials and sentences, that it should have a parliamentary flavour. At all events, there was certainly no parliamentary deposition and, as he undoubtedly preferred, Henry IV was given no parliamentary title.[1]

A commission had been appointed to consider the procedure for removing Richard to make way for Bolingbroke and this determined that he should first abdicate and then be deposed. But that Richard resigned 'cheerfully' is impossible to believe, and in any case we have the contrary testimony from the lawyer, Adam of Usk who, though a Lancastrian, was an eyewitness to some of the proceedings and was himself a member of the commission giving advice on Richard's deposition and the manner of Bolingbroke's accession. This witness relates how he was with Richard in the Tower and was 'present at his dinner'. Adam continues: 'I marked his mood and bearing.... And there and then the king discoursed sorrowfully in these words: My God! a wonderful land is this, and a fickle; which hath exiled, destroyed or ruined so many kings, rulers and great men, and is ever filled and toileth with strife and variance and envy.' Adam notes with some compassion the 'trouble of his mind' and how he had none of his own people but only spies to serve him and 'musing... on the fickle fortune of the world, I departed thence much moved at heart...'[2]

The members of Parliament summoned by Richard reassembled as Henry IV's first Parliament on 6 October, and the parliamentary rolls for that occasion begin with a version of the events leading up to and including the deposition in Westminster Hall. Much of what was said about the events leading to the abdication was, as we have seen, false, and much was omitted to distort the picture, but the scene in Westminster Hall was no doubt accurately enough described.[3] The hall was 'prepared for the holding of Parliament' with lords and 'a great multitude assembled for the holding of Parliament'. The throne stood vacant, 'in the absence of any presiding officer', and was covered with gold. Lancaster was in his due place. The

---

[1] G. Lapsley, 'The Parliamentary Title of Henry IV', E.H.R. XLIX (1934), pp. 423–449 and pp. 577–606.

[2] *Chronicon Adae de Usk*, ed. E. M. Thompson, pp. 141ff.

[3] The events concerning the deposition are in *Rot. Parl.* Vol. III, pp. 415–432.

Archbishop of York then read Richard's statement of abdication after which the 'estates' and people were asked separately if they wished to accept the abdication. They did. It was then decided that 'to remove all suspicion' it would also be expedient that the misdeeds for which Richard deserved deposition should be written down and read. He was accused of giving the possessions of the crown to unworthy persons, breaking his coronation oath, setting aside the laws, misusing Parliament, terrorising the judges in 1387, and of having Gloucester murdered and Arundel beheaded. He was also accused of having his own nominees sent to Parliament, of claiming that the lives and property of his subjects were at his disposal, and of saying 'that his laws were in his own mouth, or occasionally, in his own breast and that he alone could establish and change the laws of the realm'. In short, he was accused of tyranny and was declared deposed, a commission being established to carry out the sentence.

Then, the throne being vacant, Henry of Lancaster stood up, crossed himself and claimed the throne 'in the mother tongue' in these words, and the record breaks into English: 'In the name of Fadir, Son, and Holy Ghost, I Henry of Lancastr' chalenge yis Rewme of Yngland and the Corone with all ye membrs and ye appurtenances, als I yt am disendit be right lyne of the Blode comyng fro the gude lorde Kyng Henry therde, and thorghe yat ryght yat God of his grace hath sent me, with helpe of my Kyn and of my Frendes to recover it; the whiche Rewme was in poynt to be undone for defaut of Governance and undoyng of the gode Lawes.' The estates and the people accepted the claim and Henry showed the signet as a sign that Richard approved his claim. Arundel then placed him on the throne and preached a sermon on the text 'a man shall rule his people' (*vir dominabitur populo*). Henry thanked all the lords and estates, reassuring them that he wished that 'no man thynk yt be waye of Conquest I wold disherit any man of his heritage, franches, or other ryghtes that hym aght to have . . .' except for those who had been against the common good of the realm.

The precise nature of Bolingbroke's claim was left unclear. Even though the eight year old Earl of March had the strict right to succeed nobody supposed that another boy king was feasible. Henry, however, would have liked to establish a legitimate claim and to that end had tried to resurrect an old legend that Edmund Crouchback, from whom he was descended through his mother, had really been the elder son of Henry III but had been set aside because of infirmity in favour of Edward I. Had that been true, all previous kings since Henry III would have had no legitimate claim and his advisers would not accept it. Nor were Henry's advisers prepared to agree with the suggestion that the throne might be his simply by right of conquest. Some of them would rather have had a specifically parliamentary title but Henry preferred Richard's deposition and his recognition to be by a non-parliamentary assembly of the estates and populace on grounds left deliberately vague. The transfer of the crown did not quite go uncontested. The Bishop of Carlisle, Thomas Merke, is said to have registered a protest in these words before the deposition: 'I maintain that there is not one present who is competent and fit to judge such a sovereign as my lord the King whom we have acknowledged our (liege) lord for the space of twenty years and more', declaring that even the falsest traitor and wickedest murderer would be brought before the judge to hear his sentence.[1] But neither this protest nor any other is recorded in the partisan Parliament roll, though it was probably to answer such protests that the articles of deposition were prepared and published.

The day after the deposition, Sir William Thirning, the chief justice pronounced the sentence to Richard in the Tower on behalf of the 'Procurators to all thes States and Poeple forsayd'. He concluded with the declaration that none of these estates or people 'fro this tyme forward ne bere zowe feyth, ne do zowe obeisance os to thar Kyng'. Richard was said to have replied that 'he loked not ther after; Bot he sayde, that after all this he hoped that is Cosyn wolde be goode Lord to Hym'.[2] Within five months Richard was murdered.

[1] Evidence for the Bishop of Carlisle's protest is compared in Clarke and Galbraith, op. cit.
[2] *Rot. Parl.* Vol. III, p. 424.

CHAPTER 7

— * —

Henry IV:
Parliament and a Hobbled King

I

THE deposition of Richard II marked the end of the period during which the fundamentals of Parliament were formed by the interaction of monarchical, baronial and representational politics. Important developments of parliamentary privilege and practice lay ahead in the final eighty-five years of what are conventionally called the middle ages of English history. Yet the essential groundwork of medieval parliamentary power had been laid, and on it during the sixteenth and seventeenth centuries would be built the basic structure of the modern Parliament. For the crown itself, Richard's overthrow was even more sharply the end of a chapter. Seeking an escape from the tensions between the crown and the magnates, the king had resorted to government which was in some degree authoritarian if not absolutist. He had tried and failed to construct a system in which Parliament functioned in apposition not in opposition to the crown. With his overthrow it was settled that henceforth the monarchy would in practice be in some degree limited. But little else was resolved. The crown had been seriously weakened by the loss of the legitimacy which was the norm of the time and its weakness was a new stimulant for strife. Whereas the replacement of Edward II by Edward III had merely hastened the natural succession, the installation of Henry IV had set aside the legitimate line and made the crown a prize for competition. The right of inheritance was fundamental in medieval morality and if Richard had done wrong to deprive Lancaster of his dukedom, Lancaster was seen to have done a greater wrong when he robbed Richard of his realm. The first half of Henry's reign was therefore ravaged by rebellion; under his grandson there was to be an eruption of civil war and a change of dynasty, the end of the medieval period being scarred by that caricature of all usurpations when Richard III took his nephew's crown. The major themes of politics during much of the fifteenth century were worked out not in Parliament but on the battlefield and scaffold. Against the clamour of civil strife, the stubborn insistence of the Commons on their privileges resounds like a determined but independent descant.

It was nevertheless a period of great achievement in the development of the corporate identity of the House of Commons. During the fifteenth century the Commons' right to assent to legislation was established (indeed, for a time they became virtually the sole initiators of law-making); they themselves became the recipients of petitions (previously addressed to the king); their privileges were widened and strengthened and there were attempts to regulate the franchise. The Commons now understood even more clearly the power they had through their control of taxation and they did not hesitate to exert it. Conscious of the weakness of Henry IV's authority, they spoke to him with a degree of bluntness never used to his predecessors. All these changes, however, were clarifications and embellishments of what had gone before. Important though these decades were in the constitutional history of Parliament, the broad shape of the institution had already been cut by the hammer and chisel of political contest.

As the stuff of political action became more disconnected from Parliament, the number of Parliaments held also diminished. During the twenty-three years of Henry IV and Henry V twenty-two Parliaments were summoned. Under Henry VI there were several intervals without Parliaments: between 1439 and 1442, between 1450 and 1453, and between 1455 and 1459. In the twenty-two years of Edward IV only seven Parliaments were held and in Richard III's two years on the throne only one.

Henry IV had done his best to make the grounds of his succession both broad based and conveniently vague. When Richard was removed for breaking his coronation oath, the better claim of Edmund Mortimer had been set aside, almost without a thought, because he was a child. Archbishop Arundel had preached in the deposition assembly on the text 'A man shall rule his people' and he had spoken of the sufferings of a kingdom ruled by a child, with the clear implication that Richard had never ceased to rule childishly. Henry's own claim was vaguely grounded on his descent from Henry III, on conquest and on the assent of the 'estates and the people' given in the assembly which had deposed Richard. Later, his dynasty was also to have implicit parliamentary recognition when the first Parliament of the new reign recognized his eldest son as heir to the throne. Henry however had no formal parliamentary title and the Lancastrian monarchy was not, as Bishop Stubbs saw it, a 'great constitutional experiment', a 'premature testing of the parliamentary system'. Nor was it a parliamentary monarchy in which Henry stood for the parliamentary and constitutional traditions handed down to his family by Thomas of Lancaster. The truth is rather that Henry IV became king in circumstances not unlike those in which his ancestor had unsuccessfully threatened the reigning monarch of his time and, once installed, Henry himself faced precisely the same sort of aristocratic challenge.

Immediately after he had been installed on the throne in the assembly which made him king, Henry IV had announced that he had issued new writs summoning those who had been called there by Richard's writ to come to Parliament on 6 October. He apologized for the shortness of notice. On that day, the first of Henry's Parliaments met at Westminster.[1] Of ninety-seven Lords Spiritual and Temporal summoned, at least sixty-three attended, most of the absentees being abbots and priors. Of sixteen dukes and earls summoned only two were absent; of thirty-four barons, eleven were not there. All seventy-four knights from the thirty-seven shires attended and claimed their expenses; only about a sixth of the 173 citizens and burgesses from eighty-five cities and boroughs seem to have received writs for expenses, but many more probably attended. Few of the Commons present seem to have been in Richard's last Parliament though most had been in one or another Parliament during his reign.

Opening the proceedings, Archbishop Arundel began by explaining how Richard II's summons had become invalid (*ne feust du null force*) because of his deposition, and went on to describe how the realm had been brought near destruction by being governed by 'children' and how Almighty God had now provided a wise and discreet man to govern it. He said that the king intended 'to be counselled and governed by honourable, wise and discreet persons of his kingdom' and not by 'his own will, voluntary purpose or singular opinion'. In other words, Henry was bidding for support as a king who had renounced Richard's arbitrary ways, although he was to claim and receive all his predecessor's prerogatives. In the usual manner, the king promised to protect the liberties of the church, maintain the laws and respect liberties and franchises. The chancellor then requested the Lords to agree to the adjournment of Parliament until 14 October, the day after the coronation. That event took place with great splendour and the king was anointed with a specially holy oil which, according to Walsingham, had been entrusted by the Blessed Virgin to Thomas Becket with the prophecy that future kings of England anointed with it should be defenders and

---

[1] *Rot. Parl.* Vol. III, pp. 415–453. Some extracts from the petitions of this Parliament are in E.H.D. Vol. IV. 184–187.

friends of the church. It was said to have been hidden at Poitiers until it had been providentially delivered to Henry of Lancaster, the new king's grandfather. Whatever ceremony and sacrament could do to make good Henry IV's title was done.

Parliament then returned for business on 14 October and before the record of this begins, the parliamentary roll gives its account, which has already been described, of 'the Record and Process of the Renunciation of King Richard the Second after the Conquest, and the acceptance of the same Renunciation together with the Deposition of the said King Richard'. The business of the Parliament proper began with the presentation of the Speaker, one Sir John Cheyne who, however, had immediately to withdraw on the pretext of ill health, but actually because he was suspected of involvement with Lollardy. Behind this retirement was a vigorous new attempt on the part of the congregation of the clergy, which was meeting at the same time, to extirpate heresy. Cheyne's place as Speaker was taken by Sir John Dorewood. Parliament then voted a subsidy on wool and woolfells for three years and also a tenth and fifteenth promised to Richard II. The clergy were not asked for taxation; the king was more anxious for their prayers and favourable influence abroad where he faced some difficulties, most awkwardly in France, about the recognition of his dynasty.

Parliament's first business was the reversal of the actions of Richard's final years, and the new king used the Commons petitions for his purpose, precisely as Richard had done. The first petition granted was for the repeal of 'all that was done' in the Parliament of 1397–98, which was to be held as 'no Parliament'. But any statute 'profitable' for the realm should be enacted. The Commons then prayed that the Merciless Parliament should be considered valid and its acts enforced, which was granted. The king also accepted a petition condemning Richard's parliamentary committee as 'very derogatory to all the estates of the realm'. He declared his will that no such power 'should ever be granted henceforth by such authority of Parliament' and that it should be no precedent.[1] Petitions dealing with the restoration of those who were said to have been wrongfully deprived or exiled and putting right the wrongs of the remaining Appellants or their heirs followed. The blank charters were annulled, being later burned on Henry's orders, and the judgement against Thomas Haxey was reversed. The question was then put to the Lords and Commons whether the king's son Henry should be created Prince of Wales, Duke of Cornwall and Earl of Chester, and recognized as heir to the throne. The recognition was given and the king put a circlet on the prince's head and gave him the ring and

---

[1] *Rot. Parl.* Vol. III, p. 425.

staff. A kind of parliamentary ratification was thus given to the new dynasty. Later the Prince was made Duke of Aquitaine and given the franchise of Lancaster though that duchy was now merged permanently in the crown.

Among the acts of this Parliament was one which prohibited any subject from using or giving liveries. From this prohibition the king himself was exempted, but anyone to whom he gave his livery could only wear it in his presence, abroad, or at war. The ordinary households of magnates were also exempt. The object was simply to curb the abuse of livery and to prevent the crown from following the example set by Richard's Cheshire archers. In both respects the attempt failed. The same act provided that nobody who had come to Henry's aid against Richard II should be proceeded against in the courts 'for the pursuit of the said king, taking and withholding his body', nor for the pursuit of any of his adherents.[1]

At the beginning of the Parliament a storm broke out with demands for the arrest of Richard's councillors and friends, including the new Dukes of Aumale, Surrey and Exeter, the Marquis of Dorset, the Earl of Gloucester and the survivor of Richard's three most unpopular chamber knights, Sir William Bagot. Proceedings against them continued through much of Parliament. There were charges and counter-charges. Bagot implicated Aumale in the Duke of Gloucester's murder and said that Richard had spoken of Henry as an enemy of the church and of Aumale as his successor. Denying it, Aumale challenged his accuser to single combat. The plea of the accused men was that whatever they had done had been under duress and that they 'dyd it fore drede of dethe'. The three dukes were arrested but the whole business was awkward for the new king in view of his own part on Richard's side in the 1397 Parliament. The business dragged on until 29 October when the chief justice finally pronounced that the appellants of that Parliament were guilty of something short of treason. Aumale, Surrey and Exeter were reduced to their former earldoms of Rutland, Kent and Huntingdon, the Marquis of Dorset became again Earl of Somerset and Lord Despenser lost the earldom of Gloucester.[2] Henry had done enough to annoy these men and raise them as enemies against him but not enough to render them harmless.

In this he manifested the indecisive caution which seemed to characterize him as king and which is, superficially at least, in contrast with his earlier life

---

[1] The statutory enactments of Henry IV's first Parliament are embodied in *Stat. R.* Vol. II, pp. 111–119.

[2] *Rot. Parl.* Vol. III, pp. 449–453, elaborated in *Annales Henrici IV*, ed. Riley, Rolls Series iii, pp. 303ff.

as a brave and successful crusader and a man of principle in domestic politics. On the face of it, there appears to be some difficulty in reconciling Henry's behaviour as a king with his behaviour as Derby and Hereford. As a magnate he was gallant and highly regarded abroad. At home he had stood against Richard in 1387 on constitutional grounds but had refused to follow Gloucester in carrying opposition to the crown to extremes. He had won the throne by acting boldly. Yet once he became king his touch was very often hesitant and uncertain. For this his decline into illness and neurosis was partly responsible, but the uneasiness of his rule was evident before that. The truth is probably that the contrast between Henry as duke and Henry as king was more apparent than real. Whatever his feats as a crusader, as Hereford he had vacillated in domestic politics. He had supported the Lords Appellants of 1387, even when they fell into an extremism in which he probably did not believe, perhaps because his father's guiding hand was absent at the time. In Richard's ascendancy he turned against his former friends and after his curious betrayal of Norfolk's confidence (more, perhaps, on his father's advice than his own judgement) he was finally stimulated to action against the king only by the loss of his duchy. The symptoms of a certain irresolution were early apparent; they simply became more prominent under the stress of kingship and illness. Inevitably they made him enemies.

While the accusations against the offenders in the 1397 Parliament were still hanging fire, Parliament turned to deal with the former king. The Commons, it seems, wanted Richard to be brought to answer for his wrongdoing in Parliament, which would have been a precedent unwelcome to the king. So on 23 October, Archbishop Arundel charged the Lords Spiritual and Temporal to keep secret what was to be put to them, after which the Earl of Northumberland asked each of them what should be done with Richard to put him in safe keeping 'saving his life, which the king wishes to safeguard in every way'. Fifty-eight of them, whose names are listed in the parliamentary rolls and who include the prince of Wales, the Duke of York, the two archbishops, thirteen bishops and seven abbots, answered that Richard should be 'put in safe and secret custody' in a place where there were few people, that he should be closely guarded and waited on by none of his former servants. After a delay the king came to the Parliament in the great hall at Westminster where, with the assent of the Lords Spiritual and Temporal 'Richard, lately king of England' was sentenced to 'perpetual prison, to remain there secretly in safe custody'. Richard was subsequently transferred to the Lancastrian castle of Pontefract.[1]

[1] *Rot. Parl.* Vol. III, pp. 426–427.

It was clearly a decision which had been taken in private conclave between the king and the Lords, and the Commons' reaction to it and to the proceedings against the late king's former friends was a precursor of the attitude they would adopt towards future dynastic changes. They did not dissent from what was done, but they were not going to be involved in the dangerous acts of revenge committed by the aristocratic faction fighters if they could possibly help it. Their principal concern was self-protection. They therefore petitioned that 'since the judgements of the Parliament belong solely to the king and lords, and not to the Commons . . . no record may be made in Parliament against the said Commons that they are or will be parties to judgements given or to be given hereafter in Parliament'. Replying for the king, the archbishop said that the Commons were 'petitioners and demanders' (askers) and that judgement was a matter for the king and Lords. But he added that in making statutes, grants or subsidies, or in things 'to be done for the common profit of the realm, the king especially wishes to have their advice and assent'. It was a very clear and important recognition not only of the Commons' rights over taxation but also of the essential part they now played in law-making and politics more generally.[1]

One further action of this Parliament was indicative of the Commons' self-confidence. Recalling that, when they had 'granted' Richard the 'full liberty' of his progenitors' prerogative, he had abused this by 'turning the laws to his own will', they nevertheless petitioned, because of their confidence in the new king, that he should 'be in as great royal liberty' as his predecessors. In granting this, Henry replied that it was 'not his intention or wish to pervert the laws, statutes or good usages nor to take advantage in other way of this grant'. He can hardly have been enthusiastic about the wording of the petition or the terms in which he was constrained to reply. From the outset of his reign, partly because of his questionable legitimacy and partly because of his financial dependence, he was treated almost as a king ruling on conditions. Indeed, his reaction to the Commons' requests often seemed to indicate his tacit acceptance that this was the reality. Moreover, immediately Parliament began he was faced with petitions criticising grants he had made to individuals as rewards for their help when he had landed. In response to these he was obliged to make some concessions, one of which was his agreement to accepting the advice of his council when bestowing grants.

Parliament was dissolved on 19 November, the king having done what he could to conciliate the important men of his realm. Yet virtually half his

[1] *Rot. Parl.* Vol. III, p. 427.

reign was to be spent in fighting off rebellion. Before Christmas, Rutland, Kent, Huntingdon and Bishop Merke, although they had places at court, were conspiring to destroy Henry and his sons. The plans were revealed by Rutland to York and hence to the king. The rebels seized Windsor but Henry had already left and the revolt was quickly suppressed. Kent, Salisbury and Despenser were murdered by mobs and there were nearly thirty executions but Aumale, having revealed the plot, escaped unharmed. Bishop Merke was pardoned because the Pope refused to agree to his degradation. The only result of this abortive revolt was Richard's murder at Pontefract. It was said that he had starved himself to death; Henry was a pall bearer at his funeral.

The disturbances of the next eight years can conveniently be surveyed together before we turn to the Parliaments held during this time. In Henry IV's first Parliament, agreement had been given to an invasion of Scotland. In the summer of 1400, supported by the dissident Scottish Earl of the March, George Dunbar, the king led an expedition to force the Scottish king to do him homage and keep the peace. It achieved nothing and on the way south Henry learned that a quarrel between Lord Grey of Ruthin and Owen Glendower, the largest Welsh landowner and a descendant of princes, had developed into a more general Welsh revolt. An English march through north Wales temporarily quietened the principality but order quickly broke down again and what had begun as a private quarrel developed into a Welsh national uprising as castles and also boroughs settled by the English were successfully attacked. With the French hostile to the king who had supplanted Richard, the Lancastrian dynasty seemed increasingly shaky, not least because Henry was having to ask for more taxation, which he had promised not to do. English expeditions against the Welsh in 1401 and 1402 achieved nothing. To quieten the French Henry had agreed to the return to France of Richard's widow and her dowry, but once she had gone there was no longer any reason for the French to refrain from making deals with Henry's Celtic foes. In 1402, Glendower took prisoner Edmund Mortimer, uncle of the Earl of March. After the failure of a third English expedition, Mortimer changed sides, married Glendower's sister and made a treaty with his captor either to restore Richard if he were alive, which he was repeatedly rumoured to be, or to make the young Earl of March king. Glendower had also been treating with the Scots who invaded England but they were defeated by the Percys, Northumberland and his son Henry Hotspur, at Homildon Hill in September 1402, which was the one English success at this time.

It was indeed a famous victory but it only brought Henry IV more trouble and it contrasted uncomfortably with his own failure against the

Welsh. The Percys then quarrelled with him, apparently over ransoms, and joined Glendower. Their declared purpose was to place the Earl of March on the throne, the Percys maintaining that Henry had sworn an oath on first coming to England that he had come only for his own lands and not for the crown. It is, indeed, possible that Henry had at first felt obliged to give some such guarantee in order to get general support and that, for their own convenience, the Percys had fallen in with him, as his designs on the crown became overt, just as they now fell out with him in their disappointments over money and their rights on the border. In the background there was still talk of Richard, and discontent simmered. In July 1403 at Shrewsbury, however, Henry defeated Hotspur who was killed, and Northumberland's brother and other prisoners were beheaded. Northumberland himself submitted but in the Parliament of 1404 was found not guilty of treason but only of trespass, and was subsequently freed.

Yet there was still no peace. In 1405, in which year Henry's fortunes were at their lowest, he faced a multiple attack. Glendower, whose position in his country was now much stronger and who had declared himself Prince of Wales, made an alliance with both the French, who sent an expeditionary force to Wales, and with the Earl of Northumberland. Most incredibly there was even an agreement of a sort, though its status is uncertain, to divide England up, with Northumberland ruling the north, Glendower a larger Wales stretching into the West of England to Worcester, and the Earl of March reigning over the rest. Henry was in great danger and Archbishop Scrope of York joined the rebellion supporting a manifesto which accused Henry of bad government, heavy taxation and of failing to defend the country against French raids. But Henry was able to march north and take the rebels unprepared. Northumberland fled to Scotland and later moved to safer refuge with Glendower. Despite Archbishop Arundel's protests, Archbishop Scrope who had been tricked into submission, was executed, as were many others. The greater danger from Glendower in alliance with a French force remained, but these allies made no progress into England. Eventually the French gave up and went home. Over the next three years the English recovered the Welsh castles and control of the country. Glendower took to the hills but was never found. Finally, in yet another rebellion Northumberland was killed at Bramham Moor near Tadcaster in February 1408. At last the Lancastrian dynasty seemed secure.[1]

During these eight years, six Parliaments were held. The underlying themes of them all were the disturbances in the country, the insecurity of the

---

[1] For a general account of the reign see especially J. L. Kirby, *Henry IV of England* (1970) and E. F. Jacob, *The Fifteenth Century, 1399–1485* (1961).

king and his constant vulnerability through lack of money. Henry's income was significantly less than Richard's and the costs to be covered were greater. Throughout these years the Commons showed their awareness of the financial leverage they could exert, yet they also, quite naturally, showed no inclination to reverse Henry's *coup d'état*. Quite apart from their natural disposition to follow the power of the day in dynastic matters, their overriding concern was to avoid further disturbance. Yet they cherished their freedom to debate before reaching their conclusions, and the individuals among them were as varied in competence, energy and rectitude as in any future House of Commons. We know nothing of the manner of their proceedings from the rolls of Parliament, but a convincing glimpse of their characteristics is provided by a satirist's description of the Commons in session, almost certainly based on knowledge. It is written with a derision resembling that of a 'parliamentary sketch writer' in a twentieth century newspaper and although it purports to relate to Richard's last Parliament, the description is no doubt fully applicable to Henry IV's first, and may, indeed, have been written early in the new reign. It tells how, when the Commons were sent away to grant money, some of them went through the motion of arguing about it to justify the salaries paid by the shires so that their representatives should expound their grievances, and then goes on to describe types of members that are found in Parliament in any age. 'Some members sat there like a nought in arithmetic, that marks a place but has no value in itself. Some had supped with simony the previous evening so that the shire they represented lost all value from their presence. Some were tattlers who went to the king and denounced as his foes men who were really good friends of his and deserved no blame from king, council, or Commons, if one listened carefully to the very end of their speeches. Some members slumbered and slept and said very little. Some mumbled and stammered and did not know what they meant to say. Some were hired men and would not take any step for fear of their masters. Some were so pompous and dull-witted that they got hopelessly muddled before they reached the close of their speeches. . . .'[1] There is no category in this list which has not had its counterpart in the House of Commons of any age, including our own, and although the fifteenth century versifier, like the modern sketch-writer, was more interested in frailties than merit, this simply reminds us how effectively the institution can function despite shortcomings of individual members.

---

[1] *Mum and the Soothsegger*, passus IV ed. Mabel Day and Robert Steele (Early English Text Society, 1936); written in alliterative verse. The modern English version used here is that in *E.H.D.* Vol. IV, p.453.

Henry IV: Parliament and a Hobbled King

The second of Henry IV's Parliaments met at Westminster on 20 January, 1401, having originally been intended for York the previous autumn.[1] It was opened by Sir William Thirning, the chief justice, who had delivered the sentence of deposition to Richard II in the Tower. Money was badly needed and Henry was asking for as much as £130,000, to the Commons' dismay. Their Speaker was Sir Arnald Savage, a knight of the shire for Kent whose loquacity, not to say long-windedness, resounds over the centuries thanks to the parliamentary roll which records his words extensively. His ambition was evidently to compete with the biblically embroidered rhetoric customarily used by chancellors who opened Parliament. Yet beneath the verbosity lay a hard-edged understanding of Henry IV's vulnerability. Thus on 22 January, Savage asked the king on the Commons' behalf that they should be given reasonable time to debate what was put to them 'without being called upon suddenly to reply concerning the weightiest matters at the end of Parliament, as has been the custom in the past'. The king replied that it was not his intention to follow that sort of procedure 'or to imagine any such subtlety'. The Commons, he promised, would have the time needed for their business.[2] A few days later the Speaker was successfully insisting that the king should not listen to any unauthorized account of the Commons' debates since 'it might happen, in regard to certain matters which were moved among them, that one of their members should tell the king about such matters to make himself agreeable to the king and obtain advancement, before these matters had been determined and discussed and agreed upon between the Commons themselves'. The king might thus, said the Speaker, be 'grievously disturbed in mind towards the Commons, or some of them' and they hoped he would not receive such a person or give him hearing. To this official confirmation of the satirist's observations about those who tattled to the king, Henry replied by saying that the Commons should have 'deliberation and advertisement' so that they could 'commune on and treat about all their own business between themselves' to reach a better conclusion. He agreed not to listen to any person wishing to tell him about debates among the Commons before such matters were shown to him 'by the advice and consent of all the Commons according to the purport of their prayer'. It was a clear and conceded demand for the Commons' freedom of speech in their own house, with the privilege that the king should not judge what any individual reported but should take heed only of their agreed conclusion.[3]

---

[1] *Rot. Parl.* Vol. III, pp. 454–479.

[2] Ibid., p. 455; B. Wilkinson, *Constitutional History of England in the Fifteenth Century*, (trans.) p. 299.

[3] *Rot. Parl.* Vol. III, p. 456; Wilkinson, op. cit., pp. 299–300.

The Speaker was also making a hard political point under his oratory when he observed on 25 January that the king had 'the entire hearts of his people' since his return to England and that 'to have the hearts of his people is the greatest treasure... to every king'. For Savage added that 'if he should possess their hearts, it appears to be true that he will have that which he needs of their goods'.[1] He did not add 'and *vice versa*'. Yet the implied point that if a king did not please his people he might not have all the funds he wanted was no doubt taken. Indeed, the Commons went on to make that claim more explicitly a month later. On 26 February, they complained that 'in several Parliaments in the past their common petitions were not replied to before they had made their grant of a subsidy' and they asked to have this knowledge before grants were made. The king said he would 'commune with the Lords' but after so doing announced on the last day of Parliament that this had not been the procedure under his ancestors and that he would not change the good customs of the past. The Commons had failed to establish formally the dependence of supply on the redress of grievances but they had already virtually established it in practice.

Each side showed a certain wariness of the other. The government was unwilling to be rushed into decisions and when faced by 'word of mouth' petitions from the Commons, the king and Lords insisted that petitions must be in writing before being considered. Refusing to act on verbal petitions was perhaps also the king's way of safeguarding himself from being rushed into unintended concessions by the incessant flow of the Speaker's words.[2] Likewise, the Commons obviously had suspicions about the extent to which the record could be doctored, and with some reason. On 26 February they asked that business done in Parliament should be enacted and engrossed before the departure of the judges as in the past, that is to say enrolled and properly witnessed. To this it was replied that the clerk of Parliament would endeavour to do this and would show it to the king and Lords in Parliament 'to obtain their advice'.[3]

Speaker Savage was forward with his opinions and advice on a wide range of political matters, though the parliamentary roll does not name him, his speeches in this Parliament being always ascribed simply to the Commons. His grandest flights of rhetoric were reserved for the end of the proceeding. He had already compared the estates to a Trinity, namely king, Lords and Commons. Now he likened a parliamentary session to the Mass, with the chancellor beginning the Office, the king at the centre of the Mass,

---

[1] *Rot. Parl.* Vol. III, p. 456.
[2] Ibid., p. 456; Wilkinson, op. cit., p. 300.
[3] *Rot. Parl.* Vol. III, pp. 457–458; Wilkinson, op. cit., p. 301.

declaring his will to maintain religion and the laws and finally the Commons saying, as at the end of the Mass, *Ite missa est* and with a special obligation to add *Deo gratias* because the king had acted to prevent the destruction of the church by evil doctrine. This was a reference to the most important enactment of the Parliament, which was directed against the Lollards.

Since the early days of John Wycliff's comparative respectability under John of Gaunt's patronage, the movement he had started had become gradually more extreme. It inveighed against the papacy and clerical property, divided mankind harshly into the elect who were saved and the rest who were fore-known to damnation and denounced the remission of sin by absolution and indulgences, and also the worship of saints. It asserted that people had the right to read the Bible in their own tongue and offered a different interpretation of the sacrament of the Mass. Throughout Richard's reign the influence of Lollardy had grown and the doctrines had become progressively more eccentric. Neither university learning nor ecclesiastical authority was regarded as necessary for preaching and Lollardy took on some of the characteristics of the later puritanism, both in attacking church decorations and in ordaining their own successors as preachers. By the time of Henry IV's accession, therefore, the church was thoroughly alarmed and the Lollards no longer had the protection of those of Richard's chamber knights who had sympathized with them.

Responding to pressure from the clergy, therefore, and on the petition of the Commons, the Parliament of 1401 was responsible for the enactment known as *de Heretico Comburendo* forbidding unlicensed preaching and books and the holding of conventicles. This required that heretics who refused to recant should be handed over to the civil courts and 'burned on a high place' so that 'such punishment may strike fear in the minds of others'.[1] The burning of a Lollard priest at Smithfield followed immediately, though the extreme penalty for heresy was at first not much used. This enactment was part of an omnibus statute on a wide range of topics, which included forbidding Welshmen to buy lands in English marcher towns, and likewise restraining them in English boroughs planted in Wales itself.

The Commons in this Parliament were intensely active politically. They inquired about the inventory of Richard's jewels and sought an inquiry about Welsh-born servants of the crown. This was also the first of Henry's Parliaments to ask that the king's council should be named, appointed and charged with their duties in Parliament, to which the king agreed.[2] It was a

---

[1] *Stat.* R. Vol. II, 2 Hen. IV cl. XV, pp. 125–128.
[2] This is not recorded in the parliamentary rolls; the documentary evidence is described in A. L. Brown, 'The Commons and the Council in the Reign of Henry IV,' *E.H.R.* LXXIX (1964), pp. 1–30, reprinted Fryde and Miller, op. cit. Vol. II, pp. 31–60.

sign that the Commons were again concerned about the cost of the household, waste and the management of government, and the king's agreement to the naming of his council in Parliament may well have been their price for the grant they made of a tenth and a fifteenth for a year, with tunnage and poundage for two years. On the other hand no new council was appointed nor did the Commons try to control the council. Their purpose was rather to see that the money they were being asked for was well spent and that the councillors should be properly, formally and publicly charged with what was expected of them. As for the Speaker, Sir Arnald Savage, although he had served Richard as a chamber knight he was also on Henry's council from about 1402 to 1406, apparently finding no incompatibility between his duties as a councillor and his role in leading the Commons and presenting their criticisms to the king. The king also evidently found it convenient to accept the duality. The Parliament of 1401 was dissolved on 10 March.

No further Parliament was called until September 1402.[1] When it met, the chancellor, Bishop Stafford, Richard's old servant, opened proceedings by speaking of the disastrous state of the country to which, he said, God was administering punishment. In this Parliament distinguished Scottish captives taken at Homildom Hill appeared before the king, but there was nothing but disaster from Wales. The country was in distress and the Commons, whose Speaker was now Sir Henry de Retford, asked in their old manner to have communications with some of the Lords. This seemed to be disagreeable to Henry since he pointedly granted it as a favour rather than as a right and not as a matter of 'duty or custom'.[2] The subsidy on wool was continued for three years and tunnage and poundage for a year and a half. The unease which permeated this Parliament is indicated by the revival of all the old grievances and complaints, including those concerning grants to the king's supporters and demands for old statutes to be enforced. Nevertheless, the Parliament ended convivially on 25 November, with Henry giving a great feast to Lords and Commons.

The next Parliament met on 14 January, 1404, some six months after the defeat of the Percys at Shrewsbury.[3] It was the longest of Henry's reign so far and quite the most disagreeable for him. Opening the proceedings, the chancellor, Henry Beaufort, Bishop of Winchester, the king's half-brother, observed that each realm should be governed by good counsel, and likened

---

[1] *Rot. Parl.* Vol. III, pp. 485–511.
[2] Ibid., p. 486 and Wilkinson, op. cit., p. 303.
[3] *Rot. Parl.* Vol. III, pp. 522–544. Some of the most important passages from the parliamentary rolls are translated in *E.H.D.* Vol. IV, pp. 456–459 and Wilkinson, op. cit., pp. 303–306.

it to the body of a man. The right side was like the holy church, the left like the temporality and the 'other members' like the Commons. He went on to explain to the Parliament that after the Percys' rising and attacks by the Welsh, Scots and French, the king wished for the advice and general assent of the estates of the realm. When received, however, the advice amounted to nothing more than an outpouring of criticism to which the king had to submit uncomplainingly. How unpopular he and his reign had become after five years of disorder was made very plain. Yet, though the Commons could grumble, there was little to be done about it. King, nobles and Parliament might be in a state of reciprocal dislike, mistrust and recrimination but they were nevertheless held together by complicity in the overthrow of Richard II and there was no general wish to change matters by more disturbance.

This time the Speaker was once more Sir Arnald Savage who began by asking to be excused from that office for various unstated reasons. One of them may have been that he was also a councillor. But the king would not excuse him. The Speaker then went on not only to ask for forgiveness for any offence he might give through ignorance or negligence but also to claim the right of the Commons to complain about the king's government (*compleindre de la Governance mesme nostre Seigneur le Roi*) without its being taken amiss on account of any 'sinister information'. Henry accepted the claim. At Savage's request, the chancellor then repeated an order he had already given the Commons to assemble in their 'house' at eight each morning at the latest. The parliamentary record says nothing about the next ten days but it is clear from the subsequent record, which resumed on 25 January, that there had been much negotiation in the meantime. The product was an outpouring of requests and complaints by the Commons. They spoke of the unsafety of the coast, which had suffered from French raids, and of the Welsh rebellion; of the sudden diminishing of the customs and other revenues and, resentfully, about grants of annuities made by the king. Henry, we are informed, had sent the chancellor and treasurer to explain such financial matters to them 'in their House of Assembly, namely, in the Refectory of Westminster Abbey' (*en lour Maison d'Assemble, c'est a ditz, en la Refectorie deinz l'Abbeie de Westm'*). Some of their questions were answered verbally by the chancellor and treasurer, but others, notably those concerning Wales, were still unanswered. The Commons therefore asked that the Speaker and some of their members should be allowed to consult with the Lords, to which the king agreed.

Savage then went on to make complaints, calling his colleagues to witness that he was putting forward their views, not his personal unauthorized opinions which, he said, he had been accused of doing in the past. He asked that the statute against liveries should be enforced and added on behalf of the Commons that not only this but all other statutes should be kept and enforced. Furthermore, he said, if any statute needed to be abridged or enlarged, it should be shown to the Commons so that they could commune among themselves about the matter and so that their assent might be had, as was the past custom. In other words the Commons were determined that they should not be excluded from assenting to any amendments of existing law. The Speaker also complained of the ruinous condition of the king's castles and manors, especially Windsor, about the number of unjustified grants and the cost of the household. The Commons asked that the Lords should give their advice without dissimulation, and the king echoed this request 'with his own mouth'. All this cannot have made pleasant hearing for Henry and still less can he have liked the manner in which Parliament dealt with the next business, the petition of the Earl of Northumberland who stood at risk of condemnation for treason and who asked for the king's grace for any trespasses he might have committed in respect of liveries or other matters. It might have been supposed that after the Percys' rebellion and the king's victory at Shrewsbury Parliament would have been congratulating Henry and condemning the earl, but it was not so. Northumberland was found guilty not of treason but only of trespass, and duly given the pardon he sought. The Commons seem to have played a part in bringing this about. We know from a contemporary source that it was in response to a Commons' petition that Northumberland was allowed to clear himself of treason, and they seem to have overcome the king's resistance to this by indicating that the grant of money he sought might well depend on what happened to Northumberland. Likewise, when Northumberland was pardoned, the Commons went out of their way to thank the king, as the Parliament roll records.[1] They also pressed for and secured a reconciliation between Northumberland and his rival, the Earl of Westmorland; the disturbances in the north were treated almost as though they were a private war rather than as a threat to the king.

The Commons then resumed the attack on the king's household asking for four people to be removed from it, one of them the king's confessor. Although the king said that he saw no reason for this he nevertheless agreed. Henry was also asked to appoint his servants in Parliament who were only to be men who were honest, virtuous and well thought of. The Commons further called for the removal of aliens from attendance at court, with special reference to Bretons attending the new queen, Joan of Navarre, duchess of Brittany, whom Henry had recently married as his second wife.

---

[1] C. M. Fraser, 'Some Durham documents relating to the Hilary Parliament of 1404', B.I.H.R. 34 (1961), pp. 197–199.

The king gave his general agreement to these requests and the Commons agreed that the queen should keep a given number of her attendants. An ordinance was made for the financial regulation of the household and £12,000 from specified sources was to be set aside for it. It was further ordained, in the interests of good government and remedying complaints, and at the 'special requests' made 'at various times in this Parliament by the Commons' that certain lords and others, twenty-two men whose names are listed, were appointed to be 'his great and continual council'. It was the earliest formal statement we have of the king's council which included six bishops, the Duke of York (Edward of Rutland who had now succeeded his father), two earls and various lords and knights including Savage and the former Speaker John Doreward. The purpose of the appointment of a formal council in Parliament was not, however, in order that the Commons should control it but rather that charging the council in Parliament to attend to the grievances voiced by the Commons was seen as the best way of securing the necessary remedies.[1]

Among the other business of this active if ultimately unproductive Parliament, two items of interest concern parliamentary privileges. One was the first assertion to be made of the future demand for parliamentary control of elections. The Commons claimed that the sheriff of Rutland had not properly returned the writ of summons to Parliament, and the king asked the Lords to look into it. They found that the sheriff had not satisfactorily returned the writ for one Thomas Thorp, who had 'been elected in the shire for the Parliament'. The sheriff was now directed to do so, and was committed to the Fleet prison pending a fine and ransom.[2] Secondly, the Commons raised the general question of the molestation, murder, mayhem and battery of lords, knights and burgesses attending Parliament, and particularly injury that had been done to a certain Robert Cheddar (Cheddre), a servant of a parliamentary knight from Somerset, who had been wounded near to death. The Commons claimed that all Lords and Commons and their servants were 'under the king's protection' when 'coming, remaining and returning' to Parliament, and said that anyone who murdered one of them should be guilty of treason and that maiming should be punished with loss of a hand. The reply, however, was simply that the accused man named in Cheddar's case should submit himself within three months and if he did not do so should be attainted of the deed and pay double damages to the injured party.[3]

---

[1] *Rot. Parl.* Vol. III, p. 530, and A. L. Brown, op. cit.
[2] *Rot. Parl.* Vol. III, p. 530.
[3] Ibid., p. 542.

There was also prolonged discussion in this Parliament about money. There was nothing unusual about that; what was exceptional was that it seems to have led to a direct argument between the Commons and king personally. According to a chronicler, the king asked for 'a great tallage' for his wars with the Welsh, Scots and with the French in Gascony, only to be told that these things did not much trouble England. Besides, it was argued, he should have money enough from his customary revenues and the duchy of Lancaster. The king replied that he did not wish to lose the lands of his fathers and ought to be given the money, to which the Commons insisted that if he was to have a direct subsidy, the customs should be reduced in compensation. So Parliament 'remained in London at heavy expense until Easter disputing in this fashion'.[1] After ten weeks and much compromise including that concerning the household, a grant was made in the novel form of five per cent on income from land, though it was not to be enacted before the next Parliament. In order to avoid a precedent, no records were to be made of the tax, even on the parliamentary roll. So ended a Parliament in which the king was forced to tolerate a sustained inquisition and in which the Commons flexed their muscles although the constitutional consequences amounted to little.

The following months brought new dangers, a French attack on the Isle of Wight and further advances by Glendower, who was even able to call together his own Welsh Parliament. There were desperate calls for money from the Prince of Wales who was in charge of the campaign against the Welsh, whom the French were preparing to aid. So empty was the treasury that the payment of annuities was suspended. On 6 October, the second Parliament of the year opened at Coventry.[2] It was called the 'unlearned Parliament' because the writs required that no lawyers should be returned. The reason given for their exclusion was the old one that they concentrated on their clients' business in Parliament rather than the king's. It is also likely, however, that it also had something to do with attempts by Henry to influence the composition of Parliament through the sheriffs. At all events, one of the demands of the rebels in the subsequent rising, in which Archbishop Scrope was implicated, was for a free Parliament without the arbitrary exclusion the king was said to have practised at Coventry.

As usual, Parliament began with requests by the king for money, the chancellor exhorting the Commons, who now had another councillor as their Speaker, Sir William Sturmy, to make haste in considering supply. Far

---

[1] *Eulogium Historiarum*, ed. F. R. Haydon, Rolls Series, iii, (1863), pp. 399–400, trans. Wilkinson, op. cit., pp. 305–306.
[2] *Rot. Parl.* Vol. III, pp. 545–559.

from hurrying, the Parliament, which seems to have had some Lollard sympathies, chose at first to concentrate on its own interests. To the distress of the Archbishop of Canterbury, it attacked the wealth of the clergy, and (according to the St Albans chronicler) some knights and burgesses demanded the temporary appropriation of church property.[1] It also demanded the resumption of royal grants given since 1366 and persuaded the king to agree in the meantime to the surrender of a year's income from all royal lands leased out and also a year's suspension of pensions given by himself and Richard II.[2] Eventually, however, the Commons gave way and provided the king with a larger than usual grant of two tenths and two fifteenths, as well as new subsidies on wool. But the grants were conditional on the appointment of two treasurers of war, Lord Furnivall and Sir John Pelham, who were to oversee the expenditure and ensure that it went only on the war. They were to receive the money and 'render account to the community of the realm in the next Parliament'.[3] The land tax of the previous Parliament was also confirmed, this time being included in the roll, as being made by 'lords temporal' for themselves and for 'ladies temporal' (*dames temporelx*) at the rate of 5 per cent (expressed as 20s. on each £20) on land yielding rents of 500 marks a year. On 14 November, the Parliament was dissolved.

The next year was the worst of Henry's reign, beginning with the attempt to abduct the two Mortimer boys from Windsor. The danger from Wales intensified and Henry's fortunes reached their lowest ebb with a new revolt by the Earl of Northumberland, this time with, among others, the Earl Marshal, Thomas Mowbray (the son of Henry's old associate and adversary) and Archbishop Scrope. They declared Henry to be a usurper who was guilty of the deaths of Richard II and others, and of bringing misery to the land. Behind these complaints lay the grievances of heavy taxation, of loans raised in anticipation of revenue and suspended annuities and payments. The king quickly broke the rebellion, but the execution of Archbishop Scrope, who had been tricked into disbanding his men and was then arrested, was Henry's worst mistake so far. Among the many who were deeply offended was Archbishop Arundel, who had travelled to York to intercede for his fellow primate and who was himself tricked when Scrope's trial and execution were accomplished swiftly while Arundel was resting after his exhausting journey north. No bishop had been sentenced to

---

[1] Walsingham: trans. extracts in Wilkinson, op. cit., pp. 306–308.
[2] B. P. Wolffe, 'Acts of Resumption in the Lancastrian Parliaments, 1399–1456', *E.H.R.*, Vol. LXXIII (1958), pp. 586–590, reprinted in Fryde and Miller, op. cit.
[3] *Rot. Parl.* Vol. III, p. 546.

death before in defiance of the protection of his cloth, and beheading Archbishop Scrope was a sign that the king's patience was strained to breaking point. Moreover, Henry's health was now seriously impaired with the incapacitating but undiagnosed illness which was to kill him, while the growing opposition was extending even to some on the council.

By the end of the year, the worst of the danger was over but the Welsh were still unsubdued and the king was in desperate need of money. On 1 March, 1406, therefore, the longest Parliament ever held assembled at Westminster and lasted until three days before Christmas with two adjournments.[1] Its length was entirely due to the prolonged political bargaining the king had to endure before he was given funds. Such was the danger that the meeting place of this Parliament had twice had to be changed; it had been intended first for Coventry, then for Gloucester. The proceedings were opened by the chancellor, Thomas Langley, who explained why the king had summoned 'the Estates of the Realm . . . in Parliament': for the defence of the kingdom. The themes of this Parliament were the old ones, greatly intensified. The Commons were determined to associate their money grants with the redress of grievances, to see that there was appropriate control of the government's accounts and to exercise a degree of parliamentary surveillance of the king's council. The Speaker was a young unmarried knight of the household, Sir John Tiptoft (Tibetot), who wished 'to excuse himself from this occupation, as much on account of his youth, and lack of sense and discretion, as for other reasons' (*se vorroit avoir excusez de celle occupacion, si bien par cause de sa juvente, & pur defaute de seen & discrecion, come par plusours autres voies*). The king, however, insisted that his election be upheld. Tiptoft had been attached to Henry in one way or another since 1397 and the king may well have felt that he would make as friendly a Speaker as could be expected in all the circumstances. Subsequently, on 23 March, after making his protestation and requesting the same liberties as his predecessors, Tiptoft asked, and the king agreed, that if the Commons put anything in writing they should be allowed to have it back for amendment during the Parliament. The tone of the proceedings was set when Tiptoft went on to say that the Commons expected 'good and abundant governance' and on 3 April he elaborated the policies they wanted.

These were that the Prince of Wales should personally be in command on the Welsh border and that a body of merchants should be given charge of the protection of the sea and be provided with the tunnage and poundage and a quarter of the wool subsidy to pay for it. The Bretons should be

[1] *Rot. Parl.* Vol. III, pp. 567–603 and Stephenson and Marcham, op. cit., pp. 262–263.

removed from court and the king should retain, at least for a time, the lands and castles forfeited by Welsh rebels. In reply, the king said that these things would be done as soon as possible. All that was settled at this stage, however, was an agreement, duly enrolled, between the council and certain merchants for safeguarding the seas. A committee was appointed, which included Tiptoft, to manage the details. Something of the hostility felt towards the king is revealed by the fact that Tiptoft felt it necessary to say during these discussions that some members of the Commons were alleged to have spoken of the king's person with disrespect ('otherwise than they should'). The Speaker insisted that they had done nothing of the sort and asked that they should be excused on declaring their loyalty. To this the king agreed, accepting them as loyal subjects. Nevertheless, whatever precisely had been said in the Commons' private discussions and reported adversely to the king, it was clearly something capable of being interpreted as an improper attack on Henry himself.

Parliament then adjourned for five weeks over Easter, the king still without the money he needed. During the recess, Henry was too ill to ride from Greenwich to Windsor for the feast of St. George and may have made the journey by river. When Parliament resumed on 30 April he was still not well enough to attend and sent a letter explaining his absence as due to a malady of his leg; he arrived early in May. A day was fixed for the aliens' departure and Tiptoft reminded the king of his earlier request for 'abundant governance' (*governance habundante*), adding that Archbishop Arundel had already said that the king wished to be advised by wise councillors who would oversee the good government of the realm.[1] This promise had presumably been made before the adjournment, and the insistence of the Commons on action which is recorded at this stage was probably only the culmination of an argument between the king and Commons which had persisted throughout the first session, more or less unrecorded.

The king now agreed that this promise of 'abundant governance' had been indeed made by the archbishop, adding 'with his own mouth' that this was also his own wish. A 'bill' was then read, on 22 May, which was said to have been made freely by the king himself, giving the names of a council of seventeen (most of them had been on the previous council) and setting out rules by which they should act. It provided, for instance, that certain instructions to the chancellor, treasurer and keeper of the privy seal, all of whom would themselves be on the council, would only be valid if endorsed as being by the advice of the council. This stipulation related particularly to financial matters concerning the profit of the crown and its financial rights

[1] *Rot. Parl.* Vol. III, p. 572.

and grants.[1] Behind the bill lay the assumption that if the king was well advised and did not grant away his properties loosely, he would be rich enough to live of his own without repeatedly asking the Commons for money. It was a theme which had recurred since the beginning of the reign and Henry seems to have acknowledged the claim in principle. During the Coventry Parliament, for instance, the king had replied in English as follows to a petition on the subject: 'And for als muche that the Communes desiren that the Kyng shulde leve upon his owne, as gode reson asketh, and all Estates thynken the same, the Kyng thanketh hem of here gode desire, willyng put it in execution als sone as he wel may.' To meet the 'Commons' desire' that the crown should resume all grants made since the fortieth year of Edward III, Henry had on that occasion promised to set up a committee to determine what properly belonged to the crown and to act accordingly. Nothing seems to have been done but the king had already conceded the point in theory.

Despite the bill for the appointment of the council in Parliament and the concessions made to the Commons by laying special financial duties on the councillors, money was still not forthcoming. Instead, there followed a curious episode in which the chancellor said that Lord Lovell had several times asked to be excused from the council; to which the king agreed. Other councillors then also asked to be excused but were pressed to serve. They agreed to do so but only on condition that it was recorded on the parliamentary roll that the bill was of the king's own will and not their own seeking. In all this, it seems that the object of the Commons was not to change the composition of the council as such nor control it closely but rather to give it instructions publicly so that it would govern by generally accepted criteria and so that the money granted was well spent on the defence of the realm. Yet the Speaker was apparently still not satisfied. At the beginning of the following week, he went over the previous proceedings again, asking whether the Lords named would serve, to which Archbishop Arundel replied that they would if money enough was provided for the maintenance of good government. In other words, he reminded the Commons of their side of the bargain: taxation. The Commons would not grant the money without the understandings they wanted, but equally the councillors designated at the Commons' request would not assume their duties unless they had the taxation they needed.

Yet even now, the money was not forthcoming. Instead, the Commons remonstrated with the king on such matters as the inadequately safeguarded

---

[1] The whole of this episode and the significance of the bill of 22 May is described best by A. L. Brown, op. cit.

coasts and overseas possessions of the crown, to which Henry replied simply that he would order the council to do their best. On 7 June the Speaker was even more blunt, asserting that the king was being defrauded by the tax collectors, that the Calais garrison consisted of sailors and youths who could not ride and that the government of Ireland was as expensive as it was ineffective. Worst of all, the king's household, he said, was less honourable and more expensive than it had been and consisted not of suitable persons of substance but 'for the most part of rascals' (*de raskaile pur la greindre partie*). Later the Speaker returned to his main theme: good and abundant government was what the realm required. Underlying these complaints was an argument about supplies which had continued throughout the Parliament though not always recorded on the parliamentary roll. According to an annalist, the Commons wanted the accounts of Pelham and Furnivall to be audited, to which Henry seems to have replied that kings did not render accounts and his ministers declared that they did not know how it should be done.[1] The Commons still did not trust the concessions they had obtained and before an adjournment for the summer they made only a small grant to be going on with: an extra poundage of a shilling for a year and a fraction extra on the wool subsidy. This, however, was virtually on condition that the aliens were instantly dismissed; that the household should be modified so that its outrageous expenses were reduced; that grants made since the beginning of the Parliament should be revoked; and that there should be no more grants until household debts had been repaid. There was also to be an attempt to increase the farm, or profit, from leased lordships and lands.[2] These requirements of the Commons were specified in articles submitted on 19 June, on which day Parliament was adjourned until 13 October.

During the summer recess, Henry's health seems to have deteriorated further. Parliament resumed after the usual wait for late arrivals on 18 November and the Speaker asked the king to charge the Lords with giving their opinion on what was wrong with the kingdom and to act to reform it, to which Henry agreed. The Speaker then made such detailed requests as that an English captain and garrison should replace a foreign garrison which was defending a certain castle of Aquitaine, and that treasurers and controllers should be appointed for Wales. So the session dragged on and it was not until three days before Christmas that the Commons made their grant of a tenth and a fifteenth, and of tunnage and poundage, 'for the great confidence which they had in the lords elected and ordained to be of the

---

[1] *Eulogium Historiarum*, ed. F. R. Haydon (Rolls Series 1863) iii, p. 409.
[2] *Rot. Parl.* Vol. III, pp. 578–579.

continual council'. It was done in exchange for the king's acceptance on the same day of thirty-one articles which conceded most of the demands made on 19 June. Some of them simply required named officials to observe certain standards, but the essential articles were those regulating the work of the council by whose advice the king was to govern and which had already been appointed.

The members of the council were to be paid; some were always to be with the king, individual councillors were to leave meetings when things in which they were involved were for discussion and so on. Above all, the household officials must do their duty and obey the existing regulations, and there must be economy so that the king could live of his own. The councillors were given specific instructions to observe for the spending of revenues. Further grants were to be prohibited until the end of the next Parliament.[1] The concessions had been wrung out of the king slowly and against his will and it was a considerable victory for the Commons which seems, for a time, to have somewhat reduced the number of grants.[2] It was a further sign of Henry's need to propitiate the Commons that their Speaker, Sir John Tiptoft, was appointed treasurer of the household on 8 December. As for the council itself, the Commons had succeeded between 1401 and 1406 in excluding from it first esquires and then knights, presumably on the assumption that grander men would be more likely to have the independence from the king which was needed for the job to be done, and that men of a humbler sort would be too concerned with their own profit. The Commons did not seek closely to control the council, but behind their campaign lay the idea that if the councillors were sworn and appointed publicly and given clear instructions they would act honestly and give the king good advice for the running of his household, which advice in all the circumstances he would take. They were moved not by constitutional theory but by a practical ambition to reduce the amount of money which they themselves must produce. It was a sign of their thinking that the council recommended the king to withdraw after Christmas to a dwelling where the expenses of the household could be reduced: for a short stay, the court went to Eltham.

There were, of course, other provisions by this remarkable Parliament. In June, the crown had been settled on the heirs male of each of the king's sons in turn. Just before the Parliament finished this was amended to give the succession to heirs general of each of the princes in turn, allowing for female succession. Second, a further petition for the punishment of Lollards

---

[1] The thirty-one articles are recorded in *Rot. Parl.* Vol. III, pp. 585–589.
[2] A. L. Brown, op. cit.

was accepted. But in parliamentary history the most important enactment was one reforming county elections, which were 'sometimes made by the partiality of the sheriffs', or 'against the form of the writ'. Henceforth, at the first shire court after the delivery of the writ, proclamation of the day and place of Parliament was to be made in full court. All who were present, 'suitors duly summoned for the same cause and others as well, shall attend the election of their knights for the Parliament; and then in full shire court they shall proceed to the election freely and indifferently, notwithstanding any request or commandment to the contrary'. After the representatives had been chosen, their names, whether they were present or absent, were to be written on an indenture 'under the seals of all those who chose them, and tacked to the same writ of Parliament, which indenture, so sealed and tacked, shall be held for the sheriff's return of the said writ touching the knights of the shires'.[1] The procedure laid down for the process of election was presumably that which was already supposed to operate, but this was not the significance of the enactment. What was new was the stipulated arrangements for checking the validity of the sheriff's return, which had hitherto consisted of a simple endorsement of the writ, made in theory to the king in Parliament. A subsequent act of 1410 imposed a fine of £100 on any sheriff breaking this requirement.

After 1406, Henry's circumstances improved at home and abroad. In the earlier years, his possessions were always at risk from potential French attack even though quarrelling factions around the mad King Charles VI had vitiated effective action against the English. Then, in 1407, the Duke of Orleans, brother of the French king, was assassinated by followers of Duke John of Burgundy. This brought France to the edge of civil war and ended the fear of serious attacks on the English king's French possessions. Instead, the question was now whether the English should intervene on one side or another in the French civil strife. The danger from Scotland had also diminished with the capture at sea in 1406 of James, heir to the Scottish throne, who was brought to London where he remained in captivity for 18 years. When the old king of Scots died shortly afterwards, there was an immediate outbreak of civil conflict in Scotland. In any case the governor of Scotland, the Duke of Albany, was not anxious to take any action which might lead to the return of the young royal captive. Above all, Henry IV was henceforth free of rebellions, and although Glendower still held out in Wales it was now only a matter of time before the principality was again subdued.

On the other hand, Henry IV's health now became so much worse that

---

[1] *Stat. R.* Vol. II, p. 156; *E.H.D.* Vol. IV, pp. 459–460.

during his final six years he was very often obliged to let the council do much of the business of governing for him. How far he himself managed affairs depended on his condition at any time, but the characteristic feature of these years was a struggle between parties in the council rather than arguments between crown and Parliament. For the rest of the reign, two parties which were divided by both policies and personal rivalries came to office and were dismissed from it, much as partisan ministries were in later centuries. For the next three years, the dominant figure on the council was Archbishop Arundel who, in January 1407, became chancellor. Despite his anger with Henry over Archbishop Scrope's execution, Arundel was far too deeply committed to the Lancastrian dynasty to remain at odds with it and he was the most loyal of Henry's ministers. At the same time, Henry, Prince of Wales, who was now 19 and who had been active in the fight against Glendower for six years, became increasingly a figure of political substance and a much more frequent attender at the council. His popularity is indicated by requests in Parliament that he should have authority on the Welsh marches. There was, perhaps, already something of the aura of political leadership about him which was to make him so successful a king.

Arundel and Prince Henry apart, the most important group in the council was that of the three Beauforts, the king's half-brothers, who were the sons of John of Gaunt by Catherine Swynford. The eldest, the Earl of Somerset, was high chamberlain; the second and the ablest, Henry, was Bishop of Winchester; the third was Sir Thomas Beaufort. All were ambitious with great influence at court and were close to the king. However, when in 1407 Henry confirmed the act of Richard II which had legitimatized their birth, he pointedly excluded them from the royal succession by inserting the words *excepta dignitate regali*. It was not a point of great substance since the king had four sons; nevertheless, it was felt by the Beauforts as a snub and they held Arundel responsible for it. Henceforth they grew closer to the Prince of Wales in their opposition to the archbishop and to some extent away from the king. The seeds of court faction had been set.

Nevertheless, Arundel remained the chief minister and it was he as chancellor who opened the next Parliament which met at Gloucester on 20 October 1407.[1] The improved confidence of the Lancastrian court was indicated by the sermon Arundel preached at the opening on the text 'honour the king' which was presumably intended as a rebuking reminder that this had not been the attitude of recent Parliaments. Lauding Henry for his care in upholding the charters and the laws, Arundel spoke of the subject's duty to help the king in times of need, reminding them of the

---

[1] *Rot. Parl.* Vol. III, pp. 608–621.

threats to Wales, Guinenne, Calais, Ireland and the Scottish border. The Commons then elected as their Speaker Thomas Chaucer, one of the knights for Oxfordshire, who was the son of the poet Geoffrey. Chaucer was a cousin of the Beauforts on their mother's side and his election was perhaps encouraged by them as helpful in securing the Commons to their interest and that of the court. Chaucer was several times to be Speaker and in the next reign his loyalty was invaluable to Henry V.

On the whole, the Parliament of 1407 was more amenable than its predecessors. When the Speaker reminded the king that the grants made in the previous Parliament had been given on condition that certain lords should be members of the council and that they should ensure good governance, Arundel simply said that he had dealt with these matters both in a speech and in a schedule given to the Commons in their meeting place, the frater of the abbey. The councillors had performed their duties honestly and had voluntarily submitted the accounts of the recent grants to the inspection of the Commons. They had been obliged to borrow large sums (needed especially to pay for the garrison at Calais) and they now wished to be relieved from the oaths sworn in the previous Parliament and from any blame for what had been done. The king agreed to this, though no change was actually made to the council. What it amounted to was that the oath of responsibility imposed in the previous Parliament was now dispensed with. This seems to have brought no protest from the Commons.

The Speaker then complained about illegal purveyance by the royal household, but this too was shrugged off with the reply by the steward and treasurer of the household that if anyone had any specific charges these would be investigated and punished. After raising various other complaints, including the failure to guard the coasts and Welsh marches, the Commons turned to the main purpose of the Parliament, the supply of money, and at this point there erupted a dispute which throws a powerful light on their determination to entrench all their evolving privileges. On 13 November, the Commons were given leave to commune on matters concerning 'the common good and profit of all the realm' (that is to say, about money) with certain of the councillors they had named: the Archbishop of Canterbury, the Bishops of Winchester and Durham, the Duke of York, the Earl of Somerset and Lords Roos and Burnell. Then, a week later, the Lords were asked by the king in the council chamber what grant they considered necessary for the defence of the kingdom. They replied that it should be one and a half tenths and fifteenths and the continuation of the wool subsidy, on which the king summoned a number of the Commons (twelve of them came) to hear the Lords' opinion. They were instructed to report this to their colleagues 'in order that they might approach as near as possible to conformity with the intention of the Lords'. This caused great alarm in the lower house. It had come to be taken for granted that money grants should be initiated from the Commons (albeit often after intercommuning with the Lords on what was necessary) and also that the poorest estate should have the last word over the maximum of the grant. That principle now seemed to be infringed by the king's action in passing the initiative publicly to the Lords. Although the sum named by the Lords was granted, together with the wool subsidy and tunnage and poundage for two years, the Commons protested strongly at the consultation with the Lords over the amount.

So, on the last day of Parliament, 2 December, the Commons came before the king and the Lords in Parliament, where 'there was read a schedule of indemnity with regard to a certain altercation which had arisen between the Lords and the Commons' and this was 'entered as of record on the roll of Parliament'.[1] After describing what had happened in detail, it concluded that the Commons had been 'greatly disturbed' and had said that what had happened 'was to the great prejudice and derogation of their liberties'. The king, therefore, 'in no wise wishing anything to be done, either now or in the future, which could turn in any way against the liberty of the estate on whose behalf they had come to Parliament, or against the liberties of the above-mentioned Lords', set out the rights of the matter as follows. The Lords could always commune among themselves, in the absence of the king, about the state of the realm and remedies for it. This was also 'fully permitted to the Commons'. But neither Lords nor Commons should report to the king on any grant 'made by the Commons and agreed to by the Lords, nor on the communications about the said grant, before the Lords and Commons have come to an agreement and accord in that matter. And then it shall be made in the accustomed manner and form; that is to say, through the mouth of the Speaker of the Commons.' Finally, the king declared that what had happened should not be an example or precedent for the future. Although nothing much had been changed by the Commons' protest, they had made permanent a practice which the king had apparently attempted to change: namely that the last word over the amount of taxation would be with the Commons even though they were often willing in practice to be guided by the Lords. It may well have been Henry's hope that, by a procedural device, he could diminish the Commons' control over money which had been such a bane to him in previous Parliaments but in failing to do so he established the opposite of his intentions. The Commons'

---

[1] *Rot. Parl.* Vol. III, p. 611. (Trans. B. Wilkinson, *Const. Hist. of England in the Fifteenth Century*, pp. 309–310.)

ultimate control over the grant of taxation has remained the fundamental feature of the parliamentary constitution.

The Gloucester Parliament lasted no more than six weeks and during the course of it Prince Henry arrived from Wales and attested publicly the great services of the Duke of York about whom, he said, he had heard some malevolent accusations. (York, not surprisingly in view of his record, was almost chronically suspected of disloyalty.) There were also suggestions by the Commons that the king's younger sons, Thomas, John and Humphrey, should be given titles and land, but the king took no notice. Finally, Henry announced that he would ask for no further parliamentary grant for two years from the following feast of the Annunciation, 25 March, 1408, a promise he nearly fulfilled. The next Parliament did not meet until January 1410, the longest interval during the reign.

Arundel remained chancellor for over two years while the Prince of Wales and the Beauforts grew closer together and the king himself increasingly relied on the loyalty of his second son, Thomas, who was hostile to the Beauforts. Early in 1408, the last feeble attempt of the Earl of Northumberland to overthrow Henry by invading from Scotland was defeated on Branham Moor. Northumberland was killed and some of his associates were captured. Shortly afterwards, Henry went north and had one of the insurgents, the Abbot of Halesowen, hanged at York, though others were pardoned. In the winter of 1408-9, Harlech castle was captured and Glendower's rebellion was virtually over. Meanwhile, the chancellor-archbishop was concentrating on the suppression of Lollardy at home and attempting to end the Great Schism in the church by negotiations abroad. But gradually some sort of crisis developed in the council between the rival parties and in December 1409, just before Christmas, first the treasurer Tiptoft, and then the chancellor Arundel resigned. What precipitated this is not clear but it was brought about by criticism of some sort from the Prince of Wales about the handling of affairs. No new chancellor was appointed, but on 6 January, Lord Scrope of Masham became a treasurer. He was a relation of the late archbishop and was himself later executed for plotting against Henry V.

The resignations took place a month before Parliament met on 27 January 1410 at Westminster, to which place it had been diverted from Bristol. Arrangements had already been made to send the rolls and records to Bristol and the king had intended to spend Christmas at Gloucester to be near at hand. It is quite likely that his unfitness to travel led to the change of meeting place. In the absence of a chancellor, Bishop Beaufort opened the proceedings in the usual manner, speaking of affairs at home and abroad including the threat to Calais from the Duke of Burgundy who was now effectively ruling France.[1] Once again the Commons elected Thomas Chaucer as Speaker and four days after Parliament began the great seal was given to a new chancellor, Sir Thomas Beaufort, in the Archbishop of Canterbury's palace of Westminster where the king was in residence.

The new Parliament was distinctly anti-clerical in mood; at least the Commons were, since they began by submitting a request for the return to them of an unsuccessful petition which had apparently sought for some relaxation of the laws against the Lollards. They seem also to have petitioned for the confiscation of the wealth of bishops and abbots but nothing of this was entered on the record, presumably because the idea was so outrageous. The king agreed to let the Commons have back the petition for which they had asked provided this was understood not to be a precedent. No business of substance was dealt with before Easter when there was an adjournment until 7 April. A fortnight later the Commons published a series of eighteen articles, most of which were similar to those previously agreed for regulating the work of government.[2] The first asked the king to 'ordain and assign in the present Parliament the most valiant, wise and discreet lords of the realm to be of his council', who should be sworn into their offices together with the judges. Answering this, the king said that certain lords whom he had selected had excused themselves, presumably a reference to the resignation of Arundel and his colleagues. The new council consisted of the Prince of Wales, Bishops of Winchester, Durham and Bath and Wells, the Earls of Arundel and Westmorland and Lord Burnell, together with the new chancellor and new keeper of the privy seal, John Prophet. There is no doubt that the leader of the new administration was Prince Henry, and his friends were predominant on it.

When the councillors' names were announced, the prince followed an example set by Arundel in the previous Parliament and said that the councillors would serve if, and only if, a grant was made by the Commons.[3] All the members of the new and more aristocratic council (it included no knights other than the professionals) were sworn in except for the prince himself who was excused because of his royalty. (Later on the Bishop of St David's and the Earl of Warwick were added to the council because it was thought that the Bishop of Durham and the Earl of Westmorland might have to be away on the northern border). Since both Prince Henry and Arundel had made their 'ministries' willingness to serve dependent on adequate parliamentary supply, and since supply was dependent on parliamentary satisfaction with the government's willingness to redress

[1] *Rot. Parl.* Vol. III, pp. 622–646.
[2] Ibid., pp. 623–627.
[3] Ibid., p. 632.

grievances, it is tempting to discern here a very faint foreshadowing of future governments' need for parliamentary majorities. But we must, of course, beware of such an anachronistic comparison. The circumstances were exceptional, brought about largely by the king's increasing dependence on his council because of ill health and by the persistence of his financial need. Although there were rival parties vying for power in the council, they were not parliamentary parties as we understand the term, despite having sympathisers and supporters in the lower 'house'. In the fifteenth century what the Commons wanted was simply effective government and they did not mind which aristocratic party, or which government, provided it. They tended to take the latest offer, which is why they accommodated themselves so easily to the swings of faction later in the fifteenth century.

The new administration asked that the king should be allowed to collect a fifteenth and tenth every year for the rest of his life, even when no Parliament was sitting. This request that he should have freedom from parliamentary accountability was refused. Instead, Henry was given one and a half tenths and fifteenths spread equally over three years. As for the rest of the articles submitted to the king, most (such as those requesting the enforcement of statutes, properly guarded frontiers and the assignment of any grant to defence) were accepted. Others were agreed to with qualifications. The Commons had claimed that the revenue from customs and subsidies had fallen since Richard's time on account of evasion which Henry doubted; but he did consent to the application of any subsidy to defence. Finally, this Parliament produced a further statute (already referred to) imposing penalties on sheriffs who did not hold elections in the legal manner and making the conduct of elections a matter for inquiry by justices of assize. This Parliament ended on 9 May, leaving the prince and the Beauforts to administer the country under the king for the next two years.

During this time there was apparently a personal quarrel between the prince and Arundel. Dissension also arose in the council between Thomas, the king's second son, and the Beauforts, who had the support of Prince Henry; this was caused by Thomas's marriage to the widow of John Beaufort, Earl of Somerset. But there were much deeper differences over policy. At the time Prince Henry took over leadership of the council, Calais was under threat from the Duke of Burgundy. By 1411, however, civil war had broken out in France, and Burgundy himself, now under pressure from the Armagnacs, or Orleanists, switched policy and sought English help. An agreement with Burgundy had the support of the Prince of Wales, though the Beaufort family favoured an arrangement with the Armagnacs. Negotiations for his marriage with the Duke of Burgundy's daughter were set in train and with Henry IV's agreement, an English expeditionary force was sent to France which inflicted a defeat on the Orleanists in November 1411 and then returned to England. In the same month a new Parliament met at Westminster.[1]

It was effectively the last Parliament of Henry's reign. His health was now so bad that his grip on power seemed at first to have almost gone. Yet, as it happened, this Parliament was the scene of something very like a personal *coup* on the part of the king in which he wrested power back from his son and the Beauforts with all of whom he now had reason enough to be angry. Because of Henry's illness, Parliament was opened in his absence by Bishop Beaufort who expatiated on the importance of prompt parliamentary provision to meet the government's pressing financial need. Henry himself, however, arrived only a day late and, we may reasonably guess, was fuelled into activity by anger, having just frustrated an attempt of some kind by the Beauforts to produce his resignation of the crown to Prince Henry on grounds of ill health. Little is known about the plot but the evidence from the chroniclers is enough to make it almost certain that some scheme of this sort was mooted. Having repulsed it, Henry arrived at Parliament stimulated to rid himself of the councillors who had contemplated his resignation.

Again the Commons chose as Speaker Thomas Chaucer, who asked to be excused. Henry, however, said simply that he accepted the Commons' choice. The Speaker then asked for the right to speak openly and Henry displayed his mood by replying shortly that Chaucer could speak as other Speakers had, but in no other way. He added that he wanted no kind of 'novelty' (*novellerie*) in this Parliament and that he wished to preserve his liberties and prerogatives as fully as his predecessors.[2] Henry was clearly bent on restoring the royal authority that previous Parliaments had battered. Parliament then dealt with a case which well illustrates the kind of lawlessness with which society was permeated. Lord Roos had petitioned the king in Parliament against William Tirwhyt, a justice of the king's bench, who had assembled armed men to lie in wait for Lord Roos with whom he had a quarrel. The matter was referred to Archbishop Arundel and the chamberlain as arbiters but they decided that it was enough for the offending justice to make a formal apology to Roos. Tirwhyt continued on the bench for the rest of his life.

On 30 November, the Speaker asked the king to thank the Lords

[1] *Rot. Parl.* Vol. III, pp. 647–666.
[2] Ibid., p. 648.

appointed to his council in the previous Parliament and this, it seems, was the moment when the king struck. As asked, he thanked the councillors and expressed satisfaction with their service during the time they *were* on the council (*pur le temps qu'ils estoient de son Counsail*) thus indicating that they had now ceased to be councillors.[1] This virtual dismissal was not followed by the announcement and enrollment of a new council in Parliament. As for taxation, the king was given the usual wool subsidy for a year and tunnage and poundage. No tenths and fifteenths were asked for; instead there was a new and low yielding version of the land tax which the Commons again asked should not set a precedent. The Parliament ended on 19 December with a curious incident. The roll records that the chancellor had been to the Commons to show them an article, whose nature is undescribed, which they had submitted in the last Parliament and about which the Speaker had now asked the king to let his will be known. The king's reply was that he wished to maintain his prerogative on all points as fully as his noble ancestors, the Commons were 'all agreed' and the king annulled the article absolutely. It had clearly been derogatory to him and the episode shows that in a determined mood the king could turn the Commons to obedience when they did not have the support of a party in the Lords.[2]

Immediately after the Parliament was dissolved, the chancellor, Sir Thomas Beaufort and the treasurer, Lord Scrope were dismissed. Sir John Pelham became treasurer straight away and on 5 January Arundel again returned to the chancery. It was the beginning of a new ministry and the council was reconstituted, though not in Parliament. Neither the Prince of Wales nor the Beauforts were part of it, though shortly afterwards Henry rewarded Sir Thomas Beaufort for his service by creating him Earl of Dorset. So matters remained until Henry's death a year and a half later. In several respects policy changed with the ministry; for example support was switched from Burgundy to the Armagnacs and in 1412 Prince Thomas, now Duke of Clarence, led a brief expedition to France which, after a single victory, was bought off by the French who had reached a temporary accommodation with their opponents. At home, rumours that the Prince of Wales might seize the throne were specifically denied by him.

Henry IV died in March 1413, having been more or less incapacitated since the previous autumn. A Parliament had been called to meet on 3 February but it probably never opened and there is no record from it. Henry had preserved his dynasty and, when in a corner, had fought well for it. Yet

[1] *Rot. Parl.* Vol. III, p. 649.
[2] Ibid., p. 658.

for more than half the reign the kingdom was convulsed by rebellion and Henry was forced to an extent none of his predecessors had been to depend on Parliament for money simply to remain on the throne. This and the weakness of his title gave the Commons a degree of self-confidence which was not equalled by their successors during the rest of the medieval period. The consciousness of their potential power was never lost. Dynasties would come and go but every king would in some degree have to come to terms with the institution of Parliament in order to govern effectively.

CHAPTER 8

— * —

Henry V:
Parliament Pays for Glory

JUDGED by the magnitude of his military achievement and his success in keeping the aristocratic peace at home, Henry V was a great king. Judged by their lack of durability and by the malignant consequences for his dynasty, his achievements were a disaster. That he was an exceptional leader of men and a great general is beyond argument. He was also by temperament a healer of wounds in his own realm. At the outset of his reign, he caused the body of Richard II (for whom as a boy he had had some attachment) to be brought for burial with due royal honour at Westminster. He restored the Percys to their earldom of Northumberland and allowed the Earl of March, whose claim to the throne had been a threat to Henry IV, freedom of his lands and a place at court. Likewise he gave the earldom of Cambridge to Richard, brother of the Duke of York. Henry's policy, like that of Edward III, was to conciliate and unify the aristocracy behind him and like Edward he used war in France as the agent of unity.

Yet he was greater than Edward both in the conception of his aims and because he achieved more in a shorter time. He had learned the craft of soldiering on the Welsh border and every detail of military art and preparations concerned him. The immediate importance of his reign was almost entirely in the foreign field and Parliament did not develop in any fundamental way during the course of it. The conspicuous feature of most of his Parliaments was the wholehearted support they gave to his French enterprise. His father had faced constant parliamentary opposition as he was forced to ask for money to put down rebellions which were themselves a source of resentment. The speedy success of Henry V's French war, however, ensured that he had no difficulty in obtaining parliamentary money. Nor did his subjects have cause to complain, as Edward III's had, of the length of his wars or an initial long period of failure. If we judge Henry by the standard of our time he is condemned by wasted bloodshed, the ephemeral nature of his empire and the religious intolerance with which he persecuted the Lollards. Yet by the standards of his own time he was brave, chivalrous, honourable, just and also a man of religious conscience and personal rectitude.

On becoming king, Henry immediately made Bishop Beaufort chancellor, in place of Archbishop Arundel (who then concentrated with ferocity on eliminating Lollardy). The Earl of Arundel became treasurer in place of Sir John Pelham. The first Parliament of the new reign met on 15 May, after the coronation.[1] The king sat on his throne in the Painted Chamber and as well as the Lords Spiritual and Temporal, there were present (as the Parliament roll records) 'the knights of the shire, the citizens and burgesses, who had come to Parliament on behalf of the whole *commune* of the realm' (*pur tout la Commune du Roialme*), a new and comprehensive definition of the breadth of the Commons' representative role. The proceedings were opened by Beaufort, who spoke of the king's 'wish to be counselled by the wisest and most discreet men of the realm' for which reason he had sent for 'the said lords, knights, citizens and burgesses to be at his Parliament in order that he might have their advice on what seems best'. (Thus the Commons were specifically recognized as advisers as well as petitioners.) 'To begin anything,' the bishop continued, 'there is need of good counsel,' and he took as his text *Ante omnem actum consilium stabile* (before all action, stable counsel). The king, he said, particularly wanted advice about 'the due and competent sustenance of his high and royal estate', the good government of the realm, the maintenance of law, and cherishing those foreigners who were his friends and resisting those who were his external enemies. 'Our lord the king would not wish,' the bishop added, 'to act without opinions and good counsel from the said Lords Spiritual and Temporal and also from the Commons aforesaid. . . .'[2]

The Parliament lasted no more than four weeks: most of Henry's Parliaments were very short. Generous tax grants were made. A wool subsidy was given for four years, tunnage and poundage for one; and a fifteenth and tenth were allowed for guarding the seas. £10,000 was appropriated for the royal household. Nevertheless, the Commons spoke plainly about the failure in the previous reign to provide the good governance which had so often been requested, of which (they said) the king was well aware. They were welcoming a new broom, for, after all, Henry V came to power with the attractive freshness of a politician who had been in respectable opposition at the end of his father's reign.

---

[1] *Rot. Parl.* Vol. IV, pp. 3–14.
[2] Ibid., p. 3.

The Speaker first chosen was a lawyer, William Stourton, who was, however, immediately replaced by John Doreward who had also been the second choice in Henry IV's first Parliament. This change was made on the interesting grounds that the Speaker initially chosen had agreed, without referring the matter to his colleagues in the Commons, to the king's demand that the complaints about the state of the government should be put in writing. There was still a certain prickliness in the Commons which was left over from the previous reign. Much more significant, however, was the re-enactment in this Parliament of the law of 1406 on the regulation of elections, together with a new provision, made at the Commons' request, that no knights of the shire should henceforth be elected, in each shire, 'unless they be resident in the shire where they shall be elected on the day of the date of the writ of summons of the Parliament', and that elected citizens and burgesses should be 'resident, dwelling and enfranchised in the same cities and boroughs'.[1] This provision against carpet-bagging was, however, to be ineffective. There had ceased to be any wish to avoid the duties of a member of Parliament; on the contrary they were increasingly sought after as giving prestige and influence. The 'house' of Commons was given a quasi-aristocratic prestige by the social predominance in it of the gentry, by the presence of junior members of noble houses and by the speed with which wealthy merchants turned themselves into country gentlemen as fast as they could. (In the parliamentary rolls of the fifteenth century the word *gentils* increasingly appears as a description of members of the Commons.) In the rush for seats, those for the boroughs in particular were increasingly obtained by country gentlemen and rising lawyers unable to find a place in their shires.

Much of the next two years was taken up by a renewed attack on the Lollards and in 1414 it was necessary to fend off a Lollard uprising aimed at the person of the king after the escape from prison of the Lollard knight, Sir John Oldcastle, who had been one of Henry's own former associates. (Oldcastle was captured and executed three years later.) The second Parliament of the reign met at Leicester (a centre of Lollardy) in a hall specially built for the purpose (*en une graunde Sale ... de novel ordeignee par le Roi pur celle cause*) near the Greyfriars church.[2] The principal purpose of the Parliament was to deal with the heretics (Henry was asking for no direct taxation) and a statute was passed for discovering and destroying them. Among other acts was one for the confiscation of non-conventual alien priories. In this Parliament the king also created his brothers, John and

---

[1] *Stat. R.* Vol. II, p. 170 and *E.H.D.* Vol. IV, p. 461.
[2] *Rot. Parl.* Vol. IV, pp. 15–26.

Humphrey, Dukes of Bedford and Gloucester respectively. It seems to have been a generally placid assembly in which tunnage and poundage were granted for another three years. But it also produced a petition of the Commons, concerning their own privileges, which can at the very least be called, as it has been, 'a signpost on the constitutional highway'.[1]

The Commons began their petition (which is in English, here modernised) with the assertion that 'it has ever been their liberty and freedom that no statute nor law be made unless they have thereto (given) their assent'. Further, they said, they were and always had been 'both assentors and petitioners'. This was more than stretching the truth. They had originally been petitioners but not assentors. Yet in practice they had already come to have an assenting role and they were now trying to assert this pragmatic claim on a fictitious historical basis. From that premise, they now petitioned that in future, no law should ever be made on their petition and engrossed as a statute, 'in which additions or diminutions ... change the sentence and intention asked for by the Speaker's mouth'. (They added, however, that they did not mean by this to suggest that if they asked for two or three things, the king could not grant them what he pleased and refuse the rest.)

In reply, the king granted that nothing be enacted to the petitions of his Commons 'contrary to their asking'.[2] Bishop Stubbs, in his great constitutional history, had concluded from this that the Commons had long been seeking and had now obtained a firm agreement that their petitions should be enacted, if at all, in precisely the form in which the Commons had submitted them. This conclusion has been much qualified by later historians. For one thing it has been established that the Commons had not been engaged in a long struggle on this point because there was no need. During the reigns of Edward III, Richard II and Henry IV, petitions had been enacted more or less in the original form without fundamental changes. All that seems to have underlain the Commons' request was the fact that in Henry V's first Parliament several petitions had been drastically altered. It was simply to ensure that this breach of previous practice did not take root, that the petition of 1414 was devised.[3] It has further been emphasized that the king, in his reply, did not accept that petitions, if enacted, must not be amended at all; the concession was simply that they

---

[1] S. B. Chrimes *English Constitutional Ideas in the Fifteenth Century* which discusses in detail the significance of the Commons' petition in 1414, pp. 159–164.

[2] *Rot. Parl.* Vol. IV, p. 22. B. Wilkinson, *Const. Hist. of England in the 15th Century*, pp. 311–312 and *E.H.D.* Vol. IV, pp. 461–462.

[3] H. L. Gray, *The Influence of the Commons on Early Legislation*, (1932), pp. 261ff.

could not be amended in an opposite sense without the Commons' assent.[1] Finally, no doubt deliberately, the king refrained from acknowledging the Commons as assentors. All this puts the matter in proper perspective; parliamentary privilege always grew pragmatically and often without clear definition.

Yet the fact remains that it had come to be accepted in practice by the crown itself, partly for its own convenience, that the Commons had an assenting role. Thus Henry IV had gone out of his way to state in 1409, at a moment when it had suited the Commons to emphasize that they were merely petitioners, his own wish 'specially to have their advice and assent' in making statutes and granting taxation, then and for the future. It might also be argued that an undertaking not to amend petitions in a contrary sense without the Commons' assent would cover not only contradictory amendments, but any which might subtly undermine the essential purpose of the petition. No doubt the Commons knew well that the king and Lords could still, in the last analysis, make law without them. Moreover, during the fifteenth century there was an increasing tendency to amend petitions in the ensuing enactment in a significant though not a fundamental way without the Commons' assent, despite the petition of 1414; for instance, to reconcile them with existing law or to exempt certain persons. Yet when all such qualifications are made the petition was a significant step towards the emerging convention that every aspect of an act of Parliament should have been passed and agreed by the Commons, both the original bill, and amendments to it. The petition of 1414 has also to be assessed in the light of the fact that during the early fifteenth century the initiative for legislating passed, for a time, to the Commons. The procedures by which bills should be read by both 'houses' was taking root and it was now also the general practice for them to be enacted 'by the advice and assent of the Lords Spiritual and Temporal at the instance (or request) of the Commons' and not simply, as hitherto, by the assent of the Lords.[2] It was also during the reigns of Henry IV and Henry V that external petitioning groups and individuals increasingly came to address their petitions to the Commons rather than directly to the king, asking the Commons to adopt these as a common, or public petition, that is, as a petition on a matter of general concern. This too assisted the process by which at this time, it became clear that the Commons' assent was necessary for the validity of an act of Parliament.

During the Leicester Parliament it is likely that the question of the king's

[1] S. B. Chrimes, op. cit.
[2] Ibid., pp. 101-104.

ancestral claims to the French crown were raised, though this is not officially recorded. Civil war still raged in France between the ducal parties of the Burgundians and Armagnacs (or Orleanists), the French king Charles VI being mad and politically impotent. Shortly after the Leicester Parliament, therefore, Henry began negotiations with both sides in the French conflict about his own claims, initially demanding in full sovereignty only the territories ceded to Edward III. When this was refused events moved inexorably towards a war which had the support of all classes, Commons as well as Lords, both for glory's and for profit's sake. A second Parliament in November 1414 settled the matter and a decision was taken that Henry should seek the recovery of his rights, by negotiation if possible, but by war if necessary. Two tenths and fifteenths were granted in two instalments, one payable a year later, which suggests that the Commons still hoped for a negotiated settlement. This Parliament lasted only four weeks.[1] Thomas Chaucer, who was close to the king, was again the Speaker and he was undoubtedly instrumental in helping Henry to get the supply he needed.

In the following April, Henry laid claim to the French crown. But as he prepared to embark for France with 1,500 ships and nearly 10,000 men, he was faced with the revelation of a plot by Richard, Earl of Cambridge, York's brother, to seize the Earl of March, take him to Wales and proclaim him as Richard II's heir. The plot was apparently divulged by March himself, and Cambridge and other conspirators, including Lord Scrope, were executed. Cambridge, however, had been married to Anne Mortimer and it was their four year old son who, as a later Duke of York, was to carry forward the Mortimer claim into the dynastic conflict popularly known as the Wars of the Roses.

In August 1415 war began. Henry landed his expeditionary force without opposition on the north bank of the Seine and after a six day siege took Harfleur. Although his men were sick with dysentery, he then marched them to Calais and, as it turned out, to his greatest victory. Finding his route to Calais beyond the Somme barred by a much larger French army, Henry achieved a spectacular victory at Agincourt, inflicting devastating losses on his enemy. Many noble French prisoners were taken, including the Duke of Orleans himself, the Armagnac leader. The English suffered few losses, though the Duke of York was killed. The glory and the ransoms ensured that Henry faced no further conspiracies at home. Between 1417 and 1420 he set about the conquest of Normandy and the subjugation of the French kingdom. His instruments were an efficient and well prepared military machine and the driving force of his will.

[1] *Rot. Parl.* Vol. IV, pp. 34–54.

Henry V: Parliament Pays for Glory

Writs for the autumn Parliament of 1415 had been issued by the Duke of Bedford, as guardian of England, the day after Henry sailed for France. It met at Westminster on 4 November, after the great news of Agincourt had reached London.[1] It was an exceptionally short Parliament, lasting only nine days. But what was there to say and do except 'to give all honour to the king', as Bishop Beaufort expressed it on behalf of Bedford, just as 'the king gave all honour to Almighty God', and, of course, to provide Henry with ample funds to continue the war? There were, said Beaufort, two causes of summons: first, the good government of the kingdom and second, to aid the expedition to recover the king's royal rights in France. So the Commons granted that the outstanding tenth and fifteenth voted in the previous Parliament should be brought forward by several months and that there should be a further subsidy in less than a year's time. Most remarkably, they voted the king a subsidy on wool and tunnage and poundage for the rest of his life – the latter having been given to no former sovereign, though Richard II had been granted the wool subsidy alone for life in 1398. The only conditions made were that the king should not dispose of the proceeds by grants and that it should not be taken by his successors as a precedent. The Speaker was another knight close to the Lancastrian family, a Sir Richard Redmayne, who in the glow of Agincourt can have had no difficulty in managing the Commons on the king's behalf.

After Agincourt, and a triumphant return to London, Henry concentrated on bargaining with all the parties in France and on preparing for a new offensive which was designed, at worst, to recover the lands ceded to Edward III at Brétigny, and at best to obtain the French crown. In May 1416, the Emperor Sigismund came to London, at first to mediate, but finally to ally himself with Henry against the Armagnacs. He paid a formal visit to a Parliament, which met in the spring of 1416 in two short sessions, beginning in March and with an Easter adjournment.[2] This Parliament also brought forward the subsidy voted by its predecessor which was not due to be paid until the autumn. A second Parliament met in the same year on 19 October and lasted for a month.[3] Again the chancellor asked for help in securing the king's rights in France, which could now only be achieved by war. A grant of two tenths and fifteenths was made in two instalments of three-quarters and a quarter. The king was also allowed to raise a loan on the security of this taxation. Altogether, it was an exceptionally generous grant, although the Commons made it on condition that no further tax should be

---

[1] *Rot. Parl.* Vol. IV, pp. 62–69.
[2] Ibid., pp. 70–86.
[3] Ibid., pp. 94–105.

levied before all the present tax had been collected. They also stipulated that this time the instalments should not be brought forward. In four years, however, Henry V had had nearly as much as his father had been granted in the whole of his reign. Among other business, a treaty which Henry had made with the Emperor Sigismund was published and discussed before being duly 'ratified, approved and confirmed by all the estates'.

The treaty bound Sigismund and Henry and their heirs and successors, to prosecute a war for their rights in France. They then set about associating Duke John of Burgundy with their alliance, and made some sort of agreement with him by which he undertook that, at the least, he would not oppose an English invasion. At the same time, Henry also negotiated with the French princes he had captured at Agincourt. In preparation for an invasion, large loans were raised and plans were made for supplying the army so that it did not have to live off, and thus devastate, the country Henry intended to rule, which was in contrast to the military tactics of Edward III. In August the expedition sailed for Normandy and beginning with the capture of Caen steadily took possession of a succession of towns. With the capitulation of Rouen at the beginning of 1419, the English king took care to govern the province largely through Normans, though he also encouraged some English settlement.

In the meantime, the Duke of Burgundy had taken possession of Queen Isabella of France who then went over to his side, and declared herself regent on behalf of her insane husband. In May 1419, both the Duke of Burgundy and the queen came to Henry, bringing with them the Princess Catherine, the French king's daughter, in order to negotiate for some sort of arrangement whereby Henry would marry Catherine and be given the ancient Angevin possessions. Although it appears that Henry fell in love with the princess at this meeting, the negotiations came to nothing. Burgundy and the queen then effected a reconciliation with the opposing party headed by the dauphin, but this was aborted when John the Fearless was treacherously murdered by the Armagnacs. His successor, Philip the Good, immediately changed sides and agreed to support Henry's claim to the French crown on the understanding that Henry would marry Catherine and that Charles VI would remain king for life, with Henry as his regent and successor to the French crown. Thereafter the two kingdoms were to remain separate, but under one king. To this arrangement Henry committed himself in May 1420 by the treaty of Troyes, where a month later he married Catherine. In February 1421, after an absence of three years, he returned to England with his new queen for her coronation. Their son, the future Henry VI, was born in December; his mental instability was almost certainly derived from his French grandfather and the deficiences of his character led to the Wars of the Roses. By his conquests and his marriage, Henry V had brought about the downfall of his dynasty.

Four Parliaments had been held during the three years of Henry's absence. The Parliament which met in November 1417 lasted a month and voted him another double subsidy of a tenth and a fifteenth to be levied at Candlemas in 1418 and the same amount a year later.[1] It also agreed to a guarantee safeguarding the repayment of a large loan made by Bishop Beaufort, who had ceased to be chancellor and had been replaced by Bishop Langley of Durham. Still more money was asked for at the next Parliament in October 1419, since the new alliance with Burgundy made a still greater war effort essential.[2] The Commons, however, were now beginning to worry about the economic consequences of the war and they stipulated that taxation should be spent on military supplies in England so that the export of coin was diminished. A smaller tax grant was given; a tenth and a fifteenth for Candlemas 1420, but only a third of that amount for the following Martinmas.

The next Parliament met in December 1420, under the presidency of the Duke of Gloucester because Bedford was absent in France. No money seems to have been asked for.[3] Indeed, the chancellor's opening speech candidly acknowledged the poverty of the country and the scarcity of money. The Commons would plainly have been reluctant to give more. They were worried by the length of Henry's absence and petitioned for his return. The possible consequences of his gaining the French crown were also beginning to alarm them. They would instinctively have preferred the king to settle for the acquisition of French provinces rather than to take a foreign crown which might prejudice English interests. Accordingly, Edward III's statute which had provided that English liberties should not be diminished on that account was confirmed.

After the king's return, he first went on a prolonged progress through the kingdom which was in part a religious pilgrimage, and in part for loan-raising; Bishop Beaufort again made a heavy contribution. No subsidy, therefore, had to be asked from a Parliament over which the king himself presided when it assembled in the Painted Chamber on 2 May 1421.[4] Nevertheless, such was its confidence in the king that it authorized the council to give security for the repayment of the king's military loans. At the same time Parliament ratified the treaty of Troyes, and it is again indicative

[1] *Rot. Parl.* Vol. IV, pp. 106–115.
[2] Ibid., pp. 116–122.
[3] Ibid., pp. 123–128.
[4] Ibid., pp. 129–149.

of the rising influence of the Commons that so crucial a treaty was placed before them, as well as before the other higher estates. All the articles of the treaty were 'solemnly expounded and declared in detail' by the chancellor and 'the three estates ... approved, praised, authorized, and accepted the treaty...'[1] The next month Henry left for France for the last time and began a new campaign to extend his territory. A final short Parliament in December granted a fifteenth and a tenth, with its collection spread out over a period, but the Commons also showed that their alarm at the cost of the war was increasing.[2] It is notable that the form of payment of the loan (with details of the coin to be used) are set out in English, a language which now increasingly appears in the parliamentary rolls.

During that winter Henry became ill while campaigning and never recovered his health. In August 1422 he died, leaving an infant successor and having made provisions for a regency. Effectively, power would now be in the hands of his surviving brothers Bedford and Gloucester; Clarence had been killed in France a year earlier. Success in war had given Henry V political stability at home. He was free from aristocratic strife and from challenge by the Commons. A popular war policy had brought him grants of money on an unprecedented scale. He had raised loans which could be described as forced, apparently without arousing criticism, and he had used close relations with successive Speakers (none more so than Thomas Chaucer) to manage the Commons. In other words he had done much for which Richard II had been condemned, and yet he was applauded in doing it. The difference between them was in part the difference between an unpopular peace policy compared with a popular and successful war. But it was also a matter of political style, not least in the care Henry took for reconciliation and the forms of consultation. Throughout the reign, he and his ministers spoke to Parliaments as though they took them seriously. It is also clear that he intended to govern France through Frenchmen and not to amalgamate his two kingdoms. It was expected as well that France itself would provide for the king's military expenditure there. Yet the French dominion he bequeathed to his son proved impossible to hold. It is fruitless to speculate on how Henry would have acted had he lived; the simple fact of history is that the political and social tensions caused by the collapse of his conquests destroyed the Lancastrian monarchy.

[1] *Rot. Parl.* Vol. IV, p. 135.
[2] Ibid., pp. 150–157.

CHAPTER 9

———— * ————

Henry VI:
Parliament, Faction and Civil War

I

EVEN if Henry V had lived it is unlikely that England and France could have been held together in a dual monarchy. For all his military genius, resistance in France to the rule of the Lancastrian dynasty was too great for the country to be conquered without an unacceptable call on English money. The hope that the conquest of France would be self-financing was never realistic and without Henry's will-power and military skill the enterprise was doomed. The dauphin who was to be Charles VII held all France south of the Loire except for Gascony and had greater reserves of material resources and loyalty to draw on than the Lancastrians. What is more, the direction of the English interest in France was weakened by being divided from the government of England where the exercise of the royal authority during the minority of Henry VI was from the outset a matter of contest.

Until a few days before he died Henry V had made no provision for the governing of his possessions during his infant son's minority. Just before he left England in 1421 he had revised his general will but that concerned only his personal land and property. Had he died childless, as he was when the will was made, the crown would have passed to the older of his brothers John, Duke of Bedford. It was not until 26 August, that, in a codicil to his will drawn up at Bois de Vincennes, the dying king had set down his intentions for the government of England until the infant born nine months earlier was of an age to rule. Under this codicil, Henry V's younger brother, Humphrey, Duke of Gloucester, was to be principal guardian and protector of the infant king and his kingdom; he would have *tutelam et defensionem principales*, the word *tutela* (guardianship) indicating responsibility for an estate, in this case the realm, during a minority. In other words, Humphrey would act as regent with full royal authority. The charge of the person of the king, on the other hand, was to be given to Thomas Beaufort, Duke of Exeter, one of John of Gaunt's sons by Catherine Swynford, who would be assisted in this task by Henry's household steward, Sir Walter Hungerford, and the chamberlain, Lord Fitzhugh, both knights of the Garter. The codicil said nothing about the government of Henry V's French territory but on his deathbed he gave verbal instructions, which were witnessed, placing his responsibility in the hands of the elder of his brothers, John Duke of Bedford, who was to hold and govern Normandy and the other conquered land as though it were his own until Henry VI came of age.

The fact that the younger brother was to govern England was not a sign that Henry V had any less trust in the elder. It simply reflected Henry's wish that each should continue in the role he had recently played: Gloucester had been keeper of England in his absence, Bedford had fought with Henry V in France. The dying king trusted both of them equally to guard his son's inheritance and that trust was not misplaced. Although Gloucester was quarrelsome and ambitious for power, he never made the slightest move to usurp the rights of his nephew. Indeed, it is possible that his worst qualities were heightened because he was frustrated of the power of regency Henry had intended him to have in England. John of Bedford was equally loyal and a good deal more responsible and solid.

Bedford's government of the English territory in France with the power of a regent presented no political problem. In England, however, it was a very different matter. The regency which Henry V intended for Gloucester was quite unacceptable to the English magnates. Duke Humphrey was a man of will and energy and he had a subtle and cultivated mind. He also had an ability to make himself popular. For most of his political life he enjoyed the support of the Commons, and the Londoners in particular were behind him because he shared their protectionist instincts. But his ambition, rashness and habit of pushing his cause to extremes bred distrust. The magnates on the council and in Parliament were therefore unwilling, when they came to think about it, to give him a regent's delegated royal authority. Almost certainly they were decisively influenced by Bedford's unconcealed reluctance to see his brother as regent of England. It was not that he was unduly suspicious of Gloucester's intentions; they seem to have got on well enough. What principally influenced Bedford was the fact that if Henry VI did not survive infancy, which was always a strong possibility in medieval conditions, he himself would inherit the crown. He had no wish to do so with his position diminished by the fact that Gloucester had been ruling

England with the full royal power of a regent, while Bedford himself was locked up in the difficult affairs of France.

When Henry V died, few of the lay Lords were in England. A number of others came home with the late king's body, but it was still a small gathering of magnates which, in September, met to swear loyalty to the infant king. They decided that parliamentary sanction should be obtained for the arrangements for government during the minority, and writs were despatched for a Parliament on 9 November. The writs were sent out in the name of the king and council, not in the name of Gloucester as guardian of England. The clear implication of this was that, regardless of Henry V's will, the exercise of the royal authority, including the power to summon Parliaments, had devolved not on Gloucester but on the council of magnates. A few days before the Parliament, a larger gathering of magnates met on 5 November. The Lords Spiritual present were the Archbishop of Canterbury, Bishop Beaufort of Winchester and six other bishops. Of the lay peerage, there were the Dukes of Gloucester and Exeter, two earls and nine other lords. The most important question before this meeting of the council was the terms of Gloucester's commission to open, preside over and dissolve the coming Parliament and much against his will he was forced to accept that he exercised this function with the assent of the council.

This had not been the formula used when he had previously acted as guardian of the realm in his brother's absence, and in Gloucester's view, the change prejudiced his status. However, his case was weakened by the fact that he himself had already accepted the writ sent to him simply as Duke of Gloucester to come to the Parliament over which he would preside. Implicitly, therefore, he had acknowledged that the king's council stood higher than he himself in the matter of summoning Parliaments. The council also specifically rejected Gloucester's claim that in accordance with the late king's will he should be guardian of the king and of his royal kingdom. The most influential opponent of the power Gloucester sought was his uncle, Bishop Beaufort, John of Gaunt's son, whose long experience of politics during the previous two reigns made him a formidable opponent. Yet Beaufort could not have succeeded in his opposition if the majority of the lords had not shared his misgivings. So began the long contest about Gloucester's claims to power and his feud with Beaufort which bedevilled Henry VI's minority.

The Parliament which met on 9 November was opened by Archbishop Chichele of Canterbury.[1] The archbishop said that since the king was of tender age, Parliament had been summoned to provide for 'the good

[1] *Rot. Parl.* Vol. IV, pp. 169–191.

governance of the very excellent person of the king' (*la bone governance de tres excellent persone du Roi*) and also for the maintenance of peace, administration of the law and the defence of the realm. Arrangements must be made, he said, for government to be undertaken by honourable and discreet persons from each estate of this kingdom (*honurables & discretes persones . . . et ceo de chescun estate de ceste Roialme*). In other words, royal authority must be exercised by an appointed council representative of the estates. Chichele embellished his argument by reference to a text from Exodus in which Jethro (by which Chichele clearly meant himself) had found Moses (in other words, Gloucester) overworked and had advised that he should have continuing assistance from among the most powerful and worthy men, namely a continual council. After triers and receivers of petitions had been appointed in the usual manner, Roger Flore, a knight from Rutland, was elected Speaker, an office he had held three times previously, and other comparatively ordinary business was dealt with.

Some days later, a deputation of knights from the Commons went to see Gloucester to ask him to disclose to them the names of those appointed to be chancellor, treasurer and keeper of the Privy Seal. In response, the archbishop and a few other spiritual and lay peers went to the Commons' house to announce the names of these ministers: Thomas Langley, Bishop of Durham, William Kynwolmarsh and John Stafford respectively. At about the same time, though it is not recorded in the official roll, the Commons apparently asked in Parliament to be told who would have 'the gouernance of this Reme undre our souverain lord (the king) bi his high auctorite'.[1] Gloucester then proceeded to use this request to further his claim to a higher authority than that which the Lords were willing to give. What happened is told not in the parliamentary roll for 1422 but in a Lords' account of these events in the roll for 1427–8, at a time when Gloucester was again pressing his claim for increased power by asking for a definition of his authority as protector and defender of the land.[2]

When, in 1422, the Commons asked to know who had the government of the kingdom, Gloucester submitted his claim to the regency, both by right of birth and by the late king's will. This was rejected by the Lords as being against precedent and law, and also on the grounds that a dead king could not make such a provision without the assent of the three estates. 'The Kyng that ded ys, in his lyf ne migzt by his last will nor otherwyse altre, change nor

---

[1] This request by the Commons is quoted in a memorandum submitted by Gloucester to the Lords printed by S. B. Chrimes, 'The Pretensions of the Duke of Gloucester in 1422' E.H.R. Vol. XLV, 1930, pp. 101–103. For a full analysis of these events see especially J. S. Roskell, *The Commons in the Parliament of 1422*, Ch. VI.

[2] See pp. 510–11.

abroge (abrogate), with oute thassent of the thre Estates, nor committe or graunte to any persone, governaunce or rule of this land lenger thanne he lyved.'[1] The precedent in the minds of the council was the avoidance of a regency for Richard II's minority. The Lords, therefore, simply granted Gloucester the title 'Defensor of this Reme and chief Counseiller of the kyng', which was less than he wanted. His response was to submit a memorandum to the Lords in which, quite accurately, he declared that 'bi vertue of the codicill' he 'shuld haue *tulelam et defensionem principales* of the kyng', adding that this had been read and agreed by the council, as no doubt it had been before its members had changed their minds.[2] He also disingenuously interpreted the Commons' request to be told 'who should have the governance of the realm' as meaning that their wishes would not be met by the proposed title of Defender (Defensor) of the realm. 'It semeth to my lord that by the word Defensor the peticion of the commune nys nat satisfied.'[3] Instead, recalling that William Marshal in Henry III's minority was designated *Rector Regis et Regni Anglie*, Gloucester's memorandum suggested that he himself should be called *Rector Regni*, 'but nat Regis for that he vil nat desire', with the word 'Defensor' added to meet the Lords' wish. In other words, he would be regent of the kingdom but not governor of the king's person. There is no evidence, other than Gloucester's assertion, that the Commons sought a higher title for him than the Lords proposed. Yet his evident belief that if he could convincingly assert the Commons' support it would give a plausible reason for the Lords to change their minds reveals the now generally accepted importance ascribed to the opinions of the lower 'House'.

The Lords had their way, however, and Gloucester was obliged simply to accept the title 'Protector and Defender of realm and church in England and principal councillor of the lord king'. This title was granted by the advice and assent of the Lords in Parliament and also by the Commons 'in the same' (*et auxi de la Commune d'Engleterre assemblez en al mesme*).[4] The duke was to preside over the council but not for life and the magnates would be able to revoke the appointment. Moreover, Bedford would become protector when he was in England. It was made quite clear that ultimate disposal of the royal authority was intended to be with the lords in council and in Parliament. It was for them to determine how long these arrangements

[1] *Rot. Parl.* Vol. IV, p. 326.
[2] A copy of the codicil, confirming Gloucester's assertions about Henry V's intention, was discovered in the archives of Eton College in 1978. P. Strong, *E.H.R.* XCVI, 1980.
[3] S. B. Chrimes, 'The Pretensions of the Duke of Gloucester in 1422,' *E.H.R.* Vol. XLV, 1930, pp. 101-103.
[4] *Rot. Parl.* Vol. IV, p. 175.

should last and they would be able to revoke them. An important reason for denying Gloucester the regency in England was to ensure that nothing was done that might seem to detract from the position of Bedford who would succeed to the throne if the infant king did not survive.

The Parliament roll for 1422 then records the nomination, at the request of the Commons, of seventeen councillors for government (*conseillers assistentz a la governance*) with Gloucester and the Duke of Exeter at their head and including representatives of the estates. In addition to the two dukes, there were five lords spiritual, five earls, two peers of Parliament (one of whom was Lord Cromwell, a young man of nineteen who played a consistently prominent part in council business and was eventually to become treasurer), and three knights who were former Speakers, but were neither summoned as peers nor were elected members of this Parliament. These three knights were Sir Walter Beauchamp (Speaker in 1416) who had been treasurer of Henry V's household, Sir Walter Hungerford (Speaker in 1414) who had done Henry V high military service as an admiral and on land, and had been his household steward, and Sir John Tiptoft (Speaker in 1406) who had served both Henry IV and Henry V in various posts. Five articles written in English stated the conditions on which the councillors were willing to take office.[1] After the Lords had approved them, the articles were taken to the Commons for their examination, the Lords wishing for their views (*lour entent*). The Commons suggested a minor amendment (which they wrote in French) to one article concerned with appointments, and this was agreed. The other articles were accepted unchanged. They included requirements that the chamberlains of the Exchequer should swear to divulge to nobody what the king had in his treasury ('that for no frendship they schul make no Man privee, but the Lordis of the Counseill, what the Kyng hath withynne his Tresour'); that the clerk was required on oath to record each day the names of those lords present ('to see what, howe, and by whom, eny thyng passeth') and that, for business to be done, at least six or four of the council must be present, though if 'grete maters' were to be considered, all of them, or a majority, should be there. The councillors were to consult the protector of the moment (either Bedford or Gloucester) on occasions when they would in ordinary circumstances consult the king.

In these political matters the Commons put their point of view when they thought it appropriate. They were not a tame body and they included men of political and administrative experience and talent, most of whom had been in previous Parliaments. Most of the knights of the shire were well connected, and among them were four previous and five future Speakers.

---

[1] *Rot. Parl.* Vol. IV, p. 176.

Many of the burgesses too were 'gentilmen'. Yet the outstanding characteristic of the arrangements made for government at the start of the minority was that they constituted an essentially aristocratic dispensation in which the Commons had no significant part. This established the political tone for the years ahead. The leading members of the nobility had turned themselves to the practical business of government as members of the council more assiduously than ever before. They also continued active in conciliar business to an extent that contrasted sharply with their predecessors' habit in some former reigns (Richard II's, for instance) of sporadically and acrimoniously holding the king to account for his conduct of the business of the realm while being themselves unwilling to devote much sustained effort to it. During the long minority of Henry VI the monarchy was put into aristocratic commission and the council, whose members were paid salaries for attendance according to their rank, represented different groups and connections and were held together by their understanding that the system must be made to work because failure would bring disaster for them all. That is what underlay the various arrangements that business was only to be done by a quorum of the membership. In practice these precautions were far from inculcating rectitude. The council was lavish in its spending and its members abused their position by making liberal use of its power and patronage in grants and assignments to themselves. In the earlier years of the minority, during which Parliament ceased to give direct taxation, this produced an accumulating deficit which led eventually to financial crisis. Moreover, the council was repeatedly riven by faction and some of its members sometimes came to the brink of open strife, especially Gloucester and Beaufort. Nevertheless, throughout the minority the council remained remarkably stable in its grip on public affairs and despite the feuds within it, there were few drastic changes of membership.

This aristocratic dominance represented a setback for the political influence of the Commons, although their power over money remained and their privileges continued to grow. In Henry VI's first Parliament the Commons failed to follow the precedent of their predecessors and to insist on a degree of parliamentary oversight of the council, as the 1406 Parliament had done. In 1422, it is true, the names of the councillors were read and recorded in Parliament, though they were not publicly sworn there. But even the announcement of names generally ceased after 1423. By 1430, the council was able to change its own membership freely without reference to Parliament. Thus the Commons acquiesced in the domination of both the council and Parliament by the Lords and by so doing they lost much of the considerable political initiative that they themselves had exerted in the Good Parliament, in the early Parliaments of Richard II and in most of the Parliaments of Henry IV's reign.[1] It was not to be recovered for over two centuries. The domination of the rest of the medieval period by the factions of magnates was followed by the powerful monarchy established by the Tudors which remained free to appoint and dismiss its ministers without reference to Parliament until well into the seventeenth century.

The explanation of the Commons' comparative docility is not that they had become hesitant to protect what they saw as their essential concerns. It was rather that they were generally content with the Lords' dispensation because they increasingly identified themselves with the aristocratic interest with which the knights of the shire, the dominant element among the Commons, had so many social ties. They remained, however, jealous guardians of their control over taxation, and the terms of the grants announced by the Speaker on the final day of the first Parliament of the minority were far less generous than those given to Henry V. The grants made to the late king for life having lapsed, the wool subsidies were renewed at lower rates and tunnage and poundage was to be levied on foreign merchants only, and not on English. The purpose was clearly protectionist. These grants were, moreover, restricted to two years until November 1424, and no subsidy of a tenth and fifteenth was granted, whether or not one was asked for. Until the reverses inflicted on the English by Joan of Arc, Parliament gave no significant support for the French war, in sharp contrast to its help to Edward III. One consequence was that the Commons did not have the opportunities of their predecessors for making political terms in exchange for money.

No legislation of importance came from this Parliament, though several common petitions were granted in part and, in one case, in whole. Henry VI's first Parliament was concerned primarily with arrangements for his minority. Conciliar government had been firmly established on the principle that only the king of the moment could devolve his authority to a regent and that Henry VI as an infant was unable to do so. All acts of government were in Henry's name, and the most important acts of state, including the transfer of the great seal, were ceremonially performed in his presence. Moreover, despite their quarrels about the exercise of power during Henry's minority, his uncles and other relations were scrupulous in their determination to safeguard his rights, preserve the dynasty, and deliver the exercise of regal authority to the king when he came of age.

The key to domestic politics for the next quarter of a century was France,

---

[1] Roskell, *The Commons in the Parliament of 1422*, pp. 108–110. For a discussion of the council during Henry VI's minority see also, J. F. Baldwin, *The King's Council during the Middle Ages*, Ch. VIII.

and it is convenient to survey the outline of events there before we return to the politics of Parliament. For the better part of a decade the English managed to hold and even, with the conquest of Maine and Anjou, to extend their French territory. The essential struggle was for that part of France which lies between the Seine and the Loire. The English held the north with better organized forces but central and southern France was loyal to the dauphin who had in the long run greater financial resources. By 1429, the tide of success began to turn against the English with the appearance in the field of Joan of Arc who, guided by her divine voices, gave not only inspiration but also tactical coherence to the French effort. After relieving Orleans from the English siege, her series of victories in Champagne culminated in the crowning of the dauphin at Rheims, which as she rightly saw was, for the moment, even more important for the French cause than the recovery of Paris. The coronation of Charles VII not only gave sacramental inspiration to the French but amounted to a repudiation of the treaty of Troyes, which was highly damaging to the English cause. So much had French morale recovered that even Joan's failure to take Paris and her subsequent capture by the Burgundians could not undermine it. She was sold to the English, charged with sorcery and witchcraft and in May 1431 was burned at Rouen. The purpose of this appalling act was to discredit what had been achieved under her inspiration, but it was too late to stop the French recovery. In December, the ten-year-old Henry VI was crowned with propagandist splendour in Paris (it was the only visit he paid to his French dominion) but a coronation there could not compete with the sacramental ceremony at Rheims. All that Henry's coronation achieved was to commit the English to the virtually impossible task of keeping the French crown. Had they limited their aim to Henry V's originally declared objective of obtaining Normandy and his other ancestral lands this might have been feasible.

The blow which wrecked the English cause was, however, the defection of Burgundy. In 1423 Humphrey of Gloucester had deeply offended the Duke of Burgundy by marrying Jacqueline, who was Countess of Hainault and Holland in her own right, and who was the estranged wife of John of Brabant. A dissolution of her first marriage was obtained from the schismatic Pope. The estranged couple were childless and Philip of Burgundy, who was John of Brabant's heir, had expected to inherit the possessions of both of them. But Duke Humphrey raised forces to take possession of Jacqueline's inheritance, and Philip immediately prepared to assist John of Brabant to defend them. In the event, although Gloucester took his forces to the Low Countries, there was no fighting and Bedford, who married Duke Philip's sister to strengthen the Burgundian alliance, managed to damp down the quarrel. But permanent damage had been done to the Burgundian alliance on which, as Bedford and Beaufort, but not Gloucester, understood, English hopes in France depended. Though the Duke of Burgundy remained the ally of the English, he began to have contacts with Charles VII. Little by little the Anglo-Burgundian alliance was loosened as successive efforts were made in the French court to draw Duke Philip out of it.

In August 1435, under the auspices of papal mediators, a peace conference met át the abbey of St. Waast at Arras. It was the decisive point in the war since Philip of Burgundy had been persuaded to enter the negotiations on the understanding that if peace could not be made he would extricate himself from the English alliance, provided an honourable way of doing so could be found. Peace did, indeed, prove to be out of the question. The French would concede Henry's possession of Normandy and Guienne but only as fiefs of the French crown. They inevitably could not accept the Lancastrian claim to the throne of France. The English, on the other hand, could not, after Henry's coronation, abandon their claim to the French throne and would offer only a long truce. The conference failed and Burgundy immediately began to draw towards the French. Finally, Duke Philip, in a ceremony at St Waast's, was released by the church from his oath of alliance at Troyes. The grounds for this momentous event were that the oath had always been invalid since Charles VI had had no power to alienate the French succession and the duke was therefore immorally committed by the oath to inevitable and useless bloodshed. Philip of Burgundy did not immediately turn actively against the English and for the moment was committed only to bring them to peace. Nevertheless, this desertion finally destroyed any hope of a Lancastrian dynasty in France and in the same year the English suffered the further blow of the death of the Duke of Bedford. Yet committed to the Lancastrian claim to France by the annointing of Henry at Paris and outraged by Burgundy's desertion, they could only continue the struggle, thus driving themselves further down the road to political disaster.

During most of these years, politics in England were dominated by the rivalry and the personalities of Gloucester and his uncle Beaufort. The rich and politically shrewd bishop, to whom the crown was heavily indebted for sums of money lent to Henry V, was as strong an advocate of the Burgundian alliance as he was an opponent of Gloucester's claims to fuller power. Gloucester, on the other hand, had not only offended the Burgundians by his dubious second marriage but was also in favour of the protectionist policy of levying the wool subsidy on foreign merchants only, which was damaging to the Low Countries and therefore to the interests of the Duke of Burgundy. Probably with good reason, Beaufort saw the duke's hand in an outbreak of hostility and propaganda against Flemish merchants in 1424 and seemed even to fear more dangerous disturbances. During Gloucester's absence on his fruitless expedition to Hainault, Beaufort, who had become chancellor in July 1424, installed one of his own adherents as governor of the Tower of London and then went so far as to instruct him to refuse Duke Humphrey admission on his return to England. To defend his interest, Beaufort then brought forces to London and Gloucester accused him of trying to seize the person of the king. Subsequently, a pitched battle on London Bridge between the duke's Londoners and the bishop's retainers from Cheshire was only narrowly prevented. Bedford was hastily summoned home by the bishop to take charge of affairs as the only way of preventing civil strife.

Before this dangerous state of conflict was reached, the second Parliament of the reign had met on 23 October, 1423. To support the notion that in some real sense Henry VI reigned, the infant king was brought from Windsor to London in November, despite the winter weather (the journey made him ill), to be present in Parliament. As the Speaker is reported to have put it, the Commons wished to see 'your high and royal person to sit and occupy your own rightful seat and place in your Parliament to whom our recourse of right must be to have every wrong reformed'.[1] It was perhaps because it was thought unnecessary to do so that the parliamentary rolls do not record the royal presence on this occasion.[2] They begin, however, with a statement of the understood constitutional position, namely that a commission of the king, under the great seal, had given power to the Duke of Gloucester to hold the Parliament. The existing council was then, for the most part, reappointed and announced in Parliament. In addition to the confirmation of the previous arrangements for the conduct of the council's business (including the recording of those present at the transaction of business) additional rules were made to protect collective responsibility. Several of them reveal the suspicion which Gloucester aroused. Thus the first of the new provisions stated that neither 'my Lord of Gloucestre, ne noon other Man of the Counsaill' should grant favours in any suit, in respect of Bills, (that is, petitions) for rights, offices or benefices where the decision belonged to the council. Such Bills should only receive the answer that they should be 'seen by all the Counsaill' after which the party suing should receive an answer. Another provision was almost certainly directed at Gloucester and was a response to the trouble he was making for the Anglo-

[1] B. Wolffe, *Henry VI* (1981).
[2] *Rot. Parl.* Vol. IV, pp. 197–260.

Burgundian alliance by his tactics over Hainault. It recorded that it was 'to greet a shame' that, when the king wrote his letters to foreign countries by the council's advice in one sense, individuals wrote in a contrary sense. No man was in future to do this 'on peyne of shame and reproef'.

A considerable part of this Parliament's business was concerned with unpaid debts incurred by the previous two kings, their executors' business and their creditors' petitions. Money for the French war was badly needed, and when Parliament was prorogued for the Christmas recess in December, the Commons were told that this was not only so that everyone could enjoy the festive season in his own home but also in order that the Commons could tell their 'neighbours' (that is, their constituents) of the crown's pressing financial needs.[1] But when the Parliament resumed at the end of February (altogether it sat for fifteen weeks) all that was granted was an extension until November 1426 of the wool subsidies and tunnage and poundage on aliens alone. The Commons continued to take literally the late king's theory that the French war should be supported by the French dominions. The political atmosphere remained uneasy during the Parliament, which no doubt had something to do with Gloucester's marriage to Jacqueline of Hainault, though it was by a declaration in this Parliament that she was naturalized as English.[2] It was also a sign of dynastic nervousness that it was enacted that for a person accused of treason to try to escape was itself treason; at this time a certain Sir John Mortimer, who bore a name feared by Lancastrians, was in prison and he was duly drawn and hanged for allegedly trying to escape and for plotting to make the Earl of March king. The Lancastrians were still fearful of the Mortimer claim to the throne and it was said that Gloucester was alarmed by the large number of retinue brought to this Parliament by Edmund Mortimer, Earl of March. After this Parliament, March was sent to Ireland where he died soon afterwards of the plague. His unexpressed claim to the throne was inherited by his sister's son, the young Duke of York who was eventually to stake it in war against Henry VI. The only solid achievement of foreign policy during this Parliament was a peace with Scotland. In November a deputation from the Commons thanked Gloucester and the Lords for a statement by the chancellor on the peace negotiations. Early in the new year, James I, who had been a captive since 1406, was released and married to a niece of the Duke of Exeter.

The next Parliament met on 30 April, 1425 after Gloucester's return from the Low Countries, and sat until 14 July, with a short recess at Whitsun.[3]

[1] *Rot. Parl.* Vol. IV, p. 200.
[2] Ibid., p. 242.
[3] Ibid., pp. 261–308.

The political tension between the duke and Beaufort was now so great that Gloucester was not even given a commission to hold Parliament on the king's behalf. Instead, Henry VI, who was now three, was brought in to preside at the opening ceremony. Yet on the whole, it was not a difficult Parliament for Duke Humphrey. After his unsuccessful expedition to Hainault, he was, for instance, allowed to borrow from the king 20,000 marks over four years, by the advice and assent of the Lords and by the assent of the Commons and on security given by the council. 'We the Comune of this Reaume... yeve oure assent, that the Lordes Spirituell and Temporell of the Kyng's Counseill beyng, make the seurtees aforesaide, by the said auctorite.'[1] A dispute over precedence between the Earl of Warwick and John Mowbray, the Earl Marshal, who was one of Duke Humphrey's friends, was settled in the latter's favour by the return to him of the dukedom of Norfolk at the petition of the Commons. At the same time, however, Beaufort was given security for the repayment of his loans and in the council itself Gloucester was on the defensive.

The principal concern of the Commons, however, was taxation and according to a London chronicler: 'In that parlyment was moche altercacyon bytwyne the lordys and the comyns for tonage and poundage.'[2] For the first time since Henry V's death, this tax was reluctantly levied on English merchants, though for one year only. The wool subsidy and tunnage and poundage paid by alien merchants were, however, extended for three. The grants were made on condition that aliens should be 'put to hoste', that is to say that restrictions were to be placed on their movements. This stipulation, about which there had been much argument, was subsequently broken by the pro-Flemish chancellor Beaufort, and 'therefore there was moche hevynesse and trowbylle in thys londe'. Bishop Beaufort's unpopularity was intensified by this and other grievances among which was an act of this Parliament which forbade assemblies of masons on the grounds that they were in breach of the statute of labourers. (From this Parliament, the basic 'framework' language of the parliamentary rolls reverted from French to Latin, except that French continued to be used for naming the triers of petitions. But henceforth, English was more and more used in petitions, memoranda and certain utterances.)

The strife between the royal duke and bishop was brought to a head by the exclusion of Gloucester from the Tower and the subsequent confrontation on London Bridge in October when Londoners, instructed by Gloucester and the mayor, kept the bridge for the duke on the city side. On

---

[1] *Rot. Parl.* Vol. IV, p. 289.
[2] Gregory: *Collections of a London Citizen*, edited J. Gairdner. Camden Soc. p. 157.

the Southwark side the bishop's men, including archers, were drawn up making ready for battle, using casks for barriers and barricading windows. The citizens shut their shops and came down to keep the bridge, hostilities only being averted by the mediation of the Archbishop of Canterbury and a visiting Portuguese prince. Beaufort's immediate response was to write desperately to Bedford, urging him to come home on the grounds that if he tarried 'we shall put this land in peril with a battle. Such a brother you have here...'[1] For the moment, Gloucester, who had the king in his possession, dominated the council, and Beaufort withdrew from the city until Bedford's arrival in England just before Christmas in response to the alarmed bishop's urgent summons. The elder royal duke reached London early in January 1426, where he made a treaty with his brother to act loyally together in allegiance to the king and not to aid each other's enemies. A Parliament was essential and it was clear to Bedford, who was Protector for so long as he remained in England, that to avoid risk of disturbances, it should not be held in London whose citizens were Gloucester's partisans. Accordingly, writs were sent out for a Parliament to meet on 18 February at Leicester, which was safely in the midst of Lancastrian territory. Before the Parliament assembled, efforts were made to bring Gloucester to a preparatory council at Northampton. But he refused to come on the grounds that it meant meeting his uncle the bishop, even though he was assured that Beaufort had undertaken to keep the peace. The quarrel would have to be settled in Parliament.

On the due date the Parliament met in the great hall of Leicester castle with the infant king seated on his throne.[2] Such was the atmosphere of crisis that Gloucester and Beaufort were specially instructed to restrict the size of their retinues and all present were forbidden to carry weapons. Instead, according to one chronicler, they carried bludgeons or clubs, from which this assembly became known as the Parliament of Bats.[3] The proceedings were opened by Bishop Beaufort, as chancellor, with a sermon describing the causes of summons, which included the protection of God's people from heretics and Lollards, (Leicester being a Lollard centre) and the usual references to good government. The king then departed and Bedford was given his commission under the great seal to act for him. For over a week nothing seems to have been done to settle the quarrel. Then, on 28 February, the Commons sent in a petition asking that the divisions among the Lords should be resolved, on which an oath was taken by the Lords to

---

[1] Beaufort's letter is printed in *E.H.D.* Vol. IV, p. 240.
[2] *Rot. Parl.* Vol. IV, pp. 295–308.
[3] Gregory, op. cit., p. 160.

assist Bedford in fair arbitration between Gloucester and Beaufort and to do their best 'to putte the said parties to reson' and suffer nothing to be done against the king's peace.[1] A commission of nine spiritual and temporal lords was appointed for the purpose and Gloucester and Beaufort both agreed to put their cases to it and accept the arbitration and its terms of peace. The commissioners examined the rivals' cases and pronounced that Gloucester and Beaufort should never thereafter 'tak cause, querele, displeasance nor hevynesse' against each other but that Gloucester should have affection for Beaufort as his kinsman and uncle, and that Beaufort should have 'trewe and sad' (that is, serious and steadfast) love and affection towards Gloucester. The duke's charges against the bishop had apparently included the allegations that the bishop had tried to deprive Henry IV of the government and had plotted the death of Henry V as Prince of Wales. These were formally denied by Beaufort and Gloucester accepted his denial.

Likewise the bishop denied having taken any action against Gloucester, defending his action on London Bridge as self-protection. Beaufort declared that he 'never imagined or purposed' anything against the duke, and, in words prescribed by the Commission, Gloucester accepted this also: 'Beal Uncle, sithen ye so declare you such a man as ye say, I am ryght glad that hit is so, and for such I tak yowe.'[2] The two adversaries then took each other by the hand, as instructed. All this was done in the presence of the king. Three days later Beaufort, who had had to defend himself as though he were on trial, resigned the great seal and was succeeded by Bishop Kemp of London. John Stafford, the treasurer, likewise resigned. The Commons then agreed that the council should raise loans up to £40,000, but some of them objected to the fact that the conditions for the restriction of aliens which had been attached to the last grant had not been observed; the roll states that there were 'diverse opinions' on the matter. Bedford, nevertheless, insisted that the subsidy should be paid, and it may have been a sign of the Commons' displeasure that when they came to taxation in a second session after Easter, they renewed tunnage and poundage on English merchants for only one year whereas for aliens this tax and the wool subsidy were renewed for two.

Early in the following year Beaufort went abroad on a pilgrimage in Bohemia against the Hussites, on the way taking the Cardinal's hat he had been offered some years before but had been prevented by Henry V from receiving. Gloucester seemed to be the victor in their quarrel, if there was one. Yet it was also clear that Bedford expected the council to restrain his

---

[1] *Rot. Parl.* Vol. IV, p. 296.
[2] Ibid., p. 298–299.

brother and wished conciliar government to continue. Once Bedford had left the country, however, which he did at the same time as Beaufort, Duke Humphrey felt strong enough to press his claim to increased power again when the Parliament next met. In the meantime, he secured the consent of the council to raise funds for garrisoning towns in Hainault but no expedition was launched and Gloucester eventually accepted a papal decision declaring the validity of Jacqueline's marriage to John of Brabant and abandoned her.

The next Parliament met in October 1427, the king himself presiding over it.[1] In the first session, for which no significant business is recorded, the duke raised the question of his powers but nothing was done. In the second session which began in January, he became more insistent, demanding that the Lords should define his powers, to which they gave the long answer, which has already been referred to, in which they harked back to his similar demand in 1422 and their negative response to it. Meanwhile, in the hope of putting pressure on the Lords, Gloucester had absented himself from Parliament, telling the Lords, as their answer notes, 'that we myzt wel comune matiers of Parlement in youre absence, but we schuld non conclude witht outen you; affermyng also that ye ne wolde in eny wyse come in to the house accustumed for the Kyng and the Lordes in Parlement, unto the tyme that ye knewe what youre auctorite and pouoir were therynne.' In other words, as one historian has put it, Gloucester had gone on strike to obtain the power he wanted.[2]

The Lords, however, remained unmoved and told him that he had no cause for his action since they had answered his question in 1422.[3] They reminded him that in order to keep the peace in that year they had 'devised ... a name (Protector and Defensor) ... different from other counsaillers' which imported a 'personal duty of attendance' to the defence of the land. If, they said, they had intended more than that they would have said so. They told him that he had stated that his argument was not intended to derogate from Bedford's position and that both dukes had accepted the powers as defined in the articles. He had been summoned to Parliament as Duke of Gloucester, just as any other lord would be, and they knew no other power that he had than that. In view of his power when Bedford was out of the country, they 'marvelled with all their hearts' that 'ye shuld in any wyse be steryd (stirred) or moeved noght to contente yow therwith'. They pointedly invoked Bedford's better behaviour, requiring Gloucester to be content

[1] *Rot. Parl.* Vol. IV, pp. 316–334.
[2] S. B. Chrimes, 'The Pretensions of the Duke of Gloucester in 1422', *E.H.R.* Vol. XLV.
[3] See above p. 498.

with the power that satisfied 'the King's eldest Uncle' for, they said, they would not vary their answer. Eleven bishops, four abbots and twelve lay peers, headed by the Duke of Norfolk, subscribed to this declaration.[1]

Three points of parliamentary interest are attached to this episode. First, there was the determination of the Lords to maintain conciliar government in the king's name. Second, the Lords alone were dealing with a matter concerning the chief magnate among them yet they also considered that the case should be fully recorded on the Parliament rolls. During the previous century, the rolls had indicated comparatively little of the Lords' and king's internal deliberations, recording more about matters put by the Commons to the king and Lords and the answers given. Finally, the Commons clearly played no part in the aristocratic politics of the protectorate comparable to that which they had had in the high politics of the preceding reigns. However, they were evidently quite content with the Lords' snub to the duke. They may well have been influenced in this by their evident disapproval of Gloucester's recent abandonment of his former duchess Jacqueline, on whose behalf the mayor and alderman came to Parliament to make representations. The duke had now begun a relationship with Eleanor Cobham whom he subsequently married, and when the Commons gave grants of tunnage on English merchants and also a new tax on parishes and knights' fees, they coupled with them a request that measures should be taken for the safety of the duchess of Gloucester, who lived 'in so greet dolour and hevynesse'.

On the last day of this Parliament, the Commons petitioned successfully that, since a number of their petitions had not been dealt with, it should be ordained by the advice of the Lords and the assent of the Commons that such petitions should be delivered to the 'lords of your very wise council' who should determine them taking legal advice if necessary. Those petitions that were accepted should be enacted as law and placed on the Parliament roll. This device of delegating to the council the full parliamentary power to answer outstanding petitions resembled that which had been attacked as unconstitutional when Richard II used it.

When Beaufort returned to England later in the year, it was with papal authority for preaching a crusade against the Hussites, for which he began raising forces. This gave Gloucester the opportunity to exploit anti-papal sentiment in his campaign against the new cardinal, making use of the differences between Rome and the English government over papal provisions. However, as a result of the English reverses in France, it was agreed that Beaufort should have these forces but that he should first take

[1] *Rot. Parl.* Vol. IV, pp. 326–327.

them to reinforce the English siege of Orleans. The next Parliament met in September 1429.[1] During the course of it, Henry was crowned king of England, preparatory to his coronation in France, and Gloucester was thereupon obliged by the Lords to give up his title of Protector, on the grounds that the boy king had himself taken on the duties of protector and defender of the realm and the church. Gloucester evidently protested insistently and the Lords heard 'many important reasons and allegations made on his behalf'. But such was their suspicion of him that they still insisted that he should relinquish the role of protector though he was allowed to bear the title of chief councillor for 'as long as it pleased the king'.[2] The emergency in France was now so grave that this Parliament was generous with taxation for the war. Before Christmas the Commons voted one tenth and fifteenth, the first grant of the traditional taxation on movables for eight years. Almost immediately afterwards they doubled it, as well as granting tunnage and poundage until the next Parliament. After Christmas, the Commons voted a wool subsidy and hastened the tax on movables, as well as authorizing the council to give security for loans up to £50,000.

For all their generosity, however, the Commons wanted something in return: remedies for the increasing lawlessness in the land. A request was therefore attached to the grant of a tenth and fifteenth recording that it was made in the trust that 'we shull have knowelech of gode, and sadde governance in every partie of this your seid Roialme...'[3] Maintenance was at the root of the abuse of law, and among a number of new articles regulating the conduct of members of the council was a provision requiring them to set an example of 'restful rule'. None of the Lords was to receive, keep in his household or maintain, any robbers, oppressors of the people, ravishers of women or other offenders. The lords of the council were to swear to this and also not to practice maintenance in matters of law by word, message or writing to any officer, judge or jury, or by gift of livery. In other words, they were not to use their power to corrupt justice. Despite Gloucester's opposition, the Lords also decided that Beaufort, notwithstanding his cardinal's hat, should be a member of the king's council, absenting himself only when relations between the English government and Rome were discussed. The Commons plainly approved of this since they prefaced their second tenth and fifteenth with a recommendation of the cardinal.

[1] *Rot. Parl.* Vol. IV, pp. 335–362.
[2] Ibid., pp. 336–337.
[3] Ibid., p. 337.

In constitutional history, however, the most outstanding act of the Parliament of 1429–30 was one fixing the qualification for the franchise in the shires on a restricted basis of property which endured until 1832. Henceforth, parliamentary knights were to be chosen only by people dwelling in the shire with 'a freeholding to the value of forty shillings by the year at the least above all charges'. Sheriffs were to have power 'to examine on the Holy Gospels every such elector, how much he may expend in a year', that is, whether he fulfilled this condition.[1] There was more than one explanation for this enactment, which was made in response to a petition of the Commons in virtually the same terms as the act itself.[2] For one thing, the government and probably most of the Commons wished to put a stop to the disorderly conditions which bedevilled some shire elections. As we have already seen, enactments had previously been made, notably in 1406 and 1410, to secure free elections unimpeded by corruption on the part of the sheriff. Election was intended to be in the full shire court, with a free choice of representatives and a proper check to ensure that the sheriff made a valid return. This return was drawn up by the sheriff and attested by some but not all (the number varied greatly) of those who had been present at the election.

The number of electors in a full and open shire court could often be as high as several hundreds. Indeed, the worry now was that there were too many electors, some of whom came from outside the shire. The act restricting the franchise may well, therefore, have been encouraged by the belief that over-full shire courts led to improperly conducted and disorderly elections. At all events, the grounds for the new restriction given in the act itself were that 'the elections of knights . . . have lately been made by too great and excessive a number of people dwelling in the same shires, of which the most part were folk of small means or no worth, yet each of them claims to have a voice equivalent, in such elections, to the most valiant knights or squires dwelling within the same shires, whereby manslaughters, riots, batteries and divisions will most probably arise . . .'[3] During the Parliament of 1432, the act was amended to provide that the property qualifying a man for the franchise must be held within the shire itself. The act may also have been prompted by particular cases of disputed and invalid elections, of which there had been one in 1427 and three in 1429, since imprisonment was prescribed for sheriffs guilty of breaches of the law in respect of elections.

---

[1] *Stat. R.* Vol. II, p. 243. (English translations in *E.H.D.* Vol. IV, p. 465 and B. Wilkinson, *Const. Hist. of England in the Fifteenth Century*, document XXXIV).

[2] *Rot. Parl.* Vol. IV, p. 350.

[3] This motive is emphasized by Roskell, *The Commons in the Parliament of 1422*, Ch. I. See this for a discussion of the 1429 Act, the number of attestors, the sizes of full shire courts, and the disputed elections of 1427 and 1429.

Yet it is hard to be confident that disorderly elections were not more of an excuse than a genuine justification. The act disenfranchised the poorer freeholders and freemen who owned no land, and the scorn poured in the statute on the claims to the voting franchise of those below the level of squire and knight suggests a deliberate wish to exclude them on social grounds. It is true that a freeholding worth forty shillings was not great wealth; its modesty has been inferred on the grounds that it was no more than two-fifths of what Sir John Fortescue, the Lancastrian author of the *Governance of England*, was a few decades later to describe as a fair living for a yeoman.[1] Yet the restriction of the franchise to the better-off was probably intended to prevent its spread down the social scale, and this may well have been a reflection of the Commons' growing self-identificaion with the aristocratic interest. They now seldom argued with the Lords; they were willing to restrict their electors to their own class, and they were to become increasingly interested in the social standing of their own members. Thus in 1445 a further statute enacted that elected knights of the shire should be knights, squires or men whose estate would support a knight's dignity. Although by the time of the 1832 Reform Act inflation had substantially lowered the real value of the property qualification for the franchise, the elected members of the shire were to remain representative of the gentry.

Another petition dealing with the internal affairs of elected members of Parliament was not, however, successful. Representatives of the shires, cities and boroughs summoned to Parliament had always received payment as wages and to cover expenses. The communities were responsible for finding the money on receiving the king's writs for expenses. By custom the official rate had come to be 4s. a day for knights and 2s. a day for burgesses for each day of a Parliament and of the journeys to and from it. But the practice did not always match the theory. Some towns paid above the rate (most notably, London); others seemed to find difficulty in raising it, and paid less. How parliamentary wages were raised, and also the amount, were matters of local custom and decision. It was in practice up to them to decide whether they would levy a local tax on movables, set aside part of the town's rents or give their representatives privileges and powers instead of money. Sometimes MPs were paid in advance, sometimes by instalments and sometimes they were underpaid or unpaid.[2] The consequential grievance led to the submission of a petition from the Commons, drawing attention to the failure in some boroughs to pay the 2s. a day which elected burgesses

---

[1] Roskell, ibid.
[2] May McKisack, *The Parliamentary Representation of the English Boroughs during the Middle Ages*, Ch. V.

'ought by ancient custom to receive' and asking for a remedy. These wages, it was stated, 'in various cities and boroughs for a bad example are now recently withdrawn, so that whereas various notable and wise persons, formerly sustained by wages, used to come to Parliament, for the good of you (the king) and all the realm, they are not elected and do not come, and in their place come most enfeebled, impoverished and impotent persons, and while Parliament meets they stay at their own charges, to their perpetual impoverishment...' The remedy asked for was that they should have their writ from the sheriff for the 2s. payment to be levied, as the knights do, 'notwithstanding any usage, custom or ordinance, usurpation or subtraction of wages, made to the contrary...' The government, however, was not willing to interfere with local discretion; the petition was refused with the customary formula: *Le Roi s'advisera*.[1]

During the next few years the position of the English in France worsened and discord continued at home. In April 1430, accompanied by Beaufort, the king set off for France and his intended coronation there. It was, however, a year and a half before the coronation was feasible. During the king's absence, Gloucester at last achieved the power of regency he had long wanted, having been appointed guardian (*custos*) of the realm. The next Parliament met in January 1431.[2] The Commons were now beginning to show themselves interested in the possibility of a peace and it was ordained and advised by the Lords, and 'the Commons being present in this present Parliament' that Bedford, Gloucester and the council might treat about peace on the king's behalf. The terms of that authorization, after referring to various international efforts to secure a peace treaty, left no doubt about Parliament's thinking. It declared that 'as every man endowed with reson may well considere, it nys nought covenable ne suting, ne lyke to be the plesire of God, ne of the world' for a Christian prince to refuse peace on reasonable terms. That was especially so, considering 'howe grevous and hevy' the burden of war was to the land.[3] Nevertheless, the Commons were quite generous with taxation. They not only granted one and a third tenths and fifteenths, to be levied in instalments, but also extended tunnage and poundage and the wool subsidy and imposed a new land tax of 20s. in every £20 income from land (a knight's fee). During the course of the year Gloucester suppressed a Lollard conspiracy, secured an increase in his own salary despite the opposition of the chancellor, Archbishop Kemp of York and the treasurer, Lord Hungerford, and launched yet another attack on

---

[1] *Rot. Parl.* Vol. IV, p. 350.
[2] Ibid., pp. 367–387.
[3] Ibid., p. 371.

Beaufort. Legal precedents were put to the council to support the argument that, as a cardinal, Beaufort ought to surrender the bishopric of Winchester and that by holding it he was, being a papal official, in breach of the Statute of Praemunire. Writs of praemunire against Beaufort were prepared but action against him was postponed until he returned from France. Gloucester also caused the seizure of jewels and plate which Beaufort held from the crown as security for his loans.

On Henry's return in February 1432 Gloucester also secured the replacement of the chancellor, Archbishop Kemp, the treasurer, Lord Hungerford, who was a partisan of Beaufort's, and other officials who had in some way annoyed him, including Lord Cromwell, the chamberlain. A Parliament was summoned to meet on 12 May and Beaufort returned to answer the case against him.[1] Gloucester was obviously determined to keep the effective power of regency if he could, and as a tactical move to this end he addressed the Lords on the second day of the proceedings, saying that it seemed to him that the Parliament would be more effective if the Commons could be reassured that a spirit of concord and unity existed among the Lords. He declared that although he was the king's nearest kinsman and the chief councillor appointed by act of Parliament, he wished and intended to act with the advice and consent of the other lords and council. He then invited them to help him govern the kingdom, a clear indication that he had it in mind to continue, in practice, wielding the authority he had enjoyed as regent in the king's absence. When the Speaker was presented on the following day, the Commons duly heard from the chancellor a declaration of the Lords' concord and unity.

This demonstration of Gloucester's influence did not, however, deter Beaufort from launching an immediate counter-attack against the charges that had been made against him. The cardinal said that he had come back to England because he heard he had been accused of treason, and he now challenged anyone to make that charge. The matter was discussed by Gloucester and the Lords in the king's presence and Gloucester himself then announced that nobody had accused Beaufort of treason. On the contrary, he was recognized as a faithful subject, a statement which was formalized, at Beaufort's request, under the great seal. The matter of the seized jewels, however, was settled rather less satisfactorily, or at any rate more expensively, for the cardinal bishop, who was constrained to make further loans in exchange for their return. His willingness to do so perhaps helped him to defeat the accusations under Praemunire, which were the real substance of the case against him. (Loose talk of treason may have arisen

---

[1] *Rot. Parl.* Vol. IV, pp. 388–413.

because Praemunire involved a conflict of allegiances to king and pope.) At all events, the Commons now came out on the side of this conveniently generous lender and petitioned successfully that in view of his 'many great and notable services' Beaufort should be free of any charges under the laws of Praemunire and Provisors.[1] Encouraged by the cardinal's success in refuting any suspicion of treason, Lord Cromwell, the former chamberlain, then also challenged anyone who had made charges against him leading to his dismissal to declare them. He, however, was easily rebuffed with the answer that he had been removed not because there were charges but simply because his dismissal was the pleasure of the duke and council. The difficulties of the government, however, were worsening and the Commons, disillusioned with the cost and failure of the war, made a niggardly grant of half a tenth and fifteenth, also annulling the land tax of the previous Parliament as impracticable, although the usual indirect taxes were renewed.

It was in this Parliament that Richard, Duke of York, heir to the Mortimer claim and Henry VI's future opponent, received possession of his estates, having now come of age. Then, on the last day of the Parliament, a peerage was created for services rendered to the crown; John Cornwall was made baron of Fanhope 'with a place in the Parliaments and councils of the king'. This creation, made with the advice and assent of Gloucester, Beaufort and the other Lords, was the first creation of a baronage not related to land tenure since Richard II's patent to Lord Beauchamp of Holt, though that had been made outside Parliament whereas Cornwall's was made inside Parliament. It again carried the significance that a man who did not hold land directly from the crown, and was not on that account called to Parliament, could nevertheless be created a baron by the crown, just as a duke or an earl could be created, and that such a baron would have the same privileges as existing barons who were tenants-in-chief called to Parliament by prescriptive right. However, the device of creating a baron by parliamentary 'advice and assent' did not occur again.

During the following months Gloucester tightened his grip on the government until the next Parliament met in July 1433, exactly a year after the dispersal of its predecessor.[2] Both Bedford and Beaufort came to England for it. They had been in Calais where they had hoped in vain to have discussions with the French. It was Bedford's first visit to England for six years and he had good reason for coming. The English were on the defensive and the alliance with Burgundy was now still more fragile

---

[1] *Rot. Parl.* Vol. IV, p. 392.
[2] Ibid., pp. 419-457.

because, after the death of Bedford's Burgundian wife, he had quickly made a second marriage of which Duke Philip disapproved on political grounds. It was imperative, therefore, for Bedford to raise funds for the war effort and especially for the defence of Normandy. At home, moreover, there was growing concern about lawlessness and deep discontent with the cost and failure of the war. There was also murmured criticism, in which Gloucester may have been involved, of Bedford's generalship in France and he came determined to confront them openly. Early in the Parliament, therefore, he protested before both Lords and Commons against charges of negligence which he had heard were being made against him. After the Lords had discussed his complaint, he received the assurance from the chancellor that neither the king nor the council had ever heard of such scandalous words. But the burning question was money for the war Bedford was trying to win and that could not be dealt with so easily. Within four weeks Parliament had been prorogued for two months on several grounds. One was that there was plague in London and the suburbs; another, that the Commons wanted more information about riots, extortions, oppressions, maintenance and other defects in the kingdom which deeply worried them. Finally, as the Parliament roll recorded, the Lords needed their autumnal sport.[1] But the principal need was time to consider the lack of money. The extent of the government's financial plight was startingly revealed by the final item of business before the recess. To pay for the king's and royal household's needs until Parliament met again, the treasurer was authorized to reduce some assignments from the exchequer by £2,000.

When the next session began in October, however, the Commons first directed attention to the grievance of lawlessness. Specific reference was made to murders, rapes, robberies and other crimes in the counties of Salop, Herefordshire, Yorkshire, Nottingham, Derbyshire and Sussex. Apparently in despair of obtaining effective secular action, they suggested that, following a precedent of Edward II's time, recourse might be had to the church for excommunication. Bedford, Gloucester and the council were, however, reluctant to turn to the clergy to rescue lay authority, and so the Speaker suggested that the magnates, lay and spiritual, should publicly swear to preserve the peace and good government, taking the same oath to uphold the law and eschew maintenance as that which had been sworn in 1429. The repetition of the oath could be partly justified on the grounds that Bedford had been absent at that time. But it was more to the point that, whereas in 1429 it had been taken simply by the lords of the council, this

---

[1] *Rot. Parl.* Vol. IV, p. 420.

time it was sworn not only by the Lords generally but also (since it was now to apply to all people of whatever estate and condition) by the Commons.[1]

The Commons, however, took their concern about the state of the country even further. After debating among themselves, they appealed to Bedford to stay in England. Making their case through the Speaker, they recalled that he had remained in France after Henry V's death because the people in the conquered lands were not then so 'fermid, stablisshid and assurid' in their loyalty as they had since become. They declared that the duke had done his duty and had achieved great things in France. His coming to England, they said, had been 'full fructuous' and had led to 'restfull rule' and government. He had obeyed the king's peace, brought wrong-doers to punishment, assisted the king 'with his grete wisdom and prudence' (surely a dig at Gloucester) as well as setting a good example by 'payng also trewly for his vitailys and all maner of thing that he hath had' from the king's subjects. It would be to the king's greatest security if he stayed in England and they besought the king to desire him to do so. The chancellor then asked the Lords, including Gloucester, for their advice which was that it would be 'expedient' for Bedford to stay. So the chancellor, on behalf of the king, asked him to do so and Bedford, saying modestly that he would do what little service he could wherever he was needed, expressed his particular pleasure that the Commons held him in such affection. On the following day, in the Star Chamber, he brought up the question of his salary before the council, recalling that in the past he or Gloucester had been paid as much as 8,000 marks annually, nearly £5,500. Now he suggested that in view of the king's financial needs, he should be paid only £1,000, with an additional £500 for each journey to and from France. It was a clear repudiation of the recent greedy increase in pay taken by his brother who now, with other councillors, had to follow Bedford's example of pay restraint. Then in December Bedford placed before Parliament the conditions on which he was willing to serve, the essence of which was that he wanted full discretion to govern, including in respect of patronage. The Lords spiritual and temporal agreed, and for practical purposes Bedford was given precisely the kind of power that Gloucester had sought.[2] It was the clearest possible indication of their anxiety about the divisions in the council and the ambitions of the younger royal uncle.

Parliament then turned to the financial crisis. Just before the recess, Lord Cromwell had been given his revenge for his recent dismissal as chamberlain, when, under Bedford's new administration, he was appointed

[1] *Rot. Parl.* Vol. IV, pp. 421–422.
[2] Ibid., pp. 423–425.

treasurer in place of Gloucester's adherent Lord Scrope. Cromwell who, as a councillor, had feathered his nest with the benefits of patronage at least as much as any of his colleagues, now faced a grievous financial crisis in the crown's business. He had already informed the king and Parliament that 'all the Revenuz and Proffitz, ordinarie and extraordinarie, certain or casuell' did not suffice to meet the king's ordinary yearly charges falling short by the sum of £35,000 annually, or more. This was quite apart from the cost of the war. He had asked for the accounts of the exchequer to be examined so that the state of affairs would be understood and proper parliamentary provision made for government and defence. Otherwise, he informed the Lords, 'I neither can, may, ne dare take uppon me, to labour forthe to procede in occupation of the said Office.'[1] In October, the exchequer records were laid before the Lords with a detailed summary of revenues and expenditure. This remarkably comprehensive 'budget statement' was read to the Commons and included in the parliamentary roll. The crown was shown to be grossly in debt, with the next two years' revenue already assigned to creditors. The debt would continue to rise and there was no money to pay for the war. Yet at the end of the session the Commons voted no more than one tenth and fifteenth, from which £4,000 was to be deducted for the relief of 'desolate, wasted or destroyed, or over-greatly impoverished' towns, with the tax payments spread over two years. Again indirect taxation was made to fall only on aliens. It was obvious that both the government's financial and military situations could only get worse.

The Commons, however, were more preoccupied with domestic disorder than interested in the pursuit of the French war. At the end of the Parliament (quite probably encouraged by Bedford) they petitioned that it was 'necessary and profitable' for the assurances given by Lords, knights, citizens and burgesses, to be extracted from all subjects. They asked that the oath to uphold the king's peace should be taken by absent lords and that parliamentary knights and burgesses should be required to swear the oath in their shires and localities in the coming three months.[2] By this national oath-taking it was hoped to bind the nation to internal peace. The intensity of the Commons' concern with violence in 1433 seems to have been a response to the increase in this kind of crime during the previous few years. This raises two questions. First, to what extent had disorder worsened during the minority of Henry VI compared with the preceding reigns? Second, had conditions already been created which would lead inexorably to the

---

[1] *Rot. Parl.* Vol. IV, pp. 432–440. Cromwell's petition and his estimates of revenue and expenditure, tabulated, are in *E.H.D.* Vol. IV, pp. 516–522.
[2] *Rot. Parl.* Vol. IV, pp. 455–457.

breakdown of government and the civil strife known to history as the Wars of the Roses?

There was, of course, nothing new in the existence of widespread crime and disorder. Medieval society had always been plagued with violence against persons and property, and every king's standing depended to a large extent on his ability to maintain his peace within the realm. As well as the ordinary criminals of the type present in every age and community, there were robbers who sprang from the forest upon wayfarers and preyed on villages, and criminal gangs which terrorized whole districts. But the law was also frequently flouted by men from the very classes which had a local duty to uphold it, and sometimes in the most flagrant manner. It was the increase in this last category of crime which was the principal cause for concern as the minority of Henry VI was drawing to its close.

Conflicts over property rights, which were a matter of passionate concern to medieval men, were often the origin of such lawlessness. They led to feuds between landowners and to the raiding of property by a foe and his retinue, sometimes with loss of life. Men with any force behind them seemed ever more ready to resort to fighting rather than go to law. Even among the magnates there were bitter and ferocious feuds. In 1428, to take one example, riots occurred in East Anglia as a result of a notorious quarrel between the Duke of Norfolk and the Earl of Huntingdon which again erupted in 1430 when the Earl of Warwick also became a party to it. Norfolk and Huntingdon were among a number of lords, including Cromwell, who were required not to bring retinues to the Parliament of 1432. There was to be similar violence in 1435 between the followers of the Duke of Norfolk and the Earl of Suffolk in East Anglia.

Worse still, some of the upper classes engaged not simply in feuds among themselves but in downright criminal intimidation of their hapless neighbourhoods, making money from threats, ransoms and 'protection'. A notorious instance of such aristocratic brutality was that of Lord Talbot in Herefordshire, whose retinue terrorized the district, holding some of his victims to ransom in the dungeons of his castle at Goodrich on the Welsh border. A petition was, in consequence, adopted and presented by the Commons in 1423, no doubt after having been first brought into Parliament by the elected knights of the shire for Herefordshire. It declared that numbers of the king's subjects 'piteously and dolorously' had shown by various bills how the people of the hundred of Wormelowe had been subjected to 'extortion, oppressions, murders and homicides' and were held in prison by Talbot's followers. A list of those implicated included his brother and a large number of other men, many with Welsh names. On this occasion a special commission of oyer and terminer was appointed to hear and determine the cases and try to restore order so as to prevent an uprising.[1] In 1426, Talbot and his followers were engaged in a prolonged conflict with Joan Beauchamp, Lady Abergavenny, in which Talbot's brother was killed. She herself was a formidable and combative woman who was again involved in private warfare between 1431 and 1433 when her activities were brought before Parliament.[2]

Yet even more ominous than this type of outrage was the deliberate undermining of legal processes by men of means who had particular responsibility to maintain justice. Those guilty included not only members of the king's council who misused their power for profit and magnates who quarrelled but many other men of influence who deliberately corrupted justice in their own localities. This was the more easily done because the administration of justice had become increasingly local. The decline and unpopularity in the fourteenth century of the general eyre, which at least in theory had taken the king's impartial justice out into the country, had placed more and more responsibility for justice and law enforcement on local assizes and justices of the peace, who could be influenced by self-interest. By and large, local lords and influential gentry dominated local justice and made it serve themselves. Even the Commons, although they might collectively be on the side of the angels, had individuals among them with the opposite allegiance. Thus a certain Sir Henry Threlkeld, a knight of the shire for Westmorland in 1433, was involved in threatening jurors to prevent them from speaking the truth about local breaches of the peace. Underlying this kind of mischief was the abuse of livery which was now spreading faster than ever. Not only lords but men lower down the social scale gave their livery to followers who abused it to commit crimes and to maintain causes and quarrels of their own factions in the courts. Juries were intimidated and true verdicts stifled. Justice was undermined not so much by wrongful convictions or even by the failure to bring accused persons to court, as by the unjust acquittal of guilty men.

Such was the state of disorder in the realm. Yet civil war was not an inevitable outcome. Nor did the quarrels of magnates during the minority make the coming dynastic conflict inevitable. The inadequacy of Henry VI in his adult years and defeat in France were to be the causes of the Wars of the Roses. Nevertheless, the lawlessness and disorder which increasingly disfigured society during the minority created the kind of social conditions in which faction and dynastic conflict very easily thrive.

[1] *Rot. Parl.* Vol. IV, p. 254.
[2] Ibid., pp. 410–413 and 445–446.

II

Despite the Commons' expressed wish in 1433 that Bedford should stay in England to restore good government, his time in the country was short. Within seven months the needs of war had drawn him back to France from which he was never to return. During his time as protector in England his relations with his brother fell to a lower level than ever before, eventually erupting into an open quarrel at a meeting of the great council in April 1434. It was a large gathering, consisting of nearly seventy lay and spiritual lords and including a number of summoned knights. Its purpose was to consider how to pursue the war in the light of repeated appeals from Normandy for help and the desperate shortage of money. To this assembly, which met in the hall of the Bishop of Durham's house in London, Gloucester immediately proposed that he himself should now lead an expedition to France, and he produced plans for doing so. Given the decision that Bedford was to stay in England it does not seem to have been a particularly unreasonable suggestion. But Bedford saw it as an attack on both his regency and his conduct of the war. Stung to anger, he insisted on his right to deliver a considered reply, which Gloucester in turn took as a personal slight. With each prince claiming that his honour was impugned, the quarrel was only settled when the king, who was now approaching thirteen years old, intervened to assure them, and particularly Bedford, that their honour was not questioned. He implored his uncles to settle their differences, which they did. Gloucester's plan, which would apparently have cost the impossible sum of £50,000, came to nothing. Proposals by Bedford, which involved, among other devices, assigning to the war certain revenues from the duchy of Lancaster, were eventually adopted and in June Bedford informed the council that he was returning to France. Nevertheless, he still intended to keep his grip on the government of England, travelling between the two realms. Oaths were taken that the articles agreed to when he took over the government should remain in force. Backed with new loans from Beaufort, the duke set out, but before he left it was agreed that Charles, Duke of Orleans, who had been the prisoner of the Earl of Suffolk since 1415 should be allowed to try to negotiate a peace.

For a short time, Bedford had some success in slowing down the English decline but the general tide was running strongly for the French. In August 1435 Bedford was forced by papal pressure and military and political needs to participate in the conference of Arras, to which reference has already been made.[1] In September, a week after the end of the collapse of this peace conference, Bedford died at Rouen and it was shortly afterwards that the Duke of Burgundy renounced his alliance with the English crown. With Bedford's death, the Lancastrian dynasty had lost not only an honest and respected man who had given his life to an unwinnable struggle, exhausting himself in the process, but also the one member of the royal family who was the buttress of such unity as existed among the English magnates. Henceforth, the nobility was increasingly riven by a struggle between those who wished for peace and those who were determined to intensify the war effort. The peace party was headed by Cardinal Beaufort, who had always understood that a successful war depended on the now defunct Burgundian alliance, and by William de la Pole, Earl of Suffolk, who had been the steward of the king's household since 1433. Gloucester, who had distinguished himself as a soldier in France in Henry V's time before becoming guardian of England, was leader of the war party, in which he was to be strongly supported by Richard, Duke of York. The reality was, however, that with Burgundy's defection any hope of making good the English conquest of France was at an end.

When the next Parliament met in October 1435 it was opened by the chancellor, the Bishop of Bath and Wells, with a speech calculated to inflame political opinion against the perfidious Burgundian duke.[2] Gloucester's personal position was apparently strengthened in that he was now heir presumptive and free from his brother's restraint. On the other hand, the body politic was gravely weakened because Bedford was no longer there to insist on the maintenance of conciliar government, the best defence of stability during Henry's minority. Still worse, the bitter hatred aroused by what was seen as Burgundy's treachery led to an unreasoning determination on the part of the majority in Parliament to continue the struggle. There was a refusal to face reality and even the Commons, now that it was too late, were somewhat more willing to find the money they had been reluctant to provide when it might have been put to better use. As well as granting a tenth and a fifteenth (again subject to the deduction of £4,000 for the relief of poor localities) the Commons continued the usual indirect taxes, authorized the council to give security for loans up to £100,000 and, most remarkably, imposed an entirely new form of income tax. This was to be paid on a graduated scale on incomes of £5 a year or more on *freehold* land. (Incomes of £5 paid 2s. 6d., each further pound paid 6d. up to £100, when the rate was 8d. in the pound up to £400, and so on.)[3] In fact, the tax brought

[1] See above, p. 504.
[2] *Rot. Parl.* Vol. IV, pp. 481-494.
[3] Ibid., pp. 486-487.

in only about £9,000 and was paid mostly by the well-off. Even now, what the Commons were willing to pay nowhere near matched what was needed.

It was nearly two years before Parliament met again in January 1437.[1] The young king was now fifteen and for the previous year and more had increasingly taken some part in the activities of government. Although the French had retaken Paris and captured some territory in Normandy during 1436, the English had succeeded in relieving Calais from a Burgundian siege and Gloucester had conducted a successful raid into Artois. The Duke of York, who was now twenty-four, had been appointed lieutenant in Normandy and was showing signs of an energetic response. These limited successes assisted Gloucester in Parliament where he was lavishly praised by the Commons. Again a tenth and fifteenth were given (less £4,000) and indirect taxes were renewed for three years, though the income tax was not. Taxation was specially appropriated to Calais where soldiers from the garrison were deserting for lack of their pay.

During the following eighteen months the English achieved some successes in Normandy but it was increasingly clear, especially to Cardinal Beaufort, that there must be an attempt at least to secure a truce and if possible a renewed agreement with Burgundy. In 1438 the French even dared to invade Gascony. A preliminary Anglo-Burgundian meeting took place at Calais in January 1439 and was followed by a conference between English, Burgundian and French representatives meeting in specially erected wooden and canvas constructions at Oye, between Calais and Gravelines. Although Archbishop Kemp, the leader of the English delegation, went to the conference with strict official instructions that there was no question of giving up the Lancastrian claim to the French crown, Beaufort was privately given discretion to act for the king as he thought fit having been made party to Henry's private thinking. What the king's thinking amounted to is not known but Henry seems to have vacillated between an inclination to peace and, under the influence of his French coronation, a wish not to renounce his claim to France. The uncertainty engendered by a weak-minded king, added to the existing divisions in the council, was already beginning to frustrate any hope of a consistent policy.

At the conference, to which the Duke of Orleans came on parole, an arrangement was proposed for a long truce of fifteen years or more, during which time Henry would abstain from using the title 'king of France'. During that period he would have been free to renew the war at a year's notice or make a final peace by doing homage for the French lands he held and renouncing his claim to the crown. This suggestion was taken back to

[1] *Rot. Parl.* Vol. IV, pp. 495–510.

England by Archbishop Kemp and recommended to the king but Gloucester and other lords easily persuaded Henry to reject it. To the war party, a truce of this nature would simply provide an opportunity for the French to re-conquer Normandy, and they were probably right. According to his own testimony, Gloucester told the king that he would rather die than give up the Lancastrian claim to France.

Yet this reverse did not dislodge the grip of Beaufort and his friends on government. When the next Parliament met in November 1439, they were in the ascendant both in the council and the household, using their power of patronage, with the support of the young king, to build up their party. The first session of this Parliament was at Westminster; the second, after an adjournment for Christmas, met at Reading, in all probability for fear of the pestilence in London.[1] The Commons were only moderately generous with money, giving one and a half tenths and fifteenths (less £6,000) spread over two years. Indirect taxation was extended for three years in exchange for a poll tax on foreign merchants. There were strong complaints against the failure of the royal household to make ends meet and a quarter of a tenth and a fifteenth had to be appropriated to maintain the household. The abuse of purveyance was also a subject of protest. When there was a shortage of ready money, it invariably led to a failure of the household to pay for produce taken for its use.

A great deal of this Parliament's proceedings, however, consisted of complaints against particular well-born criminals, with demands that they should be penalized with forfeiture if they could not be brought to justice. Thus a complaint from Derbyshire told how one Piers Venables, Gentleman, after certain deeds of violence, 'havynge no liflode' (livelihood) nor a sufficiency of goods, gathered together 'many misdoers beynge of his clothinge' (that is, livery) and 'wente into the wodes in that Contre, like as it hadde be Robynhode and his meyne (fellowship)'.[2] A similar complaint was made against another band of raiders under a certain Philip Egerton in Shropshire. The anxiety about lawlessness was all the time increasing and it was no doubt the hope that the king would be spared to lead the nation out of trouble that especially inspired a manifestation in this Parliament of the political nation's concern for his health.

Among the Commons petitions is one referring to the highly infectious pestilence that was about and drawing attention to the danger to the king from the kiss during the ceremony of a knight's homage. The Commons petitioned the king that knights 'in the doyng of thair said homage, may

---

[1] *Rot. Parl.* Vol. V, pp. 3–33.
[2] Ibid., p. 16.

omitte the said kissyng of you and be excused thereof at youre will, the homage beying of the same force as though they kissed you, and have thair lettres of doyng of thair homage, the kyssyng of you ommitted not withstondyng'. The petition received the royal assent: *Le roy le voet*.[1] The legalistic and bureaucratic drafting of such petitions is a reminder of the influence in the Commons of the lawyers who imported the language of the Inns of Court into the preparation of bills and petitions. This Parliament, it may be noted, also saw the creation, by letters patent, of Lord Beaumont as the first English viscount, assigned 'a place in our Parliaments, councils and other assemblies above all the barons of our realm'.[2] Beaumont was given an annual grant of twenty marks to sustain his position. The title was influenced by the French connection; Beaumont held the rank of viscount in France.

Parliaments were now consistently less frequent. None was called for another two years. In the interval, the balance of war in France continued to be against the English, despite a notably successful campaign in Normandy by the Duke of York in 1441. York's initiative could not be followed up because of the lack of money and men. The search for peace had therefore continued and in 1440, despite a strong personal protest from Gloucester, the Duke of Orleans was released to promote negotiations with the French king. Gloucester's complaint to the king spilled over into a bitter personal attack on the cardinal. He censured him for taking the cardinal's hat which Henry V had refused to allow him, for usurping the 'governance' of the king and estranging Gloucester, York, and other kinsmen from Henry and for depriving them of influence in important public affairs. He also accused the cardinal of lending money to the crown at inordinate profit and of foreclosing on crown jewels and land held as security.[3] As so often happens in politics, the personal hatred between the two rivals had reached that point at which it becomes virtually impossible for either to doubt that any policy promoted by his opponent must be opposed.

The most sensational domestic event of this period, however, was a public scandal which struck the final blow at Duke Humphrey's already badly damaged prestige. In 1440 his new wife Eleanor Cobham, who had been a lady-in-waiting to Jacqueline of Hainault, was charged with witchcraft. Two clerks, Roger Bolingbroke and Thomas Southwell, had previously been charged with sorcery directed against the king's life and

---

[1] *Rot. Parl.* Vol. V, p. 31.
[2] *Report on the Dignity of a Peer*, Vol. V, p. 235.
[3] *Letters and Papers illustrative of the Wars of the English in France*, ed. J. Stevenson (Rolls series 1864), II ii, p. 440. Extracts printed in *E.H.D.* Vol. IV, pp. 254–256.

were said to have asserted that they had been instigated to do so by the Duchess of Gloucester. She was tried before an episcopal court and admitted her involvement in sorcery but denied any attempts against the king. She was sentenced to public penance and to walk barefoot, carrying a lighted taper through the city to St Paul's and two other churches, thereafter to be imprisoned for life. Bolingbroke was hanged; Southwell died in prison and Margery Jourdemain, known as the witch of Eye, who was said to have used her craft to cause Duke Humphrey to fall in love with Eleanor, was burned. It seems likely that Suffolk's hand lay behind this extraordinary episode which inevitably had the effect of discrediting Duke Humphrey even though he was not involved.

The Parliament which met in 1442 was opened by the usual speech on the need for good order in the realm but also making particular reference to the unusual degree of perjury.[1] At the end of March, grants of a tenth and a fifteenth, with the usual deduction, and payable in instalments over nearly two years were made for the defence of the realm. Associated with it was an act in response to a Commons' petition for the provision and equipment of a specified number of ships of various kinds, appropriating to the upkeep of this fleet a proportion of the direct tax grant.[2] The indirect subsidies were extended for two years, as was the poll tax on foreigners. But the Commons again asked for reform of the king's household and for its more efficient financial management. Their hostility to foreign merchants was also again made manifest in various ways; for example, the king was asked to suspend the privileges of Prussian and Hanseatic merchants because of their alleged wrongful behaviour but the government's reply was simply that the king would do so if negotiations to be undertaken with the merchants achieved nothing. No such statute was made.

It was nearly three years before another Parliament met, the longest interval between Parliaments since the reign of Edward I. That interval was itself an ominous sign of new times. The government evidently saw no purpose in calling another Parliament which would only have led to more complaints about the latest outbreaks of disorder in parts of the realm, probably without producing the money so desperately needed for France.

Both Gascony and Normandy were under heavy attack but it was only possible to raise one expedition. This was placed under the command of the cardinal's nephew, John Beaufort, now Duke of Somerset, and it was at first intended for Gascony. It was then switched to Normandy to help York, though that was far from being the outcome. For one thing, in order to

---

[1] *Rot. Parl.* Vol. V, pp. 35–65.
[2] Ibid., pp. 59–60.

provide for Somerset's expedition, York was denied the money he needed to pay his own men. But as well as being given a financial preference, Somerset, who had the advantage of belonging to the dominant Beaufort faction on the council, also obtained a command wholly independent of York. As a military leader, Somerset was incompetent. After crossing the channel he made no contact with the embittered York and instead led a useless and damaging raid into Brittany, which was at peace with Henry VI, and then indulged in a wasteful invasion of Maine where he at no time fought any major battle with the French. He then withdrew to Rouen from where he came home, leaving York to manage as best he could in Normandy and to nurse a new and personal grievance against the Beaufort clan. In the following year Somerset, who had long been sick, died leaving behind him the seeds of the personal feud which was to develop between the House of York and the Beauforts who managed the House of Lancaster.

In this disastrous situation the government's search for peace became ever more desperate, and in 1443 the Beaufort-Suffolk party listened favourably to a proposal by the Duke of Orleans that Henry VI should be married to Margaret, the daughter of Henry of Anjou, in exchange for some kind of accommodation with the French. Although Suffolk was somewhat fearful of the consequences of being involved in such unpopular negotiations, he nevertheless accepted the council's wish that he should lead them. The royal engagement was agreed to in 1444 but on terms far from satisfactory to the English. All that they secured in exchange was a two years' truce, with both sides maintaining their existing positions until April 1446. For the English, there was still no question of abandoning the Lancastrian title which was the French requirement for a peace treaty. Nor would the French even cede full sovereignty of Gascony and Normandy. So, in exchange for nothing better than the truce of Tours, the marriage was agreed and Margaret reached England in April 1445. Suffolk was created a marquess as his reward for negotiating a marriage which was to be useless as a means of reaching a settlement with France and disastrous for the peace of the kingdom at home.

The king that Margaret of Anjou had come to marry was now twenty-three. In Tudor mythology, Henry VI became a kind of saint, a man of blameless personal life, mild, holy and selfless, who had been unjustly supplanted by the Yorkists. The Tudors inherited the Lancastrian claim by overthrowing the last ruler representing the House of York, and they had every reason to support the rehabilitation of the last Lancastrian king. The historical evidence, however, lends no support to the view of Henry as a victimized holy man. It is true that he was much concerned with religious observance, that he was virtuous and puritanical in his personal life and that he was by inclination a man of peace, at least in the sense that he was reluctant to take part in war personally. His memorials are the two colleges he founded, Eton and King's College, Cambridge, work on which had begun when he was eighteen. His interest in education is incontrovertible, even though the religious motivation originally took precedence over the educational in his two great foundations. But the later picture of a sanctified king who even wore monkish garb as a sign of self-denial and holiness was bogus. Henry was a king who in his prime dressed as richly as any other, who was foolishly extravagant and who dispensed patronage lavishly and without wisdom. He was a king infirm of purpose who wanted the throne of France but showed not the slightest inclination to follow his father's footsteps and lead an army to secure it.

Nor did he appear to have any concern for the growing lawlessness at home. Unfit to rule, he was perceived by many about him from his early adult years to be childish and he eventually became insane. Within these facts, there is some room for disagreement about his personal disposition. It is possible to argue that though he was incompetent, he was not wilfully perverse and untrustworthy but was rather a well-meaning and virtuous man who was over-credulous, unwise and unsubtle and who was handicapped by coming too early to government.[1] On the other hand, it has also been contended that Henry was perverse and vindictive as well as inept and vacillating and that he bears responsibility with Suffolk for a number of such incidents as the treatment of Eleanor Cobham and downfall of Gloucester himself.[2] But however the nuances of Henry's disposition are interpreted, the simple fact remains that his incapacity as a ruler was the cause of the Wars of the Roses and of the loss of the crown which his kinsmen, for all their quarrelling, had kept safely for him until he began to assume authority around about the age of sixteen. Nor did he improve with maturity. Once more civil strife was the direct consequence of the character of the king.

The Parliament which met on February 1445 was of exceptional length and sat in four sessions.[3] It was opened by the chancellor who preached on the text 'righteousness and peace have kissed each other' and in praise of Suffolk's successful negotiation of the French marriage. In the first session the Commons granted half a tenth and half a fifteenth, less the customary deduction. But neither indirect taxes nor the tax on aliens had been renewed

---

[1] This is the gist of the appraisal of the king's personality in Ralph A. Griffith's *Henry VI*, 1981, a compendious account of the reign and one of two recent biographies.
[2] This is the interpretation of the king's character in Bertram Wolffe's *Henry VI*, 1981.
[3] *Rot. Parl.* Vol. V, pp. 66–117.

when Parliament was prorogued for Easter. During the recess, Henry and Margaret were married with exceptional quietness and the new queen was crowned during the second session. In June, Suffolk made two statements in Parliament on his negotiations for peace and the king's marriage, one to the Lords and then another to the Commons separately, a clear indication of the acceptance that there were now two 'Houses'. It was a sign of Suffolk's defensiveness that he felt it advisable to say that, though the French had promised to send ambassadors to discuss peace, the best way to peace was preparation for war. He also denied that he had uttered a single word in France on the details of the peace to be considered.[1] Afterwards, the Speaker, William Burley, a knight well connected with both the government and with Gloucester and York, specifically 'recommended' Suffolk on account of his services and asked the Lords to beseech the king to take the new marquess into his grace and favour. Possibly reassured by Suffolk's stated willingness to prepare for war, Gloucester and the other lords rose in their places and made the recommendation to the king which the chancellor, replying on the king's behalf, said that it would be a 'joy' to accept. Parliament was then prorogued until October.

When it reassembled the Commons still failed to produce more money despite the fact that talks with French ambassadors in London had meanwhile led to nothing better than a continuation of the truce for a few more months. Even the arrival from Normandy of the Duke of York to testify to his dire necessity did not persuade them. Not until an unprecedented fourth session was held from January to April 1446 were further grants forthcoming. Indirect taxes were given, backdated to cover four years, and a further grant of one and a half tenths and fifteenths in instalments was made over three years, but minus a larger than usual deduction. In the end, this Parliament had proved financially amenable to the government and it had approved, among other things, the patents for the endowments of Eton and Kings. It also distinguished itself by further action to restrict the franchise socially. In answer to the Commons' desire, the king willed that, in future, elected parliamentary knights must be 'notable Knyghtes of the same Shires for the which they shall so be chosen; other ellys (or else) such notable Squiers, Gentilmen of birth, of the same Shires as be able to be Knyghtes; and no man to be it, that stondeth in the degree of Yoman and bynethe'.[2]

Yet the Parliament was also clearly sceptical of the government's peace policy. On the final day, the chancellor announced that King Henry

[1] *Rot. Parl.* Vol. V, p. 74.
[2] Ibid., pp. 115–116.

intended to meet Charles VII in France in the autumn and a Lords' bill was approved repealing the clause in the treaty of Troyes requiring the assent of the three estates of each country to any such discussion. But a significant rider was added by the chancellor speaking on behalf of all the Lords and dissociating them from the meeting between the two kings which was Henry's own private idea, inspired by the Almighty. It had pleased the Lord, said the chancellor, 'to emprynt yn your Highnesse' the idea of a meeting in October with his uncle of France, for the good of both realms; 'Which seid motions and sterings onely oure Lorde hath liked to ster and meve you too, he knoweth (i.e. 'as He knows'), withoute that any of the Lordes or other of your suggettes . . . in any wise have stered or meved you soo to doo.'

The chancellor went on to express the Lords' wish for an acknowledgement that they had done everything they could in this Parliament for the accomplishment of the king's 'blissid entent'. They wished him to hold them 'discharged and excused' and to command that their request be entered on the Parliament roll.[1] The entry was made but no reply by the king was recorded. It was not necessary. The Lords had made their point, virtually washing their hands of Henry's negotiations. They suspected that concessions were being contemplated of which they would disapprove and they were right. But they could have had no idea that the king had already gone so far as to agree privately to the surrender of Maine to the new queen's father, whose family were its hereditary counts, as a first stage of a settlement with France.

The surrender of Maine seems to have been very much Henry's personal policy, formed under the influence of the queen, and it demonstrates his characteristic political folly. To enrage English opinion by surrendering so much for so little and yet still to expect support for his claim to the French crown was the height of inconsistency. Meanwhile, the hand-over in Maine was delayed for as long as possible by the English representatives appointed to arrange it on Henry's behalf, for it was bitterly resented by the English in France. Indeed, Suffolk personally secured from the king exoneration from any responsibility in the matter. Henry had promised the surrender to Charles VII in a private letter. Although he favoured peace, Suffolk disapproved of the king's precipitate policy of appeasement but connived at it in his pursuit of self-aggrandizement. That was to cost him his life.

King Henry never went to France, peace was not made and the policy he was pursuing threatened to provoke strife at home. The man most feared was Gloucester, and Suffolk and his party decided to strike at the duke before he could strike at them. The method was to be impeachment. Less

[1] *Rot. Parl.* Vol. V, p. 102.

than a year after the last Parliament had been dissolved a new one was called to meet in February 1447, 'the which Parliament was made only to slay the noble duke of Gloucester', as a contemporary chronicler accurately recorded, ascribing the intention to 'the false duke of Suffolk' and his party.[1] The Parliament was called to Bury St Edmunds, in an area where Suffolk was strong, and it assembled in the refectory of the abbey.[2] Duke Humphrey arrived a week late and was directed to go straight to his lodgings, where he was arrested after his dinner by a group of noblemen, Buckingham, Dorset, Salisbury and the new Viscount Beaumont, who was constable of England. The intention was to charge him with treason but within a week he was dead, either of a stroke or a heart attack brought on by the stress of arrest: he was fifty-seven.

The suspicion that Suffolk and his party were responsible for the duke's murder was inevitable but was probably not justified. Gloucester's body was publicly exhibited and viewed by members of the Parliament to prove that he had died of natural causes. But his death added to the unpopularity of Suffolk's party, whose old leader, Cardinal Beaufort, himself died at Winchester some weeks later. The Bury St Edmunds Parliament lasted no more than three weeks. No money was asked of it so soon after the recent grants, though it agreed that the government could raise loans of up to £100,000. With Gloucester's death, the parliament had no significant business except to bar his widow Eleanor from any dower from the late duke's estate. Several members of Gloucester's household, including his bastard son, were subsequently sentenced for high treason, hanged, cut down alive and just as they were about to be beheaded and quartered, spared by the dramatic arrival of Suffolk bearing a pardon from Henry granted on a religious pretext.[3] It was not a performance to inspire respect.

With the death of Gloucester and the king as yet childless, the Duke of York became heir presumptive, though it is very likely that Suffolk had other ideas about the succession. If the king had a child, the marquess could expect to maintain his now dominant position in the council through his influence with Queen Margaret. If Henry had no issue, then Suffolk would presumably have preferred Somerset, the Lancastrian candidate. It is even possible that there was something in later suspicions that Suffolk contemplated a union between his own son and the Lady Margaret Beaufort, the young daughter of the late Duke of Somerset, through whom the Lancastrian claim was eventually to be transmitted to the Tudors. Meanwhile, Suffolk set about diminishing York's influence, causing him to

[1] *An English Chronicle*, ed. J. S. Davies, p. 62. Extract in *E.H.D.* Vol. IV, p. 257.
[2] *Rot. Parl.* Vol. V, pp. 128–140.
[3] B. Wolffe, op. cit., p. 132.

be brought back from Normandy and appointed lieutenant of Ireland, though the duke managed to delay his departure. In York's place, Edmund Beaufort, Marquess of Dorset, who now had his late brother's rank of Duke of Somerset, became lieutenant of France.

The logical development of policy so far would have been for Suffolk to use his now unchallenged power in the council, subject to Henry's private policy-making, to make a permanent peace by giving up the claim to the French crown. Had he done so he might have restored stability to England. Instead, he and the king embroiled themselves with Brittany and by so doing at once brought the weight of France against them to the final ruin of their cause. The conditions leading to this folly were created when the fortress town of Le Mans in Maine was finally handed over to the French. This was done only after long procrastination by those Englishmen charged with arranging the hand-over, for there was bitter hostility to the surrender among the English in France as well as at home. With good reason, the English settlers in Normandy saw it as an omen of their own fate. In clear resistance to Henry's will, therefore, the negotiations were dragged out as long as possible. It was not until March 1448 that Le Mans was finally surrendered to the French, and it was only handed over then because the forces of Charles VII were investing it to force a conclusion. In return, the truce was extended for two years until 1450.

The surrender of Maine laid Normandy open wide to French invasion. During the procrastination over Le Mans nothing had been done either to build up strength in Normandy or to negotiate a peace on any such feasible terms as retaining the duchy as a fief from the French king. The respite was wasted and the surrender of Maine, which had been intended to pave the way to a settlement acceptable to the English, simply ensured a total French victory. Moreover, when they surrendered Le Mans, the English took a step which provided the trigger for their own ultimate humiliation. There was an exchange of documents and the one which was handed by the English to the French included the name of the Duke of Brittany as an English adherent. The French document, however, correctly described him as owing allegiance to the French crown. The French seem to have accepted the discrepancy without protest in order to get their hands on Le Mans; the evidence does not support a French claim some years later that they had failed to notice the change in the English document because it had been hastily handed over by candlelight. To Henry and Suffolk, however, the claim to the feudal allegiance of Brittany had more than formal significance. For reasons that are less than clear they foolishly contemplated using their claim to overlordship of Brittany to justify a military adventure which was finally to ruin the English cause in France.

Francis, Duke of Brittany, had imprisoned his brother Giles, an English adherent who had been brought up in the English court close to Henry VI, and the king and Suffolk now formed the crazy design of trying to rescue him. English soldiers who had been turned out of Maine had already occupied fortresses in the disputed border area between Normandy and Brittany, which the French regarded as a breach of the truce. Then, in March 1449 an English force under Francois de Surienne, a captain from Aragon who was also a knight of the garter, invaded Brittany and captured the town of Fougères. The expedition was supposed to lead to the rescue of Giles, and there is no doubt that it was authorized by the king and by Suffolk, who had in the meantime been made a duke. The consequence was an appeal by the duke of Brittany to the French king who declared that the Anglo-French truce had been broken. The English, on the other hand, claimed that it was a purely internal affair between Henry and the Breton duke who owed him allegiance. Yet despite their responsibility for the adventure, Henry and Suffolk did nothing to respond to de Surienne's pleas for help and he was forced to withdraw. The only consequence of this folly, which had Henry's stamp on it as much as Suffolk's, was that Charles VII declared the truce at an end and unleashed the final invasion against Normandy in the summer of 1449. The English were wholly unprepared and town after town fell. By October, Rouen had been lost and the English were driven back to the coastal area, holding only Cherbourg, Bayeux, Caen, Falaise and Honfleur. The battle of Formigny on 15 August 1450 followed by the surrender of Cherbourg ended English control of Normandy. Of all the former English lands in northern France, nothing remained save Calais.

III

The outcome of defeat in France was a revolution in England, which was already seething with unrest.[1] Within a few months, Suffolk and the two unpopular bishops who had recently been dominant on the council with him were dead, not by judicial decree but by the rage of the mob. In the space of one year, 1449, two Parliaments had already been called. The first had met at Westminster in February, after which it was prorogued twice, from 4 April to 7 May and from 30 May to 16 June when it met at

[1] For an account of the end of the reign see, R. L. Storey, *The End of the House of Lancaster*, (1966).

Winchester on account of the plague.[1] There exists a 17th century transcript of notes of a discussion in the Lords of the possibility of sending help to France. But some lords considered that commissions of array would only increase disorder at home and the conclusion was simply that the 'usual grant' should be taken for the defence of the land. The surrender of Maine had by then already badly damaged the Duke of Suffolk's reputation, though the Commons still elected a Speaker, Sir John Say of Cambridgeshire, who was directly associated with Suffolk's policy. Even so, the court's adherents in the Commons could produce no more in the first session than half a tenth and fifteenth payable in two instalments (less the usual deduction) and an extension of tunnage and poundage for five years. Although Somerset himself came home from Normandy during this Parliament, just before the final collapse, to explain the desperate situation, nothing more was forthcoming. In the second session, all that was granted was sanction for the government to raise a loan, but in the third session another half of a tenth and fifteenth was granted, again by instalments, with a poll tax on aliens and a continued wool tax appropriated to Calais, in the retentions of which the merchants in the Commons had a special interest. But the Commons were still unwilling to raise the sort of money needed for Normandy and, in the light of the government's conduct of policy, they can hardly be blamed. Disaster was imminent and within weeks after the first Parliament had been dissolved another, the most traumatic of the reign so far, was called to meet on 6 November, 1449 at Westminster.[2]

It was a sign of changed times that the Commons first elected as their Speaker a retainer of the Duke of York, Sir John Popham, an elected knight from Hampshire and an old soldier who had been at Agincourt and had himself lost estates in Normandy. He, however, asked to be excused the Speakership on grounds of age (he was sixty) and in his place the Commons chose William Tresham from Northamptonshire, a lawyer who was both one of York's retainers and also acceptable to the government; he had been Speaker three times before, once at Bury St Edmunds. York himself did not return from Ireland but he was inevitably seen as the leader of the opposition to a discredited government and the natural claimant to remedial power. That the Commons wanted change was instantly clear and in any case the government was already disintegrating. The treasurer, the Bishop of Carlisle, had resigned and just before the end of the first session in December Bishop Moleyns of Chichester, keeper of the privy seal, who had probably been the most influential figure in the council after Suffolk,

[1] *Rot. Parl.* Vol. V, pp. 141–153. A. R. Myers, 'A Parliamentary Debate of the Mid-Fifteenth Century', *B.J.R.L.*, XXII (1938).
[2] *Rot. Parl.* Vol. V, pp. 171–203.

Henry VI: Parliament, Faction and Civil War

followed him. His resignation is a sign that the first session was deeply disturbed, though little of this is recorded. The unrest in the country was shockingly revealed when Bishop Moleyns was murdered at Portsmouth by soldiers who accused him of withholding their pay. A few days afterwards a disturbance in London and an uprising in Kent had to be quelled.

When Parliament resumed, Suffolk anticipated his impeachment. For one thing, it was rumoured that the murdered Bishop Moleyns, just before he died, had said something to implicate Suffolk in treason. So on the first day of the session Suffolk made a protest before the king and Lords referring to 'the odious and horrible langage' which ran through the land about him 'almoost in every Commons mouth'. Suffolk spoke of his own and his family's service to the crown, denied the rumours absolutely, and challenged anyone who thought him guilty of treason to charge him with it.[1] A few days later the Commons petitioned the Lords for Suffolk to be placed in custody because of the rumoured charges but the Lords rejected this because no definite charge had been made against him. On 28 January, therefore, the Commons made that charge, accusing Suffolk of selling the realm to Charles VII and saying that he had 'stuffed' the castle of Wallingford with guns and gunpowder to succour the French when they landed. The duke was committed to the Tower.

Detailed charges followed some days later. He was accused of conspiring with the French king to depose Henry VI and invade England; of seeking to marry Margaret Beaufort to his own son and place her on the throne; of responsibility for the release of the Duke of Orleans; of surrendering Maine; of preventing the sending of reinforcements to France and of much else besides. He was also accused of being a party to an attempt to murder Lord Cromwell at the door of the Star Chamber in the first session, which was alleged to have been made by one of Suffolk's retainers, William Tailboys. A further bill of charges in March included maladministration, peculation and the misuse of power and maintenance.[2] Of these last charges he was certainly guilty; one of the Paston letters in 1448 declared that no-one in Norfolk dared risk saying anything against Suffolk and his people.[3] He was also, like Henry himself, guilty of being a foolish politician. But the charges of a plot against Henry VI and of treasonable relations with France were plainly absurd.

Brought from the Tower, Suffolk strongly denied all the accusations, saying that as to any matters of fact, the whole council bore equal

---

[1] *Rot. Parl.* Vol. V, p. 176.
[2] Ibid., pp. 177–182.
[3] From Margaret Paston, *Paston Letters*, No. 56, ed. Gairdner.

responsibility. How far his impeachment was an independent decision of the Commons and how far they were moved to it by Suffolk's enemies on the council cannot be known. But it seems likely that there was instigation; there was need of a scapegoat. In particular, Lord Cromwell, motivated by his personal resentment after the attempts to assassinate him, probably encouraged the charges. As the political wind blew the Commons could often be swayed by the parties among them that followed greater men. But Suffolk escaped impeachment by the king's personal intervention. Henry sent for 'all his Lordes' to come 'into his Innest Chambre, with a Gavill Wyndowe over a Cloyster', in Westminster palace and then called Suffolk in to hear, on his knees, the royal judgement. Declaring that there was no case against Suffolk in respect of the heinous and treasonable charges, Henry banished his former minister for five years. He had removed the judgement from the Lords in Parliament and delivered his own. It was a sign of changed times that although his government's authority was in ruins, Henry VI was able to intervene personally to save a friend, whereas Richard II was powerless to do so though his government was by no means so discredited. The difference was that Richard had faced an almost united aristocracy, which was determined to uproot the lesser men who served him; Henry, on the other hand, was dealing with a nobility divided by faction. It was in some respects an extra-parliamentary judgement, though it was entered on the parliamentary roll; and on behalf of all the Lords spiritual and temporal, Viscount Beaumont formally recited that what Henry had done was decreed by the king's own rule, not by their advice.[1] Yet many of the Lords must have had as much reason as the king not to have this embarrassing case thrashed out in Parliament.

At the end of March, Parliament was adjourned, and after putting his affairs in order, Suffolk sailed from Ipswich at the beginning of May, 1450. But his ship was intercepted by a vessel named *Nicholas of the Tower*, sailed by an unknown captain. Suffolk was seized and beheaded with a rusty sword on behalf of the 'community of the realm'. His body was taken to lie on the sands at Dover. That, however, was not the end of the violence. Kent was now the source of the most serious rising since the Peasants' Revolt, perhaps because the men of that county were threatened by reprisals for Suffolk's murder, for which they were blamed.

In June a rebel force led by a man known as Jack Cade, whose real identity is not known but who was said to claim that he was a Mortimer, marched on London and encamped at Blackheath. This time, however, it was not simply an uprising of unorganized peasants seeking to put right their social grievances but a political rebellion with specific and published

[1] *Rot. Parl.* Vol. V, pp. 182–183.

demands for remedies for misgovernment. It included a considerable contingent of gentry (one of whom, Robert Poyning, served in the next Parliament), a mayor, yeomen and peasants, and it is possible that the Duke of York had knowledge of it. At any rate, one of the political demands of the rebels was that York and other noblemen should be taken on to the king's council. The manifestos of the rebels also demanded the punishment of those who had lost France and put good Duke Humphrey to death, declaring that the common people had been destroyed and the king himself reduced to such a level that he could no longer even pay for his meat and drink.

For a time the rebels controlled London. There they took Lord Saye, the detested former treasurer who had been one of Suffolk's close associates, and executed him; he had been sent to the Tower by Henry in the hope of appeasing the rebels. In Salisbury the third of the unpopular former councillors, Bishop Ayscough, the king's confessor, was dragged from Mass and killed. Eventually the rebels were driven from London, and most of them dispersed in response to a free pardon. Cade was among others who continued to fight but he was killed in action and the rebellion broke up. However, there were still to be sporadic outbursts of disorder in Kent and in other southern counties, since the king had done nothing to redress the grievances about which the rebels petitioned him. Henry and the council no longer had any real control over the kingdom.

At the time of Suffolk's murder Parliament had just begun its third session at Leicester, whither Henry had retreated to be well away from the unrest in London. Desperate though the government was for money, the Commons refused any ordinary subsidy, saying that they dare not give more because of the poverty of the country. Instead, they conceded a graduated income tax rising from 6d. in the pound on land worth less than £20 annually. But as the king's debt now stood at £372,000, this was conditional both on the appointment of special treasurers and on a massive Resumption Act to oblige the king to take back lands and revenues alienated by grants since Henry's accession. It was an ineffective piece of legislation since Henry was able to use the power it gave him to make certain exceptions so that its application to men of the household was largely avoided. Nevertheless, the Act of Resumption in this Parliament, which was followed by a similar but more effective enactment in the next, is an important reminder that the demand for the crown to take back alienated royal lands was now almost the only important political initiative with which the Commons still persisted.[1] They were convinced that if the crown

---

[1] B. P. Wolffe, 'Acts of Resumption in the Lancastrian Parliaments, 1399–1456', *E.H.R.* LXXIII (1958), reprinted in Fryde and Miller, op. cit., Vol. II, pp. 61–91.

ceased to give away its revenues lavishly it could live from its own resources, not entirely but sufficiently to reduce its need for parliamentary taxation, which was their primary concern. This apart, the one area of parliamentary activity in which the Commons predominated at this time was the initiating of legislation. In the first half of the fifteenth century that function fell almost entirely to them rather than to the government for reasons which will be discussed in the final chapter. The Lords were not interested in doing so since the law-making of this period hardly touched the great political questions which mattered to them.

In virtually every important political question the Lords now determined the course of events. What was decided depended on which faction among them was uppermost. The magnates dominated not only Parliament but also the king's council, as they had done throughout Henry's minority. During the fourteenth century, professional officials and councillors below the rank of lord who were personal servants of the king had been more important in the daily running of affairs than the magnates, whose interventions were sporadic and frequently oppositional. Throughout both Henry VI's minority, however, and now during his ineffectual adulthood, the magnates actively participated in the council, often holding offices themselves. Lesser men were left with little influence. Moreover, whereas in the fourteenth century the composition of the working continual council had been the same whether or not Parliament was sitting, in the fifteenth the entire peerage now effectively claimed conciliar authority when a Parliament or great council was in session.

In June 1450 the Parliament at Leicester was hastily dissolved because of Cade's rebellion, and by the end of the month the political nation was reeling under the shock of the abandonment of Normandy. York now decided to act. During August he returned to England, gathered forces on the Welsh border and marched to London where he insisted on seeing the king and demanded changes in the council. The popular opinion of Henry's incapacity at the time is revealed in an indictment of two men of Sussex who were alleged to have said in open market that the king 'was a natural fool and would often hold a staff in his hands with a bird on the end, playing therewith as a fool, and that another king must be ordained to rule the land . . .'[1]

Another Parliament was called for November and the political tension was heightened by the arrival home from Calais of Edmund Beaufort, Duke of Somerset. For the remainder of Henry VI's reign, Parliament, like the political nation, was a prey to faction which began with the strife between

[1] *E.H.D.* Vol. IV, p. 264.

Somerset and York. Although civil war did not break out until 1455, their struggle at the political centre from now on echoed the physical conflict of lesser magnates out in the country, where Nevilles fought Percys in the north and the Earl of Devon was locked in conflict with Lord Bonville in the west. Nothing, however, was said about the succession, and York always protested his loyalty to Henry VI. Nevertheless with a childless and useless king the question of the succession lurked beneath every argument.

Richard of York, the richest man in England, represented the old Mortimer claim, which he had inherited through his mother Anne Mortimer. Given that the succession could pass through a woman, he had a better right to the throne than Henry VI and certainly the best claim to be heir presumptive. He also had good reason, as we have seen, to be angered by the personal treatment he had received from the Beauforts as well as by the chaotic state of the realm. If, on the other hand, the Lancastrians were the legitimate dynasty, Edmund Beaufort, Duke of Somerset, could claim to be male heir presumptive as a direct descendent of John of Gaunt. His disadvantage was that the Beauforts had been specifically barred from the crown. There was also his late elder brother's daughter Margaret, but she was hardly a convincing Lancastrian candidate, even though she was to transmit the Lancastrian claim to the Tudors.

In 1450, Somerset's standing was diminished by his involvement with a discredited government and his own poor showing in France. Yet, on his return to England, Henry immediately made him constable, which in all the circumstances was provocative. York, on the other hand, had an unblemished political record and was denied any place on the council. He was therefore the natural leader of the opposition. In September 1450, therefore, he decided to act and landed from Ireland gathering troops on the Welsh border. (It was a sign of the troubled times that when William Tresham, the Speaker of the previous Parliament, went to meet him he was murdered by retainers of the Lancastrian Lord Grey of Ruthin.) York then marched to London with a large force and demanded from the king a place on the council, reform of government and the calling to account of all who had committed treason. He claimed that he had come to clear his own name of treasonable charges and to deal with his accusers, protesting his own loyalty. He then devoted his energies to securing the election of his supporters to the next Parliament. It met on 6 November and remained in being, in three sessions, until the following April.[1]

York arrived at Parliament with a large force of retainers, as did his nephew the Duke of Norfolk. When he reached Westminster one of his

[1] *Rot. Parl.* Vol. V, pp. 210–226.

supporters, William Oldhall, a famous soldier in the French wars, had already been elected Speaker. In this Yorkist Parliament, an assault on the Beauforts began immediately. A bill of attainder against the late Duke of Suffolk was brought in but vetoed by the king. A bill for the removal of Somerset and others from the council was also virtually nullified by the king's exclusion from it of the duke and all other peers. There was, however, a new Act of Resumption which was more effective than that of the last Parliament and had fewer exceptions. But the most dramatic event of the Parliament was an open clash between York and Somerset. An attempt seems to have been made to arrest Somerset, but he eluded it, though his house, like those of some other Lancastrian noblemen, was pillaged. He was then placed by the king in the Tower for his own protection. The Speaker, William Oldhall, participated in this attack on Somerset and also seems to have organized a tumult in Westminster Hall, even when the courts were sitting there, and eighteen months later he was to be accused of inciting men to kill some of the Lords.

Nevertheless, the court somehow managed to recover influence during the recess and York to lose it. Henry was at the start of a short interlude of more effective personal government, which he began by undertaking a judicial eyre himself, accompanied by judges, in some of the shires to restore order by the administration of justice. Somerset's influence was strengthening. In a second session from January to April, little was done in Parliament but in a third session in the summer, a lawyer MP for Bristol, Thomas Yonge, moved a petition in the Commons for the recognition of Richard, Duke of York, as the king's heir. This presumption (which was too shocking to be mentioned on the current Parliament roll, though it was recorded retrospectively in a later Yorkist Parliament) immediately precipitated the dissolution. Yonge was incarcerated in the Tower.[1] Angered and snubbed, York withdrew from Westminster.

Henry still seemed to have some grip on government, undertaking further judicial eyres to restore order. But in the autumn Oldhall began organizing support for York and in the following February, the duke denounced Somerset's rule over the king and marched south. At Dartford in Kent he found himself faced by a larger royal army and was tricked into disbanding it on an understanding that, if he did so, Somerset would be held in arrest to answer charges. But when York's men had dispersed, he found his rival still the king's councillor while he himself was taken to London virtually as a prisoner, though he was subsequently released under promise of good behaviour. In the meantime, Gascony, England's last remaining

---

[1] See p. 555.

French province, had been invaded by the French and after the people of Bordeaux had appealed to Henry, an English force under John Talbot, Earl of Shrewsbury, relieved the city. That success improved the standing of Somerset and the court party further.

The Parliament that met in the abbey at Reading in March 1453 was dominated by the court.[1] It had been heavily packed by members of the household (seventeen per cent of the Commons were men of the royal household compared with six per cent in 1450) and with other Lancastrians. Influence had been exerted over elections.[2] An associate of Somerset's, Thomas Thorpe, a Baron of the Exchequer, was chosen as Speaker and he did a good job for the Lancastrians for which he was well paid. The Commons virtuously asked for their petition against Somerset in 1450 to be cast into oblivion and for grants made to Yorkists to be taken back, or 'resumed' by the crown. A tenth and a fifteenth were voted and the king was given the wool subsidy for life. Most remarkably a unique provision was given to the king to raise 20,000 archers at a wage of 6d. a day for six months, which were perhaps intended to help control unrest at home. This was subsequently reduced to 13,000 but another tenth and fifteenth was granted for Gascony. The king then decided to prorogue Parliament in order to go on a new judicial perambulation, this time to bring some order to the north where Percys were once more fighting Nevilles.

On 2 July, after the second tax grant, Henry thanked the Commons 'with his own mouth' telling them (the parliamentary roll records the solemn moment in Latin) not to doubt that he would be a gracious and benevolent lord to them (*Nos vobis intime regratiamur, & ne dubitetis quin vobis erimus graciosus & benevolus Dominus*). This was the last public speech to be heard from him for a long time. The chancellor then went on to explain that the king intended to go, in person, to divers regions of the kingdom and work for the uprooting of maintenance, extortion, oppression, riots and other misdeeds. The Parliament was then prorogued to meet again at Reading in November. But the perambulation never took place. Shortly afterwards, while at his hunting lodge of Clarendon near Salisbury, Henry suddenly became deranged, losing his memory, all sense of time and place and his capacity for speech.

It is possible that a brain already on the brink of madness was finally unhinged by the shock of doom-laden news from France. After Talbot's initial success at Bordeaux, his army had been defeated at Castillon where Talbot himself was killed. The English were at last driven from France. The

---

[1] *Rot. Parl.* Vol. V, pp. 227–271.
[2] J. S. Roskell, *The Commons and their Speakers*, op. cit., p. 248.

loss of Gascony after 300 years was a tremendous blow to English prestige and now that the English no longer controlled the French northern provinces there was also renewed danger from French raiders on the south coast. English settlers and soldiers were driven from France and former property-owners suddenly found themselves adrift. Men who had lost land and occupation, and soldiers returning home with nothing to do except make mischief added greatly to the already unstable social conditions. It was no coincidence that two years after the loss of France, civil war broke out in England. Such disasters could not have been foreseen by Henry VI but it is not impossible that the shock of losing his cherished second crown in France destroyed his reason.

For a month or two every effort was made to keep quiet about the king's condition, but the processes of government quickly ceased to function as Henry remained in his stupor. The magnates now had to determine how to organize government, not least because the quarrels between factions in the north were worsening. At first there was an attempt not to summon York to the council but it was inevitable that he should return to become its leader. In October he was asked to come to the council by a group of bishops who apologized for the oversight in not calling him sooner. Indeed, logic suggested that he should become regent. But at this very time he ceased to be heir presumptive because Queen Margaret gave birth to a son, Prince Edward, and it was quickly made clear that this intensely political consort wanted to claim the regency herself on her son's behalf. Such was Margaret's unpopularity, however, that this ambition simply rallied the Lords to York, who was soon in control of the government. When Parliament reassembled in November, it was immediately prorogued again until February 1454, formally by the king, who because he could not himself be present for various 'just and reasonable causes' nominated York to act for him by letters patent under the great seal. A week or so later York secured a declaration from the council that all men were free to attend and serve him, apparently on the grounds that he had been deprived of the help of his personal counsellors; he seems to have alleged that Queen Margaret and Somerset had tried to cause men to shun him in the past year or two. Shortly afterwards Somerset, on the grounds that he was guilty of treasonable acts in the events leading to the loss of France, was imprisoned in the Tower.

Parliament had been due to sit again at Reading on 11 February but it was immediately diverted to meet at Westminster three days later. But now the political scene had radically changed. A gathering of Lords in the council chamber had appointed York as the king's lieutenant to open and preside over Parliament. Answers to petitions were in the name of all the council.

But it was clear that many peers were reluctant to take sides in this uncertain struggle; when Parliament met so few Lords attended it that a system of fines was imposed on absentees according to rank.[1] The most startling indication of the new political climate was that the Lancastrian Speaker Thorpe was now in prison, accused by York of having gone to the Bishop of Durham's London house and taken possession of some undescribed goods and chattels belonging to the duke. (Many years later it was claimed by Thorpe's son that the goods were harnesses and warlike chattels seized on the king's order.) The arrest of the Speaker immediately raised the privileges of the Commons and the new session began with a petition from the Commons to the king and Lords that they should have all their liberties and privileges and that Thomas Thorpe, 'their common Speaker' (*lour commune Parlour*), should be set at liberty. A statement was then made on behalf of York explaining the case against Thorpe and requiring that he be kept in custody until he had satisfied the duke as to damages. However, the Lords, who said that they did not wish to hurt the liberties and privileges of the Commons but simply to uphold justice, were sufficiently wary of the Commons to refer the matter to the judges to find out whether Thorpe should be freed 'by force and vertue of the Privilegge of Parlement or noo'.

After 'sadde communication and mature deliberation', the justices said 'that they ought not to aunswere to that question, for it hath not be used afore tyme, that the Justicez shuld in eny wyse determine the Privilegge of this high Court of Parlement; for it is so high and so mighty in his (sic) nature, that it may make lawe, and that that is lawe it may make noo lawe; and the determination and knowlegge of that Privilegge belongeth to the Lordes of the Parlement, and not to the Justices'. But, they said, it was customary for any persons arrested in cases other than treason, felony or breach of the peace, or for a condemnation before Parliament time, to be released so that they should be free to attend Parliament. Even so, the Lords concluded that Thorpe should remain in prison, 'the Privilegge of the Parlement ... notwithstondyng'.[2] The Commons, who presumably felt in no position to argue against the dominant Lords, were directed to choose a new Speaker and Sir Thomas Charlton was elected, a man acceptable to both Lancastrians and Yorkists. In the session from 14 February to 17 April 1454, the infant prince was created Prince of Wales and Earl of Chester in acknowledgement of his right to succeed.

The Commons, however, had not lost all interest in the king's council. Recalling their generous grant in the first session, they said they could

---

[1] *Rot. Parl.* Vol. V, p. 248.
[2] Ibid., pp. 239–240.

afford no more and reminded the government that in the first session at Reading the chancellor had promised, in response to their request, that there should be established 'a sadde and a wyse Counsaill' of lords to which all could have recourse for the administration of justice. But, they concluded, they had no knowledge that this had been done as yet and would like to be told. The chancellor, Cardinal Kemp, replied that 'they shuld have good and comfortable aunswere, without eny grete delay or tariyng'.[1] But three days later this moderate man died, leaving the country without either a chancellor or an Archbishop of Canterbury. With nobody able to use the great seal, the processes of government and of the law were at a halt. The seals were 'closed in a Coofre, and . . . sealed with diverse Lordes Seales, and . . . leide uppe' in the treasury, and a delegation of lay and spiritual peers was then sent to the king at Windsor. They were instructed to try to discover his will on this matter and also to convey the Commons' request concerning the council. The candid account they brought back of the pathetic state of the king, who could neither speak nor control his limbs, is one of the most vivid entries in any Parliament roll.[2]

They related how, after the king's dinner, they put to him the matters entrusted to them but could get no word from him 'for no prayer ne desire, . . . ne eny thyng that they or eny of theim cowede do or sey, to theire grete sorowe and discomfort'. So the peers went away to their own dinner and returned to Henry afterwards 'and there they moeved and sturred hym, by all the waies and meanes that they cowede thynke, to have answere of the matiers aforeseid, but they cowede have noon'. They then had the king taken into his bedroom, to which 'he was ledde betwene II men', where they tried for the third time to get a response from him to their questions, or even an indication of whether he wished them to wait upon him any longer, 'but they cowede have no aunswere, worde ne signe; and therfor with sorowefull hartes come theire way'. The delegation asked that their report should be enacted in the parliamentary record. It was painfully clear that the role of the king must be filled and accordingly, on 27 March, the Lords appointed York Protector and Defender of the Realm and chief of the king's council. At his request, it was recorded on the parliamentary roll that he had not sought this authority but had been besought by the peers to accept it. They in turn had it recorded that they were compelled by circumstances to make the appointment.[3] Anything was now possible. The king might become sane again, but it was also possible that York might

[1] *Rot. Parl.* Vol. V, p. 240.
[2] Ibid., pp. 240–242.
[3] Ibid., p. 242.

remain Protector until Prince Edward could either himself act as Protector or, if his father died, rule as king. No more money was granted by this already very generous Parliament, but on the Commons' petition the king's two half-brothers Edmund and Jaspar Tudor were legitimated and created Earls of Richmond and Pembroke respectively, endowing them with lands accordingly. They were the sons of Henry V's widow Queen Catherine from her second marriage to a Welsh gentleman, Owen Tudor. It was by Edmund Tudor's marriage to Margaret Beaufort that the Lancastrian claim was passed to Henry VII. The Parliament ended just before Easter.

So began a year's competent administration by Richard of York. The Earl of Salisbury, his brother-in-law, became chancellor, being the first layman to hold that office during the reign, and Thomas Bourchier, Bishop of Ely, who was acceptable to both parties, was made Archbishop of Canterbury. Somerset remained in prison but it was evidently not thought possible to bring him to trial. York then set off for a judicial visit to the north, just as Henry himself had intended, with the particular purpose of putting a stop to the quarrel between the Nevilles and Percys. Their forces were dispersed but the intervention was more favourable to the Nevilles, who were York's relations through his wife Cecily, than to the Percys, and the quarrel was not ended. The Percys' ally, the Duke of Exeter, came to London and took sanctuary but was seized and imprisoned.

Early in 1455, however, the king began to recover his sanity and was told that he had a son, of whom he said he had no memory. Nor did he remember anything else during his illness. The Duke of York ceased to be Protector and at the beginning of February Somerset was released, declared loyal and once more made captain of Calais, an appointment York had assumed. Exeter too was set free and Salisbury resigned as chancellor, unable to withstand the pressure of Somerset and his party. He was replaced by Archbishop Bourchier, and the Earl of Wiltshire became treasurer. The court party then decided to call a great council dominated by Lancastrian partisans at Leicester, a place chosen because the Londoners supported York as they once had Duke Humphrey. The proclaimed purpose of the great council was to provide for the king's safety and to it knights sympathetic to the court were summoned. It never met. Convinced that Somerset and Exeter would strike at him if he did not act first, York gathered his allies and his forces and marched towards London, intending to prevent Henry from reaching Leicester. Meanwhile, on 21 May, the king, with Somerset, Buckingham and their retinues had set out from London on their way north.

York's principal allies were both Nevilles; his brother-in-law Richard Earl of Salisbury, and Salisbury's son, Richard Earl of Warwick, later the so-called 'king-maker.' Salisbury had acquired his earldom through marriage to the Montagu heiress and Warwick had acquired his by marriage to Anne Beauchamp. Salisbury had long been a great power in the north as warden of the west march on the Scottish border and as the holder of vast estates; Warwick's greatest days of power were yet to come. Both outshone the Earls of Westmorland who represented the senior line of Nevilles. From generation to generation the Nevilles were locked in bitter feuding with their rivals the Percys and in competition for the wardenships of the marches; at this time a Percy, the son of the Earl of Northumberland, governed the eastern march. Since 1453, the two clans had again been in open conflict and inevitably the Nevilles had turned to York for help when Somerset as chief councillor proved reluctant to intervene. In return, the Nevilles supported York when during his protectorate he imprisoned Somerset.

In these circumstances, and after the failure of their alliance with the Duke of Exeter, who was a distant connection of the Lancastrian royal family, the Percys had gravitated to Somerset. Following Henry VI's return to sanity, the Earl of Northumberland, the head of the Percys, had decided to end his practice of avoiding Westminster and came south to throw in his lot with Somerset. So when the crisis at the apex of politics came in 1455 the Nevilles were in no doubt that they must help York. It was the clash between the alliance of York and Neville against that of Somerset, the court and the Percys which precipitated the first battle of the civil war.

On the road south in 1455, York was supported only by the two Neville earls and Viscount Bouchier, but nevertheless had a far larger force than that with which Henry was progressing northwards from London, although the king was accompanied by more noblemen. Somerset appears to have been taken by surprise by York's advance and only set about raising an army when, just before the royal party left Westminster, he heard something of York's movements. Meanwhile, York sent two letters to the court, one to the chancellor-archbishop, the other to the king himself, protesting his loyalty and declaring that his only purpose was to protect Henry from the enemies who had estranged him from his cousin. What he wanted was the dismissal of traitors in the council and the calling of a properly representative council as the conditions for laying down their arms. To justify his conflict with the king's forces, York was to claim later that both letters had been deliberately withheld from the king and chancellor. At all events, the king, the court and their retinues had just left Watford on the way to St Albans, where they intended to break their journey, when they heard that York had arrived outside the town. The question then was whether the king and his retinues should stay where they were in open country and prepare defences, which was Somerset's proposal, or go on to St Albans and hope that once there they could negotiate a settlement with York, as the Duke of Buckingham suggested.

Unwisely, Henry chose the second course and took up his position in the centre of St Albans. Attempts to negotiate came to nothing and what was to be called the first battle of St Albans, which would be better described as an affray, followed in the streets and the gardens. The Lancastrians were overcome, Henry himself was wounded and taken, and the Yorkists made sure that Somerset was killed fighting. There were very few casualties, although Northumberland and Lord Clifford were also killed on the Lancastrian side. The first stimulus was thus given to the blood feuds of the Wars of the Roses. Great care was taken by York, however, to ensure the safety of the king; the last thing he wanted was the death of Henry which would only have inaugurated another long minority while bringing upon York the disrepute of killing a king to whom he had protested loyalty.

The fight at St Albans altered the complexion of government. In an age when governments could not be removed by an organized elected parliamentary majority, force of some sort was the only way of dismissing unacceptable ministers if the king could not be prevailed upon to do so. Kneeling before the king, York assured him of his loyalty and of his regret at what had happened. Henry pardoned him and they returned to London. Two days later at Whitsuntide, Henry wore his crown at St Paul's as a demonstration that he still reigned. But for practical purposes York now ruled, albeit very much on the Lords' sufferance, and there were changes in the administration. Bourchier became treasurer in place of the Lancastrian Earl of Wiltshire and Somerset's posts of constable and captain of Calais were taken by York and Warwick respectively. The Yorkist hold of Calais henceforth was to be of cardinal importance in the coming conflict as a redoubt when the tide of conflict flowed against the Yorkist party.

It was clear that there must be a Parliament. York was far from having a majority among the peers and he had to move warily. A change of dynasty was not a practical proposition; too many peers had a vested interest in the Lancastrian establishment, quite apart from questions of loyalty to the dynasty. Parliament met on 9 July at Westminster.[1] Henry had almost certainly never made a complete recovery after his first illness and his condition had evidently been worsened by the shock of his first experience of a battlefield at St Albans and by the neck wound he had sustained there. It

---

[1] *Rot. Parl.* Vol. V, pp. 278–344. For commentaries on this Parliament see especially J. R. Lander, 'Henry VI and the Duke of York's Second Protectorate, 1455 to 1456', *B.J.R.L.*, XLIII (1960) and B. Wolffe, *Henry VI*.

was, however, important for York that the king himself should be present on his throne to preside over the opening of Parliament and great care was taken to get Henry as fit as possible to enable him to do so. Special payments were made to three surgeons for their special care of the king at this time, in addition to which the Dean of Salisbury, who was also a distinguished physician, had been summoned to Windsor in June to deal with Henry's sickness and infirmities. All the evidence suggests that the king's condition was worse than it had been but that he had not returned to his former state of insanity and that, although he was to suffer a serious and incapacitating relapse later in the Parliament, this did not amount to his previous total stupor.[1]

The reluctance of many peers to commit themselves to either side is indicated by the fact that only twenty-seven out of a possible fifty-three temporal lords turned up. On the other hand, there was a larger than usual attendance of spiritual peers so that altogether sixty members of the peerage were present. The Commons, however, were distinctly fewer, numbering only 204 compared with 278 in the previous Parliament. They included more Yorkists and fewer members of the household. There is evidence, including from the Paston letters, the great family correspondence which sheds so much light on English life in the fifteenth century, that the Yorkists exerted pressure to secure the election of their adherents, and to influence elections, notably in Norfolk.[2] Even so there was still a strong Lancastrian element in the Commons during this Parliament.

On the second day of the session, the chancellor-archbishop announced the causes of summons, the first of which was 'to establish an ordinate and a substantial rule for the Kynges honourable Houshold, and to ordeigne where redy paiement shall growe for th'expenses of the same'. Provision should also be made for the needs of Calais and Berwick, the defence of the realm against external enemies and the keeping of the seas. The impoverishing export of gold and silver should be prevented, a decision needed to be taken on how to employ the 13,000 archers granted in the previous Parliament and provision must be made for restoring order in Wales after recent disturbances. But the most important cause of summons in the

---

[1] J. R. Lander, who cites the summonses to the doctors, concludes from them that there was no evidence of a sudden return of Henry's insanity and suggests that the summons to Kremer was no more than could be expected as Henry suffered from a 'chronically poor state of health'. B. Wolffe, op. cit., has, however, shown convincingly that Henry did not suffer from *physical* ill-health and that throughout most of his life enjoyed remarkable stamina. The probability must be that the king's mental condition was significantly worse after St Albans.

[2] K. B. McFarlane, 'Parliament and "Bastard Feudalism"', *T.R.H.S.* 4th ser. XXVI (1944).

chancellor's list was that which came last: 'to sette a parfite love and rest amonge the Lordes of this lande' to bring them together in union and accord for the welfare of king and people. Five committees of Lords and officials were established to consider the household, Calais and Berwick, the safety of the seas, money and bullion and the condition of Wales.[1] The Commons then presented their Speaker, Sir John Wenlock from Bedfordshire, a later Yorkist who was nevertheless at this time still loyal to King Henry and a member of the household.

Parliament then turned to the main business of the first session, clearing York, Neville and Salisbury from any blame for their action at St Albans. It took the form of a statement on behalf of the king putting the blame on the late Duke of Somerset, together with York's old opponent Thomas Thorpe and an unimportant member of the royal household, one William Joseph. The declaration described how the king's enemies had moved him to distrust York, Warwick and Salisbury, estranging them from him, and how, in order that Henry should not 'wondre nor mervaille' at their coming south towards him, they had written a letter from Royston to the archbishop declaring their loyalty, complaining that they had not been called to the council at Westminster because of the jealousy of their enemies and asking the archbishop to acquaint the king with their case. The following day they had written to the king himself, enclosing a copy of the first letter to the archbishop (not knowing, it was said, whether the king had seen it) and declaring that they were his 'true liegemen'. The general purport of both letters was that they would lay down their arms if a representative council was called from which traitors were banished. The statement in Parliament then went on to record that neither letter had reached the king, having been intercepted, with the result that there had come about the encounter at St Albans in which it 'happened' (as it was dishonestly put) that Somerset was slain.

The recital concluded with a declaration of the king's pardon to his cousins and their supporters for 'any thyng that happened' at St Albans, and this was enacted by the advice of Lords and Commons.[2] After this crucial business was over, all the lords who were present in Parliament, led by the two archbishops and the Dukes of York and Buckingham, took their personal oaths of allegiance to the king and it was required that those absent should do likewise. Subsequently, York also had the good name of Duke Humphrey cleared in response to a Commons' petition. The other most significant business of this first session was a radical bill for the resumption

[1] *Rot. Parl.* Vol. V, pp. 279–280.
[2] Ibid., pp. 280–282.

of alienated crown property, which would have hit the Lancastrian interest particularly hard and which was to have a crucial political impact in the second session. Parliament was then prorogued so that the Commons could deal with the harvest and because of plague in London and the suburbs. The next session, said the chancellor, would be concerned with peace.

Just before the new session began in November, a great council meeting on 6 November appointed York as the king's lieutenant to open and preside over Parliament as the king could not be present for certain 'just and reasonable causes'.[1] Once again Henry was unfit to attend Parliament and there is every reason to suppose that his relapse related to his mental condition and was genuine. No sooner was Parliament in session than a campaign began from the Commons for York's appointment as Protector for the restoration of peace in the land.[2] Three times the Commons petitioned to this effect. Their first delegation came to the Lords on 13 November, the day after the session began. It was led by a staunch Yorkist, William Burley, instead of the Speaker, a sign, perhaps, of some disagreement in the Commons on the matter. A protector should be appointed, they said, in case the king 'heraftre (in other words, from now on) myght not entende to the protection and defence of this lande.'[3] In support of their request they cited grievous riots, murders and fights in the feud between the Earl of Devonshire and Lord Bonville in the west country, which had been exceptionally brutal. The followers of Devonshire's son had even seized from his house Nicholas Radford, an old man who was recorder of Exeter, and had murdered him.

Even though York must have encouraged them, the Commons would automatically have been worried by the absence of the king from Parliament and by what they had heard about his health, for it was essential, as they said in their petition, that the people they represented should know whom they could petition for remedies for injuries and wrongs done to them. On the Lords' behalf, the archbishop promised them an answer. Two days later, however, Burley was back, this time accompanied by a 'grete nombre of the Communes, in name of all theire felawes' to ask the same question because they had had no response. This time the reference to the king's condition

---

[1] *Rot. Parl.* Vol. V, p. 284.

[2] Ibid., pp. 284–286.

[3] Ibid., p. 284. Lander, op. cit., deduces from the fact that the Commons did not specifically say that the king was incapable, but only observed that he might become so, that the real reason for the campaign for a protectorate was York's wish to take advantage of the disturbances in the west. York may well have exploited these with a well organized parliamentary campaign, but that seems to be no reason for doubting other evidence that Henry was incapable of functioning as a king.

was even more pointed. If, said Burley, 'the Kyng shuld be vexed and troubled with suche matiers' as the riots, and if the people came to him with their grievances it would be 'overe grevous and tedious to his Highnesse' and therefore there must be some person to whom they could have recourse. The state of the king's mind could hardly have been more clearly indicated. The archbishop promised them a good and comfortable answer, and immediately asked the Lords to provide it. Inasmuch, said the chancellor, as the Commons had twice asked their question, and since it was understood they would not proceed with parliamentary business until they had an answer, he put it to the Lords: 'What is thought to your wysdomes that shuld be done in this behalfe?' The Lords then discussed the matter and appointed York Protector and Defender of the land, which he accepted after making the conventional protestation of his unfitness. But even before they could announce the appointment, Burley and the Commons were back with the same request for the third time, again citing the conditions in the west as a reason a protector 'must be had'. The holy feast of Christmas was approaching, they said, and Parliament should be prorogued so that the riots could be resisted.[1] The same day, the chancellor went himself to announce the royal assent to York's appointment to all the Commons, 'beyng in theire house accustumed'.

York then named his conditions for accepting, which were much the same as before, except that he wanted certain conditions of salary (he complained that he was still owed money from last time) and was also not prepared to accept the appointment simply at the king's pleasure. Instead, he wanted tenure until he was relieved of his post by the king in Parliament. This last was agreed and he was given a guaranteed salary with an advance payment. The terms in which York accepted his appointment clearly illuminate the general understanding that the peers collectively were the ultimate repository of the crown's authority when there was no king who was able to govern. York went out of his way to declare that in taking on the protectorate he did so out of obedience to the king and 'to you as the Parage of this lande, the Lordes Spirituelx and Temporelx ... takyng uppon you th'excercise of his auctorite' for urgent and necessary causes.[2] At the same time, the Lords made it quite clear that there was no general support for a change of dynasty since it was specifically provided that the Prince of Wales should take over the protectorate when he came of age. The peers did not wish York, whom they clearly accepted as protector with some reluctance, to construe his appointment as the thin edge of a wedge of kingship. But the

[1] *Rot. Parl.* Vol. V, pp. 285.
[2] Ibid., p. 286.

arrangement made for eventually passing the protectorate on to a prince who was now only two years old clearly showed that the Lords realized that Henry was suffering from something more than a temporary minor ailment and were calculating that he might never be able to rule again. The terms in which York's appointment as protector was formally made under letters patent are also clear evidence of the peers' recognition that Henry was mentally ill. It was stated that the 'politique governaunce and restfull reule of this his Realme apperteneth (requires) grete diligence and actuell laboure, the which is to his moost noble persone full tedious and grete to suffre and bere'. The government of the realm was therefore handed over to the decisions of the council, of which York was head, but the king was to be informed of the 'direction' that the council was taking in all matters touching his personal honour and welfare.[1] Mentally ill though Henry was, it was clearly not impossible to communicate with him as it had been during the previous Protectorate. On 13 December, Parliament was prorogued until the New Year.

York's power lasted no more than three months. Henry had been at Hertford during his relapse but he now returned to Westminster, presumably because his condition had improved. York's hold on power was shaky and even before Parliament met it was rumoured that he would be dismissed from office. A letter to Sir John Fastolf reporting this rumour stated that York and Warwick came to Parliament with 300 men in coats of mail and that it was said that the duke would have been attacked if he had not done so. The queen, it was added, was an 'intensely active woman' who spared no pains to bring her 'business' to an end that favoured her power.[2] That business was to get rid of York and she probably encouraged the Lords in what followed. On 25 February, Henry came to Parliament and there, in accordance with the agreed procedure, he relieved the duke of the post of protector, instructing him specifically not to intervene with any of his former duties. The explanation of the king's sudden action was that he had been called in by the Lords, most of whom would have been adversely affected by the withdrawal of grants under the proposed drastic Act of Resumption as it then stood before Parliament. (Even the endowment of Eton and King's would have been affected.) With the end of York's protectorate, the act as passed had many exceptions to frustrate the Yorkist intentions.[3] York, however, remained on the council, to the queen's chagrin, and Warwick kept the captaincy of Calais.

---

[1] *Rot. Parl.* Vol. V, pp. 289–290.
[2] *Paston Letters*, ed. J. Gairdner, Vol. I, pp. 337–338.
[3] B. Wolffe, *Henry VI*, pp. 297–301 for a discussion of this measure.

As it happened, this partisan Parliament was the occasion of a petition which stated with great clarity one of the Commons' most important and abiding rights. Thomas Yonge, who had been imprisoned in 1451 for suggesting that York be named as heir presumptive, petitioned for redress on the grounds that sinister reports had been made of what he had said in the Commons' house, notwithstanding that, by the liberties enjoyed by the Commons of the land from time out of mind, 'all such persons as for the time being are assembled in any Parliament for the same Commons ought to have their freedom to speak and say in the house of their assembly what they think convenient or reasonable, without any kind of challenge, charge or punishment therefore to be laid to them in any wise'.[1] The matter was referred to the lords of the council.

IV

With the end of York's second protectorate, the political nation was set firmly on the road to civil war. The fundamental reason was that the king, for all practical purposes, was a puppet and since there was no practical possibility of his removal there was inevitably a desperate struggle to control him. For a time, it is true, he seems to have been involved to a limited extent in the business of government and he exerted his influence, such as it was, to encourage peace through compromise. Thus to the queen's great annoyance, York and Warwick remained on the council and Warwick retained Calais. But Queen Margaret was now the undisputed leader of the court party and she made peace impossible because she acted as a partisan and dragged Henry after her.

Medieval government hung on the authority of the king and since Henry VI was personally non-functioning there had long been a political vacuum which was filled by the Lancastrian court party, successively led in the past by Cardinal Beaufort, Suffolk and Somerset. This party, with its network of connected magnates, gentry, officials and maintained supporters, was now controlled by the queen. By the nature of any party, some people are in it and some are excluded from it. The party which came to be known as Yorkist was that of the excluded and when the government's policies failed there was no way in which the incumbents of office could be removed by political

---

[1] *Rot. Parl.* Vol. V, p. 337 (modern English version, used here, *E.H.D.*, Vol. IV, pp. 472–473).

procedures if the king, as was the case, was incapable of taking action. Twice, therefore, York had tried to bring about change by a show of force, and once by using it. On returning from Ireland in 1450, he had led his retinue to London, demanded a place on the council and had attacked Somerset in the ensuing Parliament. The second attempt had been in 1452 when he published a detailed manifesto attacking Somerset's control of the king and the misgovernment of the country, only to be tricked into disbanding his forces at Dartford. Finally, blood was shed at St Albans. On all these occasions York appealed to a wider public than the connections of friendly magnates. His base in the nobility was narrow but the extent to which he represented the widespread popular grievances caused by bad government was shown by the strong support he had in the prosperous south and especially in London, whose citizens in the end were to be decisive in putting his dynasty on the throne. In each of his attempts to secure power York promised better government and 'restful rule'.

There was no single cause of the Wars of the Roses but several, among which one had primacy. There was first the political and social breakdown resulting from the rivalry of magnates, gentry and their followers, and the abuse of patronage and maintenance. One historian, producing a mass of evidence to show how deeply this disorder had eroded political cohesion, has described the Wars of the Roses as 'an escalation of private feuds', which in the immediate sense it was.[1] There was also the humiliating failure of the government's policy in France which damaged national morale and spread political grievances throughout the English realm. But central to everything else was the character and inadequacy of the king which was responsible both for disaster abroad and the failure to check anarchy at home. A clear-minded and resolute king pursuing more rational policies could almost certainly have avoided the worst of the French collapse, either by mounting a more consistent effort in pursuit of feasible objectives or by withdrawing before there had been so much waste of national spirit and money. It is even conceivable that Normandy could have been retained and there had certainly been a good chance of keeping Gascony where the ancient English tie commanded much loyalty. But most important of all, a strong and functioning king could have checked the aristocratic feuding at home before it caused disaster. Neither quarrels between noblemen nor maintenance were new but they had got much worse because of weak government. It is true that if the bitter conflicts among the nobility had been

---

[1] R. L. Storey, *The End of the House of Lancaster*, p. 27, who observes that if Henry VI had been of the same calibre as his father 'the drift to anarchy would have been checked'. For accounts of the Wars of the Roses see under that title studies by C. Ross, J. R. Lander, A. Goodman and especially K. B. McFarlane in *Proc. Brit. Acad.* 50 (1964).

checked, there was always the risk of a return to the old conflict between the king and a united baronage. But a wise king could have found solutions for that too; after all even Richard II had almost succeeded in bringing the baronage into control and had only failed by over-reaching himself.

Beneath the difficulties caused by the king's inadequacy there also lurked the problem of the succession. That too would not have existed had Henry been an effective ruler. The old notion that the Wars of the Roses were the culmination of a long dynastic struggle in which the House of York sought to unseat the House of Lancaster in revenge for the usurpation of 1399 has long been discredited. Yet, long before York dared to put up a claim to the throne, the question of the succession was in men's minds simply because Henry was both weak and for so long childless. If, as had seemed likely, he had no heir, the successor would either be York or Somerset, and neither would have accepted the claim of the other without resistance. There was, therefore, a sense in which the dilemma did arise from the deposition of Richard II, even if not in the sense of cosmic retribution suggested by Shakespeare.

After St Albans, there was some attempt by such moderates as the Duke of Buckingham and Archbishop Bourchier to restore concord by holding the balance between the parties. But the land was not at peace and there were severe disturbances in the north and west of England and especially on the Welsh border where the Lancastrian Earl of Richmond fought with Yorkists led by Sir William Herbert. The queen's power was increasing but knowing that London supported the Duke of York she left for the Lancastrian Midlands in the summer of 1456 where Henry soon joined her. There she moved between Lancastrian castles, building up her party's strength, and in the autumn the court was established in Coventry. The queen also filled the ministry with her adherents. One of the officials of her own court, Laurence Booth, became keeper of the privy seal, which gave her power to issue instructions. In October 1458, the moderate chancellor and treasurer, Archbishop Bourchier and Viscount Bourchier were both replaced. William Wayneflete, Bishop of Winchester, became the new chancellor. The Earl of Shrewsbury was now treasurer until a more extreme Lancastrian, the Earl of Wiltshire took his place two years later. The court concentrated on building up its strength for the coming struggle and went on to develop connections with the sheriffs of at least sixteen counties who took wages from the royal household in return for which the household received crown revenues from their shires direct, by-passing the exchequer with the treasurer's agreement.[1] By such means the need for a Parliament

[1] E. F. Jacob, *The Fifteenth Century*, pp. 513–514.

was avoided. But the land remained disturbed and French raids harassed the south coast, doing so much harm that in the autumn of 1457 there was some kind of temporary reconciliation between the rival parties. As a result Warwick was made admiral to guard the seas, a significant addition to the power he already had as captain of Calais, which he ruled like a personal fief. In January 1458, a final effort for peace was made by the moderates with Henry's encouragement, and a great council assembled in London. The huge size of the magnates' retinues indicated the emptiness of what followed. Eventually the mediation of the chancellor and Archbishop Bourchier produced a supposed settlement by which York, Salisbury and Warwick were to establish a chantry at St Albans for the celebration of masses for the souls of those killed there. They were also to pay compensation to the families of the slain but since this was to be done by the renunciation of crown debts owing to them it was no financial hardship. Finally, the accord was celebrated by what was called a Loveday when the king and queen and the rivals, York, Salisbury and Warwick, and the new young Earls of Somerset and Northumberland, ardent Lancastrians brooding on revenging their slain fathers, went arm-in-arm to St Paul's Cathedral.

It was all to no purpose. In November Warwick, who was in trouble with the court for practising piracy in the Channel as a way of supporting his Calais garrison, was attacked in a brawl at Westminster which started between one of his servants and one from the royal household. He only narrowly escaped from what he saw as a plot to murder him, and to avoid arrest fled to Calais. In the following April of 1459 Queen Margaret and her party began to call up their followers and order arms, apparently encouraged by the fact that such moderates as Buckingham were now at odds with Warwick because of his aggressive acts. In June there was a great council of Lancastrian partisans from which York, Salisbury and their friends were excluded. This prompted York to summon a rival meeting at his castle of Ludlow. Warwick was sent for and returned with his sons and retainers in September. In the same month Salisbury, leading a force to join his friends at Ludlow, was intercepted at Blore Heath and in the encounter which opened the principal phase of the civil war the Yorkists won, and subsequently York published a manifesto addressed formally to the king but actually to the political nation justifying his actions. But it was a shortlived triumph. In October the Lancastrians marched on Ludlow, bringing the king with them. The Yorkists included no peers of importance outside the York-Neville family group, and York's son and heir Edward of March, now aged 17. The king on the other hand was supported by a large number of peers and their followers. The Yorkists were overcome at

Ludford Bridge and their leaders forced to flee. It was said that the Lancastrian victory hinged on the desertion of Warwick's men from Calais who were unwilling to fight when they learned that King Henry was on the opposite side, but it is as likely that the reason was the larger Lancastrian forces. York fled to Ireland where he had wholehearted support, and both the Nevilles accompanied by Edward of March took refuge in Calais.

Queen Margaret celebrated her victory by summoning to Coventry the most systematically contrived partisan Parliament in English history save that of the Rump in 1649.[1] The Parliament in which the Duke of York made his claim to the throne in 1460 was to describe the Coventry Parliament as having been designed solely for the destruction of certain great lords of the king's blood and to assert that a great part of the elected knights of the shires and many of the citizens and burgesses were named, returned and accepted 'som of theym without dieu and free election, and som of theym withoute any election'.[2] That was not a lampoon by political opponents but the simple truth. The Lancastrian leaders had simply nominated those knights of the shire who were to be returned and instructed the sheriffs accordingly. Virtually the sole business of what became known as the Parliament of Devils was the attainder of York and his friends, twenty-seven of them in all, and the history of York's alleged misdeeds, from his alleged involvement in Cade's rebellion to the breach of his oath and his recent battles with the king, was recited. Estates were confiscated and heirs disinherited. Attainder involved not only the death of an individual but the legal extinction of a family and the Parliament of Coventry made unprecedented and totally ruthless use of a procedure which was to be a major characteristic of the Parliaments between 1459 and the end of the reign of Henry VI. Under Edward IV and Henry VII attainders and the reversal of attainders were to form the largest group of parliamentary acts. It was a simple procedure; all that was required was the reading of a bill of attainder in the Parliament chamber, the silent acquiescence of the Commons and the royal assent.[3] There was no judicial procedure as there was in impeachment and men could be condemned for any of their past actions that were construed as treason by their enemies, if those enemies (formally led by the king) controlled Parliament. It was retroactive legislation for the destruction of political opponents. In this instance a few who had submitted had their lives spared but forfeited their lands and the

---

[1] *Rot. Parl.* Vol. V, pp. 345–372.
[2] Ibid., p. 374.
[3] For a discussion of the political significance of attainder and its reversal at this period see J. R. Lander, 'Attainder and Forfeiture, 1453–1509' *Hist. J.* (1961), pp. 119–151 and reprinted in Fryde and Miller, op. cit., Vol. II.

king reserved his prerogative of mercy; it has to be said for Henry that he was genuinely reluctant to impose the barbaric penalties inflicted for treason. After the acts of attainder, oaths of loyalty were sworn to Henry VI and Edward, Prince of Wales, but nothing else of substance occurred at Coventry. Yet it is worth noting the terms of one petition which even in this politically corrupt Parliament described the nature of maintenance with startling candour and clarity, complaining that 'universally' through the realm, the people suffered from robberies, rapes, extortions, riots and wrongful imprisonments. It recorded that in breaking the law the culprits were 'favoured and assisted with persons of grete myght, havyng towardes theym of their lyverey', and that those who suffered, even though they were people of good repute, dared not complain for fear of their lives.[1]

The possession of Calais saved the Yorkists and it was impossible to drive them from it. At home, the majority of Lords still adhered to the king but there was a good deal of Yorkist popular feeling and there was persecution on that account. In the summer of 1460, York published a detailed manifesto to the archbishop and the commons of the land. He attacked the abuses of purveyance which arose from the king's poverty, the waste of royal revenue granted to 'destroyers of the land' which prevented the king from living of his own and obliged him to impose heavy taxation, and the perversion of justice. Among many more complaints was one against the conscription of men from every habitation for the defence of the Lancastrian government. Words were immediately followed by action when in June Salisbury, Warwick and Edward of March landed in Kent from Calais, accompanied by a papal legate. They were joined by Archbishop Bourchier and a large number of supporters. After some hesitation the Londoners admitted them, and a number of prominent Lancastrians took refuge in the Tower. Warwick then went with a force to seek the king, who had gone to Northampton where, after abortive negotiations, there was a short battle in which the Lancastrians were defeated, the Yorkists being much assisted by the treachery of Lord Grey of Ruthin who came over to them. The Lancastrians suffered heavy losses, including the deaths of the Duke of Buckingham, the Earl of Shrewsbury and Viscount Beaumont, who were deliberately killed outside the king's tent. It was policy in this battle, as in others during the civil war, that nobles and gentry should be slain but the common soldiers should generally be spared. Henry himself was captured, assured by Warwick of the Yorkists' loyalty and taken to London. The Tower was then captured and although Lords Scales and Hungerford, who had been besieged therein, were freed

[1] *Rot. Parl.* Vol. V, p. 367.

some more minor persons were condemned to death for treason. (Lord Scales, however, was promptly murdered by some Londoners.)

There was now a clean sweep of the Lancastrian party from both the government and the household, from the top to the lower levels. Warwick's brother, George Neville, Bishop of Exeter, became chancellor and Viscount Bourchier was once more treasurer. The new keeper of the privy seal was Robert Stillington, Archdeacon of Wells, a later chancellor who played a curious part in Richard III's usurpation. Though the Yorkist magnates were numerically a small party they dominated the council and faced no opposition from Henry who seems to have been wholly passive; indeed, he presented so little problem that he was even allowed to go on a pilgrimage to Canterbury. Once the political establishment had been changed, the time had come to summon what was to be the last Parliament of the reign. The Yorkists had inevitably done their best to influence elections though not, it seems, so systematically as the Lancastrians had done at Coventry. As for the peers, the writs sent were not so selectively inclined towards York as those of Coventry had been Lancastrian. Almost all the peers called to Coventry (apart from the Lancastrians killed at Northampton) were summoned but with the addition of York and his friends. On the other hand such committed Lancastrians as Somerset, Exeter and Northumberland stayed away. The balance of opinion among the peers present was middle-of-the-road but anxious to accommodate the Duke of York.

It met at Westminster on 7 October.[1] Three days later York arrived from Ireland accompanied by about 300 armed men and determined at last to claim the crown. He came, according to the abbot of St Albans, who was a probable eyewitness of the dramatic scene, with horns and trumpets, men-at-arms and many servants. When he arrived at the palace the duke marched straight through Westminster Hall and went on to enter the Parliament chamber. He then moved forward to the throne and laid his hand on the cushion 'like a man about to take possession of his right, and kept his hand there for a short while. At last, drawing it back, he turned his face towards the people, and standing still under the cloth of state, he looked attentively at the gazing assembly.' Then Archbishop Bourchier of Canterbury approached him with a greeting and asked the duke whether he wanted to come and see the king.

It was a crushing question, showing not only that the peers knew why York had come but also that they disapproved of it and still regarded Henry as their king. The duke, according to the abbot's account, 'seemed irritated, and replied curtly: "I know of no one in the realm for whom it would not be

[1] *Rot. Parl.* Vol. V, pp. 373-388.

more fitting that he should come to see me rather than that I should go to visit him." ' This startling assertion caused the archbishop to retire in haste to the king. The account then states that Richard went to the principal chamber in the palace, which was reserved for the king, broke open the locks and stayed there 'in the manner of a king'.[1] Henry himself was occupying the queen's apartments at the time.

York's irritation with the archbishop was understandable since it was immediately obvious that the peers generally, even those tending to the duke's side, were, as contemporaries recorded, dismayed by his action. The Nevilles seem to have been taken by surprise and it is very likely that Warwick's declaration of loyalty to Henry VI at Northampton had been made in good faith. The invasion from Calais had not been undertaken with the intention of changing the dynasty but with securing the control of the puppet king from Queen Margaret and her party. The Nevilles had originally associated themselves with York not out of reverence for his legitimatist claim to the throne but as an extension of their feud with the Percys and whatever the duke's private ambitions, he had hitherto been in no doubt about the danger of demanding a change of dynasty. He now judged that circumstances had changed but underestimated the reluctance of the majority of peers, including his supporters, to repudiate sixty years of allegiance to the Lancastrian dynasty and successive oaths of loyalty to a king who was not personally their opponent and who could as well be controlled by them as by Queen Margaret – if they could only keep hold of him. Besides, there were ties of material interest with the existing dynasty. The Nevilles themselves did not approve of York's action and it was quickly clear to him that he could not simply take the crown by force but must make and justify his case in Parliament.

Nine days into the Parliament (which had already reversed the attainders of Coventry) York's counsel brought in a 'wryting' setting out the genealogical basis for the duke's claim as being descended, albeit through a female line, from Lionel, third son of Edward III, whereas Henry VI was descended from Edward's fourth son, John of Gaunt.[2] Asked by the chancellor whether they wished the duke's case to be read, the Lords agreed that it should be, inasmuch as every person, high or low, who sued in the high court of Parliament must, of right, be heard. It was not exactly an enthusiastic response, besides which the Lords added that, after it had been

---

[1] *Registrum Abbatiae Johannis Whethamstede*, ed. H. T. Riley (Rolls Series, 1872), Vol. I, pp. 376–377. (A short extract in English is in *E.H.D.* Vol. IV. pp. 283–284.)

[2] For York's case, the reference to the justices and law officers, the Lords' initial opinions, York's reply to the Lords and the final agreement, see *Rot. Parl.* Vol. V, pp. 375–380.

read, it should not be answered except with the king's commandment. Then, when pressed by York for an answer, the Lords decided that it was not for any of the king's subjects even to enter into discussion about the case without his high commandment. Accordingly, they decided all to go to the king and present the matter to him. (It is impossible to think of any other king with whom the Lords could safely have discussed theoretically his right to the crown.) Henry's response was to instruct the Lords to go and find anything that could be laid against the duke's claim. In turn they asked him to recall what he could of the matter as one who had read divers writings and chronicles.

The Lords then summoned the justices to the Parliament chamber, gave them York's submission and asked their opinion. Several days later the judges replied that their function was to determine matters of law between party and party and that it was not customary to call the judges to give counsel in such cases. This, they said, was a question between the king and the duke. Besides, it was a matter so high, touching the king's high estate, that it was above the law and it was past their learning to meddle with it. It was therefore the business of the Lords of the king's blood and the peerage of the land to deal with it. The same question was then put to the law officers who gave a similar answer, on which the Lords told them that they could not be excused as they were the king's particular counsellors 'and therefore had their fees and wages'. But the law officers remained adamant and the Lords were driven back to produce their own arguments against York's claim after they had debated the matter among themselves in private.

The first and foremost objection advanced by the peers was that they and York had taken great oaths to Henry VI. As recently as the Coventry Parliament most of them had sworn allegiance to Henry, and also to protect the queen and to accept Prince Edward as heir. They also spoke of 'grete and notable' acts of Parliament which could be laid against York's case, acts which had 'moche more auctorite than any Cronycle' and which had the authority to defeat any (other) manner of title. Since the Lords also made a specific reference to entails of the crown to the male line, this looks very much like an acknowledgement of a Lancastrian title to the throne by acts of Parliament. Yet the words have a certain ambiguity and it is very far from certain that the Lords' considered opinion was that strict inheritance by birthright, the only argument on which York based his claim, could be over-ridden by acts of Parliament. Indeed, their eventual decision in favour of York was to suggest that they held the contrary opinion. The Lords also thought that York's claim was undermined by the fact that hitherto he had only borne the arms of his father and not those of his forbear Edward III's son Lionel, the forbear through whom he based his claim to the crown. For good measure, they even threw in Henry IV's (spurious) claim to have a prior descent from Henry III.

York had no great difficulty in rebutting most of these arguments. He asserted that their oaths were invalid because every man (under pain of everlasting damnation) was bound by God to uphold truth and therefore that since his own title was undoubtedly true, the Lords' duty was to uphold him in it. He also denied, quite accurately, that there were any statutes entailing the crown apart from the one which had entailed it to Henry IV's sons, which, he pointed out, would not have been necessary if Henry had been king by right. As for his own failure to bear Lionel's arms, he said he could rightfully have borne them, and those of the English king, and had abstained for well-known reasons. But, he added 'though right for a tyme rest and bee put to silence, yit it roteth not ner shall not perish'. It was a strong case and the Lords came to the conclusion that York's title 'can not be defeted'.[1] Many of them must have been influenced in that direction by the prospect of either a conflict-ridden continuance of Henry's incompetent reign or a minority dominated by Queen Margaret. Yet they were still hesitant to depose Henry and so, to avoid trouble, they devised a compromise 'to save the Kyngs honour and astate, and to apease the seid Duc, yf he wuld'. Henry was to keep the crown for his life but York and his heirs would succeed him. When this had been agreed, the Lords decided to go to tell the king in his room. As they left the Parliament chamber, the chancellor, George Neville, warily asked the Lords whether since he personally was to put the matter to the king, they would stand by him, however the king took the matter, to which they 'answered and seid yee'.

They need not have worried about Henry's reaction. No king ever went more quietly. Inspired by the Holy Ghost and to avoid the effusion of Christian blood, as the official record puts it, the king accepted the compromise and a concord was made between himself and the duke. York agreed that Henry should be named, taken and reputed king for his life, as he had been reputed to be hitherto, and promised to honour him as such. The duke and his sons also swore never to do anything to 'abridge' the king's natural life or in any way to act against him. York was then given the principality of Wales for life with most of its revenues, half of which was to go to his two sons, and all royal officials were sworn under pain of treason to obey him as they would the king. The statute entailing the crown on Henry IV's male heirs was repealed. In none of this great aristocratic business do the Commons seem to have had the slightest part.

---

[1] York's case is discussed by S. B. Chrimes, *English Constitutional Ideas in the Fifteenth Century*, pp. 26–32.

It was, of course, a settlement that could not possibly last. Queen Margaret would never give up the claim of her young son and York could not abandon a right that had been formally 'auctorized by . . . Parlement'.[1] On 1 December, Parliament was prorogued (a second session of no significance was to meet for a few days at the end of the following January) so that York could go north to put down the Lancastrian magnates concentrated there. But during the Christmas holiday, after he was foolish enough to come out of his castle at Sandal to confront a force of the enemy which he regarded as breaking the seasonal truce, he was defeated and killed in an encounter at Wakefield Bridge with a much larger force led by Somerset, Exeter, Northumberland and other Lancastrian lords. York's second son Edmund was also slain and Salisbury was taken alive and beheaded; York's head, decked with a paper crown, was placed on the city gate of York. The moment had come for Queen Margaret to attack. After her husband's capture at Northampton she had gone at first to north Wales, then to the north of England and finally to Scotland where she negotiated for an alliance with the Scottish king. She now advanced to the south with an army of Lancastrians, wild northerners and Scotsmen spreading terror as they went on their plundering way down the great north road. In a second battle of St Albans on 17 February, the Lancastrians defeated Warwick and captured the hapless king. Warwick escaped to the Welsh border to join Edward of March. In the meantime, at Mortimer's Cross on the Welsh border, Edward had defeated the forces of the Earls of Pembroke and Wiltshire. They both escaped, though Owen Tudor, who was Queen Catherine's second husband, the Earl of Pembroke's father and the grandfather of Henry VII, was taken and beheaded. The initiative, however, now seemed to be with the queen who advanced on London. But the Londoners were reluctant to admit her and her wild forces. She hesitated and then withdrew to the north, taking King Henry with her.

The Londoners had no such reluctance to admit Edward of March who had inherited his father's claim to the throne and there was no future for Warwick and the Yorkists in continuing to recognize Henry VI now that he was again in the queen's hands. The situation was very different from that after the first battle of St Albans when nobody dared question Henry VI's title. This time, Parliament had already pronounced against its legitimacy and in favour of York's. Besides, though Henry had been passive, his side of the bargain could be regarded as broken by the queen's actions, thus releasing the Yorkists from their commitment to let him wear the crown for life. They must now have their own king. After a rally of Londoners had

[1] *Rot. Parl.* Vol. V, p. 378.

demonstrated willingness to accept Edward as king, his proclamation was approved by a council meeting attended by the Duke of Norfolk, Warwick, the chancellor and other Yorkists. Edward then went in solemn procession from St Paul's to Westminster. There he wore the royal robes, sat upon the coronation chair and received the regalia. But the coronation must wait until his kingship was consolidated by the defeat of Queen Margaret.

Financed by the Londoners and much borrowing, Edward set off after her, recruiting as he went. On 29 March, 1461, at Towton near York, the final and biggest battle of this phase of the civil war was fought in a fierce snowstorm which helped Edward by blowing against the Lancastrians. The greater part of the baronage was on the battlefield, most of them on the Lancastrian side. The outcome was a victory for the Yorkists. Many Lancastrian peers, chief among them the Earl of Northumberland, were slain and the Earls of Wiltshire and Devon were captured and beheaded. The old king, Queen Margaret and their son Prince Edward fled to Scotland. The new king went to his coronation and his first Parliament. For the first time in thirty-nine years England had a king capable of ruling.

CHAPTER 10

———— * ————

Edward IV: The King's Independence

I

EDWARD IV was the first English king since the beginning of Parliaments who seriously attempted to do what the Commons had persistently asked of his predecessors; namely, to 'live of his own' financial resources without regularly asking his subjects for taxation. This was to be his openly and proudly declared aim and it had the support of the Commons.[1] They had repeatedly tried, with some very limited success, to force the Lancastrian kings to take back crown lands and revenues which had been alienated as gifts to friends of the court. They believed that if the king thus maximized his own resources these would be enough to pay for much of the ordinary business of the court and government, freeing the Commons and those they represented from the need to find much parliamentary taxation. Edward was to adopt the practice of 'resuming' royal grants with enthusiasm and by combining it with efficient financial organization and non-parliamentary revenue-raising devices, he managed to call far fewer Parliaments than had been customary, especially in the latter part of his reign. The same policy was to be pursued even more successfully by Henry VII and if it had been sustained thereafter the course of subsequent English parliamentary history might have been very different. Indeed, it is not altogether inconceivable that Parliament might have fallen into disuse as the assembly of the States General did in France, even if the different historical tradition of England makes this seem unlikely. The reality was that little though the Commons liked granting taxation, it was the source of their own power and when the king ceased to ask them for

[1] See below, p. 595.

money their own influence over the king's politics diminished. No such theoretical forebodings, however, bothered the Commons during the closing decades of the fifteenth century. They were more than content with the new government compared with the old, grateful for the gradually emerging sense of order under a king who knew his own mind, and pleased to be governed by a ruler who favoured the merchant interest.

Although he was a successful and vigorous leader in war, Edward IV was by disposition (other things being equal) more inclined to peace than to wasteful military adventure. He had come to power by faction but he ruled as a unifier, hard though that proved to be in the first years of the reign. Edward was a man of considerable personal presence and charm. He knew how to handle the Commons and his is the first voice of an English king which authentically comes down to us through the speeches which he made in Parliament in a manner which very clearly reflects his character. In previous reigns only a few impersonal sentences, sometimes in indirect speech and usually in Norman French or Latin, had been officially recorded as from the king's own mouth, Henry IV's claim to the throne, spoken in English, being the most notable exception.[1] Political utterances were normally made by the chancellor and other ministers on the king's behalf. Edward, however, is recorded on several occasions as speaking easily and eloquently in the national tongue, combining regality with familiarity and authority with persuasiveness. After years of watching a mentally ill king being manipulated by others the Lords and Commons could not fail to be impressed.

Edward was not quite twenty years old when he met his first Parliament. He had spent some weeks receiving the submission of towns and localities in the north, though when he eventually turned south the Lancastrians, operating from their Scottish base and Northumbrian castles, still remained a serious threat. On 28 June Edward was crowned at Westminster. It was initially intended that Parliament should meet in July but because of conflict on the northern border and the Welsh marches it was not until 4 November, 1461 that it assembled at Westminster.[2] Of the peerage as it stood at the beginning of the reign only forty-five Lords were summoned compared with fifty-six in 1453, the year of the last more or less normal Parliament. The higher ranks of the peerage were particularly depleted; the peers originally summoned included only one duke, Norfolk, who died just before Parliament assembled and four earls, Warwick, Oxford, Arundel and Westmorland. Before Parliament met, however, the number of peers of all

---

[1] Henry IV's challenge to the throne, however, was not delivered to a true Parliament.
[2] *Rot. Parl.* Vol. V, pp. 461–495.

ranks was increased with Yorkist supporters. At his coronation, Edward had made his brothers, George and Richard, Dukes of Clarence and Gloucester respectively. The number of earls was also increased. Viscount Bourchier became Earl of Essex and Lord Fauconberg, one of the Nevilles, became Earl of Kent. In addition John Tiptoft, Earl of Worcester, returned home from Italy a few weeks before the Parliament. He was a man of scholarly tastes and merciless disposition who, as constable of England, was to be guilty of inflicting arbitrary and, even by the standards of the time, obscenely cruel punishment. Finally, writs were sent summoning to Parliament eight new Yorkist barons with William, Lord Hastings at their head. Hastings was a former knight retainer of Richard of York and was to become Edward IV's close friend and councillor. The Yorkists numerically dominated the House of Lords in this Parliament though a number of Lancastrian sympathizers was present. The Dukes of Somerset and Exeter, the Earl of Pembroke and other active Lancastrians were, of course, absent and fighting in Queen Margaret's cause. The Commons were also predominantly Yorkist sympathizers, not only because pressure was exerted by local magnates to ensure that this was so but also because of the contingent of members of the royal household which had been a rising component of their membership from the latter part of Henry VI's reign.[1]

The Parliament was opened by the chancellor, Bishop Neville, with a sermon on the text 'Amend your ways and your doings' (Jeremiah VII, 3) and Sir James Strangeways, a close connection of the Neville family, was chosen as Speaker. Immediately afterwards, Strangeways delivered a notably long speech on behalf of the Commons in which he thanked God for Edward's victories and the king for his 'prowesse and corage' in the redemption of the realm. Summarizing recent events, Strangeways spoke of the lamentable death of Edward's father York, 'in right kyng', and of Edward's courage in securing victory over the Earls of Pembroke and Wiltshire, even 'though all the sorowe and lamentacion for the deth of the seid noble and famous Prynce was nat a litle in your noble and naturall remembraunce'. He recalled the atrocities inflicted by the armies of the 'late called Quene of Englond' as they came south, how Edward had put aside all weariness and had come to succour London, and his great victory at Towton. The Speaker then complimented the king on his princely and knightly courage, on 'the beaute of personage that it hath pleased Almyghty God to send you' and on his wisdom. Who can doubt that this was not idle flattery but a manifestation of sincere pleasure at having a vigorous king who looked the part in place of the vague and distracted Henry VI? Noting

[1] J. S. Roskell, *The Commons in the Parliament of 1422*, p. 135.

that Edward had been called by God to reign by virtue of his 'naturall birth', the Speaker ended by beseeching him to take into his trust and favour people of experience who had supported his 'recovery' of the crown, and other trustworthy people (there was here a flickering reminder of the Commons' past interest in the king's councillors) and to put down all offenders guilty of extortion, murder, rape, rioting, violence and other offences.

The essential purposes of this Parliament were to recognize that Edward was king by right of inheritance (not by parliamentary decree), to declare once more that the Lancastrian dynasty had been a usurpation and to annul the compromise which had allowed Henry VI to retain the crown for life. A petition was immediately presented in the name of the Commons for the declaration of these things, but it was a bill clearly promoted by the government.[1] It began, in the manner of such bills, 'Forsomoch . . .' and included such phrases as 'Be it declared and juged . . .' The more normal way of introducing bills that were spontaneously produced in the lower house was with the words 'Prayen the Commons', though even this formula sometimes introduced Commons bills prompted by the government. The bill again rehearsed the descent of the crown to Edward by right of inheritance and cited the capture, deposition and murder of Richard II, and the ousting of the rightful line, as the causes of the 'persecution, punicion and tribulation' which England had since suffered, 'wherof the lyke hath not been seen or herde in any other Cristen Reame'. Thus the rolls of Parliament proclaimed the theme of Shakespeare's history, for which there is rather more to be said than is commonly allowed, the Lancastrian usurpation having led to the adventure in France which for several reasons was the largest single cause of the troubles that had smitten the kingdom.

The Commons then went on to declare that, having themselves sufficient knowledge of the usurpation, and knowing without any doubt Edward's right by the laws of God and nature, they took him as their rightful king and petitioned for his title to 'be declared, taken, accepted and reputed, true and rightwise'. The previous Parliament's recognition of Richard of York's claim was recalled and the compact he had made allowing Henry VI to keep the crown for life for the sake of the peace of the realm was declared to have been broken and nullified by Henry through the murder of Richard of York, who had been protected by the law of treason. Edward was therefore declared to be discharged from the compact. Henry, however, was not deposed since he was reckoned never to have been king, besides which the entire procedure was designed to establish that Edward IV did not owe his

[1] *Rot. Parl.* Vol. V, pp. 463-467.

crown to Parliament's decision. The petition further asked that gifts of castles, lands, possessions, rents or services by the Lancastrians should be invalidated and resumed by the crown. In enacting the bill, however, the king did so 'with certeyn moderacions, provisions and exceptions, by his Highnes theruppon made'. There is no reason to doubt that Edward's own hand was to be seen in this wary conciliation. By preserving the individual rights of a large number of people who had obtained them from the Lancastrians he sought to avoid making enemies. The modifying formula used was that the act of resumption should 'extend not nor in any wise be prejudiciall unto' all the particular persons named.[1]

The Parliament then went on to confirm the reversal of the attainders inflicted on the Yorkists at Coventry and to attaint for treason the Lancastrians who had resisted the Yorkist claim. Once again it was done by an officially initiated bill presented by the Commons. Bills of attainder against the late King Henry, Queen Margaret and other Lancastrians were enacted and the Duchy of Lancaster was permanently attached to the crown, as it has remained ever since.[2] Among those attainted were the new king's great enemies in the high nobility, including the Dukes of Somerset and Exeter, as well as very many less elevated men. One of these was the Lancastrian chief justice, Sir John Fortescue, who was in exile with Queen Margaret, still struggling in the old cause, and who has bequeathed us his invaluable concept of the proper constitution of England in his time. Another was John Morton, the future Archbishop of Canterbury and Henry VII's servant. Altogether about 113 persons were attainted and until comparatively recently historians had tended to interpret what was done as sweeping and vindictive. In fact, there was no wholesale elimination of opponents; the new king, not yet securely established, was more concerned to win over as many of his former opponents as possible rather than to take revenge. Several aristocratic Lancastrians who were uninvolved in the recent fighting were not attainted (among them the Earls of Westmorland and Oxford) and even some who had fought for Henry VI (Lord Rivers and Lord Scales, for instance) were allowed to come to Parliament. Others were pardoned later on, even after they had again changed sides. During the reign a large number of attainders was reversed, though not always immediately, so that even when the head of a family was attainted on death in battle or by execution, the family was not permanently ruined. Among those to be forgiven in the later part of the reign were both Fortescue who

---

[1] *Rot. Parl.* Vol. V, pp. 467–475.
[2] Ibid., pp. 476–483.

(renouncing his defence of the Lancastrian claim) became a councillor, and John Morton who became Edward's Master of the Rolls.[1]

As well as acting firmly to declare the new king's right, it was also essential, if social disintegration was to be avoided, for Parliament to validate the judicial acts of the Lancastrians 'late Kings of England successively in Deed and not of Right' which was done for the 'eschewing of Ambiguities, Doubts and Diversities of opinions which might arise'. The same applied to Lancastrian creations of nobility (except for rebels) and grants to towns, corporate bodies and spiritual bodies and so on.[2] Laws passed in Parliament during the Lancastrian period were not specifically covered because of the complexity in doing so but clearly it was tacitly intended that they should stand. Such was the intention to uproot Lancastrian politics, however, that the Parliament even annulled the sentence on the king's grandfather, Richard of Cambridge, who had been executed for plotting against Henry V, and Henry IV's attainders of the Earl of Shrewsbury and Lord Despenser. Yet the Parliament was not too busy with politics to be without time for ordinary matters. One such instance was a dispute between Bishop William Wayneflete of Winchester and his tenants of the manor of East Meon who claimed to be free of work and other dues on the grounds that they were freeholders not copyholders. This case was brought to Parliament at the suggestion of Edward himself when the plaintiffs approached him on one of his first royal progresses. The Lords, however, having heard a report from a committee appointed to look into the case, found for the bishop though the tenants still continued their struggle.

The Parliament was prorogued on 21 December. This was its virtual end since when it reassembled in the following May it was immediately dissolved. No money had been asked for and the tone of the government had been distinctly conciliatory. For the most part the only persons to suffer by attainder were those who had died as rebels or were still in rebellion. Just before prorogation Edward personally addressed the Commons in terms characteristic of his good sense of public relations. It was the first surviving utterance by a king that can reasonably be described as a 'king's speech' in Parliament, and the record in the rolls is clearly the transcript of a living voice and not simply a copy of a drafted speech or a clerk's paraphrase. The parliamentary roll for 1461 records an address by the king directed to the Speaker by name. In its directness it seems to anticipate the personal style of Queen Elizabeth I.

[1] J. R. Lander, 'Attainder and Forfeiture, 1453–1509', *Historical Journal*, IV (1961); republished in Fryde and Miller, Vol. II, especially pp. 97–102.
[2] *Stat. R.* Vol. II, p. 380ff., 1 Edw. IV c. I.; *Rot. Parl.* Vol. V, pp. 489–493.

'James Strangeways, and ye that be comyn for the Common of this my Lond, for the true hertes and tender considerations that ye have had to my right and title, that Y, and my Auncestres, have had unto the Coroune of this Reame, the which from us have been longe tyme witholde; and nowe, thanked be Almighty God, of whos grace groweth all Victory, by youre true hertes and grete assistens, Y am restored unto that that is my right and title; wherfore Y thanke you as hertely as Y can.' Edward then expressed his gratitude to them for remembering the cruel death of his father and brother, promised to be as good a sovereign as any of his predecessors, and thanked them for their love and assistance. He finished by saying: 'and yf Y had eny better good to reward you withall then my body, ye shuld have it, the which shall alwey be redy for youre defence, never sparyng nor lettyng for noo jepardie; praying you all of youre herty assistens and good contynuance as Y shall be unto you youre veray rightwisse and lovyng Liege Lord.'[1]

It so happens that there has also survived from this Parliament a fragment of the earliest journal of the Lords' proceedings of whose existence we are aware. The regular Lords' Journals do not begin until 1510; the Commons' Journals not until 1542. The record for 1461 therefore provides an invaluable and unique insight into the way in which the Lords conducted their business in Parliament towards the end of the fifteenth century.[2] There is evidence suggesting that the 'Fane fragment', as it is known, may well be a later medieval copy of part of the original journal. But the business and legislation discussed, and the confirmation available from the rolls of Parliament, leave no doubt that this is an authentic account of some of the Lords' discussions in Edward IV's first Parliament. In taking note of this we have a convenient opportunity to pause and look at Parliament and its procedures as it was at the end of the medieval period.

II

The Fane fragment covers the minutes of eight sitting days of Parliament. It may be a survival from an evolving series of Lords' Journals which had existed before and continued after 1461, quite possibly on an occasional

---

[1] *Rot. Parl.* Vol. V, p. 487.
[2] W. H. Dunham Jr., *The Fane Fragment of the 1461 Lords' Journal*, New Haven, Yale University Press, 1935 with a commentary by the editor on the manuscript, persons, procedure and business involved. Some extracts are printed in *E.H.D.* Vol. IV, p. 473–474.

basis. Since the minutes of business are recorded in English, the spoken language of Parliament, and not in Latin which was used in the regular Journals after 1510, it was possibly an experimental document kept on the clerk of Parliament's own initiative. In other respects, however, it corresponds closely with the form of the future Lords' Journals. Thus the heading of each page is in Latin, as is the list of Lords Spiritual and Temporal, which was the style of the future Journals. The Fane fragment also resembles the future Lords' Journals in giving both the calendar date and the day of the Parliament.

On each page is a list of the possible attenders (seventy-six Lords Spiritual and Temporal in all) according to their rank and individual order of precedence, with a dot placed against the name of each peer who was actually present. At the head of each day's list is the word *Rex*, though no dot indicates when Edward was personally present at any meeting. His presence was logical since the Lords were the king's great council in Parliament, but it was not automatic. Henry IV had agreed in 1407 that the Lords were free to discuss business without him[1] and during Henry VI's long minority and periodic imbecility the king had not been present in the Lords. Edward was now resuming an older practice. His presence is established by the content of the minutes on at least three of the seven days covered by the fragment and he may have attended every day. On 9 December, for instance, a bill to provide remedies for the 'hurtes' of London merchants 'was put in by the kings owne hande & red'. Edward's personal sponsorship of a bill which had first been presented to the Commons in the interest of the city's merchants was an early instance of his friendship towards the commercial interest which was to be a characteristic of his reign. There is evidence to suggest that the bill was drafted outside Parliament by lawyers paid by the craft companies for that purpose.[2] It was then included among the 'Communes petitiones', but it clearly represented the policy of the paternalist and nationalist Yorkist government as well as the wishes of the merchants' lobby. It sought protection against the import of various kinds of merchandise, whether by English or foreign merchants, and its scope was broadened in Parliament. During discussion in the Lords, it was considered together with a bill to give protection to the silkwomen of London and their 'mysteries' against the import of wrought silk, ribbons and laces. (Illegal imports were to be forfeit and the importer fined £10, the Lord Mayor of London having a power of search.) Both of these were private group bills put forward by the Commons and then (in respect of the

---

[1] *Rot. Parl.* Vol. III, p. 611.
[2] W. H. Dunham, op. cit., p. 65f.

merchandise bill at least) adopted by the king himself, which may have been his intention from their initiation. But neither bill was enrolled as a statute (or in the rolls of Parliament) until the Parliament of 1463.[1] The same was true of a third bill which regulated the apparel of commoners according to their rank.[2] For whatever reason the government was unable to complete these three bills in the Parliament in which they were first submitted. Nevertheless the government was actively involved in all of these enactments. It is recorded in the journal, for instance, that the chancellor informed the king of the work he had done and the advice he had taken on the 'Reformacions of excesse Array'. The drafting of this bill on apparel was of as much interest to the aristocrats in the Lords as to the quasi-aristocratic Commons who submitted it and it is quite possible that the council instigated or encouraged the Commons' bill.

Immediately following the record that the king had 'put in' the bill to protect English merchandise, the journal also provides an insight into the informal way in which consultations could take place between Lords and Commons. Although ministers occasionally went to the lower house bearing particular messages, the old style of inter-communing at the request of the Commons had gone out of use and had last been recorded in 1407.[3] In 1461, however, immediately after the reading of the merchants' bill, the journal records: 'Item this day there come up from the lower house a notable nomber of the substans of the same house. And in the Parliament chamber without the barr, had communicacion with my Lords the Chauncellor, Archbysshops of Cant' & Ebor' (York), therles (the earls) of Warr' & Worcester & other Lords spirituelx & temporelx.'[4] Whether or not this discussion between Lords and Commons beyond the bar of the House of Lords concerned that bill or another is not clear but the business was plainly important; the two archbishops and Warwick and Worcester were among the most powerful councillors.

On the same day, 9 December, the Lords also discussed two bills concerned with sheriffs, each of which illuminates the methods of discussing legislation. One entry in the journal reads: 'Item this day the bill made against Shirrefs was red but not agreed without there be a provicion made that the Lordes take no hurte thereby in their Leetes (private courts) & ffranchises.' The bill asked that all indictments and presentments to the sherriff's tourn (that is, his circuit to the hundred courts) should in future be

---

[1] *Rot. Parl.* Vol. V, pp. 506–508; *Stat. R.* Vol. II, pp. 395–398, 3 Edw. IV c. 3 & 4.
[2] *Rot. Parl.* Vol. V, pp. 504–506, *Stat. R.* Vol. II, pp. 399–402, 3 Edw. IV c. 5.
[3] *Rot. Parl.* Vol. III, p. 610.
[4] W. H. Dunham, op. cit., p. 19.

delivered to the justices of the peace at their next session. This was enacted and the sheriff's power to arrest and imprison was removed. The abuses behind the change were described in the petition and in the act as being an 'inordinate and infinite' number of indictments and arrests, jurors without conscience who obeyed the sheriff and his men instead of delivering honest verdicts, and the heaviness of fines.[1] This statute was an important step in the decline of the sheriff's power. Henceforth he was to be a shire administrator, not a judge. However, there was obviously discussion and some dissent, and provision was made to protect the special rights of lords with private jurisdictions. On the following day 'the kinges highnesse gave his Royall assent with a provision unto the Bill made against Shirrifs'. In other words, he assented to the bill as amended in the Lords.

The second bill concerned with sheriffs, did not, however, pass the Lords. The journal records: 'Item an other bill was red for the ease of Shirrifs.' This asked for certain charges on the sheriff's farm to be cancelled and the Lords did not like it. Later in the day (after the bill for the protection of merchandise had been discussed) the journal notes that four peers, the Earls of Worcester and Essex, and Lord Audley and Peter Ardern, a justice, were 'assigned to ouer se (oversee) the bill made for the ease of Shirriffs. And therupon to make reporte to the Kinge.' The bill was thus passed to a Lords' committee, perhaps so that it should be killed. At all events, its rejection is recorded in the parliamentary roll: *Le Roy s'advisera*.[2] Another example of the use of committees was recorded the same day when a committee of nine was assigned to 'have communicacion with the marchaynts of the Staple', possibly to discuss a bill to protect the woollen interest which was not enacted until 1463.

Finally, the journal gives an illuminating account of the way in which the Lords dealt with the bill which became the act confirming the judgements and charters of the Lancastrian kings.[3] The peers went through it clause by clause, agreeing to some clauses in such terms as 'it is thought reasonable' but not to others. Thus they described as 'vnresonable & right preiudiciall' the third article which would have confirmed by parliamentary authority the grants of certain franchises and liberties made by the Lancastrians. Certain lords were therefore deputed to tell the Commons that the king would not authorize their franchises and liberties by 'authority of Parliament' any more than his progenitors would have done but that they could have these benefits of the king's liberality and free disposition, as far

---

[1] *Stat. R.* Vol. II, pp. 389–391, 1 Edw. IV, c. 2.
[2] *Rot. Parl.* Vol. V, pp. 494–495.
[3] *Rot. Parl.* Vol. V, p. 489–493; *Stat. R.* Vol. II, pp. 380–389, and Dunham, op. cit., p. 12.

as this accorded with reason. Likewise, Edward would only authorize the payment of judges at the king's pleasure and not by the authority of Parliament. Moreover the journal on this day records the unanimity of this decision by a note written against each peer's name, 'not etc.' (i.e., not by authority of Parliament). It is quite clear that the govenment was using the overwhelming Yorkist majority in the Lords to safeguard the royal prerogative. In summary, this fragment of a Lords' Journal shows that bills were read more than once and sometimes three times, that they were debated and sometimes given to committees, and that they were sometimes discussed with the Commons. Finally, they could be amended by the Lords without the amendment necessarily requiring the Commons' approval.

No equivalent account of the Commons' proceedings has survived. But a parliamentary diary compiled by the two members for Colchester in the first Tudor Parliament of 1485 gives a useful glimpse into their practices and it is unlikely that there had been much change in the intervening twenty-four years.[1] After the customary opening Mass of the Holy Ghost, the knights and burgesses answered to their names, went to hear the chancellor's speech and elected a Speaker. They then got down to their main business, the hearing of petitions from people high and low and the reading of bills. There was often prolonged debate upon particular bills, sometimes lasting for more than a single day. Thus on 14 November it is recorded that the day was spent in 'arguments' for a bill which led to 'non conclusyon' and on 25 November that 'ther were red certeyn bylls and therupon were arguments and nothing passed that day'. Even more interestingly, the diarists noted that on 10 November 'there was red a byll for the Subsedy betwen the kyng and the merchaunts, whiche byll was examyned amonges us and oder divers person (presumably merchants outside Parliament) . . . and non conclusyon'. This is evidence not only of debates lasting for more than a day but of recourse to some kind of committee procedure. The next day the 'same byll' was 'red afore us and there passed as an aucte. And that doon, Maister Speker commaunded iiij gentyll men for to ber it to my Lord Chaunseler, desyryng his lordship that he wold certifie the Kyngs good grace withall.' The passage of bills between the two houses, however, was a two-way business and the diarists noted that on one occasion a bill about unlawful maintenance was sent down by the king and that on another day (the text is impaired here) 'came downe ix bylls by the Kyngs . . . his lords spirituall and temporall, delyvered unto us by the clerke of . . . so they ware red for that day, with odir maters that ware resoned'. At the end of their

---

[1] Nicholas Pronay and John Taylor, *Parliamentary Texts of the Later Middle Ages*, Ch. V; A Colchester Account.

record, the diarists noted that the king sent for 'Maister Speker and all the howse' into the Parliament chamber and there the Parliament was prorogued. The reference to bills sent down to the Commons by the Lords is of particular interest as a reflection of the fact that during the Yorkist period the Commons lost the virtually exclusive role they had played in the initiation of legislation under the Lancastrians, the significance of which must now be discussed. This can best be done in an attempt to describe the law-making procedure as it stood at the end of the medieval period.

Parliament was still essentially the king's Parliament and could not exist without him. He could present bills to it and could both veto them and amend them, though he was committed not to alter them in a way contrary to the Commons' petition. Yet the making of law did not lie in the 'mouth and breast' of the king. Sir John Fortescue was not simply speaking according to the later illusory historian's concept of a Lancastrian parliamentary monarchy when he drew a distinction between the English constitution and the French king's power to make his own laws and to tax his people without their consent. Fortescue's assertion that the king of England could not rule his people 'bi other lawes than such as thai assenten unto' was as true under York as it was under Lancaster.[1] There was now no doubt that statute law stood higher than the common law (even though statute law could still be elaborated and enlarged by common law through the judges) and statute law could be made nowhere except in Parliament.

During the fifteenth century it became the established convention that legislation required the Commons' consent as well as that of the Lords. In 1455, the clerk of the rolls of Parliament, Thomas Kirkby, who had been called to the court of exchequer in connection with a particular case, was asked to explain what was necessary for a valid act of Parliament. In reply, he stated categorically that the consent of king, Lords and Commons was needed.[2] But he also showed that the Commons did not have an unqualified right to give or withhold consent to all amendments made to their bills by the Lords. If the Lords wished to alter a bill sent up by the Commons they could do so without returning it to the Commons provided the change was in harmony with the Commons' proposal. On the other hand, if the Lords wanted to extend the scope of a bill, they would endorse it accordingly and send it back to the Commons.

Kirkby offered examples. If the Commons granted tunnage and poundage for four years and the Lords granted it only for two, it was not necessary to send the bill back to the Commons for approval of the

---

[1] Sir John Fortescue, *The Governance of England* (edited by C. Plummer, p. 109).
[2] Case in the Exchequer Chamber Year Book 33 Henr. VI, Pas. plea 8, printed in S. B. Chrimes, *Constitutional Ideas of the Fifteenth Century*, pp. 361–362.

amendment since the change was within their original grant, and did not extend the bill. But if the Commons granted tunnage and poundage for only two years and the Lords wished to extend it to four years, the Commons would have to approve the change for it to be enacted. The Lords would therefore endorse the bill with the words '*Les Seigniors sont assentus a durer pour quatre ans*' and send it back to the Commons. Such an amendment proposed by the Lords would fail if the Commons did not assent to it, but if the Commons were agreeable to the change, they would endorse the bill with the statement that they assented to the Lords' schedule attached to the bill. Furthermore, although the example Kirkby gave concerned a tax grant, over which the Commons had special rights, the procedure in relation to Lords' amendments seems to have applied to bills of any sort.

So much for the Lords' right to amend Commons bills. But could the Commons amend bills sent by the Lords to them, including those drafted on behalf of the council? From the second quarter of the century, the Lords had begun to send bills down to the Commons, the earliest surviving example being an undated bill in Henry V's reign on which it was written that the Commons had given their assent (*Les communes ount donnez lour assent*).[1] A few years later, in 1429, the Commons amended a bill from the Lords by attaching to it a schedule of extra proposals with a note saying that they assented to the bill provided the conditions in their schedule were incorporated in it. The Commons' proviso was duly incorporated in the bill on enactment.[2] But this earliest surviving case of a Commons amendment to a Lords bill is also the last during the Lancastrian period save for two questionable and trivial instances towards the end of Henry VI's reign. There is no evidence of any general practice of Commons' amendments to Lords' bills comparable to the Lords' amendments to Commons' bills. Still more to the point, there is no evidence that the Commons ever rejected a Lords' bill during the fifteenth century, whether or not its origin was the council, though in theory they had the right to do so. The most obvious explanation for this is the fact that during the Lancastrian period the number of Lords' bills sent to the Commons was negligible. The Lords left the submission of bills to the Commons and their own amendments to them were comparatively minor. Yet even if the Lords had frequently sent bills to the Commons, it is uncertain whether the Commons at this stage would have had the self-confidence to be very forthright in amending or rejecting bills sent down with the authority of the Lords and king.

Yet much more important than which house originated bills or how they

---

[1] *Rot. Parl.* Vol. IV, p. 91.
[2] H. L. Gray, *The Influence of the Commons on Early Legislation* (1932), p. 194 and *Rot. Parl.* Vol. IV, p. 354.

were amended was the undoubted constitutional theory which emerged in the fifteenth century that the Commons' assent to legislation was essential and the practice that no bill became law which had not passed through their hands. What was deemed necessary to make an act of Parliament was, of course, most clearly indicated in the sanctioning clause which prefaced it. At the end of the fourteenth century, there had been a good deal of variety in these clauses. One formula used in the reign of Richard II was 'by the whole assent of the prelates, dukes, earls, barons of this our realm, at instance and request of the Commons'. Another was 'of the assent of the lords and other'. Yet another different formula used was 'of the assent of the prelates, Lords and Commons'. In 1403, however, a new form of words was adopted which gradually became the basis of the standard: 'by advice and assent of the lords spiritual and temporal at instance and request of the Commons'. In 1433 there was added the phrase 'and by authority of Parliament' and after 1444 this became a regular part of the sanctioning clause. The words did not, of course, signify that Parliament had an authority separate from that of the king, for the king was part of Parliament. The implication was rather that law was enacted by the authority of all the estates of the realm in a national assembly. After the 1440s, the formula often used referred to the 'assent' of the Commons rather than to their request, and though the form for a time reverted to 'request', the standard usage from the reign of Richard III was: 'by advice and assent of the Lords spiritual and temporal and of the Commons, and by authority of Parliament'.[1]

The convention requiring the assent of the Commons for the making of statutes grew naturally from the practice by which the elected house was itself the principal initiator of legislation during the Lancastrian period. The great parliamentary statutes of Edward I had been entirely initiated by the king and his judges, and it was not until the reign of Edward III that law-making became very substantially, though far from exclusively, based on petitions submitted to the king in Parliament, increasingly through the Commons. During different phases of the reign of Richard II, legislation had been based both on official bills, which do not seem to have needed the Commons' assent, and on Commons petitions. The role of the Commons as the initiators of legislation had been greatly encouraged during the fourteenth century by the growing practice by which petitioners sought the support of the Commons for their requests to the king, and the Commons had adopted or avowed some of these petitions.

---

[1] The preambles of all statutes from 1377 to 1485 are set out in a table by S. B. Chrimes, op. cit., pp. 101–105.

Such petitions were of two kinds, the private which sought to redress particular grievances and the common petitions which were concerned with the general interest. Both kinds were drawn up by professional scriveners in the form of potentially legal documents and bribery was often used to forward petitions through Parliament. The goodwill of the clerks was particularly useful and worth buying but even Speakers were on occasions the recipients of gifts to persuade them to smooth the passage of bills. Sometimes the petitioners themselves came as deputations to Parliament, as happened in the case of William Wayneflete's tenants at East Meon in the 1461 Parliament which has already been mentioned.[1] But increasingly petitions from individuals were presented by knights and burgesses as representatives of their constituents, and they often got extra pay for so doing. In addition, Lords and Commons themselves presented petitions on their own behalf.

Private petitions were handed to the receivers, who were clerks acting in this capacity to the triers. The triers, who like the receivers were appointed in each Parliament, replied to those petitions they thought need not be sent on and despatched the others to the council or the appropriate court. But other private petitions were delivered not to the receivers but to the Commons and thence to the clerk of the Parliament. By the fifteenth century this class of petitions had grown enormously because it was found that directing them through the Commons was more effective in producing prompt responses than passing them through the ancient channel of receivers and triers. It was a sign of both the Commons' growing influence and the developing idea of the elected parliamentarian's role as representative of his constituents. Moreover, whereas petitions in the fourteenth century had been addressed to the king or the king and lords of Parliament, the Commons had also come to be included at the turn of the century and during the fifteenth century petitions were increasingly addressed to the Commons alone. For instance, whereas no enrolled private petitions were addressed to the Commons under Richard II about thirty per cent (sixty out of 198) were addressed to them under Henry VI.

The Commons no longer described themselves as 'poor', 'mean' or 'simple' petitioners, as they had done when addressing the king in the past. As the recipients of numerous petitions themselves, they were now addressed as 'right honourable', 'right wise' or 'worthy and discreet Commons', and although more petitions were addressed to them because they were more influential, they were also made more influential by having more petitions addressed to them. What is more, those who petitioned them

[1] *Rot. Parl.* Vol. V, pp. 475–476. See p. 572.

included people of high as well of modest estate; even Cardinal Beaufort used them.

But it was on the common petitions, concerned with matters of public interest, that the role of the Commons as legislators was built. Addressed to the king, these generally, after 1423, took the form of individual petitions each concerned with a particular topic, rather than comprehensive petitions of the older sort. These were the forerunners of what became known as public bills, and when submitting them to the king the Commons no longer did so in the form of a humble supplication but with some such simple statement as that 'various common petitions were submitted in the said Parliament by the said Commons, the tenor of which and the responses are as follows...' For many of these petitions, the Commons were themselves entirely responsible. They were drawn up by the Commons' clerk and their final form was that agreed to after debate. Petitions of common interest for which the Commons themselves were entirely responsible were concerned particularly with such matters as defence, trade, the coinage or law and order. But other common petitions which were put forward as the basis for legislation were founded on petitions by outside bodies or individuals, which the Commons thought it worthwhile to adopt in the common interest. Sometimes, the Commons in their petition specifically stated that they were interceding in a particular cause and in many such cases they simply approved the petition addressed to them, passing it on to the Lords almost unchanged as a 'common petition'. They may have done this because they lacked a procedure for vetting and rewording all of them, which could also explain why some common petitions in the earlier part of the century duplicated or contradicted others.

Nevertheless, by the time of Edward IV's accession, the procedure for passing bills into law had become much more systematic than it had been at the beginning of the fifteenth century. If the Commons agreed to adopt a bill after discussion, it was superscribed with the words '*soit baille aux seigneurs*' ('let it be submitted to the Lords'). In reaching their decisions to accept, amend or reject bills, both houses took majority decisions, though in precisely what form is not known. In the Lords it was certainly the practice to read a bill up to three times, and sometimes more often.[1] Though there is not equally direct evidence about the practice of the Commons, they probably by now did roughly the same. The passage of bills between the houses was (so far as there was any theory) a two-way business. But the growing importance of the Commons as petitioners in matters of the national interest and as recipients of petitions is linked with one of the most

---

[1] *Rot. Parl.* Vol. V, pp. 475–476, and J. H. Dunham, op. cit. esp. p. 65 and pp. 70–72.

notable features of parliamentary history in the first sixty years of the fifteenth century. During the Lancastrian period, the Commons themselves became overwhelmingly the initiators of those bills which were enacted into statutes.[1]

The Commons, however, did not assume this role as a result of some new accretion of power under the Lancastrian dispensation. Their initiative in promoting legislation, which was to be temporary, arose from the situations of the three Lancastrian kings. Henry IV was preoccupied with keeping his usurped throne which was constantly under threat. Henry V was too involved with France to be much concerned with legislating domestically, though he was firm and efficient when he did deal with politics at home. (There is a later tradition, which may have something in it, that every day after dinner, when he was not dining in state, Henry kept a cushion on a cupboard, where he leaned for an hour to receive bills and hear complaints from whoever wished to come.)[2] As for the council of Henry VI, this was too distracted by faction to be much interested in legislation. As a result, in the second quarter of the fifteenth century almost every new statute originated in the Commons.[3] Indeed, petitions from the Commons predominated in statute making during the whole of the first half of the century, though the government probably encouraged some of them. But in Henry VI's last few years the legislative initiative of the Commons had already begun to wane and the more active and powerful Yorkist kings resumed the royal initiative in statute-making. A symbol of this was Edward's practice of putting the royal sign manual, RE, on bills which had his approval, a practice started in respect of some bills in the last years of Henry VI.[4]

The legislative initiative of the Commons under the Lancastrians was an accident of politics. It did not indicate that the Commons had come to represent some kind of popular or quasi-democratic force in an aristocratic world. As we have seen at successive stages in this account of the medieval Parliament, although there was a social distinction (now being eroded)

[1] For accounts of the extremely complex questions of petitions, legislative procedure and the initiative of the Commons in the Lancastrian period, see especially: H. L. Gray, op. cit., A. R. Myers, 'Parliamentary Petitions in the Fifteenth Century', *E.H.R.* Vol. LII (1937), pp. 385–404 and pp. 590–613; and S. B. Chrimes, *English Constitutional Ideas in the Fifteenth Century*, esp. pp. 218–269.

[2] Stow, *The Annales of England* (1592) pp. 459–460, quoted by A. R. Myers, op. cit., who observes that Stow was usually well informed and notes that there are contemporary accounts of petitions being presented personally in the fourteenth and fifteenth centuries.

[3] R. L. Storey, op. cit.

[4] A. R. Myers, 'Parliament, 1422–1509' in *The English Parliament in the Middle Ages*, ed. R. G. Davies and J. H. Denton (1981), pp. 178–179.

between the knights and burgesses in the Commons, there was no sharp social distinction between many of the knights in the Commons and the nobility. It was a fluid society in which knights were promoted to the peerage, merchants could be knighted and new families had sprung to prominence through the French wars. The standing of the Commons in Parliament had nothing to do with any idea that they were some kind of constitutional counter-balance to the Lords or monarchy but rather reflected the growing appreciation by men of position that a seat in the Commons was well worth having. It was not only because there were some new boroughs that the number of borough members returned to Parliament increased during the fifteenth century, the figures for Edward IV's Parliament of 1478 being the highest for any medieval Parliament.[1] The number of borough members also rose because more men wanted to go to Parliament and in particular because members of the gentry began to seek borough seats. Many of the smaller boroughs, therefore, especially those in deeply rural areas, now returned members of the gentry instead of burgesses or merchants. This happened despite repeated efforts in many places to enforce the residence qualification. So, of 202 men returned in 1478 to represent 100 boroughs (London returned four members), three were knights, thirty-two were esquires (*armiger*) and two were described as 'gentlemen'. (John Paston was one of the knights.) But more members of the gentry sat in Parliament as burgesses than can be counted by those styled as such in the returns. It has been calculated that in the Parliament of 1478 at least half the borough representatives were country gentlemen who had persuaded the burgesses to elect them or who were members of the household-retainer class.[2] No longer were the burgesses in Parliament simply the merchants and townsmen of the early Plantagenet period. They were increasingly gentlemen, lawyers and rich merchants, anxious to be at Westminster, taking sides in the partisan politics of the time, and were often politically involved with the greater nobility of their region. As a consequence, there was now a much greater social homogeneity within the Commons' House itself (it is legitimate to speak of the Houses of Lords and Commons at the end of the medieval period) and between the Lords and Commons.

Inevitably magnates tried to influence the course of elections in their area, and were particularly stimulated to do so by the faction fighting of the

---

[1] M. McKisack, *The Parliamentary Representation of the English Boroughs during the Middle Ages*.

[2] M. McKisack, Ibid., pp. 106–116. See also J. S. Roskell, *The Commons in the Parliament of 1422*, Ch. VII.

time. The Paston letters are particularly revealing in this respect. They show such magnates as the Dukes of Exeter, Norfolk, Suffolk and York exerting pressure to get their candidates into Parliament, and yet by no means always succeeding.[1] Of course there were some in the Commons in the fifteenth century who were closely dependent on the nobility. The Nevilles and Percys, for instance, inevitably determined who should represent the northern marches and representatives of the Courteney family sat regularly for Devon. Yet for the most part, men in the Commons were not simply the pliant tools of factious magnates. Even during the civil war, when bands of armed men were at hand to exert persuasion and sheriffs were partisan, the electors did not always vote for those favoured by the local magnates, especially where there was a rivalry of interests. Elections were frequently tumultuous and not infrequently contested though most of them were arranged before the return.

Whether in the shires or Parliament, however, the gentry could not generally be cowed or driven but only managed and persuaded. Many were rich and in a number of counties at least there were members of the gentry with landed wealth hardly inferior to that of the local baronage. In Dorset and Sussex there were eight such and they all sat in Parliament.[2] Such men formed a nucleus in the Commons of every Parliament. At Westminster, therefore many of the Commons were worth too much in their own right to be simply subservient. Besides, though many of them belonged to the connections and parties of great lords, such allegiances could be unstable. Lordship over men had largely, though not quite entirely, ceased to be based on land and had lost the stability provided by the old feudal land tenure which persisted from generation to generation. Since the reign of Edward III allegiance had been principally a matter of indentured contract for pay or rents, either for a term of years or sometimes nominally for life. Yet such contracts, even for life, were easily broken, and men changed their loyalties when it suited them. Nor was the power in such connections concentrated solely in the magnates. Groups of local gentry could form their own power bases in the shires and have some influence with greater men. 'Parties' and retinues were not fixed entities but rather a shifting network of interlocking arrangements and interests. This was reflected in Parliament. Inevitably, however, the Commons went with the prevailing wind of power at any time, in the creation of which an important influence would have been the presence in every Parliament of a powerful group of

---

[1] K. B. Macfarlane, 'Parliament and "Bastard Feudalism"', *T.R.H.S.*, 4th series XXVI (1944), pp. 53–79.
[2] Ibid.

civil servants and members of the royal household, who in the second half of the century sat for borough seats in increasing numbers. In the Parliament of 1478 they constituted about seventeen per cent of the Commons, a formidable power block of at least fifty men. The councillors who, in Tudor Parliaments, were to manage the Commons in the king's interest were not, however, yet among them. So far, they were only in the Lords.[1]

The fifteenth century Parliament thus represented a balance of powers of which that of a king who was personally effective remained the greatest. Edward IV became an effective king. During his reign the government again began to produce bills for Parliament and although he called fewer Parliaments it was accepted that legislation was binding on all the king's subjects because, as a contemporary legal opinion put it in 1480, 'every man is privy and party to the Parliament, for the Commons have one or two for each community to bind or unbind the whole community'.[2] Increasingly too a gradual change took place by which the Commons and Lords, when drafting their own bills, began to follow a new example set by the crown in framing each bill in a form which could be enacted without alteration. Edward IV's act for the attainder of the former King Henry VI in 1461 was the first instance of this, when the Commons are recorded as giving their assent to the 'act'. The object was for the king to get precisely the act he wanted on to the statute book and this was now what Parliament wanted too. Under the old practice, the king's judges and officials were free, after the king's assent to a bill, to alter its wording, within its general intentions. Now bills began their progress through Parliament in the form of intended acts rather than as petitions, and amendments were inserted on the way. Statute law was ceasing to be based on generally worded replies to generally worded petitions and was taking the form of very precise legal statements specified in words for which Parliament as well as the king took responsibility.[3]

Henceforth, a bill could be altered only if the king himself added fresh provisos to it, though he could only limit the original proposals by exemptions, not add to them. Even this practice, however, was dropped in the early years of Henry VIII, leaving Parliament with virtually its present procedure for turning bills into statutes. Parliament was not static under Edward IV nor did he generally neglect the art of consultation.

Despite the faction and disorder which for so many decades disturbed the

---

[1] Roskell, op. cit., p. 135.

[2] Opinion of counsel for the crown in the Exchequer court, 1480, quoted by J. G. Edwards, 'Plena Potestas', *Oxford Essays in Medieval History presented to Herbert Edward Salter*; reprinted, Fryde and Miller, op. cit., Vol. I, Ch. IV, p. 149.

[3] Fryde and Miller, op. cit., Vol. II, p. 13.

government of England and the intermittent civil strife during the thirty years between the first battle of St Albans and the battle of Bosworth, the fifteenth century was not a stagnant period. It was a time of great material advance, trade and prosperity. For the better off, there were finer and more comfortable houses in which glass was coming into common use, although it was still a luxury. For the humbler too conditions were in many ways more prosperous, although for the humblest they remained bleak. Even the civil war bore comparatively lightly on the country as a whole, though not as lightly as some accounts seeking to correct the myth of a blood-soaked land have suggested.[1] The battlefield fighting occupied only about twelve or thirteen weeks in thirty-two years; care was taken not to destroy towns or countryside and for the most part revenge and decapitation were the lot only of the defeated leaders, not their followers. Would-be victors had no wish to inherit a ruined land and a sullen people.

Nor was the century aesthetically barren. In East Anglia and the Cotswolds the great perpendicular churches built on the prosperity of wool were the final burst of splendour in gothic architecture. There were Henry VI's foundations of King's College Cambridge and Eton. In Oxford some of the loveliest of that city's buildings were constructed in the second half of the century. The university built the Divinity Schools which is one of the finest buildings in the land. Later, Duke Humphrey's library was constructed above it to house the magnificent collection of books and manuscripts which the duke gave to the university and which was, alas, to be irretrievably dispersed by the commissioners of Edward VI. The dead of Agincourt were commemorated by the beauty of All Souls and even at the time when Bishop Wayneflete of Winchester was most heavily involved as chancellor in the final throes of Henry VI's government, he was busying himself with the foundation of Magdalen, perhaps the loveliest of Oxford's colleges. He became chancellor in 1456 and in the following year secured a licence from King Henry to found the new college, a charter being issued a year later. Wayneflete ceased to be chancellor on Henry's fall in 1460 but he still secured the support of King Edward for the foundation.

So political strife and building for worship and learning went paradoxically side by side. It was a century in which the number of grammar schools was increasing, and with them literacy in the national language which was the common property of all classes. Letter writing for social purposes was now being practised and the letters of the Paston family of Norfolk give a

---

[1] Anthony Goodman, *The Wars of the Roses*, corrects the view that the wars left the land virtually unscathed, which in turn corrected the older myth that they ravaged the land. He shows that more people were affected indirectly by the wars than the magnates and others directly involved.

remarkably vivid insight into the life of the time. Finally, Edward IV's reign was crowned by Caxton's introduction of printing, sponsored by the king himself, which revolutionized human communication and thinking. It is this which, perhaps more than any political change, makes 1485 an appropriate as well as a convenient date at which to conclude any account of medieval history, including that of Parliament.

III

For the three years following his first Parliament, Edward was occupied with overcoming the Lancastrian threat in the border counties of the north.[1] Queen Margaret, as unyielding in defeat as she had been politically foolish in power, strove without flagging to make foreign alliances which would help her recover the English throne for her husband and son. Important castles in Northumberland and Cumberland which were still held by Lancastrians gave her a power base and she and her family continued to be sheltered by the Scottish court. A Percy had been allowed to keep Dunstanborough castle on the Northumberland coast and during the winter of 1461-2 the Lancastrians repossessed Alnwick and Naworth near Carlisle. Wales too was a focus of Lancastrian discontent and remained disaffected even after Pembroke and Denbigh castles had been retaken by the Yorkists. In the West country there was intermittent disorder and Edward still lacked the full support of the nobility and gentry. In 1462, after they had been discovered in a Lancastrian conspiracy, the Earl of Oxford, his son and two squires were beheaded following a summary trial before the new constable, the Earl of Worcester.

Yet the Scots had failed to provide Margaret of Anjou with effective support; their participation in border raids was not enough. Indeed, the Scottish regent and queen mother, Mary of Gueldres, had even been in negotiations with Edward IV. So in April 1462 Margaret went to France to seek better help from Louis XI. His concern was above all to keep his English and Burgundian rivals in turmoil and he secretly promised her money and the facility to raise troops in exchange for her promise to cede Calais. But the scheme came to nothing. For one thing, the Duke of

---

[1] The best recent account of the complex diplomacy and military politics of these years, which can only be outlined here, is in C. Ross, *Edward IV*, an invaluable narrative and analysis of the reign as a whole.

Burgundy, whose territory was near Calais, would not allow the French king to march against it. For another, the diplomacy of the Earl of Warwick, which was crucial to Edward in these early years, succeeded not only in keeping Burgundy in the English interest but also in persuading the French king to think seriously about the benefits of a possible agreement with the Yorkist dynasty. Eventually, therefore, Margaret landed near Bamburgh (accompanied by Henry VI whom she had collected on the way) with no more than a few hundred mercenaries. The castle immediately admitted her and, since the Lancastrians also held Alnwick and Dunstanburgh, she virtually commanded Northumberland. But when Edward led a large army north, she calculated that she could not match it, and fled again to Scotland, losing her mercenaries who were trapped in Lindisfarne. The rebel castles were besieged by Warwick and on Christmas Eve the defenders of Bamborough under the Duke of Somerset and Sir Ralph Percy surrendered on condition that they would have life and limb. Taken to the king, who had been incapacitated at Durham with measles, both swore allegiance to him and were pardoned. Somerset was admitted to the king's service and Percy was again put in charge of Bamburgh and Dunstanburgh. Edward IV was politically generous by temperament but he was also pursuing a calculated policy of seeking to win adherents by conciliation. In this case it was to prove a mistake. For the time being, however, Somerset demonstrated his new allegiance by joining Warwick in a siege of Alnwick which continued until, in January 1463, a Lancastrian force from Scotland appeared near the castle, and enabled the garrison to escape across the border.

In the spring of 1463, after Edward and Warwick had returned to the south, Sir Ralph Percy again treacherously changed sides and admitted the Lancastrians and Scots to Bamburgh and Dunstanburgh. Sir Ralph Grey also secured and handed over Alnwick. Again the Lancastrians were on the offensive and it was in this situation that Edward met his second Parliament.[1] It had at first been summoned to York in February and then postponed to Leicester in March. Eventually it met at Westminster on 29 April, 1463, the king having cancelled previous elections on the grounds that some of them had been irregularly conducted, which perhaps meant that they had returned unsympathetic members. It proved a sufficiently amenable Parliament for Edward to keep it in being through several prorogations until 1465, although it was to show noteworthy tenacity in asserting its ancient right over taxation.

Apart from recording a large number of petitions, the rolls of Parliament tell us little of what was said or done in the first session. After the election of

[1] *Rot. Parl.* Vol. V, pp. 496–570.

a new Speaker, a John Say from Hertfordshire (who had also been a member of Lancastrian Parliaments), they simply record that 'for the hasty defence of this youre noble Reame' the Commons granted the king (against his and their mortal enemies) what is described as an 'aid' of £37,000 'oonly for the seid defence to be applied'. Of this sum, £31,000 was to be raised 'in manere and fourme' of the last fifteenth and tenth from shires, cities and boroughs, but exempting those with less than ten shillings yearly from lands and rents, or having chattels worth less than five marks. The £31,000 was the sum to be raised after the usual deduction of £6,000 to free from tax-paying places too poor to pay. However, on this occasion, the total grant to the king was to be brought up again to £37,000 by an extra levy on people with the means to pay more. This was to be paid by persons possessing land of more than twenty shillings or goods and chattels to the value of ten marks.[1] It was an experiment in raising money by a new method according to wealth and, as we shall see, it was abandoned in the next session, clearly because of taxpayers' resistance. When the king prorogued Parliament in June, the parliamentary roll records his undertaking, which had no doubt been given when he asked for the grant, to lead his army in person against his enemies.

The parliamentary rolls otherwise record only a large number of petitions, many of which became law. The most notable of these were protectionist. Apart from the acts for the protection of silkworkers and manufactured goods, which have already been discussed, there was legislation restricting credit to foreign buyers of wool and requiring all purchases from the wool staple at Calais to be for ready payment, half of which was to be in English money or in plate. This was both a commercial attack on the merchants of the Low Countries and a reflection of the government's concern to ensure the inflow of bullion. The export of wool by foreign merchants was also forbidden, a blow to the growing wool trade of Italian merchants to the Mediterranean. Further, all English merchants were to export their goods only in English ships when these were available. Another protectionist enactment prohibited the import of corn except when, in a dearth, domestic prices rose above given levels, an early version of the Corn Law.[2]

When Edward prorogued the first session of Parliament in June 1463, Warwick had already set off for the north with an army. By the end of the month, a Lancastrian-Scottish force was besieging Norham castle on the Tweed, but this was put to flight by a large Yorkist force and chased back to Scotland. A punitive English raid deep into the Lowlands then followed.

---

[1] *Rot. Parl.* Vol. V, p. 497.
[2] *Stat. R.* Vol. II, 3 Edw. IV. c. 1, pp. 392–395; *Rot. Parl.* Vol. V, pp. 501–504.

Queen Margaret, Henry VI and Prince Edward of Lancaster had been obliged to retire to Bamburgh castle, from which the former queen and the prince set out for Flanders with the Duke of Exeter and Sir John Fortescue, once more to beg for foreign help. Henry VI was left at Bamburgh where he 'reigned' as though still a king. Edward, meanwhile, was following Warwick northwards. When he reached Northampton he was faced with a riot against Somerset and despatched the still suspect duke to Wales for his own safety. It was also while Edward was at Northampton that he heard of the Scottish-Lancastrian retreat and the English raid into Scotland. He did not, however, follow this up, perhaps through lack of financial resources. He had been piling up debt since the start of his reign. Instead, he returned to London to discuss impending negotiations with the French which in October led to an agreement by which Louis promised to give no further aid to Margaret, her son or any other 'enemies of the English king'.

On 4 November, the prorogued Parliament met for a further session which lasted but a single day. All that is recorded is that the Commons submitted a 'schedule on paper' (*cedula in Papiro*) to the king, placing it on record that, because of the great charge laid on the Commons, he had agreed to remit the extra £6,000 on the better off granted in the previous session. It was therefore to be ordained and established by the authority of Parliament that the levy was void. Furthermore, the £31,000, previously described as an aid, was to be levied 'oonly by the name of a XVe' (which apparently meant that it was to be levied as a fifteenth in the cities and boroughs as well as in the shires and not as the usual urban tenth). It was not to be levied by any other name, order or form, the previous act notwithstanding. The Commons had evidently found resistance to the new tax on wealth but they also appear to have been reflecting public criticism of the king's failure (as it seemed) to apply the money to achieve a resounding victory over the enemy as he had promised. Even the payment of the second instalment of the £31,000 was delayed and the Commons showed their suspicion of Edward's intentions by the explanation given of the purpose of their 'paper'. They protested that 'they delyver this paper oonly as a remembraunce for their ententes' and they reserved their right 'at eny tyme duryng the seid Parlement . . . at their fredome and libertee (to) resorte and repaire to the seid remembraunce, to adde therto or to amenuse therof (to diminish) at their discretions', always keeping to the document's 'true and verray entent'. To this the king had to assent.[1] The Commons' determination to maintain their close control over taxation had clearly not weakened. This is the first reference in the rolls to the use in Parliament of paper rather than

---

[1] *Rot. Parl.* Vol. V, pp. 498–499.

parchment, and the term 'submitting a paper' seems to have been used virtually in the modern sense. It was during the fifteenth century that paper first came to England and in the closing decades that we first have evidence of its manufacture here.

On the same day Parliament was adjourned to meet at York in February 1464 and then immediately postponed to May and again until November. It was not until January 1465 that it met for its third proper session at Westminster. In the meantime, the scene had changed dramatically. Disaffection was widespread in the country and at the end of 1463 Somerset again turned coat, leaving Wales, where Jasper Tudor was trying to stir up revolt, to lead another rising in the north. The Yorkists now decided to seek peace with the Scots and John Neville, Lord Montagu, was sent with a force to escort Scottish commissioners to England. On the way he put a Lancastrian army to flight at Hedgley Moor and brought the commissioners to York where a truce for fifteen years was agreed. The Scots promised to cease helping the house of Lancaster, and Edward to end the help he had been giving to the insurgent Earl of Douglas. On 14 May 1464, this phase of the domestic conflict ended when the Lancastrian army was defeated at Hexham. Somerset, Roos, Hungerford and others were captured and executed. After flouting Edward's clemency they can hardly have expected less. For these services, Montagu was made Earl of Northumberland and endowed with Percy lands. Alnwick, Dunstanburgh and Norham were surrendered on promises of safety, but Bamburgh was taken by assault and Sir Ralph Grey was executed. When it fell, Henry VI had vanished. He was at large, sheltered by sympathisers, until he eventually fell into Edward's hands in July 1465 when he was committed to the Tower and more or less honourable captivity. His mental condition was so weak that he seemed to pose no threat to the king.

At the time of his agreement with the French in October 1463, when Louis had undertaken not to help Henry of Lancaster, Edward had hinted at an interest in marrying the French king's daughter. As she was only three, Louis had proposed instead a union with one of his wife's sisters, a princess of Savoy. The Duke of Burgundy, however, made a rival offer of one of his own daughters. Warwick had personally committed himself to a French alliance, but Edward might have been expected to accept a Burgundian marriage since he was increasingly inclining towards reviving the old alliance with Burgundy as helpful to English trade. Instead, in September 1464, the king astounded a great council at Reading by revealing that in May he had secretly married the Lady Elizabeth Woodville, the daughter of Lord Rivers and of the Burgundian Princess Jacquetta of Luxembourg. Not the least surprising aspects of Edward's choice of a queen were that she was a widow, and what is more one whose former husband, Sir John Grey, had died fighting for Henry VI at the second battle of St Albans. Although Elizabeth had noble blood, a royal marriage to a subject inevitably caused jealousy and Edward's promotion of his queen's formerly Lancastrian family by advantageous marriages raised particularly bitter and lasting enmities especially among the older Yorkists.

It was an unusual marriage by an unusual king. Edward was a shrewd pragmatist who often acted on impulse. He was a man of many contradictions. He kept his royal state with magnificence but was also affably at home with city merchants; indeed, he himself possessed the instincts of a businessman and was already exporting wool and cloth on his own behalf. He was a patron of the arts, a collector of books and manuscripts and towards the end of his reign the builder of the magnificent chapel of St George at Windsor. Yet he had the common touch and understood how to please his subjects by graciousness. He was a clever and when necessary a hard politician, but because of a certain laziness and a reputation as a libertine, he perhaps appeared to Warwick as a self-indulgent and easy-going youth who would remain dependent on the earl's more mature skills for government. Now, however, Edward had demonstrated his independence from the powerful earl by making a marriage which could only have been an affair of the heart since it was certainly against his political interest. It was a union that was to be disastrous for Edward's dynasty after his death, and its immediate effect was to enrage Warwick and inspire the French king to begin building a covert personal alliance with the proud, arrogant and offended earl against the careless young king. Warwick remained convinced that an arrangement with the French would be popular with English merchants hostile to their rivals in the Burgundian Low Countries, and in 1466 he succeeded in getting Edward's formal acceptance of an agreement with France by which Louis promised not to help the Lancastrians and Edward not to support either Burgundy or Brittany against the French crown. But Edward's inclination towards a Burgundian alliance was rapidly becoming certainty, one incentive being to procure the removal of an embargo placed by Burgundy at the end of 1464 on the import of English cloth into the Low Countries.

Some seven months after the king's marriage, the repeatedly prorogued Parliament which had begun in 1463 met for its final session at Westminster on 21 January 1465. An act of attainder was passed against the late Duke of Somerset and other recent rebels. There was also another Act of Resumption, again with many pragmatic exemptions. But the most important enactment was the grant to Edward for life of both the wool subsidy and tunnage and poundage. Although the king had already begun to collect the customs on his own authority, this parliamentary grant, together with the revenues gained from the resumption of land, was to provide an assured basis for the financial independence Edward eventually built up. At the end of March the king dissolved Parliament, calling no other until the summer of 1467.

In the meantime, Warwick's influence continued to decline though the king still used him in negotiations with both Burgundy and France. In 1466 Edward sent him on an embassy to discuss two proposed marriages. One was between Edward's sister, Margaret of York, and Burgundy's heir, Charles de Charolais, who was a widower. The other project was for a union between the Duke of Clarence and Charles's daughter. The second of these proposals was deeply resented by Warwick who wished to marry his own daughter to Clarence and it came to nothing. The years 1466 and 1467 were a time of intensive diplomacy, culminating in missions from France and Burgundy in the summer of 1467 when the king finally opted for Burgundy. In London, a Burgundian embassy was greeted with warm and lavish hospitality during Warwick's absence on an embassy to France in the summer of 1467. But a French embassy which accompanied Warwick on his return immediately afterwards was received with comparative coldness, and went back to France empty-handed. The king's favour to the Burgundians was demonstrated when, at the opening of the new Parliament on 3 June, Anthony, Bastard of Burgundy, who had come to joust in a tournament with Anthony, Lord Scales, the queen's brother, was present as Edward's guest in the Painted Chamber.[1]

In ordinary circumstances the opening speech would have been made by the chancellor, Warwick's brother George Neville, Archbishop of York, but he was not present, his place being taken by Bishop William of Lincoln. Five days after the opening of Parliament the archbishop was dismissed as chancellor and replaced by Robert Stillington, Bishop of Bath and Wells. Neville's offence was that he had been working (in Warwick's interest) to obtain a papal dispensation to enable Warwick's daughter to marry Clarence which, since they were cousins, was prohibited by consanguinity. A family tie between Warwick and the prince who was the king's possible heir was the last thing Edward wanted.

Immediately after the election of the Speaker, who was again John Say, the king delivered the celebrated speech in which he promised to live from his own revenues, except when the defence of the realm caused him to call on the Commons for money. 'John Say, and ye Sirs, comyn to this my Court of Parlement for the Comon of this my Lond. The cause why Y have called

[1] C. Ross, op. cit., p. 110.

and summoned this my present Parlement is, that Y purpose to lyve uppon my nowne, and not to charge my Subgettes but in grete and urgent causes, concernyng more the wele of theym self, and also the defence of theym and of this my Reame, rather than my nowne pleasir ...' He went on to ask the Commons, when such cases of need arose, to be as considerate to him as any Commons had ever been to his progenitors. He thanked them heartily for their good will, kindness and true hearts, promising to be a good and gracious king and to apply his person in time of need for their well-being and defence, 'not sparyng my body nor lyfe for eny Jeoparde that mought happen to the same'.[1] It was, perhaps, a double-edged undertaking, not only signifying Edward's general policy of financial independence but also preparing the minds of the Commons for the request for money for defence that he was going to make later, when his anti-French alliance was in place. For the present, however, no money was asked for and the king's speech was a preface to the chief business of Parliament, yet another and more thoroughgoing Act of Resumption, which was to help provide the king with his own resources on which he intended to live. It was, however, a sign of a new deterioration in lawfulness that the Commons complained again about riots, murders and the like, asking the king to act to enforce the law.[2] After less than a month, Parliament was prorogued and then prorogued twice more at Reading in November 1467 and on 5 May, 1468 before meeting at Westminster on 12 May for what was to be its final short session. By then Warwick was nearing the open breach with the king which all but destroyed the Yorkist cause.

At the time of the Burgundian embassy to London Duke Philip of Burgundy had died, being succeeded by Charles de Charolais. Hard bargaining between the two states had followed on commercial matters as well as over the proposed dynastic union. At the beginning of 1468 a treaty was signed and in July Margaret of York left England to marry Duke Charles. An agreement was also made with Brittany which finally brought Edward back to the anti-French posture of his Lancastrian predecessors. So, when Parliament reassembled on 12 May, it was immediately told of a peace and commercial treaty made with Spain and Denmark, of the king's commercial agreement 'with his olde frends of Almayn' (Germany), of the peace with Scotland and, above all, of the confederations with the duke of Burgundy, who was to marry the king's sister, and Brittany 'which two Dukes been the myghtyest Prynces that holden of the Croune of Fraunce'. All this, said the chancellor, had involved the great cost of embassies which

---

[1] *Rot. Parl.* Vol. V, p. 572.
[2] ibid., p. 618.

the king had borne himself, the object being to diminish the power of his old and ancient Adversary of France, the better to recover his right and title to the French crown. The chancellor spoke of the Duke of Burgundy as 'oon of the moost myghtyest Princez of the world that bereth no crowne'. The time was better, he said, than it had ever been before to attack the Adversary, and it was preferable to attack him in France quickly than to wait and suffer him to enter and occupy England. 'For douteles and the Kyng goo not thider, his seid Adversary wold come hyder.'[1] So once more the ancient scare of a French invasion of England was advanced to justify the king's declared intention to resume the war with France to recover his ancestral inheritance. As usual, the Commons responded favourably to a demand for war finance, granting two tenths and two fifteenths, less the usual deduction, and payable in two instalments.[2] The Speaker received an Exchequer payment of £200, presumably for help in securing the taxation.[3] The Parliament was dissolved on 7 June, after less than a month's session.

Serious trouble was now looming for the king at home. Warwick associated the defeat of his own pro-French policy and the undermining of his sense of personal magnificence with the rise of the Woodville family. His own brother had been removed as chancellor and the queen's father, Lord Rivers, now Earl Rivers, was treasurer. Four of the queen's sisters had been wed to great magnates and others of her relations were given similarly fine marriages. There seems to be truth in the allegation that the queen and her relations were financially grasping and to Warwick they represented a new upstart court party of precisely the kind against which magnates had rebelled in the past. In the country too there was discontent; the king's plans for war came to nothing and the Duke of Brittany was forced to make peace with Louis. There is little evidence that Edward intended himself to make a frontal assault on France; his unsuccessful intention seems to have been to operate through anti-French allies, and parliamentary money had been gained and spent to no good purpose. All that the king's policy had achieved so far was to stir King Louis once again to embrace the Lancastrian cause, for instance by helping an abortive Welsh rising instigated by Jasper Tudor.

The enmity of the frustrated and affronted Warwick was not in the least assuaged by gestures of favour by Edward. Rumours had reached the king late in 1467 that Warwick, who was absenting himself from court at the time, was intriguing with Margaret of Anjou and although Edward had

---

[1] *Rot. Parl.* Vol. V, pp. 622–623.
[2] Ibid., pp. 623–4.
[3] J. S. Roskell, *The Commons and their Speakers*, p. 281.

accepted the earl's denial, he rightly remained suspicious. The outraged earl was now making treasonable overtures to George of Clarence, the king's brother, an unstable young man of eighteen whose discontent and ambition Warwick skilfully exploited. Once again, moreover, there was general disorder in the land. But for a time Warwick concealed his intentions and, returning to the court, continued to take an active part on the council. During 1468 there were more Lancastrian disturbances and conspiracies which led to further executions. At the same time, Warwick was encouraging the discontent among the wider populace and in the spring of 1469 uprisings in the north set off two years of upheaval which, in their dramatic shifts of fortune, were unprecedented, even in the turbulent history of the fifteenth century.

The trigger was a rising in Yorkshire under a leader calling himself Robin of Redesdale which was immediately followed by another led by a Robin of Holderness. The latter was probably a Percy-inspired rebellion and was quickly put down by John Neville, Earl of Northumberland, who was Warwick's brother. The Redesdale rebellion was much more serious and its leader is thought to have been a knightly relative of Warwick, a Sir John Conyers.[1] It was a popular uprising almost certainly inspired by Warwick and it revived the old complaints against bad government which had constituted the Yorkist case against Henry VI. Though the revolt was dispersed in its first phase, it quickly revived and when in July Edward began to move north against the rebels he found their number alarmingly and unexpectedly large. In the meantime, Warwick announced the betrothal of his daughter to Clarence and the three of them, together with George Neville, Archbishop of York, crossed to Calais where the archbishop solemnised the marriage. They all then returned to England, immediately making common cause with the rebels but still protesting loyalty to Edward. Their complaint was the ancient cry of rebellious magnates that the king had taken the advice of evil councillors, the Woodvilles, and had rejected that of his own kinsmen, Clarence and Warwick, and that the commons were oppressed.

Events now moved rapidly against the king. Warwick marched on London which felt obliged to admit him, and Edward, who had lingered too long in the north, lacked time to gather a sufficient army. He was wholly reliant on the forces of William Herbert, the Yorkist Earl of Pembroke, and the Earl of Devon and his power was shattered when they were overwhelmed in a battle at Edgecote near Banbury. Devon escaped but Pembroke was executed, for which judicial murder Warwick lacked all

---

[1] C. Ross, op. cit., Ch. 7.

justification even by the standards of the time since Pembroke had fought for Edward whom Warwick still formally recognized as king. Virtually isolated, Edward fell into Warwick's hands on the way south, effectively becoming a prisoner, though he was still treated as king. Shortly afterwards, the Earl of Devon was captured and executed as were among others Earl Rivers, the queen's father, and her brother John. Warwick, however, lacked the support among the nobility to establish his victory. He caused a Parliament to be summoned to York but there was now so much disorder in the land that it had to be cancelled. Warwick had probably intended to put Clarence on the throne but he found no support for it. He was therefore forced to act through Edward, just as Edward's father had been obliged in 1460 to act through Henry VI. This, however, meant freeing the king from physical restraint, to which Edward's response was very different from that of King Henry. Summoning his loyal brother, Richard of Gloucester and others of his friends, including Hastings, the king returned to London in state. Yet despite the humiliation Warwick and his associates had inflicted on Edward and his queen, he took no direct action against them. Instead, he bided his time and issued a general pardon. But when a quarrel broke out in Lincolnshire in the summer of 1470 in which Lord Welles attacked one of his household, Edward acted to quell it with a speed and success that contrasted sharply with his laggardly response the year before.

At this stage Warwick and Clarence broke cover, leading a force to join the Lincolnshire rebels. They were put to flight and Warwick and Clarence fled by sea. Unable to secure admittance at Calais, they were obliged to have recourse to Louis XI. This was the French king's opportunity to contrive and support an alliance between the Lancastrians, Warwick and Clarence. A more improbable association can hardly have been imagined. It was a dishonest expedient which could never have endured. To Queen Margaret, Warwick was the great enemy who had destroyed her husband and shed the blood of the greatest Lancastrians. To Warwick, the Lancastrians stood in the way of his wish to see himself as the power behind his enthroned son-in-law, Clarence. To Clarence himself, it was an absurdity to have betrayed his brother to make Lancaster king.

Yet nothing else was on offer and so Margaret of Anjou and Warwick were formally reconciled. In England, Edward had failed to restore his authority, and in the hope of pacifying the north, he had made the mistake of giving the earldom of Northumberland back to the Percys' heir, taking it from Warwick's brother John Neville who had remained loyal to the king and had actively helped him in the recent troubles. Though Neville was made Marquis of Montagu in compensation, he felt deprived (especially by the loss of lands) and he turned rebelliously towards his brother. His treason was decisive. In September 1470, Warwick, Clarence, Jasper Tudor and the Earl of Oxford landed at Dartmouth with forces paid for by King Louis and immediately declared for King Henry VI. Edward was caught unawares, having gone to the north to put down another Neville rising, and as he came south to meet the invasion, he heard the news that Montagu was defecting to his brother with the troops he had assembled supposedly for the king's cause. Deserted by most of his men and accompanied only by a few loyalists including Gloucester and Hastings, the king could only flee the country. After a narrow escape from drowning while crossing the Wash, he set sail from King's Lynn for the Low Countries and the shelter of Charles of Burgundy. England had fallen to Warwick the king-maker and with no blow struck Henry VI was once again king in name.

Henry was taken from the Tower by Archbishop Neville and Queen Elizabeth took sanctuary at Westminster. But Henry's so-called 'readeption' as king was short-lived. A puppet in the hands of Warwick, who made himself governor of the realm, he summoned what was to be his last Parliament. It sat in sessions before and after Christmas but no record of it remains; the rolls were undoubtedly destroyed on Edward's return. It was virtually treated as a non-Parliament, but we know that it again settled the crown on Henry VI and his son, perhaps with Clarence next in line in the event of the failure of the Lancastrian male line. (There is, however, some doubt about the authenticity of the provision made for Clarence.) This act is known only from the details in an act of 1478 repealing the acts, treaties, communications and exemplifications made by the usurper in 'the most dolorous absence of the king' (Edward), many of which remained in writing 'whereby many inconveniences may ensue'.[1] During the readeption Parliament, Edward's attainders were repealed and the Dukes of Somerset and Exeter, and the Lancastrian claimants to the earldoms of Pembroke and Richmond (Jaspar and Henry Tudor) returned to England. Among the disparate members of the new establishment there was great distrust and a lack of confidence. Henry was visibly a pathetic though not unpopular figure whose mind, after his five years of incarceration, had little contact with reality. The disgruntled Clarence was soon in touch with the brother he had betrayed. Margaret of Anjou was so distrustful of Warwick that she would neither allow her son to come to England or come herself. The returned Lancastrians were unwilling to sustain Warwick in power. Probably the most popular act of Henry's readeption was the execution on Tower Hill of the hated John Tiptoft, Earl of Worcester.

[1] *Stat. R.* Vol. II, pp. 466–467, 17 Edw. IV c. 6; *Rot. Parl.* Vol. VI, pp. 191–193.

Warwick was now under pressure to repay King Louis for his help by joining in an enterprise against Burgundy. But the earl lacked the necessary financial resources and the only consequence of the French king's pressure was to push the Duke of Burgundy, with some reluctance, to assist the Yorkist cause. So in March 1471, Edward IV sailed to England with Burgundian ships and a small invasion force, landing just as Henry IV had done at Ravenspur in Yorkshire. Again like Henry, he was constrained at first to say that he had come only to claim his own duchy. The city of York admitted him; the Percys, in return for receiving back their earldom of Northumberland, refrained from attacking him; and his army rapidly increased as he marched towards London, now openly declaring that he had come to recover the throne. As he moved south, Clarence defected and was reconciled with the king and on 11 April Edward entered London encountering no resistance since Warwick was in the west Midlands gathering his army. Henry VI, who was said to have welcomed Edward as his cousin of York, saying in his simple way, 'I know that in your hands my life will not be in danger,' was placed in close custody. Archbishop Neville was sent to the Tower and Queen Elizabeth came from sanctuary at Westminster where she had given birth to the future Edward V. The king then set out, taking Henry VI with him, to meet Warwick.

At Barnet on 14 April Edward defeated Warwick in a hard fought battle. The earl and his brother Montagu were killed. On the same day, Margaret and Prince Edward of Lancaster landed at Weymouth too late for anything except their own ruin and gathered their supporters, marching towards Wales to join Jasper Tudor. On 4 May, Edward caught and destroyed them at Tewkesbury. There was great slaughter in which Prince Edward and the Earl of Devon were among those killed. Somerset was among the Lancastrian lords executed, and Queen Margaret was made a prisoner at Malvern. With her was Sir John Fortescue, who, however, was spared as were other Lancastrians who had been consistently loyal to Henry VI in exile and had not betrayed Edward. Apart from a shortlived Lancastrian revolt in the north, nothing now stood in Edward's way except a Kentish rebellion led by the Bastard of Fauconberg, the illegitimate son of the Earl of Kent, which was quickly put down.

On 21 May, the king entered London in triumph. All his enemies had been destroyed and all his rivals to the throne in the Lancastrian and male Beaufort lines were dead. Only Henry VI himself remained and the same night he was put to death in the Tower, to which he had been returned after the battle of Barnet; his reputation as a saint had begun. The only conceivable rival claimants to the throne now were two Tudors who carried the Beaufort blood in the female line, Jasper the Lancastrian Earl of

Pembroke who was still at large in Wales and his younger nephew Henry, the Lancastrian Earl of Richmond, the future Henry VII, whose earldom of Richmond had been given to Clarence. After 1470 Henry Tudor was safely in Brittany but neither he nor his uncle could possibly have seemed to be a menace to a king who now had his son and heir and was in undisputed command of the kingdom.

IV

The remaining twelve years of Edward's reign were a time of domestic peace and stability. Although there were inevitably attainders and executions after Edward's recovery of the throne they were not extensive. Many Lancastrians were pardoned, notably John Fortescue and John Morton the later cardinal, who entered the king's service. Edward may well have felt that Lancastrians who had remained loyal to Henry VI until the end were likely to give him more faithful service than Yorkists who had swayed with the political wind. Archbishop Neville was pardoned but in the spring of 1472 this worldly and unscrupulous prelate was suddenly arrested and confined in the castle of Hammes, near Calais. There he was later joined by John de Vere, Earl of Oxford, who had occupied St Michael's Mount in Cornwall but had been forced to surrender it. Now that he was free from dangers at home, the king again began to contemplate the prosecution of the war with France in the belief that the distraction of a successful foreign adventure would work wonders in stimulating the Commons' loyalty. It was, however, four years before he could move against the old enemy.

In the meantime, he again faced trouble with Clarence who was bitterly envious of favour shown to Edward's loyal brother, Richard of Gloucester. As the husband of Warwick's daughter Isobel, Clarence was a claimant to the Neville lands. Now he had a rival; Gloucester was preparing for a union with Warwick's younger sister, the sixteen-year-old widow of the late Prince Edward of Lancaster. At the end of 1471 the two brothers quarrelled openly about the Warwick inheritance which each claimed through his Neville bride, Clarence being particularly enraged by the grant to Gloucester of extensive Warwick lands in the north. Eventually their dispute came to council but even after an arbitration it continued, with Warwick's widow also fighting desperately for the Beauchamp inheritance which had been hers in her own right. It was not until an enactment in

Parliament in 1474 that it was provided that Clarence and Gloucester should share the Warwick properties, the Countess of Warwick being treated as though she was dead. The settlement was generous to Clarence but this silly and imprudent young man showed no more appreciation of this good fortune than he did of his escape from the penalty for his treason in 1470. Once again he was receptive to overtures from Louis XI.

In October 1472, Edward held his first Parliament since his temporary exile; the first also for four years. It was the longest Parliament ever held in England, lasting for seven sessions with six prorogations and spread over more than two years.[1] No future Parliament was to sit for so long until that which was used by Henry VIII to implement the Reformation. Altogether Edward's Parliament summoned in 1472 sat for over 300 days and its principal theme was the provision of money for war. The king's more aggressive foreign policy was made clear at the outset by an unnamed minister, possibly the chancellor, Robert Stillingford, who with good cause denounced Louis XI not only as the root of Edward's recent troubles but for still seeking by craft to disturb the English realm with 'inward werre' (civil strife). Edward's minister also spoke of the perilous and unhealed wounds from the recent civil strife and particularly of the 'multitude' of riotous men who were committing violent mischiefs throughout the land, undermining its prosperity. There was, he said, no more honourable or expedient way of restoring peace and prosperity at home than by occupying these 'idell and riotous people' with 'werre outward' (foreign war). By war, 'many gentlemen, as well yonger brothers as other' might be well rewarded and enabled to settle in France and soldiers now unoccupied could live on their pay in garrisons there instead of disturbing the English peace. Never since the Conquest had peace and prosperity endured at home save when kings had made 'werre outward.' Even the usurper Henry VI, 'notwithstandyng his simplenesse of witte, stode ever in glorie and honour while the werre was contynued by yonde . . .' The dispute between France and Burgundy now enabled England again to engage in France and the Commons were told that, if they gave generous financial help they, like their forefathers, would be rewarded by the flow of wealth into the land.[2]

Edward had an amenable Parliament to deal with, not least because care had been taken to ensure that as many as possible of those returned as members of the Commons were favourable to the king's interest. The king's friends among the nobility used their influence to secure the return of suitable knights and burgesses and Edward, now and in the future, made

[1] *Rot. Parl.* Vol. VI, pp. 3-166.
[2] *Literae Cantuarienses*, ed. J. B. Sheppard, Rolls Series, 1889, Vol. III, pp. 274-282. The Speech for the king is not given in the parliamentary rolls.

sure that he had as large as possible a cadre of members of the royal household in the Commons. In the Parliament of 1472 to 1475, the essential purpose of which was to find money for the projected French war, thirty-nine royal servants were members of the House of Commons, most of them from the household. They constituted about fourteen per cent of the total membership, whereas in the Parliament of 1467–8 royal servants had made up only five per cent of the Commons.[1] The Speaker elected in 1472 was a Cambridge lawyer, John Allington, who served the king at least as well as he did the Commons. In his first speech Allington spoke with particular warmth of the queen, expressing the particular joy in the land at the birth of the king's first son, and also praising the queen's relatives and others who had suffered during the readeption of Henry VI.

By the end of the first session of Parliament on 30 November, the Lords had granted a tenth of their incomes from land and annuities and the Commons agreed to pay for the service of 13,000 archers for a year at a rate of 6d. a man daily. The Commons' money for the archers' pay was also to be found by a special ten per cent tax on income, instead of the traditional tax on all movable property. This was another experiment in the attempts to relate taxation to the means of the taxpayer and it was a generous provision. It was not, however, given without strings. The appropriation of funds for particular purposes remained a strong principle in the Commons' approach to taxation and the grant for the archers was made on the condition that if an expedition had not departed by Michaelmas 1474 the money should be repaid. As a further precaution it was stipulated that revenue from the tax should not be handed to the exchequer but to four special commissioners, who included the Archbishop of Canterbury, and was to be kept at St Paul's until the king was ready for his expedition. Despite the fact that this was so strong a Yorkist Parliament, the Commons had not lost their self-confidence when it came to the power of the purse and they remembered their past complaints against Edward for failing to use money for the war purposes for which they had granted it.[2]

Nor were the Commons diffident about asking the king to take action against the general lawlessness which was once again acute after the recent political conflict. Through Speaker Allington they spoke of crimes and disorder in the land, even in the City and Westminster in disregard of the king's own presence and the sitting of his high court of Parliament. They wanted the enforcement of the old statutes, including those concerning maintenance made under the recent usurpant kings, and complained that the crimes of the powerful were unpunished. Particular attention was

[1] C. Ross, *Edward IV*, pp. 344–345.
[2] *Rot. Parl.* Vol. VI, pp. 4–8.

drawn to the 'outrageous' behaviour of Welshmen in the border areas, with a request for special consultations with the marcher lords. Order had broken down in Wales during the wars with the Lancastrians and Edward's eventual solution was to commit responsibility for order there to a council functioning in the name of his infant son Edward.

The prince had been created Prince of Wales in June 1471 and his title (with that of Earl of Chester) was ratified at the beginning of the Parliament of 1472, as was his grant of the Duchy of Cornwall. The first session of this Parliament was adjourned for a period at Christmas. During the second in February 1473, a committee of twenty-five was appointed to act as councillors and governors to the prince until he was fourteen. This council, of which Speaker Allington was a member, was to administer the prince's possessions, the revenues of which he was now allowed to receive, but it had at first no judicial powers. One of the Commons' petitions had asked the king to send great might and power to the Welsh marches or go himself to restore order, and an effort was made in the spring of 1473 to enforce the law. During the same summer of 1473 Edward also met the marcher lords at Shrewsbury in the course of a progress along the Welsh border (in which he was accompanied by Speaker Allington) to obtain their commitment to try to bring an end to lawlessness. But all this was ineffective. At the end of 1473 therefore, Edward decided that his infant son, with the queen's brother, Earl Rivers, and an inner body of the prince's council should take up residence at Ludlow, the York family's seat on the Welsh border, to exert the royal authority. In subsequent years the power of the prince's council to govern the Principality was gradually extended.

During the second session of Parliament in the spring of 1473, the Commons enlarged their financial help to Edward. It had not been possible to complete the collection of the special income tax of the previous session and its yield was uncertain. The Commons, however, now agreed in addition to grant a conventional subsidy of a tenth and a fifteenth in recognition of the king's urgent need, though this too was strictly appropriated to Edward's war effort. Though it was to be collected in the summer, it was not to be paid out to the king until he had begun to muster his army. The Lords, on the other hand, allowed their income tax grant to be used in advance for the purchase of weapons. In the event, however, the king deferred the collection of the Commons' grant until the autumn as he had signed what he intended to be a strictly temporary truce with France, having failed to make an alliance with Burgundy.[1] On 8 April, Parliament was adjourned until October 1473, Edward spending much of the intervening time in his progress on the Welsh border.

[1] *Rot. Parl.* Vol. VI, pp. 39–41.

Parliament met again in the autumn for a ten weeks session which lasted until just before Christmas. Its principal business was the passing of yet another Act of Resumption. A treaty with the Hanseatic League was also ratified. But the question of the war and of the money to pay for it was in abeyance. If Edward was to pursue his plan for war, an alliance with Charles of Burgundy was essential, but this continued to elude him because Charles was distracted by a scheme through which he vainly hoped to be elected King of the Romans. Parliament returned for a fourth session in January 1474 but the outlook for war remained so uncertain that Edward prorogued it after only a fortnight. It met again on 9 May for two sessions which ran continuously until 18 July save for a week's adjournment for Whitsuntide.

The Duke of Burgundy's imperial dreaming had come to nothing and Edward was now at last able to tell Parliament that the prospect for an attack on France was clear, though an invasion could not take place until the following year. One immediate difficulty was money since there had been a serious shortfall in the revenue collected to pay the 13,000 archers the Commons had agreed to support. The total cost would be about £118,000 but of this only about £31,000 had been collected because parts of the north had failed to pay. Moreover, the tenth and fifteenth granted in the previous session had not been collected. This latter grant was now renewed and would bring in about £30,600 and it was also agreed that a further £5,400 should be raised from those parts of the north which had failed to pay the special ten per cent income tax for the archers' pay. But the total of this revenue was still about £51,000 less than the cost of paying the archers and to make up the difference, a new method of assessment was used to obtain more from those who were charged little or nothing under the conventional method of direct taxation. However, to ease the burden on taxpayers, the additional £51,000 was not to be paid until 1475, half in the June of that year and the rest in November.[1]

Altogether, Edward had managed to extract from this Parliament undertakings to pay the equivalent of three and three-quarter ordinary subsidies and it was with good reason that the chancellor, the Bishop of Lincoln, thanked the Commons for their generosity when he prorogued Parliament. Only Henry V had managed to do better.[2] The date by which the king was to attack France was also put forward; to secure Parliament's money Edward now had to lead his invasion not later than midsummer (St John's day) 1476.[3] To assist the king's enterprise a statute passed in 1474

[1] *Rot. Parl.* Vol. VI, pp. 113–119.
[2] E. F. Jacob, *The Fifteenth Century*, pp. 202–4. For an analysis of Edward's financial devices for the war against France, see, C. Ross, op. cit., Ch. 9.
[3] *Rot. Parl.* Vol. VI, p. 118.

provided that all those who accompanied him to France would have the inheritance of their lands free of the customary inheritance fine.[1]

Soon after Parliament's dispersal, Edward and Duke Charles settled the terms of their alliance. Edward was to invade France with ten thousand men; Burgundy was to recognize Edward as king of France and assist the English invasion. In return, Edward would cede to Burgundy areas in the eastern French provinces, including Champagne and its coronation city of Rheims. For this enterprise, however, even more money than Parliament had already granted was necessary and so Edward began to raise funds by using the extra-parliamentary device of benevolences which were ostensibly free gifts from the better-off in place of military service. The king was the more successful in doing so because he exerted pressure reinforced by charm and persuasion rather than by bullying. By this method, as an Italian writing from London reported, he 'plucked out the feathers of his magpies without making them cry out'. Benevolences were to join the proceeds from the Acts of Resumption and the customs as the staple revenue providers to free the king from regular financial dependence on the Commons.

The Parliament which had begun in 1472 met for the final and seventh session in January 1475 when again the provision of money was the principal business. Once more the Commons had to admit that there would be a delay in producing the new type of grant for supporting the archers because its form was 'so diffuse and laborious'.[2] The collectors used to the old form of tenths and fifteenths clearly could not cope with the innovation and the income tax of 1472 had also produced less than had been expected owing to frauds. The Commons reported that the receivers were unable to collect the whole of the one-tenth income tax and that, in consequence, the king 'lakketh a grete part of such sommes of money as he shuld pay at this tyme to the Lordes, Knyghtes, Squyers, and other reteyned with his Highnes', to the hurt of these retainers and to the king's own displeasure.[3] The Commons' solution was to convert the supplementary tax of 1474 to the old and familiar form and so in place of the innovation the Commons voted the king another full fifteenth and tenth payable just after Easter and a further three-quarters of a tenth and fifteenth in the autumn.

On 14 March, Edward IV's long and friendly Parliament was at last dissolved. Its life had been prolonged entirely so that it could provide the king with money and its statutes and enactments were, like most during

[1] *Stat. R.* Vol. II, pp. 445–447, 14 Edw. IV, c. I.
[2] *Rot. Parl.* Vol. VI, p. 151.
[3] Ibid., p. 121.

Edward's reign, designed to forward business required or favoured by the king. That was true whether it was the Act of Resumption in the first session,[1] or the statute enacted to deal with 'the great scarcity of bow-staves ... in this realm' and the 'excessive Price' at which those available were sold, 'whereby the Exercise of Archery is greatly discontinued, and almost lost'. The remedial statute required that all merchant strangers, that is, alien importers, must bring in four bow-staves, where available, with every ton weight of merchandise they imported.[2] Virtually all Edward's statutes and enactments in this as in others of his Parliaments were of a severely practical nature and more often than not to do with trade. Thus commissioners of sewers were established to deal with rising waters and drowned lands and it was characteristic of the practical nature of Edward's statutes that the only part of Magna Carta re-enacted in this Parliament had to do with the hindrance done to river traffic by the levies at weirs and mills, which were to be pulled down.[3]

It was nearly three years before Edward summoned another Parliament and by then his great French adventure was over with no glory but not a little profit. Preparations for it were lavish, in weapons, men and provisions. The invasion army that landed in Calais in July 1475 was the largest ever led to France by any English king. But although Charles of Burgundy came to visit Edward he brought no army to help the English since he had it employed in besieging the city of Neuss in Germany where once again he had ambitions. After an abortive attempt to besiege St Quentin and the departure of Duke Charles, Edward IV came to the conclusion that he could expect no useful help from Burgundy and, reversing policy, suddenly made terms with King Louis. It was a decision resisted by some of the English nobility, including Gloucester, but most supported Edward. In August the two kings met on a specially built bridge over the Somme at Picquigny and agreed to a seven years truce. Their rival claims to the French crown were put into abeyance by reference to a court of English and French arbitrators which never met. Edward renounced his alliance with Burgundy and agreed to take his army back to England in return for a down payment of 75,000 crowns (about £15,000) from France and a pension of 25,000 gold crowns (about £10,000) annually to be paid by Louis to Edward as long as they both lived. (A by-product of the treaty was the subsequent release and return to France of Margaret of Anjou.)

There is no reason to doubt that Edward had embarked on the war

---

[1] *Rot. Parl.* Vol. VI, pp. 71ff.
[2] *Stat. R.* Vol. II, pp. 432, 12 Edw. IV, c. 2.
[3] Ibid., pp. 438–442, c. VI and c. VII.

seriously with the intention of at least wresting some territory, probably Normandy and Aquitaine, from the French. On the other hand his immediate willingness to come to terms with King Louis almost certainly owed something to Edward's temperamental inclination towards an easy peace rather than a hard war, as well as to the impossibility of relying on Duke Charles. As it happened, the truce was virtually the end of the Hundred Years War, though neither of the participants realized that. Two years later, Charles of Burgundy was killed at Nancy, fighting the Habsburgs and Swiss, and King Louis immediately attacked the Burgundian territories. To escape dependence on the French king Margaret of Burgundy, King Edward's sister, proposed that her daughter Mary should be married to Clarence, who was now a widower after the death of Isobel Neville. But Edward was quite unwilling to put his French pension at risk by involving the English once more in Burgundy's quarrel with France, or to put so much power in the hands of his treacherous brother. So instead Mary was married to Maximilian of Austria, the emperor's son, who obtained with her the claim to the Burgundian lands including the Low Countries. The seed had been laid for the great struggle between France and the Habsburgs, which was to be a dominant theme of the politics of mainland Europe until 1713. Edward IV's England was peacefully outside it and whatever disappointment the Commons felt at the inglorious end to Edward's French expedition, they at least had the satisfaction of having the final three-quarters of a tenth and fifteenth cancelled by the king.

Edward could now reign peacefully on his own augmented resources without resort to the Commons and when he called Parliament again in November 1477 it was for a very different purpose; to deal judicially, once and for all, with the persistent unfaithfulness of the Duke of Clarence. Once again Clarence was nurturing a grievance, this time owing to the king's refusal to allow his marriage to Mary of Burgundy and his enjoyment of her lands. What followed is complex and obscure in detail but the essence of the matter is clear. Clarence began to stay away from court, refusing to eat or drink when he did come on the grounds that his late duchess had been poisoned. What is more, in April 1477 he caused one of his wife's attendants, a woman of good repute called Ankarette Twynho, to be seized from her manor near Frome in Somerset and to be taken by force to Warwick. There he had her brought before the local justices and a jury, accused of having brought about the death of Isobel of Clarence by (as the rolls of Parliament put it) 'a venymouse drynke of Ale myxt with poyson to drynke'. The jury was allegedly intimidated into condemning her and also a John Thursby who was accused of poisoning Isobel's baby. They were indicted, tried and hanged within the space of three hours, but not before some of the jury had come to her to voice their remorse for an untrue verdict which, they said, they delivered only under threat of their own lives. This curious story is told in a petition for the verdict to be reversed, which was submitted by Ankarette's cousin and heir after Clarence's own fall. What lies behind it is unclear, but the whole tale is unlikely to be fictitious.[1]

In the summer of 1477 there was a rising in Cambridgeshire under a man pretending to be the Earl of Oxford, in which Clarence seems to have been in some way involved. At the same time, Louis of France was feeding Edward's suspicion of his brother with allegations that if Clarence had obtained Burgundy by marriage he would have used it against Edward. It was against this background that one of Clarence's servants, Thomas Burdett, was arrested, and with an alleged assistant, executed for attempting to bring about King Edward's death by magic, a charge of which they were doubtless innocent. Clarence now foolishly lent colour to Edward's suspicions by appearing suddenly before the council on the day after their execution to declare, during the king's absence, that both men were innocent. A few weeks later, Edward personally called Clarence to Westminster, accused him before the mayor and aldermen of London of breaking the laws of the realm and had him imprisoned in the Tower. In November a Parliament was summoned to deal judicially with the faithless and trouble-making duke.

It met on 16 January, 1478 and the session was opened by the chancellor, the Bishop of Lincoln, who took as his text: 'The Lord is my Shepherd, therefore shall I not want'.[2] There is clearer evidence for this Parliament than for any other of the reign of the efforts made to secure a House of Commons favourable to the king. Some twenty per cent of the Commons (fifty-seven MPs) had close connections with the court and government, and at least forty-three MPs were active members of the royal household. Once again Allington was Speaker. Most of the business recorded on the parliamentary roll was of a routine kind, including the provision for the marriage of the king's second son Richard Duke of York and of Norfolk to Anne, the six year old daughter of the late Duke of Norfolk, and for him to have her lands if she pre-deceased him. Attainders were reversed and routine petitions on such questions as the paving of Canterbury and Taunton were presented. Laws were made to maintain the quality of cloth and roof-tiles and to forbid the playing of such games as quoits, dice or football instead of practice at archery. There was a new sumptuary law and an act for sending Irishmen back to Ireland with certain specified

---

[1] *Rot. Parl.* Vol. VI, pp. 173–174.
[2] Ibid., pp. 167–195. *Dominus regit me*, literally 'The Lord rules me'.

exceptions. A petition was also enacted which pleaded a breach of parliamentary privilege because of a judgement in Parliament time against a John Atwyll, an MP for Exeter, who had been fined at the Exchequer court at the instance of an Exeter merchant.

But there was one over-riding reason for the meeting of Parliament; the condemnation of the Duke of Clarence. The king introduced his own bill of attainder which, though it is written in the third person, is virtually his utterance. What is more, the only surviving copy bears at the top and bottom Edward's sign manual.[1] (Though printed with the parliamentary rolls, the document was not part of the roll proper but is from an original in the records of the Tower of London.) In the indictment and condemnation, Edward recalled his clemency to former opponents and even to traitors, for which he had been repaid ill and declared that he now faced 'a moch higher, moch more malicious, more unnaturall and lothely Treason' than any before, not only because of its intentions but because 'it hath been contryved, imagined and conspired, by the persone that of all erthely creatures' had reason to give the king love and loyalty, the Duke of Clarence. He spoke of the gifts and grants he made to Clarence, who had nevertheless tried to destroy the king and his family and who had declared that Burdett had been unjustly put to death. He had tried to destroy the king from outside (that is, by the marriage he had sought with Mary of Burgundy) as well as from within and had even spread it abroad that 'the Kyng oure Sovereigne Lorde was a Bastard'. Further, he had secretly kept an exemplification of the agreement made at the time of Henry VI's readeption that Clarence would succeed to the throne in default of male Lancastrian heirs. Despite all this, the king said he could still have found it in his heart to forgive Clarence because of the love he had felt for him in their youth and his nearness of blood. But the duke had so persisted in his misdeeds that the safety of the realm demanded a sentence of high treason.

Witnesses were called for the prosecution, but none for the defence. Clarence made an answer for himself denying the charges and apparently claiming the right of trial by battle. But it was to no avail. He was found guilty by the advice of the Lords Spiritual and Temporal and the Commons and at the conclusion of the bill the declaration that the Commons 'assented' to it precedes the royal assent. The Duke of Buckingham was appointed steward of England to pronounce the sentence and spare Gloucester the task.[2] At this stage, however, Edward delayed sanctioning the execution

---

[1] *Rot. Parl.* Vol. VI, pp. 193–195.

[2] Ibid., p. 195. Apart from the act of attainder the parliamentary roll records nothing of the background of Clarence's case, for which see the Croyland Chronicle, 2nd continuation, trans. H. T. Riley, pp. 477ff., which was almost certainly written by an official who was an eye-witness; an excerpt is in *E.H.D.*, Vol. IV, pp. 328–329.

and some days later Speaker Allington with some of the Commons appeared in the upper house to ask for it to be implemented. Clarence was put to death privately in the Tower, nobody knows how; perhaps by drowning and perhaps even by drowning in a butt of malmsey, which was the contemporary belief.[1] That he had been repeatedly mischievous, treasonable and incorrigible cannot be doubted. He had repeatedly strained Edward's capacity for mercy. But that he was seriously a threat to Edward's kingship is much more questionable. This act of fratricide was an evil omen of the internal family bloodshed which was to destroy the Yorkist family. It was bad for Edward's reputation as well as morally repellent.

The king's position nevertheless seemed impregnable. He was still young and had two sons. His brother Richard was loyal; Clarence's infant son was disqualified by attainder; the king also had daughters. Indeed, his position, financial and political, seemed so unassailable that it might have seemed that Parliament was a disposable institution. The Parliament in which Clarence was condemned was dissolved within six weeks, having been asked for no taxation, and it was nearly five years before another Parliament was summoned. Yet the fact remained that Edward had felt it necessary to have recourse to Parliament for the condemnation of his brother and although he intended to reduce his financial dependence on the Commons there is no reason to think that he had any idea of letting Parliament fall into disuse. Likewise, though statute-making was now largely concerned with the business the king wished to promote, even when it took the form of Commons bills, there is no indication that Edward thought that the law could be made anywhere but in Parliament. Those laws with which he concerned himself were principally to do with trade and industry, weights, prices, overseas trade, and bullion, or were of a highly practical kind such as that concerning land drainage. Most of the laws were made in the interests of a prosperous society and Edward must be deemed a successful king and administrator.

Between the Parliament of 1478 and that of 1483 Edward kept out of continental affairs by carefully balanced negotiations with both Louis of France (who was proposing a dynastic marriage) and Maximilian, who sought a combination with England to help him recover the Low Countries. But in 1479 his relations with Scotland became increasingly tense and Louis did his best to encourage a breakdown to make sure that Edward was too occupied to be tempted to join his quarrel with Maximilian. In 1481 war broke out between England and Scotland, and in that year and again in 1482, the English invaded Scotland under Richard of Gloucester. Berwick

---

[1] *The Great Chronicle of London*, ed. by A. H. Thomas and I. D. Thornley, p. 226; extract in E.H.D., Vol. IV, p. 329.

was recovered for England, though nothing else of substance was achieved. Edward rewarded his brother by giving him the authority to govern the north, where he had great possessions, and palatine rights over conquests in Scotland. Edward's continental diplomacy, however, suddenly looked much less successful than it had done since Picquigny. At the end of 1482, after the death of Mary of Burgundy, Louis and Maximilian (the latter under irresistable pressure from the estates of Flanders) agreed that Mary's infant daughter Margaret of Burgundy should marry the Dauphin, a treaty which not only destroyed any question of a dynastic alliance between the French and English crowns but also brought to an end Edward's French pension and any real hope of an Anglo-French alliance. The king's response was to summon what was to be his last Parliament to meet in January, 1483.[1]

Edward had fought his Scottish campaigns without asking for money. Now he secured a grant of a tenth and a fifteenth, 'for the hasty and necessarie defence of this youre Reame', less the conventional deduction, to be paid at midsummer. He was also given a tax on resident aliens. It seems to have been in Edward's mind once more to threaten war against France. There was a number of petitions including yet another plea from the Commons for the enforcement of the law against wrong-doers and also the statutes against labourers, vagabonds and maintenance. A number of items of business concerned the property of the royal family, including ratification of the rights on the north-west border with Scotland granted to Richard of Gloucester and arrangements for the young Duke of York, married to the Mowbray heiress, to have the Mowbray estates. There were also various social and economic petitions and statutes, including a new sumptuary law restricting apparel according to social rank and a prohibition on the use of fulling mills in which more bonnets and caps could be 'fulled and thikked' in one day than could be fulled and thicked 'by the myght and strengthe' of twenty-four men using hand and foot in the same time.[2] But the Parliament lasted only thirty days, being dissolved on 18 February. Within two months, just short of his forty-first birthday, Edward was dead, of some sudden illness whose nature is unknown but was very probably brought on because he was worn out by excesses in his style of living, not the least of which was over-eating.

Edward IV's sunset years had been a time of unruffled authority in which the king lived richly, patronized the arts and ruled over an increasingly prosperous country. In an age when the success of monarchy depended on the personality of the king, Edward knew better than most how to rule

[1] *Rot. Parl.* Vol. VI, pp. 196–225.
[2] Ibid., pp. 223–224.

personally and though he made serious mistakes he was a highly professional king, as interested in economics and trade as in politics, and closely attentive to the details of administration. He left behind a strong monarchy and machine for the Tudors to develop and a Parliament which, for all its power over money and law making, was again the king's instrument in government. Not least the old aristocratic feuds had at last burned themselves out. On all the apparent evidence it seemed that the dynasty was as safe as the monarchy itself.

CHAPTER 11

Edward V and Richard III: Parliament and Usurper

THE grisly and familiar end of the Yorkist dynasty is a vivid reminder that, for all Parliament's privileges and its importance as a tax granting and law-making assembly, it was without influence on the rise and fall of governments or on the course of high politics at the end of the medieval period. Edward IV's greatest mistake as king was his failure to provide sufficient safeguards for the succession of his twelve-year-old heir. Yet care was especially needed at the onset of this particular royal minority because of Edward's politically misjudged marriage to Elizabeth Woodville and his advancement of her family. As well as being disliked for the favours they had received, particularly on account of their preferential treatment in the marriage market, the Woodvilles appeared to the older Yorkist families as yet another of the court parties by which the older aristocracy had felt plagued during the Plantagenet period. In conjunction with the fear of instability caused by another royal minority, this was a cause of dismay to many who had been firm adherents of Edward IV and whose instinct was to be loyal to his heir. Among these was Lord Hastings, who was perhaps the late king's closest friend, and it was his collaboration with the Duke of Gloucester which was to be fatal to Edward V. To those who thought like Hastings the lessons to be drawn from the troubled minorities of Henry III, Richard II and Henry VI were worrying enough, but their greater fear was that power would fall entirely into the hands of the Woodville family during the new king's early years. Gloucester, by comparison, seemed no menace. It would have occurred to very few to suspect that the boy who was now king would be in any danger from his uncle. Although three other post-Conquest kings had been deposed and then murdered, there had been substantial charges of misgovernment that could be laid against each of them and murder followed deposition because they remained dangerous politically so long as they were still alive. No previous king had been deposed without first having ruled and simply because he existed, which was to be the fate of Edward V. A notable feature of previous royal minorities had been the support given to the under-age sovereigns by their own families. The exemplary loyalty to the infant Henry VI of his two uncles, despite Duke Humphrey's political irresponsibility, could only give encouragement to those loyal Yorkists who preferred government to be conducted not by the Woodvilles but by Richard Duke of Gloucester as Protector, which was also what Edward IV's will required.

On Edward IV's sudden death, the Woodvilles appeared well placed to determine the course of events.[1] For one thing, they controlled the capital from which their two most powerful opponents, the Dukes of Gloucester and Buckingham, were absent. The queen's eldest son by her first marriage, the Marquis of Dorset, was in charge of the Tower and his brother, Edward Woodville, commanded the fleet. The king was at Ludlow castle in the safe hands of his uncle, Earl Rivers, a cultivated and chivalrous man who was the most attractive personality of all the Woodville family. Richard of Gloucester, on the other hand, was apparently handicapped by being far off at his castle at Middleham in Yorkshire. But that in no way weakened his determination to stake his claim to the office of Protector against the preference of the Woodvilles for government by a regency council over which Duke Richard would only be the principal member. The conciliar solution wanted by the Woodvilles was exactly that which had been imposed on Duke Humphrey in 1422, and like his predecessor Duke

---

[1] The best and most comprehensive modern account is by C. Ross, *Richard III* (1974), though I venture to think that Professor Ross somewhat over-emphasizes the extent to which Richard III's actions have to be understood as a characteristic manifestation of the violence of his times and particularly seen in the light of the precedent of violence in his own family, from the death of Richard of York and Henry VI to that of Clarence. Even to his own contemporaries Richard's crime (and they had no doubt of his guilt) was seen as evil beyond tolerance, which is why so many disparate forces combined to overthrow him. A good short account of these events is in E. Jabob, *The Fifteenth Century*. Biographies for the defence of Richard III are Sir Clement Markham's *Richard III; his Life and Character* (1906) which held Henry VII guilty of the princes' death and P. M. Kendall's, *Richard III* (1955) which raised the possibility that Buckingham was responsible. The most useful contemporary evidence is Dominic Mancini, *The Usurpation of Richard III*, ed. and trans. by C. A. H. Armstrong. For a valuable series of extracts from this and other contemporary evidence see *E.H.D.* Vol. IV, pp. 330–347. See also A. R. Myers, 'The Character of Richard III' (reprinted from *History Today*) in *English Society and Government in the Fifteenth Century*, ed. by C. M. D. Crowder (1967).

Richard naturally resisted it. Moreover, if Gloucester was to be Protector, the Woodville party wanted Edward V's coronation to take place as early as possible, on which event Duke Richard's power would be diminished, as Duke Humphrey's had been by the coronation of Henry VI. Once the young king was crowned it would be easier for the Woodvilles to control the government by acting through him. It was this that Lord Hastings was most anxious to prevent. He therefore wrote to Gloucester urging him to come quickly to London. The Duke of Buckingham, the richest and most powerful magnate in the land, who was out of London when Edward IV died, also sent a message to Gloucester assuring him of support. Though Buckingham was married to the queen's sister he detested the Woodvilles and resented the pressure Edward IV had exerted on him when he was young to marry beneath him.

Confident of enough support, Gloucester then set about disarming Queen Elizabeth's suspicions by writing to her offering warm assurances of his loyalty to the new king but also laying claim to the office of Protector under the terms of his brother's will and legal precedent. It is possible that Richard's loyal protestations influenced Earl Rivers and Edward V not to hurry to London. At all events, they set out from Ludlow several days later than they had first intended, fatally late as it turned out. On their way they were intercepted by Gloucester and Buckingham who found Rivers at Northampton. Edward V had gone on a few miles to Stony Stratford. The two dukes lulled Rivers into a false sense of security over a convivial dinner and the following morning had him arrested suddenly at dawn. They then went on to Stony Stratford and, in the presence of the king, arrested Sir Richard Grey, one of the queen's sons by her first marriage, and the king's Chamberlain, Sir Thomas Vaughan, alleging that there was a plot against Gloucester's life. Edward V protested but could do no more. Rivers and the others were despatched to Yorkshire and, having netted in one swoop an important group of the Woodville connection, Gloucester and Buckingham rode on with Edward V to London. When the news reached the capital, the queen was so alarmed that she immediately took sanctuary at Westminster, as she had done during Henry VI's readeption, taking with her her younger son Richard of York, her daughters and also the Marquis of Dorset, the elder son of her first marriage.

On 4 May, Edward was greeted by the mayor and aldermen at the outskirts of London, where Gloucester's war of propaganda immediately began. The citizens were shown four cartloads of weapons as evidence of the evil intents of the upstart Woodville family. Once in London, Edward V was sent to live in the Tower, which was still a royal residence, the coronation was arranged for June and Richard was accepted as Protector and also *tutela* of the king, the second of these titles enabling him to make use of the king's personal authority. Richard quickly put his friends in official positions and delegated vast power to Buckingham, who was not only made the virtual ruler in Wales and its marches but also had authority to raise forces in a number of English shires as well. A Parliament was summoned, the principal task of which was supposed to be (as we know from the first draft of a speech with which the chancellor, Bishop Russell of Lincoln, intended to open it) the establishment of Richard's authority to last until Edward was of ripe years.

It is most likely that by May Richard had already decided to usurp the throne, even if that had not been his intention from the start. How precisely he intended to go about it was perhaps not yet quite clear to him. He was a brilliantly inventive and ruthless tactician but a poor strategist who was incapable of seeing the danger that lurks in some tactical victories. His tactical successes had already been such as to diminish his future freedom of action. He had now gone so far that, whatever his original intentions, it must have been apparent to him that, when Edward V reached the age at which he could no longer be denied the exercise of power, he would punish Gloucester for the humiliation which had been heaped on himself and on his mother's family. Edward, therefore, must be prevented from ever attaining that power.

At this stage, a number of loyal Yorkists who had supported Richard's claim to be Protector evidently became worried about his real intentions. Lord Hastings was the most notable and potentially dangerous among them. So on 13 June, at a meeting of part of the council at the Tower, Richard suddenly had Hastings arrested, charging him with treason and also, most implausibly, of engaging in sorcery with both Queen Elizabeth and with Jane Shore, the late king's mistress. Lord Stanley and Bishop Morton of Ely were also arrested and detained in the Tower. Hastings was condemned on the spot and immediately sent out to be beheaded. Stanley, however, was quickly released and Morton only kept under restraint. Richard may have supposed that the death of Hastings would suffice to strike general fear without creating dangerous combinations against him, which might well have been the consequence of more executions.

It was now essential for Gloucester to stop the coronation which was fixed for 22 June. First he used the Archbishop of Canterbury as an intermediary to persuade Queen Elizabeth to let the young Duke of York leave sanctuary. The Protector's argument was that it would not be proper for the coronation to take place without the presence of the king's younger brother. The truth, however, was that it was logically necessary for both boys to be in the hands of the intending usurper. Certainly, if the older was to be killed as well as dethroned, Gloucester's possession of the crown would not be safe so long as the younger was alive. Indeed, Gloucester's determination to secure both boys before he usurped the throne is some circumstantial confirmation that he already contemplated the double murder of which some historians have sought to acquit him. The queen's decision to relinquish her son was probably taken because she suspected, with good cause, that Gloucester would take him by force if she refused. The sanctuary was surrounded by armed men and escape was out of the question. But the queen's general fears were evidently unallayed since she refused to leave sanctuary herself or to allow her daughters to go.

Once in possession of his younger nephew, Gloucester acted with ruthless speed. The boy was sent to join his brother in the Tower; orders were despatched to Yorkshire for the summary execution of Rivers, Grey and Vaughan; the Parliament was cancelled and arrangements for the coronation stopped. On 22 June, nine days after Hastings' execution, a Cambridge theologian, Dr. Ralph Shaw, a brother of the mayor of London, preached a serman at St Paul's Cross, declaring that Richard ought to be king on the grounds that Edward IV's children were bastards, their parents' marriage having been invalid because of an alleged pre-contract betrothal of Edward IV to the Lady Eleanor Butler. According to one account it was also alleged that Edward IV himself was illegitimate, an astonishing charge which, if it was made, cast a gross reflection on the honour of Dame Cecily of York, Richard's own mother. That some such allegation was at least hinted at has some support from a later complaint by Dame Cecily about the wrong Richard had done her. There is also a clearly implied reference to it in the formal 'petition' asking Richard to take the throne, which was later incorporated in the Parliament roll. 'Over this,' the petition stated, 'we considre, howe that Ye be the undoubted Son and Heire of Richard late Duke of Yorke . . . and in right Kyng of Englond,' a statement which, by carefully side-stepping any direct claim that Richard was Edward IV's heir, seems to imply doubts about his late brother's own right. The petition went on to note that Richard 'was born withyn this Lande; by reason wherof, as we deme in oure myndes, Ye be more naturally enclyned to the prosperite and commen wele of the same'.[1] This too was obviously a reference to the suggestion of Edward's pretended bastardy since it was not uncommonly assumed by medieval minds that great men born out of the country, as Edward IV had been, were more likely to have been illegitimately conceived on that account. The truth was, however, that none of the many reasons justifying Richard III's usurpation had any substance and every

---

[1] *Rot. Parl.* Vol. VI, p. 241.

effort was therefore made to compensate for what each individual argument lacked in quality by the quantity of reasons given.[1]

In the initial propaganda, however, the theory of Edward's pre-contract to Lady Eleanor Butler, told to Gloucester by the time-serving Bishop Stillington of Bath and Wells, seems to have been pre-eminent. There was nothing in it, but it sufficed for Gloucester's purpose. Then, on 24 June, Buckingham advanced Gloucester's claim before a gathering of the mayor, aldermen and leading citizens of London at the Guildhall, where those who signified their approval of his advocacy did so, as the Great Chronicle of London recorded, 'more for fear than for love'.

On the following day, Buckingham spoke in the same terms to a gathering of lords and gentry which seems to have consisted of those who had set out to attend the Parliament summoned in Edward V's name too soon to be stopped by notice of its cancellation. Whether or not the alleged pre-contract theory was the mainstay of Buckingham's rhetoric to this assembly is unknown, but it was only one of several arguments used in a petition adopted by a further gathering of the same men on the following day; this asked Gloucester to accept the crown and royal dignity 'accordyng to this Eleccion of us the Thre Estates of his Lande, and by youre true Enherritaunce'.[2] The assembly then went to Richard at Baynard's Castle, by the Thames near Blackfriars, where Buckingham read petitions (later incorporated in the parliamentary roll) in which, as we shall see, the pre-contract theory occupied a somewhat secondary place to a general assertion of the iniquity of Edward IV's government.[3]

The assembly of lords and gentry which offered the crown to Richard of Gloucester bore a marked resemblance to that in which Henry IV had secured it from Richard II. Both consisted of men summoned to Parliaments which were never held, and considered to represent the estates of the realm. Thus both usurpers were enabled to claim that they had been called to the throne by the estates of the realm without having to acknowledge that they owed their kingship to parliamentary enactment. Parliament simply confirmed and recorded what had been done. So, after a brief and formal hesitation, Richard of Gloucester accepted the petition and immediately rode to Westminster Hall, accompanied by many lords spiritual and temporal, where he formally took possession of the throne by sitting on the royal marble seat at the king's bench. The coronation was fixed for 6 July when it was celebrated with as much additional pomp as could be arranged to buttress a usurped title. There was a particularly large

[1] See below, pp. 624–6.
[2] *Rot. Parl.* Vol. VI, p. 241.
[3] See below, p. 625.

attendance of the higher nobility, with Buckingham at their head, none wishing to be excluded from the new king's favour. Between July and the early autumn of 1483, Edward IV's sons were gradually withdrawn from public view. They first ceased to be allowed to play in the grounds of the Tower and were then gradually observed less and less in their inner apartments until they were seen no more. Contemporaries had no doubt that they had been murdered and Richard III did nothing to try to contradict this belief. That is understandable. The princes were equally dangerous to him whether they were thought to be dead or thought to be alive. If Richard claimed that they were alive, they would still provide an incentive for an uprising to put Edward V back on the throne. Indeed, there would have been little point in ordering them to be killed unless it were at least tacitly understood that they were dead and that Richard III therefore had no Yorkist rivals. On the other hand, they could not be openly declared dead, since this would instantly unite all Richard's enemies, Yorkist and Lancastrian, in anger against him. It was the mark of Richard III's incomprehension of political strategy that he had failed to understand that this would be so. His usurpation had been achieved by a *coup d'état* and the capital city was intimidated by Richard's and Buckingham's troops, other lords having been told to keep their retinues down. The political atmosphere was pervaded by fear. In the distant north alone, where he had built his political reputation as an efficient governor, and where the fate of the dispossessed Edward V was made unreal by distance, Richard's credit remained good. But in the south there was no general support for his usurpation.

Moral outrage more than political interest was to raise against Richard III the combination by which he was eventually, if only by a hair's breadth, destroyed. Even by the standards of his own time, the nature of Richard's usurpation was heinous. The chancellor of France was making more than a political point when, addressing the States General of Tours in January, 1484, by which time the two princes were already thought to be dead, he spoke of the state of affairs in England since Edward IV's death and, in a reference which makes it clear that their murder was now the common assumption, declared: 'Reflect how his children, already big and courageous, have been killed with impunity, and the crown transferred to their murderer . . .'[1]

For a short time, Richard III remained unchallenged and in July he embarked on a progress to Reading, Oxford (where he was lavishly entertained at Magdalen, such is the magnet force of power, by William

---

[1] *E.H.D.* Vol. IV, p. 337.

Wayneflete) and then on to his own power base at York. He had done his best by small acts of clemency and indulgence to the relations of his victims (including Hastings' widow) to win public opinion but to no useful purpose. The south of England was irreconcilable and in the autumn a movement developed there for the rescue of Edward IV's sons, if they were alive, or if not, to take revenge for their death. It was essentially a revolt of the gentry and especially of those associated with the household and court of the late King Edward IV (including those of the Woodville connection) in alliance with disaffected Lancastrians. Into this conspiracy was drawn the Duke of Buckingham, for reasons which are obscure. He can hardly have expected to receive from Richard more power than the inordinate amount he had already been given. Nor is it altogether easy to believe that he had been genuinely outraged by the fate of the two young princes of whose murder, indeed, one modern theory has held Buckingham himself to be possibly guilty. It also seems unlikely that he can have had any hopes of gaining the throne for himself, even though he had a remote claim to it. For the key figure in the rebellion was the exiled Henry Tudor, the legatee through the Beaufort line of the Lancastrian claim, which he had inherited through his mother, Lady Margaret Beaufort, now Lord Stanley's wife. Buckingham was not only aware of Henry Tudor's part in the movement. He seems to have actively promoted the idea that Henry should have the crown and should undertake to unite the two dynasties by marrying King Edward's daughter Elizabeth of York, a scheme quite possibly invented by Bishop Morton.

Whatever the reason, when rebellions broke out right across the south from Kent to Devon, Buckingham was fully involved and Morton was with him when he marched from Wales to join the rebels. The revolt, however, misfired. The uprising in the south-east in October took place too soon and was prevented by the Duke of Norfolk from reaching London. Another rising followed in the counties from Berkshire to Somerset of which Salisbury was the centre, and Exeter was the focus of a revolt in the west. The rebellion was ill co-ordinated and easily dealt with. On his way from Wales, Buckingham was harassed by hostile forces and bad weather, found little support (for he was personally unpopular) and was faced with desertions. His ally, Bishop Morton, seeing that an ill wind blew, escaped to Flanders. Buckingham himself, after difficulties in crossing the flooded Severn, was found alone in Shropshire, captured and delivered to the king, who had moved south to Salisbury. There Buckingham was condemned and beheaded on 2 November, five years after he had pronounced sentence of death on Clarence. Henry Tudor, who had set sail from Brittany, tried and failed to land in Dorset and Devon and retreated across the Channel.

The precise purpose of the rebellion is less than clear. Some Yorkists must have gone into it in a last hope of rescuing Edward V. But for those many more adherents of the House of York who assumed that it was now too late to do so, the object was to replace Richard by Henry Tudor, who could have been involved for no other purpose than to claim the crown for himself. Assuming that Edward V was dead, Henry Tudor's accession and marriage to Elizabeth of York made good sense and although the uprising was an ignominious failure Henry derived great benefit from the large numbers of refugees, Yorkists and Lancastrians, who afterwards had no option but to escape from England and rally to his cause overseas. On Christmas Day, 1483, in Brittany, Henry Tudor solemnly took a public oath before these exiles that he would marry Elizabeth of York once he had gained the throne of England.

In the aftermath of the rebellion, Richard III was restrained in his punishments. Relatively few of those involved in the uprisings were put to death. But his failure to win the support of the people of the south led him to a great error; the plantation of northerners in the southern counties on lands he had declared forfeit by rebels. This was a further affront to the tight-knit communities of the shires affected and they became Richard's inveterate enemies. He still retained his support in the north and of most of the greater aristocracy which had politically committed itself to him. Yet there were few he could trust. The position of Lord Stanley, the powerful magnate of the north-west, symbolized that of many others. In the rising of the southern counties Stanley had remained with Richard while his wife Margaret Beaufort, the Countess of Richmond, plotted in support of her son Henry Tudor. Her lands were forfeit but Richard was so fearful of making more enemies that he allowed Stanley to keep the income from her lands for his life. Almost to the end, Stanley's position was ambiguous, until at Bosworth he opted at the last moment for the winning side.

Richard III's only Parliament met on 23 January, 1484 at Westminster, having been postponed from November because of the rising.[1] Little is known of its composition but given the political climate of the time it is impossible to doubt that every effort was made to produce a membership of the Commons favourable to the king. Certainly the performance of the Commons supports this assumption. Parliament was opened with a sermon by Bishop Russell of Lincoln, who had been Edward IV's chancellor and who evidently felt no difficulty of conscience in continuing in that post under Richard III. This was, in fact, the third draft of the speech the bishop had prepared for the Parliament he had been expecting to open since

---

[1] *Rot. Parl.* Vol. VI, pp. 237–263.

Edward IV's death, the first draft having been written for the Parliament of Edward V which was never held.[1] The text on which the chancellor eventually delivered his address was, 'We have many members in one body and all members do not have the same office.' His theme was the need every member of the body politic has of all the others. As with every member of the natural body, even 'the moste noble membre may not say to the leste or vileste of them alle, I have no nede of the . . .' Each member had its appropriate part. There were many diverse members of the 'grete body of Englonde' but they could be reduced to three, the Lords Spiritual, the Lords Temporal and the Commons. The prince was to give equal justice with mercy to all; the subjects were to labour so that 'hys roialle and necessarye charges may be supported'. Making a comparison with the need for food for the belly in the natural body, Bishop Russell said that in the body politic, the belly and womb were 'where the kynge ys hymselfe, hys courte and hys counselle'. The speech is of interest on two counts. First, it was a fascinating example of trimming to a changing political wind through successive drafts. The first draft extolled 'owre glorious prince and kynge Edward the Vth here present' but at the same time (for this was to have been a parliament under Richard's protectorate) it contained a rebuke by pun to the displaced Woodvilles. Declaring that lords were the stable element in the community, the bishop's undelivered text likened them to islands surrounded with waters whereby greater surety was to be found 'than in the see or in any grete Ryvers'. Secondly, the speech in all its drafts was a notable expression of an evolving theory of the estates of the realm as embodied in Parliament. In the first draft for Edward V's Parliament the estates are described as consisting of king, nobles and people, but the speech opening the Parliament of Richard III defined the three estates as the Lords Spiritual and Temporal and Commons, with the king as the head apart from the rest.

The Commons were then charged by the chancellor to assemble on the following morning in their accustomed house and to elect a Speaker who should be presented to the king. In order that justice should be done alike to natives and to strangers wishing to complain in Parliament, receivers and triers of petitions were appointed. On the second day of Parliament, the Commons sent some of their number to inform the Lords that they had chosen a Speaker, whom they did not yet name, and to ask the Lords so to inform the king and to ask when it would please the king for the Speaker to be presented. On the following Wednesday, as the roll records (in Latin) the

---

[1] Only a summary of the speech is given in the parliamentary roll; the detailed texts are printed in S. B. Chrimes, *Constitutional Ideas of the Fifteenth Century*, pp. 167–191.

Commons 'appearing before the lord king in open Parliament, presented to the lord king William Catesby as their Speaker, with whom the lord king was well content', as well he might be. Catesby was one of Richard's closest adherents, the 'Cat' in the well-known political rhyme describing England under Richard III:

> *The catte, the ratte and Lovell our dogge*
> *Rulyth all Englande under a hogge.*

The 'rat' was the king's closest councillor, Sir Richard Ratcliffe, Lord Lovel (promoted to the rank of viscount during the Parliament) was the king's chamberlain and the 'hogge' was Richard III himself whose heraldic device was the white boar.

A gentleman lawyer, Speaker Catesby was from a Lancastrian family, but had himself adhered to Edward IV. He had also received favours from Lord Hastings, whom he is said to have betrayed to Richard of Gloucester. Having first raised with Hastings the question whether he would support Richard's taking the crown and having ascertained that he would not, Catesby had then, according to Thomas More, encouraged the Protector to destroy Hastings. Thereafter Catesby (who became chancellor of the exchequer in place of Hastings) rose rapidly in the new king's service. He was always in close attendance on Richard and, like Ratcliffe and Lovel, he was an influential councillor. No Speaker could have been more suitable to Richard and we can only guess at the royal influence used to plant him in Parliament (for which seat is uncertain) and then to procure his election as Speaker. The simple fact of Catesby's election as Speaker is evidence enough of the pliancy of the Commons, not least because, unlike most previous Speakers, he had never sat in the Commons before and can have had no personal acquaintance with its procedure. Fifteenth century Speakers were, as we have seen, generally in the king's interest as well as in that of the Commons, and under Edward IV they were usually royal councillors. Catesby, however, stood unusually close to the king and his job was plainly to manage the Commons, virtually as a minister, in Richard's interest.

The first business of the Parliament, indeed the foremost of its purposes, was an enactment to give the stamp of parliamentary recognition to the usurpation. This was done by the presentation and enactment of a bill which incorporated and adopted the petition by which Richard had been invited to take the crown. The bill began by citing the roll of parchment containing articles written on behalf of the Lords Spiritual and Temporal and the Commons 'by many and diverse Lords Spirituells and Temporalls and other

Nobles and notable persones of the Commons in grete multitude' and delivered to Richard of Gloucester who had 'benignely assented' for the sake of the public weal.

The bill then continued with the statement that because the three estates and those drawing up the petition had not been 'assembled in the fourme of Parliament... diverse doubts, questions and ambiguitees, been moved and engendred in the myndes of divers personnes'. Therefore, 'to the perpetuall memorie of the trouth' it was ordained that the tenor of the roll and petition drawn up by the three estates 'out of Parliament' should now 'by the same three Estates assembled in this present Parliament... bee ratified, enrolled, recorded, approved, and auctorized, into removyng the occasion of doubtes and ambiguitees'. Everything in the petition was to be of the same effect as if it had been affirmed, specified, desired and approved 'in a full Parliament'.[1] Thus the 'estates' were deemed to have some sort of existence outside Parliament, in which capacity they had called Richard to the throne on account of 'right', which meant that he did not owe his throne to parliamentary election. On the other hand, the high court of Parliament, which was also the highest organized manifestation of the estates of the realm, had set its formal seal of approval on what had been done. The petition in full then followed, with its jumble of justifications.

It began by recalling how the land had once dwelt in peace and tranquillity when the king had followed the advice of certain Lords Spiritual and Temporal and of 'othre personenes of approved sadnesse'. In those days God had been honoured, the land had been well defended and trade had prospered. But subsequently those that had the government of the land (that is, Edward IV), delighting in flattery and led by sensuality and concupiscence, had followed the counsel of insolent, vicious and avaricious persons (that is, the Woodvilles) so that the prosperity of the land decreased and felicity was turned into misery. The petition spoke of the 'ungracious pretensed' marriage of Edward IV to Elizabeth Woodville, of the perversion of good rule, of a land governed by self-will and pleasure in which there were murders, extortions and oppression, no man was sure of his life, land, livelihood, daughter, wife or servant, and with 'every good Maiden and Woman standing in drede to be ravished and defouled'. (Such, men were now required to believe, had been the condition of the land in which Richard of Gloucester had flourished for twenty years as his brother's trusted henchman in the north.) The petition spoke of the Woodville marriage as made by witchcraft and celebrated in a private chamber, 'a prophane place', instead of openly in church. Only then, after

[1] *Rot. Parl.* Vol. VI, p. 240.

the ground had been well prepared by other arguments, came the allegation that before this marriage Edward had 'stode maryed and trouth plight' to Lady Eleanor Butler so that Edward and Elizabeth had lived in adultery and their children were bastards. Likewise, the issue of Clarence was disqualified from the throne by attainder. Furthermore, Richard of Gloucester, unlike Edward IV, had been born at home and therefore the Estates had 'more certayn knowlage of youre Byrth and Filiation aboveseid' an implied reference to rumours of Edward IV's bastardy. Thus the imagination was stretched to discover any conceivable justification for Richard's claim, however improbable, before the petition came to the point by beseeching him to take the crown.

The bill which sanctifies this most criminal of English usurpations then concluded with one of the most ringing declarations of the importance of Parliament ever devised, with an unconscious irony which exemplifies the paradox of the political lawlessness and the appeal to parliamentary lawfulness which was characteristic of the later Middle Ages. First, it was declared that Richard's title was founded by right in the laws of God and of nature and upon the ancient laws and customs of the realm. But the act continued by declaring that, nevertheless, 'the most parte of the people of this Lande is not suffisantly lerned in the abovesaid Lawes and Custumes, wherby the trueth and right in this behalf of liklyhode may be hyd, and nat clerely knowen to all people and thereupon put in doubt and question'. Moreover, it continued, 'the Courte of Parliament is of suche auctorite, and the people of this Lande of suche nature and disposicion, as experience teacheth, that manifestacion and declaration of any trueth or right, made by the Thre Estates of this Reame assembled in Parliament, and by auctorite of the same, maketh, before all other thyngs, moost feith and certaynte; and, quieting mens mydes, remoeveth the occasion of all doubts and seditious langage'. Therefore, at the request and by the assent of the three Estates of the realm, Lords Spiritual and Temporal assembled in Parliament, it was enacted that Richard III was the undoubted king of the realm 'as well by right of Consanguinite and Enheritaunce, as by lawefull Elleccion, Consecration and Coronacion', an unusually comprehensive statement of all the rival notions of what might be said to authenticate kingship. The act concluded by vesting the crown in Richard for his life, and in the heirs of his body thereafter and specifically declaring his son, Prince Edward, to be the heir apparent.[1]

So what parliamentary approval could do to make Richard's title good was done and Parliament was also required to deal with two other matters of

---

[1] *Rot. Parl.* Vol. VI, pp. 241–242.

political importance. The first was to pass acts of attainder confirming the forfeitures of rebels' land which he had already implemented on his own authority. The king's grants of forfeited lands to his supporters were also confirmed in law, despite the fact that they had been made arbitrarily. There were more than a hundred attainders, including twenty-eight in Kent and Surrey alone, fourteen in Berkshire, thirty-three in Wiltshire and eighteen in the west. (About a third were later pardoned.) There was also a number of enactments which reversed acts of Edward IV, including that which had settled the estates of the Duchy of Exeter on issue of a branch of the Woodville family. Edward IV's settlement on Queen Elizabeth was also overturned.

The second legislative purpose of the Parliament was the passage of statutes designed to establish Richard III's popularity as a reforming monarch who had come to the throne to redress the grievances of his brother's reign. Indeed, the recital of the corruption of government under Edward IV with which the petition calling Richard to the throne had opened had been a prelude to his attempt to buy popularity by reforms. Among the abuses now made illegal was the late king's exaction of the supposedly free-will gifts known as benevolences.[1] There was also a series of legal reforms. One of these allowed bail to persons suspected of felony, thus protecting them from imprisonment before trial, and also prevented the seizure of their goods before trial.[2] Another required that jurymen should be of good name and repute, and have a certain property qualification, though this only applied to the sheriff's tourn, which had already been largely by-passed as a court.[3] There was also a further act to reform the courts of piepowder which adjudicated summarily on disputed transactions in markets; penalties were provided against officials who misused their authority.[4] Most of the other acts of Richard's Parliament dealt (in the Yorkist tradition) with trade and commerce, one being a long and detailed set of regulations against dishonesty in the cloth trade.[5] All these enactments, initiated by the king and council, were a manifestation of Richard's wish to gain popular approval for his rule, and there was good sense in most of them. He had the makings of an effective king who understood the needs of good government. He had shown himself an efficient ruler of the north; now he sought to do the same for the kingdom as

[1] *Stat. R.* Vol. II, 1 Ric. III, c. 2.
[2] Ibid., c. 3.
[3] Ibid., c. 4.
[4] Ibid., c. 6. The courts of piepowder, or *pieds poudrés* (dusty feet), were so called because the merchants came straight in without ceremony for the settlement of differences on the day of their occurrence and for the immediate punishment of offenders.
[5] Ibid., c. 8.

a whole. Yet the way in which Richard had frightened so many into accepting his will suggests that the shadow of potential tyranny was seen to hang over the usurpation. Richard asked his Parliament for no direct taxation; to have done so would have diminished his popular appeal. Indeed, he remitted the subsidy that had been granted to Edward IV in January 1483. Yet what he sacrificed by this fiscal modesty was nothing compared to the advantage he gained by obtaining the parliamentary grant of tunnage and poundage and the wool subsidies for life. No former king had received this grant in the first year and first Parliament of his reign; even Edward IV had had to wait for it until his second Parliament which was held in his fourth regnal year. After four weeks of concentrated business Richard's Parliament was dissolved.

In government and administration as in other action Richard was swift, intelligent and thorough. His lasting organizational achievement was the Council of the North which sat at York charged with the civil administration of the border counties and their public order as well as their defence against the Scots. But he was driven forward by a gambler's temperament which apparently made him incapable of understanding others' reactions to his actions. His was a character deeply flawed in a way which is not altogether out of line with the recklessness which is perhaps the fundamental feature of Shakespeare's caricature of him. Most of his brief reign was spent in trying to bolster his throne against his enemies abroad while one by one his domestic hopes collapsed. In April 1484, to the king's great grief, his son and heir Prince Edward died, and Richard first chose as his heir presumptive Clarence's only child, the Earl of Warwick (despite the attainder) but later named instead his sister's son, John de la Pole, Earl of Lincoln. But Richard had probably not given up hope of a direct heir. In March 1484, he had made an agreement with Elizabeth Woodville which allowed her and her daughters to leave sanctuary, the king swearing a solemn public oath on holy relics that they would be safe. Then, when his queen, Anne Neville, died in March 1485, Richard was so generally believed to be contemplating marrying his niece, Elizabeth of York, that he was obliged formally to deny that any such incestuous idea had ever entered his mind. Yet it seems quite likely that it had.[1] Above all, his attempt to gain consent for his rule by offering popular government was frustrated by the enmities aroused by his usurpation.

For over twelve months before invasion came, Richard lived in expectation of it. What he did not know was where Henry Tudor would land; whether on the east coast, or in the south or in Wales. During the

[1] C. Ross, *Richard III*, pp. 144–146.

summer of 1484, therefore, Richard had made his headquarters at Nottingham castle, in the heart of England, from which he could most easily advance to repel invasion from whichever coast it came. No invasion had immediately followed and from November, and through the Christmas and winter season, the king was back again in the south where he learned that Henry Tudor was certainly planning an invasion for 1485. From the end of 1484, the Yorkist gentry were placed on the alert and commissions of array were issued. This was at least one important reason for not holding a further Parliament, despite the king's growing need for money; to have summoned sympathetic gentry to Parliament would have been to call them away from the defensive arrangements of which they were an essential part. In his need for money, therefore, Richard now began raising, or trying to raise, forced loans which were not far short of the benevolences he had recently outlawed. The whole of the political nation was uneasy and on edge, and from June 1485, Richard was back in Nottingham castle waiting to learn where his challenger had struck.

On 7 August, 1485, Henry Tudor landed at Milford Haven, accompanied by his uncle Jaspar Tudor, Bishop Morton and the Earl of Oxford, who some time before had left his imprisonment at Hammes to join Henry, accompanied by his former gaoler, the lieutenant of the castle, whom he had persuaded to defect with him. Henry brought with him, as well as a few hundred Yorkist and Lancastrian adherents, a small force of some 2,000 French mercenaries, paid for by the king of France. It had been Richard's calculation that the invading army would be resisted by those whom he thought to be his supporters among the Welsh gentry. Instead, many of those on whom Richard had counted went over to join Henry, who was able to march unopposed to Shrewsbury at the head of a growing army including recruits from north Wales. Shrewsbury surrendered and Henry went on to Stafford and then to Lichfield. While at Stafford, he had negotiations with Sir William Stanley, Lord Stanley's brother. Both Stanleys were sympathetic and had been made aware of the planned invasion, but their commitment to active support remained uncertain. In the meantime, Richard had summoned all his supporters, including the Duke of Norfolk and the Earl of Northumberland, to join him in resisting the invader. Sir Richard Brackenbury, lieutenant of the Tower, was ordered to bring a southern force. But signs of the disloyalty which was to be the cause of Richard's destruction were already apparent. Thus although Brackenbury had been specially instructed to keep an eye on any unreliable gentry he had recruited, two of the more important of them managed to get away by night to join Henry Tudor. Many others had stayed away from the beginning and only a minority of the peerage was with Richard at

Bosworth. There were signs too that Henry Percy, Earl of Northumberland, was discontented since he had made no speedy efforts to raise men in the north, and at Bosworth took no active part in the battle. The truth was that such loyalty as Richard had enjoyed, even from those he had rewarded most, had been steadily diminishing from the time of Buckingham's rebellion and the loss of support from men on whom he counted is itself tantamount to a contemporary comment on Richard's kingship.

Richard then moved on to Leicester, preparing to confront the challenger whom he had already twice proclaimed an outlaw with no claim to the throne, and whose only royal descent was from an illegitimate though legitimated son of John of Gaunt. The king's greatest uncertainty was about the intentions of Lord Stanley, whose fidelity he had reason to doubt but who could not openly adhere to Henry because the king held Stanley's son, Lord Strange, as a hostage. Henry had meanwhile left his army to have secret talks with the Stanleys and he was presumably given undertakings that they would help as and when they could.

On 22 August, the two armies fought each other near Market Bosworth, the king having a substantially larger force than his challenger and occupying higher ground. Richard commanded his centre; Norfolk and his forces were on the king's right; Northumberland on his left. Lord Stanley had placed his men in an ambiguous position between the two main armies so that neither could be certain what he would do. The king therefore summoned him to help, threatening to take his son's life if he did not. When Lord Stanley did not move, Richard seems to have given orders for Strange's execution but this was not carried out. Northumberland also hung back, not attacking in response to Richard's call for his help on the grounds that he must watch Stanley, as he had been deputed to do. Northumberland's troops were therefore never engaged in the battle. On the other hand, Henry's position was dangerous and when he appealed to Lord Stanley the only reply he received was that Stanley would move when he was able.

There is little clear evidence about the course of the battle.[1] Its climax came when Richard, perhaps to anticipate a feared attack by the troops of Sir William Stanley, decided to bring the fight to an issue by attempting to destroy Henry Tudor personally, who also commanded his own centre. From long experience in the domestic wars, Richard knew that once the commander of an opposing army was killed, its resistance would crumble. He therefore took the risk of leading his own knights and men to attack his

---

[1] For an account of the battle of Bosworth see A. Goodman, *The Wars of the Roses*, pp. 89–95.

opponent. It was the final demonstration of his gambler's recklessness and had it come off, as it almost did, all effective challenge to his kingship would have been ended. At the decisive moment, however, Sir William Stanley struck against the king and in the ensuing battle Richard was killed, fighting with a desperate courage and refusing to flee. The Duke of Norfolk, who commanded the king's vanguard, was also killed in the battle. Of Richard's three closest councillors, Ratcliffe was slain in the fighting, Lovel escaped, and the former Speaker Catesby was taken after the battle and executed. Lack of loyalty had undermined and treachery had finally undone the usurper. The crown which Richard had worn in battle was placed on Henry's head, according to tradition by Lord Stanley, who subsequently became the Earl of Derby. Richard's body was stripped and taken naked, slung across a horse, to a monastery at Leicester where, after being displayed, it was buried in a rough and ready way. When the monastery was dissolved, Richard's bones were thrown into the river Stour. So ended the Plantagenet line.

The year 1485 used, by tradition, to be taken as marking the end of English medieval history and it is as good as several other possible dates for this purpose of convenience. In respect of parliamentary history, 1485 certainly has its own logic as a stopping place. It must be emphasized, however, that this is not because the advent of the Tudors brought any change of system or in methods of government. Nor did the status of Parliament alter with the replacement of Richard III by Henry VII. The Tudors continued the highly personal government of the Yorkists, who had administered the realm through carefully chosen professional councillors, instead of by the aristocratic Lancastrian council. The practices of Parliament and its functions in the government of the nation which were characteristic of the Yorkist period also went on under Henry VII. Meetings of Parliament were often infrequent and politically it remained largely an instrument of the king's rule. As under the Yorkists, statutes continued to originate, for the most part, not from the Commons but from the king's government. The Commons still jealously guarded their privileges of freedom from arrest in Parliament time and freedom of speech in their own house, and also fully maintained their rights over taxation and the making of new law. Yet Parliament's notion of its political functions was still comparatively modest at the end of the medieval period.

The element of active opposition politics which had been a feature of parliamentary history during the fourteenth century had virtually disappeared during the fifteenth. Parliament no longer expressed a political critique of the king's government; it was more conspicuous in ratifying the power of whichever king had won the most recent battle. All it asked was that its traditional rights and privileges should be reaffirmed and these the dominant faction was invariably ready to grant. However much they fought among themselves, the magnates of medieval England were always concerned to avoid the inconvenience of popular unrest and they needed the support of the communities of the land and their representatives in Parliament to do so. Besides, they had no need to be niggardly about the traditional privileges of the Commons now that the practice had been acquired of packing the lower House with a sufficient number of followers of the king's court to make it pliable on major political questions. So, content with the position it had, Parliament did not begin to take a larger view of its political significance until the long Parliament of Henry VIII, which first met in 1529 and was used by the king to bring about the nationalization of the church in England by statute. This lasted not for the few weeks which, with some notable exceptions, was the customary life of a medieval Parliament, but for seven years, with repeated prorogations, as the instrument for legalizing an ecclesiastical revolution. During its long life, members of the House of Commons began to acquire the heightened sense of corporate identity and importance which was to be the strength of the modern Parliament. Its spirit of self-confidence was to be strengthened by Henry VIII's employment of Parliament to pass three successive statutes determining the succession to the throne and by the use his Tudor successors made of it for their own ecclesiastical counter-revolutions. The powerful parliamentary instrument which challenged the Stuarts by using the precious fiscal, legislative and procedural privileges inherited from the medieval period was forged in the fire of Tudor ecclesiastical politics.

Parliament, therefore, did not change in 1485. What makes 1485 something more than an arbitrary dividing line in its history is that the challenge of the aristocracy to the royal authority, which had been the persistent theme of medieval politics, virtually petered out after Bosworth. Hitherto, the magnates, feudal and post-feudal alike, though they never questioned the monarchical principle, had persistently acted on the assumption that if the king paid insufficient regard to their interests he must be resisted for flouting the tradition that he should govern by the advice of his natural counsellors. They and their struggles, and in the end their rival dynasties, had come to dominate Parliament. After Bosworth, however, the old nobility seemed exhausted in spirit. It was not that it had destroyed itself in the Wars of the Roses, though it had been badly depleted both on the battlefield and by the executioner's axe. The reality was rather that the nobility as a whole seemed to have no heart for continuing in the old manner. There was a new passivity in face of the crown's authority. It was symbolic of a changed political climate that Henry VII could assume the crown simply on the grounds that he was king because he had become king by battle. There were none of the old elaborate justifications of inherited right and election by the estates of the crown which had characterized the previous changes of dynasty. No explanations and no apologies were offered. Henry VII did not allow even the slightest suggestion that his kingship was in any way strengthened by his marriage to Elizabeth of York, important though this was for supporters of the former dynasty in its transmission of Yorkist legitimacy. On the contrary, everything possible was done to establish the independence of his own right.

The political mood of the time was favourable to a strong monarchy, to which Edward IV's reign had been a prelude. Although there were still to be a few abortive insurrections, and Henry VII was vulnerable in the north where Richard III had been strong, the Tudor kings *de facto* had no dangerous challengers. When a challenge to the authority of the crown and a critique of its government once more emerged under the Stuarts, it was not provided by the kind of arrogant combination of magnates which had dominated medieval politics. The revival of opposition politics in Parliament came rather from combinations of the gentry with parts of the nobility. In this parliamentary opposition it was not the Lords but the Commons, exploiting their inherited privileges, who were to be dominant.

As the forum of the nation, the medieval Parliament was repeatedly sullied by being called on to legitimize change achieved by violence. No other way of removing governments had yet been discovered. Yet alongside the blood-stained politics of medieval England ran a constant thread of reverence for lawfulness and lawful procedures. Often the ideal was mocked by the reality but the ideal represented the instincts of a law-seeking people and the understanding of its governing classes that no society can for long be ruled without some degree of consent. Even the painstaking and elaborate attempts to clothe lawless politics in the garments of law testify to this, and the contrast which Chief Justice Fortescue drew between the government of France and that of England, whatever it may owe to his theoretical notion of Lancastrian monarchy, is based on a personal observation of the facts in both countries.

There were, he said, two kinds of kingdoms, the one called *dominium regale* (absolute monarchy) and the other *dominium politicum et regale* (roughly, constitutional monarchy). 'The first kynge mey rule his peple bi suche lawes as he makyth hym self. And therefore he may sett vppon thaim tayles (taxes) and other imposicions, such as he wol hymself, with owt thair assent. The secounde kynge may not rule his peple bi other lawes than such as thai assenten unto....' Fortescue, servant of both Henry VI and Edward IV, placed the French king firmly in the category of absolute monarch, able to tax his subjects at will, a state of affairs which had arisen, he thought, from the English wars when the three estates dared not come together and the French king had learned to do as he pleased, taxing his commons into poverty.

'But blessyd be God, this lande (England) is rulid vndir a bettir lawe; and therfore the peple therof be not in such peynurie, nor therby hurt in thair persons . . . Lo this is the fruyt of *jus polliticum et regale*, under wich we live . . .'[1] Fortescue recognized elsewhere that there would be occasions when even the English kings would have a practical discretion to act absolutely. What he wrote was perhaps a veiled warning in Yorkist England against moving too far towards stronger kingly power. Yet what Fortescue correctly observed in England was the presence of a spirit of consent to government which had never been lost and of which Parliament had become the prime instrument.

The monarchy was to enjoy a greater power under the Tudors than it had had during most of the medieval period and their rule was often arbitrary and cruel. Yet they could not dispense with the procedures of lawful government by consultation which they had inherited from medieval England and Parliament was now at the heart of them. Like the ordinary law courts, it met still in the huddle of ancient buildings which constituted the king's palace of Westminster or, in the case of the Commons, in the abbey nearby, and the king was at its centre. The medieval Parliament, for all its limitations, had created the powerful weapons of privilege, procedure and the control of the king's supply of money with which English political liberty could be defended.

---

[1] Sir John Fortescue, *The Governance of England*, ed. Charles Plummer, pp. 109–115.

Select Bibliography

Even for the purpose of a select bibliography, the potential list of references for a book covering such an extensive period of history is so long that I have thought it sensible to restrict it to the following three categories: (1) the principal collections of printed original sources for medieval parliamentary history: (2) a short list of the most useful collections of constitutional and general historical documents (or excerpts from them) for the period; (3) a restricted selection of books and articles on constitutional and parliamentary history relevant to the period as a whole, or relating to a sustained part of it. This last section includes a number of recent collections of papers written by historians who have made seminal contributions to the study of medieval parliamentary history.

In cases where secondary authorities are important but relate only to specific topics or short or limited periods, they are referred to only in footnotes, so that each reference is related strictly to its appropriate context. To give an example, the reference to G. T. Lapsley's article on 'Archbishop Stratford and the Parliamentary Crisis of 1341', which is of immediate relevance only to that particular crisis, appears in the footnotes at the appropriate part of the text but is not repeated in the select bibliography. The same applies to references to chronicles and secondary authorities cited at various points in the narrative. The latter often provide more extensive bibliographies to particular subjects.

Thus the footnotes are used not simply to provide references to the sources of all important quotations but also in many cases as the only form of bibliographical reference.

For the chronicle sources for the political history of the period, reference can most conveniently be made to the bibliographies (with evaluations) in the five volumes of the *Oxford History of England* which cover the period and which also still provide a useful general background. They are Vol. II, *Anglo-Saxon England, c. 500–1087*, by Sir Frank Stenton; Vol. III, *From Domesday Book to Magna Carta, 1087–1216*, by A. L. Poole; Vol. IV, *The Thirteenth Century, 1216–1307*, by Sir Maurice Powicke; Vol. V, *The Fourteenth Century, 1307–1399*, by May McKisack; Vol. VI, *The Fifteenth Century, 1399–1485*, by E. F. Jacob.

For more extensive references to studies relating specifically to the medieval Parliament, see especially the bibliographies provided in the two volumes of *Historical Studies of the English Parliament*, Vol. I, *Origins to 1399* and Vol. II, *1399–1603*, edited by E. B. Fryde and Edward Miller (see below).

For lists of all Parliaments and general councils held during the medieval period and afterwards, with dates and places of assembly, prorogations, categories of persons summoned etc., see the invaluable *Handbook of British Chronology*, ed. by Sir

F. M. Powicke and E. B. Fryde, and published by the Royal Historical Society, which also includes lists of the principal officers of state. For details of regnal years, legal chronology and the law terms (to which the earlier Parliaments were related), saints' days and festivals and reckonings of time, see *Handbook of Dates for Students of English History*, published by the Royal Historical Society.

The Dictionary of National Biography is, of course, an invaluable source for further information on individual persons, especially those comparatively minor characters who appear fleetingly in the book, and for whom no individual biography exists.

1 PRINCIPAL PRINTED ORIGINAL SOURCES FOR MEDIEVAL PARLIAMENTARY HISTORY

Rotuli Parliamentorum, Vols. I–VI, 1767–83.
Rotuli Parliamentorum Anglie Hactenus Inediti, 1279–1373, ed. H. G. Richardson and G. O Sayles (Camden Society, 3rd series, LI, 1935).
Memoranda de Parliamento, 1305; the parliamentary roll for 1305, edited by F. W. Maitland (Rolls series, 1893). Reprinted in Maitland, Selected Essays, Cambridge, 1936. (Most of Maitland's introduction is reprinted in Fryde and Miller, Vol. I, see below.)
The parliamentary roll for 12 Edward II is printed in *Documents Illustrative of English History in the Thirteenth and Fourteenth Centuries*, ed. H. Cole (Record Comm., 1844).
Statutes of the Realm, ed. by A. Luders and others (1810–28), Vols. I and II.
Parliamentary Writs and Writs of Military Summons, ed. F. Palgrave (Rec. Comm., 1827–34).
Reports from the Lords' Committees . . . touching the Dignity of a Peer. 5 volumes (1820–29).
The Anonimalle Chronicle, ed. V. H. Galbraith (1927).
The Fane Fragment of the 1461 Lords' Journal, ed. W. H. Dunham, jnr. (Yale Univ., 1935).
A Parliamentary Debate of the Mid-Fifteenth Century, A. R. Myers. Bulletin of the John Rylands Library xxii (1938).
Modus Tenendi Parliamentum and *A Colchester Account of the Proceedings of the Parliament of 1485* are printed in *Parliamentary Texts of the Later Middle Ages*, ed. N. Pronay and J. Taylor (1980).

2 SOME COLLECTIONS OF HISTORICAL DOCUMENTS RELEVANT TO THE HISTORY OF PARLIAMENT AND POLITICS IN THE MIDDLE AGES

Stubbs Charters from the beginning to 1307, revised by H. W. C. Davies (1962). Anglo-Saxon excerpts with translations; Latin and Norman French untranslated.
Select Documents of English Constitutional History, 1307–1485, ed. S. B. Chrimes and A. L. Brown (1960). Untranslated.
English Historical Documents, Vol. I, *c. 500–1042*, ed. Dorothy Whitelock; Vol. II,

1042–1189, ed. David C. Douglas; Vol. III, *1189–1327*, ed. Harry Rothwell; Vol. IV, *1327–1485*, ed. A. R. Myers (all translated).

Sources of English Constitutional History, ed. C. Stephenson and F. G. Marcham (New York, 1937) (translated).

Constitutional History of Medieval England, 1216–1399, 3 volumes, B. Wilkinson. Select documents, bibliographies and commentaries (1958).

Constitutional History of England in the Fifteenth Century, 1399–1485, B. Wilkinson, with illustrative documents and bibliographies (1964).

3 A RESTRICTED LIST OF STUDIES RELEVANT TO THE HISTORY OF PARLIAMENT IN THE MEDIEVAL CENTURIES AS A WHOLE, ROUGHLY ACCORDING TO DATE OF PUBLICATION

(a) General constitutional and parliamentary histories

W. Stubbs, *Constitutional History of England*, 3 volumes (first published 1874–78, several editions to 1906).

C. Petit-Dutaillis and G. Lefebvre, *Studies and Notes Supplementary to Stubbs' Constitutional History*, trans. (Manchester, 1929).

F. W. Maitland, *Constitutional History of England* (1908).

C. H. McIlwain, *The High Court of Parliament and its Supremacy* (1910; reprinted 1962).

J. F. Baldwin, *The King's Council in England during the Middle Ages* (1913).

A. F. Pollard, *The Evolution of Parliament* (1926).

T. F. Tout, *Chapters in the Administrative History of Medieval England*, 6 vols. (1920–33).

H. L. Gray, *The Influence of the Commons on Early Legislation* (Cambridge, Mass., 1932).

M. V. Clarke, *Medieval Representation and Consent* (1936).

J. E. A. Joliffe, *Constitutional History of Medieval England* (3rd ed., 1954).

G. O. Sayles, *The King's Parliament of England* (1975), a brief account with a good bibliography.

(b) Some studies of particular periods or topics. The list includes collections of articles which, taken together, cover an extended period of the history of the medieval Parliament. (There are references in footnotes to many of the individual articles in these collections, with notes of their original place of publication.)

L. O. Pike, *Constitutional History of the House of Lords* (1894).

D. Pasquet, *The Origins of the House of Commons* (translated R. G. D. Laffan) (1925; reissued, 1964).

Historical Studies of the English Parliament, Vol. I, *Origins to 1399* and Vol. II, *1399 to 1603*, ed. E. B. Fryde and Edward Miller (1970). (A collection of seminal essays on the English Parliament by a number of authors.)

H. G. Richardson and G. O. Sayles, *The English Parliament in The Middle Ages*.

(Collected articles by the authors written at various dates on medieval parliamentary history.)

May McKisack, *The Parliamentary Representation of the English Boroughs during the Middle Ages* (1932).

J. C. Wedgwood and D. Holt, *History of Parliament*, 1439–1509, 2 volumes (with biographies of the members of the Commons) (1936).

S. B. Chrimes, *English Constitutional Ideas in the Fifteenth Century* (1936).

B. Wilkinson, *Studies in the Constitutional History of the 13th and 14th centuries* (1937).

A. R. Myers, *Parliamentary Petitions in the Fifteenth Century*, E.H.R. LII (1937).

D. Rayner, *Forms and Machinery of the 'Commune Petition' in the Fourteenth Century*, E.H.R. LVI (1941).

H. M. Cam, *Law-Finders and Law-Makers in Medieval England* (1962). (Collection of reprinted papers on the medieval Parliament, including 'The Theory and Practice of Representation in Medieval England') (1953).

J. S. Roskell, *The Commons in the Parliament of 1422* (1954).

J. S. Roskell, *The Commons and their Speakers in the English Parliament* (1965).

J. G. Edwards, *The Commons in Medieval English Parliaments* (Creighton Lecture, 1957).

J. Enoch Powell and Keith Wallace, *The House of Lords in the Middle Ages* (1968).

G. L. Harriss, *King, Parliament and Public Finance in Medieval England to 1369* (1975).

J. G. Edwards, *The Second Century of the English Parliament* (1979).

K. B. McFarlane, *England in the Fifteenth Century*. Collected essays (written over a period of years), introduced by G. L. Harriss (1981).

J. S. Roskell, *Parliament and Politics in Late Medieval England*, 2 volumes (1981). (A collection of important papers and articles on the medieval Parliament written over a number of years.)

The English Parliament in the Middle Ages, ed. R. G. Davies and J. H. Denton (1981). (A collection of essays by various authors on the medieval Parliament.)

Authorities on the Old Palace of Westminster

The History of the King's Works, Vol. I, the Middle Ages, ed. R. Allen Brown, H.M. Colvin and A.J. Taylor, HMSO (1963).

The Meeting-Places of Parliament in the Ancient Palace of Westminster, by Ivy M. Cooper, Journal of the British Archaeological Association, 3r ser. vol III (1938).

Architectural History, Journal of the Society of Architectural Historians of Great Britain, Vol. 9, 1966 (School of Architecture, Newcastle-upon-Tyne.)

Antiquities of Westminster; the Old Palace, (with 246 engravings) by J.T. Smith (1807).

The Topography of the Old House of Commons, by Orlo Cyprian Williams (an unpublished monograph of which a copy is in the Westminster Record Office.

The Parliament House, by Maurice Hastings, 1950.

The Painted Chamber at Westminster, by Paul Binski, Occ. Paper (New Series) IX Soc. of Antiquaries of London, Burlington House.

Index

Abergavenny, Lady *see* Beauchamp
Adam of Usk, 448
Adolf of Nassau, King of Germany, 156
Agincourt, battle of (1415), 490, 491, 492, 587
Airmyn, William, (Chancery clerk; Bishop of Norwich) 202, 220
Albany, Robert Stewart, 1st Duke of, 475
Aldred of York, Archbishop, 17
Alençon, Duke d', 307
Alexander III, King of Scotland, 148
Alfred the Great, King, 7–8, 11
Allington, John, Speaker, 603, 604, 609, 611
Alnwick castle, 588, 589, 592
Amiens, Mise of (1264), 108
Anarchy of the disputed succession, 26, 31
Anglo-Saxon Chronicle, 10, 13, 14, 16, 23, 24, 25, 29
Anglo-Saxons, 1–18, 41, 43, 93, 117; consultative customs, 1–2; Witan, 2, 3, 4–18; and Normans, 3–4, 19–21, 27; royal succession, 15–17
Anjou, 50, 54, 57, 104, 320, 503
Anne of Bohemia, Queen, 380, 413, 421
Anonimalle Chronicle, 337 &n, 339–41, 343–6, 347, 349, 372, 374
Anselm, Archbishop, 25, 28
Anthony, Bastard of Burgundy, 594
Appellants (Lords Appellant), 394–401, 402–3, 404, 409–10, 413, 419, 427, 429, 430, 431–2, 433–4, 435, 441, 455, 456
Aquinas, St Thomas, 120
Aquitaine, 44, 45, 57, 332, 336, 412, 415, 423
Armagnacs or Orleanists, 481–2, 490, 491, 492
Arras (St Waast) peace conference (1335), 504, 523–4

Artevelde, Jacob van, 305
Artevelt, Philip van, 382
Arthur of Brittany, 50, 53
Articles of the Barons (1215), 58
Articles of 1309 (Statute of Stamford), 181–3
Arundel, Earls of *see* Fitzalan
Arundel, Sir John, 369
Arundel, Thomas, Bishop of Ely, Archbishop of York and Archbishop of Canterbury, 390–1, 392, 394, 396, 402, 410, 415, 421–2, 423–4, 425, 426, 456, 459, 469, 471, 472, 480, 482, 486; impeachment of (1397), 423; and deposition of Richard II, 445, 446, 447, 452, 453; appointed Chancellor, 476–7, 479; and resignation, 479, 480; personal quarrel between Prince Henry and, 481; returns as Chancellor, 483
Ashton, Sir Robert, 352–3
Assize of Arms (1181), 39–40, 49, 72
Assize of Clarendon (1166), 40, 41
Assize of Northampton (1176), 40–1
Assize of *Novel Disseisin* (1166), 39, 40
Athelstan, King, 8–9, 10
attainder, bills of, xviii, 180, 400, 452, 572, 609, 628; against Yorkists, 559–60, 562, 571; against Lancastrians, 571, 586, 599; against Duke of Somerset, 593; against Duke of Clarence, 608, 610–11; against Richard III's opponents, 627
Atwyll, John, 610
Audley, Hugh, 209, 212, 221
Aumâle, William de Forz, Count of, 70
Aumâle, Duke of *see* Edward of York
Avignon papacy, 206, 238, 302, 305, 334, 335, 367–8, 383
Ayscough, William, Bishop of Salisbury, 539

Bacon, Roger, 74
Baddlesmere, Baron Bartholemew de, 203, 205, 206, 209, 210, 212, 213, 221, 222
Bagot, Sir William, 427, 433, 444, 445, 455
Baldock, Robert, 222
Ball, John, 372, 373, 374, 375
Balliol, Edward *see* Edward I of Scotland
Balliol, John le, 149, 155
Bamborough (Bamburgh) castle, 589, 591, 592
Bannockburn, battle of (1314), 196–8, 204, 209, 210, 242
Barnet, battle of (1471), 600
barons (magnates: tenants-in-chief, 250–4; Norman, 20, 21, 22, 23, 24–5, 26, 27, 28; under Henry II, 30, 34, 38, 40, 43, 44, 45, 46, 47, 55; under King John, 44, 45, 51, 52, 55–6, 57–64, 68, 71, 96; under Richard I, 45, 46, 47; and Magna Carta, 51–2, 58–63, 66–8, 96; Articles of the Barons, 58; under Henry III, 65, 66, 67–71, 73–4, 76–7, 78–9, 81, 87, 88–92, 95–116, 119; Council of Twenty-Five, 68; royal castles restored to Henry III by, 69–70; Petition of the Barons, 98; and Provisions of Oxford, 99–100, 101, 102, 107; Council of Fifteen, 99–100; Provisions of Westminster, 102–3, 104; under Edward I, 126–7, 131–2, 134–5, 147, 148, 152–4, 156–64, 176; under Edward II, 175–6, 178, 179–96, 198–217, 219–20; Articles of 1309, 181–3; Ordinances of 1311: 181, 186–93, 194, 196, 197, 198; and election of Ordainers, 184–6; Middle Party, 209–10, 212; and Treaty of Leake, 210–11; and death of Lancaster, 214; Statute of York and repeal of Ordinances, 215–217, 218; and deposition of Edward II, 224–30, 231; decreasing role in Parliament, 234; under Edward III, 237, 246, 247, 250, 252, 276, 277; Disinherited invade Scotland, 240–1; armed forces accompanying, 246–7; class distinction between knights and, 250–1, 252, 254–5; choice of parliamentary representatives, 251–2; creation of order of dukes (1337), 265; control of ministerial appointments by, 294–5; crisis between Richard II and (1386–8), 395–401; and Merciless Parliament, 395–401; abuse of maintenance and livery, 404–7, 412, 413; dispute over regency (during Henry VI's minority), 496–501, 510–11, 512; after 1485; 632; *see also* Church/clergy; Lords; peers
Barons' Wars (1264–7), 107–15
Bastard of Fauconberg, 600
Bath and Wells, Bishops of *see* Stafford; Stillington
Baynard's Castle, 374, 619
Beatrice, Princess (Henry III's daughter), 105

Beauchamp, Anne *see* Warwick
Beauchamp, Guy, Earl of Warwick, 185, 191, 193, 194, 195, 197, 198, 199
Beauchamp, Joan, Lady Abergavenny, 522
Beauchamp, Lord John, Baron of Kidderminster, 392; impeachment and execution of, 398
Beauchamp, Roger, 347
Beauchamp, Richard, Earl of Warwick, 521
Beauchamp, Thomas, Earl of Warwick, 394–5, 401, 402, 410, 428, 431; arrested, 429; trial of, 432–4
Beauchamp, Sir William, 500
Beauchamp of Holt, Lord, 517
Beaufort, Edmund, Marquess of Dorset and 2nd Duke of Somerset, 536, 540, 542, 543, 547, 548, 549, 551, 555; appointed Lieutenant of France, 534; conflict between York and, 541, 542, 544, 556; claim to royal succession, 541; appointed Constable, 541; imprisoned in Tower, 544, 547; released and made captain of Calais, 547; killed at battle of St Albans (1455), 549
Beaufort, Edmund, 4th Duke of Somerset: attainder against, 593, 599; execution of (1471), 600
Beaufort, Cardinal Henry, Bishop of Lincoln, Bishop of Winchester, 425, 464–5, 476, 477, 479, 480, 481, 482, 486, 491, 493, 497, 510–11, 512, 515, 517, 523, 524, 525, 526, 533, 555, 582; appointed Chancellor, 486, 505, 507; conflict between Gloucester and, 497, 504–5, 507–9, 510, 515–17, 527; and London Bridge confrontation, 507–8, 509; pilgrimage in Bohemia, 509, 511
Beaufort, Henry, 3rd Duke of Somerset, 558, 565, 569, 589, 591, 592; attainder of (1461), 571; captured and executed at Hexham (1464), 592
Beaufort, John, Earl of Somerset and Marquis of Dorset (died 1410), 425, 429, 435, 455, 476, 477, 479, 481, 533
Beaufort, John, (d. 1442, Father of Lady Margaret Beaufort) 1st Duke of Somerset, 528–9, 533
Beaufort, Lady Margaret, Countess of Richmond, 533, 537, 541, 547, 621, 622
Beaufort, Sir Thomas, Earl of Dorset and Duke of Exeter, 476, 477, 479, 480, 481, 483, 496, 497
Beaumont, William, Viscount, 533, 538, 560
Becket, Thomas, Archbishop of Canterbury, 357, 433; Henry II's dispute with, 31–8, 48
Bede, the Venerable, 6–7
Bedford, Duke of *see* John of Lancaster
Bereford, Sir Simon, 235, 239
Berkeley Castle, 237, 445
Berners, Sir James, impeachment and execution of (1338) 398

Berwick, 211, 242, 611–12
bigamy *see* Statute *de Bigimis*
Bigod, Lord Hugh, 98–9, 105, 156
Bigod, Robert, Earl of Norfolk, 156, 158, 159, 160, 176
Black Death, 243, 311–12, 313, 314, 315, 317, 324, 372
Black Prince *see* Edward the Black Prince
Blanche, Duchess of Lancaster, 324, 330
blank charters, 442–3, 454
Blore Heath, battle of (1459), 558
Bohun, Humphry de, Earl of Hereford, 156, 158, 159, 160, 176, 183, 185, 193, 195, 198, 205, 207, 209, 211, 212, 214, 218
Bohun, William de, Earl of Northampton, 289, 293, 298
Bolingbroke, Henry *see* Henry IV
Bolingbroke, Roger, 527–8
Boniface, Pope, 155
Boniface of Savoy, Archbishop of Canterbury, 78
Bonville, William, Lord, 541, 552
bookland, Anglo-Saxon, 10
Booth, Laurence, 557
Bordeaux, truce of (1356), 321
Boroughbridge, battle of (1322), 214, &n, 215, 222
boroughs, 115, 122–4; representation in Parliament, 49, 65, 110, 111–12, 123–4, 127–8, 132–3, 135–8, 150–1, 258–9, 584; burgage tenure in, 122–3; taxation, 123–4, 128, 130, 146, 150, 151; franchise, 123 &n; *see also* burgesses; Commons
Bosworth, battle of (1485), 587, 622, 630–1
Bourchier, Henry, Viscount, Earl of Essex, 548, 549, 557, 561, 569
Bourchier, Sir Robert, Chancellor, 289
Bourchier, Thomas, Bishop of Ely and Archbishop of Canterbury, 547, 557, 558, 560, 561–2, 617
Bouvines, battle of (1214), 57
Bowet, Henry, Archbishop of York, 441
Brackenbury, Sir Richard, 629
Bracton, Henry de, 120–1
Bramham Moor, battle of (1408), 459, 479
Brantingham, Bishop of Exeter, 345, 410
Braose, William de, Gower property of, 212
Braybrook, Robert, Bishop of London, 382
Breauté, Fawkes de, 70
Brembre, Sir Nicholas, Mayor London, 375, 383; trial and death of (1388), 394, 395–8, 399
Brétigny, Treaty of (1360), 323, 491
Brian, Baron Guy, 334, 347
Briouze, William de, 56
Bristol, 124, 445; council meeting (1216), 66
Brittany, 50, 57, 303, 304, 335, 348, 362–3, 370, 529, 534, 593; captured by Philip Augustus (1214), 54; rival claimants to, 298; and Edward III's campaigns, 298–9, 305, 306, 307, 315, 317, 336; English expedition to (1449), 535; Edward IV's agreement with, 595
Brittany, Francis, Duke of, 534, 535
Brittany, John, Duke of, 298 *see also* John of Brittany; Montfort
Bruce, Edward, 197
Bruce, Robert, 149, 163, 169
Bruce, Robert the younger *see* Robert I
Bruges: abolition of staple (1344), 318; truce of (1375), 335–6; captured by Burgundians, 383
Buckingham, Henry Stafford, Duke of, 615, 616, 617, 619, 620; passes sentence on Clarence (1478), 610; joins rebellion against Richard III, 621; captured and executed, 621
Buckingham, Humphrey Stafford, Duke of, 547, 551, 557, 558, 560
Buckingham, Earl of *see* Thomas of Woodstock
Burdett, Thomas, execution of, 609
burgage tenure, 122–3, 124
burgesses, 13, 39, 122–3, 250, 584; first summons to Parliament by Simon de Montfort (1265), 65, 110, 111–12; and attendance at Parliament, 119–20, 121–2, 123, 124, 127–8, 130, 131, 132–3, 135–8, 150–1, 153, 154, 163, 166, 233–4 and *firma burgi*, 122n; election of parliamentary representatives, 123, 258–9; and customs duty, 130–1, 132; re-election of members to Parliament, 171–3; political role, 172, 233; and deposition of Edward II, 224–5, 228; conjoined as single unit with knights, 241 &n; security when travelling, 247; merchant gilds, 250; wages and expenses, 514–15; *see also* Commons; merchants
Burgh, Hubert de, justiciar, 66, 69 &n, 75, 77
Burghersh, Bartholomew de, 275, 299, 300, 307, 316, 319–20
Burghersh, Henry, Bishop of Lincoln, 222, 223, 229, 276, 278
Burgundy, 475, 479–80, 481–2, 492, 505, 525, 588–9, 602; breakdown of English alliance under Henry VI, 503–4, 517–18, 524; Edward IV's alliance with, 593, 594, 595–6; and Margaret of York's marriage to Charles of, 595; Edward IV escapes to, 599; and help given to Yorkists by, 600; *see also* France
Burgundy, Dukes of *see* Charles de Charolais; John the Fearless; Philip the Good
Burke, Edmund, 2
Burley, Simon, 376, 381, 392, 435; impeachment and execution of (1388), 398
Burley, William, 531, 552–3
Burnell, Hugh, Lord, 477, 480
Burnell, Robert, Bishop of Bath and Wells, 137, 144, 159
Bury, Adam, 348
Bury, Richard, Bishop of Durham, 238, 239

Bury St Edmunds Parliaments: 1267: 115; 1296: 155; 1447: 533, 536
Bussy, Sir John, Speaker, 419, 424, 426, 427, 431, 432, 433, 434, 435, 436, 438, 444
Butler, Lady Eleanor, 618, 619, 626
Butler, William, 139-40
Buxhill, Sir Alan, 363

Cade, Jack, rebellion of (1450), 538-9, 540, 559
Calais, 320, 322, 323, 333, 415, 418, 423, 473, 479, 490, 517, 525, 535, 550, 558, 559, 560, 562, 590, 607; siege of (1346-7), 307, 312; and truce of (1347), 307, 310, 317; treaty of (1364), 324, 328; removal of wool staple from, 340, 345, 347, 348; Gloucester imprisoned at, 429; and murder of Gloucester, 434; threat of attack by Burgundy, 479, 481; Yorkists' hold on, 549, 560
Cambridge Parliament (1388), 402-4, 405-9, 411
Canterbury, 87, 373; provincial council (1283), 146; Convocation of, 353
Canterbury, Archbishops of see Arundel; Becket; Bourchier; Chichele; Courtney; Kemp; Langton; Morton; Reginald; Reynolds; Rich; Stigand; Stratford; Sudbury; Walden; Walter; Winchelsey
Carlisle, Bishop of, 536; see also Merke
Carlisle, Earl of see Harclay
Carlisle Parliament (1307), 173-4
carucage (tax), 48-9, 71
Carlyle, Thomas, 3n
Castille 333; battle of Najera (1367), 328; John of Gaunt's claim to, 357, 380, 382, 387, 410
Castillon, battle of (1453), 543
castles, 100, 106; restoration to Henry III of royal, 69-70, 75
Catesby, William, Speaker, 624, 631
Catherine of Valois, Queen, 492, 447, 565
Cavendish, John, fishmonger, 386
Caxton, William, 588
Cecily of York, Dame, 618
Chapter House, Westminster Abbey, Commons' meetings in, xxii, 266, 267, 315, 337-8, 339-41, 342-3, 347, 353, 424, 465
Charles I, King, 88, 231, 262-3
Charles IV, King of France, 223, 245
Charles V, King of France, 322, 323, 328, 329, 331, 335
Charles VI, King of France, 423, 475, 492
Charles VII, King of France, 492, 495, 503, 504, 532, 534, 535
Charles the Bad of Navarre, King, 317, 320, 322
Charles de Blois, 298, 307, 328
Charles de Charolais, Duke of Burgundy, 594, 595, 599, 605; Margaret of York's marriage to, 595; Edward IV's cause helped by, 600; and alliance with Edward IV, 606, 607, 608, killed at Nancy, 608
Charlton, Sir Thomas, Speaker, 545
charter of liberties, Henry I's, 25, 57-8
Charter of the Forest, 68-9 &n, 158, 163
Chaucer, Geoffrey, 477, 325
Chaucer, Thomas, Speaker, 477, 480, 482-3, 490, 494
Cheddar, (Cheddre), Robert, 467
Cheshire, 446; insurrection (1393), 418; made principality by Richard II, 435
Chester, Earl of, 70
chevauchée (military tactic), 299, 306, 320, 321, 330, 333, 387
Cheyne, Sir John, Speaker, 454
Chichele, Henry, Archbishop of Canterbury, 497-8, 508
Chichester, Bishop of, 109; see also Moleyns; Robert; Stratford
Chinon, truce of (1214), 78
Chronicle of Lanercost, 214n
Church/clergy, 62, 169, 221, 469; Henry II's dispute with Becket over jurisdiction of, 30-8; Pope's Interdict (1208) and King John's excommunication, 54-5, 56; Magna Carta on, 60; and Provisions of Oxford, 67, 87, 88; and taxation, 72, 73, 92, 93-4, 97, 115, 116, 135, 146, 150, 151, 155-6, 157, 159, 161, 162, 164, 260-1, 327, 332, 334-5; Statute *de bigimis*, 126, 133; Statute of Mortmain, 135; *circumspecte agatis* writ, 141; attendance at Parliament of representatives of, 138, 149, 152, 153, 155, 163, 166, 180, 242, 259-60, 307; *Clericis Laicos*, papal bull, 155-6, 159, 161, 162, 261; financial exactions of papacy, 173-4, 260-1, 327, 330, 334-5, 338; dispute between Archbishops of Canterbury and York, 180-1; and deposition of Edward II, 224-30; withdrawal from Parliament of representatives of, 259-62; *praemunientes* clause, 261; conflict between Edward III and Archbishop Stratford, 289-94, 296; right of trial by peers, 291, 293-4, 296; 1343 parliamentary complaint against papacy, 301-2; Statute of Provisors, 313-14; Statute of Praemunire, 318-19; Statute of 1363 against jurisdiction of papal courts, 327; property dispute, 330; dismissal of clerical ministers by king, 331; English *concordat* with Pope, 336; Good Parliament's attacks on papal demands (1376), 338-9; trial of John Wyclif, 353; violation of sanctuary at Westminster Abbey, 363, 367; Great Schism between Rome and Avignon, 367-8, 383, 479; 1382 Statute against heretics, 382; 1390 Statute of Provisors, 412, 415, 416, 417-18; and 1393 new Statute of Praemunire, 418; and Lollards, 463, 479; *De Heretico Comburendo*, 463

circumspecte agatis writ (1285), 141
civil servants in Parliament, 585–6
Clare, Gilbert de, 8th Earl of Gloucester, 98, 104, 105, 109, 112, 113, 115
Clare, Gilbert de, 9th Earl of Gloucester, 176, 183, 185, 197, 198, 203, 209, 212
Clare, Thomas de, 113
Clarence, George, Duke of, 569, 594, 597, 598, 599, 600, 601, 608–11; quarrel over Warwick inheritance between Gloucester and, 601–2; Edward IV prevents marriage of Mary of Burgundy to, 608, 610; arrested and imprisoned in Tower, 609; bill of attainder against (1478), 610–11; and put to death in Tower, 611
Clarence, Isobel Neville, Duchess of, 601, 608
Clarence, Lionel, Duke of, 307, 313, 330, 342, 562, 563, 564
Clarence, Thomas, Duke of, 479, 481, 483, 494
Clarendon: great council (1164), 31, 33, 34–5; *colloquium* (1317), 206, 207
Clarke, M. V., 446
Clement VI, Pope, 302
Clement VII, Pope, 367–8, 383
clergy *see* Church
Clericis Laicos (papal Bull, 1296), 155–6, 159, 161, 261
Clerk of the House of Commons, 81
Clerk of the Parliaments, 81, 268, 269
Clifford, Lord de, 62
Clifford, Lord, killed at St Albans (1455), 549
Clinton, William, Earl of Huntingdon, 288
Cnut (Canute), King, 11, 14, 16, 18
Cobham, Eleanor, Duchess of Gloucester, 511, 530, 533; charged with witchcraft, 527–8
Cobham, Lord, 435
colloquium (colloquies), 80, 82, 87, 105, 115; Clarendon (1317), 206, 207; Westminster (1317), 207; *see also* great councils
commendation, Anglo-Saxon practice of 6 &n,20
commission of 1386 to control Richard II's household, 392, 393, 431–2
commissions of array and taxes, 257, 309, 310, 629
commissions of trailbaston, 289
Common Law, 42–3 &n, 103, 125, 129, 349, 400, 412, 413–14, 416, 578
Commons, xv, xvi, xvii, xviii, xxi, xxii, 28, 37, 49, 81, 86, 101, 111, 112, 125, 127–8, 132, 140, 146, 189, 216; meeting places for, xxii, 266, 267, 315, 337–8, 347, 353, 363, 370, 424, 465, 477; shire and borough representatives called for 1st time to Parliament, 65, 92–3, 110, 111–12; medieval functions, 86, 95, 121; knights attend for first time, 92–3; composition of, 131–2, 154; full powers called for in summons to Parliament, 150, 154 &n; becomes integral constituent of Parliament, 153; political role of knights, 164–5; re-election of members to, 172–3, 257; impeachment, 180, 329, 348–50, 351, 361, 385, 386, 397, 398, 432, 435, 537–8; consultation between magnates and, 181–2; regular attendance at Parliament from 1311: 189–90; not represented at York Parliament (1320), 190, 211–12; and Statute of York's recognition of role of, 216–17; growing importance under Edward II of, 216–17, 218–19 &n, 220–1, 230; *Modus Tenendi Parliamentum* on, 220; and Edward II's deposition, 224–5, 231, 233; political role, 233, 241, 359, 362, 366, 416, 434, 457, 463; knights and burgesses conjoined as single unit, 241 &n; choice and election of knights to, 253–8; sheriffs and lawyers disqualified from membership of, 254, 333, 468; election of burgesses and citizens to, 258–9; intercommuning between Lords and, 266–7, 315, 334, 344, 346, 353, 370, 378, 575; common petitions and bills leading to statutes, 268–72, 274, 301, 302; and reference back to constituencies, 282–4; separate procedure for common petitions, 311; social standing, 328, 329, 346, 583–4; Good Parliament, 337–51; first account of debate in 'House' of, 339–41, 342–3; granting of poll tax by, 369, 370, 371–2, 378; petition on livery and maintenance (1388), 404–7; right to assent to legislation established, 452; control of taxation by, 452, 457, 462, 473, 478–9, 502, 567–8, 631; satirist's description of, 460; reform of county elections by, 475, 481, 487; freedom of speech in, 461, 555, 631; assenting role of, 478, 488, 489, 580; social predominance of gentry in, 487, 585; role as initiators of legislation, 489, 540, 578, 580–3, 631; and loss of political initiative, 501–2; property qualification for franchise in shires, 513–14; wages and expenses, 514–15; social restrictions on franchise in shires, 531; arrest of Speaker raises privileges of, 545; Journals of proceedings, 573; Colchester members' diary of proceedings, 577–8; amendments to bill, 578–9; petitions, 580–2; increased number of borough members, 584; social composition of, 584–6; members of civil service and royal household in, 585–6, 602–3, 609; 'schedule on paper' submitted to Edward IV, 591–2; under Henry VII, 631; and under Henry VIII, 632
'community of bachelors', 102–3
community of the realm, 77, 127, 180, 181–2, 219, 233–4
compurgation, 41
Comyn, John, 173, 174

Index

Confirmatio Cartorum, 161–3
Constitutions of Clarendon, 33–5, 37, 38
consultation and consent, concept of, 1–2, 13, 17, 27, 28, 43–4, 71, 86, 87, 92–3, 117, 120–1, 129, 154n, 216, 218
Conyers, Sir John, 597
copy-holders, 248
Cornwall, John, Lord Fanhope, 517
Council of Regency, Edward III's, 235, 237
Council of the North, York (1484), 628
councils, king's smaller (inner, executive), Norman *curia regis*, 4, 22–4, 38; Henry II's, 30, 42; Henry III's, 66, 74, 78, 82, 88, 90 &n, 109, 110; Council of Fifteen (1st permanent council, 1258), 99–100, 104, 107, 109, 185; Edward II's 204–5, 206; Edward III's Council of Nine, 347–8, 351; Richard II's, 358, 361, 362, 368, 369, 392, 393–4, 402, 431; Henry IV's, 463–4, 467, 470, 471–4, 477, 479, 480–1, 483; Henry VI's, 497, 498, 499–500, 501, 505, 511, 512, 539, 540, 541, 544, 545–6; *see also* great councils; Parliament
county courts *see* shire courts
county elections, reform of, 475, 481, 487
court of chivalry, 364, 400, 412–13
court of common pleas, xx, 42, 167, 426
Court of Requests (White Hall), xxi, xxii
Courtenay family, 585
Courtenay, Edward de, Earl of Devon, 414
Courtenay, Thomas, Earl of Devon, 541, 597, 598, 600
Courtney, Philip and Peter, 384
Courtney, William, Bishop of London and Archbishop of Canterbury, 347, 353, 363, 377, 379, 380
Coventry: Parliament (1404), 468–9, 472; Henry VI's court moved to (1456), 557, 559; Parliament of the Devils (1459), 559–60, 561, 563, 571
Crécy, battle of (1346), 306–7, 308, 312
crime, 32, 129, 139, 141, 518, 521–2, 603; royal pardons of, 272–3; murder fine, 20, 103; Statute of 1352: 316; homicide and murder, 414; well-born criminals, 526
Crocker, Edward, xxi
Cromwell, Lord, 500, 516, 517, 519–20, 521, 538; attempted murder of, 537, 538
crown property, bill for resumption of alienated (1455), 551–2
crusades, 45, 115, 414, 415
curia regis or *consilium* (king's council), 4, 17, 21–3, 24, 42, 79, 81
customs duty, 130 &n, 131, 157, 161, 181, 187, 275, 436, 481; maletote, 130, 149, 157, 161, 277, 280–1, 282, 283, 286, 287, 301; *ad valorem* tax, 130n; tunnage (tax on wine) and poundage (tax on merchandise), 130, 333, 334, 382, 464, 470, 478, 483, 486, 488, 491, 507, 512, 515, 536, 593–4, 628; *see also* taxation; wool

Dalyngryg, Edward, 417
D'amory, Richard, 224
D'Amory, Roger, 209, 210, 212, 214, 221
Danegeld, 10, 23, 71
Danelaw, 8
Darcy, Sir John, 292, 293, 307
Daverill, Sir John, 239
David II Bruce, King of the Scots, 236, 240; takes refuge at French court, 242, 244; taken prisoner at Neville's Cross, 307, 310
David, Prince of Wales, 143, 186; trial of (1283), 136, 137, 138, 143, 150
De Heretico Comburendo Statute (1401), 463
De Tallagio non Concedendo draft charter (1297), 161–2
Derby, Earls of *see* Henry IV; Henry de Grosmont; Stanley, Lord
Despenser, Henry, Bishop of Norwich, 383, 384–5; impeachment of, 385
Despenser, Hugh, justiciar, 106
Despenser, Hugh, the elder, Earl of Winchester, 179, 198, 199, 209, 212, 213, 215, 218, 221–2, 223, 224, 270, 271
Despenser, Hugh, the younger, 203, 209, 212, 213, 215, 218, 221–2, 223, 224, 270, 271
Despenser, Thomas, Earl of Gloucester, 429, 435, 438, 455, 458
Devon, Earls of *see* Courtenay
Dialogue of the Exchequer, 20, 28–9
Dictum of Kenilworth (1266), 114
the Disinherited, 240–1
Domesday Book, 4n, 20, 24, 49
Dordrecht bonds, 280
Dorewood, Sir John, Speaker, 454, 467, 487
Dorset, Thomas Grey, Marquis of, 615, 616; *see also* Beaufort
Douglas, Earl of, 592
Dunbar, George, Scottish Earl of, 458
Dunstable tournament, 182 &n
Dunstanborough castle, 588, 589, 592
Durham, Bishops of, 45, 308; *see also* Fordham; Langley

Eadric, Ealdorman, 10
ealdormen (later earls), 5, 6, 9, 10, 11, 12, 19, 26
Eastry, Prior Henry, 226–7
Edgar, King, 9, 11
Edgar the Atheling, 15, 16 &n, 17
Edgecote, battle of (1469), 597
Edington, William, Bishop of Winchester, 307
Edmund I, King, 9
Edmund (2nd son of III Duke of York), 565
Edmund of Cambridge, Prince, 332
Edmund 'Crouchback', Earl of Lancaster, 449
Edmund II Ironside, King of Wessex, 15, 16 &n
Edmund, Earl of Lancaster and Leicester, 97, 104, 114, 193

Index

Edmund Langley, Earl of Cambridge and 1st Duke of York, 358, 364, 380, 383, 387, 397, 398, 422, 435, 444, 445

Edmund Rich *see* Rich

Edmund of Woodstock, Earl of Kent, 223, 224; arrest and execution of, 237–8

Edward I, King (reigned 1272–1307), xxii, 13, 70, 81, 82, 83, 102, 104, 105, 110, 111–12, 115, 116, 117–74, 176, 178, 188, 251, 253, 260, 261, 269, 442, 449; statute laws of, 83, 117–18, 122, 125, 126–7, 129–30, 133–42, 169–70, 171, 269; Barons' Wars, 107, 108, 113; crusade of, 115, 116, 131; accession to throne (1272), 116, 119; first Parliament (1275), 119–200, 121, 125, 127–8, 130, 131–2, 153; French campaigns, 119, 143, 149, 152, 155, 175; Welsh campaigns, 119, 142–3, 146, 148, 149–50; Jews expelled by, 147; death of Queen Eleanor, 149; baronial and clerical opposition to, 149, 155–63, 178; 'Model' Parliament, 152–5; Scottish wars, 155, 159, 160, 162, 166, 168–9, 173, 174, 175; Flanders expedition, 156, 158–9, 162; Lincoln Parliament, 163–5; and Lenten Parliament, 166–7, 168–70; death of (1307), 174

Edward II, King (reigned 1307–27), xvii, 53, 148, 154n, 158, 159, 172, 173, 174, 175–230, 238, 246, 251, 252, 253, 254, 256, 258, 259–60, 261, 268, 272, 362, 416; character and appearance, 176–7; coronation, 177–8, 179; and Piers Gaveston, 178–80, 182–3, 191, 192; Articles of 1309, 181–3; Scottish wars, 184, 188, 195, 196–8, 199, 203, 204, 205, 206, 208, 210, 211, 222; New Ordinances, 186–93, 194, 196, 197, 198, 215; revocation of royal grants of lands and castles, 187, 199, 201, 210, 211; conflict between Thomas of Lancaster, 187, 193–4, 195, 198–9, 201–14, 215; execution of Gaveston, 193–4, 205; battle of Bannockburn, 196–8, Lincoln Parliament, 202–4; committee to reform royal household, 205, 207, 211; and Middle Party, 209–10; Treaty of Leake, 210–11; siege of Berwick, 211; execution of Lancaster, 214; Statute of York and repeal of Ordinances, 215–17, 218, 220–1; and the Dispensers, 221–2; opposition of Queen Isabella and Roger Mortimer, 223–4; capture of, 224; deposition of (1327), 61, 217, 224–30, 231, 232, 233, 356, 391, 393, 447; and secret murder of, 237

Edward III, King (reigned 1327–77), xviii, xix, xxii, 20, 28, 63, 73, 83, 152, 157, 177, 184–5, 223, 224, 228, 231–354, 406, 485, 488, 490, 493, 562; 'elected' as guardian of the realm, 224; and Edward II's deposition in favour of, 224–32; and government of Mortimer, 232, 235, 236–8; coronation, 234; Scottish wars, 235–6, 240–2, 243–4; marriage to Philippa of Hainault, 236; downfall and death of Mortimer, 238–9; character and abilities, 239–40; moves government to York, 241; magnification of peerage by, 252, 276, his claim to French crown, 245–6, 279, 298, 323, 329, 381; statute laws of, 268–74, 286–7, 295–6, 302, 305, 312–13, 316, 321–2, 324–7; taxes needed to meet cost of French wars, 274–87, 296–7, 304–5, 308, 309, 313, 355; conflict with Archbishop Stratford, 289–94, 296; Brittany expedition (1342), 298–9; invasion of Normandy, 306–7; and Treaty of Brétigny (1360), 323; Castillian expedition, 328; dismissal of clerical ministers forced on, 331; truce of Bruges (1375), 335–6; Good Parliament, 337–51; and Council of Nine appointed, 347–8, 351; death of (1377), 354

Edward IV, King (reigned 1461–70 and 1471–83), Earl of March, 443, 452, 558, 559, 560, 565, 567–613, 614, 616, 621, 625–6, 627, 628, 633; proclaimed king (1461), 565–6; and victory at battle of Towton, 566; coronation, 568, 569; financial independence sought by, 567, 594–5; character and abilities, 568, 593, 612–13; speeches in Parliament, 568, 572–3, 594–5; and first Parliament (1461), 568–77; war against Lancastrians in the north, 588–9, 591, 592; and agreement with French (1463), 591, 592, 593; marriage to Elizabeth Woodville, 592–3; and alliance with Burgundy, 593, 594, 595–6, 605, 606, 607; Warwick's breach with, 595, 596–7; and rebellion against, 597–600; battle of Edgecote, 597; and captured by Warwick, 598; escapes to Burgundy (1470), 599; returns to England and defeats Warwick and Lancastrians (1471), 600; and his throne secure, 600–1; plans to attack France, 601, 602, 604, 605–6; Parliament of 1472–5: 602–7; seeks to restore order in Wales, 604; French expedition (1475), 607; and treaty of Picquigny, 607–8; trial and condemnation of Duke of Clarence, 608, 609–11; Scottish wars, 611–12; death (1483), 612, 615

Edward V, Prince of Wales (1470–?83), xix, 600, 603, 604, 614; Council of Twenty-five appointed (1473), 604; takes up residence at Ludlow, 604, 615; and Richard of Gloucester's usurpation of throne, 614–20; sent to Tower, 616, 620; and alleged murder of, 620, 621

Edward VI, King, xxii, 587

Edward, Prince (Richard III's son), 628

Edward Balliol, Edward I, King of

Scotland: invades Scotland and crowned king (1332), 240–1; driven out of Scotland, 242; and restored to throne by Edward III (1334), 243
Edward, the Black Prince, 1st Duke of Cornwall, xxii, 252, 276, 281, 328, 330, 341–2, 376; knighted by Edward III, 306, 308, 310, French wars, 306, 307, 320, 321, 332; battle of Poitiers (1356), 321; and Treaty of Brétigny (1360), 322; made ruler of Aquitaine, 324; battle of Najera, 328; taxation levied in Gascony by, 328, 329; death (1376), 342, 350
Edward the Confessor, King (reigned 1042–66), xx, xxi, 11, 14, 15, 16, 18, 19, 20, 25, 58, 73, 219; bones removed to Westminster Abbey, 115–16
Edward the Exile, 16n
Edward, Prince of Wales (Henry VI's son), 544, 545, 547, 560, 563, 566, 588, 591, 600
Edward of York, Earl of Rutland, Duke of Aumâle and Duke of York, 417, 422, 423, 429, 435, 445, 455, 458, 467, 477, 479, 485, 490
Edwin, Earl, 17
Edwin of Northumbria, King, 6–7
Egerton, Philip, 526
Eleanor (Simon de Montfort's wife), 88, 89, 114
Eleanor (Simon de Montfort's daughter), 143
Eleanor of Castille, Queen, 149
Eleanor of Provence, Queen, 77, 78, 92
elections: Statute of Westminster I on, 129–30; of knights, 255–6, 475; parliamentary control of, 467; statutes (1406/1410/1413) on regulation of, 475, 481, 487, 513–14; property qualification for franchise in shires, 513–14; disputed and invalid, 513; social restrictions on franchise in shires, 531
Elizabeth Woodville, Queen (Edward IV's wife), 592–3, 596, 600, 614, 617, 625, 627, 628; takes sanctuary at Westminster (1470), 599, 603; birth of son Edward, 600, 603; takes sanctuary again (1485), 616
Elizabeth of York, Queen, 621, 622, 628, 633
Ely, Bishops of see Arundel; Bourchier; Fordham; Hotham; Longchamp; Morton
Elys, William, 348
Emma of Normandy, Queen, 14, 15
English language, 29, 46, 102, 324–5, 574, 587
Erghum, Ralph, Bishop of Salisbury and of Bath and Wells, 358
Espléchin, truce of, 288
Essex, Earls of see Bourchier, Viscount; Thomas of Woodstock
Ethelbert, 8
Ethelred the Unready, King, 10, 41
Ethelred II, King, 11

Eton College, 530, 531, 554, 587
Evesham, battle of (1265), 96, 113, 156
Exchequer, xx, 22, 23, 32, 49, 70, 75, 76, 292; removed by Edward II to York, 185; returned to Westminster, 276
Exeter, Bishops of see Brantingham; Neville; Stafford; Stapledon
Exeter, Dukes of see Beaufort; Holland

Falkirk, battle of (1298), 163
famine, 200, 205, 247, 248
Fane fragment (Journal of Lords' proceedings), 573–7
Fastolf, Sir John, 554
Favent, Thomas, 394, 396, 398
Fieschi, Cardinal Ottoboono, 114
firma burgi, 122n
Fitzalan, Edmund, Earl of Arundel, 193, 195, 211
Fitzalan, Richard, Earl of Arundel, 293, 334, 347
Fitzalan, Richard, Earl of Arundel, 377, 378, 379, 380, 381, 392, 393, 399, 401, 402, 404, 405, 410, 431; quarrels between Richard II and, 385–6, 421–2; public outburst against Lancaster (1394 Parliament), 419–20, 421; Richard II's suspicions of, 427–8, 429; imprisoned in Carisbrooke castle, 429; trial and execution of (1397), 432–3
Fitzalan, Thomas, Earl of Arundel, 486
Fitzalan, William, Earl of Arundel, 568
Fitzhugh, Lord, 496
Fitz-Osbern, William, 20
Fitz-Peter, Geoffrey, justiciar, 48, 50
FitzWalter, Robert, 58
Flanders, 249, 305; Edward I's expedition to, 156, 157, 158–9, 162; Edward III's embargo on export of wool to, 244–5, 278; 1383 'crusade' to, 383–5
Fleta, legal writer, 83 &n, 88
Flore, Roger, Speaker, 498
Florence of Worcester, 9
Foliot, Gilbert, Bishop of London, 36
folkland, Anglo-Saxon, 10
folkmoots, 4–5, 7, 255
Fordham, John, Bishop of Durham and of Ely, 391
forests, forest law, 21, 37, 75, 163–4, 170, 173, 188, 221, 232–3, 270; Charter of the Forest, 68–9 &n, 163
Formigny, battle of (1450), 535
Fortescue, Sir John, 514, 571–2, 578, 591, 600, 601, 633–4
France, French wars, xix, 44, 47, 50, 56, 66, 71, 75n, 78, 87, 98, 107, 109, 174, 517–18, 588–9, 594; Henry I's conquest of Normandy, 25–6; rebellions against Henry II, 44; John defeated and loses territories in, 53–4, 57; battle of Bouvines (1214), 57; Louis acknowledges Henry III and returns to, 68; truce of Chinon (1214), 78;

parlements, 80, 84, 329; Henry III's Gascony expedition, 92, 93-4, 95; Treaty of Paris (1259), 104; Edward I's campaigns, 119, 143, 149, 152, 155, 156, 175; Scottish treaty of alliance with (1295), 155; Edward II's conflict over Gascony with, 222-3; Scots supported against Edward III by, 244; Edward III's claim to throne of, 245-6, 279, 298, 323, 329; Brittany expedition (1342-3), 298-9; truce of Malestroit (1343), 299, 300, 302, 304; Edward III's invasion of Normandy, 306-7; and truce of Calais (1347), 307, 310; draft treaty of Guines (1354), 319-20; battle of Poitiers (1356), 321; and truce of Bordeaux, 321; and breakdown of government in, 322; Jacquerie, peasant rising, 322; Treaty of Brétigny (1360), 323, 491; John of Gaunt's disastrous expeditions in, 333, 362-3; truce of Bruges (1375), 335-6; attacks on south coast of England, 358, 362; and threat of invasion by, 388; Richard II's truce with, 402, 410, 415, 423; and peace negotiations, 414-15, 417, 418, 420-1; Treaty of 1396 (28-year truce), 422-3; Richard II's marriage to Isabella of, 423; Glendower's alliance with, 459; attack on Isle of Wight, 468; civil war in, 481, 490; English defeat Orléanists (1411), 482; Henry V's campaigns, 485, 490-1, 492, 493, 494, 495; battle of Agincourt (1415), 490, 491, 492; and conquest of Normandy, 490, 492; treaty of Troyes (1420), 492, 493-4, 532; Henry V's marriage to Catherine of Valois, 492; Bedford's administration of English territories in, 496; and Joan of Arc, 502, 503; and coronation of Charles VII, 503; and coronation in Paris of Henry VI, 503, 515; defection of Burgundy, 503-4, 524; failure of Arras peace conference (1335), 504, 523-4; death of Bedford in Rouen, 524; Oye conference (1439), 525-6; Somerset's expedition to Normandy (1442) 528-9; Henry VI's marriage to Margaret of Anjou, 529, 531; and truce of Tourçe (1444), 529, 531, 534; surrender of Maine (1448), 532, 534, 536; English invasion of Brittany (1449), 535; battle of Formigny (1450), 535; and French conquest of Normandy, 535, 540; battle of Castillon (1453) and English driven out of, 534-5; Edward IV's relations with, 591, 592, 593, 594, 595-6, 601, 602, 604, 605-6, 612; and Warwick's alliance with Louis XI, 593, 598, 599; and Edward IV's expedition to, 607; treaty of Picquigny (1475), 607-8; Henry VII supported by, 629; *see also* Hundred Years' War
freemen, freeholders, 5, 6, 17, 21, 29, 60, 62, 63, 95, 124, 151, 250

Frescobaldi, bankers, 186, 187
Furnivall, Lord, 469, 473

Galbraith, V.H., 446
Garter, Order of the, 240, 253, 303, 317, 496
Gascony, 71, 107, 119, 144, 148, 169, 234, 320, 328, 332, 333, 382, 415, 421, 422-3, 468, 495, 529; Henry III's expedition in, 92, 93-4, 95; French confiscation of, 149, 151, 155; Edward I's campaigns, 149, 150, 152, 156, 157, 161; Charles IV of France's confiscation of (1324), 223; Edward III's campaigns, 305, 306, 307, 321; Treaty of Brétigny, 323; taxation levied by Black Prince in, 328, 329; French attacks and conquest of, 525, 528, 542-3, 544
Gaveston, Piers, Earl of Cornwall, 181, 183-4, 185, 186, 191, &n, 192, 193, 196, 197, 198, 199, 205, 209; forced into exile by magnates (1308), 178-80; and return of, 182-3, 191; banishment of (1311), 186, 192; and reinstated by Edward II, 192; execution of (1312), 193-4, 195, 205, 210, 218
Gelderland, Duke of, 417
gentry, 102, 108, 252, 405, 487, 584, 585; *see also* knights
Geoffrey Plantagenet, Archbishop of York, 46
George of Clarence *see* Clarence, Duke of
Gilbert, John, Bishop of Hereford and of St David's, 391, 410
Gildesborough, Sir John, Speaker, 369, 370
gilds and fraternities, 62, 111, 249-50; Commons seeks suppression of (1388), 407-8
Giles of Brittany, 535
Glanville, Ranulf, justiciar, 45
Glendower, Owen, Prince of Wales, 458, 459, 468, 475, 476, 479
Gloucester, Duchess of *see* Cobham, Eleanor
Gloucester, Dukes of *see* Humphrey of Lancaster; Richard III, King; Thomas of Woodstock
Gloucester, Earls of *see* Clare, Gilbert de; Despenser
Gloucester Abbey (St Peter's): Parliament (1278), 134; Edward II buried in, 237; Parliament (1378), 363-8; Parliament (1407), 476-9
Godwin, Earl, 14-15
Good Parliament (1376), 329, 337-51, 501
Grand Assize, 39, 42
Gray, John de, 54
Great Charter *see* Magna Carta
great councils, xv, 4, 13, 82; Norman *magnum consilium*, 4, 22, 23-4, 38, 279; distinction between Parliaments and, 13, 276-7 &n, 318-19; Henry I's, 25; Henry II's, 30-1, 32, 34-6, 38, 43; attributes associated with Parliaments of, 38;

Richard I's, 45, 46, 47–8, 49–50; Magna Carta provides procedures for summoning members of, 61–2; Henry III's, 65, 66, 67, 71, 72, 73, 77, 78, 91, 93–5; described as 'Parliament' for first time (1237), 77, 79; atrophy from 14th century onwards, 88; Edward III's, 276, 277–8, 281; and privy councils, 417; *see also curia regis*; Parliaments; Witan

great councils: list in chronological order: 1163 (Westminster), 32; 1164 (Clarendon), 31, 33–5; 1164 (Northampton), 31, 35–6; 1194 (Nottingham), 47; 1198 (Oxford), 47–8; 1199 (Northampton), 50; 1212: 93; 1213 (Oxford), 92–3; 1215 (Staines), 80; 1218 (Worcester), 80; 1220: 71; 1224: 72; 1234 (Westminster), 77; 1236 (Merton), 77; 1237 (Westminster), 77, 79–80; 1242: 78–9, 91; 1244 (Westminster), 87, 91–2; 1246 (London), 80; 1248 and 1249: 92; 1254 (Westminster), 93–5; 1265 (Winchester), 114; 1267 (Marlborough), 115; 1268: 115; 1294: 149; 1309 (York), 183; 1317 (Nottingham), 207; 1330 (Nottingham), 238–9; 1336 (Nottingham), 244, 276, 277–8; 1337 (Stamford), 278; 1338 (Nottingham), 281; 1342 (Westminster), 298; 1344: 303; 1347: 309; 1352: 317; 1353 (Westminster), 317–19; 1371: 352; 1376 (Westminster), 351–2; 1379: 368; 1386 (Oxford), 389; 1392 (Stamford), 417; 1434 (London), 523; 1455: 552; 1458 (London), 558

Great Schism, 367–8, 383, 479
Green, Sir Harry, 427, 433, 438, 444, 445
Green, Sir Henry, Chief Justice, 325
Green, John Richard, 52, 53
Gregory IX, Pope, 78
Gregory X, 120, 133
Gregory XI, 334–5; English *concordat* with, 336
Grey, Sir John, 593
Grey, Sir Ralph, 589, 592
Grey, Sir Richard, 616, 618
Grey, Thomas *see* Dorset, Marquis of
Grey of Ruthin, Reginald, Lord, 458, 541, 560
Grosseteste, Robert, Bishop of Lincoln, 92
Gui, Cardinal, 108, 110–11
Guines, 313, 317, 324; draft treaty of (1354), 319–20
Guthrum, King of Danes, 8
Guy de Blois, 307

Hales, Sir Robert, 374, 376
Halesowen, Abbot of, 479
Halidon Hill, battle of (1333), 242
Hanseatic League, treaty with (1473), 605
Hapeton, Walter de, 139
Harclay, Sir Andrew, Earl of Carlisle, 314, 222
Harcourt, Godfrey de, 306

Harfleur, siege of (1415), 490
Harlech castle, capture of (1409), 479
Harold II Godwinson, King, 14, 15, 16, 17, 18
Harold III Hardrada, King of Norway, 15
Hastings, battle of (1066), 17, 18, 19
Hastings, John, Earl of Pembroke, 330, 331, 332
Hastings, William Lord, 569, 598, 599, 614, 616, 621, 624; arrest and execution of (1483), 617
Hawley, Robert, 363
Haxey, Sir Thomas, 424, 425, 426, 427, 428, 455
Hedgley Moor, battle of (1463), 592
Hengham, Chief Justice Ralph de, 140–1, 144
Henry I, King (reigned 1100–35), 25, 28, 30, 33, 40; 'charter of liberties', 25, 57–8; conquest of Normandy, 25–6
Henry II, King (reigned 1154–89), 26, 28–44, 45, 50, 54, 66, 79, 117; dispute between Becket and, 31–8, 48; great councils of, 30, 31, 32, 34–6, 38, 43; and land ownership, 38–9; and Assize of Arms, 39–40; administration of justice, 39, 40–3; rebellions against, 44, 55
Henry III, King (reigned 1216–72), xxi, 13, 65–116, 121, 151, 162, 184, 210, 231, 253, 449, 564; Magna Carta reissued, 51n, 61, 63, 66–9, 71, 72–3, 78, 87; crowned at Gloucester, 66; Louis of France acknowledges his title to throne, 68; crowned for second time (1220), 69; restoration of royal castles to, 69–70; personality, 73, 74; Peter des Rivaux's administration, 75–6; 1st barons' rebellion against, 76–7, marriage to Eleanor of Provence, 77; involvement with papal politics, 78, 97–8; 2nd barons' rebellion, 88–9; Gascony expedition, 92, 93–4, 95; and regency in his absence, 92; Petition of the Barons, 98; and Provisions of Oxford, 99–100, 101, 102, 106, 107; and Provisions of Westminster, 102–3, 104; Treaty of Paris (1259), 104; charges against de Montfort dropped, 105–6; Barons' Wars (1264–7), 107–15; defeated at Battle of Lewes, 108; defeat and death of de Montfort, 112–13; Dictum of Kenilworth, 114; and Statute of Marlborough, 115
Henry IV Bolingbroke, King (reigned 1399–1413), Earl of Derby, Duke of Lancaster, xx, xxi, 395, 398, 410, 414, 423, 424, 432, 435, 442, 444, 451–84, 488, 489, 502, 509, 564, 572, 583; first Parliament attended by (as Earl of Derby), 388; Richard II bestows dukedom of Hereford on, 435; quarrel with Norfolk, 437–8, 439, 440–1, 456; banished and estates taken from 441, 443; usurpation of throne

by (1399), 445–50, 452–3; first Parliament of his reign, 448, 453, 454–7, 458; coronation, 453–4; his son Henry recognized as heir to throne, 454–5; proceedings against Richard II's friends, 455; character and behaviour, 455–6; ill health of, 456, 470, 471, 473, 475–6, 479, 481, 482; rebellions against, 458, 459, 466, 469; Scottish expedition (1400), 458; and Welsh revolt, 458–9; and battle of Shrewsbury (1403), 459, 464, 466; marriage to Joan of Navarre, 466–7; Parliament of 1406: 470–5; and execution of Archbishop Scrope, 469–70; excludes Beauforts from royal succession, 476; and Beauforts' plot against, 482; death of, 483

Henry V, King (reigned 1413–22), 452, 468, 470, 479, 480, 482, 483, 485–94, 495, 509, 519, 527, 572, 583; created Prince of Wales and recognized as heir to throne, 454–5; popularity of, 476; as leader of Henry IV's council, 480, 481; personal quarrel between Arundel and, 481; and agreement with Duke of Burgundy, 481; French campaigns, 485, 490, 492, 493, 494; coronation, 486; first Parliament of, 486–7, 488; claim to French crown of, 490, 492, 493; plot against, 490; and battle of Agincourt (1415), 490, 491; treaty with Emperor Sigismund, 492; marriage to Catherine of Valois, 492; death of (1422), 494; provisions for regency, 494, 495–6

Henry VI, King (reigned 1422–61 and 1470–71), xix, 452, 492–3, 494, 495–566, 583, 589, 601, 602, 615, 616; dispute over regency during his minority, 495–502; coronation in Paris (1430), 503, 515; attends Parliament (as infant), 505, 507, 508; coronation at Westminster (1429), 512; marriage to Margaret of Anjou (1445), 529, 531; character, 529–30; French policy, 532, 534–5; saves Suffolk's life, 538; and feud between York and Somerset, 540–1, 542–3, 544; York demands government reforms and council changes, 541; judicial eyres undertaken in country, 542, 543; insanity of, 543, 544, 546, 550 &n, 552–3, 554, 555, 574, 592; birth of son Edward, 544, 547; 1st battle of St Albans, 549, 551; and causes of Wars of the Roses, 556–7; court established at Coventry, 557; battle of Ludford, 558–9; captured at Northampton (1460), 560, 565; York's claim to the throne, 561–4; and concord between York and, 564; captured at 2nd battle of St Albans, 565; and deposed by Edward IV (1461), 565–6; bill of attainder against, 571, 586; committed to Tower, 592; readeption of (1470), 599, 603, 610; captured by Edward IV, 600; put to death in Tower (1471), 600

Henry VII, King (reigned 1485–1509), 137, 547, 559, 567, 571, 601, 633; joins rebellion against Richard III, 621–2; invasion of England by, 629–30; battle of Bosworth, 630–1; assumes crown, 631, 632–3; marriage to Elizabeth of York, 628, 633
Henry VIII, King, 30, 37, 262, 586, 602, 632
Henry of Almain, 108
Henry of Grosmont, Earl of Derby, 239, 306
Henry of Keighley, 164–5, 171, 172
Henry of Lancaster, 1st Duke of Lancaster, 224, 225, 229, 235, 237, 238, 239, 288, 321, 324, 454
Henry of Trastamara, 328
Henry of Winchester, Bishop, 35
Herbert, Sir William, 557
Herbert, William, Earl of Pembroke, 597–8
Hereford, Bishops of see Gilbert; Orleton
Hereford, Duke of see Henry IV
Hereford, Earl of see Bohun, Humphry de
heregeld (Anglo-Saxon tax), 10
heretics/heresy, 454, 487, 508; 1382 Statute against, 382; *De Heretico Comburendo* (1401), 463; 1414 Statute against, 487
Hexham, battle of (1464), 592
Holland, Henry, Duke of Exeter, 547, 569, 571, 591, 599
Holland, John, Earl of Huntingdon and Duke of Exeter, 381, 386, 387, 417, 422, 435, 455, 458
Holland, John, Earl of Huntingdon, 521
Holland, Thomas, Earl of Kent, and Duke of Surrey, 429, 435, 438, 455, 458
Holland, Thomas, Earl of Kent, 381, 417
Homildon Hill, battle of (1402), 458, 464
Hotham, Bishop of Ely, Chancellor, 235
Hugerford, Lord, 560
Hugh of Lincoln, Bishop, 47–8
Humphrey of Lancaster, Duke of Gloucester, 479, 487–8, 493, 494, 505–6, 507, 517, 519, 524, 525, 526, 527, 530, 531, 532, 551, 587, 615–16; dispute over regency, 495–501, 508, 510–11, 516; conflict between Bishop Beaufort and, 497, 504–5, 507–9, 510, 515–17, 527; given title of Protector and Defender, 499, 510; marriage to Jacqueline of Hainault, 503, 504, 506; exclusion from Tower, 505, 507; and London Bridge confrontation, 507–8, 509; marriage to Eleanor Cobham, 511; obliged to give up title of Protector (1429), 512; Guardian of the realm in absence of King (1430), 515; quarrel with Bedford, 523; his wife Eleanor accused of witchcraft, 527–8; arrest and death of (1447), 533, 539
hundred courts, 7, 21 &n, 31, 40
Hundred Years' War (1337–1453), 240, 244–6, 273, 288, 297–300, 302–3, 304, 305–7, 308–9, 313, 315, 317, 319–20,

322–4, 327–30, 331, 332, 333, 335–6, 358, 369, 384–5, 387, 393, 404, 502, 607–8; taxes needed to meet costs of, 274, 275–87; battle of Sluys, 288; Brittany expedition, 298–9; truce of Malestroit (1343), 299, 300, 302, 304; Edward III's invasion of Normandy, 306; battle of Crécy (1346), 306–7, 308; truce of Calais (1347), 307, 310, 317; draft treaty of Guines (1354), 319–20; battle of Poitiers (1356), 321; truce of Bordeaux (1356), 321; treaty of Brétigny (1360), 323, 491; truce of Bruges (1375), 335–6; Richard II's peace negotiations, 402, 410, 414–15, 417, 418, 420–1, 423; treaty of 1396: 422–3; during reign of Henry V: 485, 490–1, 492, 494; battle of Agincourt (1415), 490, 491, 492; treaty of Troyes (1420), 492, 493–4, 532; under Henry VI, 502–4, 506, 515, 523, 525, 527, 528–9, 532, 534–5, 542–4; truce of Tours (1444), 529, 531, 534; surrender of Maine (1448), 532, 534, 536; battle of Formigny (1450), 535; French conquest of Normandy, 535, 540; battle of Castillon and loss of Bordeaux (1453), 543; treaty of Picquigny (1475), 607–8
Hungerford, Sir Thomas, 352, 359
Hungerford, Walter, Lord, 496, 500, 515, 516, 592
Huntingdon, Earls of see Clinton; Holland

impeachment, 180, 329, 385, 386, 397, 435; in Good Parliament, 348–50, 351, 361; defined, 349n; of Richard II's knights (1388), 398; of Archbishop Arundel, 432; of Duke of Suffolk (1449), 537–8
income tax, 524–5, 539, 603, 604, 605
Ine of Wessex, King, 7, 8
'infamous tract' (libellus famosus), 290
Inge, William, 202
Ingham, Sir Oliver, 235, 239
inheritance, 39, 55, 59, 441, 443, 451; taxation and fines, 55, 56, 135, 606
Innocent III, Pope, 54–5, 56, 58, 64, 70
Innocent VI, Pope, 317
intercommuning (between Lords and Commons), 266–7, 315, 334, 338, 344, 346, 353, 366, 370, 378, 478, 575
Interdict (1208), 54–5, 56
Ireland, 418, 422, 436, 444, 445
Isabella of Angoulême, Queen (John's wife), 53, 210
Isabella of France, Queen (Edward II's wife), 174, 179, 211, 213, 245, 271; and Edward II's deposition, 223–30; government by Mortimer and, 232; downfall of Mortimer, 238, 239; takes habit of Poor Clares, 239
Isabella of France, Queen (Richard II's wife), 423, 492
itinerant justices, 40, 42, 49

Jacqueline, Countess of Hainault, 503, 504, 506, 510, 511, 527
Jacquerie (peasant uprising), 322
Jacquetta of Luxembourg, Princess, 592
James I, King of Scots, 475, 506
James II, King, 232
Jewel Tower, xx
Jews, 68, 91, 101, 147
Joan, Princess of Wales, 381
Joan of Arc, 502, 503
Joan of Navarre, Queen (Henry IV's wife), 466–7
Joan of the Tower, 236, 242
John, King (reigned 1199–1216), 44, 45, 46, 47, 50–64, 66, 67, 69, 70, 71, 74, 76n, 78, 80, 92, 120; accession to throne, 50; coronation (1199), 50; and Magna Carta, 50, 51–2, 53, 57, 58–63, 87, 188; character and abilities, 52–3, 56; rebellions, and defeats in France, 53–4, 57; Pope's Interdict and excommunicated, 54–5, 56; barons' conflict with, 55–6, 57, 59, 64, 68, 71, 93, 96, 231; and revolt against, 57–8; Articles of the Barons (1215), 58
John II the Good, King of France, 315, 316, 317, 320; captured by English (1356), 321, 322, 323; death in captivity (1364), 328
John of Bohemia, 307
John of Brabant, 503, 510
John of Brittany, 105
John the Fearless, Duke of Burgundy, 475, 479–80, 481, 492
John of Gaunt, Duke of Lancaster, 330, 332, 336, 348, 351–2, 353–4, 356–8, 359, 360, 361, 364, 365, 369, 370, 373, 376–7, 378, 379, 381, 384, 386, 387, 411, 418, 423, 426, 427, 438, 442, 463, 476, 541, 562, 630; disastrous French expeditions, 333, 362–3; Good Parliament (1376), 339, 341, 342, 343, 345, 346–7, 350, 351–2; London citizens turn against, 353–4; and coronation of Richard II, 357; government, during king's minority, by, 357–8; abuse of sanctuary at Westminster Abbey, 363, 367; Northumberland's quarrel with, 377; Castillian enterprise, 357, 380, 382, 383, 387, 410; Richard II's relations with, 386, 410, 427; goes to Portugal (1386), 388; returns to England (1389), 410; rules Aquitaine as Duke of Guienne, 412, 415–16, 421; Arundel's public outburst against (1394), 419–20, 421; trial of Gloucester, Arundel and Warwick, 433, 434, 435; death (1399), 441
John of Lancaster, Duke of Bedford, 479, 487–9, 491, 493, 494, 495, 503–4, 508–9, 515, 517, 518, 519, 523–4; government of French territories by, 496; dispute over Regency, 496–7, 499, 500; Commons appeal to him to stay in England as Protector, 519, 523; Gloucester's quarrel with, 523; death in France (1435), 504, 524

John the Marshall, 35
John of Northampton, Mayor of London, 383
Joseph, William, 551
Jourdemain, Margery, witch of Eye, 528
Journals of Lords' proceedings: Fane fragment, 573–7
judges, king's, 166, 167, 392–3, 436, 563; law-drafting function of, 126, 140–1
jury, 41–2, 49, 63, 129, 139, 273, 349, 406, 414, 522, 627
justices of the peace, 257, 273, 406, 414
justiciar, office of, 26, 30, 33, 37, 45, 46, 47, 48, 50, 57, 60, 69, 70, 72, 75, 90, 95, 98–9, 105, 106

Kemp, Cardinal John, Bishop of London, Archbishop of York and of Canterbury, 509, 515, 516, 525, 526, 546
Kenilworth castle, 113, 114, 193; Edward II imprisoned in, 224, 237; and parliamentary delegations visit him, 225, 226, 227, 229, 230
Kenilworth Parliament (1266), 114
Kent, William Neville, Earl of, Lord Fauconberg, 569
Kent, Earls of see Edmund of Woodstock; Holland; Thomas
Kilsby, William, 281, 288, 289, 290, 293
king's bench, xx, 125, 167
King's College, Cambridge, 530, 531, 554, 587
Kirkby, John, mercer, 370
Kirkby, Thomas, clerk of the Rolls, 578, 579
knights, 13, 42, 252–8; shire responsibilities and duties, 42, 43, 49, 93, 100–2, 103, 125, 257–8; military service, 47–8, 109, 124; as representatives of shires at Parliament under Henry III, 65, 86, 101–2, 108–9, 110, 112; summoned to attend Parliament for first time (1254), 92–4; assessment and collection of taxes by, 93; functions at Parliament, 95, 108–9, 131–2, 163, 171–2; representation at Parliament under Edward I, 119–20, 121–2, 125, 127–8, 131–3, 135–6, 144–6, 147, 150–1, 153, 154, 160, 163, 164, 166; first used in political role (1301), 164–5; re-election of, 171–3, 257; and deposition of Edward II, 224–5, 228, 229, 233; enhanced role under Edward III, 233–4; conjoined as single unit with burgesses, 241 &n; security when travelling, 247; blurred class distinction between barons and, 250–1, 252, 254–5; defined, 252–3; king's household, 253; property qualification for obligation to knighthood, 253; election of, 255–8, 475, 481, 487, 513–14; social standing, 329, 346, 584; property qualification for franchise (1429), 513–14; wages and expenses, 514–15; social restrictions on election of (1446), 531; see also Commons
Knights of the Star, French Order of, 317
Knyvett, Sir John, 331, 333–4, 337
Knywolmarsh, William, 498

labour policy/legislation, 312, 314, 316, 322, 368, 372, 407, 413
Lancaster, Duchess of see Blanche
Lancaster, Dukes of see Henry IV; Henry of Lancaster; John of Gaunt
Lancaster, Earls of see Edmund; Thomas of Lancaster
land, land tenure, 252; Anglo-Saxon transfer of, 10; Domesday survey, 20; Norman, 19, 20–1; under Henry II, 38–9, 40, 42; carucage tax on, 48–9, 71; under Henry III, 74; title-deeds to, 74; burgage tenure, 122–3, 124; under Edward I, 122, 124, 125, 134–5, 141–2
land tax, 468, 469, 483, 517
Langland, William, *Piers Plowman*, 325, 327
Langley, Thomas, Bishop of Durham, 470, 477, 480, 493, 498, 545, 550
Langton, John, 159
Langton, Stephen, Archbishop of Canterbury, 54, 55, 56, 57, 58, 70
Langton, Walter, Bishop of Coventry and Lichfield, 173, 176, 193
Lateran Council (1215), 41
Latimer, Lord, 337, 340, 345–6, 347–8, 349, 351, 352, 353, 358, 361
law and order, law-enforcement, 69, 141, 170–1, 200, 232, 236, 404, 405
law courts, 42; at Westminster Hall, xx, 40, 42, 55, 167; hundred, 7, 21 &n, 31, 50; shire, 5, 7, 21, 27, 40, 43, 49, 72, 93, 234, 251; ecclesiastical v. lay, 31–2; itinerant justices, 40, 42, 49; baronial, 250; use of English language in (1362), 324, 325
lawlessness, 200–1, 205, 222, 246, 247, 512, 518–19, 521–2, 526, 530, 595, 603–4
lawyers, 527; disqualified from membership of Commons, 254, 333, 468
Lee, Sir John de la, 329, 349n
Leeds castle, Edward II's siege of, 213
Leicester, Earl of see Montfort, Simon de
Leicester Parliaments: 1414: 487–90; 1426 (Parliament of Bats), 508–9; 1450: 539–40
letter writing, social, 587–8
Lewes, battle of (1264), 108
Lincoln, battle of (1217), 68
Lincoln, Bishops of see Beaufort; Grosseteste; Hugh; Rotherham; Russell; William
Lincoln, Henry de Lacy, Earl of, 179, 183, 185, 193
Lincoln, John de la Pole, Earl of see Pole
Lincoln Parliaments: 1301: 163–5, 172; 1316: 202–4, 207; 1327: 236
Lionel, Prince see Clarence, Duke of
Lister, Geoffrey, 375
livery and maintenance, abuse of, 404–7,

413–14, 415, 416, 421, 424, 465, 512, 518, 522, 560, 603; Statute against (1390), 412; 1399 Act against, 455, 465
Llywelyn, Prince of Wales, 103, 113, 143, 146
Lodden Bridge great council (1191), 46
Lollards, Lollardy, 454, 463, 469, 474, 479, 480, 486, 487, 508, 515
London, 29, 49, 105, 114, 115, 124, 249, 264, 619; Witan meetings 12, 13; taxation, 49, 61, 91; Simon de Montfort's occupation of, 107; and Edward II's deposition, 223, 225, 227–8, 231; request for annual Parliaments at Westminster (1327), 263; and effect of regular Parliaments, 264; John of Gaunt's unpopularity, 353–4, 357; Peasants' Revolt in, 373–5; fishmongers' monopoly, 383; Richard II's bad relations with, 417; disturbance in (1449), 537; Jack Cade's rebellion (1450), 538–9; Yorkists take over (1460), 560–1; Edward IV accepted as king by, 565–6; and enters in triumph (1471), 600; see also Westminster
London, Bishops of see Beaufort; Braybrook; Courtney; Foliot; Kemp; Stratford; Sudbury
London Bridge: Gloucester–Beaufort confrontation on, 507–8
Longchamp, William, Bishop of Ely, deposition of, 45–7
Lord Chancellor, 81
Lord Chief Justice, 266
Lords (House of), xvi, xvii, xxi–xxii, 81, 153, 167 &n, 180, 208, 252, 254, 259, 268, 285, 361, 489; peers rights to be tried by, 62, 291, 293–4, 296; judicial role, 167 &n, 329; intercommuning between Commons and, 266–7, 315, 334, 338, 344, 346, 353, 366, 370, 378, 478, 575; Good Parliament, 337, 343–51; attack on court of Richard II, 385; Merciless Parliament, 395–401; trial of Gloucester, Arundel and Warwick (1397), 430–5; deposition of Richard II, 447–50, 456–7; dispute over regency (1422), 497–502, 510–11, 512; Fane fragment, 573–7; right to amend Commons' bills by, 578–9; see also barons; Parliament; peers
Lords of Appeal, 81
Lords Appellant, see Appellants
Louis VII, King of France, 64, 66, 68, 71, 80
Louis IX (St Louis), King of France, 104, 105, 107, 108, 126
Louis X, King of France, 245
Louis XI, King of France, 588, 591, 593, 596, 602, 609, 611, 612; Warwick's alliance with, 593, 598, 599, 600; treaty of Picquigny (1475), 607–8
Lovel, Lord, 472
Lovel, Francis, Viscount, 624, 631

Low Countries (Netherlands), 244–5, 275, 276, 281, 286, 288, 504, 506, 590, 593, 611
Ludford, battle of (1459), 558–9
Ludlow castle, 558; Edward, Prince of Wales resides at, 604, 615, 616
Ludwig IV, Emperor, 245
Lusignan family of Poitou, 53, 103–4, 210
Lusignan, Aymer de, Bishop of Winchester, 103
Lusignan, Hugh de, 54
Luton, meeting of Witan at (931), 9
Lyons, Richard, 337, 340, 345–6, 347, 348, 349

McIlwain, C.H., 43n
Magna Carta (Great Charter: 1215), 21, 25, 27, 42, 49, 50, 51–2, 53, 57, 58–63, 67, 77, 78, 87, 96, 158, 162, 184, 221, 231, 290, 607; notion of liberties enshrined in, 59–60, 62–3; first reissue of (1216), 66–8; second reissue of (1217), 68–9; third reissue of (1225), 71, 72–3, 112, 130, 213
magnum consilium (council of magnates), 4, 22, 23–4, 38, 279; see also great councils
Maine, surrender to French of (1448), 532, 534, 536, 537
Maitland, F.W., *Introduction to the Memoranda de Parliamento*, 81–2, 83, 86, 166, 170–1
Malestroit, truce of (1343), 299, 300, 302, 304
maletote (duty), 130, 149, 157, 161, 277, 280–1, 282, 283, 286, 287, 301
Manny, Walter, 289, 298, 309, 320
Mansell, John, 90
manumission, 375, 377, 378
March Earls of see Dunbar; Edward IV; Mortimer
Marcolf's chamber, xxii
Mare, Sir Peter de la, first Speaker of the Commons, 339, 340–1, 342, 343–6, 347, 351, 352, 357, 359, 360–1
Margaret, Princess, the Maid of Norway, 148
Margaret of Anjou, Queen (Henry VI's wife), 529, 531, 532, 533, 544, 554, 562, 563, 564, 565, 569, 588–9, 591, 596; birth of son, Prince Edward (1453), 544; court party controlled by, 555, 557, 558; summons partisan Parliament to Coventry (1459), 559; alliance with Scottish king, 565, 588; second battle of St Albans (1461), 565; defeated at battle of Towton (1461), 566; bill of attainder against, 571; seeks foreign help, 588–9, 591; Warwick's alliance with, 598, 599; imprisoned at Malvern (1471), 600; released, and returns to France (1475), 607
Margaret of Burgundy (daughter of Mary of Burgundy), 612
Margaret of York, Duchess of Burgundy (sister of Edward IV), 594, 595, 608
Marlborough Parliament (1267), 115

Index

marriage-aid (1290), 145, 148
Marshall, Richard, Earl of Pembroke, 76, 77
Marshall, William, Earl of Pembroke, 58, 66, 69, 71, 80
Mary of Burgundy (daughter of Margaret of York, duchess of Burgundy), 608, 610, 612
Mary of Gueldres, Queen Mother and Scottish Regent, 588
Matilda, Empress, 26
Maximilian of Austria, 608, 611, 612
merchants, 123, 124, 195; Statute of Acton Burnell (1283), 136–8, 141; Statute of Merchants (1285), 141; bills to give protection to (1461 and 1463), 574–5, 590; *see also* burgesses; customs duty; wool trade
Merciless Parliament (1388), 395–401, 403, 404, 410, 431, 436, 439, 454
Merke, Thomas, Bishop of Carlisle, 450, 458
Middle Party, 209–10, 212
military service, 248; Norman *servitium debitum*, 20; Assize of Arms (1181), 39, 49; under Henry II, 39–40, 47–8; under Richard I, 47–8; under John, 57; under Henry III, 93–4, 97, 109–10; under Edward I, 124, 146, 156, 160; under Edward III, 234–5, 270, 271, 308, 309; under Henry VI, 361
Model Parliament (1295), 132, 152–3, 154–5
Modus Tenendi Parliamentum, 219–20
Moleyns, Adam, Bishop of Chichester, 536–7
monetagium ('sales' tax), 25
money, legislation on, 163, 273, 302
Montagu, John, Earl of Salisbury, 445, 458
Montagu, John Neville, Marquis of, Earl of Northumberland, 592, 597, 598–9, 600
Montagu, Sir William, 209
Montagu, William, Earl of Salisbury, 238, 239, 293
Montagu, William, Earl of Salisbury, 334, 417, 429, 438
Montfort, Joan de, Duchess of Brittany, 298
Montfort, John de, Duke of Brittany and Earl of Richmond, 298, 306, 317, 328, 335
Montfort, Simon de, Earl of Leicester, 65, 81, 88–9, 90, 95, 98, 103, 104, 105, 107–13, 114, 116, 122, 143, 156; King's charges dropped against (1260), 105–6; Barons' Wars, 107–8; 1264 and 1265 Parliaments of, 108–10, 111–12, 123, 153; defeat and death (1265), 112–13
Montfort, Simon de, Jr, 113
Moray, Thomas Randolph, Earl of, 240, 244
Morcar, Earl, 17
Mort d'ancestor, assize of, 39
Mortimer family, Earls of March, 212, 213, 214, 221, 341
Mortimer, Anne (Richard of York's wife), 490
Mortimer, Edmund, 3rd Earl of March, 334, 341, 342, 344, 347, 348, 350, 352, 360, 364, 368
Mortimer, Edmund, 5th Earl of March, 444, 449, 452, 458, 459, 485, 490, 506
Mortimer, Edmund (uncle of 5th Earl), 458
Mortimer, Sir John, 506
Mortimer, Roger de, 1st Earl of March, 235, 240, 267, 271; Edward II's deposition, 223–4, 225, 227, 228, 230; and government of, 232, 235, 236–8; takes title of Earl of March, 235; secret murder of Edward of Carnarvon by, 237; and arrest and execution of Edmund of Kent, 237–8; downfall and death (1330), 238–9
Mortimer, Roger de, 4th Earl of March, 342, 387, 422, 436, 438, 444
Mortimer, Sir Thomas, impeachment of, 434–5
Mortimer's Cross, battle of (1461), 565
Morton, Cardinal John, Bishop of Ely and Archbishop of Canterbury, 571, 572, 601, 617, 621, 629
Mowbray, John, 169
Mowbray, John, Duke of Norfolk, 507, 511, 521, 541, 568, 609
Mowbray, Thomas, Earl of Nottingham and 1st Duke of Norfolk, 395, 398, 410, 419, 422, 423, 426, 428, 429, 432, 434, 435, 436, 438; quarrel with Henry Bolingbroke, 438, 439, 440–1; banished for life, 441; and estates taken from, 441, 443
Mowbray, Thomas, 469
murder fine, 20, 103
Murimith, Adam, 289

Najera, battle of (1367), 328, 363
Netherlands *see* Low Countries
Neville family, 562, 585; feud between Percys and, 541, 544, 547, 548, 562
Neville, Alexander, Archbishop of York, 364, 393, 413, 417; trial of (1388), 394, 395–7, 398
Neville, Anne (Richard III's wife), 628
Neville, George, Bishop of Exeter and Archbishop of York, 561, 562, 564, 566, 569, 594, 597, 600; imprisoned in Hammes castle (1472), 601
Neville, John *see* Montagu, Marquis of
Neville, Ralph *see* Westmorland, Earls of
Neville, Richard, Earl of Salisbury *see* Salisbury
Neville, Richard, Earl of Warwick *see* Warwick
Neville, William *see* Kent, Earl of
Neville of Raby, Lord, 337, 347, 348, 351
Neville's Cross, battle of (1346), 307
Norfolk, John Howard, 1st Duke of, 621, 629, 630, 631; *see also* Mowbray
Norfolk, Earls of, 207, 224; *see also* Bigod
Norham castle, 592; siege of (1463), 590
Norman Conquest, 3, 5, 6, 11, 15, 17, 18–19, 20, 21, 27, 29, 248

Normandy, 50, 57, 104, 323, 504, 518, 523, 525, 534, 536; Henry I's conquest of, 25–6; Philip II's capture of, 54; Edward III's campaigns, 306–7, 321; Henry V's conquest of, 490, 492; Duke of York's campaign (1441), 527, 528–9; Somerset's expedition to (1442), 528–9; French conquest of (1450), 535, 540
Normandy, John, Duke of, 306
Normans, 18–28, 29, 41; and Anglo-Saxons, 3–4, 19–21, 27; English rebellions against (1068–72), 20; land ownership and legislation, 20–1; councils or courts, 4, 17, 21–4, 25, 26, 38; baronial revolts, 24–5, 26; Anarchy of disputed succession between Matilda and Stephen, 26; evolution of constitutional government, 26–8
Northampton, battle of (1264), 108
Northampton, battle of (1460), 560
Northampton, Earl of see Bohun, William de
Northampton great councils: 1164: 31, 35–6; 1199: 50
Northampton Parliaments: 1307: 179; 1328: 236, 247; 1338: 279; 1380: 369–72
Northumberland, Henry Percy, 1st Earl of, 347, 353, 445, 446–7, 456, 458; John of Gaunt's quarrel with, 377; and rebellions against Henry IV, 459, 466, 469, 479; found guilty of trespass and pardoned (1402), 466; killed at Bramham Moor (1408), 459, 479
Northumberland, Henry Percy, 2nd Earl of, 548; killed at St Albans (1455), 549
Northumberland, Henry Percy, 3rd Earl of, 558, 561; killed at Towton (1461), 566
Northumberland, Henry Percy, 4th Earl of, 629, 630; Edward IV restores earldom to (1469), 598
Northumberland, John Neville, Earl of see Montagu, Marquis of
Norwich, Bishops of see Despenser; Salmon
Nottingham, 12, 13, 393, 629; Earl of see Mowbray; Parliament (1336), 244
Nottingham great councils: 1194: 47; 1317: 207; 1330: 238–9; 1336: 276, 277–8; 1338: 281; 1397: 429

Odo, Bishop, 20
Offa, King of the Mercians, 8
Offord, John, Dean of Lincoln, 307
Old Palace Yard, xx
Oldcastle, Sir John, 487
Oldhall, William, Speaker, 542
Oleson, Tryggvi, J., 11
opposition, legal, legitimization in Magna Carta of, 60–1
ordeal by battle, 39, 41
ordeal by water, 41
Ordainers, 183, 191, 196, 198, 204, 208, 209, 215–16, 218, 251; election of (1310), 184–6, 187, 189

Ordinance of 1363 (on apparel and diet), 326–7
Ordinance of Labourers (1349), 312, 314
Ordinance of the Staple (1353), 318
Ordinances, New (1311), 181, 186–93, 194, 196, 197, 198, 199, 201, 204, 205, 206, 207, 210–11, 263, 362; Edward II's repeal of, 215–216, 221
Orleans, Charles, Duke of, 523, 525, 527, 529, 537
Orleans, Dukes of, 475, 490
Orleton, Adam, Bishop of Hereford and of Winchester, 222, 223, 224, 225, 228, 229, 235, 290
Otterburn, battle of (1388), 402
Oxford, 64, 74, 107, 620; architecture, 587; Parliament (1258), 98–9, 101, 102, 103; Provisions of (1262), 67, 87, 88, 99–100, 101, 102–3
Oxford, Earls of see Vere, de
Oxford great councils: 1198: 47–8; 1213: 92–3; 1386: 389
Oye (Calais) conference (1439), 525–6

Painted Chamber (*Camera Depicta*), Westminster Palace, xxi–xxii, 265, 266, 292, 293, 300, 327, 330, 333, 334, 337, 391, 430, 486, 493, 594; opening of Parliament in, xxi, xxii; medieval paintings in, xxi, 184, 185; Commons meetings, xxii, 266; election of Ordainers in (1310), 184–5; intercommuning, 266–7, 315, 338
papacy, 97–8, 106, 108, 115, 165, 415, 416, 417–18; Avignon, 206, 238, 302, 305, 334, 335, 367–8, 383; see also Church; individual popes
Papal Legate, 66, 69, 108, 110–11, 114, 152, 174
Papal Provisions, 78
pardons, royal, 236, 272–3, 380, 413, 430–2, 433, 436, 437, 442, 466
Paris, Matthew, chronicler of St Albans (1200–59), 50, 52, 80; *Chronica Majora*, 78, 89, 91 &n
parlement, French, 80, 84, 329
Parliament: emergence under Henry III, 65, 77, 79–88; earliest uses of term, 65, 77, 79–80, 82, 88; composition of, 65, 131–2, 138, 153; judicial functions, 81–2, 83–6, 87, 88, 147, 148, 166, 167–8, 171, 267–8; political functions, 86–8, 120, 121, 122, 127, 142, 147–8, 168–9, 172, 220; Provisions of Oxford (1258), 100; de Montfort's partisan Parliament 110–12; attendance expenses, 110, 171, 172, 257, 403–4, 514; legislative functions, 117–18, 122, 125–7, 140–1, 169–71, 268–74; Model Parliament (1295), 132, 152–3, 154–5; full powers called for in summons to, 150, 154 &n; Scottish representation, 169, 173; continuity of membership, 171–3;

consultation between magnates and Commons, 181–2; Ordinances require annual holding of (1311), 188–9, 190–1, 263; regular attendance of Commons, 189–90, 233; armed attendance of members forbidden, 194–5, 247, 264; royal power v. estate, 217–18; *Modus Tenendi Parliamentum* on, 219–20; deposition of Edward II, 224–30, 231; lists of magnates chosen for, 251–2; withdrawal of representative clergy from, 259–62; first provision for annual (1330), 262–4, 272; proceedings in Westminster, 265–7; intercommuning, 266–7, 315, 334, 338, 344, 346, 353, 366, 370, 378, 478, 575; king's officials cease to attend regularly, 293; Stratford affair, 292–4, 296; control of ministerial appointments by, 294–5; meetings of Lords and Commons in separate 'houses', 301; separate procedure for common petitions, 311; English language used in (1363), 325; dismissal of clerical ministers forced on king by, 331; Good Parliament (1376), 337–51, 354; impeachments, 348–50, 351, 361, 385, 386, 398, 432, 435; level of attendance, 364; poll tax, 369, 370, 371–2; punishment for absenteeism, 382; 1386–8 crisis between Richard II and, 389–401; and Merciless Parliament (1388), 395–401; trial of Gloucester, Arundel and Warwick (1397), 430–5; and parliamentary committee, 438–42; deposition of Richard II, 447–50; diminishing number of, 452; control of elections by, 467; protection of members attending, 467; bills to be read by both 'houses', 489; dispute over regency during Henry VI's minority, 497–502, 510–11; wages and expenses, 514–15; amendments to bills, 578–9; and Commons assent to legislation, 580; *see also* attainder; Commons; great councils; petitions; Rolls of Parliament; statutes; taxation
Parliament chamber *see* White Chamber
Parliament House, xxii
Parliament of the Devils (Coventry, 1459), 559–60
parliamentary committee (1398–9), 438–40, 441–2
parliamentary privileges, 133n, 451, 467, 477–8, 488–9, 545, 610
Parliaments, chronological list of (held at Westminster except when meeting place is given): 1237: 77, 79–80; 1242: 78, 91 &n; 1244: 87, 91–2; 1246: 80; 1248: 92; 1249: 92; 1254: 93–5; 1257: 97–8; 1258: 98, 101, 102; 1258 (Oxford), 98–9, 101, 102, 103; 1259: 102–3, 104; 1260: 105–6; 1264: 108–9; 1265: 110, 111–12, 123; 1265 (Winchester), 114; 1267 (Bury St Edmunds), 115; 1267 (Marlborough), 115; 1268: 115; 1269: 115–16; 1270: 116; 1275: 119–20, 121, 125, 127–8, 130, 131–2, 153; 1276: 133–4; 1278 (Gloucester), 134; 1279: 135; 1281 (Worcester), 143; 1283 (Shrewsbury), 135–8, 143, 146, 150; 1285: 138; 1290: 134, 144–6, 147, 148; 1292: 139; 1294: 150, 151; 1295: 132, 152–3, 154–5; 1296 (Bury St Edmunds), 155; 1297 (Salisbury), 130, 156, 157; 1297: 159–60, 161; 1298 (York), 162, 165; 1299: 163; 1300: 163; 1301 (Lincoln), 163–5, 172; 1302: 166; 1305: 81–2, 83, 86, 117, 120, 128, 166–7, 168–70, 173; 1306: 173; 1307 (Carlisle), 173–4; 1307: (Northampton), 179; 1308: 179–80; 1309: 180–2; 1309 (Stamford), 182–3; 1309 (York), 183; 1310: 183–4; 1311: 186, 189–90, 192, 195; 1312: 194, 195; 1313: 195, 218; 1314 (York), 198, 199; 1315: 199–200; 1316 (Lincoln), 202–4, 207; 1318 (York), 211; 1320 (York), 190, 211–12; 1320: 212, 213; 1322 (York), 215–16, 219, 222; 1324: 223; 1325: 190; 1327: 224–30, 231, 234–5, 270, 271; 1327 (Lincoln), 236; 1328 (York), 236; 1328 (Northampton), 236, 247; 1328 (Salisbury), 237; 1330 (Winchester), 238; 1330: 239; 1332: 241; 1332 (York), 241–2; 1333 (York), 242; 1334 (York), 242; 1334: 242–3; 1335 (York), 243–4; 1336: 244; 1336 (Nottingham), 244, 276, 277–8; 1337: 252, 275–6, 278, 283; 1338: 279, 280; 1338 (Northampton), 279; 1339: 282, 283, 284; 1340: 285; 1341: 292–3; 1343: 296, 299, 300–1; 1344: 303–5; 1346: 307–8; 1348: 309, 310–11; 1351: 313–14; 1352: 315–17; 1354: 319–20; 1355: 320; 1357: 321–2; 1362: 324, 325; 1363: 325, 326, 327; 1364: 327; 1366: 327; 1368: 328–9; 1369: 329; 1371: 330–2; 1372: 332–3; 1373: 333–4, 335; 1376: 329, 337–51; 1377: 352–3, 359–62; 1378 (Gloucester), 363–8; 1379: 368; 1380: 369; 1380 (Northampton), 369–72; 1381: 377–9; 1382: 380, 382–3; 1383: 384, 385; 1384 (Salisbury), 385–6; 1384: 386; 1385: 387, 388; 1386: 389–92; 1387: 395; 1388: 395–401, 404; 1388 (Cambridge), 402–9; 1390: 406, 411–13, 414; 1391: 414, 415–16; 1393 (Winchester), 417–18; 1394: 419–21; 1395: 422; 1397: 423–7; 1397: 429–35; 1398 (Shrewsbury), 430, 432, 435–9; 1399: 448, 453–7, 458; 1401: 461–4; 1402: 464; 1404: 459, 464–8; 1404 (Coventry), 468–9, 472; 1406: 470–5; 1407 (Gloucester), 476–9; 1410: 479–81; 1411: 482–3; 1413: 486–7; 1414 (Leicester), 487–90; 1414: 490; 1415: 491; 1416: 491–2; 1417: 493; 1418: 493; 1419: 493; 1420: 493; 1421: 493–4; 1422: 497–502; 1423: 505–6; 1425: 506–7; 1426 (Leicester), 508–9; 1427: 510–11; 1429–30: 512–15; 1431: 515; 1432:

513, 516–17; 1433: 517–20; 1435: 524–5; 1437: 525; 1439: 526; 1440 (Reading), 526–7; 1442: 528; 1445: 514, 530–1; 1446: 531–2; 1447 (Bury St Edmunds), 533; 1449: 535; 1449 (Winchester), 535–6; 1449: 536–8; 1450 (Leicester), 539–40; 1450: 540, 541–2; 1451: 542; 1453 (Reading), 543; 1454: 544–7; 1455: 549–54; 1456: 554; 1459 (Coventry), 559–60, 563; 1460: 559, 561–5; 1461: 568–77, 581; 1463: 575, 589–90, 591–2; 1464 (York), 592; 1465: 592, 593–4; 1467: 594–5; 1467 (Reading), 595; 1468: 595–6; 1470: 599; 1472: 602–4; 1473: 604–5; 1474: 605–6; 1475: 606–7; 1477: 608–9; 1478: 584, 599, 609–11; 1483: 612; 1484: 622–8; 1485: 577
Parning, Robert, 289
Paston, John, 584
Paston letters, 537, 550, 585, 587–8
patronage, 382, 387, 405, 418, 425, 519, 520, 526
Paulinus, 6
Peasants' Revolt (1381), 339, 368, 370, 371, 372–5, 376, 377, 378, 380, 383, 408, 538
Peche, John, 348
Pedro the Cruel, 328, 330
peers, peerage, 61, 81, 207–8, 252, 254–5; right of trial by Lords, 62, 291, 293–4, 296; composition under Edward I of, 153–4; of the realm (earliest use of term), 207–8; Edward II's magnification of, 252; order of seniority in Parliament, 265; Richard II creates new type, unrelated to land, 392; and rewards his supporters, 435; *see also* barons; Lords
Pelham, Sir John, 469, 473, 483, 486
Pembroke, Earls of *see* Hastings; Herbert; Jaspar; Marshall Tudor; Valence
Percy family, 585, 588, 600; Henry V restores earldom of Northumberland to, 485; feud between Nevilles and, 541, 544, 547, 548; Edward IV returns earldom of Northumberland to, 598
Percy, Henry Hotspur, 402, 458, 459
Percy, Henry *see* Northumberland, Earls of
Percy, Sir Ralph, 589
Percy, Sir Thomas, Earl of Worcester, 432, 435, 445, 447
Perrers, Dame Alice, 330, 346, 347, 348, 352, 362
Petition of the Barons, 98
Petition of Rights (1637), 161
petitions, xviii, 82, 84–5, 86, 140, 147, 166, 167, 168 &n, 169, 171, 181, 184, 199–200, 233, 234, 283, 338, 349n, 350, 351, 362, 403, 404, 406, 407–8, 436, 454, 580–2; 583, 590; private, 82, 268, 269, 581–2; common, 82, 83, 164, 168n, 171, 268–72, 274, 294–5, 301, 302, 305, 581, 582; new procedure for (1348), 311; parliamentary committee to deal with outstanding, 438–40; on privileges of Commons (1414), 488–9; legalistic and bureaucratic drafting of, 527, 581
Petty Jury, 42
Philip II Augustus, King of France, 44, 54, 56, 64, 71
Philip IV the Fair, King of France, 149, 155, 245
Philip V, King of France, 245
Philip VI, King of France, 244, 245, 281, 298, 303, 304, 305, 306, 307, 310, 315, 317
Philip the Good, Duke of Burgundy, 492, 505, 517–18, 525, 588–9; defection to Charles VII of, 503–4, 524; death (1467), 595
Philipot, Sir John, 358, 361, 365, 366, 375
Philippa of Hainault, Queen (Edward III's wife), 223, 236, 244, 289, 330
Pickering, Sir James, Speaker, 365–6, 384
Picquigny, treaty of (1475), 607–8
Pipewell Chronicle, 226
Plessyngton, Sir Robert, 441
Poitiers, battle of (1356), 321, 322
Poitou, 56, 57, 71, 320, 323
Pole family, 259, 436
Pole, John de la, Earl of Lincoln, 628
Pole, Michael de la, 1st Earl of Suffolk, 380–1, 382, 385, 387, 388, 389–90, 391, 392, 393, 402, 413; impeachment of, 386; trial of (1388), 394, 395–7, 400
Pole, William de la, 289
Pole, William de la, 4th Earl of Suffolk and 1st Duke of Suffolk, 521, 524, 528, 530, 542, 555; peace negotiations with French, 529, 530, 531, 532, 534, 536; and death of Gloucester, 533; and Duke of York, 533–4; Brittany expedition, 535; impeachment and arrest of (1449), 537; murder of, 535, 538, 539
poll tax, 353, 369, 370, 371–2, 373, 375, 378, 528, 536
Pollard, A.F., *Evolution of Parliament*, dv, 3–4n
Pontefract castle, 209, 211, 214, 445; assembly of magnates (1320), 212–13; Richard II imprisoned in, 456; and murder of Richard II, 458
Popham, Sir John, Speaker, 536
Poyning, Robert, 539
Presentment of Englishry, abolition of, 287
prices and incomes (wages), 200–1, 203, 312, 313–15, 326, 372, 407
Prince's Chamber, xxii
printing, Caxton's introduction of, 588
prises, taking of, 157, 181, 184, 187–8, 189
Prophet, John, 480
Provisions of Oxford (1262), 67, 87, 88, 99–100, 101, 102, 108, 109–10, 111, 156; Henry II's abandonment of, 106, 107
Provisions of Westminster (1258), 102–3, 104, 114, 115
purveyance, 181, 272, 283, 287, 305, 313, 316, 325, 379, 477, 526, 560

quo warranto legislation, 70, 134-5
Quo Warranto, Statute of (1290), 134-5, 141-2

Radcot Bridge, battle of (1387), 395, 438
Radford, Nicholas, 552
Ragman Rolls, 126
Ratcliffe, Sir Richard, 624, 631
Readeption Parliament (1470), 599
Reading Parliament: 1440: 526-7; 1453: 543
Redesdale rebellion (1468), 597
Redmayne, Sir Richard, 491
Refectory, Westminster Abbey: Commons' meetings in, xxii, 266, 424, 465; great council (1244), 91
Reginald, Archbishop of Canterbury, 54
representation, concept of parliamentary, 2-3
Resumption Acts, 539, 542, 554, 593, 594, 595, 605, 607
Retford, Sir Henry de, Speaker, 464
Reynolds, Walter, Archbishop of Canterbury, 225, 226, 228
Rich, Edmund, Archbishop of Canterbury, 77, 78
Richard I Coeur de Lion, King (reigned 1189-99), 44-50, 53, 66; 3rd crusade, 45; deposition of Longchamp, 45-7; Bishop Hugh's resistance to military service and scutage, 47-8; and taxation, 48-9, 72
Richard II, King (reigned 1377-99), xix, xx, xxii, 341, 342, 352, 354, 355-450, 451, 488, 499, 501, 456, 538, 557, 619; appointed guardian of the realm (1372), 332; comes before Parliament (1376), 350; coronation, 356, 357, 358; first Parliament (1377), 359-62; Peasants' Revolt (1381), 373-5; character, 376, 381 &n, 385-6, 408, 443-4; committee to examine household and government of, 379-80, 387-8, 393-4, 431; marriage to Anne of Bohemia (1382), 380; personal rule of, 381-2, 384, 388, 392-3, 399, 401-2, 409-11, 413, 425-7, 430-44, 451; Arundel's quarrels with, 385-6, 421-2; John of Gaunt's relations with, 386, 388; Scottish expedition, 387; crisis of 1386-8: 388-401; and 1386 Parliament, 389-92; takes refuge in Tower, 395, 396; Merciless Parliament (1388), 395-401; and Cambridge Parliament (1388), 403, 406-7, 408; maintenance and livery, 406-7, 412-14, 416, 421; declares himself of age and assumes government (1389), 409-11; adopts badge of white hart as livery, 414, 425; private army of, 414, 427, 430; defends Lancaster against Arundel's accusations, 430; death of Queen Anne (1394), 421; Irish expedition, 422; marriage to Isabella of France, 423; Commons questions cost and power of his court, 424-7; loans raised under pressure by, 428-9, 444; arrest and trial of Gloucester, Arundel and Warwick, 429-35; rewards his supporters with peerages, 435; Shrewsbury Parliament (1398), 435-9; oaths of loyalty used by, 436, 437, 443; and Hereford-Norfolk quarrel, 437-8, 440-1; parliamentary committee (1398-9), 438-42; blank charters used by, 442-3; mental instability, 443; Irish expedition (1399), 444, 445; deposition of (1399), xviii, xxi, 61, 231, 356, 428, 429, 438, 445-50, 451, 452, 461; imprisoned in Tower, 446, 447, 448; transferred to Pontefract, 456-7; murder of, 450, 458
Richard III, King (reigned 1483-5), Duke of Gloucester, xix, xxi, 231, 452, 611, 614-31, 633; as Duke of Gloucester, 569, 598, 599, 601, 607, 614, 615; quarrel over Warwick inheritance between Clarence and, 601-2; English invasions of Scotland led by (1481-2), 611-12; and granted authority to govern the north, 612; usurpation of throne by (1483), 561, 615-20; becomes Protector, 616-17; coronation, 619-20; alleged murder of Princes in the Tower, 620, 621; rebellion against, 621-2; Parliament of (1484), 622-8; character, 628; Henry Tudor's invasion of England (1485), 629-30; killed at Bosworth, 630-1
Richard of Cambridge, 572
Richard of Cornwall, 89, 90, 92, 105
Richard of Devizes, 45
Richard of York, Earl of Cambridge (Edmund of Langley's son), 485, 490
Richard, 3rd Duke of York, 490, 506, 517, 524, 525, 531, 533-4, 536, 539; Normandy campaign (1441), 527, 528-9; Lieutenant of Ireland, 534; conflict between Somerset and, 540-1, 542, 544, 556; his claim to royal succession, 541, 542, 544; appointed king's lieutenant to preside over Parliament, 544, 552; first Protectorate of (1454-5), 546-7; first battle of St Alban's, 548-9, 551, 556; pardoned by King, 549, 551; second Protectorate of (1455-6), 552-4, 555; battles of Blore Heath and Ludford (1459), 558-9; flees to Ireland, 559; attainder of (1459), 559-60; publishes manifesto (1460), 560; and makes his claim to throne (1460), 561-4, 570; concord between Henry VI and, 564; assigned principality of Wales, 564; killed at Wakefield Bridge, 565, 569
Richard, Duke of York (Edward IV's son), 609, 612, 616, 617-18, 620; joins his brother Edward in Tower, 618; and alleged murder of, 620, 621
Richardson, H.G., 83-4
Richmond, Earl of, 176, 205, 211; *see also* Montfort, John de; Tudor, Edmund

Rickhill, Justice William, 434
Rivaux, Peter des, 75-6, 89
Rivers, Richard Woodville, Earl, 571, 592, 596, 598, 604, 615, 616, 618
Robert I the Bruce (reigned 1306-29), King of the Scots, 167, 180, 205, 211, 221, 222, 235-6, 240; coronation, 173; battle of Bannockburn (1314), 196-8; recognized by English as King of the Scots, 236
Robert IV, King of the Scots, 475
Robert, Duke of Normandy, 25
Robin of Holderness, 597
Robin of Redesdale, 597
Roches, Peter des, Bishop of Winchester, 57, 66, 69, 75, 89
Rochester, Bishops of, 133, 346
Roger of Bethune, mayor of London, 227
Rolls of Parliament, xvii-xviii, 145, 147-8, 166, 168 &n, 169, 199, 200, 202 &n, 241, 265, 266, 270, 271, 283, 295, 303, 311, 317, 318, 325, 326, 327, 329, 345, 349, 351, 352, 360, 380, 386, 388, 391, 396, 398, 419, 438, 454, 461-2, 498-9, 500, 511, 546, 572-3, 589-90; first account of day-to-day proceedings (1316), 202; falsification of, 439, 441, 446, 448; English language used in, 494
Roos, Lord, 477, 482, 592
Ros, Sir John, 203
Rotherham, Thomas, Bishop of Lincoln, 605, 609
Runnymede, 58-9, 87
Rusbrook, Thomas, 379
Russell, John, Bishop of Lincoln, 617, 622-3
Rutland, Earl of see Edward of York

Sadlington, Sir Robert, 289, 304
St Albans: great council (1212), 93; first battle of (1455), 548-9, 551, 556, 565, 587; second battle of (1461), 565, 593
St Albans chronicler, 357, 469, 561; see also Paris, Matthew
St David's, Bishop of, 352, 364-5
St Paul's Cathedral, 46, 155; Convocation (1344), 303; Convocation (1371), 332; Convocation (1373), 335
St Stephen's Chapel, xx, xxii
Salisbury, 24, 79
Salisbury, Bishop of see Erghum
Salisbury, Dean of, physician, 550
Salisbury, Sir John, 398
Salisbury, Richard Neville, Earl of, 547-8, 551, 558, 559, 560; captured at Wakefield and executed (1460), 565; see also Montagu, Earls of
Salisbury Parliaments: 1297: 130, 156, 157; 1328: 237; 1384: 385-6
Salmon, John, Bishop of Norwich, 204
Savage, Sir Arnald, Speaker, 461-3, 464, 465-6, 467
Say, Sir John, Speaker, 536, 590, 594

Saye and Sele, James Fiennes, Lord, 539
Sayles, G.O., 83-4
Scales, Anthony, Lord, 560, 561, 571, 594
Scone, coronation stone of, 155
Scotland, 56, 119, 143-4, 159, 179, 214, 234, 358, 377, 402; royal succession in, 148-9; wars under Edward I, 155, 159, 160, 162-3, 165, 166, 168-9, 173, 174, 175, 188; French treaty of alliance with, 155; battle of Stirling Bridge (1297), 160; battle of Falkirk (1298), 163; Robert Bruce crowned king of (1306), 173; Edward II's visit to (1307), 179; wars under Edward II, 184, 188, 195, 196-8, 199, 203, 204, 205, 206, 208, 210, 211, 222; battle of Bannockburn (1314), 196-8; siege of Berwick (1318), 211; truce with Edward II (1323), 222, 235; wars under Edward III, 235-6, 240-2, 243-4; 'The Shameful Peace', 236, 240; Edward Balliol crowned as Edward I of (1332), 240-1; battle of Halidon Hill (1333), 242; defence of border, 282, 283, 424, 425; battle of Neville's Cross (1346), 307; wars under Richard II, 358, 369, 370, 404; and Richard's expedition to, 387; battle of Otterburn (1388), 402; truce with (1389), 410, 422; Henry IV's expedition against (1400), 458; battle of Homildon Hill (1402), 458, 464; James I captured by English (1406), 475; battle of Branham Moor (1408), 479; peace with (1423), 506; Margaret of Anjou's alliance with, 565, 588; English raid into, 591; Edward IV's truce with (1463), 592; war with (1481-2), 611-12
Scrope, Geoffrey, Chief Justice, 242
Scrope, Henry le, 334
Scrope, Henry, Lord of Masham, 479, 483, 490, 520
Scrope, Richard, Lord of Bolton, 331, 345, 347, 365, 366, 368, 369, 378, 380, 382, 388, 391, 392, 395, 402
Scrope, Richard, Archbishop of York, 459, 468, 469-70
Scrope, William, Earl of Wiltshire, 417, 423, 429, 435, 438, 444, 445, 547, 557
scutage (shield money), 40, 47, 48, 55, 57, 58, 59, 61, 67, 68, 71, 91, 92, 146, 280
Seagrave, Hugh, 377
Segrave, Nicholas, 167
servitium debitum, 20
Shackell, John, 363, 364
Shameful Peace (treaty with Scotland, 1328), 236, 240
Shareshill, William de, Chief Justice, 315, 318, 319
Shaw, Dr Ralph, 618
Sherburn-in-Elmet assembly (1320), 213
sheriffs (shire-reeves), 5, 21, 22, 27, 39, 49, 72, 76, 92, 94, 101, 107, 119, 123, 126, 139, 198, 255, 256, 258, 405, 424, 425,

475, 481, 513; appointment of, 103, 106; disqualified from membership of Commons (1372), 254, 333; statutes against, 286–7, 575–6
shire/county courts, 5, 7, 21, 40, 43, 49, 72, 93, 234, 251, 255–6, 475, 481, 487, 513–14
shires: representation at Parliament by knights, 42, 86, 92–3, 94–5, 101, 102, 127–8, 131–3, 135–6, 144–6, 147, 150; taxation, 48–9, 72, 76, 121, 146, 150–1; military levy of knights and men from, 109–10; statute on military service outside (1327), 234–5; property qualification for franchise (1429), 513–14; and social restrictions on franchise (1446), 531
Shore, Jane, 617
Shrewsbury, 629; Parliament (1283), 135–8, 143, 146; Parliament (1398), 430, 432, 435–9, 443, 444; battle of (1403), 459, 464, 466
Shrewsbury, John Talbot, Earl of, 543, 557; killed at Northampton (1460), 560; *see also* Talbot
Sigismund, Emperor, 491, 492
Simon, Earl *see* Montfort, Simon de
Sluys, battle of (1340), 288
Somerset, Dukes and Earls of *see* Beaufort
Southwell, Robert, 527–8
Speaker of the Commons, xviii, xxii, 300–1, 359, 360, 365, 369, 384, 419, 427, 436, 437, 454, 461–3, 464, 465–6, 468, 470, 472, 473, 476, 477, 480, 482–3, 487, 491, 494, 498, 500, 536, 542, 545, 551, 569, 581, 590, 603, 623–4; first appointed (1376), 340–1, 344
Stafford, Edmund, Bishop of Exeter, 410, 414, 423–4, 444, 464
Stafford, Henry and Humphrey *see* Buckingham, Dukes of
Stafford, Hugh, Earl of, 347
Stafford, John, Bishop of Bath and Wells, 480, 498, 509, 524
Stafford, Lord, 292, 293
Staines 'Parliament' (1215), 80
Stamford great council (1337), 278
Stamford Parliament (1309), 182–3
Stamford Bridge, battle of (1066), 18, 19
Stanley, Thomas, Lord, Earl of Derby, 617, 621, 622, 629, 630
Stanley, Sir William, 629, 630, 631
Stapledon, Walter, Bishop of Exeter, 222, 223, 225
staples, 195, 249, 274, 278, 317–18, 319, 340, 345, 347, 348
Star Chamber, 168, 519, 537
statute law, statutes, 30, 38, 77, 79, 83, 163, 216–17, 218, 221, 232, 234–5, 512–14, 526–7, 624–8, 631; Magna Carta reissued, considered as first Act (1225), 71; Edward I's use of Parliaments to promulgate, 117–18, 122, 125, 126–7, 129–30, 133–42, 169–70, 171, 269; *de Bigimis* (1276), 126,

133, 136; first provision for annual Parliaments (1330), 262–4, 272; under Edward III, 269–74, 286–7, 295–6, 302, 305, 316, 321–2, 324–7; difference between ordinances and, 312–13, 326; under Richard II, 367–8, 382, 412–13, 439–40; under Henry IV, 454–5, 463, 465–6, 471–2, 474–5; under Edward IV, 570–2, 574–83, 586, 590, 605–6, 607, 611; *see also* Assizes; attainders; Magna Carta; Ordinances; Resumption Acts
Statute of Acton Burnell (1283), 136–8, 141
Statute of Cambridge (1388), 403, 407, 408–9
Statute of Carlisle (1307), 174
Statute of Gloucester (1278), 134, 138
Statute of Gloucester (1378), 368
Statute of Labourers (1351), 243, 313, 314, 316, 372; amendments to, 322; confirmed (1378), 368
Statute of Labourers (1388), 407, 413
Statute of Marlborough (1267), 103, 115
Statute of Merchants (1285), 141
Statute of Merton (1236), 77
Statute of Mortmain (1279), 135
Statute of Praemunire (1353), 318–19, 516–17
Statute of Praemunire (1393), 418
Statute of Provisors (1351), 313–14, 517
Statute of Provisors (1390), 412, 415, 416, 417–18
Statute of *Quia Emptores* (1290), 141, 142, 145
Statute of *Quo Warranto* (1290), 134–5, 141–2
Statute of Ragman (1276), 133–4
Statute of Stamford (1309), 182–3
Statute of the Staple (1354), 319
Statute of Trailbastons (1305), 170
Statute of Treasons (1352), 316, 394, 397, 398–9, 436
Statute of Westminster I (1275), 125–6, 127, 128, 129–30, 256
Statute of Westminster II (1285), 134, 138–9; *De Donis Conditionalibus* (1st clause), 138–9, 142
Statute of Winchester (1285), 141
Statute of York (1322), 215–17, 218, 221, 442
Statute of York (1335) 274
Stenton, Sir Frank, 11
Stephen of Blois, King, xxii, 26, 31
Stigand, Archbishop of Canterbury, 19
Stillington, Robert, Bishop of Bath and Wells, 561, 594, 595–6, 619
Stirling Bridge, battle of (1297), 160
Stirling castle, siege of, 197
Stothard, Charles, xxi
Stourton, William, Speaker, 487
Strange, Lord, 630
Strangeways, Sir James, Speaker, 569–70
Stratford, John, Bishop of Winchester and

Archbishop of Canterbury, 222, 223, 228, 229, 261, 275, 279, 281-2, 288, 307; Edward III's conflict with, 289-94, 296; 1344 Convocation at St Paul's, 303
Stratford, Ralph, Bishop of London, 292, 303
Stratford, Robert, Bishop of Chichester, 282, 288, 289, 292, 303
Stubbs, Bishop, *Constitutional History of England*, xvi, 79, 92, 152, 153, 438, 452-3, 488
Stury, Richard, 417
Sturmy, Sir William, Speaker, 468
subinfeudation, 125, 142, 248
Sudbury, Simon, Bishop of London and Archbishop of Canterbury, 334, 336, 359, 364, 368, 369, 370, 373, 374, 376
Suffolk, Earls of *see* Pole, de la
Surienne, François de, 535
Surrey, Duke of *see* Holland, Thomas
Surrey, Earl of *see* Warenne, Earl
Swynford, Catherine, 425, 476

Tailboys, William, 537
Talbot, John *see* Shrewsbury, Earl of
Talbot, Lord, 521-2
Talbot, Sir Thomas, 419
tallage, 49 &n, 91, 111, 124, 159, 161, 287, 316
taxation, xv, xvi, xvii, 2; heregeld, 10; Danegeld, 10, 23, 48, 71; Norman, 19, 22-3, 25; murder fine, 20, 203; *monetagium*, 25; under Henry II, 30, 40, 47; scutage, 40, 47-8, 55, 57, 58, 59, 61, 67 &n, 68, 71, 91, 92, 146, 280; under Richard I, 45, 46, 47-9; carucage, 48-9, 71; tallage, 49 &n, 91, 111, 124, 159, 161-2, 287, 316; under King John, 55, 57, 61, 71; aids, 55, 61, 67, 68, 73, 78, 79, 80, 92, 95, 115, 145, 220, 282-3; inheritance tax, 55, 56, 135; and Magna Carta, 61, 67, 68, 73, 78; under Henry III, 65, 67, 71-2, 73, 78-9, 91-5, 97-101; 115-16; consent of community principle, 71; granted in return for redress of grievances, 73; marriage-aid, 92, 145, 148; papal taxes, 97, 327; under Edward I, 119, 121, 128, 130, 131, 135, 146-7, 150-2, 154-6, 157, 158-62, 164, 166, 169; of boroughs, 123-4, 128, 130, 146, 150, 151; under Edward II, 179, 180, 181, 187, 188, 195, 204, 209; under Edward III, 240, 241, 242-3, 244, 249, 261, 274, 275-87, 294, 295, 296-7, 304-5, 308, 309, 310, 313, 315, 316, 317, 320, 324, 327, 329, 331, 333, 334-5, 338-9, 340, 344-5, 346, 350, 351, 353; new system of collection (1334), 242-3; clerical liability to, 260-1, 327, 332; feudal aid for knighting Black Prince, 306, 308, 310, 316; poll tax, 353, 369, 370, 371-2, 373, 375, 528, 536; under Richard II, 358, 359-60, 361, 366-7, 368-9, 370-2, 373, 380, 382, 383, 386, 394, 404, 410, 412,
414, 415, 421, 422, 424, 436, 437, 452; Commons' control of, 452, 457, 462, 473, 478-9, 502, 567-8, 631; under Henry IV, 454, 458, 459, 460, 461-2, 464, 465, 468, 469, 472-3, 477-8, 481, 483; land tax, 468, 469, 483, 517; under Henry V, 486, 490, 491-2, 493, 494; under Henry VI, 502, 506, 507, 512, 515, 517, 518, 520, 524-5, 526, 528, 530, 532, 536, 539, 543, 560; income tax, 524-5, 539, 603, 604, 605; under Edward IV, 567, 589-90, 591, 593-4, 596, 602, 603, 604, 605, 606, 608, 612; wealth tax, 590, 591; *see also* customs duty; wool
Teutonic Knights, 414
Tewkesbury, battle of (1471), 600
thegns, Anglo-Saxon, 4, 5, 6, 9, 11-12, 20
Thirning, Sir William, 450, 461
Thomas, Duke of Clarence *see* Clarence
Thomas, Earl of Lancaster, 176, 179, 182, 183, 184, 185, 191, 196, 197, 200, 218, 239, 270, 453; refuses to attend York Parliament, 190, 212; conflict between Edward II and, 187, 193-4, 195, 198-9, 201-14, 215; appointed chief of council (1316), 204-5; abduction of his wife, 206-7; and Middle Party, 209-10; Treaty of Leake (1318), 210-11; execution of (1322), 214, 221; reversal of sentence on (1327), 235
Thomas of Woodstock, Earl of Buckingham, Duke of Gloucester, xxii, 357, 364, 369, 370, 371, 377, 378, 386, 387, 388, 390-1, 392, 402, 405, 410, 411, 418, 419, 423, 425, 431, 444, 456; and trial of Richard II's courtiers (Merciless Parliament), 394, 395, 396, 398, 399, 400, 401, 403; abortive crusade of, 414, 415; Cheshire insurrection, 418-19; Irish expedition (1394), 422; Richard II's suspicions of, 427-8, 429; arrest and imprisoned in Calais, 429; trial of (1397), 432-3, 434; murder of, 434, 435; and alleged confession, 434
Thorp, Thomas, 467
Thorpe, Robert, 331
Thorpe, Thomas, Speaker, 543, 545, 551
Thorseby, John de, 307
Threlkeld, Sir Henry, 522
Thursby, John, 608-9
Tiptoft, Sir John, Earl of Worcester, Speaker, 470, 471, 474, 479, 500, 569, 599
Tirwhyt, Justice William, 482
Tostig (Harold II's brother), 15
Tours, truce of (1444), 529, 531, 534
Tower of London, 46, 107, 108, 176, 223, 289, 310, 329, 363, 374, 421, 429, 539, 599, 600; Henry of Keighley imprisoned in, 165; Richard II takes refuge in, 373, 395, 396; and imprisoned in (1399), 446, 447, 448, 450; Gloucester's exclusion from, 505, 507; Suffolk imprisoned in (1449),

537; Somerset imprisoned in (1454), 544; captured by Yorkists (1460), 560–1; Henry VI put to death in (1471), 600; Duke of Clarence imprisoned and put to death in, 609, 611; Princes Edward and Richard imprisoned in (1483), 616, 618, 620; and alleged murder of princes, 620
Towton, battle of (1461), 566, 569
Treaty of Leake (1318), 210–11
Treaty of Paris (1259), 104, 105
Tresham, William, Speaker, 536, 541
Tresilian, Sir Robert, 392, 393; trial and death of (1388), 394, 395–7
Triennial Act (1641), 262–3
Tristram, Professor Ernest, xxi
Troyes, treaty of (1420), 492, 493–4, 503, 532
Trussell, William, 229
Trussell, William, son, 300
Tudor, Edmund, Earl of Richmond, 547, 548, 599
Tudor, Henry *see* Henry VII
Tudor, Jaspar, Earl of Pembroke, 547, 565, 569, 592, 596, 599, 600–1, 629
Tudor, Owen, 547, 565
Twynho, Ankarette, 608–9
Tyler, Wat, 373, 374

'unknown charter of liberties', 57
Urban V, Pope, 327
Urban VI, Pope, 367–8, 383, 398

Valence, Aymer de, Earl of Pembroke, 193, 194, 196, 198, 199, 203, 206, 207, 209–10, 211, 212, 213, 221
Valence, William de, Earl of Pembroke, 103
Vaughan, Sir Thomas, 616, 618
Venables, Piers, 526
Vere, John de, 12th Earl of Oxford, 568, 571, 599, 601, 629
Vere, Robert de, Earl of Oxford (1296–1331), 185
Vere, Robert de, Earl of Oxford (1372–92), 376, 381, 382, 386, 388, 389, 392, 398, 413, 417; trial of, 394, 395–7
Vesci of Alnwick, Eustace de, 57
villeins, 29, 62, 63, 72, 124, 247–8, 362, 372, 375, 408; work-service of, 247–8, 249
Vita Aedwardi Regis, 16
Vita Edwardi Secundi, 205–6, 207

Wake, Lady Blanche de, 320
Wakefield Bridge, battle of (1460), 565
Waldegrave, Sir Richard, 377
Walden, Roger, Archbishop of Canterbury, 432
Wales and Welsh Marches, 56, 103, 105, 107, 111, 112, 113, 130, 158, 212, 217, 596; Edward I's campaigns in, 119, 142–3, 146, 148, 149–50; trial of Prince David (1283), 136, 137, 138; war in Marches (1321), 212; Welshmen summoned to Parliament, 217, 224–5; national uprising led by Glendower, 458, 459, 468, 469, 470, 475, 476, 479; lawlessness in Marches, 603–4
Wallace, William, 160, 163, 168
Wallingford, Sir William, 283
Walsingham, Thomas of, 346, 370, 410, 435, 446, 453
Walter, Hubert, Archbishop of Canterbury, 47, 48–9, 50, 54
Walter of Coutances, Archbishop of Rouen, 46, 47
Walton Ordinances (1338), 281, 283, 286, 288
Walworth, Sir William, 358, 361, 365, 366, 374, 375
Warenne, Earl (Earl of Surrey and Essex), 78, 185, 193, 194, 195, 197, 199, 207, 208–9, 229, 288, 293
Wars of the Roses (1455–85), 342, 405, 444, 493, 521, 522, 530, 541, 547–66, 587, 588–9, 590–1, 592, 598–600, 632; 1st battle of St Albans (1455), 548–9, 551, 556; causes of, 556–7; battle of Blore Heath (1459), 558; battle of Ludford (1459), 558–9; battle of Northampton (1460), 560; battle of Wakefield Bridge (1460), 565; 2nd battle of St Albans (1461), 565; battle of Mortimer's Cross (1461), 565; battle of Towton (1461), 566; siege of Alnwick (1462–3), 589; battle of Hedgley Moor (1463), 592; battle of Hexham (1464), 592; battle of Barnet (1471), 600
Warwick, Anne Beauchamp, Countess of, 548, 601–2
Warwick, Richard Neville, Earl of (Warwick the Kingmaker), 547–8, 551, 554, 558, 560, 566, 568, 589, 590, 593, 594, 596–600; captaincy of Calais, 549, 554; attacked at Westminster, 558; and escapes to Calais, 558, 559; battle of Northampton, 560; declaration of loyalty to Henry VI, 560, 562; defeated at 2nd battle of St Albans, 565; Louis XI's alliance with, 593, 598, 599, 600; Edward IV's breach with, 595, 596–7; and rebellion against Edward IV, 597–600; alliance with Lancastrians, 598, 599; governor of the realm (1470), 599; killed at battle of Barnet (1471), 600; Clarence/Gloucester quarrel over inheritance of, 601–2
Warwick, Edward, Earl of (Clarence's son), 628
Warwick, Earls of *see* Beauchamp
Waynflete, William, Bishop of Winchester, 557, 572, 581, 587, 620–1
wealth tax, 590, 591
Welles, Lord, 598
Wenlock, Sir John, Speaker, 551
wergild, 62

Wessex, royal house of, 2, 4, 16n, 18
Westminster Abbey, 17, 132, 401, 435; Chapter House, xxii, 266, 267, 315, 337, 339–41, 347, 353; Refectory, xxii, 91, 266, 424, 465; consecration of (1066), 15; rebuilt by Henry III, 73; Edward the Confessor's bones translated to (1269), 115–16; Edward I crowned at (1274), 119; Stone of Scone brought to, 155; Richard II's coronation, (1377), 357; violation of sanctuary, 363, 367; Edward IV's coronation (1461), 568; Elizabeth Woodville takes sanctuary in (1470 and 1483), 599, 616
Westminster *colloquium* (1317), 207
Westminster chronicler, 384, 385, 403, 421
Westminster great councils *see* great councils
Westminster Hall, xx–xxi, xxii, 32, 110, 167, 264, 321, 327, 430, 447; law courts, xx, 42; hammer beam roof, xx; throne, xx–xxi; proclamation of opening of Parliament in, xxi; Richard II's reconstruction of, 425; deposition of Richard II in (1399), 447–50
Westminster, Old Palace of, xx–xxiii, 167, 409–10; destroyed by fire (1834), 185; *see also* Painted Chamber; Parliaments
Westmorland, Earls of, 548
Westmorland, Ralph Neville, Earl of, 435, 445, 480
Westmorland, Ralph Neville, Earl of, 568, 571
White Chamber, xxii, 266, 267, 300, 301, 304, 313, 316, 318, 326, 327, 329, 334, 338, 389
White Hall or Less Hall, Westminster, xxi, xxii, 167, 396
White Ship, wreck of 26
Wihtred of Kent, King, 7
Wilkinson, Professor B., 399
William I the Conqueror, (reigned 1066–87), 2, 13, 14, 15, 16, 17, 18, 19, 20, 21–4, 25, 31, 38, 103, 219
William II Rufus, xx, 24–5
William of Lincoln, Bishop, 594
William of Malmesbury, 3n
Wiltshire, Earl of, 547, 557, 565, 566, 569; *see also* Scrope, William
Winchelsey, Robert, Archbishop of Canterbury, 155, 158, 165, 174, 176, 183, 199
Winchester, 103; Witan meetings, 12, 13; great council (1265), 114; Statute of (1285), 141; Parliament (1330), 238; Parliament (1393), 417–18; Parliament (1449), 535–6
Winchester, Bishops of *see* Beaufort; Edington; Kemp; Lusignan; Orleton; Roches; Stratford; Waynflete; Wykeham
Winchester, Earl of *see* Despenser, Hugh
Windsor castle, 107, 108, 392, 458, 466; Edward III's rebuilding of, 324; parliamentary committee (1398), 440; attempted abduction of Mortimer boys from (1405), 469; St George's Chapel, 593
Windsor tournament (1344), 303
wine *see* customs duty: tunnage
Witan (Anglo-Saxon council), 2, 3, 4–18, 23, 88, 117, 171
Woodville family, 596, 597, 614–16
Woodville, Edward, 615
Woodville, Elizabeth *see* Elizabeth Woodville
Woodville, John, 598
Woodville, Richard *see* Rivers, Earl
wool trade, 149, 247, 249, 305, 309, 321, 383, 384, 415, 590; tax/subsidy on, 128, 130, 149, 157, 159, 161, 259, 277–8, 279, 280, 282, 287, 295, 308, 309, 310, 313, 315, 320, 324, 329, 332, 333, 367, 368, 412, 436, 454, 464, 470, 477, 478, 483, 486, 491, 507, 512, 536, 543, 593–4, 628; staples, 195, 249, 278, 317–18, 319; Edward III's embargo on exports to Flanders, 244–5, 278; export monopoly scheme, 278, 280; removal of Calais staple, 340, 345, 348
Worcester, Bishop of, 352
Worcester, Earls of *see* Percy; Tiptoft
Worcester Chronicle, 137
Worcester great council (c.1218), 80
work-service, commutation for rent of, 247–8, 249
Wulfstan, Bishop, 23
Wyclif, John, 330, 335, 353, 367, 384, 463
Wykeham, William of, Bishop of Winchester, 334, 342, 347, 352, 353, 357, 392, 410, 411

Yonge, Thomas, 542, 555
York, 12, 124, 185, 193, 211, 236, 600, 621; provincial council (1283), 146; Edward III moves government to (1332), 241; Council of the North (1684), 628
York, Anne, Duchess of, 609
York, Archbishops of *see* Aldred; Arundel; Geoffrey; Kemp; Neville; Scrope
York, Dukes of, 342; *see also* Edmund Langley; Edward of York; Richard, 3rd Duke of York; Richard, Duke of York
York House, London, 180, 181
York Parliaments: 1298: 162; 1309: 183; 1314: 198, 199; 1318: 211; 1320: 190, 211–12; 1322: 215–16, 219, 222; 1328: 236; 1332: 241–2; 1333: 242; 1334: 242; 1335: 243–4; 1464: 592

THE PLANTAGENETS

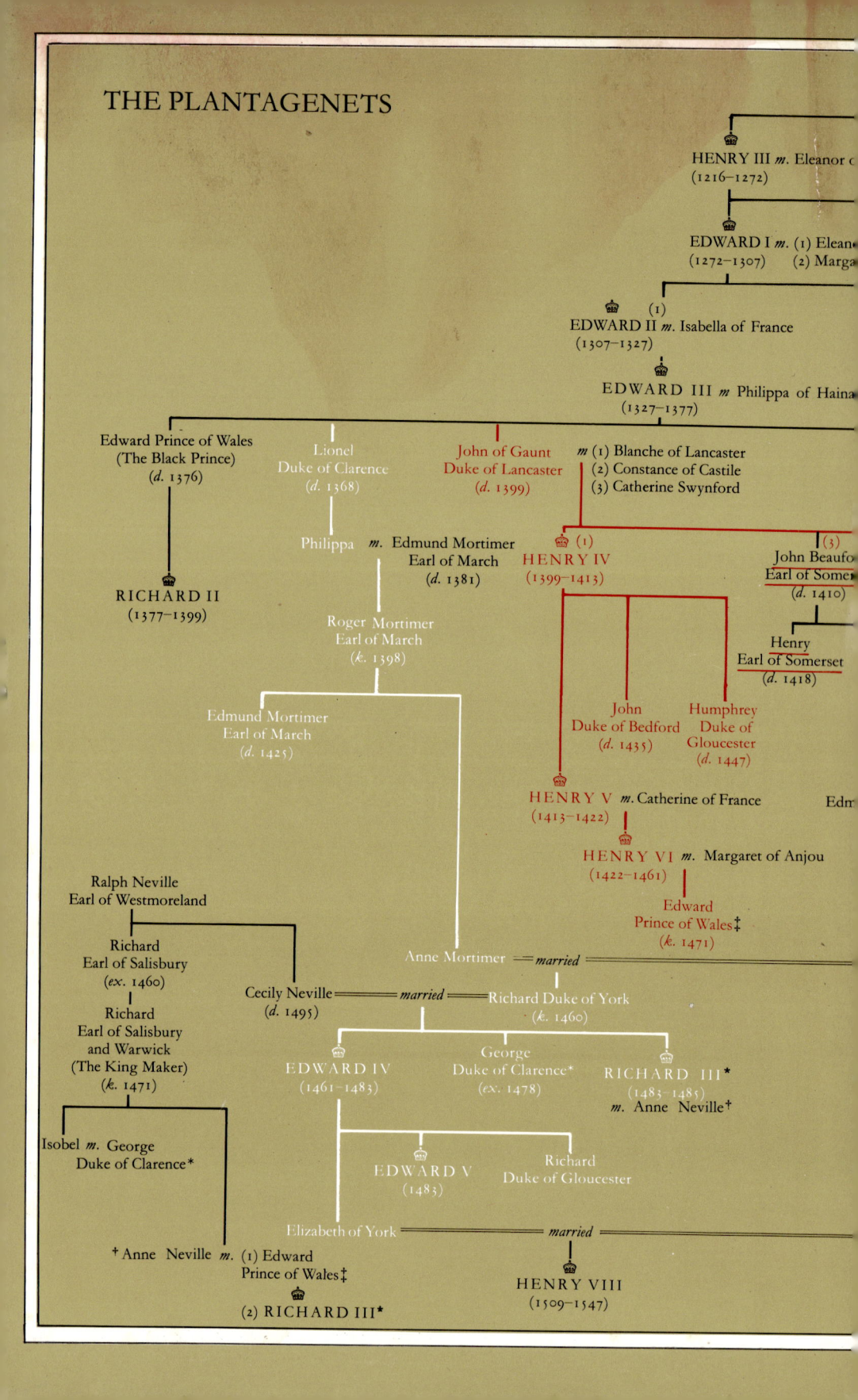

HENRY III *m.* Eleanor
(1216–1272)

EDWARD I *m.* (1) Eleanor
(1272–1307) (2) Margaret

(1)
EDWARD II *m.* Isabella of France
(1307–1327)

EDWARD III *m* Philippa of Hainault
(1327–1377)

Edward Prince of Wales (The Black Prince) (*d.* 1376)

Lionel Duke of Clarence (*d.* 1368)

John of Gaunt Duke of Lancaster (*d.* 1399) *m* (1) Blanche of Lancaster (2) Constance of Castile (3) Catherine Swynford

Philippa *m.* Edmund Mortimer Earl of March (*d.* 1381)

HENRY IV (1399–1413)

John Beaufort Earl of Somerset (*d.* 1410)

RICHARD II (1377–1399)

Roger Mortimer Earl of March (*k.* 1398)

Henry Earl of Somerset (*d.* 1418)

Edmund Mortimer Earl of March (*d.* 1425)

John Duke of Bedford (*d.* 1435)

Humphrey Duke of Gloucester (*d.* 1447)

HENRY V *m.* Catherine of France (1413–1422)

HENRY VI *m.* Margaret of Anjou (1422–1461)

Edward Prince of Wales‡ (*k.* 1471)

Ralph Neville Earl of Westmoreland

Richard Earl of Salisbury (*ex.* 1460)

Anne Mortimer = married

Richard Earl of Salisbury and Warwick (The King Maker) (*k.* 1471)

Cecily Neville (*d.* 1495) = married = Richard Duke of York (*k.* 1460)

Isobel *m.* George Duke of Clarence*

EDWARD IV (1461–1483)

George Duke of Clarence* (*ex.* 1478)

RICHARD III* (1483–1485) *m.* Anne Neville†

EDWARD V (1483)

Richard Duke of Gloucester

† Anne Neville *m.* (1) Edward Prince of Wales‡

Elizabeth of York = married = HENRY VIII (1509–1547)

(2) RICHARD III*